Lecture Notes in Computer Science 16574

The series Lecture Notes in Computer Science (LNCS), including its subseries Lecture Notes in Artificial Intelligence (LNAI) and Lecture Notes in Bioinformatics (LNBI), has established itself as a medium for the publication of new developments in computer science and information technology research, teaching, and education.

LNCS enjoys close cooperation with the computer science R & D community, the series counts many renowned academics among its volume editors and paper authors, and collaborates with prestigious societies. Its mission is to serve this international community by providing an invaluable service, mainly focused on the publication of conference and workshop proceedings and postproceedings. LNCS commenced publication in 1973.

José Manuel Ferrández Vicente ·
Mikel Val-Calvo · Hojjat Adeli
Editors

Artificial Intelligence for Neuroscience, Mental Health, and Neurodegenerative Disorders

11th International Work-Conference on the Interplay Between Natural and Artificial Computation, IWINAC 2026
Canary Islands, Spain, May 26–29, 2026
Proceedings, Part I

Springer

Editors
José Manuel Ferrández Vicente
Universidad Politécnica de Cartagena
Cartagena, Murcia, Spain

Mikel Val-Calvo
Universidad Politécnica de Valencia
Valencia, Spain

Hojjat Adeli
Ohio State University
Columbus, OH, USA

ISSN 0302-9743 ISSN 1611-3349 (electronic)
Lecture Notes in Computer Science
ISBN 978-3-032-27313-0 ISBN 978-3-032-27314-7 (eBook)
https://doi.org/10.1007/978-3-032-27314-7

This Springer imprint is published by the registered company Springer Nature Switzerland AG
The registered company address is: Gewerbestrasse 11, 6330 Cham, Switzerland

Preface

The main topic of these IWINAC/ICINAC 2026 books is to study intelligent systems inspired by the natural world, in particular biology. Several algorithms and methods and their applications are discussed, including evolutionary algorithms. Bio-inspired intelligent systems have thousands of useful applications in fields as diverse as machine learning, biomedicine, control theory, telecommunications, and why not music and art. This book covers both the theory and practice of bio-inspired artificial intelligence, along with providing a bit of the basis and inspiration for the different approaches. This is a discipline that strives to develop new computing techniques through observing how naturally occurring phenomena behave to solve complex problems in various environmental situations. Brain-inspired computation is one of these techniques that covers multiple applications in very different fields. Through IWINAC/ICINAC we provide a forum in which research in different fields can converge to create new computational paradigms that are on the frontier between neural and biomedical sciences and Information technologies.

As a multidisciplinary forum, IWINAC is open to any established institutions and research laboratories actively working in the field of natural or neural technologies. But beyond achieving co-operation between different research realms, we wish to actively encourage co-operation with the private sector, particularly SMEs, as a way of bridging the gap between frontier science and societal impact.

In this edition, four main themes outline the Conference topics: Neuroscience and Mental Health, Affective Computing, Robotics, and Translational Systems.

1) Machine learning holds great promise in the development of new models and theories in the field of Neuroscience, in conjunction with classical statistical hypothesis testing. Machine learning algorithms have the potential to reveal interactions, hidden patterns of abnormal activity, brain structure and connectivity, and physiological mechanisms of brain and behavior. In addition, several approaches for testing the significance of the machine learning outcomes have been successfully proposed to avoid "the dangers of spurious findings or explanations void of mechanism" by means of proper replication, validation, and hypothesis-driven confirmation. Therefore, machine learning can effectively provide relevant information to take great strides toward understanding how the brain works. The main goal of this field is to build a bridge between two scientific communities, the machine learning community, including leading scientists in deep learning and related areas within pattern recognition and artificial intelligence, and the neuroscience community. Artificial Intelligence has become the ultimate scale to test the limits of technological advances in dealing with Life Science challenges and needs. In this sense, the interplay between Natural and Artificial Computation is expected to play a most relevant role in the diagnosis, monitoring, and treatment of Neurodegenerative Diseases, using the advanced computational solutions provided by Machine Learning and Data Science. This requires us to interchange new ideas, launch projects and contests, and eventually create an inclusive knowledge-oriented network with the aim of empowering

researchers, practitioners, and users of technological solutions for daily life experience in the domains of Neuromotor and Linguistic competence functional evaluation, clinical explainability, and rehabilitation by interaction with humans, robots, and gaming avatars, not being strictly limited to only these, but inclusively open to other related concepts. The use of Machine Learning-based Precision Medicine in monitoring daily life activity and providing well-being conditions to especially sensitive social sectors is one of the most relevant objectives. Case study descriptions involving neurodegenerative diseases (Alzheimer's disease, fronto-temporal dementia, cerebrovascular damage and stroke, autism, Parkinson's disease, amyotrophic lateral sclerosis, multiple sclerosis, Huntington's chorea, etc.) are included. Mild cognitive impairment (MCI) is considered the stage between the mental changes that are seen between normal ageing and early stages of dementia. Indeed, MCI is one of the main indicators of incipient Alzheimer's disease (AD) among other neuropsychological diseases. The growth of these diseases is generating a great interest in the development of new effective methods for the early detection of MCI because, although no treatments are known to cure MCI, this early diagnosis would allow early intervention to delay the effects of the disease and accelerate progress towards effective treatment in its early stages. Although there have been many years of research, the early identification of cognitive impairment, as well as differential diagnosis (to distinguish significant causes or typologies for its treatment), are problems that have been addressed from different angles, but are still far from being solved. Diverse types of tests have already been developed, such as biological markers, magnetic resonance imaging, and neuropsychological tests. While effective, biological markers and magnetic resonance imaging are economically expensive, invasive, and require time to get a result, making them unsuitable as a population screening method. On the other hand, neuropsychological tests have a reliability comparable to biomarker tests, and are cheaper and quicker to interpret.

2) Emotions are essential in human-human communication, cognition, learning, and rational decision-making processes. However, human-machine interfaces (HMIs) are still not able to understand human sentiments and react accordingly. With the aim of endowing HMIs with the emotional intelligence they lack Affective Computing science focuses on the development of artificial intelligence by means of the analysis of affects and emotions, such that systems and devices could be able to recognize, interpret, process, and simulate human sentiments.

Nowadays, the evaluation of electrophysiological signals plays a key role in advancements towards that purpose since they are an objective representation of the emotional state of an individual. Hence, the interest in physiological variables like electroencephalogram, electrocardiogram, or electrodermal activity, among many others, has notably grown in the field of affective states detection. Furthermore, emotions have also been widely identified by means of the assessment of speech characteristics and facial gestures of people under different sentimental conditions. It is also worth noting that the development of algorithms for the classification of affective states in social media has experienced a notable increase in recent years. In this sense, the language of posts included in social networks, such as Facebook or Twitter, is evaluated with the aim of detecting the sentiments of the users of those media tools. Affective Computing and Sentiment Analysis is intended to be a meeting point for researchers that are interested in any of those areas of expertise related to sentiment analysis, and want to initiate their studies or are currently working on these topics. Hence, manuscripts introducing new proposals based on the analysis of physiological measures, facial recognition, speech recognition, or natural language processing in social media are examples of affective computing and sentiment analysis.

3) Over recent decades there has been an increasing interest in using machine learning and in the last few years, deep learning methods, combined with other vision techniques to create autonomous systems that solve vision problems in different fields. This special session was designed to allow researchers and developers to publish original, innovative, and state-of-the art algorithms and architectures for real-time applications in the areas of computer vision, image processing, biometrics, virtual and augmented reality, neural networks, intelligent interfaces, and biomimetic object-vision recognition.

This workshop provided a platform for academics, developers, and industry-related researchers belonging to the vast communities of **Neural Networks**, **Computational Intelligence**, **Machine Learning**, **Deep Learning**, **Biometrics**, **Vision Systems**, and **Robotics**, to discuss, share experience, and explore traditional and new areas of computer vision, machine and deep learning combined to solve a range of problems. The objective of the workshop was to integrate the growing international community of researchers working on the application of Machine Learning and Deep Learning Methods in Vision and Robotics into a fruitful discussion on the evolution and the benefits of this technology to society.

4) Finally, Artificial Intelligence (AI) has become a catalyst for innovation in a wide variety of disciplines, playing a pivotal role in solving contemporary challenges. This session focuses on the translational applications of AI in multiple fields, highlighing how the technology is transforming key sectors in response to the needs of today's society. Grid and power infrastructure management is one of the domains where AI is revolutionizing efficiency and reliability. Through predictive analytics, optimization, and proactive maintenance, AI enables a smarter and more resilient power grid, crucial in a world seeking decarbonization and the use of renewable energy. In agriculture, AI drives precision farming, improving agricultural production, water resource management, and crop quality. In civil engineering, AI-assisted planning and design streamline construction projects and optimize infrastructure. Smart cities and urban planning benefit from AI to optimize transportation, waste management, and the quality of life of inhabitants. In education, AI personalizes teaching and assessment, tailoring learning to the individual needs of students. In nutrition and food science, AI algorithms are used for creating healthy diets and detecting contaminants in food. This topic explored how AI fosters innovation and transformation in these diverse areas, highlighting the solutions this technology offers to address current challenges and improve the quality of life in modern society. From smarter power grids to safer food, AI is paving the way to a more efficient and sustainable future in a variety of multidisciplinary fields.

The wider view of the computational paradigm gives us more elbow room to accommodate the results of the interplay between nature and computation. The IWINAC/ICINAC forum thus becomes a methodological approximation (set of intentions, questions, experiments, models, algorithms, mechanisms, explanation procedures, and engineering and computational methods) to the natural and artificial perspectives of the mind embodiment problem, both in humans and in artifacts. This is the philosophy that continues in IWINAC meetings, the "interplay" movement between the natural and the artificial, facing this same problem every two years. This synergistic approach will permit us not only to build new computational systems based on natural measurable phenomena, but also to understand many of the observable behaviors inherent to natural systems.

The difficulty of building bridges between natural and artificial computation was one of the main motivations for the organization of IWINAC 2026. The IWINAC/ICINAC 2026 proceedings contain the 99 works selected by the Scientific Committee from more than 187 submissions, after the refereeing process. The type of peer review used was single blind with an average number of reviews received per submission of 2.5, and an average number of papers per reviewer of 3 with external reviewers involved, outside the PC. The first volume, entitled Artificial Intelligence for Neuroscience, Mental Health and Neurodegenerative Disorders, includes all the contributions mainly related to new tools for analizing neural data for mental health or detecting emotional states, or interfacing with physical systems. The second volume, entitled Bioinspired Intelligent Systems: From Robotics and Computer Vision to Trustworthy Applications, contains the papers related to bioinspired programming strategies and all the contributions oriented to the computational solutions to engineering problems in different application domains, such as biomedical systems, or big data solutions.

An event of the nature of IWINAC/ICINAC 2026 cannot be organized without the collaboration of a group of institutions and people who we would like to thank now, starting with Universidad de Granada and Universidad Politécnica de Cartagena. In addition to our universities, we received financial support from Red Nacional en Inteligencia Artificial para Neurociencia y Salud Mental (IA4NSM) and Apliquem Microones 21 s.l We also would like to express our great gratitude to Ibero-American network **Red Cyted New Technologies for Mental Health (NT4SM) 225RT0169**, to **Cátedra UGR-Endesa en IA**, and to the European Comission **Marie Curie Action MSCA-SE EPISTEAM (101129655)** for organizing their sessions in the Conference.

We want to express our gratefulness to our invited speakers Hojjat Adeli, from Ohio State University (USA), Pablo Laguna Lasaosa from Universidad de Zaragoza (Spain), and Pedro Gómez Vilda, from Universidad Politécnica de Madrid (Spain) for accepting our invitation and for their magnificent plenary talks.

We would also like to thank the authors for their interest in our call and the effort in preparing the papers, condition sine qua non for these proceedings. We thank the Scientific and Organizing Committees, in particular the members of these committees who acted as effective and efficient referees and as promoters and managers of pre-organized sessions on autonomous and relevant topics under the IWINAC/ICINAC global scope.

Our sincere gratitude goes also to Springer, for their continuous receptivity, helpfulness, and collaboration in all our joint editorial ventures on the interplay between neuroscience and computation.

Finally, we want to express our special thanks to BCD eventos, our technical secretariat, and to Ana María García de Alba, for making this meeting possible, and for arranging all the details that comprise the organization of this kind of event.

We want to dedicate these two volumes of the IWINAC proceedings to the memories of Professors Rodellar, Sánchez-Andrés, and Mira. We deeply miss them.

May 2026

José Manuel Ferrández Vicente
Mikel Val Calvo
Hojjat Adeli

Organization

General Chair

José Manuel Ferrández Vicente	Universidad Politécnica de Cartagena, Spain

Organizing Committee

Mikel Val Calvo	Universidad Politécnica de Valencia, Spain

Honorary Chairs

Hojjat Adeli	Ohio State University, USA
Rodolfo Llinás	New York University, USA
Zhou Changjiu	Singapore Polytechnic, Singapore

Invited Speakers

Hojjat Adeli	Ohio State University, USA
Pablo Laguna	Universidad de Zaragoza, Spain,
Mariano Alcañis	Universidad Politécnica de Valencia, Spain

Field Editors

Sung-Bae Cho	Yonsei University, South Korea
Emilia Barakova	Eindhoven University of Technology, Netherlands
Gema Benedicto	Universidad Politécnica de Cartagena, Spain
María Paula Bonomini	Instituto Tenológico de Buenos Aires, Argentina
Diego Castillo-Barnes	Universidad de Granada, Spain
Enrique Dominguez	Universidad de Málaga, Spain
Félix de la Paz	Universidad Nacional de Educación a Distancia, Spain
Antonio Fernández-Caballero	Universidad Castilla-La Mancha, Spain
Jose García-Rodríguez	Universitat d'Alacant, Spain
Andrés Gómez-Rodellar	University of Edinburgh, UK

Pedro Gómez-Vilda	Universidad Politécnica de Madrid, Spain
Juan Manuel Górriz	Universidad de Granada, Spain
David Guijo-Rubio	Universidad de Córdoba, Spain
Marina Jodra	Universidad Complutense de Madrid, Spain
Vicente Julián-Inglada	Universitat Politècnica de València, Spain
Caroline Konig	Universitat Politécnica de Catalunya, Spain
Krzysztof Kutt	Jagiellonian University, Poland
Fco. Jesús Martínez Murcia	Universidad de Málaga, Spain
Rafael Martínez Tomás	Universidad Nacional de Educación a Distancia, Spain
Jiri Mekyska	Brno University of Technology, Czechia
Ramón Moreno	Grupo Antolin, Spain
Ioana Moldovan	Technical University of Cluj Napoca, Romania
Silivan Moldovan	Technical University of Cluj Napoca, Romania
Grzegorz J. Nalepa	Jagiellonian University, Poland
Andrés Ortiz	Universidad de Málaga, Spain
Daniel Palacios-Alonso	Universidad Rey Juan Carlos, Spain
José T. Palma	Universidad de Murcia, Spain
Jorge Pérez-Aracil	Universidad de Alcalá, Spain
Javier Ramírez	Universidad de Granada, Spain
Mariano Rincón Zamorano	Universidad Nacional de Educación a Distancia, Spain
Sancho Salcedo	Universidad de Alcalá, Spain
Jose Santos Reyes	Universidade da Coruña, Spain
Fermín Segovia	Universidad de Granada, Spain
Antonio Tallón	Universidad de Huelva, Spain
Ramiro Varela	Universidad de Oviedo, Spain
Alfredo Vellido	Universitat Politécnica de Catalunya, Spain

International Scientific Committee

Amparo Alonso Betanzos, Spain
Jose Ramon Álvarez-Sánchez, Spain
Margarita Bachiller Mayoral, Spain
Francisco Bellas, Spain
Emilia I. Barakova, Netherlands
Guido Bologna, Switzerland
Paula Bonomini, Argentina
Enrique J. Carmona Suárez, Spain
José Carlos Castillo, Spain
Germán Castellanos-Dominguez, Colombia
Sung-Bae Cho, Korea

Ricardo Contreras, Chile
Jose Manuel Cuadra Troncoso, Spain
Félix de la Paz López, Spain
Javier de Lope, Spain
Enrique Domínguez, Spain
Eduardo Fernández, Spain
Richard J. Duro, Spain
Antonio Fernández-Caballero, Spain
José Manuel Ferrandez, Spain
Victor Fresno, Spain
Jose Garcia-Rodriguez, Spain
Javier Garrigós, Spain
Pedro Gómez-Vilda, Spain
Pascual González, Spain
Juan M. Gorriz, Spain
Manuel Graña, Spain
César Hervás Martínez, Spain
Tom Heskes, Netherlands
Joost N. Kok, Netherlands
Krzysztof Kutt, Poland
Markus Lappe, Germany
Emilio Letón Molina, Spain
Maria Teresa López Bonal, Spain
Tino Lourens, Netherlands
Angeles Manjarrés, Spain
Jose Manuel Molina Lopez, Spain
Rafael Martínez Tomás, Spain
Juan Morales Sánchez, Spain
Grzegorz J. Nalepa, Poland
Elena Navarro, Spain
Andrés Ortiz García, Spain
José Palma, Spain
Francisco Peláez, Brazil
Maria Pinninghoff, Chile
Javier Ramírez, Spain
Andoni Razvan, USA
Mariano Rincón Zamorano, Spain
Victoria Rodellar, Spain
Camino Rodríguez Vela, Spain
Pedro Salcedo Lagos, Chile
Ángel Sanchez, Spain
Eduardo Sánchez Vila, Spain
José Luis Sancho-Gómez, Spain
José Santos Reyes, Spain
Antonio Sanz, Spain

Luis M. Sarro, Spain
Andreas Schierwagen, Germany
Guido Sciavicco, Italy
Fermín Segovia, Spain
Antonio J. Tallón-Ballesteros, Spain
Jan Treur, Netherlands
Ramiro Varela Arias, Spain
Hujun Yin, UK
Yu-Dong Zhang, UK

Contents

NeurDis: "Functional Evaluation of Neuromotor and Cognitive Disorders. Hommage to Victoria Rodellar"

NT4SM: "Intelligent Systems for the Study and Support of Youth Mental Health (CYTED)"

"Socio-Cognitive, Affective and Physiological Computing"

"Intelligent Systems for Assessment, Treatment, and Assistance in early stages of Alzheimer"

"Neuroprosthesis, Ethics. EPISTEAM"

ECTLAB: "European Culture and Technology Lab (EUT+). EPISTEAM"

MALENE: “3rd Workshop on Machine Learning in Neuroscience”

Extracting Circadian Rhythms from Continuous Glucose Monitoring via Physics-Constrained Empirical Mode Decomposition

Diego Castillo-Barnes[1(✉)], Ignacio Rodríguez-Rodríguez[2], Nelsa González[1,3], Andrés Ortiz[2], Claudio Laudani[4], Luis Ortega-Paz[4], and Francesco Costa[1,3]

[1] Instituto de Investigación Biomédica de Málaga y Plataforma en Nanomedicina (IBIMA Plataforma BIONAND), Málaga, Spain
diego.castillo@ibima.eu
[2] Communications Engineering, University of Malaga, Málaga, Spain
[3] Hospital Universitario Virgen de la Victoria, Málaga, Spain
[4] Division of Cardiology, University of Florida College of Medicine, Jacksonville, FL, USA

Abstract. Continuous glucose monitoring (CGM) provides high-resolution metabolic time series that exhibit strong nonlinearity, nonstationarity, and multiscale temporal structure. Conventional CGM metrics summarize variability but fail to explicitly characterize the underlying physiological rhythms and long-term trends.

We propose a physics-constrained signal decomposition framework for CGM analysis based on empirical mode decomposition and Hilbert transform principles. By estimating characteristic periods of intrinsic mode functions through Hilbert-based instantaneous frequency analysis, the method enables robust separation of ultradian components, circadian rhythms, and long-term residual behavior at the individual level. A stopping criterion grounded in physiologically meaningful time scales prevents overdecomposition and ensures interpretability.

The framework is demonstrated on CGM recordings from patients with recent acute coronary syndromes, illustrating its ability to extract stable circadian profiles and subject-specific residual dynamics suitable for phenotyping and longitudinal modeling. The proposed methodology is general and can be applied to a wide range of biomedical time series where adaptive, physics-informed decomposition is required.

Keywords: Continuous glucose monitoring · Empirical mode decomposition · Holo-Hilbert spectrum · Circadian rhythms · Time series

J. M. Ferrández Vicente et al. (Eds.): IWINAC 2026, LNCS 16574, pp. 3–14, 2026.
https://doi.org/10.1007/978-3-032-27314-7_1

1 Introduction

Continuous glucose monitoring (CGM) has transformed the assessment of glucose dynamics by providing dense, real-world time series sampled over multiple days. These signals reflect the interaction of physiological regulation, behavioral patterns, and pathological processes, resulting in pronounced nonlinearity and non-stationarity.

However, while current CGM analyses rely predominantly on summary statistics, such as time-in-range or glycemic variability indices, these metrics do not explicitly model the multiscale temporal organization of glucose dynamics [1,4]. In particular, circadian rhythms, ultradian fluctuations, and slower metabolic trends are typically aggregated into global descriptors, limiting the ability to disentangle physiologically distinct processes at different time scales [6].

From a signal processing perspective, CGM recordings are characterized by the superposition of oscillatory components with variable amplitude and frequency embedded in long-term trends and subject-specific baseline shifts. Capturing this structure requires analytical tools capable of adapting to non-stationary behavior without imposing a priori assumptions on signal linearity or periodicity. Adaptive signal decomposition methods, such as empirical mode decomposition (EMD), provide a natural framework for this purpose by decomposing signals into intrinsic mode functions that reflect data-driven temporal scales [3].

Nevertheless, standard EMD-based approaches applied without explicit constraints may suffer from overdecomposition, mode mixing, and limited reproducibility across subjects. In the absence of physiologically grounded stopping criteria, the number and interpretation of extracted modes can vary substantially, hindering comparability and clinical interpretability. This is particularly relevant in CGM analysis, where differences in recording duration, noise characteristics, and glycemic variability may lead to inconsistent decompositions [8].

In this work, we introduce a physics-constrained, Holo-Hilbert–guided framework for the analysis of CGM time series that explicitly links adaptive signal decomposition to characteristic temporal scales. By estimating dominant oscillatory periods through Hilbert-based instantaneous frequency analysis and constraining the decomposition according to physiologically meaningful time ranges, the proposed method enables robust extraction of circadian glucose rhythms and long-term residual behavior at the individual level while preserving interpretability and reproducibility.

2 Methods

2.1 Study Population and CGM Dataset

The data analyzed in this study were obtained from the ORACLE project, a prospective multicenter study investigating cardiometabolic risk in patients following acute coronary syndromes, coordinated by coordinated by IBIMA Plataforma BIONAND. The study protocol was approved by the corresponding institutional ethics committees and conducted in accordance with the Declaration of Helsinki and Good Clinical Practice guidelines. Written informed consent was obtained from all participants.

CGM was initiated at hospital discharge using factory-calibrated wearable sensors (Freestyle Libre 3 or Freestyle libre 3 plus, Abbott) providing interstitial glucose measurements at five-minute intervals.

The present work focuses on baseline CGM data from patients with type 2 diabetes mellitus[1] and nondiabetic controls.

Overall, CGM data from 242 subjects were initially available. After applying the signal-quality and temporal-consistency control procedures described in Sect. 2.2, the final analysis included 154 participants: 69 patients with type 2 diabetes and 85 nondiabetic controls. The diabetic group had a mean age of 67.7 $\pm$ 11.1 years and included 18 women and 51 men, whereas the control group had a mean age of 65.3 $\pm$ 11.1 years and included 11 women and 74 men.

2.2 Preprocessing and Quality Control

CGM recordings were processed using a strict signal-level quality-control pipeline designed to ensure temporal continuity and physiological plausibility while preserving intrinsic glucose variability. Raw data were first sorted by timestamp, duplicate entries were removed, and invalid glucose values were discarded (NaNs, non-positive values, or values exceeding 600 mg/dL).

Problematic signal segments were then identified based on predefined criteria: temporal gaps of at least 3 hours, prolonged flat segments (standard deviation < 0.5 mg/dL or ≤ 2 unique values) lasting ≥ 3 hours, strictly monotonic ramps (increasing or decreasing) persisting for ≥ 3 hours, and implausible single-step glucose jumps exceeding 50 mg/dL between consecutive 5-minute samples. Entire calendar days intersecting any of these segments were removed from the analysis.

After cleanup, CGM recordings were required to span at least 12 consecutive days. Signals not meeting this minimum duration were excluded. Remaining data were processed using a sequence-based resampling strategy that preserved original timestamps and interpolated only short gaps (>5 and ≤ 15 minutes) by linear interpolation. Longer gaps were not interpolated. Data quality was further enforced by requiring an average of at least 75% of the expected daily samples (approximately 216 measurements per day) and that at least 80% of days met this criterion.

Signals passing quality control were aligned to a circadian reference (midnight) by discarding leading partial days and subsequently trimmed to a fixed analysis window of exactly 12 complete days to ensure comparability across subjects. Recordings exhibiting near-zero variance or loss of physiological variability at any processing stage were excluded.

[1] Diabetes was defined as a previous clinical diagnosis of diabetes mellitus and a current treatment with antidiabetic medications at the time of hospital discharge.

2.3 Physics-Constrained Empirical Mode Decomposition

Each preprocessed CGM signal was decomposed using Complete Ensemble Empirical Mode Decomposition with Adaptive Noise (CEEMDAN), which represents a noise-assisted extension of empirical mode decomposition designed to mitigate mode mixing and improve decomposition stability [8]. Given a glucose signal $x(t)$, CEEMDAN produces a finite set of IMFs $\{c_k(t)\}_{k=1}^{K}$ and a residual $r(t)$ as follows in (1):

$$x(t) = \sum_{k=1}^{K} c_k(t) + r(t). \tag{1}$$

In contrast to conventional CEEMDAN applications that iterate until numerical convergence or a predefined residue energy threshold, we imposed a *physics-constrained stopping criterion* based on the characteristic temporal scale of the extracted modes. This constraint explicitly reflects the physiological time scales of interest in CGM data and prevents the overdecomposition of slow metabolic trends.

For each IMF $c_k(t)$, a characteristic period T_k was estimated from its instantaneous frequency obtained via the Hilbert transform. Let $f_k(t)$ denote the instantaneous frequency of $c_k(t)$; the characteristic frequency $\bar{f}_k$ was computed as the energy-weighted average in (2), and the corresponding characteristic period was defined as $T_k = 1/\bar{f}_k$. When instantaneous frequency estimation was unstable, a spectral fallback based on the dominant Fourier component was used.

$$\bar{f}_k = \frac{\sum_t f_k(t)\,|c_k(t)|^2}{\sum_t |c_k(t)|^2}, \tag{2}$$

The CEEMDAN decomposition was terminated when the characteristic period of the newly extracted IMF exceeded a predefined upper bound ($T_{\text{stop}} =$ 48 hours in our context). This threshold was selected to separate oscillatory components operating on ultradian and circadian time scales from slower, non-oscillatory metabolic trends. All signal components with $T_k > T_{\text{stop}}$ were therefore aggregated into the residual term $r(t)$ rather than decomposed further.

Additional safeguards were applied to ensure physically meaningful decompositions. Specifically, (i) at least three IMFs were always extracted before allowing energy-based stopping, (ii) IMFs contributing less than 0.5% of the total signal energy were discarded, and (iii) the monotonic ordering of IMF characteristic periods ($T_1 < T_2 < \cdots < T_K$) was enforced; violations resulted in the truncation of higher-order modes.

This physics-constrained CEEMDAN strategy yields a compact and interpretable representation of CGM signals, in which oscillatory dynamics are explicitly separated from long-term residual behavior, providing a principled basis for circadian rhythm extraction and inter-subject comparison.

2.4 Circadian and Residual Components

Following physics-constrained CEEMDAN decomposition, IMFs were grouped according to their characteristic periods to obtain physiologically interpretable signal components [2]. IMFs with characteristic periods within the circadian range (8–24 hours) were aggregated to form a subject-specific circadian component, representing daily glucose oscillations driven by endogenous and behavioral regulatory mechanisms.

All slower signal components, including IMFs with characteristic periods exceeding the circadian range and the final residual returned by the decomposition, were retained as a residual component capturing long-term glycemic behavior beyond daily rhythmicity, such as baseline shifts and slow metabolic trends not attributable to oscillatory dynamics.

This separation yields a compact representation of CGM signals in which circadian rhythmicity and long-term trends are explicitly disentangled at the individual level, as illustrated in Fig. 1 for a representative subject.

2.5 Feature Extraction from Circadian and Residual Components

To enable quantitative comparison between type 2 diabetic and nondiabetic subjects, a predefined set of 33 features was extracted from the circadian and residual components of each individual CGM signal. Feature extraction was performed at the subject level, ensuring that each participant contributed a single feature vector to subsequent analyses. All features were defined *a priori* based on physiological interpretability, and no feature selection or dimensionality reduction was applied before statistical testing.

Circadian Temporal Features (16 features) were derived from the 24-hour average profile of the circadian component and characterized the amplitude, timing, and shape of daily glucose rhythms. These included descriptors of peak and trough behavior, variability and asymmetry, and area-under-the-curve measures across standard time segments.

Circadian Frequency Features (8 features) summarized the distribution of characteristic periods within the circadian range, capturing inter-individual variability in rhythmic periodicity and decomposition structure (e.g., summary statistics of circadian periods, number of modes, and mean IMF period).

Residual Features (6 features) quantified slow, non-oscillatory glucose trends beyond daily rhythmicity, describing the magnitude and variability of baseline changes and long-term fluctuations over the analysis window.

Finally, **composite features** (3 features) assessed the relative contribution of circadian dynamics to overall glucose variability, including the variance fraction explained by the circadian component, the circadian-to-residual variability ratio, and a normalized measure of circadian strength.

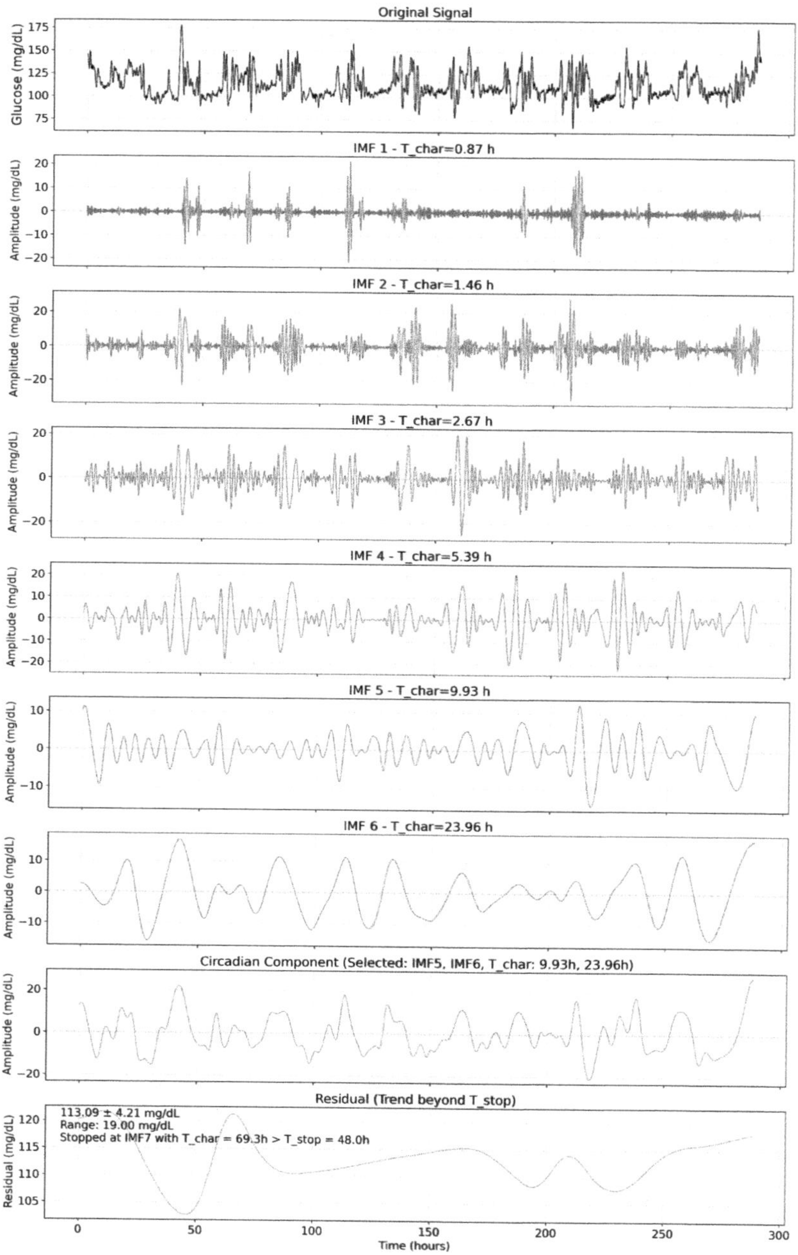

Fig. 1. Example of physics-constrained CEEMDAN decomposition for a representative nondiabetic subject. The original CGM signal is decomposed into IMFs ordered by increasing characteristic period. IMFs with characteristic periods in the circadian range are aggregated to form the circadian component, while slower dynamics are retained in the residual signal. This decomposition explicitly separates daily glucose rhythmicity from long-term glycemic trends at the individual level.

3 Results

Group-level differences between type 2 diabetic and nondiabetic subjects were assessed using univariate statistical testing on the 33 predefined features extracted from circadian and residual components. Normality was evaluated independently within each group, and features meeting normality assumptions in both groups were compared using Welch's t-test, whereas the Mann-Whitney-Wilcoxon U test was used otherwise. Multiple comparisons were controlled via false discovery rate (FDR) correction, and effect sizes were computed for all comparisons.

Figure 2 summarizes mean differences between groups for all features, highlighting those remaining significant after FDR correction.

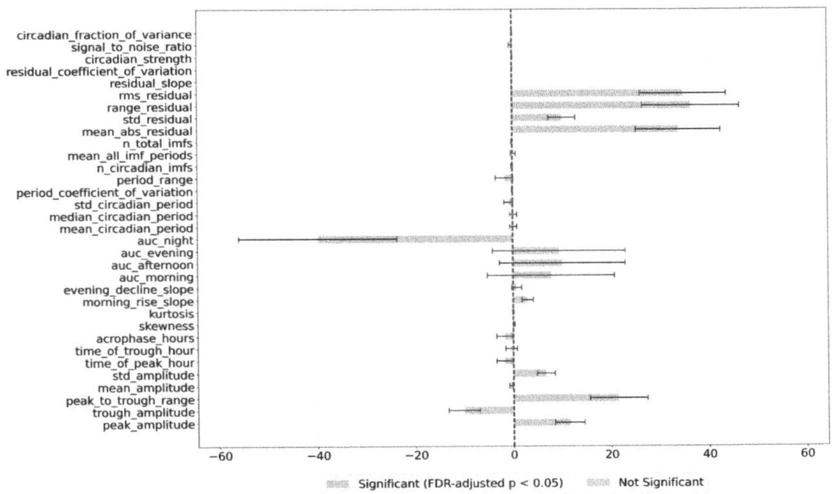

Fig. 2. Forest plot showing the mean differences between type 2 diabetic and nondiabetic subjects for all extracted features. Bars represent group mean differences, with error bars indicating 95% confidence intervals. Features highlighted in red remain statistically significant after false discovery rate (FDR) correction ($p < 0.05$).

Circadian Temporal Features: revealed marked amplitude-related differences between groups. Type 2 diabetic subjects exhibited higher peak amplitude, lower trough amplitude, and consequently a larger peak-to-trough range, as well as increased standard deviation of the circadian component. The morning rise slope was significantly steeper in diabetic subjects, and the evening decline slope showed a smaller but consistent difference. Time-resolved area-under-the-curve measures reflected a reduced nocturnal AUC and an increased morning AUC in the diabetic group, whereas higher-order shape metrics, such as skewness and kurtosis, did not differ significantly.

Circadian Frequency Features: indicated that mean and median circadian periods were comparable between groups, but dispersion-related metrics differed. Diabetic subjects showed greater variability in their circadian periods, reflected by higher standard deviation and coefficient of variation, while the total number of circadian intrinsic mode functions remained similar across groups.

Residual Component Features: exhibited the strongest group-level contrasts. Type 2 diabetic subjects showed higher mean absolute residuals, residual standard deviation, range, and root-mean-square amplitude, together indicating greater magnitude and variability of slow background glucose dynamics. Both the residual coefficient of variation and the residual slope differed significantly, with diabetic subjects displaying increased relative variability and more negative long-term trends over the analysis window.

Composite Circadian/Residual Metrics: also showed clear group differences. Diabetic subjects presented a higher fraction of total variance explained by the circadian component and greater overall circadian strength, accompanied by a reduced circadian-to-residual signal-to-noise ratio, suggesting an altered balance between rhythmic and background glycemic variability.

4 Discussion

4.1 Circadian and Residual Dynamics in CGM Signals

The proposed decomposition consistently identified one or two IMFs within the circadian range (8–24 hours) across subjects, which were aggregated to define a subject-specific circadian glucose rhythm. Despite inter-individual variability in the exact characteristic periods of these modes, the resulting circadian component proved robust at the individual level. Group-level comparisons revealed that differences between type 2 diabetic and nondiabetic subjects were driven primarily by changes in the amplitude, variability, and temporal organization of this circadian component, rather than by systematic shifts in the mean circadian period.

Beyond circadian oscillations, the residual component captured slow, non-oscillatory glucose dynamics that are not accessible through standard circadian analyses. Residual-derived features exhibited the strongest group-level differences, highlighting the relevance of long-term background trends for characterizing glucose regulation. These differences are illustrated in Fig. 3, where diabetic subjects display higher residual magnitude and variability than nondiabetic controls.

4.2 On the Interpretation of CEEMDAN-Derived Modes

A common concern when applying empirical mode decomposition techniques is the absence of fixed frequency bands across subjects, as the characteristic period

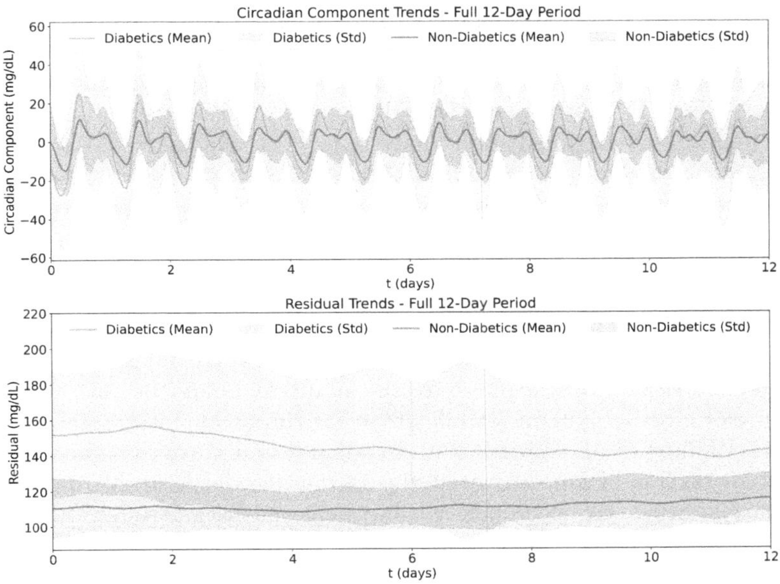

Fig. 3. Group-averaged circadian (top) and residual (bottom) component trends over the full 12-day analysis window. Solid lines indicate group means, and shaded areas represent one standard deviation. The residual component exhibits substantially larger magnitude and variability in type 2 diabetic subjects compared to nondiabetic controls.

of a given IMF index (e.g., IMF3 or IMF4) may vary between individuals. In the present framework, this variability does not represent a limitation, as the identification of circadian dynamics is based on the characteristic period of each mode rather than its ordinal position within the decomposition. The circadian component is therefore defined as the aggregation of all modes falling within the circadian band, irrespective of IMF index.

Characteristic periods themselves constitute subject-specific descriptors of intrinsic temporal organization. While not exploited as primary features in this study, these periods provide a natural basis for individualized characterization and may offer additional discriminatory power in future analyses.

4.3 Methodological Generalizability and Comparison with Existing Approaches

Although illustrated here using CGM data from patients with acute coronary syndromes, the proposed framework is agnostic to both disease context and sensor modality. The separation of circadian and residual components is applicable to any setting in which daily rhythmicity and slower trends coexist, including controlled dietary interventions, sports performance monitoring, sleep, and activity analysis [9]. The use of adaptive, data-driven decomposition combined with explicit time-scale constraints enables application to heterogeneous real-world signals without imposing rigid model assumptions.

Beyond scalar metrics, several studies have sought to preserve the temporal organization of CGM signals through functional or statistical modeling. [6] applied multilevel functional data analysis to postprandial CGM trajectories, revealing structured physiological variability invisible to conventional indices. Likewise, [4] used functional principal component analysis to uncover interpretable temporal profiles, such as nocturnal hyperglycemia and postprandial oscillations.

Compared to these approaches, our framework introduces a physics-constrained, CEEMDAN-based strategy that extracts intrinsic oscillations according to physiologically meaningful time scales. Unlike functional approaches based on basis expansions, it preserves the adaptive, nonlinear, and nonstationary nature of glucose dynamics while enforcing time-scale interpretability.

In [7], Phillips et al. showed that circadian baseline rhythms account for a substantial fraction of glucose variability in multimodal wearable data, a finding consistent with our decomposition but achieved here through a fully data-driven approach. The observed modulation of circadian rhythmicity aligns with evidence linking disrupted biological timing to impaired glucose regulation in diabetes [5]. In this sense, our framework complements these existing temporal analyses by embedding physiological time-scale constraints directly into the decomposition, enabling interpretable characterization of both circadian rhythmicity and slower metabolic trends.

4.4 Limitations and Future Directions

This study focused on methodological development and proof-of-concept group discrimination. The feature set was predefined and univariate in nature, and no multivariate modeling or predictive analysis was performed. Future work will explore the integration of circadian and residual features into multivariate models and the longitudinal stability of extracted components.

5 Conclusions

In this work, we presented a physics-constrained signal decomposition framework for CGM data, designed to separate daily circadian rhythms from slower background dynamics. By integrating adaptive empirical mode decomposition with physiologically informed time-scale constraints, the method yields an interpretable, subject-specific representation of glucose variability without imposing fixed frequency bands or parametric assumptions.

Applied to baseline CGM recordings from type 2 diabetic and nondiabetic subjects, the framework effectively distinguished circadian oscillations from long-term residual trends. Group differences were mainly driven by increased circadian amplitude and variability, together with enhanced residual magnitude and instability in diabetic subjects, while mean circadian periodicity remained largely preserved.

Beyond CGM, the approach is applicable to other physiological signals combining rhythmic and slow components, offering a compact and interpretable tool for multiscale analysis of nonstationary biomedical data.

Acknowledgments. The study is part of the ORACLE project (ClinicalTrials.gov: NCT06993415), funded by the European Union through the European Research Council (ERC) under the Horizon Europe programme (ERC-2023-STG-101117469). F.C. is funded by the European Union (ERC, ORACLE, ERC-2023-STG-101117469). Views and opinions expressed are however those of the author(s) only and do not necessarily reflect those of the European Union or the European Research Council. Neither the European Union nor the granting authority can be held responsible for them. D.C.-B. is supported by a Sara Borrell postdoctoral contract (CD25/00046) from the Instituto de Salud Carlos III (ISCIII), under the Strategic Action in Health (AES), co-financed by the European Social Fund Plus (ESF+) and the European Union. Work by I.R.-R. is part of the grant RYC2023-045296-I funded by MICIU/AEI/10.13039/501100011033 (Spain) and by ESF+. This work is also supported by the Spanish Ministry of Science and Innovation under project PID2022-137461NB-C32, funded by MICIU/AEI/10.13039/501100011033; and part of the TIC251-G-FEDER project, funded by ERDF/EU.

Disclosure of Interests. The authors have no competing interests to declare that are relevant to the content of this article.

References

1. Battelino, T., Alexander, C.M., Amiel, S.A., et al.: Continuous glucose monitoring and metrics for clinical trials: an international consensus statement. Lancet Diabetes Endocrinol. **11**(1), 42–57 (2023). https://doi.org/10.1016/s2213-8587(22)00319-9
2. Carroccia, A., Grasso, M., Maggioni, M., Colosimo, B.M.: Improved signal characterization via empirical mode decomposition to enhance in-line quality monitoring. Procedia CIRP **41**, 717–722 (2016). https://doi.org/10.1016/j.procir.2015.12.094
3. Civera, M., Surace, C.: A comparative analysis of signal decomposition techniques for structural health monitoring on an experimental benchmark. Sensors **21**(5), 1825 (2021). https://doi.org/10.3390/s21051825
4. Fraser, R.A., et al.: Mon-544 uncovering temporal patterns in CGM data for personalized diabetes care. J. Endocr. Soc. **9**(Supplement 1) (2025). https://doi.org/10.1210/jendso/bvaf149.911
5. Lee, D.Y., et al.: Attention to innate circadian rhythm and the impact of its disruption on diabetes. Diabetes Metab. J. **48**(1), 37–52 (2024). https://doi.org/10.4093/dmj.2023.0193
6. Matabuena, M., Sartini, J., Gude, F.: Beyond scalar metrics: functional data analysis of postprandial continuous glucose monitoring in the aegis study (2024). https://doi.org/10.48550/ARXIV.2405.14690
7. Phillips, N.E., Collet, T.H., Naef, F.: Uncovering personalized glucose responses and circadian rhythms from multiple wearable biosensors with Bayesian dynamical modeling. Cell Rep. Methods **3**(8), 100545 (2023). https://doi.org/10.1016/j.crmeth.2023.100545

8. Torres, M.E., Colominas, M.A., Schlotthauer, G., Flandrin, P.: A complete ensemble empirical mode decomposition with adaptive noise. In: 2011 IEEE International Conference on Acoustics, Speech and Signal Processing (ICASSP). IEEE (2011). https://doi.org/10.1109/icassp.2011.5947265
9. Yao, J., et al.: Diet, physical activity, and sleep in relation to postprandial glucose responses under free-living conditions: an intensive longitudinal observational study. Int. J. Behavioral Nutr. Phys. Act. **21**(1) (2024). https://doi.org/10.1186/s12966-024-01693-5

Hilbert Spectrum-Based Approach for fNIRS Interhemispheric Functional Connectivity Analysis

Nicolás J. Gallego-Molina[1,2(✉)], Andrés Ortiz[1,2], Diego Castillo-Barnes[1,2,3], and Ignacio Rodríguez-Rodríguez[1,2]

[1] Communications Engineering Department University of Málaga, 29004 Málaga, Spain
[2] Andalusian Data Science and Computational Intelligence Institute (DaSCI),Granada, Spain
njgm@ic.uma.es
[3] Instituto de Investigación Biomédica de Málaga y Plataforma en Nanomedicina (IBIMA Plataforma BIONAND), Avenida Severo Ochoa, 35, 29590 Málaga, Spain

Abstract. Functional Near-Infrared Spectroscopy (fNIRS) is a promising neuroimaging technique due to its non-invasive nature and tolerance to movement. However, its interpretation is often hindered by physiological and systemic artifacts that mask neural activity. In this work, we propose a data-driven framework to extract neural components from fNIRS signals and to analyze interhemispheric functional connectivity in language disorders. The approach is based on Complete Ensemble Empirical Mode Decomposition with Adaptive Noise (CEEMDAN) combined with Hilbert spectral analysis to isolate oscillatory components associated with neural hemodynamics without relying on predefined frequency filters. Then, functional connectivity is computed between channels across hemispheres and statistically significant connections are identified through Mann–Whitney U test and subsequently used as features within a nested classification framework based on XGBoost. The results reveal altered interhemispheric connectivity patterns and demonstrate the discriminative potential of the extracted features, achieving stable classification performance across cross-validation folds.

Keywords: fNIRS · EMD · Hilbert spectrum · Functional connectivity

1 Introduction

Noninvasive neuroimaging techniques, as Functional Near-Infrared Spectroscopy (fNIRS), allows to measure the hemodynamic response arisen from the brain processes. Furthermore, we can determine the neural activity based on the neurovascular principle [7] in which when a brain area becomes active its demand for oxygen an glucose increase, causing a rise in the cerebral blood flow (CBF), and an increment in oxygenated hemoglobin (HbO) and a reduction in deoxygenate

J. M. Ferrández Vicente et al. (Eds.): IWINAC 2026, LNCS 16574, pp. 15–24, 2026.
https://doi.org/10.1007/978-3-032-27314-7_2

hemoglobin (Hbr). However, in the fNIRS signals there are present other components originating from multiple physiological causes such as cardiac, respiratory and muscle activity [9]. Thus, we need to remove these components in order to correctly process the fNIRS signal for the analysis of neural activity.

The most commonly adopted strategy to mitigate these effects is frequency-based filtering. In particular, band-pass filters with cut-off frequencies typically ranging from 0.01 to 0.09 Hz , or low-pass filters with an upper limit around 0.09 Hz [8], are widely used to suppress cardiac, respiratory, and Mayer wave components while preserving neural linked hemodynamic fluctuations. Although the exact cut-off values may vary across studies [5,8], these physiological interferences are known to occupy relatively stable frequency ranges, with cardiac activity usually appearing around 1–2 Hz, respiratory oscillations in the range of 0.2–0.4 Hz, and Mayer waves around 0.1 Hz. For example, in [2] a band pass filter with cut-off frequencies of 0.01 Hz to 0.08 Hz were used to provide evidence that fNIRS is capable of providing comparable resting state functional connectivity measures to functional Magnetic Resonance Imaging (fMRI).

Beyond conventional filtering, multivariate decomposition techniques such as Principal Component Analysis (PCA) and Independent Component Analysis (ICA) have been employed to isolate neural-related components from systemic noise. For example, in [12] ICA was employed to analyze resting-state functional connectivity and PCA was used in [14] to isolate task-related hemodynamic responses from physiological noise by exploiting the dominant variance components of the recorded signals. However, the performance of theses methods depends on assumptions such as signal stationarity or statistical independence, which are not always satisfied in fNIRS recordings.

In this context, Empirical Mode Decomposition (EMD) has emerged as an attractive alternative due to its fully data-driven nature and its suitability for analyzing nonlinear and non-stationary signals. Allowing physiological components to be separated according to their intrinsic time scales rather than predefined frequency bands. Several studies, such as [13] and [3] have demonstrated the effectiveness of EMD and its ensemble variants in reducing motion artifacts and isolating neural-related hemodynamic fluctuations in fNIRS data. In this work, we propose a Hilbert spectrum-based framework to quantify interhemispheric functional connectivity using a dataset from a language disorder experiment. The proposed methodology exploits the advantages of EMD, specifically Complete Ensemble Empirical Mode Decomposition with Adaptive Noise (CEEMDAN) [1,10], to directly isolate the neural component of the hemoglobin concentration time series from the fNIRS signals without relying on conventional band-pass filtering. Then, we performed an exploratory functional connectivity analysis on the processed signals containing the components reflecting neural activity. Revealing significant interhemispheric pattern with a diagnostic capability and supporting the ability of the proposed approach to effectively extract meaningful neural information from fNIRS signals.

The rest of the paper is organized as follows. First, Sect. 2 describes de dataset and the proposed methodology. Then, Sect. 3 discussed the results and finally, Sect. 4 depict the conclusions and future work.

2 Materials and Methods

2.1 Database

The data analyzed in this study were obtained from a longitudinal research project conducted by the LEEDUCA group at the University of Málaga, Spain [6]. This large-scale study includes more than 1,400 children between 4 and 8 years of age and was approved by the Medical Ethics Committee of the University of Málaga (05/02/2020, PND016/2020). Authorization was also granted by the Andalusian Education Authority to carry out assessments in public schools. As part of the study protocol, participants completed a comprehensive battery of cognitive and linguistic assessments administered on a quarterly basis. Based on these evaluations, a subset of children was selected to participate in a fNIRS experiment.

The final sample comprised 34 children, including 13 diagnosed with dyslexia and 21 typically developing controls, all matched in age (4 years) and socioeconomic background. During the experiment, participants were exposed to amplitude-modulated white noise stimuli presented at modulation rates of 4.8, 16, and 40 Hz, which correspond to the characteristic temporal scales of key speech units in Spanish. Each recording session lasted approximately 15 minutes, with stimuli delivered in both ascending and descending sequences (4.8–16–40 Hz and 40–16–4.8 Hz), each lasting 2.5 minutes.

fNIRS data were acquired using a NIRSport system equipped with eight sources and eight detectors, resulting in a total of 20 measurement channels per wavelength. The optodes were arranged with an average source-detector separation of approximately 3 cm, ensuring sensitivity to cortical hemodynamic activity. Signals were sampled at 7.8125 Hz and preprocessed using the MNE-Python library, which was employed for channel interpolation to address detector saturation, conversion from light intensity to optical density, and subsequent transformation into hemoglobin concentration.

2.2 Empirical Mode Decomposition (EMD)

EMD [4] is a data-driven technique designed for the analysis of nonlinear and non-stationary signals. Unlike traditional filtering approaches, EMD adaptively decomposes a signal into a finite set of intrinsic mode functions (IMFs), each representing an oscillatory component with well-defined instantaneous frequency. Thus, each IMF represents a narrowband signal satisfying two conditions: (i) the number of extrema and zero crossings differs by at most one, and (ii) the local mean of the upper and lower envelopes is zero. Given a signal $x(t)$, EMD expresses it as

$$x(t) = \sum_{k=1}^{K} c_k(t) + r_K(t) \tag{1}$$

where $c_k(t)$ denotes the k-th IMF and $r_K(t)$ is the final residual. The IMFs are obtained through an iterative sifting process, in which local extrema are interpolated to form envelopes whose mean is subtracted from the signal until the IMF conditions are met.

Although EMD provides a flexible representation, it is sensitive to noise and may suffer from mode mixing. To address this limitation, Ensemble Empirical Mode Decomposition (EEMD) [11] was introduced by averaging decompositions obtained from multiple noise-perturbed realizations of the signal

$$x^{(i)}(t) = x(t) + \beta n^{(i)}(t) \tag{2}$$

where $n^{(i)}(t)$ is white noise and β controls its amplitude. Each realization is decomposed independently, and the final modes are obtained by averaging corresponding IMFs across all realizations.

While this approach improves robustness, it does not guarantee exact signal reconstruction and may produce an inconsistent number of modes. To overcome these drawbacks, CEEMDAN was introduced [10]. CEEMDAN ensures completeness by extracting each mode from a uniquely defined residual while controlling the noise contribution at every stage. This results in a stable decomposition in which the original signal is exactly reconstructed as the sum of all modes and the final residue.

$$x(t) = \sum_{k=1}^{K} \tilde{c}_k(t) + r_K(t) \tag{3}$$

At each iteration, noise is adaptively scaled and added to the residual, and the first IMF of the resulting signal is computed and averaged across realizations. This strategy guarantees both stability and exact reconstruction, while significantly reducing mode mixing.

2.3 Hilbert Spectrum-Based Extraction of Neural Component in fNIRS Signals

Due to the described properties, CEEMDAN is particularly well suited for biomedical signal processing, where signals are highly non-stationary and often contaminated by physiological artifacts. In this work, CEEMDAN is employed to isolate neural-related oscillatory components from fNIRS recordings, providing a robust basis for reliable estimation of interhemispheric functional connectivity without relying on predefined frequency filters.

First, for each fNIRS channel of a subject CEEMDAN is used to decompose the signals into a set of IMFs as shown in Fig. 1. Then, each IMF is analyzed computing the marginal Hilbert spectrum [4]. For this we apply the Hilbert transform to each IMF and compute the instantaneous frequency as

$$\omega = \frac{d\theta(t)}{dt} \tag{4}$$

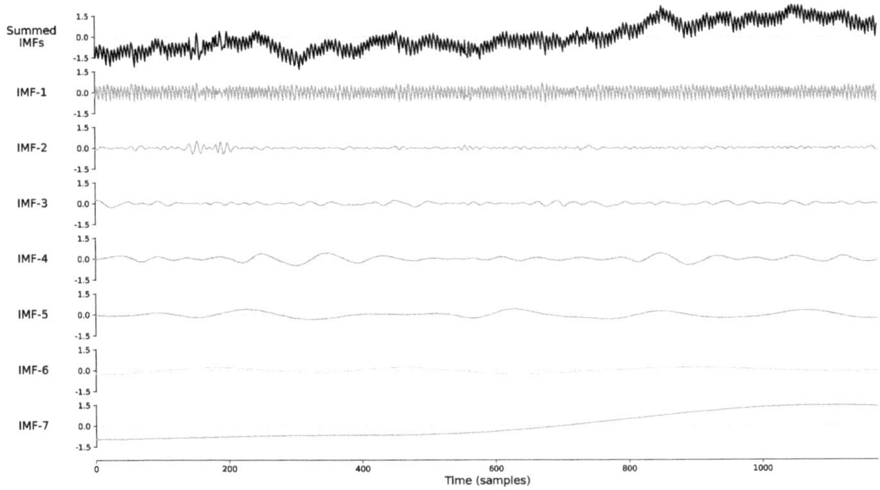

Fig. 1. IMFs computed with CEEMDAN of a fNIRS signal.

where $\theta(t)$ is the instantaneous phase. Then, by applying the Hilbert transform on each IMF component, the original signal can be expressed as

$$x(t) = \sum_{j=1}^{n} a_j(t) \exp\left(i \int \omega_j(t)\, dt\right), \tag{5}$$

From Eq. 5 we can represent the amplitude and the instantaneous frequency as functions of time in a three-dimensional plot known as Hilbert spectrum. Based on this representation, the Hilbert marginal spectrum can be defined as

$$h(\omega) = \int_0^T H(\omega, t)\, dt \tag{6}$$

Fig. 2 illustrates the marginal spectrum derived from the IMFs shown in Fig. 1. This representation summarizes the overall contribution of each frequency component by integrating its amplitude over time, thereby providing an estimate of the total energy associated with each frequency across the signal duration.

Finally, considering the information from the marginal Hilbert spectrum we proceed to select the IMFs with neural activity information. It is established that the hemodynamic response linked to neural activity measured with fNIRS is mainly represented within the low-frequency range between 0.01 and 0.08 Hz. Based on this criterion, the IMFs whose dominant spectral peak falls within this interval are retained. The selected IMFs are then summed to reconstruct a signal that represents the neural component of the original fNIRS recording.

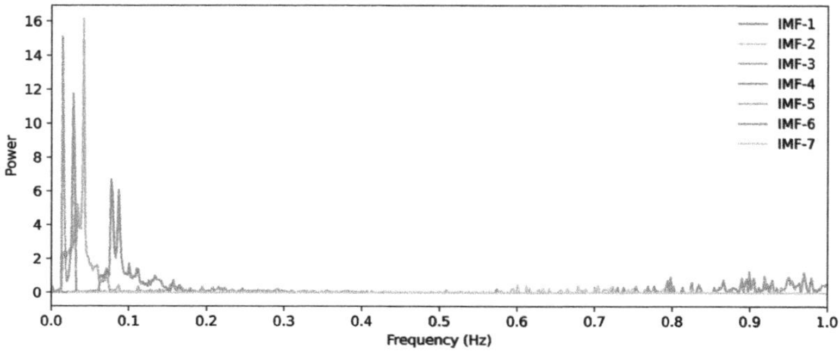

Fig. 2. Marginal Hilbert spectrum of the IMFs computed in Fig. 1.

2.4 Revealing Interhemispheric Functional Connectivity Patterns

The proposed methodology aims to characterize interhemispheric functional connectivity by first isolating the neural component of the fNIRS signals. Once the neural activity is extracted, functional connectivity is computed between channels located in the left and right hemispheres using the Pearson correlation coefficient. This approach allows the quantification of synchronization patterns between both hemispheres. To identify connectivity differences between typically developing children and those with dyslexia, a non-parametric test, the Mann–Whitney U test is employed, enabling the detection of statistically significant interhemispheric connections without assuming data normality.

Then, we have revealed discriminative patterns of interhemispheric functional connectivity and evaluated their diagnostic capability in a nested classification framework. This framework consist of a K-fold cross-validation scheme for training an XGBoost model. Within each fold, the model is trained exclusively on statistically significant connections selected using the Mann–Whitney U test computed on the training set, thereby preventing data leakage.

3 Results and Discussion

The proposed framework enabled the extraction of neural-related fNIRS components through CEEMDAN decomposition followed by Hilbert spectral analysis. The selected IMFs, whose dominant frequencies lay within the expected neurovascular band (0.01–0.08 Hz), provided a stable representation of neural activity while attenuating physiological and instrumental noise. This preprocessing step proved essential for improving the interpretability of the functional connectivity patterns derived from the data. In this work, we have focused on the fNIRS signals from the 40 Hz, given its well-established relevance to phonological processing. Accordingly, the results presented in this section correspond to this stimulus. Figure 3 shows a graph representation of the mean connectivity matrix of control subjects on the left and participants with dyslexia on the right. The connectivity matrices represent the functional connections measured with Pearson correlation coefficient between the fNIRS channels in left and right hemisphere. These channels are numbered from 1 to 20, being the first 10 in the left hemisphere and from 11 onward in the right hemisphere. Therefore, for each subject we have a total of 100 possible connections.

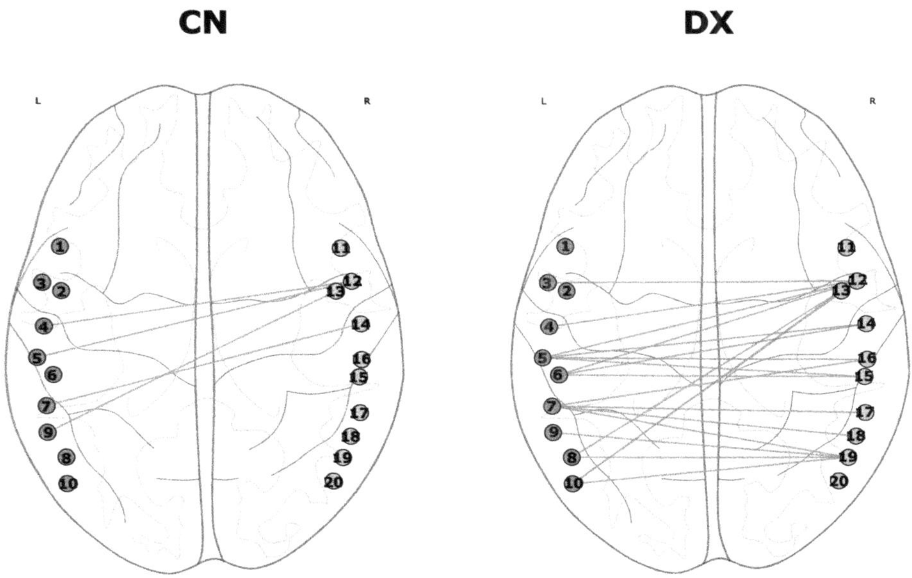

Fig. 3. Mean interhemispheric functional connectivity for control (left) and participants with dyslexia (right).

Interhemispheric functional connectivity analysis revealed consistent differences between the control and dyslexic groups. Several channel pairs exhibited statistically significant alterations, as identified by the Mann–Whitney U test. Figure 4 depicts the connections with significant differences between control and dyslexic groups. We can identify significant functional connections from left fronto-temporal area to right parietal area (channel 1 to 18), from left and right temporoparietal area (channel 5 to 16), from left temporoparietal to right parietal area (channel 5 to 19), from left temporoparietal to right temporal area (channel 7 to 14), and from left temporoparietal to right parietal area (channel 7 to 19).

Finally, in Table 1 we present the classification results obtained with the nested approach combining Mann–Whitney U test and XGBoost. The results assess the discriminative potential of the significant interhemispheric functional connectivity features. The XGBoost classifier achieved stable performance across folds, reaching a balanced accuracy of 0.71, and demonstrating that interhemi-

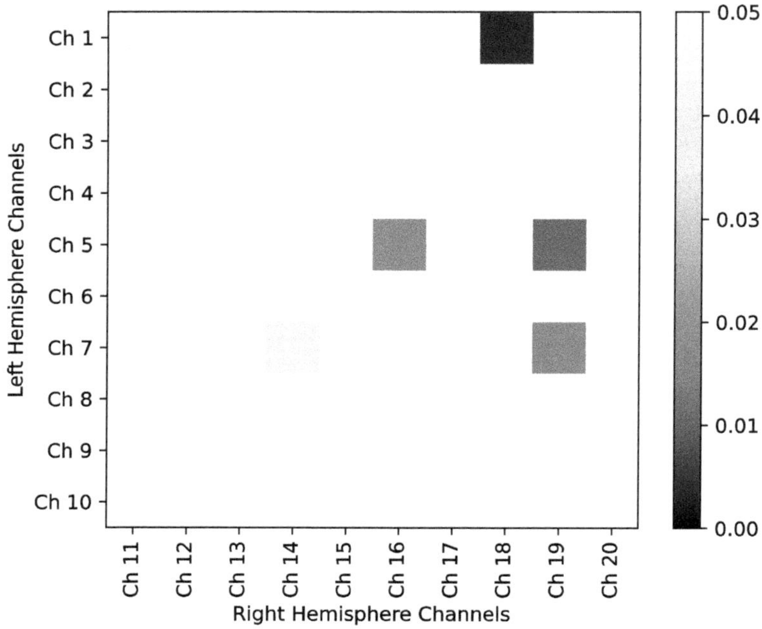

Fig. 4. Significant interhemispheric functional connections from Mann–Whitney U test.

spheric connectivity derived from extracted neural fNIRS components with the Hilbert spectrum based approach contains relevant diagnostic information.

Table 1. Performance of the nested classification framework using XGBoost.

Metric	Mean	SD
Balanced Accuracy	0.71	0.09
AUC	0.69	0.13
Sensitivity	0.60	0.08
Specificity	0.82	0.16

4 Conclusions

The proposed methodology enables the evaluation of the diagnostic potential of interhemispheric functional connectivity derived from the neural components of fNIRS signals extracted using the proposed Hilbert spectrum-based approach, providing insight into its ability to discriminate between groups. The findings confirm the suitability of CEEMDAN combined with Hilbert spectral analysis for isolating meaningful neural activity in fNIRS data. Furthermore, the observed differences between groups support the role of interhemispheric connectivity as a sensitive neurophysiological marker associated with dyslexia. These results not only validate the robustness of the proposed methodology but also highlight its potential applicability to other experimental paradigms and neurological conditions, including disorders characterized by altered neural synchronization such as epilepsy.

Acknowledgments. This research is part of the PID2022-137461NB-C32 funded by MICIU/AEI/10.13039/501100011033 and by ERDF/EU and TIC251-G-FEDER project, funded by ERDF/EU (Universidad de Málaga). Work by I.R.-R. is part of the grant RYC2023-045296-I funded by MICIU/AEI/10.13039/501100011033 and by ESF+.

References

1. Colominas, M.A., Schlotthauer, G., Torres, M.E.: Improved complete ensemble EMD: a suitable tool for biomedical signal processing. Biomed. Signal Process. Control **14**, 19–29 (2014). https://doi.org/10.1016/j.bspc.2014.06.009
2. Duan, L., Zhang, Y.J., Zhu, C.Z.: Quantitative comparison of resting-state functional connectivity derived from fNIRS and fMRI: a simultaneous recording study. Neuroimage **60**(4), 2008–2018 (2012). https://doi.org/10.1016/j.neuroimage.2012.02.014
3. Hemmati Berivanlou, N., Setarehdan, S.K., Ahmadi Noubari, H.: Evoked hemodynamic response estimation using ensemble empirical mode decomposition based adaptive algorithm applied to dual channel functional near infrared spectroscopy (fNIRS). J. Neurosci. Methods **224**, 13–25 (2014). https://doi.org/10.1016/j.jneumeth.2013.12.007
4. Huang, N.E., Shen, Z., Long, S.R., Wu, M.C., Shih, H.H., Zheng, Q., Yen, N.C., Tung, C.C., Liu, H.H.: The empirical mode decomposition and the Hilbert spectrum for nonlinear and non-stationary time series analysis. Proc. R. Soc. Lond. Ser. A Math. Phys. Eng. Sci. (1998). https://doi.org/10.1098/rspa.1998.0193
5. Naseer, N., Hong, K.S.: fNIRS-based brain-computer interfaces: a review. Front. Hum. Neurosci. **9** (2015). https://doi.org/10.3389/fnhum.2015.00003
6. Ortiz, A., et al.: Dyslexia diagnosis by EEG temporal and spectral descriptors: an anomaly detection approach. Int. J. Neural Syst. **30**(07), 2050029 (2020). https://doi.org/10.1142/S012906572050029X
7. Phillips, A.A., Chan, F.H., Zheng, M.M.Z., Krassioukov, A.V., Ainslie, P.N.: Neurovascular coupling in humans: physiology, methodological advances and clinical implications. J. Cereb. Blood Flow Metab. **36**(4), 647–664 (2016). https://doi.org/10.1177/0271678X15617954
8. Pinti, P., Scholkmann, F., Hamilton, A., Burgess, P., Tachtsidis, I.: Current status and issues regarding pre-processing of fNIRS neuroimaging data: an investigation of diverse signal filtering methods within a general linear model framework. Front. Hum. Neurosci. **12** (2019)
9. Scholkmann, F., et al.: A review on continuous wave functional near-infrared spectroscopy and imaging instrumentation and methodology. Neuroimage **85**, 6–27 (2014). https://doi.org/10.1016/j.neuroimage.2013.05.004

10. Torres, M.E., Colominas, M.A., Schlotthauer, G., Flandrin, P.: A complete ensemble empirical mode decomposition with adaptive noise. In: 2011 IEEE International Conference on Acoustics, Speech and Signal Processing (ICASSP), pp. 4144–4147 (2011). https://doi.org/10.1109/ICASSP.2011.5947265
11. Wu, Z., Huang, N.E.: Ensemble empirical mode decomposition: a noise-assisted data analysis method. Adv. Adapt. Data Anal. **01**(01), 1–41 (2009). https://doi.org/10.1142/S1793536909000047
12. Zhang, H., et al.: Functional connectivity as revealed by independent component analysis of resting-state fNIRS measurements. Neuroimage **51**(3), 1150–1161 (2010). https://doi.org/10.1016/j.neuroimage.2010.02.080
13. Zhang, Y., Sun, J., Rolfe, P.: Monte Carlo study for physiological interference reduction in near-infrared spectroscopy based on empirical mode decomposition. J. Mod. Opt. **57**(21), 2159–2169 (2010). https://doi.org/10.1080/09500340.2010.531152
14. Zhang, Y., Brooks, D.H., Franceschini, M.A., Boas, D.A.: Eigenvector-based spatial filtering for reduction of physiological interference in diffuse optical imaging. J. Biomed. Opt. **10**(1), 011014 (2005). https://doi.org/10.1117/1.1852552

Schizophrenia Detecting Using Reinforcement Learning-Based Active Learning and Hyperparameter Optimization

Mohammad Mahdi Motevalli[1(✉)], Seyed Vahid Moravvej[2], Roohallah Alizadehsani[3], and Juan M. Gorriz[4]

[1] Faculty of Engineering, Islamic Azad University, Central Tehran Branch, Tehran, Iran

[2] Department of Electrical and Computer Engineering, Isfahan University of Technology, Isfahan, Iran

[3] Institute for Intelligent Systems Research and Innovation (IISRI), Deakin University, Waurn Ponds, Australia

[4] Data Science and Computational Intelligence Institute, University of Granada,Granada, Spain

Abstract. Schizophrenia is a severe mental health condition that requires prompt and precise diagnosis. Traditional methods rely on deep convolutional neural networks (CNNs) and require large, pre-labeled image datasets, which are time-consuming and costly to compile. To solve this problem, we propose a novel active learning (AL) model that leverages deep reinforcement learning (DRL) to improve performance with fewer labeled samples. Unlike conventional methods that use heuristic selection independently of training, our approach dynamically integrates DRL to select unlabeled images for labeling. The model features multiple CNNs for feature extraction and fully connected layers for classification, trained on a limited set of labeled data and iteratively expanded via DRL-guided annotation. We also integrate a mutual learning-based artificial bee colony (ML-ABC) algorithm for optimized hyperparameter tuning. The algorithm modifies the selected food source by choosing the one with better fitness. This choice depends on a shared learning parameter between two agents. Tested on the COBRE and BrainGluSchi datasets, our model demonstrates robust accuracy with average F-measures of 93.092% and 91.238%, highlighting its efficacy and versatility in diagnosing schizophrenia.

Keywords: Schizophrenia · active learning · reinforcement learning · hyperparameter optimization · artificial bee colony

1 Introduction

Early detection of mental health conditions is a complex undertaking. Schizophrenia, a persistent mental health disorder, usually emerges in late ado-

J. M. Ferrández Vicente et al. (Eds.): IWINAC 2026, LNCS 16574, pp. 25–34, 2026.
https://doi.org/10.1007/978-3-032-27314-7_3

lescence or early adulthood and impacts approximately 1% of the global population. It is marked by symptoms such as hallucinations, delusions, and negative behaviors, including social withdrawal and self-neglect [1]. This paper aims to develop a deep learning model for schizophrenia detection.

In recent years, CNNs have significantly transformed schizophrenia research [2–7]. For example, SupriyaPatro et al. [8] developed a lightweight 3D CNN framework for classifying schizophrenia using MRI images, which boosts accuracy with an ensemble bagging classifier. Guo et al. [9] merged three-dimensional (3D) and 2D CNNs to classify schizophrenia using multimodal magnetic resonance imaging (MRI). This improves detection with squeeze-and-excitation blocks and a support vector machine. CNN models perform well only when they are trained on large and accurately labeled image datasets. However, preparing such datasets requires significant time, effort, and cost. For this reason, researchers need methods that either reduce annotation costs or limit the number of training samples needed. AL helps solve this problem. It selects the most useful unlabeled images for experts to label. These labeled samples are then used to train the model. Nevertheless, many traditional AL approaches rely on fixed criteria such as uncertainty or representativeness. These rules do not change as training progresses. A sample may seem uncertain early on, but later becomes easy to classify. Static methods ignore this shift, leading to redundant labeling, poor efficiency, and slower convergence, especially in medical imaging tasks where CNN learning patterns change notably across stages.

DRL modifies its data selection strategy over time by learning from training feedback. Unlike static approaches, it assesses the usefulness of labeling each instance and updates its policy to suit the model learning stage. This mechanism enables DRL to ignore samples that seem uncertain in early stages. Later, when these samples become easier to classify, labeling is no longer needed. This reduces redundant annotation and speeds up training [10]. Despite its benefits, DRL is vulnerable to changes in hyperparameters, which can affect its stability. To address this, researchers have used optimization methods such as grid search and genetic algorithms. Grid search works for simple parameter spaces but performs poorly in complex ones. Genetic algorithms adapt to difficult setups but require discrete parameters, limiting their flexibility. As a solution, metaheuristics like the ABC algorithm offer a compromise between exploration and exploitation. However, the performance of ABC weakens when it explores less and exploits in an unstable manner. To solve this, the present work introduces a mutual learning module into ABC. This enhancement improves collaboration among solutions, increases search diversity, boosts performance consistency, and helps avoid local optima, leading to more effective optimization outcomes [11].

This paper introduces an active learning framework designed for schizophrenia detection. It combines deep reinforcement learning for selecting samples with the ML-ABC algorithm for tuning hyperparameters. The main contribution is the combination of DRL and ML-ABC. This setup helps the model pick important samples and keep the training process stable and efficient. To the best of our knowledge, no prior research has applied this combined approach to schizophrenia diagnosis.

This paper is organized as follows: Sect. 2 presents the design and methods of the proposed model. Section 3 discusses datasets, evaluation measures, and a comprehensive analysis of results. Section 4 concludes with a summary and potential avenue for future work.

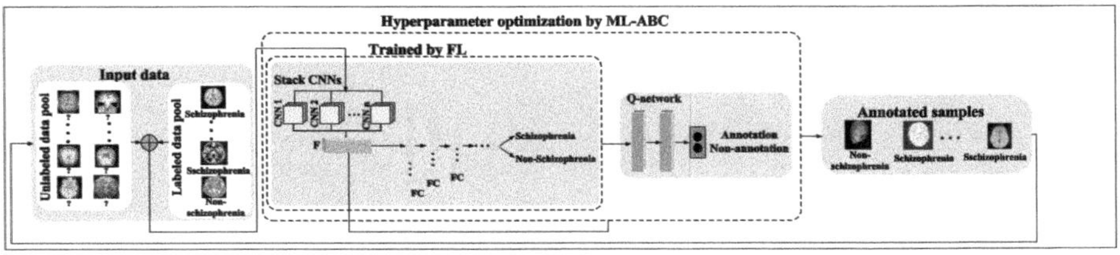

Fig. 1. Overview of the proposed schizophrenia detection framework. The system includes a classification module with parallel CNN branches and a Q-network for sample selection. Extracted features are fused and classified through FC layers. RL selects informative unlabeled samples, while ML-ABC optimizes hyperparameters to achieve stable, accurate training.

2 Materials and Methods

Figure 1 illustrates the proposed schizophrenia detection model, which uses a classifier with multiple CNN layers and a DRL to select crucial unlabeled data, and is optimized by an ML-ABC algorithm.

In this study, we examine an image dataset designated as $X = \{x_i\}_{i=1}^{N}$, where x_i represents the i-th image in our collection, and N denotes the total number of training images. Each image is associated with a class from a set $c = \{c_i\}$, with c_i corresponding to one of the C distinct classes. The subset of our dataset with labeled images is defined as $X_L = \{(x_{L_i}, y_{L_i})\}_{i=1}^{N_L}$, where x_{L_i} is the i-th labeled image, and y_{L_i} is its class label, and N_L is the number of labeled images. Meanwhile, the unlabeled images are grouped into $X_U = \{x_{U_i}\}_{i=1}^{N_U}$, with x_{U_i} identifying the i-th unlabeled image, and N_U indicating their total number.

The DRL model employed for sample selection is organized as follows:

State: At each decision-making point, the agent evaluates the current context, which encapsulates critical and pertinent information. The state is crafted by amalgamating feature vectors extracted by CNNs, f_i, along with their corresponding predicted scores, $f(x_i)$. These states are collectively represented as $S = \{s_i^t\}$, where $s_i^t = (f_i^t, f(x_i^t))$ and t marks the specific time instance.

Action: The possible actions in this model decide whether a human should label a sample. These options are represented as $= \{0, 1\}$. An action of $a_i^t = 1$ signals that the sample x_i^t should be labeled. Following this, a human annotates the sample, which is then added to the labeled dataset. The AL process continues until all potential samples are labeled or the labeling budget is exhausted.

Reward: Our reward mechanism, which significantly enhances the evaluation of the agent's actions, differs from traditional methods that delay rewards until the conclusion of a sequence. This approach ensures immediate feedback, effectively linking each decision to its long-term consequences. The reward system is divided into two segments:

1) For actions that lead to annotation ($a_i^t = 1$): The reward function applies a slight penalty of -0.2, $R(s_i^{t-1}, a_i^t) = -0.2$, which discourages unnecessary annotation and helps conserve resources.

2) For actions that avoid annotation ($a_i^t = 0$): The model defines m_c as the centroid of the feature vector for class c, calculated as follows:

$$m_c = \frac{1}{n_c} \sum_{i \in \pi_c} f_i \tag{1}$$

where $n_c = |\pi_c|$, represents the number of sample indices associated with class c. The calculated class centroids are then used to derive the entropy loss function for the unlabeled samples:

$$L(x_{U_i}, c) = -\sum_{j=1}^{C} \frac{e^{-(f_{U_i} - m_{c_j})^2}}{\sum_{j=1}^{C} e^{-(f_{U_i} - m_{c_j})^2}} \log \frac{e^{-(f_{U_i} - m_{c_j})^2}}{\sum_{j=1}^{C} e^{-(f_{U_i} - m_{c_j})^2}} \tag{2}$$

Here, f_{U_i} represents the feature vector of the i-th unlabeled image extracted by the CNNs. The reward function for the scenario where $a_i^t = 0$ is then defined as follows:

$$R(s_i^{t-1}, a_i^t) = \begin{cases} 1 & \text{if } L(x_{U_i}, c) < \partial \\ -1 & \text{if } L(x_{U_i}, c) > \partial \end{cases} \tag{3}$$

Here, $L(x_{U_i}, c)$ measures the entropy loss for the unlabeled image x_{U_i}, while ∂ serves as an adjustable parameter that dynamically adaptss based on the model's improving accuracy. This reward mechanism drives the model to label low-confidence samples, reflecting an evolution from traditional uncertainty-based methods. Early in training, when the model's reliability is low, ∂ is assigned a lower value, reflecting the initial unreliability of features extracted. As training progresses and the model annotates more samples, ∂ gradually increases, signaling improved dependability in feature extraction. This adaptive approach optimizes resource use by focusing annotations on samples crucial for learning as the model's accuracy improves.

Our model employs an array of CNNs, each featuring five 2D convolutional layers, progressively reducing the filter size from 128 to 8 to finely tune feature detection capabilities. Each convolutional layer uses 2 × 2 kernels, strides of 3, and padding of 4, optimizing the balance between feature extraction efficiency and spatial resolution. Following the convolutional stages, a 2 × 2 max-pooling layer minimizes the spatial dimensions of the feature maps while retaining essential features, thus boosting processing speed. The outputs from all CNNs merge into a single vector, F, which diverges into two separate pathways: the Q-network, which makes decisions about annotating data, and the classification channel, focused on detecting schizophrenia. To train the classifier, we apply focal loss (FL) [?] to address imbalances in classification. The Q-network's training commences with defining a sequence $(s_i^t, a_i^t, r_i^t, s_i^{t+1})$, representing a state transition in the reinforcement learning agent's experience. This sequence captures the process where the agent, upon executing action a_i^t in state s_i^t, receives a reward r_i^t and moves to the next state s_i^{t+1}. Subsequently, we employ the deep Q-learning technique to learn the data selection policy.

Table 1. Overview of hyperparameters used in the study

Hyperparameter	Range	Best
Batch size	16 to 1024	74
Learning rate	[0.0001 to 0.1]	0.005
Epoch	32 to 2048	253
Activation function	{ReLU, Leaky ReLU, Tanh, Sigmoid}	ReLU
Dropout rate	[0–1]	0.3
Number of stacked CNNs	1 to 8	3

2.1 Optimization of Hyperparameters

Hyperparameter tuning is critical in DRL, as it significantly impacts model performance and accuracy. Table 1 shows the hyperparameters used in the proposed model. The ranges for these parameters were determined based on previous research on detecting schizophrenia. To identify the most suitable configuration, we used the random key technique in combination with the ML-ABC algorithm.

The random-key method encodes hyperparameters as numeric vectors, known as keys, which are then manipulated by evolutionary algorithms to find optimal solutions. Each vector represents a potential solution, with its elements corresponding to different hyperparameters. These vectors undergo operations like mutation, crossover, and selection to explore and exploit the search space. The random key technique simplifies the adaptation of continuous search strategies to discrete hyperparameter settings, ensuring a diverse exploration of possibilities and improving the robustness and efficiency of the optimization process. This method is particularly useful in complex models where traditional optimization approaches may need help to converge or find global optima.

The ML-ABC algorithm. In this study, a modified ABC algorithm is applied to strengthen the random key mechanism. The standard ABC method maintains a balance between exploration and exploitation. This property makes it suitable for optimization tasks. In the classical update rule, a new position for the i-th solution in the j-th dimension is generated as follows:

$$v_i^j = x_i^j + \varphi(x_i^j - x_k^j) \tag{4}$$

Here, x_i^j denotes the j-th dimension of the i-th candidate solution. The index k indicates another randomly selected solution such that $k \neq i$. The coefficient φ is a random number in the range $[0, 1]$. If the new position v_i^j provides better fitness, it replaces the current one. Otherwise, the original position is retained. Since this update depends only on two solutions, it may cause unstable search behavior.

To improve stability, the proposed ML-ABC incorporates fitness information from both interacting solutions. The update rule is defined as:

$$v_i^j = \begin{cases} x_i^j + \varphi(x_k^j - x_i^j), & \text{if } Fit_i < Fit_k \\ x_k^j + \varphi(x_i^j - x_k^j), & \text{if } Fit_i \geq Fit_k \end{cases} \tag{5}$$

In this formulation, Fit_i and Fit_k represent the fitness values of solutions i and k, respectively. The parameter φ is generated as a uniformly distributed integer in the interval $[0, F]$, where F is a nonnegative constant called the mutual learning factor. The new position v_i^j is influenced by the solution with better fitness. This mechanism guides the search toward higher-quality regions. The factor F controls the strength of the perturbation. Small values encourage stronger interaction, while very large values may weaken both exploration and exploitation.

3 Experiments

To assess the effectiveness of our proposed model, we utilized two public datasets: COBRE [12] and BrainGluSchi [13]. The COBRE dataset comprises 72 individuals diagnosed with schizophrenia and 75 healthy controls, with ages ranging from 18 to 65 years in each group. The BrainGluSchi dataset includes 71 individuals with schizophrenia and 80 healthy participants. Our model underwent rigorous comparisons with state-of-the-art models in the evaluation phase, including 3D Resnet [4], AI-GAN [5], 3D-CNN [8], CNN-SVM [9], T1-CNN [6], and VGG19-Adam [7]. Additionally, we conducted ablation studies to determine the contributions of the AL and hyperparameter optimization (HO) components in our model. The outcomes of these studies across both datasets are detailed in Tables 2 and 3.

For the COBRE dataset, AI-GAN outperforms the other compared models, achieving higher F-measure and AUC values, indicating better classification and predictive performance. 3D-CNN performs worst across all metrics, highlighting its limitations in this context. The proposed model demonstrates significant improvements, surpassing the best-performing comparison model (AI-GAN) by approximately 6.5% in accuracy, 4.5% in F-measure, and 4.5% in AUC, underscoring its advanced predictive capabilities. Compared to its derivatives without AL and HO, the fully equipped proposed model shows enhancement, with an increase of over 4% in accuracy and about 3% in both F-measure and AUC, validating the efficacy of integrating AL and HO. Moreover, in the BrainGluSchi dataset, AI-GAN again leads the compared models in F-measure and AUC. T1-CNN and VGG19-Adam perform notably poorly, which may reflect issues with their architectures in handling this dataset. The proposed model delivers a substantial boost, improving accuracy by roughly 6.5%, F-measure by 5%, and AUC by 3.5% over the highest scores achieved by AI-GAN, thereby highlighting its robustness. Compared to its variants lacking AL and HO, the complete proposed model achieves about 2% higher accuracy, 4% higher F-measure, and 1.3% higher AUC, underscoring the critical role of these components in improving model performance.

Table 2. Comparative performance metrics of the proposed model against established models on the COBRE dataset

Model	Accuracy	F-measure	AUC
3D Resnet [4]	87.104 ± 0.068	87.711 ± 0.059	0.812 ± 0.069
AI-GAN [5]	87.125 ± 0.065	89.003 ± 0.093	0.829 ± 0.005
3D-CNN [8]	84.552 ± 0.057	85.966 ± 0.038	0.782 ± 0.075
CNN-SVM [9]	85.965 ± 0.017	86.652 ± 0.088	0.797 ± 0.067
T1-CNN [6]	81.861 ± 0.003	83.494 ± 0.050	0.761 ± 0.029
VGG19-Adam [7]	83.330 ± 0.036	83.500 ± 0.069	0.771 ± 0.031
Proposed w/o AL	88.834 ± 0.018	89.811 ± 0.092	0.839 ± 0.087
Proposed w/o HO	90.380 ± 0.070	90.615 ± 0.076	0.850 ± 0.011
Proposed	**92.919 ± 0.011**	**93.092 ± 0.067**	**0.866 ± 0.024**

Table 3. Comparative performance metrics of the proposed model against established models on the BRAINGLUSCHI dataset

Model	Accuracy	F-measure	AUC
3D Resnet [4]	83.497 ± 0.055	84.695 ± 0.032	0.804 ± 0.009
AI-GAN [5]	84.739 ± 0.062	86.216 ± 0.093	0.822 ± 0.088
3D-CNN [8]	80.228 ± 0.004	82.047 ± 0.092	0.781 ± 0.088
CNN-SVM [9]	81.909 ± 0.070	82.716 ± 0.095	0.793 ± 0.062
T1-CNN [6]	79.955 ± 0.069	79.461 ± 0.057	0.749 ± 0.094
VGG19-Adam [7]	79.281 ± 0.008	81.199 ± 0.069	0.764 ± 0.036
Proposed w/o AL	87.726 ± 0.009	86.746 ± 0.091	0.835 ± 0.074
Proposed w/o HO	88.936 ± 0.036	87.747 ± 0.005	0.845 ± 0.072
Proposed	**90.329 ± 0.039**	**91.238 ± 0.074**	**0.858 ± 0.046**

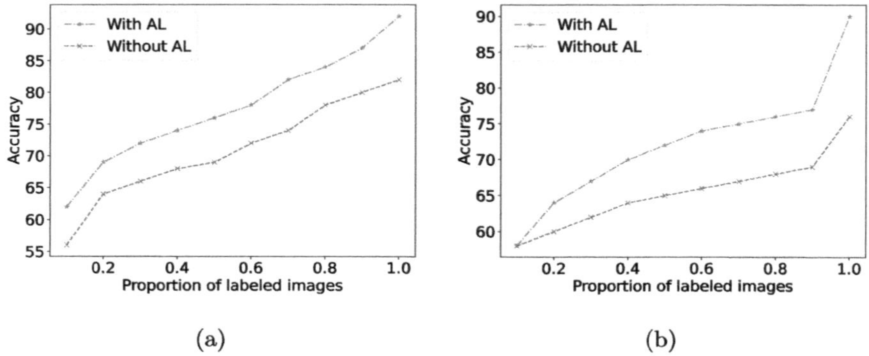

Fig. 2. Performance comparison of the model with and without AL on a) COBRE and b) BrainGluSchi datasets.

Figure 2 compares the performance of the model with and without AL on the COBRE and BrainGluSchi datasets. Active learning significantly improves accuracy across both datasets, with a particularly noticeable impact as the proportion of labeled images increases, demonstrating its effectiveness in enhancing learning efficiency and model robustness.

Tables 4 and 5 show the performance of the proposed ABC algorithm against a collection of well-established metaheuristic optimization algorithms, including the salp swarm algorithm (SSA), cuckoo optimization algorithm (COA), firefly algorithm (FA), bat algorithm (BA), differential evolution (DE), and original ABC. On COBRE, the proposed ABC outperforms the original ABC by approximately 9% accuracy and 4% F-measure. In the BrainGluSchi dataset, the proposed ABC achieves roughly 3% higher accuracy and 5% higher F-measure than the original ABC, highlighting its superior optimization capabilities.

Table 4. Comparative performance metrics of the proposed ABC against established metaheuristic algorithms on the COBRE dataset

Model	Accuracy	F-measure	AUC
SSA	79.359 ± 0.090	83.227 ± 0.089	0.755 ± 0.043
COA	80.411 ± 0.045	84.426 ± 0.002	0.768 ± 0.040
FA	81.740 ± 0.068	85.878 ± 0.096	0.784 ± 0.040
BA	83.313 ± 0.066	86.880 ± 0.007	0.794 ± 0.094
DE	84.889 ± 0.017	88.476 ± 0.001	0.810 ± 0.007
ABC	85.327 ± 0.093	89.595 ± 0.084	0.821 ± 0.080
Proposed ABC	**92.919 ± 0.011**	**93.092 ± 0.067**	**0.866 ± 0.024**

Table 5. Comparative performance metrics of the proposed ABC against established metaheuristic algorithms on the BRAINGLUSCHI dataset

Model	Accuracy	F-measure	AUC
SSA	77.524 ± 0.056	80.460 ± 0.001	0.731 ± 0.058
COA	78.230 ± 0.078	81.656 ± 0.079	0.742 ± 0.040
FA	78.475 ± 0.082	82.543 ± 0.031	0.759 ± 0.078
BA	80.431 ± 0.021	84.831 ± 0.003	0.769 ± 0.081
DE	86.973 ± 0.047	85.972 ± 0.015	0.785 ± 0.077
ABC	87.286 ± 0.061	86.373 ± 0.100	0.797 ± 0.048
Proposed ABC	**90.329 ± 0.039**	**91.238 ± 0.074**	**0.858 ± 0.046**

4 Conclusions

Our study introduces a novel AL model that leverages DRL to improve schizophrenia diagnosis with fewer labeled samples. Our approach significantly outperforms traditional methods by dynamically integrating DRL into the ML-ABC algorithm for selective labeling during hyperparameter optimization. On the COBRE and BrainGluSchi datasets, the model achieved impressive F-measures of 93.092% and 91.238%, respectively. This demonstrates the model's practical value by reducing reliance on extensive manual annotation. It also speeds up dataset construction and enables efficient training with limited labeled data.

In future work, the model should be evaluated on larger, more diverse datasets to improve generalizability. This can be achieved by collaboration with additional medical institutions to access broader imaging repositories. The second limitation is the complexity of the proposed DRL-based AL framework, which may hinder deployment in real clinical environments. Future studies can simplify the architecture, apply model compression, or explore lightweight CNN backbones. A third limitation concerns privacy risks when sharing patient images for training. This issue may be reduced by using federated learning, anonymization pipelines, or secure multi-party computation to enable training across centers without exposing sensitive data.

References

1. Gao, J., et al.: Exploring schizophrenia classification through multimodal MRI and deep graph neural networks: unveiling brain region-specific weight discrepancies and their association with cell-type specific transcriptomic features. Schizophr. Bull. **51**(1), 217–235 (2025)
2. Khan, F.S., Ninoria, S.: Schizophrenia detection from EEG spectrograms using transfer learning and self-distillation methods. In: Proceedings of the Indian National Science Academy, pp. 1–18(2026)

3. Paul, V.M., et al.: OGTCN-E-MGO: an optimized deep learning framework for EEG-based schizophrenia detection. Phys. Eng. Sci. Med. 1–15 (2026)
4. Weng, T., Zheng, Y., Xie, Y., Qin, W., Guo, L.: Diagnosing schizophrenia using deep learning: novel interpretation approaches and multi-site validation. Brain Res. **1833**, 148876 (2024)
5. Saadatinia, M., Salimi-Badr, A.: An explainable deep learning-based method for schizophrenia diagnosis using generative data-augmentation. IEEE Access (2024)
6. Zhang, J., et al.: Detecting schizophrenia with 3d structural brain MRI using deep learning. Sci. Rep. **13**(1), 14433 (2023)
7. Mudholkar, S., Agrawal, A., Sisodia, D.S., Jagat, R.R.: Deep transfer learning for schizophrenia detection using brain MRI. In: International Conference on Biomedical Engineering Science and Technology, pp. 66–82. Springer (2023)
8. SupriyaPatro, P., Goel, T., VaraPrasad, S., Tanveer, M., Murugan, R.: Lightweight 3D convolutional neural network for schizophrenia diagnosis using MRI images and ensemble bagging classifier. Cogn. Comput. **16**(4), 2019–2035 (2024)
9. Guo, H., et al.: Discriminative analysis of schizophrenia patients using an integrated model combining 3d CNN with 2D CNN: a multimodal MR image and connectomics analysis. Brain Res. Bull. **206**, 110846 (2024)
10. Patel, U., Patel, V.: Active learning-based hyperspectral image classification: a reinforcement learning approach. J. Supercomput. **80**(2), 2461–2486 (2024)
11. Danaei, S., et al.: Myocarditis diagnosis: a method using mutual learning-based ABC and reinforcement learning. In: 2022 IEEE 22nd International Symposium on Computational Intelligence and Informatics and 8th IEEE International Conference on Recent Achievements in Mechatronics, Automation, Computer Science and Robotics (CINTI-MACRo), pp. 000265–000270. IEEE (2022)
12. Center for Biomedical Research Excellence (COBRE). COBRE Schizophrenia Imaging Dataset (2026). https://fcon1000.projects.nitrc.org/indi/retro/cobre.html. Accessed Feb 2026
13. SchizConnect Consortium. BrainGluSchi Schizophrenia Imaging Dataset (2026). https://www.schizconnect.org/data. Accessed Feb 2026

Drop in Transfer Entropy between EEG Bands during Auditory Steady-State Response in Developmental Dyslexia

I. Rodríguez-Rodríguez[1,2](✉), F. J. Enamorado-Martín[1], Inês Domingues[3], D. Castillo-Barnes[1,4], Nicolás J. Gallego-Molina[1,2], and A. Ortiz[1,2]

[1] Communications Engineering Department, University of Málaga, Málaga, Spain
[2] Andalusian Data Science and Computational Intelligence Institute (DaSCI), Granada, Spain
ignacio.rodriguez@ic.uma.es
[3] Polytechnic University of Coimbra, Coimbra, Portugal
[4] Instituto de Investigación Biomédica de Málaga (IBIMA), Málaga, Spain

Abstract. Developmental Dyslexia (DD) has been associated with alterations in the oscillatory dynamics involved in the temporal sampling of speech, particularly in the hierarchical mechanisms of coupling between slow and fast rhythms. This work investigates the direction and temporal evolution of Transfer Entropy (TE) between theta phase and gamma amplitude during sustained auditory stimulation, with the aim of identifying dynamic and spatial markers that distinguish typical readers from people with DD. EEG were recorded in a control group (34 subjects) and study group (15) under a 40 Hz stimulus. Bidirectional TE time series were estimated in successive EEG windows, extracting dynamic metrics and functional domains by channel and by wide time intervals. Subsequently, XGBoost classifiers were applied by channel $\times$ bin and importance analysis by means of permutation grouped by domains. The results show a selective decrease in TE in the theta $\rightarrow$ gamma direction between $\sim$20 and 45 s in the dyslexia group, with greater expression in left perisylvian electrodes related to language. This drop does not appear in the gamma$\rightarrow$theta direction, consistent with the asymmetric nature of phase-amplitude coupling described in hierarchical models of speech processing. The classification performance reaches AUC$\approx$0.88 in that time frame. The importance analysis confirms that forward-related features sustain discrimination between groups. The findings support the value of targeted TE as a dynamic and spatially specific biomarker for DD.

Keywords: Transfer Entropy · EEG · Dyslexia · Phase-Amplitude Coupling (PAC)

1 Introduction

Developmental dyslexia (DD) is a neurocognitive disorder characterized by persistent difficulties in phonological processing and in the acquisition of decoding

J. M. Ferrández Vicente et al. (Eds.): IWINAC 2026, LNCS 16574, pp. 35–44, 2026.
https://doi.org/10.1007/978-3-032-27314-7_4

and/or reading fluency, despite adequate educational opportunities [12]. In recent decades, electrophysiological evidence has shown that these difficulties are not limited to reduced behavioral performance, but are associated with reproducible differences in brain oscillatory dynamics and in the functional organization of networks involved in language [3]. However, diagnostic and screening procedures based exclusively on behavior are conditioned by motivational, contextual and schooling factors, which favors a late and heterogeneous identification. In this context, the use of neurophysiological markers acquires relevance due to their potential to capture temporal mechanisms of speech processing and contribute to a more mechanistically informed characterization of DD [1].

Speech processing is based on the ability of the auditory-cortical system to synchronize its activity with temporal regularities of the stimulus. The so-called cortical tracking of speech describes the alignment of low-frequency neural activity with temporal features of speech, such as temporal or "enveloping" contour, and is considered a relevant functional component in the segmentation and decoding of acoustic-linguistic information [7].

An influential theoretical framework that integrates these findings is the Temporal Sampling Framework (TSF) [6], which proposes that DD involves an alteration of the temporal sampling of speech by neural oscillations, with special emphasis on slow rhythms (theta) that structure phonemic linguistic units. Within this hierarchical architecture, a key operational mechanism for multi-scale integration is phase-amplitude coupling (PAC), whereby the slow oscillation phase modulates the amplitude of faster oscillations, contributing to the segmentation and temporal gain of local assemblies [9]. It is especially relevant that theta-gamma PAC in auditory cortex has been associated with speech processing efficiency and is proven to be linked to linguistic competence [13].

A frequent limitation of coupling analyses based on static estimators or global averages is that sustained auditory processing is not strictly stationary. In controlled periodic stimulation paradigms, such as auditory steady-state response (ASSR), the response shows temporal-dependent properties and may be conditioned by time-based consistency, variability, and adaptive mechanisms under sustained stimulation. Recent work has provided mechanistic evidence in humans that ASSR around 40 Hz can be explained by greater temporal consistency (lower latency variability), rather than by trivial increases in instantaneous amplitude [8]. It supports the need to characterize not only an estimation of coupling but how it evolves during stimulation.

From a methodological point of view, the classical PAC and other synchrony metrics describe statistical dependence, but do not determine the directionality of information exchange between bands. Transfer Entropy (TE) offers a nonlinear alternative to quantify effective targeted connectivity, and its use in neurophysiological signals has been critically evaluated [17]. This, combined with further advances in computing, modelling and artificial intelligence open up possibilities for new applications of these proposals [5].

Based on these considerations, the work is situated at the intersection between oscillatory models of speech processing and DD, the need to treat dynamics as a temporally evolutionary phenomenon, and the use of directed measures to approximate mechanisms. In particular, the analysis of the flow of information between EEG frequencies relevant to speech, (theta-gamma interaction), is proposed through bidirectional TE time series estimated in successive windows, so that it is possible to identify patterns of transients and directional asymmetries over time. This approach allows us to formulate and evaluate the hypothesis that DD could manifest not only as an average difference in coupling, but as a temporally localized alteration in the consistency of slow to fast flow during sustained exposure, consistent with TSF.

2 Materials and Method

2.1 Data: Acquisition and Preprocessing

The dataset included EEG signals recorded in two groups of participants: a group with typical reading development (34 subjects) and a group with a formal diagnosis of developmental dyslexia (15 subjects). The control group had a mean age of 94.1 ± 3.3 months, and the dyslexic group, 95.6 ± 2.9 months. The families gave informed consent in accordance with international ethical standards, in the frame of the Leeduca project (University of Málaga, Spain) [11].

The experimental task consisted of passive exposure to long-duration rhythmic auditory stimulus, modulated at 40 Hz, designed to induce a stable pattern of cortical synchronization in the delta-theta bands, relevant for temporal speech sampling. The signals were acquired with a standard recording system following the 10–20 arrangement, employing a 32-channel assembly at a sampling rate of 500 Hz. Impedances remained below 10 k Ω.

Preprocessing focused on removing artifacts and obtaining clean signals for oscillatory analysis. The EEG was re-referenced to Cz and band-pass filtering was applied with zero-phase FIR filters to preserve the phase of the rhythms of interest. For the slow-fast coupling analysis, two specific bands were extracted:

- Theta (4–8 Hz): band responsible for prosodic-syllabic sampling.
- Gamma (30–80 Hz): band related to phonemic processing.

2.2 Theta-Gamma Phase and Amplitude Extraction Using the Hilbert Transform

To obtain the instantaneous phase of the theta band and the amplitude envelope of the gamma band the Hilbert transform was used. It is widely used in EEG analysis [14], producing a quadrature component that, together with the original signal, defines the analytic signal:

$$z(t) = x(t) + j\,\mathcal{H}\{x(t)\} = A(t)e^{j\phi(t)} \tag{1}$$

From this representation are derived the instantaneous phase $\phi(t)$: extracted from the theta signal, and the instantaneous amplitude $A(t)$: derived from the gamma signal.

The phase is suitable for capturing the dynamics of slow oscillations that govern cortical excitability windows, while the gamma amplitude acts as an index of the fast activity modulated by these windows. The synchronization between both series constitutes a physiologically informative measure of slow-fast hierarchical interaction.

2.3 Transfer Entropy as a Directed PAC Measure

Directed Transfer Entropy. The TE [4] is a nonlinear index of effective connectivity that quantifies the directional influence of one time series on another. Thus, TE was used to formalize the flow of information between:

- Theta phase → Gamma amplitude (forward).
- Gamma Amplitude → Theta Phase (backward).

Mathematically, let X_t and Y_t be two stochastic processes that represent, respectively, the instantaneous phase in slow band (theta) and amplitude modulated in fast band (gamma). The directed TE quantifies the information that X_t's past provides about the future of Y_t, beyond that already provided by Y_t's past. Its formal definition is expressed as a conditional mutual information:

$$\begin{aligned} \mathrm{TE}_{X\to Y} &= I\left(Y_{t+1}; X_t^{(l)} \mid Y_t^{(k)}\right) \\ &= \sum_{y_{t+1},\, x_t^{(l)},\, y_t^{(k)}} p\left(y_{t+1}, x_t^{(l)}, y_t^{(k)}\right) \log \frac{p\left(y_{t+1} \mid x_t^{(l)}, y_t^{(k)}\right)}{p\left(y_{t+1} \mid y_t^{(k)}\right)} \end{aligned} \tag{2}$$

The objective was to identify directional asymmetries (predominance of slow → fast flow), consistent with hierarchical models of auditory processing.

Symbolic Discretization. To estimate TE over continuous signals, a discretization based on quantile partitions was used. Each signal (θ phase and γ amplitude) was discretized into B categories using percentile-based binning, with B fixed a priori (here $B = 10$), allowing conditional distributions to be approximated by means of transition counts. The choice of B balances resolution and statistical stability, ensuring sufficient sample counts within each temporal window. This way noise sensitivity is reduced and robust TE estimation under short time windows is facilitated. So, let be a continuous signal $s(t)$, a partition is constructed $\{\mathcal{I}_1, \dots, \mathcal{I}_B\}$ of the $s(t)$ range. In particular, if $s(t) \in \mathcal{I}_b, \quad \text{then } S_t = b, \qquad b \in \{1, \dots, B\}$.

This procedure generates a symbolic series $\{S_t\}$ whose structure allows approximate conditional distributions by empirical counts. The quantile discretization is especially suitable in EEG due to its invariance to scale and its robustness against non-Gaussian deviations, and has been recommended in contemporary phase-amplitude directed interactions research [15].

For each time window these symbolic sequences are they also recode in a dense alphabet $\{0, \ldots, K-1\}$, eliminating empty classes and improving the identification of effective transitions. Dense recoding reduces bias in probability estimation and improves behavior in short windows, a property highlighted in recent studies on estimation frequency-dependent directed connectivity [10].

2.4 Temporal Window and Bidirectional TE Calculation

The analysis was designed to capture the temporal evolution of targeted coupling during sustained stimulation. To do this, each record was subdivided into temporally contiguous windows, creating n windows of previously specified fixed duration (2 sec) balancing temporal resolution and statistical reliability by ensuring that each window contains enough samples to produce stable TE estimates while still preserving the temporal dynamics of the coupling. The central time of each window was obtained as a temporal reference. Let S_t be a symbolic series. For windows $w_j = [t_j^{(\mathrm{ini})}, t_j^{(\mathrm{end})}]$, $j = 1, \ldots, N$, we define $X^{(j)} = \{X_t : t \in w_j\}$ and $Y^{(j)} = \{Y_t : t \in w_j\}$ and we estimate $\mathrm{TE}_{\theta\to\gamma}(w_j)$ and $\mathrm{TE}_{\gamma\to\theta}(w_j)$, Producing the series $\{\mathrm{TE}_{\theta\to\gamma}(w_j)\}_{j=1}^{N}$ and $\{\mathrm{TE}_{\gamma\to\theta}(w_j)\}_{j=1}^{N}$.

Hence two independent estimators were calculated in each window, $\mathrm{TE}_{\theta\to\gamma}$ (forward) and $\mathrm{TE}_{\gamma\to\theta}$ (backward). The result was a time series of TEs per channel and per subject for both directions. This procedure allows characterizing transient variations, temporal stability and possible decoupling episodes [8].

2.5 Derived Variables and Feature Extraction

From the series of TE forward and TE backward in each window, statistical, dynamic and spectral indicators were extracted. All characteristics were calculated in parallel for forward and backward. The final set included:

- Basic statistics: mean, standard deviation, coefficient of variation, median, interquartile range, minimum, maximum, range, asymmetry and kurtosis.
- Forward-backward asymmetries: mean ratio and mean difference.
- Directional proportions: proportion of windows with forward>backward.
- Temporal dynamics: lag-1 autocorrelation, number of change points, maximum duration of high streaks.
- Spectral (FFT): dominant frequency, dominant power and spectral entropy.
- Linear trends: slope and significance index of the temporal trend.

These characteristics were calculated both on the entire time series and on time intervals ("bins") defined in seconds.

2.6 Domain Aggregation

To facilitate interpretation, the characteristics were grouped into two conceptual domains:

- Forward: Features derived exclusively from $\mathrm{TE}_{\theta\to\gamma}$.

– Backward: characteristics from $TE_{\gamma \to \theta}$.

For each domain and each channel, average values were calculated per group (control, dyslexia). The characteristics were normalized channel-by-channel using z-scores to ensure comparability.

2.7 Supervised Classification Using XGBoost

The classificatory analysis was performed by channel and by temporal bin, using the previously described features in Sect. 2.5 as input matrix. The labels corresponded to the diagnosis (control vs. dyslexia). A nested cross-validation approach was applied to avoid overfitting, by means of external loop (repeated partitions stratified to estimate generalizable performance) and internal loop (grid search of hyperparameters of the XGBoost model [2], such as maximum depth, learning rate, regularization).

The pipeline used the area under the ROC curve as the main metric. Mean precision, balanced accuracy, and F1 were also calculated for the positive class. The decision threshold for F1 was optimized in the training set of each partition. The results by canal × bin were also represented in topographic maps showing the classification performance by cortical region.

2.8 Explainability Through Permutation-Out-of-Fold

To interpret the importance of the characteristics, an approach based on permutation-out-of-fold was used, in which the importance of each variable is estimated in the cross-validation test sets, avoiding contamination between training and evaluation [18]. The drop in performance when swapping a feature reflects its predictive contribution. For each domain (forward, backward) an aggregate importance was also calculated, facilitating a more general level interpretation. This procedure allowed the identification of both relevant individual characteristics and temporal or spatial profiles of sensitivity to differences between groups.

3 Results and Discussion

Our results show a targeted drop in forward $TE(\theta \to \gamma)$ in the dyslexia group, robustly localized between ~20 and 45 s from the onset of rhythmic auditory stimulation. This decrease appears in all locations, but is topographically reinforced in left perisylvian regions linked to language processing (T7, P7, F7, FC5, CP5, TP9) [3], as shown by the time series and topoplots of the forward domain (Fig. 1). This spatial pattern is consistent with EEG reviews that place the dyslexia-control differences in left temporoparietal sites.

The absence of a comparable decrease in the backward direction ($\theta \to \gamma$) (Fig. 1) is consistent with the physiology of $\theta \to \gamma$ phase-amplitude coupling (PAC) and with hierarchical models of temporal sampling [9]. Specifically, MEG/EEG evidence indicates that $\theta \to \gamma$ coordination increases with intelligibility and linguistic competence, supporting that the predominant functional flow for

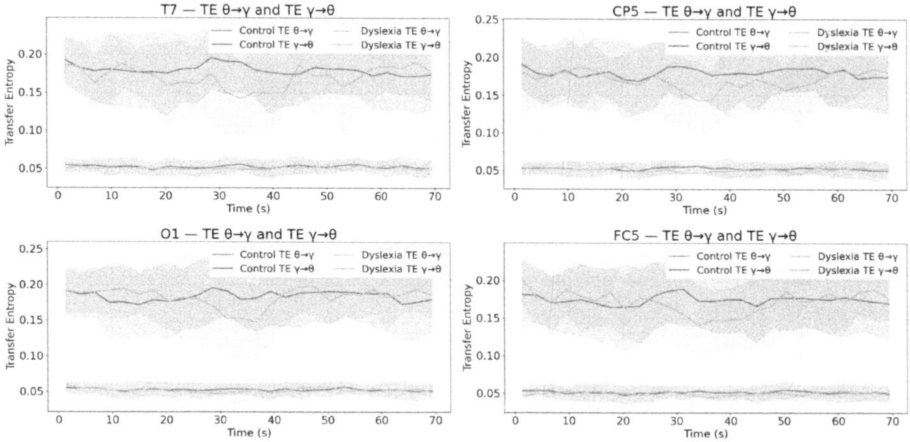

Fig. 1. Temporal evolution of TE in the control group and the study group in backward and forward. Each subplot corresponds to an electrode selected for its involvement in language processing.

phonemic parse is organized as slow $\rightarrow$ fast (θ phase modulating amplitude γ). In neural mass models and directed TE approaches (e.g., conditional TE, phase-TE), the directionality of information from slow to fast rhythms can be explicitly estimated and correlates with the effectiveness of the PAC [16]; in this framework, a reduced forward TE suggests a lower capacity of θ to "open" excitable windows that enhance γ, consistent with a functional decrease in PAC.

The temporally localized character of the alteration (20–45 s) links to recent results in steady-state auditory response paradigms (ASSR 40 Hz): the magnitude of ASSR does not depend only on instantaneous amplitude, but critically on temporal consistency (lower latency variability). A loss of consistency under sustained stimulation would degrade the functional synchronization of γ with slow rhythms in prolonged windows, especially during the 20-45 s range, and could contribute to the drop in forward TE that we observed [8].

The topomap representations of some features (Fig. 2, Fig. 3) show that the controls-dyslexia difference results in positive increases (mean controls minus

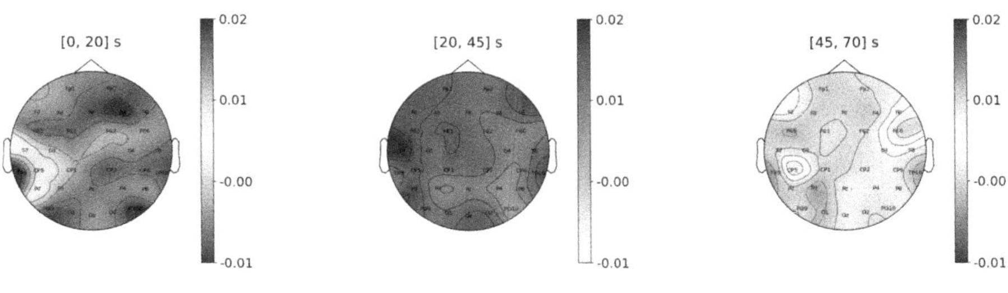

Fig. 2. Temporal evolution of the controls-dyslexia difference for TE Forward (mean per electrode).

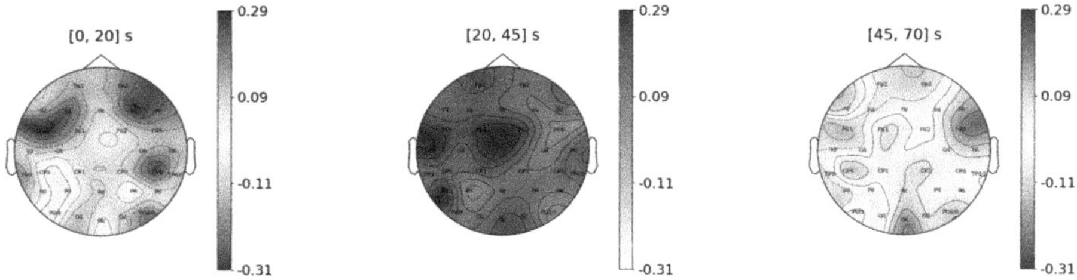

Fig. 3. Temporal evolution of the controls-dyslexia difference for Asymmetry Ratio (mean per electrode).

dyslexia mean) specifically by 20–45 s, and with slightly negative values outside that interval, indicating a greater degradation of $\theta \rightarrow \gamma$ flow in dyslexia.

Operationally, the channel × bin classifier with XGBoost overcomes AUC≈0.80 in the 20–45 s range in these near-language areas (Fig. 4). This performance is consistent with the neurophysiological pattern: the strip where the forward domain best separates the groups is precisely where the classifier obtains maximum performance, in electrodes that map regions with linguistic relevance. As a whole, the performance per channel is reflected in the maps and metrics (Table 1), and coincides with the literature that places the focus of dyslexia on the left temporoparietal and occipitotemporal nexus [3].

This pattern fits with the TSF [6], which postulates a deficit in the temporal sampling of speech by slow oscillations in dyslexia. Recent studies in nat-

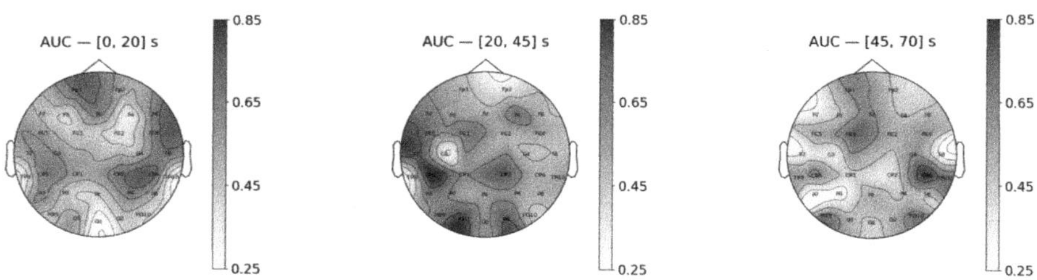

Fig. 4. AUC obtained by windows at each electrode.

Table 1. Key metrics obtained in electrodes involved in language processing [20–45]s.

Channel	AUC	Precision	F1	Balanced Accuracy
CP5	0.88	0.83	0.65	0.73
O1	0.80	0.70	0.59	0.70
T7	0.79	0.76	0.64	0.72
FC5	0.66	0.64	0.62	0.64

ural listening show atypical profiles in delta/theta that discriminate dyslexia against controls with AUC around 0.77–0.80 [1], reinforcing the causal role of slow rhythms in speech parsing. In this line, an atypical $\theta \rightarrow \gamma$ TE for 20–45 s is a plausible marker of deterioration of hierarchical coupling.

For the global interpretation, the permutation of variables by domain ("group-permutation") shows that the importance of the forward domain peaks at 20–45 s (Fig. 5), confirming that simultaneously breaking all the variables $\theta \rightarrow \gamma$ is what most degrades the AUC. Since importance by permutation measures the drop in performance when breaking relationships with the label, and does not require compensation between domains, this forward maximum demonstrates that the separation between groups is sustained by the foward set in that window.

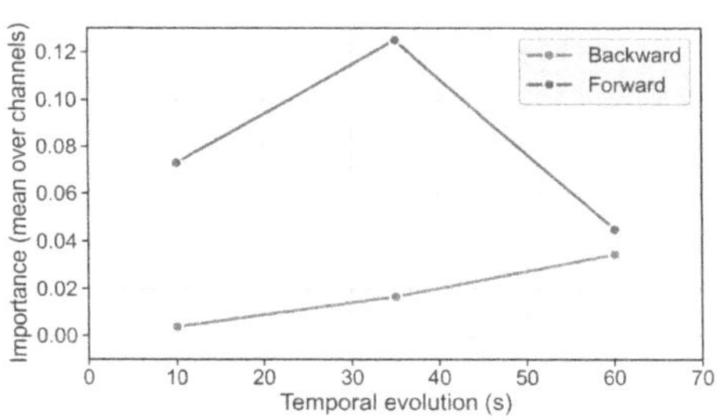

Fig. 5. Temporal evolution of importance obtained by permuting groups of features.

4 Conclusions

This study demonstrates that DD is characterized by a temporally localized alteration of the flow of theta → gamma information during sustained auditory stimulation, with maximum manifestation between 20–45 s and in left-wing language regions. The absence of changes in the reverse direction supports the hierarchical and asymmetric nature of PAC. The combination of targeted TE, domain analysis, and channel-specific classification reveals a consistent and robust pattern. These results suggest that forward dynamics is a useful biomarker for the identification and neurophysiological characterization of DD.

Acknowledments. This research is part of the PID2022-137461NB-C32 funded by MICIU/AEI/10.13039/501100011033 and by ERDF/EU and TIC251-G-FEDER project, funded by ERDF/EU (Universidad de Málaga). The work by I.R.-R. is part of the grant RYC2023-045296-I funded by MICIU/AEI/10.13039/501100011033 (Spain) and by ESF+.

References

1. Araújo, J., et al.: Atypical low-frequency cortical encoding of speech identifies children with developmental dyslexia. Front. Hum. Neurosci. **18**, 1403677 (2024)
2. Bentéjac, C., Csörgő, A., Martínez-Muñoz, G.: A comparative analysis of gradient boosting algorithms. Artif. Intell. Rev. **54**(3), 1937–1967 (2021)
3. Cainelli, E., Vedovelli, L., Carretti, B., Bisiacchi, P.: EEG correlates of developmental dyslexia: a systematic review. Ann. Dyslexia **73**(2), 184–213 (2023)
4. De La Pava Panche, I., Gómez-Orozco, V., Álvarez-Meza, A., Cárdenas-Peña, D., Orozco-Gutiérrez, Á.: Estimating directed phase-amplitude interactions from EEG data through kernel-based phase transfer entropy. Appl. Sci. **11**(21), 9803 (2021)
5. Górriz, J., et al.: Computational approaches to explainable artificial intelligence: advances in theory, applications and trends. Inf. Fusion **100**, 101945 (2023). https://doi.org/10.1016/j.inffus.2023.101945
6. Goswami, U.: A temporal sampling framework for developmental dyslexia. Trends Cogn. Sci. **15**(1), 3–10 (2011). https://doi.org/10.1016/j.tics.2010.10.001
7. Issa, M.F., Khan, I., Ruzzoli, M., Molinaro, N., Lizarazu, M.: On the speech envelope in the cortical tracking of speech. Neuroimage **297**, 120675 (2024)
8. Johnson, T.D., Gallagher, A.J., Coulson, S., Rangel, L.M.: Network resonance and the auditory steady state response. Sci. Rep. **14**(1), 16799 (2024)
9. Lizarazu, M., Carreiras, M., Molinaro, N.: Theta-gamma phase-amplitude coupling in auditory cortex is modulated by language proficiency. Hum. Brain Mapp. **44**(7), 2862–2872 (2023)
10. Lobier, M., Siebenhühner, F., Palva, S., Palva, J.M.: Phase transfer entropy: a novel phase-based measure for directed connectivity in networks coupled by oscillatory interactions. Neuroimage **85**, 853–872 (2014)
11. Ortiz, A., Martinez-Murcia, F.J., Luque, J.L., Giménez, A., Morales-Ortega, R., Ortega, J.: Dyslexia diagnosis by EEG temporal and spectral descriptors: an anomaly detection approach. Int. J. Neural Syst. **30**(07), 2050029 (2020)
12. Peterson, R.L., Pennington, B.F.: Developmental dyslexia. Lancet **379**(9830), 1997–2007 (2012). https://doi.org/10.1016/s0140-6736(12)60198-6
13. Poeppel, D., Idsardi, W.J., Van Wassenhove, V.: Speech perception at the interface of neurobiology and linguistics. Philosoph. Trans. Roy. Soc. B Biol. Sci. **363**(1493), 1071–1086 (2008). https://doi.org/10.1093/oso/9780199561315.003.0011
14. Rodríguez-Rodríguez, I., Ortiz, A., Gallego-Molina, N.J., Formoso, M., Woo, W.L.: EEG interchannel causality to identify source/sink phase connectivity patterns in developmental dyslexia. Int. J. Neural Syst. **33**(04), 2350020 (2023). https://doi.org/10.1142/s012906572350020x
15. Siebenhühner, F., et al.: Genuine cross-frequency coupling networks in human resting-state electrophysiological recordings. PLoS Biol. **18**(5), e3000685 (2020)
16. Sotero, R.C.: Topology, cross-frequency, and same-frequency band interactions shape the generation of phase-amplitude coupling in a neural mass model of a cortical column. PLoS Comput. Biol. **12**(11), e1005180 (2016)
17. Ursino, M., Ricci, G., Magosso, E.: Transfer entropy as a measure of brain connectivity: a critical analysis with the help of neural mass models. Front. Comput. Neurosci. **14**, 45 (2020)
18. Valente, G., Castellanos, A.L., Hausfeld, L., De Martino, F., Formisano, E.: Cross-validation and permutations in MVPA: validity of permutation strategies and power of cross-validation schemes. Neuroimage **238**, 118145 (2021)

Modeling and Predicting Age-at-Onset Trajectories in Genetic Frontotemporal Dementia Using Survival Methods

Juan E. Arco[1,2(✉)], Lena Marth[3,4], Sonja Schönecker[3], Francisco J. Martínez-Murcia[2,5], Catharina Prix[3], Olivia Wagemann[3,4], Elisabeth Wlasich[3], Alexander Bernhardt[3], Anna Stockbauer[3], Arabella Bouzigues[6], Lucy Chisman-Russell[6], Eve Ferry-Bolder[6], Phoebe H. Foster[6], Günter U. Höglinger[3,4,7], Jonathan D. Rohrer[6], Bradley F. Boeve[8], Adam L. Boxer[9], Howard J. Rosen[9], Hilary W. Heuer[9], Leah K. Forsberg[8], E. Marisa Ramos[9], Javier Ramírez[2,5], Juan M. Górriz[2], and Johannes Levin[3,4,7]

[1] Mind, Brain and Behavior Research Center, University of Granada, Granada, Spain
[2] Andalusian Research Institute in Data Science and Computational Intelligence (DasCI), University of Granada, Granada, Spain
jearco@ugr.es
[3] Department of Neurology, LMU University Hospital, LMU Munich, Munich, Germany
[4] German Center for Neurodegenerative Diseases (DZNE), Munich, Germany
[5] Department of Signal Theory, Networking and Communications, University of Granada, 18010 Granada, Spain
[6] Dementia Research Centre, Department of Neurodegenerative Disease, UCL Queen Square Institute of Neurology, London, UK
[7] Munich Cluster for Systems Neurology (SyNergy), Munich, Germany
[8] Department of Neurology, Mayo Clinic, Rochester, MN, USA
[9] Memory and Aging Center, UCSF, San Francisco, CA, USA

Abstract. Accurately predicting age at symptom onset in genetic frontotemporal dementia (FTD) remains challenging due to substantial inter-individual variability, even among carriers of distinct pathogenic variants within the same gene. Time-to-event models provide a natural framework to address this problem while accounting for right censoring in presymptomatic individuals. In this study, we analyze age-at-onset prediction in a multicenter cohort of individuals at genetic risk for FTD using a hierarchical survival modeling strategy. We first develop incremental Cox proportional hazards models to systematically evaluate the progressive predictive value of different covariate blocks. We then compare the best-performing Cox model with more flexible non-linear approaches, including DeepSurv and Random Survival Forests. Models are evaluated using strictly out-of-sample five-fold cross-validation, with performance assessed via the concordance index and the integrated Brier score.

The Genetic Frontotemporal Dementia Initiative (GENFI), on behalf of the ALLFTD Consortium.

J. M. Ferrández Vicente et al. (Eds.): IWINAC 2026, LNCS 16574, pp. 45–54, 2026.
https://doi.org/10.1007/978-3-032-27314-7_5

Our results show that genetic group and progenitor age at onset are the primary drivers of predictive performance, yielding clearly distinct symptom free survival trajectories across risk groups. Non-linear models do not substantially outperform the optimized Cox model, despite their increased flexibility. These findings indicate that Cox models capture most of the prognostic information available in this setting, providing a robust framework for modeling disease trajectories in genetic FTD.

Keywords: Frontotemporal dementia · Survival analysis · Age-at-onset prediction · Cox proportional hazards · Deep learning · Random survival forests

1 Introduction

Frontotemporal dementia (FTD) is a heterogeneous group of neurodegenerative disorders characterized by progressive behavioral, executive, language, and sometimes motor impairment [1]. A substantial proportion of cases are familial, most commonly involving autosomal dominant mutations in MAPT, GRN, or C9orf72 [2]. Although mutation carriers face a high lifetime risk of disease, age at symptom onset varies widely within and across genetic groups. Accurate prediction of onset is therefore clinically relevant, as it may inform patient monitoring and the timing of preventive or disease-modifying interventions [3]. However, substantial inter-individual variability and complex interactions between genetic and non-genetic factors make prognostic modeling challenging.

Previous studies have shown that genetic variants strongly influence age at onset, with *MAPT* carriers typically presenting earlier than those with C9orf72 or GRN mutations [4]. Additional factors such as sex, education, clinical phenotype, and family history may further modulate disease expression. In particular, parental age at onset has been suggested as a predictor of offspring onset, indicating partial heritability beyond the primary mutation. Time-to-event models provide a natural framework to analyze age at onset while accounting for right censoring [5]. The Cox proportional hazards model is widely used due to its interpretability [6], whereas more recent non-linear approaches, including deep neural networks and ensemble methods, aim to capture complex interactions [7].

In this work, we investigate the prediction of age at symptom onset in a large multicenter cohort of individuals at genetic risk for FTD. We adopt a principled, incremental modeling strategy in which covariates are added hierarchically to Cox proportional hazards models, allowing us to quantify the marginal contribution of genetic, clinical, and progenitor-related information. We further compare the best-performing Cox model with non-linear survival approaches, including DeepSurv and Random Survival Forests, using strictly out-of-sample evaluation. Our goal is to provide both interpretable insights into disease modifiers and a robust assessment of predictive performance across complementary survival modeling paradigms.

2 Materials and Methods

2.1 Dataset and Participants

This study used a harmonized dataset from the Genetic Frontotemporal Dementia Initiative (GENFI) and the ARTFL-LEFFTDS Longitudinal Frontotemporal Lobar Degeneration (ALLFTD) multicenter prospective cohorts, including individuals carrying pathogenic variants in C9orf72, GRN, or MAPT. GENFI comprises research centers across Europe and Canada, whereas ALLFTD is a predominantly US-based multicenter cohort including a genetic FTD sub-cohort. A total of 1376 presymptomatic and symptomatic carriers were screened. Seventy-eight individuals were excluded because both parents were affected by a neurodegenerative syndrome, 51 due to incomplete family history data, and 66 due to dataset inconsistencies or unclear symptomatic status, resulting in a final cohort of 1181 variant carriers (40.1% symptomatic). Participants either had one affected parent or no notable family history. Age at onset was retrospectively determined for most carriers and their affected parents based on medical history assessments. Diagnoses followed current clinical criteria and evaluations were conducted at specialized centers using standardized protocols. Ethical approval was obtained at all sites, and written informed consent was provided by all participants or their legal representatives.

The primary outcome was age at symptom onset. For symptomatic individuals, this corresponded to the clinically identified onset age, while for asymptomatic participants the age at last clinical assessment was used as a censoring time, resulting in a right-censored time-to-event formulation. Covariates were selected based on prior evidence and data availability. These included and years of education (demographics), genetic group, clinical phenotype at onset: dementia, Amyotrophic Lateral Sclerosis (ALS)/FTD, parkinsonism, or unaffected, and family history of neurodegenerative disease. To investigate parent-of-origin effects, parental age at symptom onset was included when available. Analyses involving parental age were restricted to participants for whom exactly one affected progenitor (father or mother) was known, and a binary indicator encoding progenitor type was included in selected models.

2.2 Data Preprocessing

No imputation of missing values was performed at any stage of the analysis. Subjects with missing values in any of the variables required for a given model were excluded from that specific analysis. This conservative strategy was adopted to avoid introducing artificial information and to ensure that all reported results rely only on observed data. Categorical variables were transformed using one-hot encoding, while continuous variables were standardized to zero mean and unit variance when required by the modeling approach. All preprocessing steps were performed independently within each training fold during cross-validation to prevent information leakage from the test data.

2.3 Cox Proportional Hazards Model

As a baseline approach, we employed the Cox proportional hazards model [8], a semi-parametric framework widely used for time-to-event analysis in the presence of right censoring. The Cox model relates individual covariates to the instantaneous risk of experiencing the event without requiring explicit specification of the baseline hazard function.

Let T denote age at symptom onset and $\mathbf{x} \in \mathbb{R}^p$ a vector of covariates. The Cox model defines the hazard function at time t as follows:

$$h(t \mid \mathbf{x}) = h_0(t) \exp\left(\boldsymbol{\beta}^\top \mathbf{x}\right), \tag{1}$$

where $h_0(t)$ is an unspecified baseline hazard and $\boldsymbol{\beta}$ is a vector of regression coefficients capturing the log-linear effect of the covariates. A key assumption of the model is proportional hazards, implying that covariate effects on the hazard are constant over time. Model parameters were estimated by maximizing the partial likelihood, which depends only on the ordering of observed event times and naturally accommodates right-censored observations. After coefficient estimation, the baseline cumulative hazard was obtained using the Breslow estimator [9], allowing individual-specific survival functions to be derived.

Cox models were fitted incrementally using different blocks of covariates to quantify the contribution of demographic, genetic, clinical, and familial information. Specifically, the covariate blocks included in each model are defined as follows:

- **Demographics (M1):** sex at birth and years of education.
- **Genetics (M2):** M1 plus genetic variant (GRN, MAPT, C9orf72).
- **Phenotype (M3):** M2 plus clinical phenotype at onset (e.g., dementia, ALS, ALS/FTD, parkinsonism).
- **Family history (M4):** M3 plus parental inheritance information (maternal, paternal, or none).
- **Progenitor age (M5):** M4 plus age at symptom onset of the affected progenitor (father or mother).
- **Progenitor type (M6):** M5 plus progenitor sex indicator (father vs. mother).

This incremental design enables a principled evaluation of how each covariate block contributes to predictive performance and risk stratification.

2.4 DeepSurv: Non-linear Cox Modeling

Although the Cox proportional hazards model offers interpretability and robustness, it assumes a linear relationship between covariates and the log-hazard, which may be restrictive in complex biomedical settings. To relax this assumption while preserving the proportional hazards framework, we employed DeepSurv [7], a deep learningâĂŞbased extension of the Cox model. In DeepSurv, the linear predictor is replaced by a non-linear function learned by a neural network. Formally, the hazard function is defined as follows:

$$h(t \mid \mathbf{x}) = h_0(t) \exp\left(f_\theta(\mathbf{x})\right), \tag{2}$$

where $f_\theta(\mathbf{x})$ denotes the output of a neural network with parameters θ. As in the standard Cox model, the baseline hazard $h_0(t)$ remains unspecified during training, and the proportional hazards assumption is preserved. Model parameters were learned by minimizing the negative Cox partial log-likelihood, with the neural network output replacing the linear risk score. After training, individual survival functions were derived using the estimated baseline hazard combined with the predicted risk scores, following the same procedure as in the Cox model.

We implemented the DeepSurv model as a fully connected multilayer perceptron with two hidden layers, using rectified linear unit (ReLU) activations and dropout regularization to reduce overfitting. The network was trained by minimizing the negative Cox partial log-likelihood with gradient-based optimization, and early stopping based on validation performance was applied to prevent overtraining. This architecture provides sufficient flexibility to capture non-linear covariate effects while maintaining a relatively compact model size.

2.5 Random Survival Forests

As a fully non-parametric alternative, we employed Random Survival Forests (RSF) [10], an ensemble method that extends random forests to right-censored time-to-event data. Unlike Cox-based approaches, RSF does not assume proportional hazards or a specific functional relationship between covariates and risk, allowing it to capture complex non-linear effects and interactions in a data-driven manner.

RSF builds an ensemble of survival trees trained on bootstrap samples of the data, using random subsets of covariates at each split. Node splits are selected to maximize survival differences, typically via a log-rank criterion. For a given individual, each tree yields a node-specific cumulative hazard estimate, which is commonly computed using the Nelson–Aalen estimator. The ensemble cumulative hazard function is obtained by averaging across trees:

$$\hat{H}(t \mid \mathbf{x}) = \frac{1}{B} \sum_{b=1}^{B} \hat{H}_b(t \mid \mathbf{x}), \tag{3}$$

and the corresponding survival function follows as

$$\hat{S}(t \mid \mathbf{x}) = \exp\Big(-\hat{H}(t \mid \mathbf{x})\Big).$$

In contrast to Cox and DeepSurv models, which explicitly parameterize the hazard function $h(t \mid \mathbf{x})$, RSF directly estimates the cumulative hazard function $H(t \mid \mathbf{x})$. Predicted survival probabilities are therefore obtained through the standard relationship between cumulative hazard and survival.

RSF models were trained using an ensemble of survival trees grown on bootstrap samples of the training data, with standard log-rank splitting criteria and a fixed number of trees. At each split, a random subset of covariates was considered to promote diversity among trees and reduce variance. Ensemble predictions were obtained by averaging tree-specific cumulative hazard estimates, yielding stable survival probability estimates across the covariate space.

2.6 Validation Strategy and Performance Metrics

All models were evaluated using stratified five-fold cross-validation to obtain an unbiased estimate of out-of-sample performance. In each fold, data were split into disjoint training and test sets, with all preprocessing steps (including feature scaling and model fitting) performed exclusively on the training data and then applied to the corresponding test set. Performance metrics were computed on each test fold and summarized as mean $\pm$ standard deviation across folds.

Predictive discrimination was assessed using Harrell's concordance index (C-index) [11], a rank-based measure that quantifies a model's ability to correctly order individuals according to their risk of experiencing the event. Formally, the C-index estimates the probability that, for a comparable pair of individuals, the subject with higher predicted risk experiences the event earlier, as follows:

$$C = \Pr(\eta_i > \eta_j \mid T_i < T_j, \delta_i = 1), \tag{4}$$

where η_i denotes the predicted risk score. To evaluate calibration and overall probabilistic accuracy, we additionally computed the Integrated Brier Score (IBS) [12]. The time-dependent Brier score at time t measures the squared error between the observed survival status and the predicted survival probability, as follows:

$$\text{BS}(t) = \mathbb{E}\left[\left(\mathbb{I}(T > t) - \hat{S}(t \mid \mathbf{x})\right)^2\right]. \tag{5}$$

To account for right censoring, inverse probability of censoring weighting (IPCW) was applied, using a Kaplan–Meier estimator of the censoring distribution. The IBS summarizes prediction error over a predefined time interval $[t_{\min}, t_{\max}]$ as

$$\text{IBS} = \frac{1}{t_{\max} - t_{\min}} \int_{t_{\min}}^{t_{\max}} \text{BS}(t)\, dt. \tag{6}$$

Lower IBS values indicate better calibrated and more accurate survival predictions.

3 Results

We first evaluated the incremental contribution of different covariate blocks using Cox proportional hazards models trained and assessed under a strictly out-of-sample cross-validation framework. Table 1 summarizes the predictive performance of the hierarchical models (M1–M6), reporting discrimination and calibration in terms of the C-index and the IBS, respectively. The baseline M1 model exhibited limited predictive ability, with a C-index close to chance level and the highest IBS among all models. The inclusion of genetic variant in M2 resulted in a substantial improvement in performance, increasing the C-index by more than 0.17 and reducing the IBS accordingly. A further marked gain was observed when adding clinical phenotype at onset (M3), yielding a C-index above 0.80 and a pronounced reduction in prediction error. In contrast, the addition of family history information in M4 did not lead to further improvements, with performance metrics remaining comparable to those of M3. Incorporating parental age at symptom onset in M5 produced the best overall performance, achieving the highest C-index and the lowest IBS across all models. Finally, adding progenitor type (maternal vs. paternal) in M6 did not provide additional benefit beyond M5, suggesting limited incremental value of this variable once parental age at onset was accounted for.

Table 1. Out-of-sample performance of incremental Cox proportional hazards models. They are built hierarchically by progressively adding blocks of covariates. Performance is reported as mean ± standard deviation across folds for the C-index (higher is better) and the IBS (lower is better).

Model	Variables	C-index (mean ± SD)	IBS (mean ± SD)
M1	Demographics	0.528 ± 0.024	0.176 ± 0.010
M2	M1 + Genetics	0.699 ± 0.018	0.152 ± 0.008
M3	M2 + phenotype	0.801 ± 0.017	0.132 ± 0.007
M4	M3 + family history	0.795 ± 0.020	0.132 ± 0.008
M5	**M4 + progenitor age**	**0.817 ± 0.016**	**0.129 ± 0.010**
M6	M5 + progenitor type	0.816 ± 0.018	0.129 ± 0.010

To facilitate the interpretation of the incremental Cox models, we focus on those model transitions that resulted in the largest improvements in predictive performance. Figure 1(a) therefore illustrates the Cox-predicted survival curves stratified by genetic group, highlighting how the addition of genetic information translates into clearly distinct age-at-onset risk trajectories. Notably, MAPT variant carriers exhibit a substantially lower survival probability compared with the other genetic groups. Around the age of 60 years, their predicted survival probability is markedly reduced relative to C9orf72 carriers and is several-fold lower than that observed in GRN carriers. These results highlight the central role of genetic status in shaping age-at-onset risk.

Figure 1(b) illustrates the Cox-predicted survival curves stratified by clinical phenotype after adding phenotype information to the demographic and genetic covariates (Model M3). The inclusion of clinical phenotype further refines the

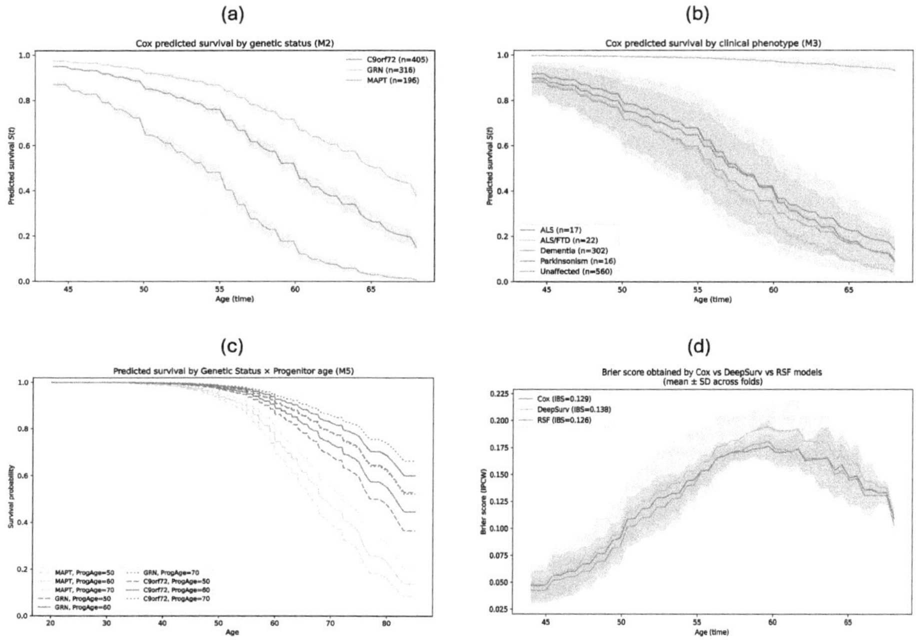

Fig. 1. Cox-based survival analyses illustrating the progressive contribution of genetic, clinical, and familial factors. (a) Survival curves stratified by genetic variant (Model M2), showing distinct age-at-onset trajectories across MAPT, C9orf72, and GRN carriers. (b) Survival curves stratified by clinical phenotype (Model M3), with more aggressive phenotypes exhibiting earlier declines in survival probability. (c) Predicted survival for representative genetic profiles at different progenitor ages (Model M5), highlighting a consistent shift toward earlier onset with decreasing progenitor age. (d) Time-dependent Brier score comparing Cox, DeepSurv, and Random Survival Forest models, with shaded areas indicating ± one standard deviation across folds.

predicted age-at-onset trajectories, revealing marked heterogeneity across phenotypic groups. In particular, more aggressive phenotypes such as ALS and ALS/FTD show substantially earlier declines in survival probability compared with dementia and parkinsonism, while unaffected individuals display the most delayed risk profile. These findings indicate that clinical phenotype provides complementary prognostic information beyond genetic status, capturing meaningful differences in disease aggressiveness and temporal progression.

To further elucidate the contribution of familial factors, Fig. 1(c) illustrates Cox-predicted survival curves for representative genetic profiles while systematically varying the age at symptom onset of the affected progenitor (Model M5). Across all genetic groups, earlier progenitor onset is associated with a marked leftward shift of the survival curves, indicating an increased risk of earlier disease onset in the offspring. This effect is particularly pronounced in MAPT variant carriers, where differences in progenitor age translate into substantial separations between survival trajectories. These findings underscore the strong influence of parental age at onset as an independent modifier of age-at-onset risk, beyond genetic status and clinical phenotype.

Table 2. Predictive performance of linear and non-linear survival models trained on the covariate set derived from M5. All models achieve comparable discrimination and calibration, with RSF yielding the highest average C-index and lowest IBS under five-fold cross-validation.

Model	Variables	C-index (mean ± SD)	IBS (mean ± SD)
Cox	M5	0.817 ± 0.016	0.129 ± 0.010
DeepSurv	M5	0.813 ± 0.013	0.141 ± 0.009
RSF	**M5**	$\mathbf{0.819 \pm 0.017}$	$\mathbf{0.126 \pm 0.008}$

We compared Cox regression with two widely used machine learningâĂŞbased approaches: DeepSurv and Random Survival Forests (RSF) to assess whether more flexible, non-linear survival models could improve predictive performance. All models were trained on the same covariate set corresponding to Model M5, and Table 2 shows that they achieved comparable discrimination and calibration performance. RSF yielded the highest average C-index and the lowest IBS, indicating a modest but consistent improvement in both ranking ability and overall prediction error. However, performance differences were minimal, and the linear Cox model performed similarly to the more complex approaches.

The time-dependent Brier score curves shown in Fig. 1(d) further illustrate these findings. Across most of the age range, RSF consistently exhibits the lowest prediction error, followed closely by the Cox model, while DeepSurv shows slightly higher error, particularly around the age interval with the highest density of events. Notably, all models display a characteristic increase in Brier score between approximately 55 and 60 years of age, reflecting increased uncertainty around the typical age of symptom onset in this cohort. Taken together, these results suggest that while non-linear models can offer marginal gains, the incremental structure and interpretability of the Cox model remain highly competitive for age-at-onset prediction in this setting.

4 Conclusions and Future Work

In this study, we investigated age at symptom onset in gFTD using a principled time-to-event framework that integrates demographic, genetic, clinical, and familial information. By progressively building Cox proportional hazards models, we showed that genetic status and progenitor-related variables provide substantial and complementary contributions to age-at-onset prediction, leading to clearly distinct survival trajectories across variant groups and family histories. Importantly, the inclusion of progenitor age at onset yielded the largest improvement in predictive performance, highlighting its relevance as a key modifier of disease timing. Comparisons with non-linear survival models, including DeepSurv and Random Survival Forests, revealed broadly comparable performance, suggesting that the main determinants of age at onset are well captured by relatively simple and interpretable models. Future work will focus on exploring longitudinal and time-varying covariates, and assessing the clinical utility of individualized age-at-onset predictions in prospective settings. Taken together, these results may contribute to improved risk stratification and prognostic assessment in genetic neurodegenerative diseases.

Funding Information. This research is part of the PID2022-137451OB-I00 and PID2022-137629OA-I00 projects, funded by the MICIU/AEI /10.13039/501100011033 and by FEDER, EU.

References

1. Rohrer, J.D., et al.: Clinical and neuroanatomical signatures of tissue pathology in frontotemporal lobar degeneration. Brain **134**(9), 2565–2581 (2011)
2. Rohrer, J.D., Nicholas, J.M., Cash, D.M., et al.: Presymptomatic cognitive and neuroanatomical changes in genetic frontotemporal dementia in the Genfi study. Lancet Neurol. **14**(3), 253–262 (2015)
3. Jiskoot, L.C., et al.: Longitudinal cognitive biomarkers predicting symptom onset in presymptomatic frontotemporal dementia. J. Neurol. **265**(6), 1381–1392 (2018). https://doi.org/10.1007/s00415-018-8850-7
4. Moore, K.M., Nicholas, J., Grossman, M., et al.: Age at symptom onset and death and disease duration in genetic frontotemporal dementia: an international retrospective cohort study. Lancet Neurol. **19**(2), 145–156 (2020)
5. Kleinbaum, D.G., Klein, M.: Survival Analysis: A Self-Learning Text. Springer, Cham (2012). https://doi.org/10.1007/978-1-4419-6646-9
6. Therneau, T.M., Grambsch, P.M.: Modeling Survival Data: Extending the Cox Model. Springer, Cham (2000). https://doi.org/10.1007/978-1-4757-3294-8
7. Katzman, J.L., Shaham, U., Cloninger, A., Bates, J., Jiang, T., Kluger, Y.: DeepSurv: personalized treatment recommender system using a Cox proportional hazards deep neural network. BMC Med. Res. Methodol. **18**(1), 24 (2018)
8. Cox, D.R.: Regression models and life-tables. J. Roy. Stat. Soc. B **34**(2), 187–202 (1972)
9. Breslow, N.: Discussion of the paper by d. r. cox. J. Roy. Stat. Soc. B **34**(2), 216–217 (1972)
10. Ishwaran, H., Kogalur, U.B., Blackstone, E.H., Lauer, M.S.: Random survival forests. Ann. Appl. Stat. **2**(3), 841–860 (2008)
11. Harrell, F.E., Califf, R.M., Pryor, D.B., Lee, K.L., Rosati, R.A.: Evaluating the yield of medical tests. JAMA **247**(18), 2543–2546 (1982)
12. Graf, E., Schmoor, C., Sauerbrei, W., Schumacher, M.: Assessment and comparison of prognostic classification schemes for survival data. Stat. Med. **18**(17–18), 2529–2545 (1999)

Feasibility of EEG-Based Bimanual Upper-Limb Exoskeleton Control for Activities of Daily Living

Y. Vales[1], E. Peral-Sempere[1], R. Martín-Batanero[1], D. Martínez-Pascual[1], J. M. Catalán[1,2], A. Blanco-Ivorra[1,3], and N. Garcia-Aracil[1,2](✉)

[1] Robotics and Artificial Intelligence Group, Miguel Hernández University, Avda. de la Universidad s/n, 03202 Elche, Spain
{yvales,esther.perals,david.martinezp,jcatalan,ablanco,nicolas.garcia}@umh.es
[2] Department of Systems Engineering and Automation, Miguel Hernández University, Avda. de la Universidad s/n, 03202 Elche, Spain
[3] Department of Materials Science, Optics, and Electronic Technology, Miguel Hernández University, Avda. de la Universidad s/n, 03202 Elche, Spain

Abstract. While brain–computer interface (BCI) controlled exoskeletons have shown promise in restoring function for paralyzed individuals, most existing systems are restricted to unilateral operation, failing to address the bimanual coordination required for real-world tasks. This paper presents a pilot study on the feasibility and functional performance of a newly developed bimanual upper-limb exoskeleton. The system integrates augmented reality and eye-tracking for intuitive object selection, and a BCI for grasping control. During the experimental phase participants completed a bimanual task in which they simulated filling a glass with water from a bottle and drinking from the glass.

Keywords: Assistive Robotics · Brain-Computer Interface · Electroencephalography

1 Introduction

Stroke affects approximately 1.1 million people in the European Union and is one of the leading causes of physical disability in adults worldwide [10,14,15]. Upper-limb motor impairment, one of the most common sequelae, occurs in up to 80% survivors and is strongly associated with dependence on activities of daily living (ADL). It is estimated that one-third of stroke survivors experience severe motor deficits, which can result in significant functional dependence [15].

Although conventional rehabilitation can mitigate motor impairments, it is frequently insufficient to fully restore function in cases of severe paralysis. In response to these limitations, advanced assistive technologies such as robotic exoskeletons and neuroprosthetic systems have been developed to support upper-limb function. In particular, brain–computer interface (BCI) controlled exoskeletons have demonstrated the potential to restore hand and finger movements even

J. M. Ferrández Vicente et al. (Eds.): IWINAC 2026, LNCS 16574, pp. 55–64, 2026.
https://doi.org/10.1007/978-3-032-27314-7_6

in cases of complete paralysis. These systems translate modulations of brain activity, such as those associated with motor imagery, into real movements of an external device, thereby re-establishing a functional link between motor intention and physical execution [8]. Among BCI approaches, electroencephalography (EEG) based systems have gained particular relevance due to their non invasive nature and practical applicability in clinical settings [8, 16].

To further enhance system performance and usability, multimodal control strategies integrating additional biosignals such as electrooculography (EOG) and electromyography (EMG) have been proposed. EEG-based control have shown feasibility for controlling autonomous upper-limb exoskeletons during daily living subtasks in stroke patients, improving decoding robustness, reliability, and the intuitiveness of human–robot interaction [4, 8].

Despite these advances, most available assistive robotic devices remain unilateral, limiting their applicability to real-world functional tasks that inherently require coordinated bimanual interaction [16]. Multimodal control architectures that integrate information from position, force, and interaction sensors alongside cortical signals enable real-time closed-loop adaptation to both the user's physical and cognitive state and the surrounding environment. Such approaches provide more natural, efficient, and personalized assistance, which is particularly critical for complex bimanual tasks [1, 9].

This paper presents a pilot study whose main objective is to evaluate the feasibility of a EEG-based control system combined with AR for operating the bimanual assistive exoskeleton in four participants. The exoskeleton's multimodal control system acts as a bridge between the user's motor intentions and the execution of physical movements. It continuously adapts assistance while encouraging active engagement, enabling users to perform functional tasks with a reasonable degree of autonomy.

2 Materials and Methods

2.1 Participants

This pilot study involved four adults (three males and one female). They were aged between 23 and 32 (26.5 ± 4.36 years). None had prior experience with BCI systems. Inclusion criteria required the absence of neurological, cognitive, or motor impairments.

All participants received detailed information about the experimental procedures and provided written informed consent before participation. The study was conducted in accordance with the Declaration of Helsinki and was approved by the Ethics Committee of Miguel Hernández University (Elche, Spain) under reference IB.NMGA.250113.

2.2 Bimanual Upper-Limb Exoskeleton

The bimanual upper-limb exoskeleton is composed of two arm exoskeletons and two hand exoskeletons (Fig. 1).

Both arm exoskeletons are powered by 5 active Degrees of Freedom (DOF): shoulder abduction/adduction, shoulder flexion/extension, internal/external shoulder rotation, elbow flexion/extension, and wrist pronation/supination. To adapt the exoskeleton for each user's anatomy, several adjustment mechanisms are incorporated. Both arm exoskeletons allow for modifications in dimensions such as shoulder width, the distance between shoulders, upper arm length, and forearm length. These adjustments ensure that the exoskeleton's axes align with the user's joints. In addition, a series of orthoses are distributed along the arm, forearm, and hand to further fit the exoskeleton to the user. These components are secured in place with straps.

To enable object grasping and controlled hand opening and closing, an Helium hand exoskeleton (iDRhA, [7]) was integrated as a distal module into each upper-limb exoskeleton of the bimanual system. Thus, both robotic arms were equipped with an independent hand module. The device allows independent actuation of the first, second, and third digits, while the fourth and fifth digits are mechanically linked and actuated synchronously as a coupled pair [6].

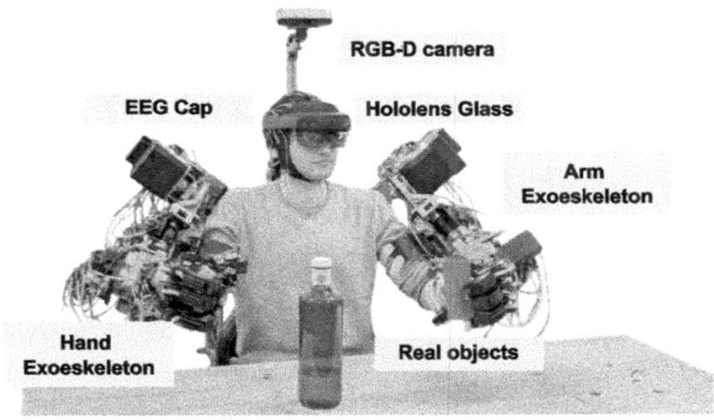

Fig. 1. Experimental setup of the Brain-Computer Interface (BCI) integrated with the bimanual upper-limb exoskeleton and the Hololens glasses for assisted task execution.

2.3 Computer Vision System and Eye Tracking

The computer vision module integrated into the system provides three core capabilities: gaze estimation, real-object classification and estimation of their three-dimensional pose. This system combines the native eye tracking capabilities of Microsoft HoloLens 2 with an external computer vision pipeline based on YOLOv8 using an RGB-D camera. In addition, taking advantage of the mixed-reality capabilities of the HoloLens 2, a human-machine interaction system was implemented in Unity using the Mixed Reality Toolkit (MRTK) package for unified access to gaze, gestures, and voice.

The HoloLens 2 eye-tracking subsystem continuously estimates the gaze ray, including the origin, direction, and the intersected element in the scene. To ensure reliable interaction, the system interprets a gaze maintained on the same target for a predefined dwell time as an intentional selection. Once the selection is confirmed, the user interface provides immediate visual and audio feedback. In parallel, the system transmits the relevant information to an external processing unit, which performs object detection, classification, and pose estimation using an RGB-D camera. The response received is then used to update the holographic content aligned with the physical environment, presenting the user with contextual information such as object identity or spatial position (Fig. 2). This cycle repeats continuously, enabling a seamless, hands-free, and gaze-driven interaction within the AR environment.

Fig. 2. Visualization in AR. The process of selecting an interactive object and displaying information to the user. During the selection process, the button's text color is displayed in cyan.

2.4 EEG Control Interface

EEG signals were recorded using a 9-channel wireless amplifier (LiveAmp®, Brain Products GmbH, Gilching, Germany). EEG electrodes were positioned according to the international 10–20 system at F3, F4, T7, T8, C3, C4, Cz, P3, and P4 using polyamide-based solid-gel electrodes. All signals were sampled at 1 kHz and band-pass filtered between 0.1–30 Hz. A customized version of the BCI2000 open-source framework was implemented for real-time signal processing and command generation, enabling control of the bimanual upper-limb exoskeleton [11, 12].

The sensorimotor rhythm (SMR) associated with motor imagery was quantified through event-related desynchronization (ERD) using a power-based method [12]. Band-power variations within the sensorimotor range were continuously estimated relative to a reference baseline (Reference Value). An optimal frequency for detecting motor imagery related SMR desynchronization (8–15 Hz) was identified through power spectrum analysis, selecting the frequency with maximal ERD during imagined or attempted hand-closing and maximal event-related synchronization (ERS) during relaxation. Based on these values, a discrimination threshold was computed for online BCI control. Detected SMR-ERDs were translated into exoskeleton closing commands, enabling real-time coupling of motor intention with device actuation.

2.5 Experimental Setup and Protocol

The experimental protocol consisted of two main phases: an EEG control interface calibration phase followed by the experimental phase.

EEG Control Interface Calibration Phase. Participants were seated and instructed to either relax or imagine grasping movements in response to visual cues displayed on a computer screen positioned on the table in front of them, as shown in Fig. 3a.

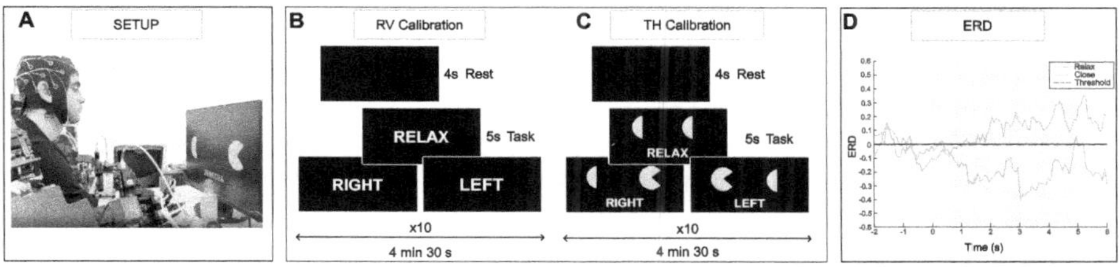

Fig. 3. Calibration EEG. **A**. Experimental setup during the calibration session. **B**. Reference Value Calibration, used to analyze the ERD offset at which the participant was instructed to imagine closing the indicated hand or to remain relaxed. **C**. Threshold Calibration, aimed at determining the threshold at which the signal was classified as ERD and triggered the closure of the indicated Pac-Man mechanism. **D**. Example of a participant's ERD following offline analysis, showing the average motor imagery–induced desynchronization in the contralateral hemisphere during task presentation (0–5 s).

Two calibration procedures were conducted following protocols adapted from previous studies [4,8]. The first procedure aimed to determine RV and establish baseline SMR-ERD levels. During this task, participants performed motor imagery of grasping with their right or left hand, or remained relaxed, in response to visual cues (Fig. 3b). The trials were randomized (10 repetitions per condition, 5 s each) and interleaved with 4 s rest periods. The second procedure consisted of a visual feedback task in which two on screen Pac-Man–shaped indicators were presented on the left and right sides of the display (Fig. 3c). Participants were instructed to perform motor imagery of the indicated hand and received real-time visual feedback through the progressive closure of the corresponding indicator as ERD activity was detected. This enabled lateralized modulation of SMR.

Post hoc analysis in MATLAB identified the optimal ERD thresholds, which were then implemented to control the HELIUM hand exoskeleton in real time. Both procedures were repeated as necessary to ensure robust threshold selection (Fig. 3d).

Experimental Phase. For the experimental phase, participants were seated comfortably in front of a desk and equipped with the bimanual upper-limb exoskeleton, a wearable EEG monitoring system, and AR glasses. An RGB-D camera was positioned above and behind the participant to capture the workspace (Fig. 1).

The experimental phase consisted of performing a bimanual activity in which participants simulated filling a glass with water from a bottle and drinking from the glass. The bottle and glass were positioned across the table surface, ensuring they remained within the field of view of the RGB-D camera. The task consisted of seven primary functional states (Fig. 4). State 1 involved object detection utilizing the RGB-D camera and AR glasses. Following detection, the system executed the grasping of the bottle (State 2) or the cup (State 3). Following each grasping action, the system executed a verification check to determine if both objects were held; if the user still had an empty hand, the sequence looped back to State 1, otherwise proceeding to the pouring (State 4) and drinking (State 5) phases. Finally, the sequence concluded with the return of the bottle (State 6) and the glass (State 7) to their initial positions. Across these states, grasping and releasing actions (States 2, 3, 6, and 7) were triggered via EEG-derived SMR-ERD thresholds, while the arm trajectories (States 2, 3, 5, 6, and 7) were managed through exoskeleton position control.

At the end of the experiment, all participants completed the Self-Assessment Manikin (SAM) [3] questionnaire. This pictorial assessment tool was used to evaluate their affective state and perceived experience.

2.6 Data Collection and Analyses

Feasibility. Each user completed four EEG-controlled tasks, resulting in a 16 sessions evaluation. System performance was evaluated using the EEG Time to Initialize (TTI) metric, as previously applied in similar studies [4,5,8]. TTI were evaluated as time since the action is visually indicated to the user until the EEG signals exceed the corresponding detection thresholds (reaction time). Control reliability was defined as achieving at least 75% successful subtask initializations; fluent control was assumed for initialization times below 3 s and reliable control for times below 5 s.

Users' Affective State and Performance Assessment. To evaluate the users' affective state and subjective experiences, participants were assessed using the SAM [3]. This non-verbal pictorial assessment technique directly measures three primary emotional dimensions: pleasure, arousal, and dominance on a nine-point scale. By employing this test at the end of the experimental sessions, the emotional impact of the system and the users' overall perceived experience were captured.

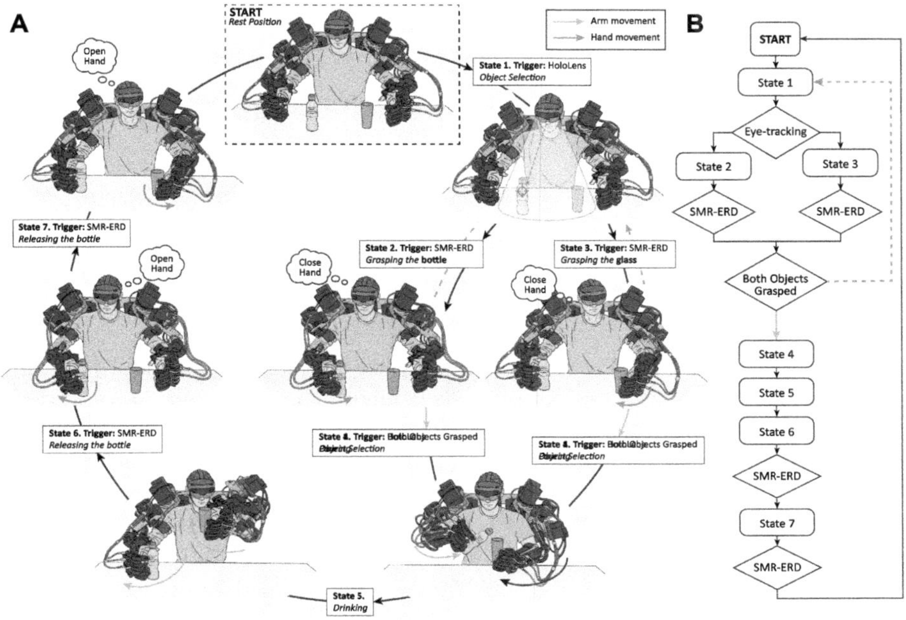

Fig. 4. Shared-human bimanual robot control strategy based on a finite-state machine for the pouring task, triggered by EEG and eye tracking. **A.** Control strategy. **B.** Control-loop flowchart of the whole-arm bimanual exoskeleton.

3 Results

The results of TTI represent the pooled data from the four participants (Fig. 5a). This values show a median of 2.60 s, with an interquartile range spanning from 0.78 s (q_{25}) to 7.50 s (q_{75}). Also in this condition, 68.75% of the values remained below 6 s. The subjective responses reported with the SAM test are represented in Fig. 5b. Participants reported a mean valence score of 6.75 ± 0.50, an arousal score of 3.25 ± 0.50, and a dominance score of 6.25 ± 0.96.

4 Discussion

This preliminary study evaluated the feasibility of a EEG-based control system combined with AR for operating the bimanual assistive exoskeleton in four participants.

Control system feasibility was assessed using the TTI metric, an indicator of the fluency of a BCI–exoskeleton system [4, 5, 8].

The TTI values observed in this study were higher than those reported in previous studies employing unimanual EEG control [4, 5], where values were tipically below 6 s, whereas in our case they reached up to 7.5 s. However, compared

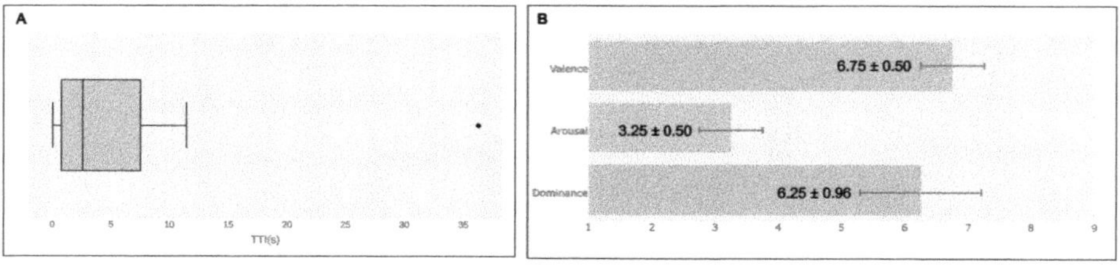

Fig. 5. A. Results of the TTI parameter. **B.** Self-Assessment Manikin (SAM) measures reported by the users involved in the experimental sessions.

with the 75% of trials below 6 s reported for unimanual EEG control [4,5], our bimanual system achieved 68.75% of trials below the 6 s threshold. Moreover, the median TTI (2.60 s) indicates that participants were generally able to initiate movements promptly and sustain SMR-ERD modulation. Therefore the results show performance acceptable, considering the complexity of the system.

However, several trials exceeded previously suggested fluency thresholds. These findings indicate that while the system demonstrates functional feasibility, temporal variability in activation remains a relevant limitation.

This variability, as well as the prolonged activation times observed in some cases, may be associated with inaccurate ERD detection during task execution due to several challenges. Previous studies have shown that the brain does not remain in a "neutral" state between tasks, but rather in an active relaxation state, which can affect ERD modulation and response timing [2]. Additionally, slow cortical potentials involved in movement preparation, known as Movement-Related Cortical Potentials (MRCPs), and intertrial phase coherence (ITPC) can change across consecutive sessions, demonstrating that prior experience influences current brain responses [2]. Additionally, it is estimated that between 15% and 30% of users exhibit BCI illiteracy, a challenge that remains unresolved by current research [13]. These findings suggest that EEG-based control cannot be considered in isolation during task execution, as it is influenced by prior preparation, task-switching, and cumulative learning from previous sessions.

Given the restricted number of sessions, the TTI results should be interpreted as preliminary. While the data suggests a consistent trend in the bimanual activity, the sample is not large enough to generalize these to a broader population.

Regarding the self-assessed user experience, the reported valence (6.75 ± 0.50) indicates that participants perceived the interaction as pleasant and satisfying, with the low standard deviation suggesting a high degree of consensus. This is complemented by a relatively low arousal score (3.25 ± 0.50), which suggests that the task was engaging without becoming a source of stress or cognitive overstimulation. Furthermore, the dominance score (6.25 ± 0.96) demonstrates that users maintained a sense of control over the bimanual exoskeleton. Therefore, the affective responses of the participants reported via the SAM test suggest a favorable user experience.

Concerning the study limitations, this is a preliminary investigation with a very small sample size. The experiments were conducted in a non-soundproof environment, and the EEG calibration was not optimal. Additionally, the intervals between subtasks were insufficient for participants' brains to return to a "neutral state", which could have affected performance due to preceding arm exoskeleton movements. To address these issues, future study will involve a larger sample size, it conducted in a quiet environment with longer pauses between tasks, and a modified protocol designed to improve SMR-ERD detection. The new protocol will include strategies to optimize user preparation before each subtask, as well as anticipatory movement planning with longer pauses between actions specifically between arm movements and object grasping, and the opening and closing of the hand via EEG control. Additionally, distributed training protocols should be implemented to facilitate stabilization of ERD across multiple sessions.

5 Conclusion

In this preliminary study, the multimodal platform was presented and evaluated, consisting of two upper-limb robotic exoeskeletons controlled via a EEG interface that combines EEG signals and AR. The integration of object detection using a augmented reality with SMR-ERD based control for grasping enabled all four participants to complete the bimanual ADL task.

System feasibility was assessed using the TTI metric, which indicates that the system achieves satisfactory performance, with observed limitations that remain within acceptable bounds and do not significantly affect stability. On the other hand, according to the SAM questionnaire, participants reported a positive experience and a good sense of control while using the device.

Acknowledgments. This research was funded by the Spanish Agency of Innovation, the European Union-Next Generation and the Generalitat Valenciana a través de los proyectos CIPROM/2022/12 y PLEC2022-009424.

References

1. Ajoudani, A., Zanchettin, A.M., Ivaldi, S., Albu-Schäffer, A., Kosuge, K., Khatib, O.: Progress and prospects of the human-robot collaboration. Auton. Robot. **42**(5), 957–975 (2018)
2. Barios, J.A., et al.: Synchronization of slow cortical rhythms during motor imagery-based brain-machine interface control. Int. J. Neural Syst. **29**(05), 1850045 (2019)
3. Bradley, M.M., Lang, P.J.: Measuring emotion: the self-assessment manikin and the semantic differential. J. Behav. Ther. Exp. Psychiatry **25**(1), 49–59 (1994)
4. Catalán, J.M., et al.: Hybrid brain/neural interface and autonomous vision-guided whole-arm exoskeleton control to perform activities of daily living (adls). J. Neuroeng. Rehabil. **20**(1), 61 (2023)

5. Crea, S., et al.: Feasibility and safety of shared EEG/EOG and vision-guided autonomous whole-arm exoskeleton control to perform activities of daily living. Sci. Rep. **8**(1), 10823 (2018)
6. Diez, J.A., Blanco, A., Catalan, J.M., Badesa, F.J., Lledo, L.D., Garcia-Aracil, N.: Hand exoskeleton for rehabilitation therapies with integrated optical force sensor. Adv. Mech. Eng. **10**(2), 1–11 (2018)
7. iDRhA: Innovative Devices for Rehabilitation & Assistance. https://idrha.es/ (2019). Accessed 28 Feb 2024
8. Nann, M., et al.: Restoring activities of daily living using an EEG/EOG-controlled semiautonomous and mobile whole-arm exoskeleton in chronic stroke. IEEE Syst. J. **15**(2), 2314–2321 (2020)
9. Novak, D., Riener, R.: A survey of sensor fusion methods in wearable robotics. Robot. Auton. Syst. **73**, 155–170 (2015)
10. Pu, L., Wang, L., Zhang, R., Zhao, T., Jiang, Y., Han, L.: Projected global trends in ischemic stroke incidence, deaths and disability-adjusted life years from 2020 to 2030. Stroke **54**(5), 1330–1339 (2023)
11. Schalk, G., McFarland, D.J., Hinterberger, T., Birbaumer, N., Wolpaw, J.R.: BCI2000: a general-purpose brain-computer interface (BCI) system. IEEE Trans. Biomed. Eng. **51**(6), 1034–1043 (2004)
12. Soekadar, S., et al.: Hybrid EEG/EOG-based brain/neural hand exoskeleton restores fully independent daily living activities after quadriplegia. Sci. Robot. **1**(1), eaag3296 (2016)
13. Thompson, M.C.: Critiquing the concept of BCI illiteracy. Sci. Eng. Ethics **25**(4), 1217–1233 (2019)
14. Tsao, C.W., et al.: Heart disease and stroke statistics–2023 update: a report from the American heart association. Circulation **147**(8), e93 (2023)
15. Wafa, H.A., Wolfe, C.D., Emmett, E., Roth, G.A., Johnson, C.O., Wang, Y.: Burden of stroke in Europe: thirty-year projections of incidence, prevalence, deaths, and disability-adjusted life years. Stroke **51**(8), 2418–2427 (2020)
16. Zhang, M., et al.: Decoding coordinated directions of bimanual movements from EEG signals. IEEE Trans. Neural Syst. Rehabil. Eng. **31**, 248–259 (2022)

Longitudinal Modeling of Alzheimer's Disease Progression Using a Bayesian Latent Framework with APOE-Dependent Genetic Effects

C. Vázquez-García[1](✉), F. J. Martínez Murcia[1], F. Segovia[1], A. Forte[2], J. Ramírez[1], I. Illán[1], A. Hernández-Segura[1], C. Jiménez-Mesa[3], and J. M. Górriz[1]

[1] Department of Signal Processing and Biomedical Applications, University of Granada, 18071 Granada, Spain
{crisvgarcia,fjesusmartinez,fsegovia,javierrp,illan,alejandrohs,gorriz}@ugr.es

[2] Department of Statistics and Operations Research, University of Valencia, 46010 Valencia, Spain
anabel.forte@uv.es

[3] Department of Communication Engineering, University of Malaga, 29071 Malaga, Spain
carmenj@uma.es

Abstract. Longitudinal modeling of neurodegenerative diseases remains a major challenge due to the complexity of the underlying processes and the strong heterogeneity of individual trajectories. Neuroimaging provides a unique opportunity to characterize disease-related alterations long before clinical onset, enabling earlier intervention. In this work, we employ a Variational Autoencoder (VAE) to compress high-dimensional neuroimaging scans into a low-dimensional latent representation (z_0) that captures dementia-related patterns. We then model the temporal evolution of this neuroimaging biomarker using a Bayesian longitudinal framework that incorporates genetic information as covariates. This approach allows us to study population-level disease trajectories while explicitly accounting for genetic risk factors. Our results show that the proposed neuroimaging biomarker z_0 and the Bayesian longitudinal model successfully stratifies subjects into genotype-dependent risk subgroups, revealing distinct baseline profiles and progression patterns consistent with known genetic effects.

Keywords: APOE · Dementia · Bayesian

1 Introduction

Neurodegenerative Diseases (NDDs), such as Alzheimer's Disease (AD) or Parkinson's Disease (PD), represent a concerning challenge affecting the entire

J. M. Ferrández Vicente et al. (Eds.): IWINAC 2026, LNCS 16574, pp. 65–74, 2026.
https://doi.org/10.1007/978-3-032-27314-7_7

global population. Studies show that approximately 55 million people suffered from dementia in 2019, a value expected to increase up to 139 million worldwide by 2050 according to the World Health Organization (WHO). This poses a burden to affected individuals, families, and the socioeconomic and health environment, reflected as an estimated annual cost of dementia to stand at US$ 1.3 trillion in 2019, predicting an increase to 2.8 trillion by 2030 [1]. Moreover, the increase of life expectancy is causing the world population to age, making dementia a major cause of mortality and impairment. Therefore, effective tools for early diagnosis and treatment are urgently required.

Functional neuroimaging is widely used in clinical setting as a diagnosis tool, as these provide relevant insights of the neurological alterations that underlie the NDDs long before the onset of clinical symptoms [2]; however, these neuroimages contain complex and high-dimensional information about the diseases that typically requires expert interpretation. Detecting these subtle changes enables the characterization of disease patterns and progression trajectories, while also potentially identifying high-risk individuals at preclinical stages.

Dimensionality reduction techniques have therefore become crucial for analysis. According to the manifold hypothesis [3] [4] [5], meaningful representations exist on a lower-dimensional manifold despite the apparent high dimensionality. By projecting data into a structured latent space, we can reveal disease-associated patterns that may be hidden in the raw images. In a previous work, in the Alzheimer's Disease Neuroimaging Initiative (ADNI) database, we proposed a framework for extracting a biomarker related to dementia directly from Positron Emission Tomography (PET) scans, allowing to obtain meaningful biomarkers that capture dementia patterns. The framework consists of a VAE that uses bayesian inference to compress the scans into a low-dimensional latent manifold, where each variable of the space encodes a pattern [8]. To encourage the model to capture dementia patterns, we also introduced a similarity between metrics related to dementia severity and latent variables. Using this setup, we can decode the latent patterns of dementia back to brain space using the same VAE, allowing visualization of dementia patterns in the brain. This framework is therefore a powerful and flexible tool for extracting dementia-related biomarkers directly from neuroimaging that contain meaningful information long before the onset of symptoms.

However, this model was not designed to explicitly exploit the longitudinal structure of neuroimaging cohorts, as its primary goal was the extraction and validation of dementia-related patterns at the population level. In the present work, we take a first step towards longitudinal modeling by introducing a Bayesian framework that characterizes the temporal evolution of this latent biomarker. The main contributions of this work are:

1. Introduce and evaluate a Population-level Bayesian longitudinal model that can predict the evolution of the dementia biomarker through time.
2. Generate and visualize temporal population trajectories of the biomarker leveraging the longitudinal database.

3. Include genetics as a covariable, allowing the identification of different progression subgroups according to their genotype.

2 Materials and Methods

2.1 Data and Neuroimaging Biomarker

Data used in the preparation of this article were obtained from the Alzheimer's Disease Neuroimaging Initiative (ADNI) database (adni.loni.usc.edu). The ADNI was launched in 2003 as a public-private partnership, led by Principal Investigator Michael W. Weiner, MD. The primary goal of ADNI has been to test whether serial magnetic resonance imaging (MRI), positron emission tomography (PET), other biological markers, and clinical and neuropsychological assessment can be combined to measure the progression of mild cognitive impairment (MCI) and early Alzheimer's disease (AD). For up-to-date information, see www.adni-info.org.

In this study, we analyze a dementia-related latent neuroimaging biomarker derived from PET scans from the ADNI database. A total of 3466 longitudinal ^{18}F-FDG PET scans were included. FDG-PET provides a measure of cerebral glucose metabolism, which is known to reflect early functional alterations associated with neurodegeneration and AD [6].

Each scan is encoded using a previously proposed Bayesian VAE framework [8], which maps high-dimensional neuroimaging data into a low-dimensional latent space. This framework is explicitly regularized to align one latent dimension, denoted as z_0, with dementia-related cognitive scores, resulting in a latent variable that links disease-relevant metabolic patterns to cognitive status.

In the present work, z_0 is treated as a continuous outcome variable, providing a compact and biologically meaningful summary of each PET scan that can be modeled longitudinally.

2.2 Bayesian Longitudinal Model

To characterize the temporal evolution of the neuroimaging biomarker, we use a Bayesian longitudinal regression model. Let z_{ij} denote the latent biomarker value for subject i at visit j, measured at time τ_{ij} relative to baseline:

$$\begin{aligned} z_{ij} &\sim \mathcal{N}(\mu_{ij}, \sigma^2), \\ \mu_{ij} &= \alpha + \beta\, \tau_{ij} + \boldsymbol{x}_i^\top \gamma + \tau_{ij}\, \boldsymbol{x}_i^\top \boldsymbol{\delta}, \end{aligned} \tag{1}$$

where α and β are the population-level intercept and the slope, $\boldsymbol{x}_i$ are the baseline covariates, γ captures their effect on baseline biomarker levels, and $\boldsymbol{\delta}$ models their interaction with time. We restrict the model to population-level fixed effects, omitting subject-specific random effects, to isolate the contribution of genetic factors while avoiding overparameterization. More expressive models with individual-level effects will be explored in future work.

2.3 Genetic Covariates (APOE Genotype)

Genetic risk was modeled using baseline covariates encoding the subjects's Apolipoprotein (APOE) genotype. APOE genotype is a well-established risk factor for AD, with the $\varepsilon4$ allele associated with increased risk and earlier onset, and the $\varepsilon2$ allele considered protective [7].

Genotype information was encoded using dummy variables corresponding to the observed genotype groups. Table 1 summarizes the number of subjects and observations for each genotype subgroups. Due to the limited number of observations in the $\varepsilon2/\varepsilon2$ subgroup, results involving this group should be interpreted with caution. The final genetic model is given by

$$\mu_{ij} = \alpha + \beta\tau_{ij} + \beta_{age}(age_i - \bar{age}) + \sum_{k=1}^{5} \gamma^{(k)} G_i^{(k)} + \sum_{k=1}^{5} \delta^{(k)} G_i^{(k)} \tau_{ij} + \epsilon_{ij}, \quad (2)$$

where $G_i^{(k)}$ denotes the dummy variable for genotype subgroup k, with genotype $\varepsilon3/\varepsilon3$ selected as the reference category due to its large sample size. The coefficients $\gamma^{(k)}$ represent deviations in baseline biomarker values relative to the reference group, while $\delta^{(k)}$ capture genotype-specific deviations in longitudinal slope.

Table 1. Number of observations for each genotype subgroup.

Genotype	# of observations	# of subjects
3/3	1623	763
3/4	1148	546
4/4	328	156
2/3	261	119
2/4	83	35
2/2	15	5

2.4 Bayesian Inference and Prior Specification

The model was implemented in Python using the CmdStanPy interface of Stan, which performs Bayesian inference via Hamiltonian Monte Carlo (HMC) [9]. All parameters were assigned weakly informative normal priors, selected to reflect plausible effect sizes while providing regularization. Table 2 summarizes the prior distributions used.

Normal priors were chosen for their interpretability and robustness, particularly in a preliminary modeling setting where strong prior information is limited. Temporal effects were assigned smaller variances to reflect the expectation of smooth longitudinal changes, whereas baseline effects were allowed greater variability to account for population heterogeneity [10]. However, the modeling framework is fully Bayesian, so alternative prior distributions (e.g., Student-t or Cauchy for heavier tails) could be used if prior knowledge or robustness considerations justify it.

Table 2. Prior distribution for the parameters of the genetic model

Parameter	Description	Prior
α	Baseline intercept	$\mathcal{N}(0, 3)$
β_{time}	Effect of time	$\mathcal{N}(0, 0.4)$
β_{age0}	Effect of baseline age	$\mathcal{N}(0, 0.2)$
σ	Observation noise SD	$\mathcal{N}(0, 0.05)$
$\gamma^{(k)}$	Effect of genotype k	$\mathcal{N}(0, 0.5)$
$\delta^{(k)}$	Effect of genotype k on time	$\mathcal{N}(0, 0.05)$

2.5 Model Diagnostics

Model convergence and sampling quality were assessed using standard Bayesian diagnostics, including the number of divergent transitions, the potential scale reduction factor $\hat{R}$, and the Effective Sample Size (ESS). Divergent transitions indicate numerical instabilities during the Hamiltonian dynamics integration and typically arise from complex posterior geometries, such as regions of high curvature or sharp boundaries. A large number of divergences suggest that the sampler may fail to adequately explore the posterior distribution. The $\hat{R}$ statistic compares within-chain and between-chain variability to evaluate convergence across multiple Markov chains. Values close to 1 indicate that all chains are sampling from the same target distribution, whereas larger values suggest lack of convergence and insufficient mixing [11]. Next, the ESS quantifies the amount of independent information contained in the correlated samples generated by the HMC algorithm. Due to autocorrelation between successive samples, the nominal number of draws overestimates the true amount of information. ESS corrects for this effect and can be interpreted as the number of independent samples that would yield an equivalent estimation precision. Low ESS values indicate poor mixing and reduced reliability of posterior summaries. In practice, we report both the bulk-ESS and tail-ESS, which respectively assess sampling efficiency in the central region and in the tails of the posterior distribution [12].

3 Results

To evaluate whether a simplified population-level Bayesian longitudinal model can capture meaningful genotype-dependent patterns, we model temporal evolution of the dementia-related neuroimaging biomarker z_0 using APOE genotype as covariate. The biomarker z_0 is extracted for each observation using the VAE encoder and treated as a continuous longitudinal outcome. Table 3 reports the main sampling diagnostics obtained during Bayesian inference. All convergence criteria indicate excellent sampling behavior, with no divergent transitions, maximum $\hat{R}$ values well below the accepted threshold, and large ESS for both bulk and tail distributions. These results confirm the numerical stability and reliability of posterior estimates.

Table 3. Metric validation table for the HMC.

Metric	Value	Significance
Divergences	0	Excellent
Max $\hat{R}$	1.0004	Excellent (< 1.01)
Min ESS (bulk)	10937	Excellent (> 400)
Min ESS (tail)	12358	Excellent (> 400)
Parameters with $\hat{R} > 1.01$	0	Excellent

Figure 1 summarizes the estimated genetic effects on the biomarker trajectory. The intercept effects reveal a clear stratification across genotype subgroups. Genotypes carrying the APOE $\epsilon 4$ allele exhibit higher baseline values of z_0, with the strongest effect observed for the 4/4 subgroup. In contrast, genotypes containing the $\epsilon 2$ allele tend to show lower baseline values, suggesting a more conservative disease profile.

Genetic effects on the temporal slope are estimated with greater uncertainty. While $\epsilon 4$-associated genotypes display, on average, steeper trajectories, variability across subgroups limits the strength of conclusions that can be drawn from slope estimates alone. This behavior is expected in a population-level model that does not explicitly account for subject-specific heterogeneity. Nevertheless, the overall direction of the effects remains consistent with known genetic risk patterns [7].

The combined impact of intercept and slope effects on the population trajectories is shown in the lower panels of Fig. 1. Subjects in the 3/4 and 4/4 subgroups exhibit a more pronounced increase in z_0 across the observed time span, indicating greater disease burden relative to the reference group. In contrast, genotypes associates with the $\epsilon 2$ allele show attenuated trajectories.

Figure 2 and Tables 4 and 5 provide a clearer visualization of genotype-specific deviations relative to the 3/3 reference trajectory. Genotypes 3/4 and 4/4 consistently display higher biomarker values across the age range, reflecting earlier disease onset. Conversely, genotypes 2/2, 2/3, and 2/4 show lower baseline values and reduced progression. Notably, the 2/4 subgroup exhibits an intermediate trajectory, suggesting a compensatory interaction between the protective $\epsilon 2$ and the risk-associated $\epsilon 4$ alleles.

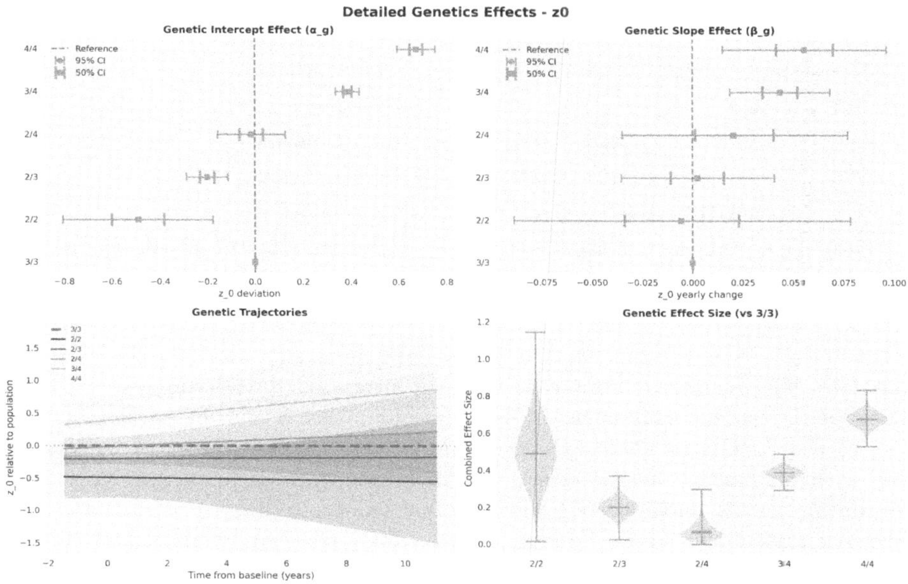

Fig. 1. Detailed genetic effects. Top left and top right panels show the effects of the genetic intercept γ and the genetic slope δ of each genotype subgroup Bottom left panel shows the genetic trajectories during the ADNI data collection span. Bottom right shows the combined effect of each genotype subgroup. Note that genotype 3/3 has been set as reference due to its large number of observations.

4 Discussion

In this work, we examined whether a dementia-related neuroimaging biomarker derived directly from FDG-PET scans preserves clinically meaningful genetic structure when analyzed longitudinally. The biomarker z_0, previously shown to encode dementia-related metabolic patterns [8], was modeled using a Bayesian longitudinal framework incorporating APOE genotype as a population-level

Table 4. γ parameter statistics for each genotype.

Genotype	γ (Effect)	SD	95% CI	Significance
3/3	0.0	—	—	Reference
2/2	**-0.495**	0.161	[-0.815, -0.176]	Significant (**protective**)
2/3	**-0.205**	0.043	[-0.291, -0.120]	Significant (**protective**)
2/4	-0.020	0.071	[-0.161, 0.120]	Not significant
3/4	**+0.381**	0.025	[0.331, 0.431]	Significant (**risk**)
4/4	**0.647**	0.040	[0.569, 0.726]	Significant (**risk**)

Table 5. δ parameter statistics for each genotype.

Genotype	$\boldsymbol{\delta}$ (Effect)	SD	95% CI	Significance
3/3	0.0	—	—	Reference
2/2	−0.007	0.042	[−0.077, 0.063]	Not significant
2/3	−0.000	0.019	[−0.032, −0.031]	Not significant
2/4	+0.018	0.029	[−0.029, 0.066]	Not significant
3/4	**+0.040**	0.013	[0.019, 0.061]	Significant (**faster progression**)
4/4	**+0.035**	0.021	[0.000, 0.070]	Marginal ($p \sim 0.05$)

covariate. The results demonstrate that the proposed model robustly captures genotype-dependent differences in baseline biomarker levels. In particular, carriers of the APOE $\epsilon 4$ allele exhibit systematically higher values of z_0, consistent with an earlier disease onset and increased risk. In contrast, genotypes containing the $\epsilon 2$ allele show lower baseline values, indicative of a more conservative trajectory. These findings closely align with well-established genetic risk profiles reported in the literature [7]. Genetic effects on the longitudinal progression are estimated with greater uncertainty. This is expected given the deliberate restriction of the model to population-level effects, without incorporating subject-specific random intercepts or slopes. Rather than aiming to fully explain individual variability, the goal of this study is to assess whether a latent biomarker extracted from neuroimaging retains sensitivity to genetic

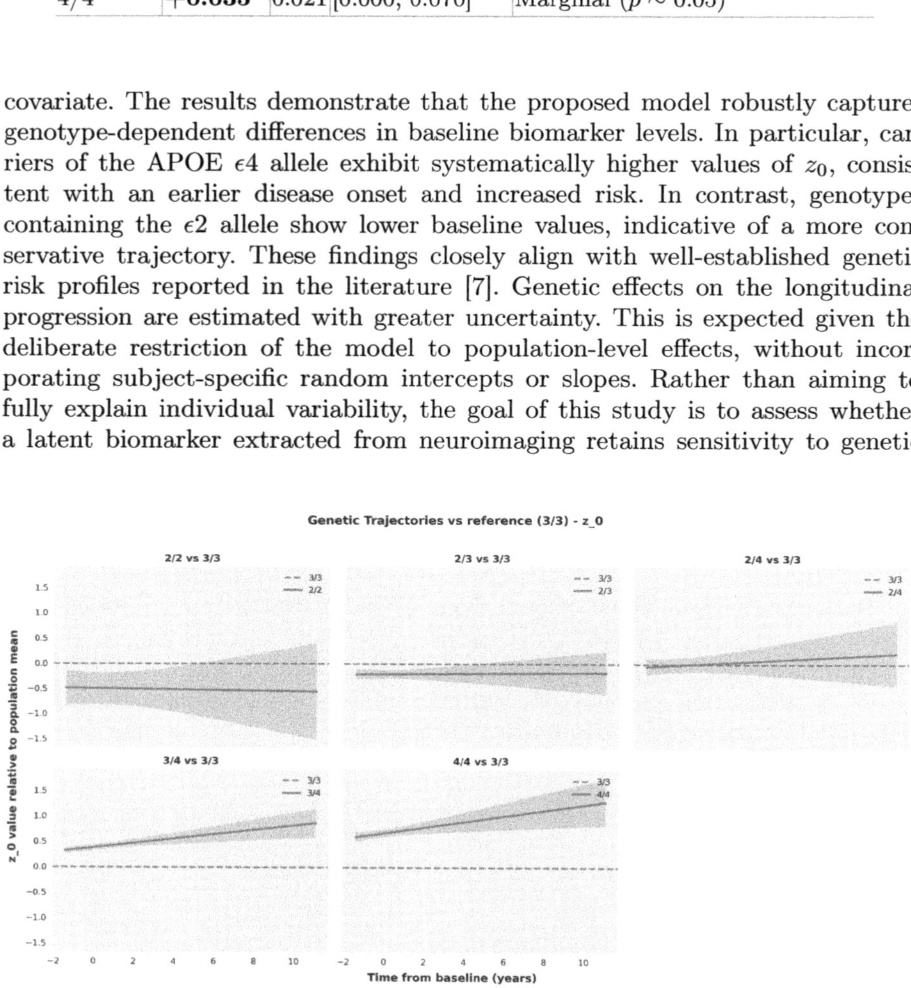

Fig. 2. Contribution of the genetic effects to the baseline trajectory for each genotype subgroup. This effect is computed as $\gamma^{(k)} + \delta^{(k)}t$, where k represents the genotype subgroup. Genotype 3/3 has been set as reference.

risk stratification at the population level. From this perspective, the observed slope effects—although modest—are directionally consistent with known APOE-related progression patterns, with $\epsilon4$-associated genotypes showing faster progression and $\epsilon2$-associated genotypes exhibiting attenuated trajectories. Based on the combined behavior of baseline and longitudinal effects, four broad genetic risk groups can be identified:

- Genotype 4/4, associated with high risk, early onset, and accelerated progression.
- Genotype 3/4, associated with elevated risk and early deviation from the reference trajectory.
- Genotypes 3/3 and 2/4, exhibiting intermediate or moderate risk.
- Genotypes 2/3 and 2/2, associated with low risk and relatively stable biomarker evolution.

It is important to interpret the insights from subgroups 2/2 and 2/4 with caution, due to the small number of subjects in each group.

Overall, these findings indicate that the proposed neuroimaging biomarker captures biologically and clinically meaningful genetic information, even within a simplified longitudinal modeling framework. This work constitutes a first step toward more expressive Bayesian models incorporating individual-level variability and additional covariates, while already demonstrating the potential of latent PET-derived biomarkers for early genetic risk stratification in AD.

Acknowledgments. This research is part of the PID2022-137629OA-I00 and PID2022-137451OB-I00 projects, funded by the MICIU/AEI /10.13039/501100011033 and by FEDER, EU, and the C-ING-183-UGR23 project, cofunded by the Consejería de Universidad, Investigación e Innovación and by European Union, funded by Programa FEDER Andalucía 2021–2027. F.J.M.M. received support from grant RYC2021-030875-I, funded by MICIU/AEI/10.13039/501100011033 and European Union NextGenerationEU/PRTR.

Data collection and sharing for the ADNI is funded by the National Institute on Aging (National Institutes of Health Grant U19AG024904). The grantee organization is the Northern California Institute for Research and Education. In the past, ADNI has also received funding from the National Institute of Biomedical Imaging and Bioengineering, the Canadian Institutes of Health Research, and private sector contributions through the Foundation for the National Institutes of Health (FNIH) including generous contributions from the following: AbbVie, Alzheimer's Association; Alzheimer's Drug Discovery Foundation; Araclon Biotech; BioClinica, Inc.; Biogen; Bristol-Myers Squibb Company; CereSpir, Inc.; Cogstate; Eisai Inc.; Elan Pharmaceuticals, Inc.; Eli Lilly and Company; EuroImmun; F. Hoffmann-La Roche Ltd.; Janssen Alzheimer Immunotherapy Research & Development, LLC.; Johnson & Johnson Pharmaceutical Research & Development LLC.; Luminosity; Lundbeck; Merck & Co., Inc.; Meso Scale Diagnostics, LLC.; NeuroRx Research; Neurotrack Technologies; Novartis Pharmaceuticals Corporation; Pfizer Inc.; Piramal Imaging; Servier; Takeda Pharmaceutical Company; and Transition Therapeutics.

References

1. Fletcher, J.: World Alzheimer Report 2024: Stigma and Awareness: Some Critical Questions. Alzheimer's Disease International, London (2024)
2. Frisoni, G.B., Fox, N.C., Jack, C.R., Jr., Scheltens, P., Thompson, P.M.: The clinical use of structural MRI in Alzheimer disease. Nat. Rev. Neurol. **6**(2), 67–77 (2010)
3. Tenenbaum, J., de Silva, V., Langford, J.A.: A global geometric framework for nonlinear dimensionality reduction. Science **290**(5500), 2319–2323 (2000)
4. Cunningham, J.P., Yu, B.M.: Dimensionality reduction for large-scale neural recordings. Nat. Neurosci. **17**(11), 1500–1509 (2014)
5. Bengio, Y., Courville, A., Vincent, P.: Representation learning: a review and new perspectives. IEEE Trans. Pattern Anal. Mach. Intell. **35**(8), 1798–1828 (2013)
6. Mosconi, L.: Brain glucose metabolism in the early and specific diagnosis of Alzheimer's disease: FDG-PET studies in MCI and AD. Eur. J. Nucl. Med. Mol. Imaging **32**(4), 486–510 (2005)
7. Bu, G.: APOE targeting strategy in Alzheimer's disease: lessons learned from protective variants. Mol. Neurodegener. **17**(1), 51 (2022)
8. Vázquez-García, C., et al.: An explainable framework for the relationship between dementia and glucose metabolism patterns. arXiv preprint arXiv:2601.20480 (2026)
9. Betancourt, M.: A conceptual introduction to Hamiltonian Monte Carlo. arXiv preprint arXiv:1701.02434 (2017)
10. Gelman, A., Simpson, D., Betancourt, M.: The prior can often only be understood in the context of the likelihood. Entropy **19**(10), 555 (2017)
11. Gelman, A., Rubin, D.B.: Inference from iterative simulation using multiple sequences. Stat. Sci. **7**(4), 457–472 (1992)
12. Kass, R.E., Carlin, B.P., Gelman, A., Neal, R.M.: Markov chain Monte Carlo in practice: a roundtable discussion. Am. Stat. **52**(2), 93–100 (1998)

Survival Modeling in the Latent Space for Alzheimer's Prognosis

F. J. Martinez-Murcia[1,4](✉), C. Vázquez-García[1,4], A. Forte Deltell[3], I. A. Illán[1,4], F. Segovia[1,4], Á. Hernández-Segura[1,4], C. Jiménez-Mesa[2,4], J. E. Arco[1,4], J. Ramírez[1,4], J. M. Górriz[1,4], and for the Alzheimer's Disease Neuroimaging Initiative ADNI[1,2,3,4]

[1] Department Signal Theory, Networking and Communications, University of Granada, Granada, Spain
fjesusmartinez@ugr.es
[2] Department of Communications Engineering, University of Malaga, Malaga, Spain
[3] Department of Statistics and Operations Research, University of Valencia, Valencia, Spain
[4] Andalusian Research Institute on Data Science and Computational Intelligence, University of Granada, Granada, Spain

Abstract. Background: Accurate prediction of dementia onset is critical for clinical trial design but often fails to capture dynamic disease progression. Methods: We benchmarked four survival architectures using latent neurodegenerative signatures (z-scores) and genetic data (APOE4) over a 15-year horizon, evaluating integrated predictive performance focused on a 10-year study period. Results: Parametric Accelerated Failure Time (AFT) models, specifically the Log-Normal architecture, achieved the highest discriminative accuracy (C-index $= 0.765$, $iAUC = 0.791$). Sensitivity analysis revealed that while APOE4 dominates late risk, latent biomarkers drive accuracy at early stages of the disease, especially the z_2 in the 2.5–10 years, eventually subsuming traditional demographic signals. Conclusion: Latent phenotypic markers are essential for short-term prognosis, requiring model architectures matched to specific clinical objectives.

Keywords: Survival Analysis · Latent Variable · Alzheimer's Disease

1 Introduction

Alzheimer's disease (AD) is one of the most formidable health and socioeconomic challenges of the 21st century [1]. As the global population ages, the prevalence

Data used in preparation of this article were obtained from the Alzheimer's Disease Neuroimaging Initiative (ADNI) database (adni.loni.usc.edu). ADNI investigators contributed to the design and implementation of ADNI but did not participate in analysis or writing of this report. A complete listing of ADNI investigators can be found at: http://adni.loni.usc.edu/wp-content/uploads/howtoapply/ADNIAcknowledgementList.pdf.

J. M. Ferrndez Vicente et al. (Eds.): IWINAC 2026, LNCS 16574, pp. 75–84, 2026.
https://doi.org/10.1007/978-3-032-27314-7_8

of dementia is projected to grow exponentially, placing an unsustainable burden on health systems and family care structures. Due to the variability of the disease, much effort has been put into research, treatment and clinical practice in the last 20 years. In this context, the focus has shifted from the diagnosis of established dementia to early identification and risk stratification in the prodromal stages, specifically in Mild Cognitive Impairment (MCI).

MCI represents a heterogeneous transitional state between normal cognitive aging and dementia [2,5]. While a significant proportion of individuals with MCI progress to AD, others remain stable or even revert to normal, raising a critical question that transcends binary classification. Other approaches focus on the prognosis of specific diagnostic categories, such as the MCI-converters (MCI-c) and non-converters [6,8]. However, dementia is, by nature, a continuous process, and the use of diagnostic classes, although useful for clinical practice, may hinder research.

In this context, newer studies are focusing on longitudinal changes in specific biomarkers [9], linking them to newer stratification that may help not only in clinical practice but also in clinical research and drug development [10]. The existence of an underlying "disease continuum" has been repeatedly proven [9, 10]. From a mathematical point of view, this disease continuum might be seen as a "latent" variable under the manifold hypothesis [11], and here, Variational Autoencoders (VAEs) stand out as promising tools to unveil this latent space [4,11,12].

This work explores the predictive ability of these latent spaces in predicting disease prognosis using "time-to-event" modelling, what is more commonly known as survival analysis [13,14]. The usage of latent features as covariates for survival models has been poorly explored in the literature, and such, it may reveal as a promising tool not only for clinical practice but also for clinical research, paving the way for novel methods of risk assessment in clinical research and practice.

2 Methodology

2.1 Latent Variable Analysis Through Variational Autoencoders

In AD, the neurodegenerative process can be viewed as a "disease continuum" that drives changes in biomarker expression and diagnostic outcomes. We captured this using Variational Autoencoders (VAEs) [15], which are probabilistic generative models that learn a continuous, structured latent space. The VAE architecture comprises a probabilistic encoder mapping input to a latent distribution $q_\phi(z|x)$ and a decoder modeling the probability of reconstructing the input $p_\theta(x|z)$. The model optimizes the Evidence Lower Bound (ELBO), balancing a reconstruction loss with a KL divergence regularization term. This forces the latent distribution toward a standard Normal prior, ensuring a continuous and smooth space for valid interpolation. It can be thought of as a regularization term. In further modifications of the VAE, other parameters and terms are added, such as the β-VAE [16], which adds a β parameter to control the regularization term.

Research has shown that the learnt μ and σ can be used as proxies of the latent space, and indeed, they are used in many works as features for further processing in neurodegeneration [12].

In this work, the encoder $q_\phi(z|x)$ was modeled using a 3-layer MLP network ($N \rightarrow 64 \rightarrow 32 \rightarrow 3$). Hidden layers used nonlinear activation (leaky RELU) and batch normalization to stabilize training. Latent space was configured in $z = 3$ dimensions for simplicity and to enable 3D visualization. The decoder $p_\theta(x|z)$ was modelled using a symmetric MLP network expanding the dimensions from the latent space ($3 \rightarrow 32 \rightarrow 64 \rightarrow N$). The model was trained on 70% of the dataset using subject stratification, saving 15% for validation and 15% for testing. We used the Mean Squared Error (MSE) for reconstruction loss and $\beta = 2$ to improve disentanglement. The training was stopped after convergence (no performance improvement in the validation set).

2.2 Survival Analysis

Survival analysis is a probabilistic framework designed to study the duration until an event of interest occurs while handling incomplete information via censoring [14]. In a longitudinal AD study, some MCI participants may experience the event of interest (conversion from a diagnosis of MCI to one of Alzheimer's-type dementia), but some others not (censored). Treating them as "non-converters" in a binary classification discards the vital information that they remained disease-free up to a certain point in time t. Survival analysis incorporates this information through the concept of censoring [13].

Formally, survival models are specified via the survival and risk functions. Let T be a non-negative random variable representing the time to conversion to AD. The survival function $S(t)$ is defined as the probability that an individual survives (does not convert) beyond time t:

$$S(t) = P(T > t)$$

Complementarily, the instantaneous risk function (hazard function), $\lambda(t)$, describes the rate of occurrence of the event at time t, given that the individual has survived until that moment:

$$\lambda(t) = \lim_{\Delta t \rightarrow 0} \frac{P(t \leq T < t + \Delta t | T \geq t)}{\Delta t}$$

This function allows us to evaluate how the risk of conversion evolves over time and how it is modulated by specific covariates. To rigorously evaluate longitudinal dementia risk, we employed a comparative framework using both semiparametric and fully parametric architectures. The semiparametric Cox Proportional Hazards (CPH) model [17] was used to evaluate relative risk, assuming that the hazard ratio between individuals remains constant over time.

To directly model expected survival times, we implemented fully parametric Accelerated Failure Time (AFT) models [18], which assume covariates multiplicatively accelerate or decelerate disease onset. We evaluated three distinct parametric distributions for the AFT error term: Weibull for a monotonic hazard, Log-Normal for a unimodal hazard, and Log-Logistic for a unimodal, heavy-tailed hazard well-suited for late-onset clinical events.

After VAE training, we froze the encoder weights, and projected all study subjects and visits into the three-dimensional latent space. For each visit, we obtain a latent $z_i = \mu_{i,0}, \mu_{i,1}, \mu_{i,2}$ vector, which will be part of the survival regression, along with variables such as gender, education or genotype (including APOE). By contrasting the CPH model with these three AFT distributions, we aimed to determine whether a proportional risk assumption or a specific parametric acceleration of disease onset best captures the progression of dementia in this cohort.

2.3 Experimental Setup

The Alzheimer's Disease Neuroimaging Initiative (ADNI). Data used in the preparation of this article were obtained from the Alzheimer's Disease Neuroimaging Initiative (ADNI) database (adni.loni.usc.edu). The ADNI was launched in 2003 as a public-private partnership, led by Principal Investigator Michael W. Weiner, MD. The primary goal of ADNI has been to test whether serial magnetic resonance imaging (MRI), positron emission tomography (PET), other biological markers, and clinical and neuropsychological assessment can be combined to measure the progression of mild cognitive impairment (MCI) and early Alzheimer's disease (AD). For up-to-date information, see www.adni-info.org.

In this work, we model tabular data derived from structural MRI (see Table 1 for demographic details). Specifically we performed cortical reconstruction and volumetric segmentation with the Freesurfer image analysis suite [19]. This generates an input vector $x \in \mathbb{R}^N$, where N typically ranges from a 50 to 150 (in our work, it was 87, as for the cortical aseg atlas). Data was afterwards normalized by the total intracranial volume (TIV) to correct for head size variations, and standardization (Z-score) of the variables.

Table 1. Demographics of the dataset, including the number of recorded events (no/yes) for each of the ApoE-4 genotypes and gender.

	N	Age	Education	MCI (N/Y)	Dementia (N/Y)	Death (N/Y)
Total	296	72.63 (±7.29)	16.10 (±2.67)	265/31	239/57	264/32
ApoE-4 0	165	72.84 (±7.71)	16.20 (±2.60)	146/19	138/27	151/14
ApoE-4 1	108	73.07 (±6.68)	15.91 (±2.81)	96/12	85/23	92/16
ApoE-4 2	23	69.07 (±6.15)	16.26 (±2.53)	23/0	16/7	21/2
Female	156	72.06 (±7.27)	15.71 (±2.52)	137/19	129/27	140/16
Male	140	73.27 (±7.29)	16.54 (±2.77)	128/12	110/30	124/16

Evaluation
We report performance metrics (C-index) within a 5-fold cross-validation approach. To evaluate the longitudinal consistency of the model's predictive accuracy, we assessed the Brier Score across a temporal grid ranging from 2 to 15 years post-baseline, as implemented in [20]. The time-dependent Brier score is an extension of the mean squared error to right censored data. Given a time point t, it is defined as:

$$\mathrm{BS}^c(t) = \frac{1}{n} \sum_{i=1}^{n} I(y_i \leq t \wedge \delta_i = 1) \frac{(0 - \hat{\pi}(t|\mathbf{x}_i))^2}{\hat{G}(y_i)} + I(y_i > t) \frac{(1 - \hat{\pi}(t|\mathbf{x}_i))^2}{\hat{G}(t)},$$

where $\hat{\pi}(t|\mathbf{x})$ is a model's predicted probability of remaining event-free up to time point t for the feature vector $\mathbf{x}$, and $1/\hat{G}(t)$ is an inverse probability of censoring weight. This approach accounts for the dynamic nature of dementia progression. Furthermore, we calculated the Integrated Brier Score (IBS) to provide a single summary metric of the model's cumulative calibration error across the entire study duration. Feature importance was verified across multiple landmarks to ensure that the identified predictors remained relevant over both short-term (5-year) and long-term (10–15 year) horizons.

To assess the time-dependent discriminative capacity of our models, we calculated the Cumulative Dynamic Area Under the ROC Curve ($AUC(t)$). Following the framework of [21], this approach defines 'cases' as individuals who experienced a dementia event by time t and 'controls' as those who remained event-free beyond that landmark. This provides a longitudinal profile of model performance, whereas the standard Harrell's C-index provides only a global summary. We further summarized this performance using the mean cumulative AUC (iAUC), representing the integrated discriminative accuracy over the entire 15-year study period.

3 Results and Discussion

3.1 Comparative Model Performance

To rigorously evaluate model performance, we used a tri-metric approach capturing both global rank-order and time-dependent probabilistic accuracy. As detailed in Table 2, the fully parametric, heavy-tailed Accelerated Failure Time (AFT) models consistently outperformed both the semi-parametric Cox framework and the monotonic Weibull model. The Log-Normal AFT model demonstrated the highest global discriminative capacity (C-index = 0.765 [0.013]). This discriminative superiority was maintained across the longitudinal horizon, with the Log-Normal model also achieving the highest Integrated Cumulative Dynamic AUC (iAUC = 0.791 [0.017]). This indicates that the Log-Normal distribution best captures the overall hierarchy of dementia risk across the disease continuum.

Table 2. Cross-Validated Predictive Performance of Survival Models. Note: Lower IBS indicates superior calibration; higher iAUC indicates superior discrimination. Both metrics integrate performance across the 10-year study horizon

	C-index	IBS	iAUC
CoxPH	0.757 [0.015]	0.130 [0.006]	0.783 [0.020]
LogLogisticAFT	0.764 [0.013]	0.127 [0.007]	0.790 [0.017]
LogNormalAFT	0.765 [0.013]	0.128 [0.006]	0.791 [0.017]
WeibullAFT	0.757 [0.015]	0.130 [0.006]	0.783 [0.020]

Furthermore, the heavy-tailed parametric models also achieved superior probabilistic calibration over time. The Log-Logistic AFT model yielded the lowest Integrated Brier Score (IBS $= 0.127 \pm 0.007$), closely followed by the Log-Normal model (IBS $= 0.128 \pm 0.006$). By comparison, the Cox Proportional Hazards and Weibull AFT models exhibited higher prediction error (IBS $= 0.130 \pm 0.006$). This demonstrates that heavy-tailed parametric assumptions not only excel at stratifying patient risk but also generate the most reliable absolute survival probabilities across the 10-year horizon. We computed the integrated AUC and BS in the 10 year due to the small population with follow-up times beyond 10 years.

By evaluating models across this tri-metric framework, we established the comprehensive superiority of heavy-tailed parametric architectures (Log-Normal and Log-Logistic AFT) for dementia risk modeling. Unlike typical survival analyses where semi-parametric models (like Cox) are favored for their lack of baseline hazard assumptions, our cohort data decisively favored specific parametric structures. The Log-Normal model achieved the highest discrimination (C-index and iAUC), whereas the Log-Logistic model achieved optimal longitudinal calibration (IBS).

Biologically and mathematically, this unified performance makes sense. The Cox model assumes proportional hazards, and the Weibull model assumes a strictly monotonic (constantly accelerating) risk over time. In contrast, Log-Normal and Log-Logistic distributions assume a unimodal hazard with heavy tails –a model that accommodates a 'peak' conversion window followed by a long tail of resilient survivors who convert much later than average. The superior performance of these models across all three metrics strongly suggests that 10-year dementia progression is best characterized by this heavy-tailed, non-monotonic hazard, establishing the Log-Normal and Log-Logistic AFT models as the optimal statistical tools for both clinical trial stratification and individualized risk prognostication.

3.2 Temporal Dynamics of Predictive Accuracy

Because dementia pathology evolves progressively, we analyzed the temporal stability of our models using time-dependent metrics.

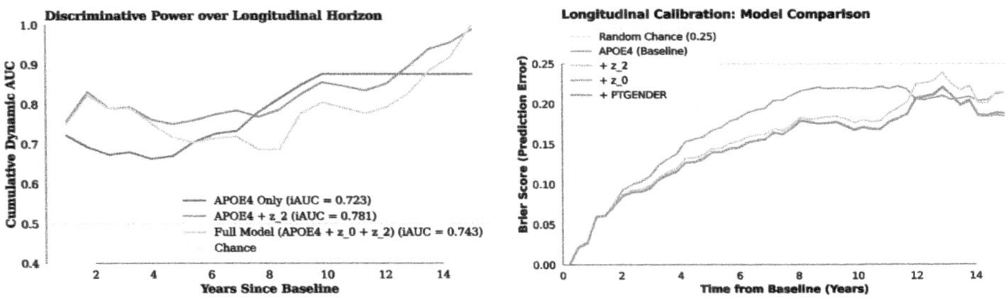

(a) Cumulative Dynamic AUC (b) Time-dependent Brier Scores

Fig. 1. Longitudinal Predictive Performance of Survival Models. (A) Cumulative Dynamic AUC ($AUC(t)$) illustrating the discriminative capacity of nested feature sets over time. The integrated AUC (iAUC) demonstrates that the inclusion of latent factors z_0 and z_2 provides superior risk stratification over the baseline *APOE4* model. (B) Time-dependent Brier Scores across a 15-year horizon; the dashed gray line at 0.25 represents the threshold for non-informative predictions.

As shown in Fig. 1a, the Cumulative Dynamic AUC reveals a slight temporal decay, indicating that baseline biomarkers are highly sensitive to proximal conversion (within 5–8 years) but experience a minor reduction in discriminative power for distal risk (up to 15 years). Nevertheless, the full model maintained an integrated AUC (iAUC) well above chance. Furthermore, longitudinal calibration remained robust; the time-dependent Brier Score (Fig. 1b) consistently stayed below the 0.25 non-informative threshold across the entire 15-year horizon, confirming the long-term reliability of the probabilistic risk projections.

3.3 Model Examination

The model was trained using lifelines [22], and the LogNormalAFTFitter class, with a training set of 683 observations (151 events observed). Each observation, even from the same participant, was treated as independent because it is identified by a genotype, latent vector, and other population features; however, during cross-validation we deliberately kept observations from a single subject within the same fold to prevent potential flaws. The training ended with a log-likelihood of -544.98, a C-index of 0.77, AIC of 1099.97 and a log-likelihood ratio test 104.81 on 3 df. Model coefficients are shown at Fig. 2a. The coefficient analysis (Fig. 2a) confirms that genetic susceptibility (*APOE4*) and latent structural/cognitive signatures (z_0, z_2) are the primary drivers of model accuracy.

More importantly, the temporal heatmap (Fig. 2b) unveils a highly dynamic 'crossover' effect in biomarker relevance. Feature importance was quantified by evaluating the change in Brier Score (ΔBS) upon the systematic removal of individual covariates. Latent structural/cognitive signatures, specifically z_2, exhibited peak predictive utility at the early and mid-term landmarks (2.5 to 10 years). In contrast, genetic susceptibility (APOE4) demonstrated a 'late-gain'

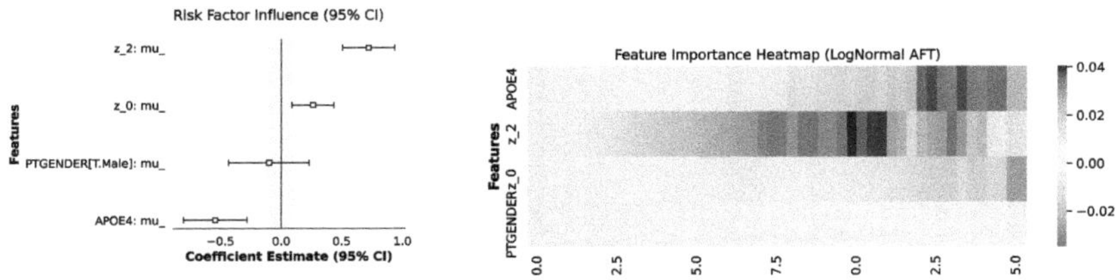

(a) Forest plot of log-hazard coefficients

(b) Temporal Importance Heatmap

Fig. 2. Predictor Significance and Dynamic Importance. (A) Forest plot of log-hazard coefficients with 95% confidence intervals; positive values indicate an acceleration of dementia onset. (B) Temporal Importance Heatmap (Δ Brier Score) across study landmarks. Note the "Late-Gain" profile of latent factor z_0, where its contribution to model calibration increases substantially at the 12- and 15-year horizons.

importance profile, dominating the predictive weighting at the 12- and 15-year horizons.

4 Conclusions

This study demonstrates that longitudinal dementia risk requires moving beyond static evaluations. We identified a predictive 'crossover': latent neurodegenerative signatures (specifically z_2) are the primary drivers for early-to-mid-term prognosis, whereas genetic utility (APOE4) peaks late, driving distal outcomes at the 15-year horizon. These findings suggest that for clinical trial enrichment, heavy-tailed AFT models provide optimal stratification, whereas the Cox model, driven by late-stage latent biomarkers, offers a more calibrated tool for personalized patient care.

Acknowledgements. This work is part of the projects PID2022-137629OA-I00 and PID2022-137451OB-I00, and by grant CNS2024-154296 funded by funded by MICIU/AEI/10.13039/501100011033 and by ERDF/EU. Work by F.J.M.M. is supported by the grant RYC2021-030875-I funded by MICIU/AEI/10.13039/-501100011033 and by European Union NextGenerationEU/PRTR.

Data collection and sharing for this project was funded by the Alzheimer's Disease Neuroimaging Initiative (ADNI) (National Institutes of Health Grant U01 AG024904) and DOD ADNI (Department of Defense award number W81XWH-12-2-0012). ADNI is funded by the National Institute on Aging, the National Institute of Biomedical Imaging and Bioengineering, and through generous contributions from the following: AbbVie, Alzheimer's Association; Alzheimer's Drug Discovery Foundation; Araclon Biotech; BioClinica, Inc.; Biogen; Bristol-Myers Squibb Company; CereSpir, Inc.; Cogstate; Eisai Inc.; Elan Pharmaceuticals, Inc.; Eli Lilly and Company; EuroImmun; F. Hoffmann-La Roche Ltd and its affiliated company Genentech, Inc.; Fujirebio; GE Healthcare; IXICO Ltd.; Janssen Alzheimer Immunotherapy Research & Development, LLC.; Johnson & Johnson Pharmaceutical Research & Development LLC.; Lumosity; Lundbeck; Merck & Co., Inc.; Meso Scale Diagnostics, LLC.; NeuroRx Research;

Neurotrack Technologies; Novartis Pharmaceuticals Corporation; Pfizer Inc.; Piramal Imaging; Servier; Takeda Pharmaceutical Company; and Transition Therapeutics. The Canadian Institutes of Health Research is providing funds to support ADNI clinical sites in Canada. Private sector contributions are facilitated by the Foundation for the National Institutes of Health (www.fnih.org). The grantee organization is the Northern California Institute for Research and Education, and the study is coordinated by the Alzheimer's Therapeutic Research Institute at the University of Southern California. ADNI data are disseminated by the Laboratory for Neuro Imaging at the University of Southern California.

References

1. 2025 Alzheimer's Disease Facts and Figures. Alzheimer's & Dementia. 21 (2025)
2. Illan, I.A., et al.: Spatial component analysis of MRI data for Alzheimer's disease diagnosis: a Bayesian network approach. Front. Comput. Neurosci. **8**, 156 (2014). https://doi.org/10.3389/fncom.2014.00156
3. Martinez-Murcia, F.J., et al.: Computer aided diagnosis tool for Alzheimer's disease based on Mann–Whitney–Wilcoxon U-test. Expert Syst. Appl. **39**, 9676–9685 (2012). https://doi.org/10.1016/j.eswa.2012.02.153
4. Martinez-Murcia, F.J., et al.: Studying the manifold structure of Alzheimer's disease: a deep learning approach using convolutional autoencoders. IEEE J. Biomed. Health Inform. **24**, 17–26 (2020). https://doi.org/10.1109/JBHI.2019.2914970
5. Górriz, J.M., et al.: Computational approaches to explainable artificial intelligence: advances in theory, applications and trends. Inf. Fusion **100**, 101945 (2023). https://doi.org/10.1016/j.inffus.2023.101945
6. Aksu, Y., et al.: An MRI-derived definition of MCI-to-AD conversion for long-term, automatic prognosis of MCI patients. PLoS ONE **6**, e25074 (2011). https://doi.org/10.1371/journal.pone.0025074
7. Górriz, J.M., et al.: Artificial intelligence within the interplay between natural and artificial computation: advances in data science, trends and applications. Neurocomputing **410**, 237–270 (2020). https://doi.org/10.1016/j.neucom.2020.05.078
8. Adaszewski, S., et al.: How early can we predict Alzheimer's disease using computational anatomy? Neurobiol. Aging **34**, 28152826 (2013)
9. McDade, E., et al.: Longitudinal cognitive and biomarker changes in dominantly inherited Alzheimer disease. Neurology **91**, e1295–e1306 (2018). https://doi.org/10.1212/WNL.0000000000006277
10. Jack, C.R., Jr., et al.: Revised criteria for diagnosis and staging of Alzheimer's disease: Alzheimer's Association Workgroup. Alzheimer's Dementia **20**, 5143–5169 (2024). https://doi.org/10.1002/alz.13859
11. Martinez-Murcia, F.J., et al.: Bridging imaging and clinical scores in Parkinson's progression via multimodal self-supervised deep learning. Int. J. Neural Syst. **34**, 2450043 (2024). https://doi.org/10.1142/S0129065724500436
12. Sauty, B., Durrleman, S.: Progression models for imaging data with longitudinal variational auto encoders. In: Wang, L., et al. (eds.) MICCAI 2022. LNCS, vol. 13431, pp. 3–13. Springer, Cham (2022). https://doi.org/10.1007/978-3-031-16431-6_1
13. Nakagawa, T., et al.: Prediction of conversion to Alzheimerś disease using deep survival analysis of MRI images. Brain Commun. **2**, fcaa057 (2020). https://doi.org/10.1093/braincomms/fcaa057

14. Orozco-Sanchez, J., et al.: Exploring Survival Models Associated with MCI to AD Conversion: A Machine Learning Approach (2019). https://doi.org/10.1101/836510
15. Kingma, D.P., Welling, M.: Auto-encoding variational bayes. arXiv preprint arXiv:1312.6114 (2013)
16. Higgins, I., et al.: β-VAE: learning Basic Visual Concepts with a Constrained Variational Framework 22 (2017)
17. Desikan, R.S., et al.: Genetic assessment of age-associated Alzheimer disease risk: development and validation of a polygenic hazard score. PLoS Med. **14**, e1002258 (2017). https://doi.org/10.1371/journal.pmed.1002258
18. Liu, E., et al.: Using the weibull accelerated failure time regression model to predict time to health events. Appl. Sci. **13**, 13041 (2023). https://doi.org/10.3390/app132413041
19. Fischl, B., et al.: Sequence-independent segmentation of magnetic resonance images. Neuroimage **23**(Suppl 1), S69-84 (2004). https://doi.org/10.1016/j.neuroimage.2004.07.016
20. Pölsterl, S.: Scikit-survival: a library for time-to-event analysis built on top of scikit-learn. J. Mach. Learn. Res. **21**, 1–6 (2020)
21. Heagerty, P.J., et al.: Time-dependent ROC curves for censored survival data and a diagnostic marker. Biometrics **56**, 337–344 (2000). https://doi.org/10.1111/j.0006-341x.2000.00337.x
22. Davidson-Pilon, C.: Lifelines: survival analysis in python. J. Open Source Softw. **4**, 1317 (2019). https://doi.org/10.21105/joss.01317

Segmentation of Traumatic Brain Injury on Magnetic Resonance Imaging

Jenifer Castaño(✉), Deisy Chaves, Maria Trujillo, Alejandro Herrera, and Pedro Amador

Universidad del Valle, Cali, Colombia
{jenifer.castano,deisy.chaves,maria.trujillo,herrera.alejandro, pedro.amador}@correounivalle.edu.co

Abstract. Traumatic brain injury (TBI) is one of the leading causes of disability and mortality worldwide, since a large proportion of the population is exposed to this kind of injury due to falls or traffic accidents. TBI can lead to short and long-term consequences, affecting the physical, mental, and functional health of individuals. These sequelae involve social, emotional, and professional challenges, directly impacting quality of life. TBI diagnosis is based on the study of injuries on Magnetic resonance imaging brain images; however, the accurate segmentation of TBI-related injuries remains challenging due to their variability in size, shape, location, and imaging characteristics, which limits the accuracy of diagnosis. This work proposes a strategy for the automatic segmentation of injuries associated with TBI based on nnU-Net, including an evaluation of different preprocessing techniques and fine-tuning to analyze their effect on the model's performance. The results show that nnU-Net combined with KDE normalization and fine-tuning achieves the best performance (DSC = 0.56). Besides, a framework integrating the entire segmentation pipeline was implemented, providing a tool to support clinical practice and future research related to TBI.

Keywords: Medical Image Segmentation · Traumatic Brain Injury · Brain MRI · Deep Learning

1 Introduction

Traumatic brain injury (TBI) remains a major global public health concern and is among the leading causes of death and long-term disability worldwide, with millions of new cases each year [9]. TBI caused injuries such as concussions, contusions, diffuse axonal injury, hematomas, and intracranial hemorrhages [8], which can lead to permanent cognitive, motor, and psychiatric sequelae [5]. Accurate and early identification of these injuries is essential for clinical diagnosis and treatment planning.

Magnetic resonance imaging (MRI), particularly $T1$-weighted images, enables detailed visualization of brain structures and TBI-associated lesions. However,

J. M. Ferrández Vicente et al. (Eds.): IWINAC 2026, LNCS 16574, pp. 85–95, 2026.
https://doi.org/10.1007/978-3-032-27314-7_9

manual segmentation is a time-consuming process, dependent on specialist expertise and prone to errors. Besides, traumatic lesions exhibit high variability in size, shape, location, and intensity, thereby complicating image registration and intensity normalization and potentially introducing both local and global errors in the segmentation process [7].

Although automatic and semi-automatic methods have been developed to address this problem [1,13,19], no model has yet been established as a reliable standard for the segmentation of TBI-associated lesions [3]. In this context, deep learning-based models, particularly U-Net architectures, have shown promising results in segmenting the brain MRI injuries [10,22]. However, most prior studies emphasize architectural design, with limited attention to the impact of preprocessing on model performance.

In this work, we systematically evaluate the influence of anatomical registration, atlas selection, intensity standardization, and the use of pretraining on the automatic segmentation of TBI lesions in $T1$-weighted MRI. Therefore, the main contributions of this study are twofold: i) the identification of an effective preprocessing configuration for U-Net–based TBI segmentation, including registration strategies, atlas selection, and intensity normalization techniques; ii) a reproducible and ready-to-use framework for the automatic segmentation of TBI lesions in $T1$-weighted images. Experimental results highlight the importance of preprocessing in traumatic lesion segmentation tasks, demonstrating that specific choices can improve segmentation performance.

2 Related Work

The identification of brain lesions in MRI has been addressed through various methods, including conventional approaches and deep learning-based models. Traditional methods include clustering techniques such as K-Means and Fuzzy C-Means [1], as well as probabilistic models based on Markov random fields and atlas-based quantification approaches [14]. Optimization strategies have also been proposed, such as Particle Swarm Optimization (PSO) and hybrid variants inspired by biological algorithms.

In recent years, convolutional neural network-based techniques have demonstrated superior performance in medical image segmentation tasks. In particular, architectures based on U-Net and its variants, both 2D and 3D, have been widely used to segment white matter lesions, hematomas, and other structural alterations [10,22]. Similarly, hybrid models combining U-Net with transformers, such as HUT [18], and architectures based on Swin Transformers, such as SwinUNETR [17], have been proposed. In addition, automated tools such as Icobrain, FreeSurfer, SPM, and FSL have been employed for structural and volumetric segmentation in various clinical contexts [4,13,21].

Regarding preprocessing, the analyzed studies report the use of techniques such as skull stripping, bias field correction, intensity normalization, noise reduction, and registration to a standard atlas [16,17]. In addition, data augmentation and multimodal registration strategies have been applied to improve model robustness. Despite these advances, most research focuses primarily on model architecture, whereas the effect of preprocessing configurations on final segmentation performance has been less explored, particularly in the context of TBI. This gap motivates the present study.

3 Proposed Strategy

The proposed strategy for TBI injury segmentation is illustrated in Fig. 1. The workflow begins with the AIMS-TBI dataset, which includes 172 subjects with lesions and 115 healthy controls. These images are preprocessed using a five-step pipeline: skull removal, image alignment, cropping based on the region of interest, intensity normalization, and finally resampling. Using the preprocessed images, the model is trained, incorporating the fine-tuned weights obtained from an external dataset. Finally, the trained model performs predictions on unseen images, and its performance is evaluated.

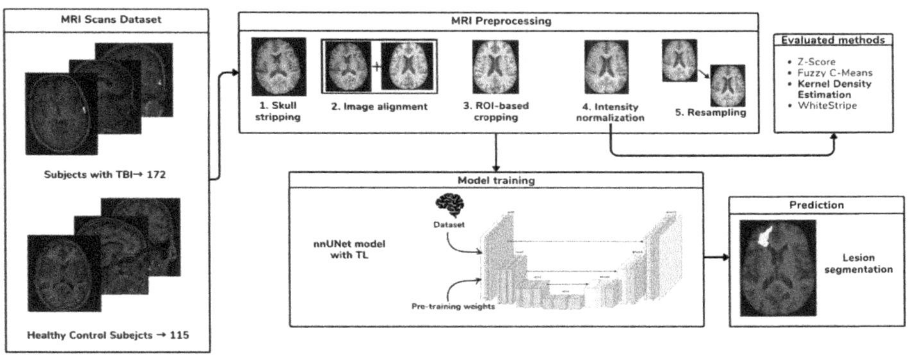

Fig. 1. Proposed workflow for segmenting TBI-associated lesions.

The proposed framework, including preprocessing scripts, normalization implementations, training configurations, and evaluation procedures, is publicly available at https://github.com/CastanoJenifer/TCEC-Segmentation. This repository provides detailed instructions for data preparation and execution.

3.1 MRI Scan Datasets

In this study, two datasets were employed: the BRATS dataset for fine-tuning and the AIMS-TBI dataset for the primary task.

AIMS-TBI 2025: The dataset used for model training and evaluation corresponds to the Automated Identification of Moderate-Severe Traumatic Brain Injury (AIMS-TBI 2025) challenge [7], organized as part of MICCAI 2025. The images were acquired at multiple centers using different 1.5T and 3T MRI scanners and include $T1$-weighted MRI scans. The ground truth annotations were generated through automated segmentation followed by manual review by two trained annotators and subsequently validated by an expert annotator [7].

The original annotations in the AIMS-TBI dataset included multiple labels which, according to a neurology specialist, correspond to different types of injuries. However, as classification was not the objective of this study, the labels were binarized into lesion (1) and non-lesion (0). The final dataset comprises 287 subjects (166 men and 121 women).

BRATS 2021 (Dataset for Fine-Tuning): The BRATS 2021 competition training set, aimed at the automatic segmentation of brain gliomas in MRI, was used for pre-training. The dataset contains 1,251 3D studies with expert-validated manual annotations. Although multiple modalities are provided ($T1$, contrast-enhanced $T1$, $T2$, and $T2$-FLAIR). In this study, only the $T1$ modality is used. The original segmentations, which include multiple tumor subregions, were converted to a binary scheme (tumor $= 1$, non-tumor $= 0$) to maintain consistency with the binary segmentation task of the AIMS-TBI dataset.

3.2 MRI Preprocessing

Preprocessing consists of five sequential steps: (i) skull removal using the ROBEX tool [11], (ii) anatomical registration using ANTs [2], (iii) cropping based on the region of interest (brain), (iv) intensity normalization, and (v) resampling to an isotropic resolution. The first two preprocessing steps (i) and (ii) were specifically incorporated into this work to improve anatomical consistency, in addition to the standard nnU-Net preprocessing pipeline (steps iii, iv, and v). In particular, the SRI24 and ICBM152 atlases were evaluated for anatomical registration.

Although nnU-Net applies Z-score intensity normalization for T1-weighted images by default, we evaluated alternative methods, including Fuzzy C-Means (FCM), Kernel Density Estimation (KDE), and WhiteStripe (WS). These normalization methods were selected based on the analysis of [6], which evaluates the effect of intensity standardization strategies on longitudinal atrophy quantification, demonstrating that normalization can improve the quantification of atrophy. Alternative normalization techniques were implemented using the Intensity Normalization library and integrated into the nnU-Net pipeline.

This allowed us to analyze the influence of preprocessing decisions, atlas selection for anatomical registration, and the impact of intensity standardization on TBI segmentation models' performance.

3.3 Models

Preprocessed images were used to train TBI injury segmentation models by employing two architectures: nnU-Net and 3D U-Net, based on the U-Net architecture, which is widely used in medical image segmentation. In particular, nnU-Net [12] was selected as the main model for the study, because it automatically adapts to the dataset, without the need for extensive manual hyperparameter tuning. As a comparative model, we used a 3D U-Net implementation proposed by Wolny et al. [20], designed for volumetric segmentation of biomedical images. Moreover, fine-tuning was explored by first training the model on the source dataset to learn general feature representations, and subsequently fine-tuning it on the target dataset using the best-performing weights from the initial training stage.

4 Experimental Setup

For the assessment of the segmentation model based on nnU-Net optimized for TBI-associated lesions, the effect of different configurations on segmentation performance was analyzed focusing on three factors: (i) the atlas used for anatomical registration (ICBM152 or SRI24) and the training configuration (2D or 3D); (ii) the intensity normalization method (Z-score, Fuzzy C-Means, WhiteStripe, or Kernel Density Estimation); and (iii) the use of fine-tuning. Models were trained on the AIMS-TBI dataset, using 80% of the data for training (n = 230) and 20% for testing (n = 57). Also, all images of BRATS 2021 dataset were used to pre-train source models for fine-tuning.

4.1 Training Configuration

nnU-Net models were trained for 1,000 epochs using the standard U-Net architecture, with 125 iterations per epoch, a patch size of [128, 160, 112], and a batch size of 2. Optimization was performed using SGD with Nesterov momentum (0.99), an initial learning rate of $1e^{-2}$, a polynomial decay scheme, and a weight decay of $3e^{-5}$. The loss function combined Dice and Cross-Entropy with a smoothing factor of $1e^{-5}$. Data augmentation included 3D rotations and mirroring along all three axes.

For fine-tuning, pretraining was performed for 1,000 epochs (250 iterations per epoch) using the same hyperparameters. The comparative 3D U-Net model was trained for up to 125,000 iterations using the Adam optimizer (learning rate $1e^{-2}$, weight decay $3e^{-5}$), with a Dice + Binary Cross-Entropy loss function, the same patch and batch size, and validation every 2,500 iterations.

4.2 Evaluation Metrics

The performance of each configuration was quantified using two standard segmentation metrics: the Dice coefficient (DSC) and the Jaccard index (IoU) [15].

Both metrics measure how similar the predicted segmentation is to the ground-truth segmentation, where scores to 1 indicate higher accuracy. For the evaluation of healthy subjects, the scoring strategy established by the original challenge was adopted: cases without ground truth were assigned a Dice score of 1 if no lesion was predicted, and a score of 0 if any prediction was made.

5 Results

Table 1 shows the model's performance under different combinations of atlas and training configuration (2D or 3D). In general terms, registration based on the SRI24 atlas and the 3D configuration achieved the best performance. In the 2D models, the ICBM152 atlas slightly outperformed SRI24, achieving a DSC of 0.4999 and an IoU of 0.4484. However, in the 3D models, SRI24 achieved higher values for both metrics compared to ICBM152, indicating that both the registration atlas and the model dimensionality influence segmentation performance.

Table 1. Segmentation Performance Across Model Configurations and Atlases.

Metric	2D-SRI	3D-SRI	2D-ICBM	3D-ICBM
DSC	0.4547	**0.5262**	0.4999	0.4619
IoU	0.4058	**0.4712**	0.4484	0.4045

Regarding the intensity normalization methods, as shown in Table 2, the KDE method achieved the best performance, with a DSC of 0.5322 and an IoU of 0.4750, positioning it as the most accurate configuration among the evaluated normalization methods. The second-best performance was achieved by the Z-score method, with a DSC of 0.5262 and an IoU of 0.4712. In contrast, WS showed the lowest values for both metrics.

Table 2. Segmentation Performance Across Intensity Normalization Methods.

Metric	Z-Score	FCM	KDE	WS
DSC	0.5262	0.4436	**0.5322**	0.0602
IoU	0.4712	0.3866	**0.4750**	0.0355

Finally, Table 3 presents the evaluation of the effect of fine-tuning and the comparative 3D U-Net model. When comparing the nnU-Net model with and without fine-tuning, it can be observed that the version with fine-tuning achieved better differentiation between control subjects and subjects with lesions, benefiting from the BRATS dataset. Although BRATS does not contain the same type of lesion, it addresses a related segmentation problem and provides a large number of MRI scans with similar characteristics, which helped compensate for the moderate size of the trauma dataset. This behavior is reflected in the obtained metrics, achieving a DSC of 0.5642 and an IoU of 0.5097, representing the best performance among all evaluated variants. In contrast, the 3D U-Net model did not perform adequately in lesion segmentation and identification, with an average DSC of 0.0207 and an IoU of 0.0119. Consequently, the fine-tuned nnU-Net achieved the best results and was selected as the final model of the study.

Table 3. Comparison of Model Evaluation Results.

Metric	nnU-Net w/o TL	nnU-Net TL	3D U-Net
DSC	0.5322	**0.5642**	0.0207
IoU	0.4750	**0.5097**	0.0119

Besides, Figs. 2, 3, and 4 present the model's qualitative results, including performance by age group and time since injury (TSI), and visual segmentation examples. Results shown that the best segmentation performance was observed in men aged 48–63 years and women aged 64–78 years (Fig. 2), in both genres during the 64–128-week period or chronic phase, whereas the lowest performance was observed between weeks 8 and 16 or subacute phase (Fig. 3).

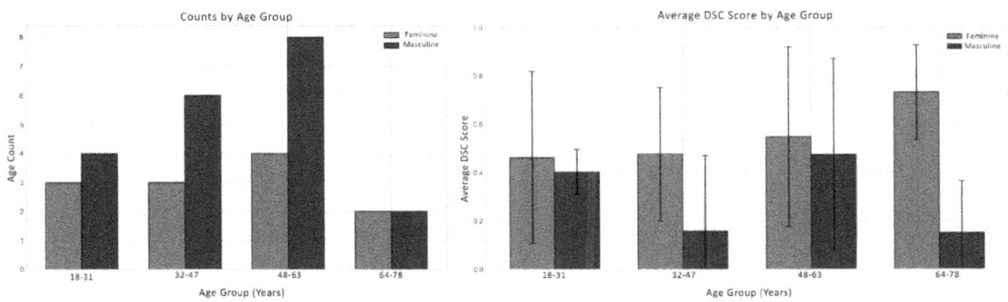

Fig. 2. Prediction performance by age group (right) and the number of patients per age group in the test data (left). All cases in which no ground truth foreground was annotated were excluded.

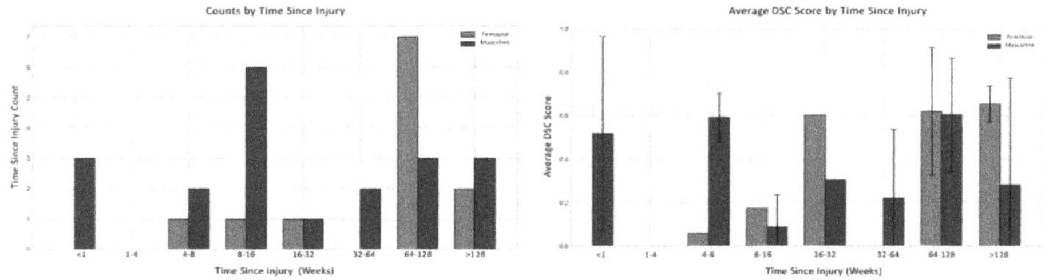

Fig. 3. Prediction performance by Time Since Injury (right) and the number of patients per TSI group in the test data (left). All cases in which no ground truth foreground was annotated were excluded.

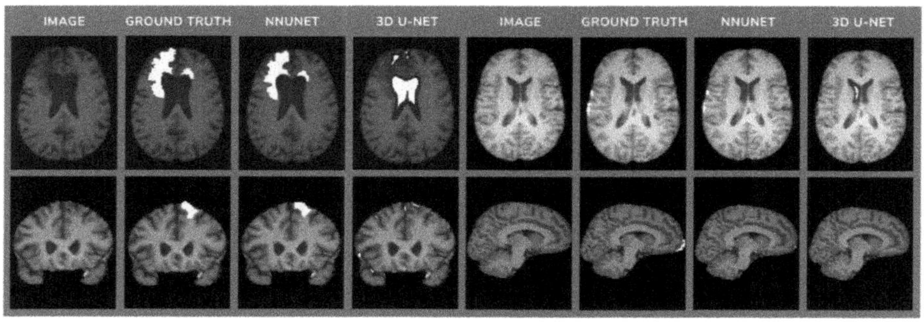

Fig. 4. Qualitative Segmentation Results. In the first two patients, nnU-Net achieved segmentations very close to the reference. In the third subject, the segmentation was partial but acceptable, and in the last subject, although the lesion location was identified, many of the corresponding voxels were not segmented. In contrast, the 3D U-Net model did not correctly segment any of the cases and misclassified anatomical structures as lesions.

6 Discussion

The experimental results show that the extended preprocessing strategy and the evaluation of different normalization methods significantly influenced the performance of the segmentation model and, specifically, that normalization based on KDE consistently outperformed the standard Z-score method used by default in nnU-Net.

One possible explanation for this behavior lies in the intensity characteristics of TBI-associated lesions. Compared to healthy brain tissue, these lesions tend to have heterogeneous intensity distributions. Since Z-score normalization assumes an approximately normal distribution, it may not adequately represent such variability. In contrast, KDE allows the intensity distribution to be modeled in a non-parametric manner, adapting to the particularities of the dataset. This could reduce inter-subject variability and facilitate more stable learning of relevant features during training.

Regarding the registration process, the use of the SRI24 atlas was found to produce better results compared to other configurations evaluated. This behavior could be explained by the population correspondence between the atlas and the dataset used in the study. The SRI24 atlas was constructed from American subjects, and most trauma dataset acquisition centers are located in North America. This demographic and anatomical similarity could have favored better structural alignment, improving the spatial consistency of the segmented lesions.

Furthermore, the use of fine-tuning also played a relevant role, especially considering the limited size of the TBI dataset. Initialization with pre-trained weights can provide more robust low-level feature representations, favor model generalization to unseen data, and improve injury detection.

Despite the results obtained, the study has some limitations. The performance of the normalization methods and the selected atlas could depend on the specific characteristics of the dataset, including variations in scanners, acquisition protocols, and demographic factors. In addition, validation was performed on a single dataset, so it would be necessary to evaluate the proposed strategy in external cohorts to confirm its generalizability.

7 Conclusions and Future Work

This study evaluated U-Net-based models for the automatic segmentation of TBI-associated lesions in $T1$-weighted MRI images. Several preprocessing and registration strategies were compared, demonstrating that the SRI24 atlas combined with KDE normalization achieved the best performance, as it more effectively captured the variability in intensity distribution compared to the Z-score normalization. Furthermore, the use of fine-tuning from the BRATS dataset significantly improved model performance, mitigating the limitation associated with the moderate size of the AIMS-TBI dataset. Among the evaluated architectures, nnU-Net achieved the best overall performance. The results showed variations according to age and time since injury, suggesting that physiological and temporal factors influence segmentation quality. However, the study is limited to the AIMS-TBI dataset and presents a gender imbalance.

Future work should include validation and adaptation of the model using more diverse datasets with different scanners, acquisition protocols, and injury types, as well as inclusion of the pediatric population to analyze model behavior in developing brains. Finally, cross-validation and post-processing techniques should be implemented to further improve the robustness and accuracy of the segmentation.

Acknowledgments. We would like to thank the University of Utah for providing access to the AIMS-TBI dataset.

References

1. Ali, E., Sadek, S., Makki, Z.: Hybrid improved fuzzy c-means and watershed segmentation to classify Alzheimer's using deep learning. IAES Int. J. Artif. Intell. **13**(4), 4080–4094 (2024)
2. Avants, B., Epstein, C., Grossman, M., Gee, J.: Symmetric diffeomorphic image registration with cross-correlation: Evaluating automated labeling of elderly and neurodegenerative brain. Med. Image Anal. **12**(1), 26–41 (2008)
3. Bennett, A.: Manual lesion segmentations for traumatic brain injury characterization. Front. Neuroimaging **2** (2023)
4. Berger, L., Holshouser, B., Nichols, J., Pivonka-Jones, J., Ashwal, S., Bartnik-Olson, B.: White matter metabolite ratios predict cognitive outcome in pediatric traumatic brain injury. Metabolites **13**(7) (2023)
5. Bernal-Pacheco, O., Vega-Rincón, M., Hernández-Preciado, J.: Consecuencias neuropsiquiátricas del trauma craneoencefálico (2009)
6. Carvajal-Camelo, E., Bernal, J., Oliver, A., Lladó, X., Trujillo, M.: Evaluating the effect of intensity standardisation on longitudinal whole brain atrophy quantification in brain magnetic resonance imaging. Appl. Sci. **11**(4), 1773 (2021)
7. Dennis, E., Tustison, N., Deutscher, E., Wilde, E., Caeyenberghs, K.: Aims TBI - automated identification of moderate-severe traumatic brain injury lesions. In: MICCAI 2024, pp. 1–15 (2024)
8. Ginsburg, J., Smith, T.: Traumatic brain injury. In: Encyclopedia of Child Behavior and Development, p. 374 (2025)
9. Guan, B., Anderson, D., Chen, L., Feng, S., Zhou, H.: Global, regional and national burden of traumatic brain injury and spinal cord injury, 1990–2019. BMJ Open **13**(10) (2023)
10. Hazarika, R., Maji, A., Syiem, R., Sur, S., Kandar, D.: Hippocampus segmentation using u-net convolutional network from brain MRI. J. Digital Imaging **35**(4) (2022)
11. Iglesias, J., Liu, C., Thompson, P., Tu, Z.: Robust brain extraction across datasets. IEEE Trans. Med. Imaging **30**(9), 1617–1634 (2011)
12. Isensee, F., Jaeger, P., Kohl, S., Petersen, J., Maier-Hein, K.: NNU-Net: a self-configuring method for deep learning-based biomedical image segmentation. Nat. Methods **18**(2), 203–211 (2020)
13. Maffei, C., Gilmore, N., Snider, S., Foulkes, A., Bodien, Y., Yendiki, A., Edlow, B.: Automated detection of axonal damage in acute severe TBI. NeuroImage: Clinical **37** (2023)
14. Mistral, T.: Automated quantification of brain lesion volume from post-trauma MR diffusion-weighted images. Front. Neurol. **12** (2022)
15. Müller, D., Soto-Rey, I., Kramer, F.: Towards a guideline for evaluation metrics in medical image segmentation. BMC. Res. Notes **15**(1), 210 (2022)
16. Muller, J., et al.: Machine learning-based classification of chronic TBI using hybrid diffusion imaging. Front. Neurosci. **17**, 1182509 (2023)
17. Rachmadi, M., Byra, M., Skibbe, H.: Instance-level loss functions for segmentation of white matter hyperintensities. Comput. Biol. Med. **174**, 108414 (2024)
18. Soh, W., Yuen, H., Rajapakse, J.: Hut: hybrid unet transformer for brain lesion segmentation. Heliyon **9**(12) (2023)
19. Wilke, M., de Haan, B., Juenger, H., Karnath, H.: Manual, semi-automated, and automated delineation of chronic brain lesions. Neuroimage **56**(4), 1–9 (2011)
20. Wolny, A., et al.: Accurate and versatile 3d segmentation of plant tissues at cellular resolution. eLife **9**, 1–34 (2020)

21. Zhang, X.: Brain age prediction using interpretable CNN in mild TBI. Neuroimage **297** (2024)
22. Zhao, X.: stbi-gan: adversarial learning for traumatic brain segmentation. Computerized Med. Imaging Graph **112** (2024)

From Regions to Manifolds: Linking Radiomic Signatures with PCA and UMAP Brain Representations in Glioma

Carmen Jimenez-Mesa[1(✉)], Yizhou Wan[2], Giulio Sansone[3,4], Nicolas J. Gallego-Molina[1,6], Andres Ortiz[1,6], Cristobal Vazquez-Garcia[6,7], Juan M. Gorriz[5,6,7], Stephen J. Price[2], John Suckling[5,8], and Michail Mamalakis[5,9]

[1] Department of Communications Engineering, University of Malaga, Malaga, Spain
carmenj@uma.es
[2] Department of Clinical Neurosciences, University of Cambridge, Cambridge, UK
[3] Department of Neuroscience, University of Padova, Padova, Italy
[4] Padova Neuroscience Center (PNC), University of Padova, Padova, Italy
[5] Department of Psychiatry, University of Cambridge, Cambridge, UK
[6] DaSCI Andalusian Institute of Data Science and Computational Intelligence, University of Granada, Granada, Spain
[7] Department of Signal Theory, Telematics and Communications, University of Granada, Granada, Spain
[8] Cambridge and Peterborough NHS Foundation Trust, Cambridge, UK
[9] Cancer Research United Kingdom Cambridge Institute, University of Cambridge, Cambridge, UK

Abstract. Surgical resection is the standard treatment for glioma patients, yet postoperative outcomes remain highly variable. In this study, we investigated structural brain reorganisation following surgery using a multiscale imaging approach. We extracted five key radiomic features from T1-weighted MRI scans within 116 anatomical regions and the tumor area and applied Support Vector Machine classification to identify regions predictive of shorter- versus longer-term survival. To characterise global structural variability, both Principal Component Analysis (PCA) and Uniform Manifold Approximation and Projection (UMAP) were applied across patients to derive low-dimensional spatial representations. Region-based analysis highlighted peri-tumoral cortices, as well as subcortical and cerebellar structures, as most discriminative. At the global level, the application of Euclidean distance computed in the embedding spaces revealed more pronounced longitudinal changes in shorter-term survivors, whereas longer-term survivors exhibited comparatively more stable patterns over time. Overlaying radiomic regions on Euclidean distance maps from the PCA components indicated partial spatial correspondence, suggesting complementary information from local and global features. These results demonstrate the utility of combining regional radiomics with global manifold learning to characterise postoperative brain changes and their association with survival. This

J. M. Ferrández Vicente et al. (Eds.): IWINAC 2026, LNCS 16574, pp. 96–106, 2026.
https://doi.org/10.1007/978-3-032-27314-7_10

multiscale framework may inform future prognostic models and guide surgical and therapeutic strategies in glioma patients.

Keywords: Glioma · Radiomic features · UMAP · Surgical resection

1 Introduction

Surgical resection is the standard treatment for primary brain tumours, aiming to remove as much tumour as possible while preserving neurological function. Despite advances in planning and intraoperative guidance, survival outcomes remain highly variable, even among patients with similar tumour grade, location, and preoperative condition [1]. Moreover, surgery can induce widespread alterations across brain networks, reflecting compensatory, disruptive, or maladaptive processes; characterising these global patterns in a robust and interpretable manner therefore remains challenging [2].

Radiomic analysis [11] provides quantitative descriptors from medical images, enabling the identification of regional biomarkers linked to diagnosis and prognosis. However, it typically focuses on individual regions and may miss broader multivariate patterns [3,4].

Dimensionality reduction techniques such as Principal Component Analysis (PCA) [7] and Uniform Manifold Approximation and Projection (UMAP) [8] can uncover dominant patterns of variability across subjects. By analysing voxel intensities across patients, these methods reveal global modes of brain organisation, capturing either principal linear axes of statistical variation (PCA) or more complex non-linear relationships (UMAP), which may not be fully identified through regional or voxelwise statistics.

In this study, we integrate regional radiomic signatures with UMAP-derived spatial components to investigate postoperative structural reorganisation in glioma patients. We aim to (i) identify the most informative anatomical regions associated with clinical outcome using radiomic features, and (ii) characterise global patterns of inter-subject structural variability through spatial components extracted via manifold learning. Together, these complementary strategies enable a multiscale assessment of both focal anatomical biomarkers and distributed structural reorganisation.

2 Materials and Methods

2.1 Glioma Dataset

The data used in this study consists of 48 patients diagnosed with high-grade glioma who underwent surgical resection, sourced from a clinical dataset (currently restricted access). All individuals gave written informed consent to participate, and the use of their data for clinical research was approved by the Research Ethics Committee (REC reference: 19/WM/0152). For each subject, T1-weighted MRI scans were acquired both preoperatively and postoperatively.

All images were spatially normalised to the Montreal Neurological Institute (MNI) standard space using SPM12 (fil.ion.ucl.ac.uk/spm/) and resampled to an isotropic resolution of $1 \times 1 \times 1$ mm, resulting in final image dimensions of $157 \times 189 \times 156$ mm. To ensure anatomical consistency and remove non-brain tissues, skull-stripping was performed using HD-BET [5]. Patients were divided into two outcome groups based on overall survival after surgery: a shorter-term survival group ($n = 25$) comprising patients who survived less than 13 months following the postoperative scan, and a longer-term survival group ($n = 23$) including those who survived 13 months or more.

2.2 PCA and UMAP-Based Brain Maps

To characterise global structural patterns across patients, we applied two complementary dimensionality reduction techniques: PCA and UMAP. In both cases, analyses were performed across the patient dimension of the T1-weighted MRI scans. Imaging data were arranged as a $V \times N$ matrix (V voxels, N patients). PCA was used to extract $K = 8$ orthogonal components, retaining at least 90% of the cumulative explained variance as in our previous work [6]. These components represent the principal linear axes of inter-subject structural variability. In parallel, UMAP was applied to obtain $K = 8$ low-dimensional representations capturing non-linear relationships in the data, thereby modelling more complex patterns of inter-subject variability.

Prior to dimensionality reduction, voxel intensities were standardised. The resulting components were reshaped into three-dimensional images in MNI space for anatomical interpretation.

To quantitatively compare conditions or timepoints, voxelwise Euclidean distances were computed in the eight-dimensional embedding space (PCA or UMAP), yielding a single three-dimensional map summarising multivariate structural differences. This unified framework enables direct comparison between linear and non-linear representations of global brain reorganisation.

2.3 Radiomic Feature Extraction

Radiomic analysis was performed to quantify region-specific structural characteristics at two complementary spatial scales: (i) atlas-based regional features and (ii) tumor-focused voxelwise features.

For the regional analysis, the brain was parcellated using the 116-area Automated Anatomical Labeling (AAL) template [10]. Within each region, radiomic features were extracted from the T1-weighted images in a segment-based configuration. Specifically, five key features were selected for analysis: the first-order metrics *Entropy* and *Energy*, as well as the texture-based descriptors *Contrast*, *Inverse Difference Moment (IDM)*, and *Correlation* derived from the gray-level co-occurrence matrix (GLCM). These features were chosen to capture both the intensity distribution and spatial heterogeneity of the tissue within each region.

In parallel, a voxel-based radiomic analysis was conducted within the tumour mask. Instead of aggregating features over predefined anatomical regions, radiomic descriptors were computed directly within the tumour area, preserving local heterogeneity patterns. This approach allowed us to capture fine-grained structural characteristics specific to the lesion itself.

Together, these two strategies enabled the investigation of both distributed anatomical alterations and focal tumour-related heterogeneity.

2.4 Classification Framework

To evaluate the discriminative power of the extracted radiomic features, we implemented a supervised classification framework to distinguish between shorter-term and longer-term survival groups.

Feature Selection. Classification was based on the five radiomic features extracted within each anatomical region. Analyses were performed independently for each region, allowing assessment of region-specific discriminative power, with each patient represented by a five-dimensional feature vector for the corresponding region (and the tumor region).

Support Vector Machine Classification. A Support Vector Machine (SVM) classifier with a linear kernel [9] was employed to perform binary classification. Model performance was assessed using stratified five-fold cross-validation to ensure that class proportions were maintained in each fold. Within each iteration, z-score normalisation was computed exclusively on the training data and then applied to the corresponding test set, preventing features with larger numerical ranges from disproportionately influencing the classifier. Classification performance was evaluated using multiple complementary metrics, including accuracy, the area under the receiver operating characteristic curve (AUC), sensitivity (true positive rate), and specificity (true negative rate).

Permutation Testing. To assess whether the observed classification performance exceeded chance level, a permutation test was conducted. Group labels were randomly shuffled across subjects while keeping the feature matrix fixed. For each permutation, the full classification pipeline was recomputed using the same cross-validation scheme. This procedure was repeated a large number of times (500 permutations) to generate a null distribution of performance values under the hypothesis of no association between features and survival group. The permutation p-value was calculated as:

$$p = \frac{\#\{\text{permuted score} \geq \text{observed score}\} + 1}{N_{\text{permutations}} + 1} \quad (1)$$

A p-value below 0.05 was considered evidence that the classifier performance was significantly above chance.

3 Results and Discussion

3.1 Region-Based Radiomic Classification

We first evaluated the predictive ability of the five selected radiomic features within each anatomical region in the different scenarios. These conditions include: the longitudinal comparison of pre- versus post-surgery scans within the shorter-term survival group (Table 1), the same longitudinal comparison within the longer-term survival group (Table 2), and the cross-sectional comparison between shorter- and longer-term survivors at both the pre-surgery and post-surgery timepoints (Table 3 and Table 4). This framework allows us to assess both intra-group changes over time and inter-group differences at each stage of the surgical process.

Table 1. Summary performance in the classification scenario of shorter survivals using pre-surgery vs. post-surgery data. Metrics for the ten most discriminatory anatomical regions identified are included.

Region name	Accuracy	AUC	Sensitivity	Specificity	p-value
Tumor Region	0.80	0.84	0.80	0.80	0.002
SupraMarginal_L	0.74	0.82	0.72	0.76	0.002
Temporal_Sup_L	0.72	0.82	0.64	0.80	0.008
SupraMarginal_R	0.72	0.78	0.80	0.64	0.008
Rolandic_Oper_R	0.72	0.68	0.60	0.84	0.016
Temporal_Mid_L	0.72	0.84	0.76	0.68	0.006
Vermis_3	0.70	0.52	0.80	0.60	0.008
Parietal_Sup_R	0.70	0.688	0.60	0.80	0.012
Vermis_1_2	0.70	0.46	0.72	0.68	0.016
Precentral_L	0.70	0.80	0.60	0.80	0.018

Across the four experimental conditions, the classifier identified distinct sets of anatomical regions as most discriminative. In the longitudinal comparison within the shorter-term survival group (Table 1), alongside bilateral supramarginal and temporal regions, as well as Rolandic and precentral areas, consistently contributed to distinguishing pre- versus post-surgery scans. For the longer-term survival group (Table 2), the most informative regions included postcentral, superior frontal, and precentral cortices, and additional opercular and temporal areas. It is notable that features extracted from the tumor region consistently contributed to classification performance across both survival groups, highlighting their relevance when comparing pre- and post-surgery timepoints.

In the cross-sectional comparisons between shorter- and longer-term survivors, pre-surgery scans (Table 3) highlighted subcortical and limbic regions such as the caudate, thalamus, insula, cingulum, angular gyrus, and rectus,

Table 2. Summary performance in the classification scenario of longer survivals using pre-surgery vs. post-surgery data. Metrics for the ten most discriminatory anatomical regions identified are included.

Region name	Accuracy	AUC	Sensitivity	Specificity	p-value
Postcentral_R	0.80	0.83	0.73	0.86	0.002
Frontal_Sup_R	0.78	0.82	0.74	0.81	0.002
Tumor Region	0.78	0.88	0.70	0.88	0.002
SupraMarginal_R	0.76	0.81	0.68	0.82	0.002
Precentral_R	0.76	0.85	0.69	0.81	0.004
Rolandic_Oper_R	0.74	0.82	0.65	0.83	0.004
Parietal_Inf_L	0.74	0.63	0.60	0.87	0.005
Frontal_Mid_R	0.72	0.65	0.56	0.85	0.008
Temporal_Pole_Sup_R	0.72	0.80	0.74	0.70	0.012
Frontal_Inf_Oper_R	0.72	0.85	0.70	0.75	0.008

Table 3. Summary performance in the classification scenario of pre-surgery scans using shorter-survivals vs. longer-survivals data. Metrics for the ten most discriminatory anatomical regions identified are included.

Region name	Accuracy	AUC	Sensitivity	Specificity	p-value
Caudate_R	0.73	0.868	0.76	0.70	0.004
Angular_R	0.72	0.67	0.88	0.54	0.002
Frontal_Inf_Oper_R	0.72	0.61	0.76	0.67	0.006
Rectus_R	0.71	0.502	0.68	0.74	0.012
Olfactory_R	0.70	0.491	0.64	0.78	0.008
Insula_R	0.69	0.43	0.76	0.62	0.014
Cingulum_Ant_R	0.69	0.728	0.64	0.75	0.012
Temporal_Mid_R	0.69	0.75	0.64	0.74	0.008
Cingulum_Mid_L	0.695	0.544	0.64	0.74	0.008
Thalamus_L	0.67	0.547	0.6	0.74	0.020

whereas post-surgery scans (Table 4) emphasised cerebellar vermis regions, hippocampus, insula, Rolandic operculum, and thalamus, along with some frontal areas. These results suggest that longitudinal changes within survival groups primarily involve peri-tumoral and adjacent cortical regions, while inter-group differences engage a broader set of subcortical and cerebellar structures.

Table 4. Summary performance in the classification scenario of post-surgery scans using shorter-survivals vs. longer-survivals data. Metrics for the ten most discriminatory anatomical regions identified are included.

Region name	Accuracy	AUC	Sensitivity	Specificity	p-value
Vermis_10	0.75	0.77	0.68	0.83	0.006
Insula_L	0.69	0.764	0.56	0.83	0.010
Cerebelum_4_5_R	0.69	0.758	0.80	0.58	0.022
Cingulum_Mid_R	0.67	0.614	0.56	0.79	0.016
Hippocampus_L	0.67	0.30	0.68	0.66	0.030
Vermis_9	0.67	0.728	0.64	0.70	0.022
Caudate_R	0.67	0.72	0.64	0.70	0.028
Rolandic_Oper_L	0.67	0.406	0.56	0.78	0.024
Frontal_Sup_R	0.66	0.67	0.6	0.72	0.046
Thalamus_R	0.65	0.684	0.76	0.53	0.016

3.2 Global Structural Patterns Using PCA

To complement the regional analysis, we applied PCA and UMAP to the T1-weighted MRI scans across the patient dimension, generating spatial components (maps) that summarise inter-subject variability. An intensity scale ranging from 0 to 1 was applied to better capture the differences between areas. Figure 1 shows the first and second components of the resulting PCA maps for all experimental

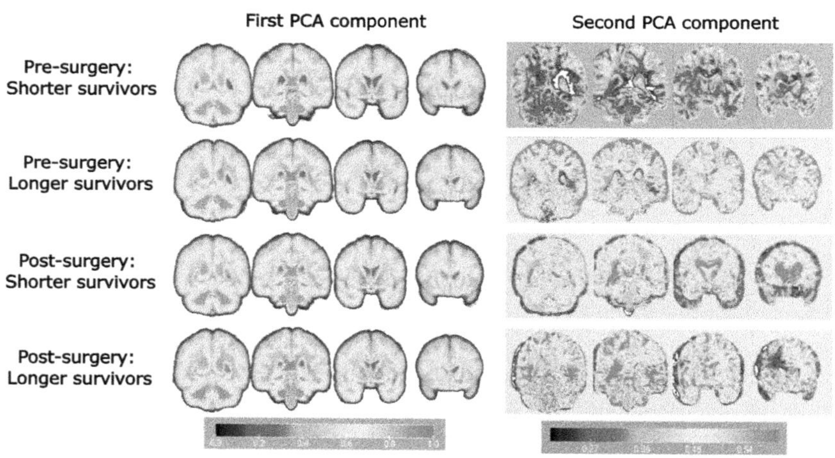

Fig. 1. Spatial representation of the first (left) and second (right) PCA-components map across survival groups and timepoints: preoperative scans for shorter-term (first row) and longer-term (second row) survivors, and postoperative scans for shorter-term (third row) and longer-term (fourth row) survivors.

conditions: pre- and post-surgery scans of shorter-term survivors (first and third rows, respectively) and longer-term survivors (second and fourth rows, respectively). Since the UMAP representation was computed in an eight-dimensional embedding space, it cannot be directly visualised in two dimensions. Therefore, Fig. 1 displays only the PCA components for visual inspection and qualitative comparison across conditions.

Visual inspection of the PCA maps reveals that the first component exhibits largely similar global patterns across the four experimental conditions. In contrast, the second component shows differences in spatial distribution, with higher intensities observed in longer-term survivors. Overall, there is a general increase in component intensity in post-surgery scans compared to pre-surgery scans, suggesting structural changes following resection.

3.3 Integration of Regional and Global Analyses

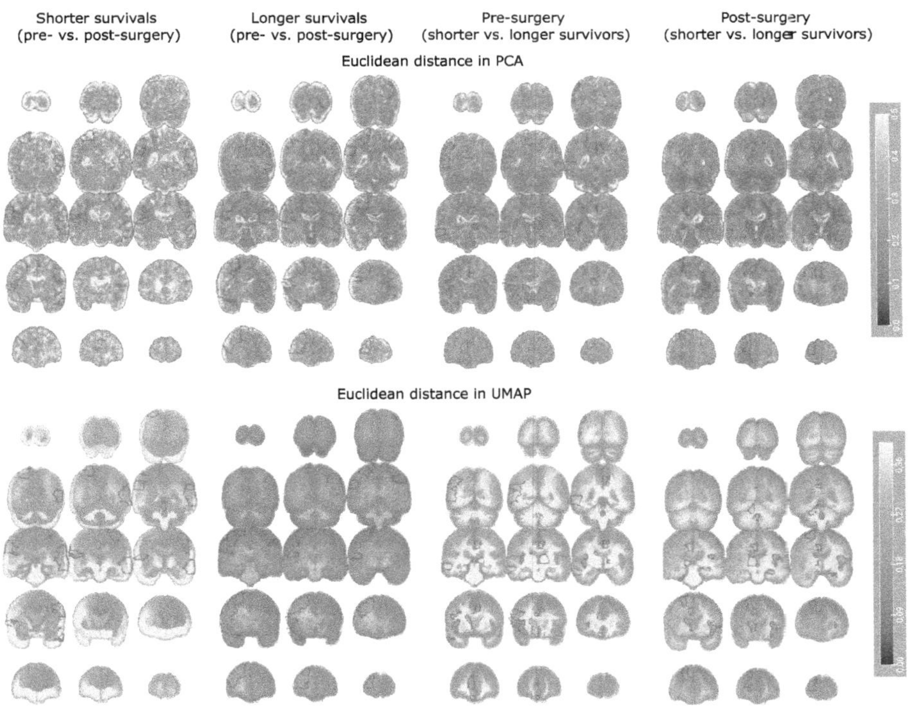

Fig. 2. Voxelwise Euclidean distance maps computed in PCA (first row) and UMAP (second row) embedding spaces. Columns 1–2 show within-group longitudinal differences (shorter- and longer-term survivors, respectively), while columns 3–4 show between-group differences at the preoperative and postoperative timepoints. Radiomic discriminative regions are overlaid in red (Color figure online).

To integrate the regional radiomic findings with the global PCA- and UMAP-derived patterns, we computed voxelwise Euclidean distance maps illustrating structural differences across time and survival groups (Fig. 2) using the 8 components generated in the manifolds. The first row corresponds to distances computed in the PCA space, and the second row to distances computed in the UMAP embedding space. The first two columns represent within-group longitudinal changes, calculated as the distance between preoperative and postoperative scans for shorter- and longer-term survivors, respectively. The last two columns depict between-group differences at each timepoint, showing preoperative and postoperative distances between shorter- and longer-term survival groups. It illustrates that shorter-term survivors exhibit more pronounced longitudinal changes between preoperative and postoperative scans compared to longer-term survivors. Additionally, between-group differences appear more marked at the preoperative stage, whereas postoperative maps show reduced separation between shorter- and longer-term survival groups. These findings suggest that structural alterations over time are more prominent in shorter-term survivors, while surgery may attenuate pre-existing inter-group differences at the global level.

The contours of the most discriminative regions identified in the radiomic analysis were overlaid (red) onto these distance maps to assess their spatial correspondence with global structural variations. Visually, several of the highlighted regions are located in proximity to areas exhibiting higher Euclidean distances (red contours), indicating partial spatial agreement between regional discriminative power and large-scale structural variability, specially in the bottom maps. However, the overlap is not exact, suggesting that regional radiomic features and global manifold-derived patterns capture complementary aspects of postoperative brain reorganisation rather than identical spatial information.

4 Conclusions

In this study, we combined regional radiomic analysis and PCA-based and UMAP-based global brain mapping to characterise postoperative structural reorganisation in glioma patients and its relationship to survival outcomes. Region-based classification highlighted specific anatomical areas, including the Tumor Region, peri-tumoral cortical regions, and several subcortical and cerebellar structures, as consistently discriminative across longitudinal and cross-sectional comparisons. These findings suggest that local radiomic features can provide robust indicators of survival-related changes.

Complementary PCA-derived and UMAP-derived spatial components revealed global patterns of structural variability across patients. Shorter-term survivors exhibited more pronounced longitudinal changes between preoperative and postoperative scans, whereas longer-term survivors showed comparatively more stable global patterns over time. Moreover, between-group differences were more evident at the preoperative stage and appeared reduced after surgery, suggesting a partial convergence of global structural patterns in the postoperative condition. Notably, UMAP representations revealed more structured and spatially coherent differences compared to the linear patterns captured by PCA, highlighting the added value of non-linear manifold learning for characterising complex postoperative brain reorganisation. Overlaying the contours of the most discriminative radiomic regions on the Euclidean distance maps demonstrated partial spatial correspondence, indicating that regional and global analyses capture complementary, rather than redundant, information.

Together, these results highlight the potential of a multiscale approach to postoperative brain assessment, combining voxel- and region-level radiomics with global manifold learning. Future work will focus on integrating additional imaging modalities (e.g., diffusion MRI, functional MRI) and clinical variables to improve prognostic accuracy. Furthermore, we plan to explore multivariate frameworks that jointly model local and global features, as well as temporal evolution, to better understand the mechanisms of postoperative brain reorganisation and their impact on patient outcome.

Acknowledgments. This research is part of the PID2022-137629OA-I00, PID2022-137451OB-I00 and PID2022-137461NB-C32 projects, funded by the MICIU/AEI/10.13039/501100011033 and by ERDF/EU. The work by C.J.M. is part of the grant JDC2023-051807-I funded by MICIU/AEI/10.13039/501100011033 and by ESF+. This study was funded from the National Institute for Health and Care Research (NIHR), Career Development Fellowship (CDF-2018-11-ST2-003 to SJP.). This publication presents independent research funded by the National Institute for Health and Care Research (NIHR). All research at the Department of Psychiatry in the University of Cambridge is supported by the NIHR Cambridge Biomedical Research Centre (NIHR203312) and the NIHR Applied Research Collaboration East of England. The views expressed are those of the author(s) and not necessarily those of the NHS, the NIHR or the Department of Health and Social Care.

Disclosure of Interests. The authors have no competing interests to declare that are relevant to the content of this article.

References

1. Dadario, N.B., Brahimaj, B., Yeung, J., Sughrue, M.E.: Reducing the cognitive footprint of brain tumor surgery. Front. Neurol. **12** (2021). https://doi.org/10.3389/fneur.2021.711646
2. Drewes, C., Sagberg, L.M., Jakola, A.S., Solheim, O.: Perioperative and postoperative quality of life in patients with glioma-a longitudinal cohort study. World Neurosurgery **117**, e465–e474 (2018)
3. Górriz, J.M., et al.: Computational approaches to explainable artificial intelligence: advances in theory, applications and trends. Inf. Fusion **100**, 101945 (2023)
4. Górriz, J.M., Ramírez, J., et al.: Artificial intelligence within the interplay between natural and artificial computation: advances in data science, trends and applications. Neurocomputing **410**, 237–270 (2020)
5. Isensee, F., et al.: Automated brain extraction of multisequence MRI using artificial neural networks. Hum. Brain Mapp. **40**(17), 4952–4964 (2019)

6. Jimenez-Mesa, C., Wan, Y.: Uncovering neuroimaging biomarkers of brain tumor surgery with AI-driven methods (2025). arXiv preprint arXiv:2507.04881
7. Jolliffe, I.T., Cadima, J.: Principal component analysis: a review and recent developments. Phil. Trans. R. Soc. A **374**(2065), 20150202 (2016)
8. McInnes, L., Healy, J., Melville, J.: Umap: uniform manifold approximation and projection for dimension reduction. In: Proceedings of the 2018 ICML Workshop on Visualization for Deep Learning (2018)
9. Schölkopf, B.: Learning with kernels: support vector machines, regularization, optimization, and beyond (2002)
10. Tzourio-Mazoyer, N., Landeau, B., et al.: Automated anatomical labeling of activations in SPM using a macroscopic anatomical parcellation of the MNI MRI single-subject brain. Neuroimage **15**(1), 273–289 (2002)
11. Van Griethuysen, J.J., Fedorov, A., et al.: Computational radiomics system to decode the radiographic phenotype. Can. Res. **77**(21), e104–e107 (2017)

Early Diagnosis of Epileptic Seizures from EEG Signals Using Graph Convolutional Network Model

Afshin Shoeibi[1(✉)], Mohammad Mehdi Barzegar[2], Marjane Khodatars[1], Mahboobeh Jafari[1], Abdoljavad Khajavi[3], and Juan M. Gorriz[1]

[1] Data Science and Computational Intelligence Institute, University of Granada, Granada, Spain
afshin.shoeibi@gmail.com

[2] Department of Biomedical Engineering, School of Electrical Engineering, Iran University of Science and Technology (IUST), Tehran, Iran

[3] Department of Community Medicine, School of Medicine, Gonabad University of Medical Sciences, Gonabad, Iran

Abstract. Epileptic seizures are among the most significant chronic neurological disorders, caused by abnormal electrical activity in the brain and accompanied by symptoms such as limb tremors, loss of consciousness, and speech disturbances. Electroencephalography (EEG) is considered one of the most important tools for diagnosing epileptic seizures due to its non-invasiveness and relatively low cost; however, it faces challenges such as artifacts and low spatial resolution. In this study, a computer-aided diagnosis system (CADS) is proposed for the detection of epileptic seizures. For this purpose, the Turkish epilepsy dataset was used for experiments. In the first step, standard preprocessing procedures were applied to the EEG signals. Then, handcrafted features were extracted from the EEG channels to provide a compact representation of the local dynamics of the signals. Next, a brain graph was constructed using an adjacency matrix based on the Pearson correlation method and was used as input to the proposed deep learning (DL) architecture. Finally, a proposed graph convolutional network (GCN) was employed to extract discriminative features from the preprocessed EEG signals. The results show that the proposed method achieved a maximum accuracy (Acc) of 95.72% using EEG signals with a 15-s time frame.

Keywords: Epileptic Seizures · Diagnosis · EEG Signals · CADS · GCN

1 Introduction

Epilepsy is one of the most common chronic neurological disorders, characterized by the occurrence of sudden, unpredictable, and recurrent seizures [1]. Epileptic seizures are classified into focal and generalized types, depending on the affected

J. M. Ferrández Vicente et al. (Eds.): IWINAC 2026, LNCS 16574, pp. 107–117, 2026.
https://doi.org/10.1007/978-3-032-27314-7_11

brain region and the pattern of neuronal activity [1]. Each type may be associated with different clinical symptoms, such as loss of consciousness, involuntary limb movements, visual disturbances, and cognitive impairment [2]. According to the World Health Organization (WHO), approximately 50 million people worldwide suffer from epilepsy, with around 5 million new cases diagnosed annually [2].

EEG recordings play a crucial role as a non-invasive diagnostic tool for identifying abnormal patterns associated with epileptic seizures [3–5]. EEG signals capture time–frequency variations in neuronal activity and enable continuous monitoring of brain function. Moreover, this method is relatively inexpensive, portable, and provides significantly higher temporal resolution compared to imaging modalities such as MRI. EEG recordings allow medical professionals to identify seizure types, and evaluate patients' responses to treatment [1]. Despite these advantages, accurate interpretation of EEG signals remains challenging. These challenges include variability in seizure patterns across individuals and environmental conditions, as well as the need for long-term data analysis [4–6]. In addition, manual EEG interpretation requires extensive expertise from neurologists and is prone to human error [4].

In recent years, deep learning (DL) models have achieved significant progress in analyzing EEG signals for epileptic seizure detection [7]. However, a key limitation of many DL approaches is their inability to capture functional connectivity between EEG channels, which plays a critical role in seizure analysis [7]. To address this issue, graph-based DL models, particularly graph convolutional networks (GCNs), have been introduced [8]. By modeling EEG signals as a graph composed of nodes (electrodes) and edges (functional connections), GCNs can effectively extract complex spatiotemporal relationships, thereby improving detection performance [8]. Zhang et al. [9] proposed a dynamic GCN with dilated convolution (DGDCN) for epileptic seizure detection, achieving an accuracy of 79.7% on the TUSZ dataset. Similarly, Hu et al. [10] introduced an iterative gated GCN (IGGCN) architecture for seizure detection using EEG signals. Other studies have also proposed architectures such as the sequential graph convolutional network (SGCN) [11], demonstrating promising results.

In this work, a proposed GCN architecture is provided for epileptic seizure detection from EEG signals. All experiments are conducted on the Turkish epilepsy [12] dataset. The preprocessing stage consists of low-level and high-level steps. Low-level preprocessing includes operations such as filtering, normalization, and windowing. In the high-level stage, node features and the adjacency matrix are extracted and used as inputs to the proposed GCN model for feature learning. Finally, a sigmoid activation function is applied for classification. The remainder of this paper is organized as follows. Section 2 describes the proposed method in detail. Section 3 reports the evaluation metrics. In the following, experiment results are presented in Sect. 4. Finally, Sect. 5 provides the discussion and conclusion.

2 Material and Methods

In Fig. 1, the block diagram of the proposed CAD system for epileptic seizure detection based on EEG signals is presented. In this study, the Turkish epilepsy dataset [12] is used. In the first step, preprocessing operations, including filtering, windowing, and down-sampling, are applied to the EEG signals. Then, each EEG channel is considered a node, and a set of handcrafted features is extracted from each channel to construct the node feature matrix. Simultaneously, the adjacency matrix is calculated using the Pearson correlation coefficient to model the functional connections between channels. Next, the resulting brain graph is fed into the proposed GCN architecture to extract distinctive features. Finally, the sigmoid activation function is used to perform the classification.

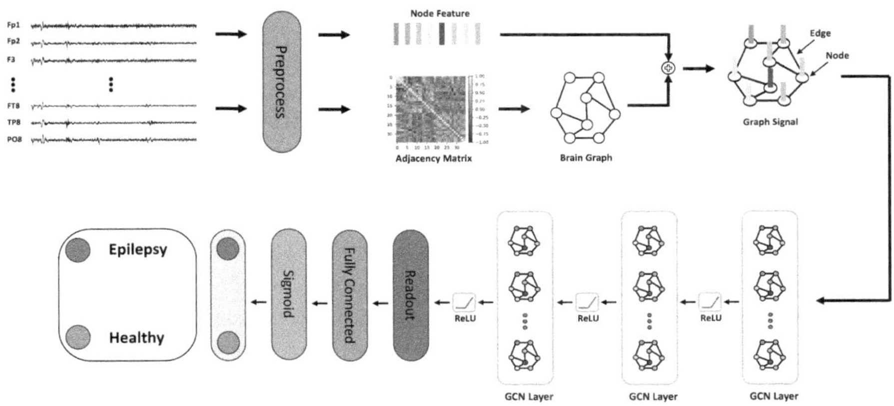

Fig. 1. General block diagram of the proposed method.

2.1 Dataset

All simulations were performed on the Turkish epilepsy dataset [12]. This dataset includes EEG signals from the parietal, frontal, temporal, occipital, frontopolar, auricular, and central regions for 50 subjects with epileptic seizures and 71 healthy control (HC) subjects [12]. The subjects include both men and women, with an average age of 46 years. In this dataset, EEG signals for all 121 subjects, across two classes, were recorded using a device with 35 channels at a sampling frequency 500 Hz, based on the 10–20 electrode placement system [12].

2.2 Preprocessing

Preprocessing of EEG signals consists of two levels: low-level and high-level. In low-level preprocessing, standard steps such as windowing and filtering are applied to the EEG signals. In contrast, high-level preprocessing includes steps such as node feature extraction and graph construction via an adjacency matrix, which are performed to prepare the data for input into the proposed GCN model.

Low-Level Preprocessing In the low-level preprocessing, first EEG signals are preprocessed using a band-pass filter in the frequency range of 0.5–48 Hz to reduce unwanted artifacts. Next, down-sampling is applied, reducing the sampling frequency 500 Hz 250 Hz. In addition, the Common Average Referencing (CAR) method [13] is employed as an important step to improve the signal-to-noise ratio (SNR) and reduce common noise across channels. Finally, the EEG signals are segmented into 5 s, 10 s, and 15 s time windows, which are then fed separately as inputs to the proposed GCN model.

Graph Construction via Adjacency Matrix To extract complex spatiotemporal patterns while simultaneously leveraging the brain's functional connectivity and intrinsic signal properties, EEG signals were modeled as a graph $G = \{V, E, A\}$, where the 35 recording channels were represented as a set of graph nodes (V), and the functional connections between them were defined as edges (E) in the adjacency matrix (A) [14]. To quantitatively measure these connections, the Pearson correlation coefficient was employed, as it captures the linear dependency between the time series of two different channels. For two signals x_i and x_j, the correlation coefficient is calculated as follows [14]:

$$r_{ij} = \frac{\sum(x_i - \mu_i)(x_j - \mu_j)}{\sqrt{\sum(x_i - \mu_i)^2 \sum(x_j - \mu_j)^2}} \tag{1}$$

The resulting Pearson correlation matrix creates a fully connected graph, with many edges having low weights and potentially containing noise [14]. To obtain an optimal and sparse network representation, a thresholding scheme was applied to the connectivity matrix [14]. The threshold (τ) was defined as the sum of the median and one standard deviation of the connectivity values [14]. Finally, the elements of the graph adjacency matrix (A) were initialized as follows, preserving stronger connections while eliminating weaker ones [14]. Figure 2 illustrates sample Pearson correlation matrices for HC and epileptic seizures patients.

$$A_{ij} = \begin{cases} 1 & \text{if } r_{ij} \geq \tau \\ 0 & \text{otherwise} \end{cases} \tag{2}$$

Node Feature Extraction. In addition to the adjacency matrix (A), which defines the topological structure, distinctive features were extracted from each channel to capture the signal dynamics at each electrode and were considered as node features. These features were organized into an $N \times F$ matrix X, where $N = 35$ represents the number of nodes and $F = 6$ denotes the number of extracted features per node. The six extracted features—mean, standard deviation (STD), sample entropy [15], approximate entropy [15], peak frequency [16], and absolute power [16]—collectively enable a comprehensive analysis of the signal across time, frequency, and nonlinear complexity domains.

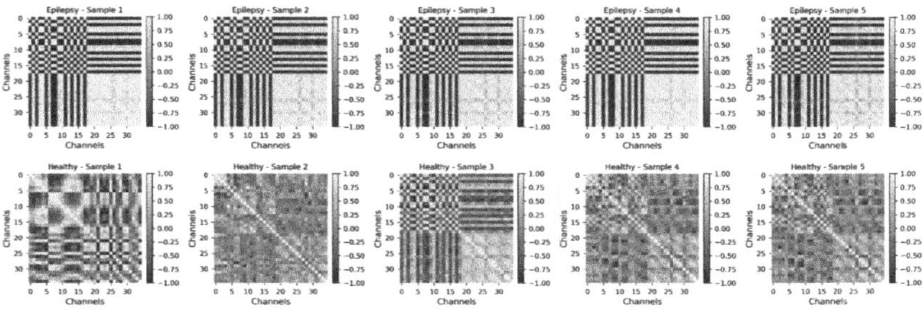

Fig. 2. Sample Pearson correlation matrices for HC and epileptic seizures patients.

2.3 Proposed Graph Convolutional Network Model

In general, GCN models learn a transformation from the initial node feature representation (matrix X) and produce an output of size $N \times d'$. For a given layer l, the feature update process can be expressed as [17]:

$$X^{l+1} = f(X^l, A) \tag{3}$$

where $l = 0, 1, \ldots, L-1$, L denotes the total number of layers, X^0 represents the input features, X^L denotes the output, and f is the function learned by the model. A basic formulation of the function f can be written as [17]:

$$X^{l+1} = \sigma(A'X^lW^l) \tag{4}$$

where W^l is the weight matrix and σ is a nonlinear activation function, such as ReLU [17]. In this formulation, to ensure that the model considers both the features of each node and those of its neighboring nodes, a modified adjacency matrix $A' = A + I$ is used, where I is the identity matrix [17].

However, repeatedly applying this operation across all graph layers may result in large values in the elements of X^l, potentially leading to model instability. To address this issue, the formulation is modified as follows [17]:

$$X^{l+1} = \sigma(D^{-\frac{1}{2}}A'D^{-\frac{1}{2}}X^lW^l) \tag{5}$$

In this formulation, the adjacency matrix is normalized using the degree matrix D, which is a diagonal matrix whose diagonal elements correspond to the row-wise sums of A'. This symmetric normalization [17] operation, defined as $D^{-1/2}A'D^{-1/2}$, prevents feature values from growing excessively and mitigates the risk of exploding values during training. The details of proposed GCN model are provided in Fig. 1 and Table 1.

Table 1. Details for proposed GCN model.

	Layer	Output Size
Input		(35×6)
Block 1	Graph Convolution	(35×64)
	ReLU	
	Graph Convolution	(35×64)
	ReLU	
	Graph Convolution	(35×32)
	ReLU	
	Average pooling	(1×32)
Block 2	Fully Connected	(1×16)
	ReLU	
	Fully Connected	(1×1)
Prediction	Sigmoid	(1×1)

3 Evaluation Metrics

To evaluate the performance of the proposed GCN architecture, accuracy (Acc), F1 score (F1), precision (Prec), sensitivity (Sens), and specificity (Spec) are calculated. Additionally, a 5-fold cross-validation [5] method is employed to assess the proposed DL model, and the mean and standard deviation (std) of the evaluation metrics on the test data are reported. In this step, the scikit-learn library in the Python environment is used to implement the 5-fold cross-validation and compute the evaluation metrics.

4 Experiment Results

This section presents the results of the proposed GCN architecture-based CAD system for detecting epileptic seizures from EEG signals. All simulations were performed on a personal computer with an NVIDIA 3090 GPU, 1 TB RAM, and a Core i9 CPU. To implement the proposed GCN architecture, software tools in the Python environment, including TensorFlow and scikit-learn, were used.

In Table 2, the performance of the GCN model for EEG signals with time intervals of 5 s, 10 s, and 15 s is reported. According to Table 2, the proposed

Table 2. Results for proposed model based on different EEG time-frames.

Segment	Accuracy	Sensitivity	Specificity	Precision	F1-Score
5 s	93.24 ± 0.53	94.06 ± 0.89	92.63 ± 1.13	90.63 ± 0.81	92.31 ± 0.47
10 s	95.56 ± 0.22	94.10 ± 0.66	96.65 ± 0.66	95.54 ± 0.81	94.81 ± 0.35
15 s	95.72 ± 0.90	95.03 ± 1.08	96.25 ± 0.89	95.05 ± 1.16	95.04 ± 1.04

model achieves superior performance for the 15 s time window compared to the 10 s and 5 s windows.

In the training step, the hyper-parameters of the GCN architecture were adjusted to achieve the highest possible accuracy in epileptic seizure detection. In this step, the model hyper-parameters, including the number of epochs, batch size, and learning rate, were set to 150, 32, and 0.001, respectively. In addition, the Adam optimizer was used. Furthermore, binary cross-entropy and the sigmoid function were used as the loss function and activation function (in the FC layer), respectively. In addition, the confusion matrices of the proposed GCN architecture for EEG signals with different time intervals are shown in Figs. 3, 4 and 5.

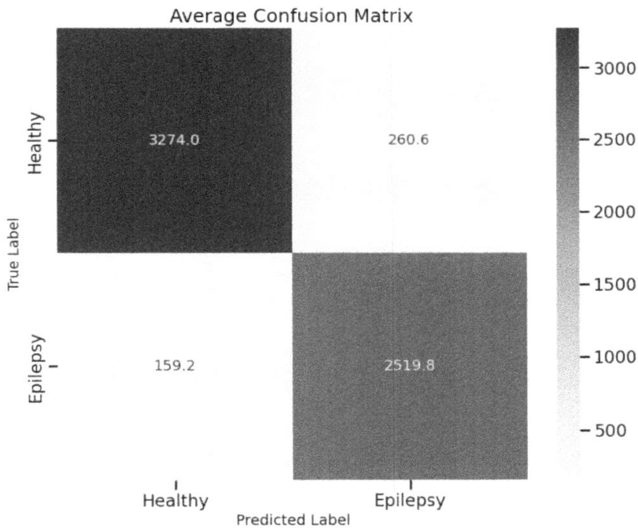

Fig. 3. Confusion matrix for proposed GCN model based on EEG signals with 5s time-frame.

The improved performance for the 15 s time window can be attributed to the fact that longer time intervals typically contain more informative patterns relevant to epileptic seizure detection. Moreover, longer segments better capture the spatio-temporal dependencies between EEG channels, which is crucial for enhancing the performance of graph-based architectures such as GCN.

5 Discussion, Conclusion, and Future Works

In this paper, a CAD system based on a GCN architecture is proposed for the automatic detection of epileptic seizures from multi-channel EEG signals. In the proposed method, EEG signals are first modeled as a brain graph, and

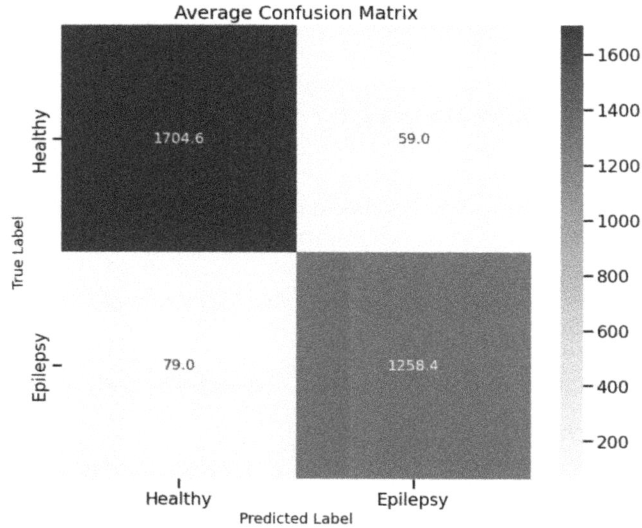

Fig. 4. Confusion matrix for proposed GCN model based on EEG signals with 10s time-frame.

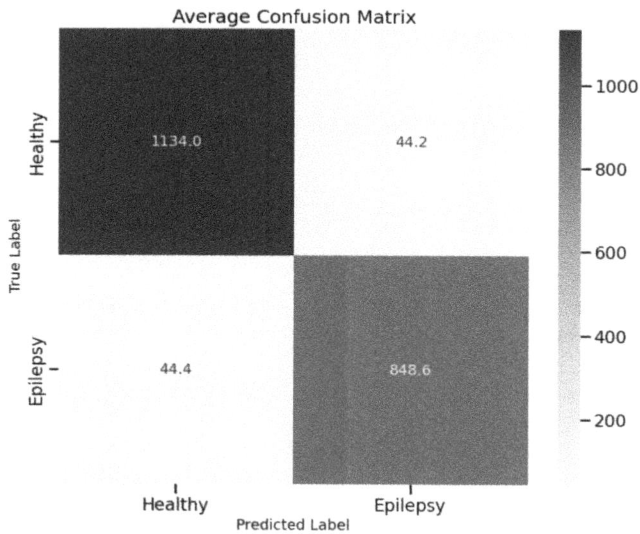

Fig. 5. Confusion matrix for proposed GCN model based on EEG signals with 15 s time-frame.

the functional connections between channels are extracted using the Pearson correlation coefficient in the form of an adjacency matrix. In addition, a set of handcrafted features is considered as node features.

Subsequently, the brain graph, along with the node features, is used as input to the GCN architecture for the detection of epileptic seizures. The obtained results demonstrate that the proposed model achieves significant performance in detecting epileptic seizures. Specifically, for EEG signals with a 15 s time frame, the model achieves an accuracy of 95.72%, indicating the effectiveness of the proposed method in extracting spatio-temporal features from EEG signals.

The proposed CAD system can be utilized as an effective auxiliary tool for the diagnosis of epileptic seizures in clinical applications. For future work, the use of advanced graph-based architectures such as dynamic GCN with RNNs [18], Graph Attention Networks (GAT) [19], and GAT-Transformer [20] is suggested. Furthermore, integrating GCN with uncertainty quantification techniques [21] could improve the robustness and interpretability of the model (Table 3).

Table 3. Comparison of the proposed model with related works.

Ref	Dataset	Preprocessing	Model	Results
[22]	University of Helsinki Hospital Dataset	Down-Sampling, Filtering, Segmentation, 7 Statistical Features, 4 Entropy Features	CNN-AE	Acc = 92.34
[23]	CHB-MIT	Denoising By DWT, PSDEDs	3D-CNNs	Acc = 92.6
[24]	CHB-MIT	Normalization, One-Hot Encoding	Multi-Channel CNN-Bi-LSTM-Attention	Acc = 94.83
[25]	Bonn	Normalization	CNN	Acc = 88.67
[26]	TUH	Filtering, STFT	Pretrained networks	Acc = 88.30
[27]	CHB-MIT	FFT	CNN	Acc = 97.1
Our	**Turkish**	**Low and High-Level Preprocessing Pipeline**	**GCN**	**Acc = 95.72**

References

1. Rasheed, K., et al.: Machine learning for predicting epileptic seizures using EEG signals: a review. IEEE Rev. Biomed. Eng. **14**, 139–155 (2020)
2. Gabeff, V., et al.: Interpreting deep learning models for epileptic seizure detection on EEG signals. Artif. Intell. Med. **117**, 102084 (2021)
3. Kunekar, P., Gupta, M.K., Gaur, P.: Detection of epileptic seizure in EEG signals using machine learning and deep learning techniques. J. Eng. Appl. Sci. **71**(1), 21 (2024)
4. Varlı, M., Yılmaz, H.: Multiple classification of EEG signals and epileptic seizure diagnosis with combined deep learning. J. Comput. Sci. **67**, 101943 (2023)
5. Huang, X., Meng, H., Li, Z.: Deep learning for epileptic seizure prediction from EEG signals: a review. Biomed. Sig. Process. Control **117**, 109518 (2026)

6. Barzegar, M.M., Ahmadi Daryakenari, N., Khodatars, M.: Explainable epileptic seizure detection from electroencephalography signals via CNN-Bi-LSTM attention hybrid model. J. Res. Health **15**(6), 779–792 (2025)
7. Prasanna, C.S., Rahman, M.Z.U.: Multi-seizure classification using transformer-based attention models and pseudo-labeling techniques in EEG analysis. IEEE Access **14**, 9594–9605 (2026)
8. Atitallah, S.B., Driss, M., Boulila, W., Koubaa, A.: Graph-based EEG analysis for seizure prediction enhanced with Kolmogorov-Arnold networks and self-supervised learning. Eng. Sci. Technol. Int. J. **73**, 102245 (2026)
9. Zhang, X., Dai, C., Guo, Y.: Dynamic graph convolutional network with dilated convolution for epilepsy seizure detection. Bioengineering **12**(8), 832 (2025)
10. Hu, Y., Liu, J., Sun, R., Yu, Y., Sui, Y.: Classification of epileptic seizures in EEG data based on iterative gated graph convolution network. Front. Comput. Neurosci. **18**, 1454529 (2024)
11. Jibon, F.A., et al.: Sequential graph convolutional network and DeepRNN based hybrid framework for epileptic seizure detection from EEG signal. Digit. Health **10**, 20552076241249870 (2024)
12. Lih, O.S., et al.: EpilepsyNet: novel automated detection of epilepsy using transformer model with EEG signals from 121 patient population. Comput. Biol. Med. **164**, 107312 (2023)
13. Tsuchimoto, S., et al.: Use of common average reference and large-Laplacian spatial-filters enhances EEG signal-to-noise ratios in intrinsic sensorimotor activity. J. Neurosci. Methods **353**, 109089 (2021)
14. Hou, Y., et al.: GCNs-net: a graph convolutional neural network approach for decoding time-resolved EEG motor imagery signals. IEEE Trans. Neural Netw. Learn. Syst. **35**(6), 7312–7323 (2022)
15. Bdaqli, M., et al.: Diagnosis of Parkinson disease from EEG signals using a CNN-LSTM model and explainable AI. In: Ferrández Vicente, J.M., Val Calvo, M., Adeli, H. (eds.) IWINAC 2024. LNCS, vol. 14674, pp. 128–138. Springer, Cham (2024). https://doi.org/10.1007/978-3-031-61140-7_13
16. Shoeibi, A., et al.: Early diagnosis of schizophrenia in EEG signals using one dimensional transformer model. In: Ferrández Vicente, J.M., Val Calvo, M., Adeli, H. (eds.) IWINAC 2024. LNCS, vol. 14674, pp. 139–149. Springer, Cham (2024). https://doi.org/10.1007/978-3-031-61140-7_14
17. Zhang, S., Tong, H., Xu, J., Maciejewski, R.: Graph convolutional networks: a comprehensive review. Comput. Soc. Netw. **6**(1), 1–23 (2019)
18. Gosala, B., Singh, A.R., Tiwari, H., Gupta, M.: GCN-LSTM: a hybrid graph convolutional network model for schizophrenia classification. Biomed. Sig. Process. Control **105**, 107657 (2025)
19. Li, Z., Zhang, G., Wang, L., Wei, J., Dang, J.: Emotion recognition using spatial-temporal EEG features through convolutional graph attention network. J. Neural Eng. **20**(1), 016046 (2023)
20. Yan, H., Guo, K., Xing, X., Xu, X.: Bridge graph attention based graph convolution network with multi-scale transformer for EEG emotion recognition. IEEE Trans. Affect. Comput. **15**(4), 2042–2054 (2024)
21. Gao, H., et al.: Graph convolutional network with connectivity uncertainty for EEG-based emotion recognition. IEEE J. Biomed. Health Inform. **28**(10), 5917–5928 (2024)
22. Wang, Y., Yuan, S., Liu, J.X., Hu, W., Jia, Q., Xu, F.: Combining EEG features and convolutional autoencoder for neonatal seizure detection. Int. J. Neural Syst. **34**(08), 2450040 (2024)

23. Gao, Y., Gao, B., Chen, Q., Liu, J., Zhang, Y.: Deep convolutional neural network-based epileptic electroencephalogram (EEG) signal classification. Front. Neurol. **11**, 375 (2020)
24. Ma, Y., et al.: A multi-channel feature fusion CNN-Bi-LSTM epilepsy EEG classification and prediction model based on attention mechanism. IEEE Access **11**, 62855–62864 (2023)
25. Acharya, U.R., Oh, S.L., Hagiwara, Y., Tan, J.H., Adeli, H.: Deep convolutional neural network for the automated detection and diagnosis of seizure using EEG signals. Comput. Biol. Med. **100**, 270–278 (2018)
26. Raghu, S., Sriraam, N., Temel, Y., Rao, S.V., Kubben, P.L.: EEG based multi-class seizure type classification using convolutional neural network and transfer learning. Neural Netw. **124**, 202–212 (2020)
27. Zhou, M., et al.: Epileptic seizure detection based on EEG signals and CNN. Front. Neuroinform. **12**, 95 (2018)

Assessing the Robustness of Clinical–Metabolic Activity Models Through SAR in the PPMI Dataset

A. Hernández[1,2(✉)], I. A. Illán[1,2], J. Ramírez[1,2], F. Segovia[1,2], C. Vázquez-García[1,2], F. J. Martínez-Murcia[1,2], and J. M. Górriz[1,2]

[1] Data Science and Computational Intelligence Institute, University of Granada, Granada, Spain
{illan,javierrp,fsegovia,crisvgarcia,fjesusmartinez,gorriz}@ugr.es

[2] Department of Signal Theory, Telematics and Communications, University of Granada, Granada, Spain
alejandrohs@ugr.es
https://dasci.es/

Abstract. Changes in dopaminergic transporter availability can be quantified using single-photon emission computed tomography (SPECT) with the ^{123}I-FP-CIT radiotracer, providing valuable biomarkers for investigating neurodegenerative processes. However, establishing statistically reliable relationships between clinical variables and dopaminergic brain patterns remains challenging, particularly when dealing with high dimensional neuroimaging data. In this work, we investigate the association between clinical variables—age, Movement Disorder Society Unified Parkinson's Disease Rating Scale total score (MDS-UPDRS$_{\text{total}}$), Montreal Cognitive Assessment (MoCA) and Geriatric Depression Scale (GDS)—and dopaminergic activity derived from preprocessed SPECT images of Parkinson's Progression Markers Initiative (PPMI) database. After intensity normalization of the filtered dataset, dimensionality reduction is performed using Principal Component Analysis to obtain compact representations of images patterns. These representations are then used to model the relationship between clinical variables and brain dopaminergic activity. Model validation is conducted using the Statistical Agnostic Regression (SAR) framework, which evaluates the existence of significant linear associations through resampling procedures and estimates an upper bound on the expected prediction risk under a worst-case Bayesian scenario. Statistical power is further assessed via Monte Carlo simulations under the null distribution. Our results demonstrate that SAR provides a principled and robust methodology for validating clinical–neuroimaging associations, effectively mitigating false positives and overfitting biases inherent to conventional validation schemes. This framework enables reproducible inference and offers strong theoretical guarantees, thereby reinforcing the reliability of machine learning-driven discoveries in neuroimaging studies of Parkinson's disease.

Keywords: Statistical Agnostic Regression · Linear Regression · Machine Learning · Support Vector Regression · Statistical Learning

J. M. Ferrández Vicente et al. (Eds.): IWINAC 2026, LNCS 16574, pp. 118–127, 2026.
https://doi.org/10.1007/978-3-032-27314-7_12

Theory · Neuroimaging · Principal Component Analysis · Parkinson's Progression Markers Initiative

1 Introduction

One of the main strengths of machine learning (ML) approaches is their flexibility in handling high-dimensional and complex data without requiring explicit assumptions about underlying distributions. This characteristic makes them particularly attractive for neuroimaging applications, but robust validation remains a critical issue. While classical statistical models provide formal hypothesis testing and residual diagnostics, ML approaches are typically validated through cross-validation (CV) strategies, data splitting, and resampling to assess stability and generalization [1,2]. Bootstrapping has been shown to improve goodness-of-fit estimation and metamodel validation [3–5]. However, unlike Ordinary Least Squares (OLS), many modern ML models lack formal significance testing procedures [6,7], and significance analysis is often insufficiently addressed in AI-driven studies [8,9]. In small-sample settings, permutation tests or CV-derived values may lead to optimistic bias in the estimation of prediction error [10–12].

These methodological considerations are especially pertinent in the study of Parkinson's disease (PD), a progressive neurodegenerative disorder with heterogeneous clinical manifestations. The development of predictive and progression models increasingly relies on ML techniques applied to large, multicenter datasets such as the Parkinson's Progression Markers Initiative (PPMI) [13]. In neuroimaging studies, high variability in CV performance across experimental designs has been widely documented [14,15], and convergence of learning curves does not necessarily ensure reliability [16]. As ML models become more complex and are applied to large, heterogeneous datasets, rigorous validation is essential to prevent overfitting and inflated predictive claims. To address this limitation, Statistical Agnostic Regression (SAR) was proposed in [17], a Statistical Learning Theory (SLT)-based non-parametric test that derives an upper bound on the expected risk of linear Support Vector Regression (SVR) models, enabling principled comparison against the null hypothesis. In this work, we apply SAR to regression-based ML models for PD, aiming to mitigate false positives and counteract the optimistic bias reported in conventional validation schemes [8–10], to ensure the generalizability, reproducibility, and statistical reliability of ML-based inferences derived from neuroimaging biomarkers.

2 Materials and Methods

2.1 SAR

The linear regression framework is intended to find linear relationships between variables $(\boldsymbol{y}, \boldsymbol{X})$, commonly expressed as $\boldsymbol{y} = \boldsymbol{\omega X} + \epsilon$, where ϵ denotes zero-mean noise with constant variance. Although classical solutions such as OLS provide unbiased linear estimates, their performance degrades under noise, nonlinearity, or high-dimensional settings. To overcome these limitations, methods derived from SLT, such as SVR [18], incorporate regularization principles to improve robustness.

Generalization performance in SLT is obtained through the expected risk over the unknown data distribution. As this quantity cannot be directly evaluated, an estimation of the generalization performance is computed through validation. The SAR methodology first estimates the training risk $\mathcal{R}_N(f_N)$ for a linear SVR model, $f(\widehat{\boldsymbol{x}}) = \widehat{\boldsymbol{x}}\boldsymbol{\omega}$, using the ϵ-insensitive loss, while simultaneously upper-bounding the true risk $\mathcal{R}(f)$ via a PAC-Bayesian inequality that incorporates model complexity [17]. The associated expected risk for the null reference case ($\boldsymbol{\omega} = \mathbf{0}$) provides a theoretical threshold for determining whether the learned linear model captures a meaningful structure beyond chance. Comparing the expected risk of the fitted SVR model with that of a null model ($\boldsymbol{\omega} = \mathbf{0}$), defines the acceptance or rejection of the null hypothesis. This test is repeated by a Monte Carlo permutation procedure: for each of the $R+1$ resampled datasets, both the null risk ($\mathcal{R}^0$) and model risk ($\mathcal{R}(f)$) are recalculated to account for sample variability. The p-value measures the likelihood that the model risk exceeds the null threshold, providing a significance estimate for the linear relationship. The empirical test power $(1-\beta)$ quantifies the probability of correctly rejecting the null and depends on sample size N, allowing assessment of the detectability of meaningful linear patterns.

2.2 Multimodal Clinical and Neuroimaging Data: PPMI Database

The Parkinson's Progression Markers Initiative (PPMI) provides a large, multicenter dataset of neuroimaging and clinical information to characterize biomarkers and progression patterns in Parkinson's disease (PD). In this study, we analyze single-photon emission computed tomography (SPECT) images acquired using the ^{123}I-FP-CIT radiotracer, which allows the assessment of dopaminergic transporter activity in the brain. In addition to imaging data, several clinical variables are considered, including age, Movement Disorder Society Unified Parkinson's Disease Rating Scale total score (MDS-UPDRS$_{\text{total}}$), Montreal Cognitive Assessment (MoCA), and Geriatric Depression Scale (GDS). To ensure methodological consistency and avoid biases due to missing data, the dataset was filtered to retain only the first medical visit of subjects with complete information across all modalities, including SPECT scans and selected clinical variables. After this filtering procedure, the final cohort comprised 176 healthy control (HC) subjects and 407 patients diagnosed with PD. Table 1 reports the mean and standard deviation of the clinical variables considered in the subsequent analysis.

Furthermore, SPECT images were preprocessed using SPM12 in MATLAB including spatial normalization and smoothing, to ensure anatomical comparability across subjects and reduce inter-subject variability. In addition, an intensity normalization step was applied to the SPECT preprocessed images in order to mitigate background intensity variability across scans and improve the comparability of the resulting signal distributions. Given the high dimensionality of

Table 1. Clinical variables available from the first medical visit in the PPMI database, including their mean values and standard deviations for the two diagnostic groups.

Clinical Variables	HC	PD
Age [yr]	61.1(11.2)	61.74(9.60)
MDS-UPDRS$_{\text{total}}$	4.01(4.00)	31.8(13.0)
MoCA	28.23(1.10)	27.12(2.34)
GDS	5.17(1.36)	5.25(1.44)

neuroimaging data, dimensionality reduction was subsequently performed using a mask generated from the mean SPECT image of HC subjects and via Principal Component Analysis (PCA). This approach enables the extraction of compact representations of the underlying brain activity patterns while preserving the dominant sources of variance in the dataset, facilitating subsequent statistical modeling and analysis.

2.3 Proposed Pipeline

In this work, a linear SVR model is trained using different sample sizes from the dataset. Statistical significance is evaluated using the SAR test, with 100 realizations whose regression results are averaged to assess the effect of sample size [19]. A Python-based pipeline is implemented to perform principal component analysis, data selection, SVR training and validation, and visualization of SAR validation statistics using the *sarlib.py* library developed by our research group and available at https://github.com/SiPBA/sar). The resulting plots are presented in the following section to discuss the validity of the obtained results. The pipeline steps are described in Fig. 1.

3 Results

A systematic SAR-based analysis demonstrates the absence of a statistically significant linear relationship ($p_{\text{value}}^{\text{SAR}}$ in Table 2) between clinical variables (age, MoCA, and GDS) and striatal activation derived from DaTSCAN, robust to variations in sample size, intensity normalization, and feature space dimensionality.

Figures 2a and 2b show the principal results of (MDS-UPDRS$_{\text{total}}$) variable analysis. The linear relationship between the first principal component (PCA$_1$), or the primary eigenbrain, and the MDS-UPDRS$_{\text{total}}$ is illustrated in Fig. 2a. The dependence between significance, power and sample size (N) is represented in Fig. 2b. Given the statistical power of the SAR test, this experiment represents an example of a positive correlation, where higher clinical motor impairment (MDS-UPDRS$_{\text{total}}$) is associated with specific patterns of dopaminergic depletion captured in the PCA_1 projection weights, that represents activity in the

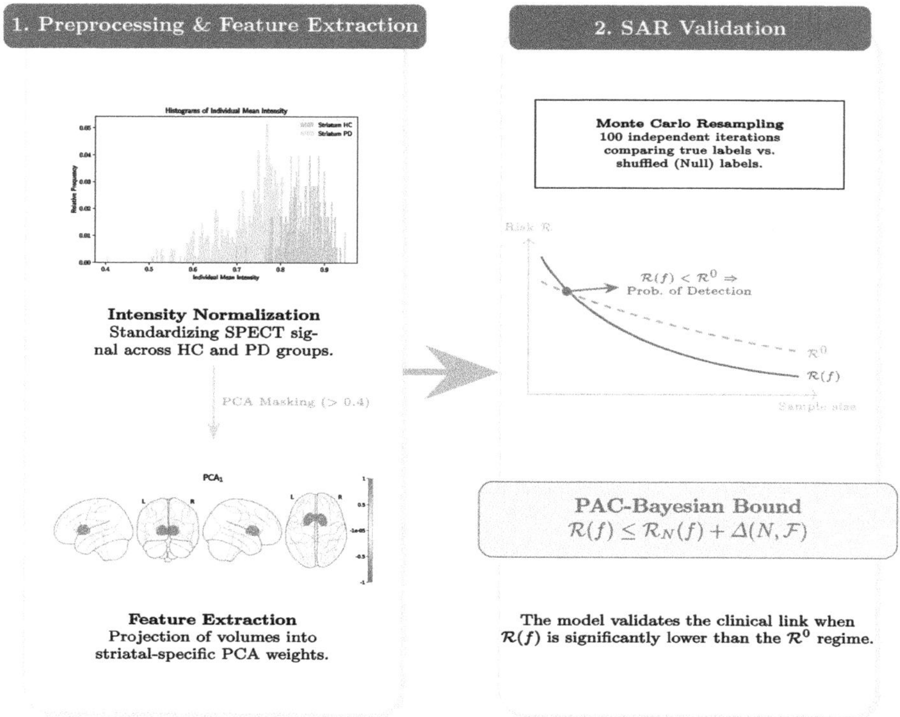

Fig. 1. Validation pipeline.

striatum. Monte Carlo simulations (100 realizations) show that at smaller sample sizes ($N < 150$), the estimated model risk $\mathcal{R}(f)$ remains above the null-model threshold $\mathcal{R}^0$, suggesting that the linear association cannot be reliably distinguished from chance in low-data regimes. As N increases, the model risk $\mathcal{R}(f)$ consistently drops below the flatness threshold $\mathcal{R}^0$. The statistical power $1 - \beta$ follows an S-shaped trajectory, rising significantly after $N = 200$ and reaching saturation at approximately $N = 400$. As stated at the beginning of this section, the SAR test fails to reject the null hypothesis for the age, MoCA, and GDS models, whereas the classical test fails to reject it only for the GDS model. This shows the ability of the SAR method to better control false positives compared to the classical F-test. On the other hand, since SAR is capable of detecting a genuine effect between MDS-UPDRS$_{\text{total}}$ and dopaminergic activity in the striatum, the statistical significance tests associated with the F-statistic tend to reject the null hypothesis due to their comparatively optimistic behavior relative to the SAR method. This excess optimism results in a higher number of rejections of the null hypothesis and, consequently, poorer control of false positives.

Furthermore, a statistical significance test is applied based on the p-value of the F-test derived from Ordinary Least Squares (OLS) predictive models.

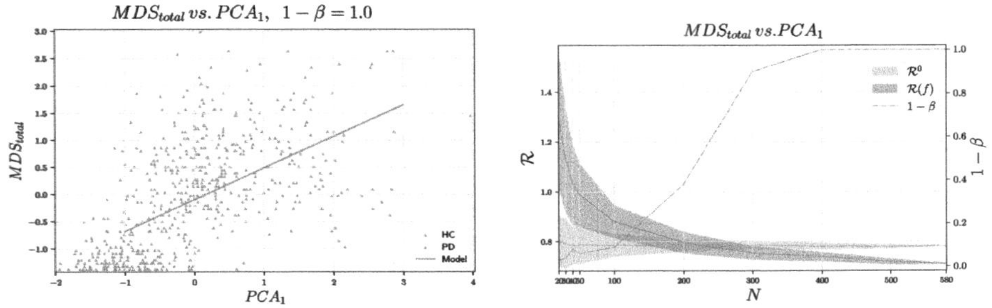

(a) Linear relationship (PCA_1 vs. MDS-UPDRS).

(b) SAR validation metrics vs. sample size (N).

Fig. 2. Experimental results of the clinical-metabolic mapping. (a) Scatter plot of MDS-UPDRS$_{\text{total}}$ against the first principal component for HC and PD groups ($1-\beta=1.0$). (b) Evolution of expected risk $\mathcal{R}(f)$ (blue) vs. null-model threshold $\mathcal{R}^0$ (green), with statistical power $1-\beta$ (red) converging to 1.0 as N increases. (Color figure online)

Table 2. Statistical significance metrics for prediction models using PCA$_1$ as predictor variable across HC and PD groups: SAR-derived p-value ($p^{\text{SAR}}_{\text{value}}$) and F-test p-value ($p^{\text{OLS}}_{\text{value}}$) obtained through OLS model. This table identifies the predictive models that exhibit a statistically significant linear relationship ($p_{\text{value}} < \alpha$) for each metric associated with each method (F-test via OLS, and SAR).

Response\ p-value	$p^{\text{OLS}}_{\text{value}}$	$p^{\text{SAR}}_{\text{value}}$
Age	$6.848 \cdot 10^{-4}$	1.0
MDS-UPDRS$_{\text{total}}$	$3.825 \cdot 10^{-54}$	0.0
MoCA	$1.218 \cdot 10^{-7}$	1.0
GDS	0.9727	1.0

This approach allows us to determine whether, for the complete set of available data, the p-value falls below the significance level of $\alpha = 0.05$ for any linear relationship ($p^{\text{OLS}}_{\text{value}} < \alpha$). Additionally, a statistical significance test based on the p-value of the SAR test is performed to assess whether, for the full dataset, the p-value is below the significance threshold of $\alpha = 0.05$ for any linear relationship ($p^{\text{SAR}}_{\text{value}} < \alpha$). The results of the p-value significance metric for each predictive model and for each significance test (classical and SAR) are reported in Table 2.

Finally, to demonstrate that the OLS method is not the Best Linear Unbiased Estimator (BLUE), the residual analysis is presented in Fig. 3. Specifically, Fig. 3a shows the p-values obtained from the Breusch-Pagan test for heteroscedasticity ($p^{\text{BP}}_{\text{value}} < \alpha$) for all proposed predictive models. Since the only model that does not exhibit heteroscedasticity is the predictive model of the GDS, Fig. 3b displays a scatter plot illustrating a strong linear relationship between the residuals and the predictor variable (PCA$_1$), indicating the presence

Response\ p-value	$p_{\text{value}}^{\text{BP}}$
Age	$2.225{\cdot}10^{-6}$
MDS-UPDRS$_{\text{total}}$	$8.667{\cdot}10^{-4}$
MoCA	$1.600{\cdot}10^{-3}$
GDS	0.748

(a) BP-test results

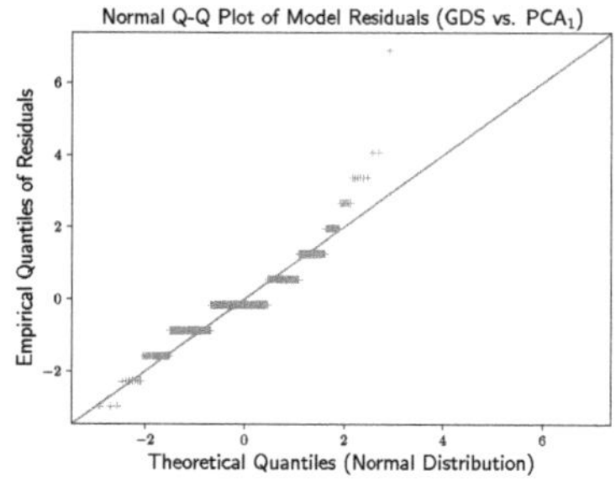

(b) Q-Q plot of model residuals

Fig. 3. (a) Summary of the p-values from the Breusch-Pagan test ($p_{\text{value}}^{\text{BP}}$) assessing heteroscedasticity in the models (i.e., when $p_{\text{value}}^{\text{BP}} < \alpha$). (b) Scatter plot of the residuals from the GDS predictive model against the predictor variable (PCA$_1$), showing a strong linear relationship, indicative of endogeneity in the model.

of endogeneity. This violates the key OLS assumption that the errors are exogenous, rendering the estimators biased and inconsistent. Because the assumptions of homoscedasticity (absence of heteroscedasticity) and exogeneity (absence of endogeneity) are necessary conditions of the Gauss-Markov theorem, their violation implies that OLS cannot be considered the BLUE.

4 Discussion

A significant body of literature in Parkinson's research focuses on identifying clinical, genetic, and imaging biomarkers to predict disease progression. For instance, the large-scale longitudinal study by Latourelle et al. [20] successfully identified multiple predictors of motor progression using a validation strategy based on conventional k-fold cross-validation. While such methods are standard in the field, they primarily estimate the generalization error of a specific model configuration rather than testing the fundamental existence of a relationship against a null-regime.

The strong linear association between the PCA$_1$ and MDS-UPDRS$_{\text{total}}$ (Fig. 2a) confirms that ^{123}I-FP-CIT SPECT imaging remains a gold-standard biomarker for motor dysfunction. However, SAR validation adds a layer of reliability to this claim, proving that the association is not a byproduct of overfitting but a stable biological signal detectable once a sufficient sample size is reached.

As shown in our analysis (Fig. 2b), conventional metrics can be deceptively optimistic in small-to-medium sample sizes. In regimes where $N < 150$, a model might achieve a seemingly acceptable mean squared error or R^2 via cross-validation, yet fail to outperform the SAR "flatness" threshold ($\mathcal{R}^0$). This suggests that many relationships reported in literature using standard CV might be susceptible to spurious correlations or false positives, especially when the signal-to-noise ratio is low or the feature space is high-dimensional.

The findings in Table 2 indicate the importance of adopting robust statistical significance frameworks when evaluating predictive models. While the classical F-test suggests a higher number of significant relationships, this behavior appears to be driven by its comparatively optimistic bias, which may lead to an increased rate of false positives. In contrast, the SAR-based approach demonstrates a more conservative behavior, failing to reject the null hypothesis in several cases (age and MoCA prediction models) where the classical test does, thereby providing improved control over spurious detections. Importantly, SAR still identifies meaningful effects, such as the relationship between MDS-UPDRS$_{\text{total}}$ and striatal dopaminergic activity. These results show the potential advantages of SAR as a more reliable tool for statistical inference in predictive modeling contexts.

Regarding the use of the classical OLS method, as discussed in the previous section, a residual analysis across all proposed predictive models (Fig. 3) clearly demonstrates that OLS is not BLUE, as the data do not satisfy the necessary conditions of the Gauss-Markov theorem. Furthermore, as shown in Table 2, the statistical significance associated with the F-test derived from the OLS models indicates that this classical test does not adequately control for false positives, as previously noted. For these reasons, in light of the results obtained for the OLS method, any conclusions drawn from it should be interpreted with caution, due to potential overoptimism and the violation of the assumptions required for OLS to be BLUE.

The validation approaches used in [20] make use of large amounts of variables to define biomarkers to characterize the disease progression. Variables such as age or sex are included in the analysis of the data, and complex models are used to construct biomarker predictors. We show here that the SAR framework provides a mathematically grounded rejection of the null hypothesis ($H_0 : \boldsymbol{\omega} = \mathbf{0}$), filtering for clinical-metabolic associations that may be reported as significant when they are, in fact, artifacts of the specific data partition or model complexity and do not possess sufficient statistical power.

5 Conclusions

This work establishes SAR as a rigorous and theoretically grounded framework for validating clinical–neuroimaging associations in high-dimensional settings. By explicitly testing learned models against a null regime and incorporating PAC-Bayesian risk bounds, SAR transcends the limitations of conventional cross-validation approaches, which may yield overly optimistic estimates—particularly in small-sample or high-variance scenarios.

Applied to the PPMI dataset, the proposed methodology not only confirms the well-known association between dopaminergic depletion and motor impairment but, critically, demonstrates that such relationships can be robustly distinguished from spurious correlations only beyond sufficient sample sizes. This highlights the importance of statistical power considerations in neuroimaging studies and calls into question the reliability of findings derived solely from standard validation protocols.

More broadly, SAR provides a unified framework for controlling false discoveries while preserving sensitivity to meaningful biological signals, without requiring longitudinal data or restrictive modeling assumptions. Its adoption can substantially enhance the reproducibility and interpretability of machine learning models in clinical research.

Future work should extend this framework to deep learning architectures, as well as longitudinal and multimodal analyses including SWEDD subjects or effects of class imbalance, further advancing the development of reliable biomarkers and predictive models in neurodegenerative diseases.

Acknowledgments. This research is part of the PID2022-137629OA-I00, PID2022-137461NB-C32 and PID2022-137451OB-I00 projects, by the MICIU/AEI /10.13039/501100011033 and by "ERDF/EU", and the C-ING-183-UGR23 project, cofunded by the Consejería de Universidad, Investigación e Innovación and by European Union, funded by Programa FEDER Andalucía 2021–2027.

Disclosure of Interests. The authors declare that they have no known competing financial interests or personal relationships that could have appeared to influence the work reported in this paper.

References

1. Snee, R.D.: Validation of regression models: methods and examples. Technometrics **19**(4), 415–428 (1977). https://doi.org/10.1080/00401706.1977.10489581
2. Kohavi, R.: A study of cross-validation and bootstrap for accuracy estimation and model selection. In: International Joint Conference on Artificial Intelligence (IJCAI), pp. 1137–1143 (1995)
3. Kleijnen, J.P.C., Bettonvil, B., Van Groenendahl, W.: Validation of trace-driven simulation models: regression analysis revisited, pp. 352–357 (1996). https://doi.org/10.1145/256562.256650
4. Miller, M.E., Hui, S.L., Tierney, W.M.: Validation techniques for logistic regression models. Stat. Med. **10**(8), 1213–1226 (1991). https://doi.org/10.1002/sim.4780100805
5. Oredein, A.I., Olatayo, T.O., Loyinmi, A.C.: On validating regression models with bootstraps and data splitting techniques. Global J. Sci. Front. Res. **11** (2011)
6. LeCun, Y., Bengio, Y., Hinton, G.: Deep learning. Nature **521**, 436–444 (2015). https://doi.org/10.1038/nature14539
7. Górriz, J.M., et al.: Artificial intelligence within the interplay between natural and artificial computation: advances in data science, trends and applications. Neurocomputing **410**, 237–270 (2020). https://doi.org/10.1016/j.neucom.2020.05.078
8. Isaksson, A., et al.: Cross-validation and bootstrapping are unreliable in small sample classification. Pattern Recogn. Lett. **29**(14), 1960–1965 (2008). https://doi.org/10.1016/j.patrec.2008.06.018
9. Górriz, J.M., et al.: Is K-fold validation the best model selection method for Machine Learning? *arXiv* (2024). https://doi.org/10.48550/arXiv.2401.16407. `[stat.ML]`. https://arxiv.org/abs/2401.16407
10. Varoquaux, G.: Cross-validation failure: small sample sizes lead to large error bars. Neuroimage **180**, 68–77 (2018). https://doi.org/10.1016/j.neuroimage.2017.06.061

11. Bengio, Y., Grandvalet, Y.: No unbiased estimator of the variance of K-fold cross-validation. J. Mach. Learn. Res. **5**, 1089–1105 (2004). https://doi.org/10.5555/1005332.1044695
12. Moore, D.S., et al.: The Practice of Business Statistics Companion Chapter 18: Bootstrap Methods and Permutation Tests, chap. 18. W. H. Freeman (2003). ISBN: 0716757265, 9780716757269
13. Martinez-Murcia, F., et al.: Bridging imaging and clinical scores in Parkinson's progression via multimodal self-supervised deep learning. Int. J. Neural Syst. **34**(8), 2450043 (2024). https://doi.org/10.1142/S0129065724500436
14. Eklund, A., Nichols, T.E., Knutsson, H.: Cluster failure: why fMRI inferences for spatial extent have inflated false-positive rates. Proc. Natl. Acad. Sci. (PNAS) **113**(28), 7900–7905 (2016). https://doi.org/10.1073/pnas.1602413113
15. Braga-Neto, U.M., Dougherty, E.R.: Is cross-validation valid for small-sample microarray classification? Bioinformatics **20**(3), 374–380 (2004). https://doi.org/10.1093/bioinformatics/btg419
16. Viering, T., Loog, M.: The shape of learning curves: a review. IEEE Trans. Pattern Anal. Mach. Intell. **45**(6), 7799–7819 (2023). https://doi.org/10.1109/TPAMI.2022.3220744
17. Górriz, J.M., et al.: Statistical agnostic regression: a machine learning method to validate regression models. J. Adv. Res. **80**, 503–533 (2026). https://doi.org/10.1016/j.jare.2025.04.026. ISSN 2090-1232
18. Vapnik, V.N.: The Nature of Statistical Learning Theory. Springer, New York (1995)
19. Friston, K.: Sample size and the fallacies of classical inference. Neuroimage **81**, 503–504 (2013). https://doi.org/10.1016/j.neuroimage.2013.02.057
20. Latourelle, J.C., et al.: Large-scale identification of clinical and genetic predictors of motor progression in patients with newly diagnosed Parkinson's disease: a longitudinal cohort study and validation. Lancet Neurol. **16**(11), 908–916 (2017). https://doi.org/10.1016/S1474-4422(17)30328-3

Ordinal vs. Nominal Classification for Alzheimer's Disease Staging Using Structural MRI

Miguel Á. Contreras-Córdoba[1](✉), Juan E. Arco[2,3], Juan M. Górriz[2,3], Pedro Antonio Gutiérrez-Peña[1], and the Alzheimer's Disease Neuroimaging Initiative

[1] Department of Computer Science and Artificial Intelligence, University of Córdoba, Córdoba, Spain
{macontreras,pagutierrez}@uco.es

[2] SiPBA at Data Science and Computational Intelligence Institute, University of Granada, Granada, Spain
{jearco,gorriz}@ugr.es

[3] Data Science and Computational Intelligence Institute (DaSCII), University of Granada, Granada, Spain

Abstract. Alzheimer's disease (AD) and its precursor stages present an inherent ordinal structure, progressing from cognitively normal (NOR) through mild cognitive impairment (MCI) to full AD. This work exploits that natural ordering by comparing nominal and ordinal classification approaches applied to structural MRI (sMRI) data from the Alzheimer's Disease Neuroimaging Initiative (ADNI). We evaluate a linear Support Vector Machine (SVM), a Logistic Regression (LR) classifier, as well as LogAT and LogIT as nominal baselines, and the Support Vector Ordinal Regression EXtension (SVOREX) as an ordinal counterpart. All classifiers operate directly on voxel-level gray matter (GM) maps and are evaluated across binary (six pairwise combinations), three-class and four-class settings using Correct Classification Rate (CCR), Mean Absolute Error (MAE) and Average Mean Absolute Error (AMAE) under a 5-fold cross-validation protocol. Results show that SVOREX consistently achieves the lowest ordinal errors, particularly in the clinically most relevant multi-class scenarios, supporting the value of incorporating class-order information in Alzheimer staging from MRI data.

Keywords: Alzheimer's disease · ordinal classification · MRI · SVM · logistic regression · SVOREX · ADNI

---

the Alzheimer's Disease Neuroimaging Initiative–Data used in preparation of this article were obtained from the Alzheimer's Disease Neuroimaging Initiative (ADNI) database [15]. As such, the investigators within the ADNI contributed to the design and implementation of ADNI and/or provided data but did not participate in analysis or writing of this report. A complete listing of ADNI investigators can be found at: http://adni.loni.usc.edu/wp-content/uploads/how_to_apply/ADNI_Acknowledgement_List.pdf.

J. M. Ferrández Vicente et al. (Eds.): IWINAC 2026, LNCS 16574, pp. 128–137, 2026.
https://doi.org/10.1007/978-3-032-27314-7_13

1 Introduction

Alzheimer's disease is a progressive neurodegenerative disorder and the most common form of dementia. In its preclinical stage, which can last decades [1], amyloid plaques and tau tangles accumulate in the brain without outward symptoms. These early morphological changes are primarily detectable through Structural Magnetic Resonance Imaging (sMRI), which offers a non-invasive window into the macroscopic brain atrophy that accompanies disease progression. A variety of machine learning methods have been applied to sMRI for AD classification, ranging from voxel-based methods using Support Vector Machines (SVM) [5] to deep convolutional neural networks [3,12], benefiting from recent advances in artificial computation and explainable AI [8,9]. Most of these works frame the problem as standard (nominal) multi-class classification, where all misclassification are given the same penalty, regardless of how "distant" the true and predicted classes are when looking at the severity of each of the stages. Ordinal regression, by contrast, is a classification paradigm in which the classes have a predefined order relationship: $C_1 \prec C_2 \prec \cdots \prec C_Q$ [11]. In the context of Alzheimer's disease, a natural ordering runs from Alzheimer's Disease (AD) (most severe), through Mild Cognitive Impairment converter (MCIc) and stable Mild Cognitive Impairment (MCI), to Cognitively Normal (NOR). Misclassifying an AD patient as NOR is substantially more harmful clinically than confusing AD with MCIc. Ordinal methods penalise distant errors more heavily, which aligns with the clinical reality of the task. In our study we compare nominal classifiers (linear SVM, Logistic Regression (LR)) with an ordinal counterpart Support Vector Ordinal Regression with Explicit Constraints (SVOREX) when applied directly to grey matter (GM) voxel maps extracted from the Alzheimer's Disease Neuroimaging Initiative (ADNI) [15] database. Unlike deep learning approaches that rely on GPU-intensive training pipelines, our study investigates whether classic linear models, benefiting from standard preprocessing and a well-established cross-validation protocol, already reveal the advantage of ordinal modelling for Alzheimer staging.

The primary objective of this study is to test the central hypothesis that ordinal classification improves the staging of Alzheimer's disease compared to standard nominal classifiers. Consequently, our main research question is whether the explicit modelling of the natural disease progression order yields lower ordinal errors, and if this advantage holds when evaluated under a robust nested cross-validation scheme using high-dimensional voxel features.

2 Dataset

Data used in the preparation of this study were obtained from the ADNI database [15]. The ADNI was launched in 2003 as a public-private partnership, with the primary goal of testing whether serial Magnetic Resonance Imagings (MRIs), Positron Emission Tomographys (PETs), other biological markers, and clinical and neuropsychological assessments can be combined to measure the progression of MCI and early AD. The dataset used in this study corresponds to the one employed in [10], and consists of 818 T1-weighted structural MRIs, considering only the first medical examination per participant. It consists of four clinical groups: 229 NOR subjects (label 3), 185 subjects with stable MCI (label 2), 216 subjects whose MCI progressed to AD (MCIc) (label 1), and 188 subjects with confirmed AD (label 0). This labelling reflects a natural ordinal ordering from most to least severe: AD $\prec$ MCIc $\prec$ MCI $\prec$ NOR. Table 1 summarises the demographic and clinical characteristics of the subjects included in the study, confirming the class distribution according to the final image selection.

Table 1. Demographic and clinical characteristics of the dataset (Mean ± Standard Deviation).

Characteristic	AD	MCIc	MCI	NOR
N	188	216	185	229
Age	75.3 ± 7.5	74.5 ± 7.0	75.0 ± 7.7	75.9 ± 5.0
Sex (M/F)	99/89	136/80	122/63	119/110
MMSE	23.2 ± 2.2	26.8 ± 1.7	27.2 ± 2.5	29.1 ± 1.0

Images are segmented GM volumetric maps, preprocessed using CAT12 [7] and SPM12 [6], resulting in whole-brain voxel feature vectors that serve as direct input to the classifiers.

3 Methodology

For this work, we compare nominal classification with ordinal classification methods. The term ordinal classification refers to supervised learning problems characterized by an inherent order relationship between classes [11].

3.1 Classification Models

We evaluate six models: a trivial baseline, nominal classifiers, and ordinal ones.

- **Dummy Classifier.** We include a dummy classifier (stratified random predictions) as a trivial baseline. This provides a lower bound of performance to calibrate whether the results obtained are informative or simply reflect the dataset's class imbalance.
- **LR.** We used a logistic regression with ℓ_2 regularisation and balanced class weights as the nominal baseline. We obtain the optimum regularisation strength C using grid search.
- **LogAT/LogIT.** We also include Logistic Regression with All-Thresholds (LogAT) and Immediate-Thresholds (LogIT) formulations as additional linear implementations [13].

- **SVM.** We used SVM with balanced class weights as a second baseline for nominal classification, using a grid search to optimize the regularisation strength C, as we did before.
- **SVOREX.** Is an ordinal extension of the SVM introduced by Chu and Keerthi [4]. It generalises the binary SVM to K ordered classes by learning a single weight vector $\mathbf{w}$ and a set of $K-1$ explicit ordered thresholds $b_1 \leq b_2 \leq \cdots \leq b_{K-1}$. A sample $\mathbf{x}$ is predicted as class k if $b_{k-1} \leq \mathbf{w}^\top \mathbf{x} < b_k$ (with $b_0 = -\infty$ and $b_K = +\infty$). The primal optimisation problem is:

$$\min_{\mathbf{w}, \mathbf{b}, \boldsymbol{\xi}, \boldsymbol{\xi}^*} \frac{1}{2}\|\mathbf{w}\|^2 + C \sum_{i=1}^{N} \sum_{k=1}^{K-1} (\xi_{ik} + \xi_{ik}^*) \tag{1}$$

subject to, for all i and k:

$$\mathbf{w}^\top \mathbf{x}_i - b_k \leq -1 + \xi_{ik}, \quad \xi_{ik} \geq 0, \quad \text{if } y_i \leq k, \tag{2}$$

$$\mathbf{w}^\top \mathbf{x}_i - b_k \geq 1 - \xi_{ik}^*, \quad \xi_{ik}^* \geq 0, \quad \text{if } y_i > k, \tag{3}$$

where ξ_{ik} and ξ_{ik}^* are slack variables that penalise violations of the upper and lower margin constraints, respectively, for each threshold b_k, and $C > 0$ is the regularisation parameter that balances margin maximisation against training error. The explicit threshold structure directly encodes the ordinal order of the classes into the margin constraints, penalising predictions that violate the natural ordering of the disease stages. In the binary case (K=2), SVOREX reduces exactly to the standard SVM. A linear kernel is used throughout, and the optimum value of C is determined via grid search as described above.

3.2 Preprocessing Pipeline

Before classification, each input matrix $X \in \mathbb{R}^{N \times D}$ (where N is the number of subjects and D is the number of voxels) passes through two steps: 1) **Variance filtering**: removing voxels with zero variance across subjects using a `VarianceThreshold(0)` filter; and 2) **Standardisation**: scaling each remaining feature to zero mean and unit variance via `StandardScaler`. All preprocessing steps are encapsulated within a scikit-learn `Pipeline`, ensuring that both variance filtering and standardisation are fitted exclusively on the training fold during cross-validation and never applied to the held-out test fold. This design prevents any form of data leakage and guarantees that the reported performance estimates reflect true generalisation on unseen data.

3.3 Experimental Settings

The selection of hyperparameters and estimation of generalisation performance are done using a nested cross-validation scheme to prevent data leakage and provide a robust estimation. The outer loop uses a 5-fold `StratifiedKFold` to estimate the final performance on unseen data. Within each training fold of the outer loop, an inner 5-fold `StratifiedKFold` is evaluated via `GridSearchCV` to optimise the hyperparameters, with Average Mean Absolute Error (AMAE) as the optimisation criterion for multiclass and Balanced Accuracy for binary cases. For the linear models, the regularisation parameter C is searched over $\{10^{-3}, 10^{-2}, \ldots, 10^{3}\}$. Final performance is reported as the mean and standard deviation across the outer test folds. All experiments use a fixed random seed for reproducibility.

3.4 Classification Scenarios

Three classification settings are considered:

- **Binary (2-class).** All six pairwise combinations of the four classes: AD vs. MCIc, AD vs. MCI, AD vs. NOR, MCIc vs. MCI, MCIc vs. NOR, and MCI vs. NOR.
- **Three-class.** A single grouping that merges MCIc and MCI into a Combined MCI (MCIcomb) group, resulting in: AD $\prec$ MCIcomb $\prec$ NOR.
- **Four-class.** The full staging problem: AD $\prec$ MCIc $\prec$ MCI $\prec$ NOR.

3.5 Evaluation Metrics

Correct Classification Rate (CCR). Standard accuracy, defined as the proportion of correctly classified samples.
Balanced Accuracy (BACC). Balanced Accuracy, calculated as the macro-average of per-class recall to account for class imbalance.
Mean Absolute Error (MAE). Average absolute distance between predicted and true ordinal labels:

$$\mathrm{MAE}(y, \hat{y}) = \frac{1}{N} \sum_{i=1}^{N} |y_i - \hat{y}_i|. \tag{4}$$

AMAE. Class-averaged MAE, introduced to handle class imbalance in ordinal problems [2]:

$$\mathrm{AMAE} = \frac{1}{Q} \sum_{q=1}^{Q} \mathrm{MAE}_q, \quad \mathrm{MAE}_q = \frac{\sum_{i=1}^{N} \mathbf{1}[y_i = q]\, |\hat{y}_i - y_i|}{\sum_{i=1}^{N} \mathbf{1}[y_i = q]}, \tag{5}$$

where Q is the number of classes.

4 Results

Tables 2 and 3 report the performance metrics (Mean $\pm$ Standard Deviation) across the outer folds for each combination and classifier. Lower MAE and AMAE and higher CCR and BACC indicate better performance. Best values per combination are shown in **bold**.

Table 2. Results for binary classification experiments (Mean ± Std).

Combination	Classifier	CCR ↑	BACC ↑
AD vs. MCI	Dummy	0.3754 ± 0.0025	0.3756 ± 0.0023
	LR	0.7320 ± 0.0240	0.7319 ± 0.0241
	SVM	**0.7345 ± 0.0354**	**0.7344 ± 0.0354**
AD vs. MCIc	Dummy	**0.6237 ± 0.0074**	**0.6223 ± 0.0074**
	LR	0.5791 ± 0.0221	0.5719 ± 0.0246
	SVM	0.5717 ± 0.0263	0.5727 ± 0.0283
AD vs. NOR	Dummy	0.6115 ± 0.0036	0.6068 ± 0.0036
	LR	**0.8442 ± 0.0164**	**0.8428 ± 0.0166**
	SVM	0.8299 ± 0.0432	0.8317 ± 0.0426
MCI vs. NOR	Dummy	0.6014 ± 0.0019	0.5956 ± 0.0015
	LR	**0.6112 ± 0.0389**	**0.6070 ± 0.0447**
	SVM	0.5725 ± 0.0154	0.5721 ± 0.0113
MCIc vs. MCI	Dummy	0.3641 ± 0.0031	0.3612 ± 0.0027
	LR	**0.5988 ± 0.0709**	**0.5977 ± 0.0733**
	SVM	0.5963 ± 0.0583	0.5969 ± 0.0593
MCIc vs. NOR	Dummy	0.6494 ± 0.0045	0.6494 ± 0.0045
	LR	**0.7528 ± 0.0396**	**0.7513 ± 0.0386**
	SVM	0.7101 ± 0.0149	0.7091 ± 0.0154

4.1 Confusion Matrices

Figures 1 and 2 show the confusion matrices obtained for the three-class and four-class experiments, respectively. Rows represent true labels and columns predicted labels; ordinal class codes are as defined in Table 1.

4.2 Discussion

Several observations can be drawn from the results.

Binary Experiments. The easiest binary problem is AD vs. NOR, where LR achieves a CCR of 0.844, consistent with the large morphological differences between these extreme stages. The hardest binary problems are those involving adjacent MCI stages: MCIc vs. MCI (best CCR $\approx$ 0.60) and MCI vs. NOR (best CCR $\approx$ 0.61), reflecting their subtle structural differences. LR and SVM show competitive performance across combinations, with SVM achieving the best CCR and BACC in AD vs. MCI. LR obtains the best results in AD vs. NOR, MCI vs. NOR, MCIc vs. MCI, and MCIc vs. NOR.

Three-Class Experiment. Merging MCIc and MCI into a single MCIcomb group simplifies the discrimination task at the cost of losing clinical granularity. SVOREX achieves the best CCR (0.5245) and MAE (0.4914), while LR obtains

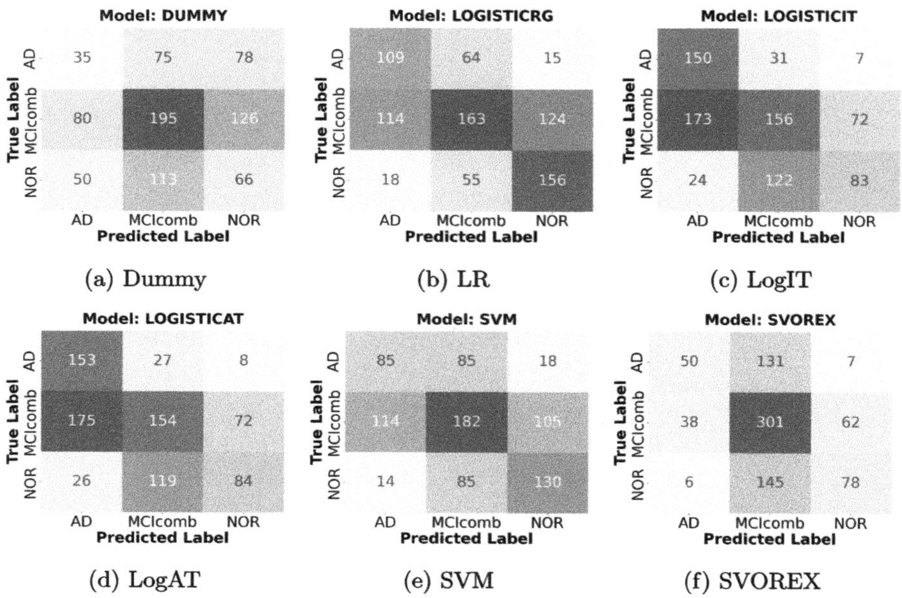

(a) Dummy (b) LR (c) LogIT

(d) LogAT (e) SVM (f) SVOREX

Fig. 1. Confusion matrices for the three-class AD vs. MCIcomb vs. NOR experiment.

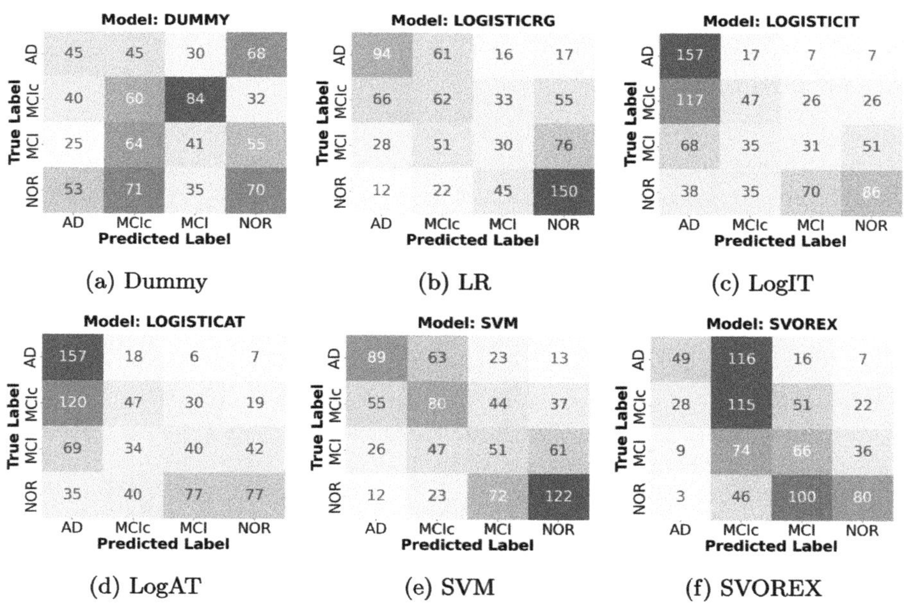

(a) Dummy (b) LR (c) LogIT

(d) LogAT (e) SVM (f) SVOREX

Fig. 2. Confusion matrices for the four-class AD vs. MCIc vs. MCI vs. NOR experiment.

Table 3. Results for three-class (AD vs. MCIcomb vs. NOR) and four-class (AD vs. MCIc vs. MCI vs. NOR) experiments (Mean ± Std).

Scenario	Classifier	CCR ↑	BACC ↑	MAE ↓	AMAE ↓
3-class(AD/MCIcomb/NOR)	Dummy	0.3619 ± 0.0032	0.3202 ± 0.0035	0.7946 ± 0.0055	0.8908 ± 0.0055
	LogAT	0.4780 ± 0.0300	0.5216 ± 0.0268	0.5635 ± 0.0347	0.5304 ± 0.0342
	LogIT	0.4755 ± 0.0245	0.5164 ± 0.0253	0.5624 ± 0.0254	0.5309 ± 0.0278
	LR	0.5232 ± 0.0176	**0.5555 ± 0.0209**	0.5171 ± 0.0165	**0.4971 ± 0.0179**
	SVM	0.4853 ± 0.0357	0.4913 ± 0.0411	0.5538 ± 0.0446	0.5608 ± 0.0590
	SVOREX	**0.5245 ± 0.0209**	0.4523 ± 0.0196	**0.4914 ± 0.0272**	0.5687 ± 0.0264
4-class(AD/MCIc/MCI/NOR)	Dummy	0.2641 ± 0.0030	0.2611 ± 0.0032	1.2249 ± 0.0083	1.2236 ± 0.0066
	LogAT	0.3924 ± 0.0234	0.4013 ± 0.0176	0.8740 ± 0.0241	0.8603 ± 0.0298
	LogIT	0.3925 ± 0.0141	0.3995 ± 0.0150	0.8837 ± 0.0577	0.8712 ± 0.0589
	LR	0.4107 ± 0.0304	0.4005 ± 0.0291	0.8080 ± 0.0321	0.8176 ± 0.0275
	SVM	**0.4181 ± 0.0173**	**0.4127 ± 0.0183**	0.7763 ± 0.0298	0.7815 ± 0.0269
	SVOREX	0.3790 ± 0.0419	0.3744 ± 0.0322	**0.7592 ± 0.0250**	**0.7598 ± 0.0244**

the best BACC (0.5555) and AMAE (0.4971) due to class-level imbalance. SVM performs worst in this setting.

Four-Class Experiment. This is the most challenging and clinically informative scenario. SVOREX consistently obtains the best ordinal performance (MAE 0.759 ± 0.025, AMAE 0.760 ± 0.024), demonstrating the benefit of explicitly modelling the ordinal structure when all four disease stages must be jointly discriminated, although nominal classifiers achieve higher nominal correctness (CCR and BACC). The gap between SVOREX and the nominal methods in terms of ordinal errors confirms that ordinal information becomes increasingly valuable as the number of classes grows.

Error Patterns and Class-Jump Minimization. A critical advantage of ordinal methods is their ability to prevent severe misclassifications, such as confusing the extreme stages of the disease (e.g., predicting NOR for a patient with AD). Analyzing the confusion matrices for the 4-class problem (Fig. 2), we observe the distribution of off-diagonal errors. Nominal baselines like the Dummy classifier, and to a significant extent the nominal SVM and LR, display more scattered predictions, leading to higher counts of "class-jump" errors ($|y_i - \hat{y}_i| > 1$). In contrast, SVOREX tightly clusters its predictions along the main diagonal. Even when SVOREX misclassifies a sample, it tends to assign it to an adjacent clinical stage (e.g., AD confused with MCIc), which is clinically less harmful. This behavior directly translates to the significantly lower AMAE and MAE scores achieved by the ordinal models (Table 3), validating the theoretical benefits of explicit thresholding in SVOREX and properly addressing the clinical priority of avoiding extreme diagnostic errors.

5 Conclusion

This work presents a comparative study of nominal and ordinal linear classifiers for Alzheimer's disease staging from gray matter voxel maps extracted from sMRI. Across three-class and four-class scenarios, SVOREX, the ordinal counterpart of the SVM, consistently achieves lower ordinal error (AMAE) than logistic regression and SVM in the majority of settings, with the advantage becoming most pronounced in the four-class full-staging problem. These results suggest that incorporating the natural ordinal structure of Alzheimer's disease progression into the learning objective is beneficial, even when using simple linear models operating on high-dimensional voxel features. The AD vs. NOR binary problem yields the highest accuracy across all experiments (CCR $\approx$ 0.85), confirming that the structural atrophy associated with end-stage AD is the most discriminative signal available in sMRI. Conversely, distinguishing adjacent MCI subtypes remains challenging, with CCR below 0.62 for all classifiers, indicating that finer-grained staging may require richer imaging features or multi-modal data. Future work will explore the combination of these classical ordinal approaches with deep feature representations, the use of additional biomarkers, and the application of ordinal loss functions within end-to-end neural architectures. Several limitations of this study should be acknowledged. First, the ADNI cohort is a convenience sample recruited at specialised academic centres, which may not be fully representative of the broader population; selection biases related to participant recruitment, imaging protocols across sites, and diagnostic criteria could affect the generalisability of the findings. Second, performance is estimated via a single 5-fold cross-validation rather than a repeated or nested scheme, which may yield higher-variance estimates, particularly for the smaller class subsets. Finally, the study relies exclusively on GM voxel maps from T1-weighted sMRI; incorporating complementary modalities or longitudinal data could substantially expand classification performance in the most challenging staging scenarios.

Acknowledgements. Data collection and sharing for this project was funded by the Alzheimer's Disease Neuroimaging Initiative (ADNI) (National Institutes of Health Grant U01 AG024904) and DOD ADNI (Department of Defense award number W81XWH-12-2-0012). ADNI is funded by the National Institute on Aging, the National Institute of Biomedical Imaging and Bioengineering, and through generous contributions from the following: AbbVie, Alzheimer's Association; Alzheimer's Drug Discovery Foundation; Araclon Biotech; BioClinica, Inc.; Biogen; Bristol-Myers Squibb Company; CereSpir, Inc.; Cogstate; Eisai Inc.; Elan Pharmaceuticals, Inc.; Eli Lilly and Company; EuroImmun; F. Hoffmann-La Roche Ltd and its affiliated company Genentech, Inc.; Fujirebio; GE Healthcare; IXICO Ltd.; Janssen Alzheimer Immunotherapy Research & Development, LLC.; Johnson & Johnson Pharmaceutical Research & Development LLC.; Lumosity; Lundbeck; Merck & Co., Inc.; Meso Scale Diagnostics, LLC.; NeuroRx Research; Neurotrack Technologies; Novartis Pharmaceuticals Corporation; Pfizer Inc.; Piramal Imaging; Servier; Takeda Pharmaceutical Company; and Transition Therapeutics. The Canadian Institutes of Health Research is providing funds to support ADNI clinical sites in Canada. Private sector contributions are facilitated by the Foundation for the National Institutes of Health [14]. The grantee organization is the Northern California Institute for Research and Education, and the study is coordinated by the Alzheimer's Therapeutic Research Institute at the University of Southern California. ADNI data are disseminated by the Laboratory for Neuro Imaging at the University of Southern California. The present study has been supported by the "Agencia Estatal de Investigación (España)" (grant ref.: PID2023-150663NB-C22/AEI/10.13039/501100011033), and by the University of Córdoba and Junta de Andalucía (grant ref.: PP2F_L1_15).

References

1. Alzheimer Europe: Alzheimer's dementia. https://www.alzheimer-europe.org/dementia/alzheimers-dementia. Accessed 21 Feb 2026
2. Baccianella, S., Esuli, A., Sebastiani, F.: Evaluation measures for ordinal regression. In: 9th International Conference on Intelligent Systems Design and Applications, pp. 283–287 (2009). https://doi.org/10.1109/ISDA.2009.230
3. Barbero-Gómez, J., Cruz, R., Cardoso, J., Gutiérrez, P., Hervás-Martínez, C.: CNN explanation methods for ordinal regression tasks. Neurocomputing (2025). https://doi.org/10.1016/j.neucom.2024.128878
4. Chu, W., Keerthi, S.: New approaches to support vector ordinal regression. In: Proceedings of the 22nd ICML, pp. 145–152 (2005). https://doi.org/10.1145/1102351.1102370
5. Cuingnet, R., Gerardin, E., Tessieras, J., et al.: Automatic classification of patients with Alzheimer's disease from structural MRI: a comparison of ten methods using the ADNI database. Neuroimage **56**(2), 766–781 (2011). https://doi.org/10.1016/j.neuroimage.2010.06.013
6. Friston, K., et al.: Statistical Parametric Mapping: The Analysis of Functional Brain Images. Academic Press, London (2007)
7. Gaser, C., Dahnke, R.: Cat12: a computational anatomy toolbox for the analysis of structural MRI data. GigaScience **13**, giae049 (2024). https://doi.org/10.1093/gigascience/giae049
8. Gorriz, J.M., et al.: Artificial intelligence within the interplay between natural and artificial computation: advances in data science, trends and applications. Neurocomputing **410**, 237–270 (2020)
9. Gorriz, J.M., et al.: Computational approaches to explainable artificial intelligence: advances in theory, applications and trends. Inf. Fusion **100**, 101945 (2023)
10. Gorriz, J., et al.: Latent space projections and atlases: a cautionary tale in deep neuroimaging using autoencoders. arXiv preprint arXiv:2509.03675 (2025). https://arxiv.org/abs/2509.03675. Accessed 13 Dec 2025
11. Gutiérrez, P., García, S.: Current prospects on ordinal and monotonic classification. Prog. Artif. Intell. 171–179 (2016). https://doi.org/10.1007/s13748-016-0088-y
12. Jain, R., Jain, N., Aggarwal, A., Hemanth, D.: Convolutional neural network based Alzheimer's disease classification from magnetic resonance brain images. Cogn. Syst. Res. 147–159 (2019). https://doi.org/10.1016/j.cogsys.2018.12.015
13. Pedregosa, F., Bach, F., Gramfort, A.: On the consistency of ordinal regression methods. J. Mach. Learn. Res. **18**(90), 1–35 (2017)
14. U.S. Congress: Foundation for the national institutes of health (1990). https://www.fnih.org
15. Weiner, M.: ADNI (2003). https://adni.loni.usc.edu/

NeurDis: “Functional Evaluation of Neuromotor and Cognitive Disorders. Hommage to Victoria Rodellar”

Perspectives on Making Sense of Complex Data: Towards Integrative Human-Aware Evaluation

Martin Atzmueller[1,2](✉), David Massanés[1], and Xiao Wei[1]

[1] Osnabrück University, Semantic Information Systems Group, Wachsbleiche 27, 49090 Osnabrück, Germany
{david.massanes,xiao.wei}@uos.de

[2] German Research Center for Artificial Intelligence (DFKI), Hamburger Str. 24, 49084 Osnabrück, Germany
martin.atzmueller@uos.de

Abstract. Making sense of data requires interpretable and explainable methods. This paper discusses perspectives on computational sensemaking on complex data towards integrative human-aware evaluation. In particular, we highlight several directions on integrative human-aware modeling and evaluation of interpretability methods. These can enable more trustworthy applications, thus providing a first step towards human-aware explainable AI (XAI) evaluation in the domain of complex data.

Keywords: Graphs · Sequential data · Hyperspectral data · XAI

1 Introduction

In order to make sense of complex data, computational sensemaking methods [2] can be applied to enhance understanding of the data, ultimately leading to interpretability and explainability of data and/or models, respectively. In particular, computational sensemaking then also tightly connects to the concepts of explainable artificial intelligence (XAI). According to [10], for example, XAI should produce details and/or reasons in order to "make its functioning clear or easy to understand" [10]. This is crucial for complex data, as its inherent complexity can lead machine learning (ML) models to incorporate specific biases or arrive at incorrect conclusions, making them considerably more opaque due to both model and data complexity. Likewise, according to [12], interpretability refers to a more model-immanent characteristic, defining systems as being interpretable "if their operations can be understood by a human, either through introspection or through a produced explanation" [12].

This paper focuses on computational sensemaking on complex data, providing first perspectives by exemplifying potential extensions and the integration of

M. Atzmueller, D. Massanés, X. Wei—The authors are in alphabetical order (equal contribution).

J. M. Ferrández Vicente et al. (Eds.): IWINAC 2026, LNCS 16574, pp. 141–151, 2026.
https://doi.org/10.1007/978-3-032-27314-7_14

explainable artificial intelligence (XAI) [4,19] methods into existing frameworks for complex data, also covering different modalities. We focus on complex network data modeled as graphs, in addition to sequential and time series data, as well as hyperspectral (image) data. In particular, we sketch first modeling approaches and discuss perspectives towards integrative human-aware evaluation.

2 Related Work

Below, we discuss related work on different types of complex data, focusing on complex networks/graphs, sequential data, and hyperspectral data.

2.1 Complex Networks and Graphs

Complex relational data occurs, e. g., directly in different forms of feature-rich networks [21] such as sensor networks, social networks, and knowledge graphs. For such networks and graphs, attributes of nodes and/or edges, as well as the dynamics of a graph capture different aspects of features and complexity. Furthermore, such complex (graph) structures can often be induced from other forms of complex data, such as log, image, or time series data. Then, abstractions of this data can be implemented via network/graph modeling, and/or higher-order approaches can be applied for capturing more complex structures, e. g., [11,38].

In general, explainability techniques have only recently been applied to complex networks and graphs, where higher-order approaches are still underexplored [4]. Explanation-aware approaches include, for example, knowledge-based methods [20], interpretable complex network mining [7], summarization techniques [13] as well as pattern mining methods [9] often building on methods for interpretable pattern mining on graphs [5].

2.2 Hyperspectral Data

Hyperspectral data provides high-dimensional spectral representations of natural systems by capturing reflected or emitted radiation. Hyperspectral imaging creates a 3D “data cube”, which contains both spatial and spectral information. The captured hundreds of narrow, contiguous spectral bands provide a rich spectral signature for each pixel. However, hyperspectral data pose substantial analytical challenges due to their high dimensionality, strong spectral correlation, and frequent noise. Here, computational sensemaking [2], in particular, methods for data interpretation and explanation can be applied [4].

Traditional machine learning methods like Gaussian models, regression, or decision-tree-based methods can be applied in this context [18], and are typically interpretable to some extent. However, for these methods there are several inherent limitations, typically including a strong reliance on handcrafted feature engineering, limited capability in modeling joint spectral–spatial information, and often insufficient capacity to capture complex nonlinear relationships. Deep learning (DL) has emerged as a powerful alternative due to its ability to automatically learn hierarchical feature representations directly from raw data, for which different deep architectures have been applied [24]. Since DL models are typically closed box (also known as black box) models, XAI techniques have been increasingly applied to provide post-hoc insights into DL decision-making processes. For example, Gradient-weighted Class Activation Mapping (Grad-CAM), SHapley Additive exPlanations (SHAP), saliency maps, and Local Interpretable Model-agnostic Explanations (LIME) have been applied to explain CNN models [1,16,28,29,35,37].

2.3 Sequential Data

Sequential data, particularly time series, exhibit several characteristics that complicate interpretation, such as irregularities, redundant yet interrelated components, and complex temporal relations. Recent work has thus focused on constructing more human-understandable representations of time series. Here, for example, methods include coupling higher-level features and symbolization techniques [31,32] for extracting meaningful features from continuous-valued series. Similarly, there have been some methods [25] leveraging the feature extraction framework tsfresh for extracting informative temporal features from spatiotemporal soil moisture recordings for crop type classification. Although those presented studies work with continuous-valued series, the same principle can be extended to other sequential modalities such as text or event logs, e. g., [7,13].

Specifically in the context of sequential data, hidden Markov models (HMMs) have recently gained more traction across a variety of research domains and applications, e. g., for sentiment analysis [30]. HMMs consist of a discrete Markov chain (hidden states) and emission distributions linked to the chains' states, thereby disentangling latent state dynamics from observation processes in a probabilistic way. Because each hidden state can be visualized and labeled, HMMs provide a natural interpretability channel via probabilistic mappings from raw measurements to human-interpretable state dynamics. Recent work therefore focused on extending the HMM architecture by (1) incorporating neural emission models such as CNNs for processing sequential image-like observations [23] and by (2) encoding history aware transitions using RNN architectures, effectively relaxing the memoryless transition restriction present in first-order HMMs while yielding interpretable latent states whose dynamics are jointly optimized with emissions [15].

2.4 XAI Evaluation

For the evaluation of XAI methods, a large number of evaluation metrics can be applied, as discussed in [17], e. g., for assessing both faithfulness to the model and robustness across data instances. For example, accuracy measures the extent to which an explanation generalizes to unseen data, while fidelity evaluates how closely the explanation approximates the original model's predictions. These exemplary criteria illustrate a technical framework for evaluating the interpretability of models, given some quantifiable metrics. However, due to differences in human cognition, background knowledge, and expectations, it is equally important to investigate how users understand these explanations. In this context, Human-Centered Artificial Intelligence (HCAI), which emphasizes user-centered evaluation of commonly applied XAI methods, has gained increasing attention [14]. In their study, the authors conducted a study which involves interviews with participants from diverse backgrounds. The results revealed significant limitations in existing XAI approaches and highlighted the need for new design principles and evaluation methodologies that better address the specific information needs and perspectives of different AI stakeholders. Consequently, integrated design and evaluation of computational sensemaking methods is required.

3 Perspectives for Sensemaking on Complex Data

Below, we highlight perspectives on the integration and extension of existing ML and XAI methods for enhancing human-aware interpretability on complex data.

3.1 Complex Networks and Graphs

Understanding and explaining complex data is critical in various domains, e. g., in the scope of complex systems. Prominent examples include cybersecurity and intrusion detection, financial fraud detection, social media, smart mobility, industrial, and Internet-of-Things (IoT) systems, etc. Beyond established work on static graphs, many real-world scenarios involve temporally evolving, feature-rich interactions [21] that reflect ongoing processes in complex systems and human behavior. Making sense of such data calls for integrative perspectives, e. g., on modeling, analysis, and human-aware explanation.

One important direction involves the development of modeling frameworks in the context of dynamic (attributed) interaction networks, e. g., [21]. When networks are viewed, for example, from a data-stream perspective, the respective models need to accommodate temporal evolution and structural variability. Conceptual representations then need to detect, e. g., deviating or drifting subnetworks and support sequence-based assessment over edges and interactions. Such representations enable, e. g., the identification of atypical developments as systems evolve, then grounding anomaly detection into structurally and temporally coherent models.

A second interesting direction centers on adequate explainability abstractions and interpretable representations. Such concepts can then provide aggregated, human-understandable insights about both data characteristics and model behavior. Emphasizing a process-oriented perspective on sequential network data, for example, can facilitate the interpretation of evolving interactions, link dynamics, centralities, and other structural indicators [6,22]. When combined with explicit (procedural) or generative models, this can then support transparent explanations, e. g., of how and why network dynamics deviate from specific expectations as captured by a model-based representation [3].

Complementing these perspectives, the development of explainable methods enabling the modeling and analysis of complex data is crucial. When considering anomaly detection, for example, identifying unexpected, irregular, or otherwise interesting structural phenomena in dynamic networks, such methods should emphasize the temporal and sequential nature of the data, exploiting appropriate model assumptions to detect evolving anomalies. Incorporating abstraction concepts can then allow for multi-level explanations, from the local node/edge-level to more system-level events, e. g., concerning structural changes [6, 9]. Visualization, prototyping, and interactive introspection can further support human-aware evaluation in general, enabling analysts to explore and understand complex patterns through intuitive and interpretable representations, e. g., [8, 27].

3.2 Hyperspectral Data

Regarding hyperspectral data, most existing studies apply only one post-hoc XAI method to interpret DL models. However, the resulting explanations are rarely validated using additional approaches. Therefore, for tackling consistency and reliability, one important perspective is to employ multiple complementary XAI methods to interpret the same DL model and to systematically compare their results. Such cross-method validation can help assess the consistency and robustness of the explanations, thereby improving their credibility and facilitating human understanding.

In addition, in the majority of studies applying XAI to HSI analysis, spectral band contributions and spatial contributions are interpreted separately. However, given that spectral and spatial information are inherently intertwined within the HSI data cube, such isolated analyses can lead to an incomplete understanding, which can be inconsistent with established real-world understanding. 3D-CNNs, for example, are capable of simultaneously extracting spatial-spectral information via three-dimensional filters, thereby preserving the intrinsic data structure and capturing material properties of varying complexity. However, the explanation of 3D-CNNs combined with the comprehension of the interplay between spatial and spectral features in HSI is still underdeveloped, while investigating these interactions is essential for achieving a more comprehensive interpretation to enhance user understanding. For example, a step-wise CNN design can extract features in sequential stages: first along the spectral dimension, then the spatial dimension, and finally fusing them, as a more interpretable option than standard CNNs. Accordingly, an important direction for future research lies in the development of XAI frameworks that can jointly consider the relationship between spatial and spectral contributions.

Furthermore, current research predominantly focuses on static HSI data, where hyperspectral images are typically acquired at a single time point, and temporal variations are not considered. However, in real-world applications, continuous observations of HSI over time are essential for monitoring dynamic processes. Relying only on static HSI analysis can therefore limit the practical relevance of the findings. Models that can jointly analyze spectral, spatial, and temporal information (such as appropriate 4D models) can then offer greater practical value. Although a few recent studies have applied DL architectures to analyze the dynamic states of HSI, interactions between spatial, spectral, and temporal dimensions remain currently underexplored. Thus, as a further interesting future perspective, the development and analysis of frameworks targeting 4D models and XAI approaches can enable deeper insights and understanding into these multidimensional and dynamic relationships of hyperspectral data.

3.3 Sequential Data

HMM-based approaches often rely on pure probabilistic modeling, typically using Gaussian mixture models (GMMs) as emission density functions. However, Gaussian components cannot capture the rich structure of modern sequential observations such as hyperspectral images obtained from satellites, limiting the ability of domain experts to reason about the underlying phenomena. Approaches integrating CNN-based emissions [23] have already been proposed. Therefore, a natural extension is to replace the density functions with multimodal neural emitters, granting the HMM access to high-dimensional multimodal data and enabling user-driven XAI explanations that make the hidden-state inference transparent.

In the context of sequential hyperspectral image data, a CNN can be used as an emission function, allowing hidden states to be directly controlled by spatial-spectral patterns that can be inspected by domain experts during model validation. Since CNNs are already equipped with well-established XAI tools, state-dependent heatmaps, obtained from methods such as Grad-CAM, can be generated for each hidden state, visualizing which pixels or spectral bands were crucial for a particular state transition, and can be presented in an interactive dashboard for expert feedback.

Similarly, since in many monitoring scenarios the observations live on graph-based structures such as (complex) sensor networks, Graph Neural Networks (GNNs) can be used as emissions to aggregate information from the topology before mapping them to the hidden states. Regarding interpretability, a natural direction is therefore the application of, e. g., GNNExplainer [39] in order to highlight which subgraph structures and subsets of node features are most relevant with respect to particular state transitions.

Embedding RNN or transformer-based encoders into the state transition network enables history-aware state encoding that can handle long-range dependencies typically found in real-world scenarios. Differentiable transition modules are interpretable, e. g., by using integrated gradients, and transformer-based architectures can be directly interpreted through their attention matrices. This complementary extension to neural emitters therefore provides a principled way to visualize and investigate temporal dependencies in depth and should therefore be researched further in the future.

In addition, hand-crafted or automatically extracted (higher-level) features can also serve as emission vectors. The integration of such observations would bridge the interpretability of feature-extraction approaches to latent state dynamics, since feeding feature vectors directly into the emission model would yield state-specific probabilities that are better understandable by humans.

4 Towards Integrative Human-Aware Evaluation

When dealing with complex data, e. g., large-scale networks, hyperspectral images, or sequential data, we need to investigate which mechanisms and properties to apply for analysis, interpretation, and explanation, in order to facilitate computational sensemaking. Then, these mechanisms should operate on, for example, multiple levels – ranging from basic entities up to more summarizing structures in a flexible way [33] and should be adaptive to the user, also connecting to human-centered artificial design principles [34].

4.1 General Considerations

For human-aware explanation, we can consider, for example, adaptive explanations, i. e., how to generate an explanation so that it enhances trust for a specific conclusion as a result of a model relative to a specific user. This, for example, requires an adequate user model capturing domain/background knowledge, preferences etc., depending on the task and explanation context. Furthermore, an important aspect relates to the explanation of heterogeneous data, since this is often observed in the context of complex data. How can we, for example, provide comprehensible explanations for the many (potentially integrated) types of complex data? Exemplary directions include, e. g., interactive visualization techniques embedded in machine learning workflows or case-based/prototype-based methods, also enabling rich user interaction. Finally, all of these methods and approaches could be embedded in direct evaluation processes, as an integrated human-aware evaluation approach, e. g., in a closed-loop setting, where user and system feedback can be directly integrated, to provide direct refinement and guidance of the analysis.

4.2 Human-Aware Modeling of Complex Data

In the following, we provide an example towards integrative human-aware evaluation, to make the perspectives discussed in this paper more concrete: We sketch a multimodal (first-order) HMM pipeline for the agricultural domain, showcasing how modeling principal BBCH [26] growth stages could look like. The proposed pipeline is illustrated in Fig. 1. We treat the ten principal BBCH stages as discrete hidden states $S = \{S_0, S_1, \ldots, S_9\}$ where the index corresponds to the respective BBCH code (0 = germination, 1 = leaf development, ..., 9 = senescence). At each time step $t = 1, 2, \ldots, T$, the model receives multimodal observations where O_t^{img} and O_t^{graph} depict hyperspectral image and graph-structured data, respectively. For example, the images could be crop-specific HSI data cubes while the graphs could represent a soil sensor network, similar to the approach from [36]. The hidden state sequence Q represents a potential BBCH stage trajectory, where q_t is the current state at time t. CNNs and GNNs could be integrated as the emission density functions $f^{(j)}(O^{\text{img}})$ and $f^{(j)}(O^{\text{graph}})$. Such a modeling approach could potentially be used for early stress detection in crops, thereby easing targeted interventions. Apart from delivering an analysis of the factors impacting the observed phenomenon, the model could also be used as a generator, providing predictions of future information.

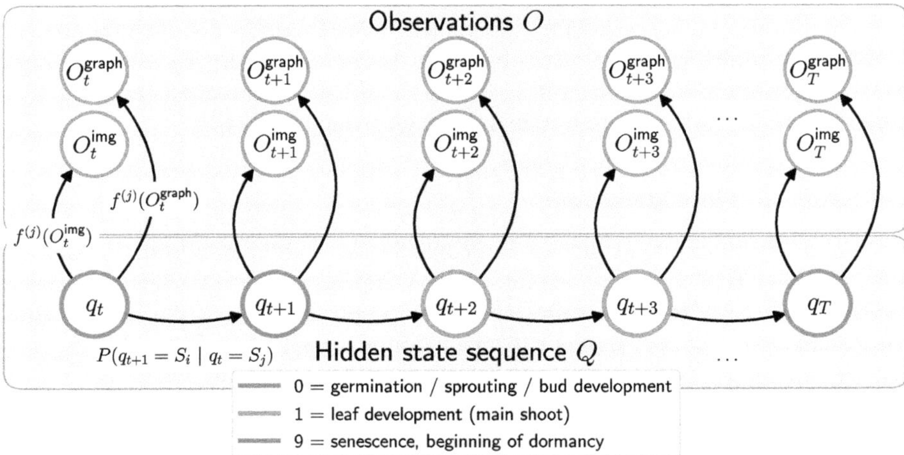

Fig. 1. Multimodal HMM example for the principal BBCH growth stages.

The given example illustrates how the hidden-state formulation naturally lends itself to both domain-expert interaction by, e. g., inserting prior knowledge, and transparent evaluation by visualizing state dynamics and quantifying observation relevance. Further, such an approach nicely combines the integrative modeling of the different complex data modalities discussed in this paper.

5 Conclusions

In this paper, we discussed different perspectives on human-aware integrative modeling and evaluation of complex data, focusing on graph/network, hyperspectral image, and sequential data modalities. We highlighted the potential of applying and/or integrating existing XAI techniques to/into complex data processing pipelines in order to enhance interpretability. Further, we sketched an interpretable HMM-based modeling approach that allows for the integrative combination of the three main data modalities discussed in this paper, showcasing a holistic human-aware modeling perspective for processing, evaluating, and interpreting complex multimodal data in a human-understandable way.

Acknowledgments. This work was partially supported by zukunft.niedersachsen, Volkswagen Foundation ("HybrInt – Hybrid Intelligence through Interpretable Artificial Intelligence in Machine Perception and Interaction"; Grant ID: ZN4219), and by the German Research Foundation (DFG), grant MODUS-II (316679917, AT 88/4-2).

References

1. Ahmed, M.T., Villordon, A., Kamruzzaman, M.: Hyperspectral imaging and explainable deep-learning for non-destructive quality prediction of sweetpotato. Postharvest Biol. Technol. **222**, 113379 (2025)
2. Atzmueller, M.: Declarative aspects in explicative data mining for computational sensemaking. In: Seipel, D., Hanus, M., Abreu, S. (eds.) WFLP/WLP/INAP -2017. LNCS (LNAI), vol. 10997, pp. 97–114. Springer, Cham (2018). https://doi.org/10.1007/978-3-030-00801-7_7
3. Atzmueller, M.: Onto model-based anomalous link pattern mining on feature-rich social interaction networks. In: Proceedings of WWW'19 (Companion). ACM (2019)
4. Atzmueller, M., Fürnkranz, J., Kliegr, T., Schmid, U.: Explainable and interpretable machine learning and data mining. Data Min. Knowl. Disc. **38**(5), 2571–2595 (2024)
5. Atzmueller, M., Günnemann, S., Zimmermann, A.: Mining communities and their descriptions on attributed graphs: a survey. Data Min. Knowl. Disc. **35**(3), 661–687 (2021)
6. Atzmueller, M., Kanawati, R.: Explainability in cyber-security using complex network analysis: a brief methodological overview. In: Proceedings of EICC. ACM (2022)
7. Atzmueller, M., Kloepper, B.: Mining attributed interaction networks on industrial event logs. In: Yin, H., Camacho, D., Novais, P., Tallón-Ballesteros, A.J. (eds.) IDEAL 2018. LNCS, vol. 11315, pp. 94–102. Springer, Cham (2018). https://doi.org/10.1007/978-3-030-03496-2_11
8. Atzmueller, M., Puppe, F.: A case-based approach for characterization and analysis of subgroup patterns. J. Appl. Intell. **28**(3), 210–221 (2008)
9. Atzmueller, M., Sylvester, S., Kanawati, R.: Exploratory and explanation-aware network intrusion profiling using subgroup discovery and complex network analysis. In: Proceedings of EICC, pp. 153–158. ACM (2023)
10. Barredo Arrieta, A., et al.: Explainable Artificial Intelligence (XAI): concepts, taxonomies, opportunities and challenges toward responsible AI. Inf. Fusion **58**, 82–115 (2020)
11. Bick, C., Gross, E., Harrington, H.A., Schaub, M.T.: What are higher-order networks? SIAM Rev. **65**(3), 686–731 (2023)
12. Biran, O., Cotton, C.: Explanation and justification in machine learning: a survey. In: Proceedings of IJCAI Workshop on XAI, pp. 8–13 (2017)
13. Bloemheuvel, S., Kloepper, B., Atzmueller, M.: Graph summarization for computational sensemaking on complex industrial event logs. In: Proceedings of MIEL 2019, International Conference BPM 2019. Vienna, Austria (2019)
14. Bobek, S., et al.: User-centric evaluation of explainability of AI with and for humans: a comprehensive empirical study. Int. J. Hum. Comput. Stud. (2025)
15. Boudaoud, A., Kabou, S.: DifferentiableHMM: neural differentiable hidden Markov model. ITEGAM-JETIA **12**(57), 124–132 (2026)
16. De Lucia, G., Lapegna, M., Romano, D.: Towards explainable AI for hyperspectral image classification in edge computing environments. Comput. Electr. Eng. **103**, 108381 (2022)
17. Dembinsky, D., Lucieri, A., Frolov, S., Najjar, H., Watanabe, K., Dengel, A.: Unifying VXAI: a systematic review and framework for the evaluation of explainable AI. arXiv preprint arXiv:2506.15408 (2025)

18. Gewali, U.B., Monteiro, S.T., Saber, E.: Machine learning based hyperspectral image analysis: a survey. arXiv preprint arXiv:1802.08701 (2018)
19. Gunning, D., Stefik, M., Choi, J., Miller, T., Stumpf, S., Yang, G.Z.: XAI - explainable artificial intelligence. Sci. Robot. **4** (2019)
20. Guven, C., Seipel, D., Atzmueller, M.: Applying ASP for knowledge-based link prediction with explanation generation in feature rich networks. IEEE Trans. Netw. Sci. Eng. **8**(2) (2021)
21. Interdonato, R., Atzmueller, M., Gaito, S., Kanawati, R., Largeron, C., Sala, A.: Feature-rich networks: going beyond complex network topologies. Appl. Netw. Sci. **4**(1), 1–13 (2019)
22. Kanawati, R., Atzmueller, M.: Modeling and mining feature-rich networks. In: Proceedings of WWW 2019 (Companion). IW3C2/ACM (2019)
23. Lei, J., Li, G., Zhang, J., Guo, Q., Tu, D.: Continuous action segmentation and recognition using hybrid convolutional neural network-hidden Markov model model. IET Comput. Vision **10**(6), 537–544 (2016)
24. Li, S., Song, W., Fang, L., Chen, Y., Ghamisi, P., Benediktsson, J.A.: Deep learning for hyperspectral image classification: an overview. IEEE Trans. Geosci. Remote Sens. **57**(9), 6690–6709 (2019)
25. Massanés, D., Atzmueller, M.: Time series feature extraction and crop type classification on spatiotemporal soil sensor network data. In: Proceedings of 46. GIL-Jahrestagung, pp. 104–115. GI e.V., Bonn (2026)
26. Meier, U.: Entwicklungsstadien Mono- Und Dikotyler Pflanzen: BBCH Monografie. Open Agrar Repositorium (2018)
27. Meinert, S., Schlinge, P., Strodthoff, N., Atzmueller, M.: ProtoMask: segmentation-guided prototype learning. In: Proceedings of IEEE ICTAI, pp. 881–888. IEEE (2025)
28. Nagasubramanian, K., Jones, S., Singh, A.K., Sarkar, S., Singh, A., Ganapathysubramanian, B.: Plant disease identification using explainable 3D deep learning on hyperspectral images. Plant Methods **15**(1), 98 (2019)
29. Oveis, A.H., Giusti, E., Meucci, G., Ghio, S., Martorella, M.: Explainability in Hyperspectral Image Classification: a study of XAI through the SHAP Algorithm. In: Proceedings of WHISPERS Workshop, pp. 1–5. IEEE (2023)
30. Perikos, I., Kardakis, S., Hatzilygeroudis, I.: Sentiment analysis using novel and interpretable architectures of Hidden Markov Models. Knowl.-Based Syst. **229**, 107332 (2021)
31. Schwenke, L., Atzmueller, M.: Making time series embeddings more interpretable in deep learning: extracting higher-level features via symbolic approximation representations. In: The International FLAIRS Conference Proceedings, vol. 36 (2023)
32. Schwenke, L., Stückemann, T., Atzmueller, M.: Evaluating higher-level and symbolic features in deep learning on time series: towards simpler explainability. In: Rojas, I., Joya, G., Catala, A. (eds.) IWANN 2025. LNCS, vol. 16008, pp. 345–357. Springer, Cham (2026). https://doi.org/10.1007/978-3-032-02725-2_27
33. Shneiderman, B.: The eyes have it: a task by data type taxonomy for information visualizations. In: Proceedings of IEEE Symposium on Visual Languages, pp. 336–343. Boulder, Colorado (1996)
34. Shneiderman, B.: Bridging the gap between ethics and practice: guidelines for reliable, safe, and trustworthy human-centered AI systems. ACM Trans. Interact. Intell. Syst. **10**(4), 1–31 (2020)
35. Thakur, S., Jain, P., Agarwal, S., Meena, J., Gupta, V.K., Singh, L.K.: Explainable deep learning models for food fraud detection and its authenticity analysis. In: Proceedings of ISCON, pp. 1–6. IEEE (2025)

36. Van Den Hoogen, J., Hudson, D., Atzmueller, M.: Graph signal processing unearths the best locations for soil moisture sensors. In: Proceedings of International Conference on Machine Learning and Applications, pp. 963–968. IEEE (2024)
37. Wei, X., Griesel, A., Atzmueller, M.: Improving transparency in machine learning for agriculture: a case study on mushroom classification using CNN and grad-cam. In: Proceedings of 46. GIL-Jahrestagung, pp. 176–187. GI e.V., Bonn (2026)
38. von Westenholz, M., Atzmueller, M., Römer, T.: Simplicial complexes in network intrusion profiling: pattern construction through simplicial centralities. Appl. Netw. Sci. **10**(1), 35 (2025)
39. Ying, Z., Bourgeois, D., You, J., Zitnik, M., Leskovec, J.: GNNExplainer: generating explanations for graph neural networks. In: Advances in Neural Information Processing Systems, vol. 32. Curran Associates, Inc. (2019)

Automatic Detection of Williams Syndrome Using Acoustic Tremor Features: A Noninvasive and Low-Cost Method

Raúl Fernández-Ruiz[1], Daniel Palacios-Alonso[1,2(✉)], Nikola Hristov-Kalamov[1], Agustín Álvarez-Marquina[2], Irene Hidalgo-delaGuía[3], Elena Garayzábal-Heinze[4], Andrés Gómez-Rodellar[5], and Rafael Martínez-Olla[2]

[1] Escuela Técnica Superior de Ingeniería Informática, Universidad Rey Juan Carlos, Tulipán S/N, 28933 Móstoles, Spain
daniel.palacios@urjc.es

[2] Center for Biomedical Technology, Universidad Politécnica de Madrid, 28220 Madrid, Spain

[3] Department of Spanish Language and Theory of Literature Universidad Complutense de Madrid, Avenida Complutense, 28040 Madrid, Spain

[4] Department of Linguistics Universidad Autónoma de Madrid, Ciudad Universitaria de Cantoblanco, 28049 Madrid, Spain

[5] Department of Engineering Computer science and mathematics, Saint Louis University, 28003 Madrid, Spain

Abstract. This study presents a non-invasive, and low-cost method to automatically detect Williams Syndrome. It addresses the diagnostic delay arising from phenotypic similarities with common neurodevelopmental disorders, such as Down Syndrome. A total of 72 acoustic features were extracted, encompassing glottal source biomechanics, tremor indicators, and voice quality parameters. Unlike conventional voice analysis methods which typically rely on features such as F0, Jitter, Shimmer, Mel Frequency Cepstral Coefficients (MFCCs), and Cepstral Peak Prominence, our approach utilizes a broader set. Using a Random Forest classifier, we achieved a detection accuracy of 93.98%, revealing that Physiological Tremor and Neurological Tremor are the most effective features for distinguishing normotypic from non-normotypic individuals. In conclusion, the proposed method effectively differentiates Williams Syndrome from a normotypic group using a minimal set of interpretable features. Future work could expand this research to include neurodevelopmental and genetic conditions, such as Down syndrome and Smith–Magenis syndrome. By incorporating a broader range of neurological disorders, the model could aid in developing more comprehensive and robust differential diagnostic tools.

Keywords: Williams Syndrome · Tremor Features · Machine Learning · Voice Analysis · Monitoring Rare Diseases

J. M. Ferrández Vicente et al. (Eds.): IWINAC 2026, LNCS 16574, pp. 152–162, 2026.
https://doi.org/10.1007/978-3-032-27314-7_15

1 Introduction

Speech analysis has proven to be one of the most effective ways to early detect neurological diseases and to monitor their progression in a cost-effective and non-invasive manner. This is due to the fact that changes in vocal performance, the rate of silent pauses, or speech fluency are often among the initial most altered speech hallmarks. Tools for speech and voice analysis can help in characterizing phonatory changes attributed to neurological disorders, as these conditions induce biomechanical irregularities that are reflected in the glottal source signal [14]. However, the data analyzed typically comes from spontaneous speech samples rather than isolated phonation tasks [5,17].

Neurological disorders that appear early in life exert a phonetic influence, as observed in cerebral palsy or genetic syndromes that compromise neurological development. These disorders include syndromes that are not widely recognized and have a low prevalence, often classified as rare diseases, which are of particular concern. In many cases, insufficient knowledge of these diseases results in delayed or incorrect diagnoses, significantly affecting the timely implementation of specific therapeutic interventions necessary to meet the current and future demands of the patients.

In the context of neurodevelopmental syndromes, phonation analysis presents a promising approach, as the unique phonatory characteristics arise primarily from neurodevelopmental delays linked to chromosomal abnormalities responsible for these syndromes. Variations among these syndromes are attributable to clinical conditions that affect laryngeal biomechanics. One example is the deficiency of collagen and elastin observed in Williams Syndrome (WS) [10,16].

1.1 Related Works

WS is a genetic disorder that affects neurodevelopment since the embryonic stage [6]. It is attributed to a microdeletion on the long arm of chromosome 7 (7q11.23). Around 25–27 genes are associated with the WS, with CLIP2, ELN, GTF2I, GTF2IRD1, and LIMK1 frequently being deleted from the critical Williams syndrome chromosomal region (WSCR). Of particular interest to our study is the elastin gene (ELN), which provides elasticity to conjunctive tissues within the vocal folds, thus playing a crucial role in phonation quality.

The prevalence of WS is estimated to be 1 in 7,500 newborns [20]. WS is diagnosed by detecting a heterozygous deletion of approximately 1.5 to 1.8 Mb within the Williams-Beuren syndrome critical region on chromosome 7q11.23. Common genetic diagnostic methods, such as fluorescent in situ hybridization (FISH) and comparative genomic hybridization (microarray CGH), provide high-resolution results. However, their effectiveness relies on the prior identification of the specific genetic anomaly. The difficulty is not rooted in the diagnostic methods themselves but rather in initially ascertaining if a child's atypical syndrome aligns with WS, which then necessitates appropriate genetic testing.

Research on linguistic abilities in individuals with WS has been productive, revealing both preserved and consistent linguistic proficiency and those that challenge these abilities [1,2,4,13,15,19]. In contrast, the study of phonation in WS individuals remains underexplored. Limited research has addressed the vocal characteristics of WS, highlighting the hoarse, deep, and sometimes coarse voice of these individuals [8]. Phonation in individuals with Williams Syndrome has not been thoroughly studied, apart from a single study [12], research on the acoustic properties of voice and the biomechanics of the larynx in this population remains sparse.

The most prevalent clinical manifestations of WS include congenital heart defects (such as supravalvular aortic stenosis), infantile hypercalcemia, and reduced muscle tone [18,21]. Existing research highlights elastin deficiency in the vocal fold connective tissue, which contributes to increased laxity, greater viscosity, and diminished elasticity [23]. In particular, Urbán et al. [22] reported deficiencies in all three forms of elastin within the lamina propria of the vocal folds in the WS patients examined.

The remainder of this paper is organized as follows. Section 2 describes the dataset, the acoustic metrics extracted, and the machine learning methodology employed. Section 3 presents the experimental results, followed by a discussion on the clinical relevance of the findings, study limitations, and future work. Finally, Sect. 4 offers the conclusions.

2 Materials and Methods

2.1 Dataset

The dataset consists of 240 individuals, divided into two groups: a non-normative group (WS) comprising 22 participants and a normative group including 218 participants. In the non-normative group, the age range is broader, spanning from 3 to 31 years. In contrast, the normative group exhibits a narrower age range, from 5 to 12 years (123 boys and 95 girls) (see Table 1).

Informed consent was obtained from all legal guardians of the participants involved in this study. This study benefited from the invaluable support of the Spanish Williams syndrome Association, which facilitated access to eligible participants and their corresponding audio recordings, thus allowing a complete data collection. All WS individuals had been diagnosed with a microdeletion in the 7q11.23 region of chromosome 7, confirmed by the FISH test. For the normative group, all samples were recorded at public schools in the community of Madrid, Spain. The inclusion criteria required that participants were free of psychological alterations or other conditions that could affect phonation, such as dysphonia.

The audio was captured at a sampling rate of 44,100 Hz inside a soundproof room, with the presence limited to the recording assistant and the participant. Each participant was asked to articulate an utterance of vowel [a:] kept as stable as possible in tone and loudness for as long as they could. The recordings were taken over multiple sessions, spaced at least one week apart. Ultimately, between four and six samples were collected from each participant [9].

Table 1. Distribution of participants and samples by group, age and gender

	Williams Syndrome				Normative			
	Male		Female		Male		Female	
	Individuals	Samples	Individuals	Samples	Individuals	Samples	Individuals	Samples
$3 \leq \text{age} \leq 8$	7	35	6	27	70	310	62	280
$9 \leq \text{age} \leq 13$	0	0	4	19	53	246	33	156
$13 < \text{age}$	0	0	5	24	0	0	0	0

2.2 Metrics

The 72 features are obtained using BioMet®Phon, a software developed for the characterization of phonation in the evaluation of voice quality [7]. An application which estimates the glottal source from voice and provides a wide feature set of this signal, including perturbation, cepstral, spectral, biomechanical, glottal open and contact intervals, and tremor features. The semantic capabilities of these biomechanical features are:

1. Fundamental frequency of a glottal cycle, the inverse of the glottal period. It helps, among others, to distinguish male from female voices.
2. Relative jitter. It is a perturbation parameter that, along with other features, detects instability in phonation, used in detection and grading of dysphonia.
3. Relative shimmer in average amplitude per glottal cycle. It helps detect instability in phonation and characterizes dysphonia.
4. Relative shimmer in area. It also contributes to detecting phonation instability and characterising dysphonia.
5. Maximum flow declination ratio (MFDR). It measures the sharpness of the glottal source minimum salience. It is used to detect emotional states in phonation and dysphonia assessment.
6. Ratio of mucosal wave to glottal wave energies, useful for detecting potential neurological alterations in a speaker.

7–20. Cepstral features form part of the speaker's compact biometric signature and help in speaker identification and verification, and forensic comparison applications.

21–34. Spectral profile features are also part of the glottal biomechanical signature, as well as indicators of normative or non-normative phonation, and they are useful in identification/verification, as well as in detecting dysphonia.

35–46. Biomechanical features provide a robust set of descriptors for the mechanical function of the glottis and contribute to the interpretability of alterations, and to quantify the degree of dysphonia. Noteworthy features include:

47–58. Phonation cycle interval features offer a complete description of relevant glottal cycle intervals (closure, return, opening).

59–62. Glottal closure defect features describe deficiencies in closure, adduction, abduction, and permanent gap of the vocal folds, contributing to the depiction of imperfections in the glottal cycle.
63–65. First- to third-order PARCOR coefficients (partial correlations) estimated from an equivalent AR model of the mean-removed vocal fold body tension. Each coefficient measures the residual correlation between the current cycle and a lagged cycle after accounting for intermediate lags, thereby characterizing the short-memory temporal structure of the signal and supporting tremor/instability detection.
66–72. Voice tremor features characterize potential alterations in the neuromotor system related to glottal closure, manifested as vocal tremor (controlled or uncontrolled). Three features serve as tremor markers; the remaining three provide information on frequency, perceptibility, and relative amplitude.

2.3 Random Forest Classifier

Random Forest (RF) is an ensemble learning method that operates by constructing a multitude of decision trees at training time and outputting the class that is the mode of the classes (classification) or mean prediction (regression) of the individual trees [3]. This approach addresses the high variance inherent in individual decision trees by averaging multiple deep decision trees, trained on different parts of the same training set, with the goal of reducing the variance [11].

The algorithm employs a bagging (bootstrap aggregating) technique. Given a training set $X = x_1, \ldots, x_n$ with responses $Y = y_1, \ldots, y_n$, the method repeatedly selects a random sample with replacement of the training set and fits trees to these samples:

$$B = \{(x_1^*, y_1^*), \ldots, (x_n^*, y_n^*)\} \tag{1}$$

For each node in the tree, a subset of features is randomly selected to determine the best split. The quality of a split is measured by an impurity criterion. In this study, we employ the Gini Impurity index, defined as:

$$I_G(p) = 1 - \sum_{i=1}^{J} p_i^2 \tag{2}$$

where J is the number of classes and p_i is the probability of an item being classified into class i at a specific node. The split that maximizes the reduction in impurity (Information Gain) is selected. This randomness in feature selection and data sampling ensures diversity among trees, making the model robust against overfitting. This is especially important in high-dimensional or imbalanced biomedical datasets. This robustness is further reinforced by the inherent feature selection mechanism of random forests, which evaluates feature contribution in terms of the reduction of impurities among decision trees. Consequently, features that are not informative tend to have a limited impact on the overall performance of the model.

2.4 Model Training and Performance Evaluation

A stratified three-fold cross-validation was used for the training process. To mitigate the risk of data leakage, the data were split at the level of individual speakers rather than at the level of audio files. The training folds are approximately formed from 70 WS and 658 normative audio files, while the testing fold has 35 WS and 329 normative audio samples. This process is repeated with thirty different random seeds to obtain robust results. The metric used to evaluate the performance of the model is the F1 score, as it is sensitive to imbalanced datasets. This is attributable to the fact that precision reflects the reliability of the model in classifying a sample as belonging to the positive class, whereas recall (also referred to as sensitivity) quantifies the proportion of actual positive samples that are accurately identified. Since the imbalance ratio (IR) in the training set is approximately 9.4, the dataset is highly imbalanced, which can lead to a biased model. This happens because decision trees choose splits that minimize an impurity criterion, and with strong class imbalance, the resulting splits may favor the majority class. In this case, RF can assign different weights to the samples of each class, specifically adjusting weights inversely proportional to class frequencies in the input data. The RF model consists of 125 estimators, with a minimum of five samples required to split a node. This constraint was introduced because working with a highly imbalanced dataset and a limited number of samples may lead to overly specific models that do not generalize well.

For measuring the impact of each feature in the model, Permutation Feature Importance (PFI) [3] was employed, which measures performance loss when a feature is randomly shuffled. At the end of each training the PFI was computed over the test fold. Table 2 shows the five features with the highest mean PFI across all the seeds.

Table 2. Top five features ranked by mean PFI across all the seeds.

Permutation Feature Importance		
Index	Feature	Importance
66	Physiological Tremor Frequency (Hz)	0.41
68	Neurological Tremor Frequency (Hz)	0.24
63	First-Order Cycle Coefficient	0.007
41	Cover Mass	0.003
40	Flutter Tremor Frequency (Hz)	0.002

3 Results and Discussion

Table 3 shows the results of the model obtained after following the training process in the previous section. The model achieves a high performance over the validation sets with a 93% F1 score. This performance is closely related to the information shown in Table 2, where the Physiological Tremor Frequency and Neurological Tremor Frequency variables showed a clear predominance over the rest, both associated with vocal tremors. Feature 66 represents the frequency of the first component (2 to 4 Hz) of unbiased vocal-fold body-tension instability, attributed to physiological tremor, while feature 68 is associated with the frequency of the second component (5 to 8 Hz) of unbiased vocal-fold body tension, attributed to neurological tremor. Figure 1 shows the relationship between these two variables, revealing a clear separation between both studied groups. Normotypic individuals display a broader range of dispersion in both variables, while the WS group is narrower distribution but consistently higher values in both characteristics.

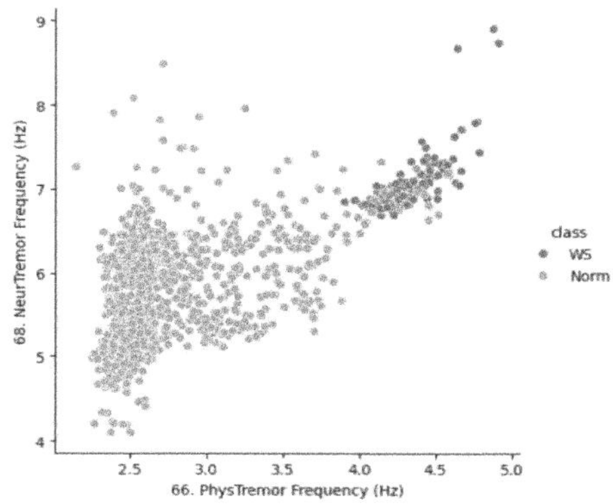

Fig. 1. Scatter plot illustrating the separation of classes using the two most discriminative features: Physiological Tremor Frequency (X-axis) and Neurological Tremor Frequency (Y-axis).

Table 3. Results obtained for the RF model, the displayed values correspond to the average performance across the three stratified folds for each seed

	Metrics	Train	Validation
RF	F1 score	$0.97 \pm 4.2 \cdot 10^{-3}$	$0.93 \pm 1.1 \cdot 10^{-2}$
	Recall	1.0 ± 0	$0.96 \pm 1.8 \cdot 10^{-2}$
	Precision	$0.95 \pm 8.1 \cdot 10^{-3}$	$0.92 \pm 9.6 \cdot 10^{-3}$

3.1 Analysis of Tremor Significance

The experimental results confirm that focusing on specific phonatory features yields high diagnostic accuracy for Williams Syndrome. Notably, the feature selection process consistently identified *Physiological Tremor* (2–4 Hz) and *Neurological Tremor* (5–8 Hz) as the most discriminative variables. This finding supports the hypothesis that the genetic deletion of *ELN* directly impacts the biomechanics of the vocal folds. The deficiency in elastin likely alters the passive tension and restorative capacity of the glottal tissue, thereby amplifying the amplitude of physiological tremor. Furthermore, the prominence of neurological tremor suggests potential alterations in the central neuromotor control of phonation, consistent with the fine motor deficits observed in WS patients. By isolating these specific frequency bands, the RF model captures the subtle phenotypic "fingerprint" of the syndrome, distinguishing it from normotypical voice patterns with high precision.

3.2 Study Limitations

The primary limitation of this study lies in the limited number of individuals available for analysis (22 WS patients), which is an expected circumstance given the rare nature of the disease (prevalence 1:7,500). Incorporating a larger cohort would permit more detailed analyses, including segmentation by age ranges, thereby enriching the interpretation of the results and facilitating the identification of developmental patterns. An important limitation is the restricted applicability of the results to populations with markedly different genetic or linguistic characteristics. Although the model is based on sustained vowel phonation to minimize sociolinguistic bias, validation in cross-cultural cohorts remains necessary. Additionally, the high class imbalance (1:10) required careful handling via stratified sampling and class weighting; while effective, this imbalance poses a persistent challenge for model generalization.

3.3 Future Work

Future research lines will focus on expanding the comparative analysis to include other supervised learning algorithms utilized in preliminary screenings, such as Support Vector Machines (SVM), K-Nearest Neighbors (KNN), and Extreme Gradient Boosting (XGBoost). The goal is to benchmark the robustness of Random Forest against these models, particularly in terms of sensitivity to class imbalance and feature selection stability.

Beyond classical ML, we aim to extend this method to multiclass classification scenarios, specifically differentiating WS from other neurodevelopmental disorders such as Down Syndrome or Smith-Magenis Syndrome, which often share overlapping phenotypes. From a methodological perspective, we plan to explore Deep Learning architectures, such as Convolutional Neural Networks (CNNs) applied to spectrograms or Recurrent Neural Networks (LSTMs) for time-series analysis, provided sufficient data becomes available. Finally, investigating the correlation between these vocal biomarkers and specific genetic deletion sizes could offer new insights into the genotype-phenotype relationship in Williams Syndrome.

4 Conclusions

WS is a rare disease, its low prevalence complicating early diagnosis, often leading to diagnostic errors. This diagnostic delays the timely application of specific therapeutic interventions that could improve the linguistic, cognitive, and adaptive development of individuals. Consequently, many people with WS encounter additional challenges in the educational, social, and emotional domains, negatively affecting both their quality of life and those of their families.

The majority of research on the automatic detection of diseases via voice analysis predominantly relies on a restricted range of acoustic features, notably including Mel frequency cepstral coefficients (MFCCs), spectrograms, and conventional metrics such as *jitter*, *shimmer*, and *pitch*. In this paper, we propose an alternative strategy based on the extraction of an expanded set of 72 phonatory metrics, encompassing less explored aspects such as tremors and alterations associated with phonation.

Given the characteristic disproportion in sample sizes between normotypical and non-normotypical cohorts commonly observed in rare diseases research, a Stratified K-Fold validation scheme at the individual level (rather than at the audio level) was chosen. This approach aims to obtain robust performance estimates and prevent any type of information leakage between training and validation sets. The most significant finding of this study is the identification of two features associated with *Physiological Tremor* and *Neurological Tremor*, which enable F1 scores exceeding 93% in the automatic identification of WS. This result highlights the importance of using specific features linked to various aspects of phonation and expands the conventional analytical framework employed in previous studies, which traditionally focused on a limited set of features.

This tendency toward reusing conventional features may be influenced by both their efficacy in diagnosing more prevalent pathologies, such as Parkinson's disease or Down syndrome, and the availability of public databases containing such metrics. However, the results obtained herein emphasize that the use of specialized phonatory features can be decisive in the case of rare diseases and that their application reduces the reliance on advanced synthetic data augmentation techniques or intensive hyperparameterization strategies.

Indeed, the present model has demonstrated the ability to achieve high levels of accuracy with minimal pre-processing and a moderate hyperparameter configuration. This finding is particularly significant in contexts where the computational resources or available data volumes are limited.

Acknowledgments. This work was supported by the State Research Agency of Spain (Agencia Estatal de Investigación – AEI) under Grant (CarHaVoz: PID2023-152984OB-I00).

References

1. Benítez-Burraco, A., Garayzábal, E., Cuetos, F.: Syntax in Spanish-speaking children with Williams syndrome. J. Commun. Disord. **60**, 51–61 (2016). https://doi.org/10.1016/j.jcomdis.2016.03.001
2. Benitez-Burraco, A., Garayzabal, E., Cuetos, F.: Morphology in Spanish-speaking children with Williams syndrome. Lang. Cogn. **9**(4), 728–740 (2017). https://doi.org/10.1017/langcog.2017.6
3. Breiman, L.: Random forests. Mach. Learn. **45**, 5–32 (2001)
4. Clahsen, H., Ring, M., Temple, C.: Lexical and morphological skills in English-speaking children with Williams syndrome. In: Williams Syndrome Across Languages, pp. 221–244. John Benjamins (2004)
5. Egas-López, J.V., et al.: Automatic screening of mild cognitive impairment and Alzheimer's disease by means of posterior-thresholding hesitation representation. Comput. Speech Lang. **75**, 101377 (2022)
6. Ewart, A.K., et al.: Hemizygosity at the elastin locus in a developmental disorder, Williams syndrome. Nat. Genet. **5**(1), 11–16 (1993)
7. Gómez Vilda, P., et al.: BioMet® Phon: a system to monitor phonation quality in the clinics. In: eTELEMED 2013: The Fifth International Conference on eHealth, Telemedicine, and Social Medicine, pp. 253–258. IARIA, IRIA, St. Maarten, Dutch Caribbean (2013)
8. Gosch, A., Städing, G., Pankau, R.: Linguistic abilities in children with Williams-Beuren syndrome. Am. J. Med. Genet. **52**(3), 291–296 (1994)
9. Hidalgo de la Guía, I., Garayzábal Heinze, E., Gómez Vilda, P.: Lo que la voz nos cuenta acerca de los síndromes genéticos: El caso del síndrome de williams. Loquens **4**(1), 0–11 (2017)
10. de la Guía, I.H.: El nivel fónico de la población con síndrome de Smith Magenis: particularidades fonatorias y fonético-fonológicas. Comparativa con síndrome de Williams, síndrome de Down y desarrollo típico. Ph.D. thesis, Universidad Autónoma de Madrid (2019)
11. Hastie, T., Tibshirani, R., Friedman, J.: The Elements of Statistical Learning. Springer, New York (2009). https://doi.org/10.1007/978-0-387-84858-7
12. Hidalgo, I., Vilda, P.G., Garayzábal, E.: Biomechanical description of phonation in children affected by Williams syndrome. J. Voice **32**(4), 515-e15 (2018)
13. John, A.E., Dobson, L.A., Thomas, L.E., Mervis, C.B.: Pragmatic abilities of children with Williams syndrome: a longitudinal examination. Front. Psychol. **3**, 199 (2012). https://doi.org/10.3389/fpsyg.2012.00199
14. Kadiri, S.R., Alku, P.: Analysis and detection of pathological voice using glottal source features. IEEE J. Sel. Top. Sig. Process. **14**(2), 367–379 (2019)
15. Mervis, C.B., Becerra, A.M.: Language and communicative development in Williams syndrome. Ment. Retard. Dev. Disabil. Res. Rev. **13**, 3–15 (2007). https://doi.org/10.1002/mrdd.20140
16. Moore, J., Thibeault, S.: Insights into the role of elastin in vocal fold health and disease. J. Voice **26**(3), 269–275 (2012). https://doi.org/10.1016/j.jvoice.2011.05.003
17. Nissar, I., Mir, W.A., Shaikh, T.A., et al.: Machine learning approaches for detection and diagnosis of Parkinson's disease-a review. In: 2021 7th International Conference on Advanced Computing and Communication Systems (ICACCS), vol. 1, pp. 898–905. IEEE (2021)

18. R Thomas Collins, I.: Cardiovascular disease in Williams syndrome. Curr. Opinion Pediatr. **30**(5), 609–615 (2018). MOP.0000000000000664
19. Stojanovik, V., Perkins, M., Howard, S.: Linguistic heterogeneity in Williams syndrome. Clin. Linguist. Phonet. **20**(7–8), 547–552 (2006). https://doi.org/10.1080/02699200500266422
20. Strømme, P., Bjømstad, P.G., Ramstad, K.: Prevalence estimation of Williams syndrome. J. Child Neurol. **17**(4), 269–271 (2002)
21. Tassabehji, M.: Williams-Beuren syndrome: a challenge for genotype-phenotype correlations. Hum. Mol. Genet. **12**(Spec No 2), R229–R237 (2003). https://doi.org/10.1093/hmg/ddg299
22. Urbán, Z., et al.: Connection between elastin haploinsufficiency and increased cell proliferation in patients with supravalvular aortic stenosis and Williams-Beuren syndrome. Am. J. Hum. Genet. **71**(1), 30–44 (2002)
23. Watts, C.R., et al.: An investigation of voice quality in individuals with inherited elastin gene abnormalities. Clin. Linguist. Phonet. **22**(3) (2008)

VR-Based Hand-Motion Assessment for Parkinson's Disease: A Prototype Adapted for Secure Privacy-Preserving Neural Classification

Nikola Hristov-Kalamov[1], Laura García-Martín[1], Raúl Fernández-Ruiz[1], Bozhidar Petrov-Valchev[1], Victoria Mora-de la Torre[1], Agustín Álvarez-Marquina[2], Rafael Martínez-Olla[2], and Daniel Palacios-Alonso[1,2](✉)

[1] Universidad Rey Juan Carlos, Madrid, Spain
{nikola.hristov,raul.fruiz,victoria.mora,daniel.palacios}@urjc.es, {l.garciamar.2021,b.petrov.2018}@alumnos.urjc.es
[2] Center for Biomedical Technology, Universidad Politécnica de Madrid, Madrid, Spain
{aalvarez,rmolalla}@fi.upm.es

Abstract. Virtual reality (VR) can elicit controlled motor behaviours and capture rich hand-motion signals for digital biomarker research in Parkinson's disease (PD). However, these recordings are clinically sensitive, motivating privacy-preserving analytics. This paper presents a prototype that combines (i) VR assessment minigames for PD-oriented motor elicitation and logging, (ii) a prototype using a fully connected neural classifier trained on standardized hand-motion features extracted from said VR software, and (iii) an adaptation for privacy-preserving inference via standard Secure Multi-Party Computation (MPC) protocols like Garbled Circuits (GCs) using fixed-point arithmetic. We demonstrate the validity of this setup for hand motion data collection, meaningful analysis inference and classification. Additionally, we provide a path forward for encrypted inference that preserves input/model confidentiality while maintaining functional classification and a practical path toward secure, reproducible VR-based motor assessment in PD.

Keywords: Virtual Reality · Parkinson's Disease · Digital Biomarkers · Privacy-Preserving Machine Learning · Garbled Circuits

1 Introduction and Related Work

Parkinson's Disease (PD) is currently the second most prevalent neurodegenerative pathology worldwide, affecting over 10 million individuals due to population aging [11]. The disease is characterized by a spectrum of motor symptoms, such as bradykinesia, resting tremor, rigidity, and postural instability, and non-motor symptoms that often manifest insidiously. Despite its prevalence, the diagnostic

J. M. Ferrández Vicente et al. (Eds.): IWINAC 2026, LNCS 16574, pp. 163–176, 2026.
https://doi.org/10.1007/978-3-032-27314-7_16

process remains challenging; definitive diagnosis relies heavily on clinical observation and subjective scales, often resulting in a significant diagnostic latency from symptom onset [10]. Consequently, there is an urgent need for objective, high-resolution metrics to support early detection and continuous monitoring.

In recent years, the integration of Virtual Reality (VR) and sensors has emerged as a transformative approach to quantify motor dysfunction objectively. Unlike traditional observation, VR enables the collection of "digital biomarkers" through immersive exergames. Recent studies have demonstrated that VR-based assessment can outperform traditional imaging techniques in detecting motor dysfunction severity [21], while offering rehabilitation benefits comparable to or better than conventional therapies [17].

The versatility of VR allows for the targeting of specific PD phenotypes. Significant research has focused on eye-tracking within VR environments to identify oculomotor impairments. Jiang et al. established diagnostic models using Support Vector Machines (SVM) to extract saccade features [6]. Similarly, Brien et al. and Reiner et al. employed video-based eye-tracking to classify disease stages and severity [4,19], while advanced deep learning models have been applied to analyze pro-saccades and smooth pursuit behaviors [7]. Beyond ocular metrics, VR has been effectively paired with motion capture to analyze gait. Ma et al. utilized high-fidelity VR replicas to study Freezing of Gait (FoG) [13], and Oishi et al. explored the use of ear-worn IMUs trained on VR motion capture data for unobtrusive monitoring [16].

Parallel to data acquisition, the application of Machine Learning (ML) and Artificial Intelligence (AI) is pivotal for processing these complex datasets. Recent literature illustrates a shift toward advanced architectures. For example, Avola et al. proposed Recurrent Neural Networks (RNN) with Long Short-Term Memory (LSTM) to estimate patient performance in immersive rehabilitation [1]. Multimodal approaches are also gaining traction; Dudek et al. analyzed voice biomarkers in Mixed Reality settings [5], while Mao et al. integrated flexible sensors with deep learning for posture recognition [15]. Other studies have expanded into cognitive and social domains, utilizing robotics and tele-rehab apps to maintain cognitive reserve and social functioning [3,14], as well as defining novel metrics like the motor-cognitive reserve index [9] and game-based digital biomarkers for well-being [18].

Nevertheless, a critical discrepancy remains between the diagnostic granularity afforded by multi-sensor fusion and the requirements for data confidentiality. Although studies such as Avola et al. [1] have successfully employed Recurrent Neural Networks to quantify rehabilitation progress, and Mao et al. [15] have demonstrated the utility of triboelectric sensors for posture recognition, these architectures necessitate the processing of plaintext kinematic identifiers. Such unencrypted handling of high-frequency motor data poses privacy risks, as the unique biomechanical signatures captured by VR systems may facilitate unauthorized subject re-identification [8]. To address this problem, the architecture proposed herein integrates a privacy-preserving inference layer based on Garbled Circuits (GCs), thereby decoupling the utility of the digital biomarker foundation from the potential exposure of the raw biometric trace. Similar works that utilize such techniques include [2,12,20].

This paper proposes a novel system that combines immersive VR minigames for symptom elicitation with a prototype for a privacy-preserving classification architecture. We present three minigames designed to trigger specific PD symptoms: *Micrography* (evaluating fine motor control), *Simon Says* (assessing bradykinesia and rigidity), and *Gravity* (testing coordination and reaction time). Unlike previous works, our approach integrates a Secure Multiparty Computation (MPC) protocol based on GCs. This framework ensures that the biometric data captured is processed by a Fully Connected Neural Network without ever being exposed in its raw form, protecting patient confidentiality while maintaining high classification accuracy. The main contributions of this work are summarized as follows:

1. The prototypical design and implementation of three VR minigames specifically tailored to capture digital biomarkers of bradykinesia, tremor, and micrographia in PD patients.
2. The development of a proof-of-concept secure inference architecture using GCs, allowing for the experimental classification of encrypted clinical data without decryption during processing.
3. A preliminary validation of the system's usability and low adverse effects in a cohort of PD patients, demonstrating the feasibility of combining the aforementioned techniques with clinical tools in a prototype environment.

The remainder of this paper is organized as follows: Sect. 2 details the materials and methods, including the design of the VR assessment suite, the participant protocol, feature representation, and the approach for privacy-preserving inference. Section 3 presents the experimental results of the proof-of-concept prototype covering some qualitative examples, plaintext classification performance and usability findings. Section 4 discusses the interpretation of these findings, threats to validity, and deployment considerations. Finally, Sect. 5 concludes the paper and outlines directions for future work.

2 Materials and Methods

2.1 VR Assessment Suite and Data Logging

The prototype integrates a Unity-based VR application that delivers three PD-oriented minigames (Micrography, Simon Says, and Gravity) to elicit controlled hand and arm behaviors under immersive guidance. The suite is designed to be accessible for participants with limited prior VR exposure by relying on simple interaction metaphors (visual cues, guided actions, and direct controller/hand interaction). The system utilizes the Meta Quest ecosystem, leveraging the XR Hands package for markerless hand tracking and standard XR controllers for precision tasks. During gameplay, the system logs raw hand-motion traces intended for downstream analysis and classification.

To clarify the experimental tasks and the intended interaction design, Fig. 1 presents conceptual mockups of the three minigames. These mockups are included as methodological aids (not as final game assets) to illustrate what participants are asked to do and how the interaction is instrumented.

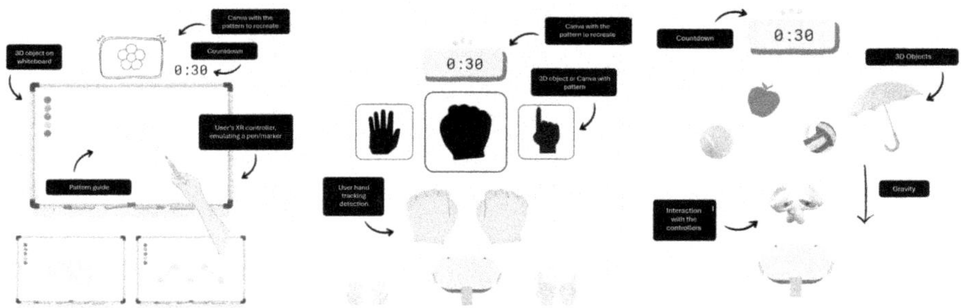

(a) Micrography (b) Simon Says (c) Gravity

Fig. 1. Conceptual mockups of the three VR minigames used for motor elicitation and data logging: (a) Micrography, (b) Simon Says, and (c) Gravity. The mockups illustrate the intended user actions and visual guidance, as well as the interaction modality: controllers in Micrography and Gravity, and headset-only interaction (no controllers) in Simon Says.

Micrography (Fig. 1a) prompts guided pattern tracing, where the participant follows a visual template using an XR controller as a pen/marker. This task is designed to elicit continuous fine motor control under visual guidance. Simon Says (Fig. 1b) presents on-screen cues that the participant reproduces as hand poses or short gestures within a time window, emphasizing coordination and pose accuracy under guided stimuli. Gravity (Fig. 1c) requires reaching and catching falling objects under time pressure, emphasizing reach-to-grasp dynamics and eye–hand coordination. Across all tasks, the goal is not to optimize game score but to elicit structured and repeatable motor behavior suitable for quantitative logging.

Table 1 summarizes the task intent and motor focus of each minigame and, crucially, specifies which signals are used as input features in the classifier reported in this paper. This avoids ambiguity between (i) raw kinematic signals used for learning and (ii) additional task-level indicators that may be recorded for future analyses.

For the proof-of-concept prototype, we represent each sample as a fixed-length segment and derive a 540-D feature vector from the raw 3D Wrist/Palm/IndexTip series. These features are standardized prior to training, and subsequently converted to Q32.32 fixed-point representation to support privacy-preserving inference via Garbled Circuits, as described in the subsequent subsections.

Table 1. VR minigames used for motor elicitation and data logging. In all tasks, the classifier uses only the raw 3D hand-motion series from Wrist, Palm, and IndexTip (x, y, z). Each sample is a fixed-length 6 s segment resampled every 0.1 s (60 instants) and serialized into a 540-D vector after standardization. Additional task-level indicators are logged by the system but are not used as input features in this paper.

Minigame	Task description and motor focus
Micrography	Guided pattern tracing using an XR controller as a pen/marker; focuses on fine motor control during continuous drawing under visual guidance.
Simon Says	Imitate on-screen hand poses/gestures within a time window; focuses on coordination and pose accuracy under guided cues.
Gravity	Catch (and, if applicable, discriminate) falling objects; focuses on reach-to-grasp dynamics and eye–hand coordination under time pressure.

2.2 Participants, Protocol, and Ethics

We collected data from two groups: 16 participants diagnosed with Parkinson's disease (PD) and 16 normative participants (controls). The PD stage ranged between 1 and 2. Exclusion criteria included inability to remain standing and lack of sufficient autonomy to complete the session. Each session lasted approximately 10–20 min depending on participants' familiarity with VR technology. All participants provided informed consent, and the protocol received approval from the Universidad Politécnica de Madrid.

2.3 Feature Representation, Labels, and Plaintext Classifier

We formulate a binary classification task where labels encode group membership: class 0 corresponds to normative participants (controls) and class 1 to participants diagnosed with Parkinson's disease (PD). The current proof-of-concept dataset comprises 32 participants (16 controls and 16 PD), from which we derive one fixed-length hand-motion sample per participant for model training and evaluation.

Each sample contains nine 3D time series capturing the wrist (`Wrist_x,y,z`), palm (`Palm_x,y,z`), and index fingertip (`IndexTip_x, y,z`). The VR application logs these signals at 0.1 s intervals over a 6 s window, yielding 60 instants per variable. The sample comprises 2 s for each of the three games. We select the smallest sample size possible to prove the validity of our concept and to minimize computational overhead when classifying under GCs. We serialize the resulting values into a single feature vector of length 540 (9 variables $\times$ 60 instants).

We perform a stratified 80/20 partition at the participant level. The split is subject-disjoint: no participant appears in both training and validation sets.

The plaintext model (`SimpleFC`) is implemented in PyTorch as a lightweight fully connected network with input size 540, one hidden layer of 16 neurons with ReLU activation, and a 2-neuron output layer producing logits for the two classes. Once more the size of the neural network is kept as small as possible, enough to provide a workable proof-of-concept prototype. ReLU is selected for simplicity and for later compatibility with the encrypted circuit implementation, where activation can be expressed via sign detection under Q32.32 fixed-point arithmetic.

Training uses cross-entropy loss with learning rate 10^{-3} and weight decay 10^{-4}. Given the proof-of-concept scope and cohort size, we report accuracy as the primary performance metric in this manuscript.

2.4 Privacy-Preserving Inference via Garbled Circuits

To address privacy concerns with sensitive data, classification is done using a MPC technique, namely GCs. A conventional fully connected neural network is trained using the acquired data. Subsequently the weights and biases of the model are used in conjunctions with GCs to classify a sample without revealing any of the underlying information.

We implement a two-party privacy scenario: one party holds sensitive patient inputs, while a second party holds a classification model and wishes to keep model details confidential. GCs enable joint evaluation such that intermediate values are never revealed in plaintext and only the final classification is recovered. Similar works include [2].

To support neural arithmetic inside boolean circuits, parameters and inputs are converted to signed 64-bit fixed-point Q32.32 representation. In this format, floating-point values are scaled by 2^{32} and stored as two's-complement integers, enabling binary additions and multiplications consistent with the circuit design.

Since the Q32.32 representation allows working with plain integers, basic arithmetic operations (addition and multiplication) are implemented using standard circuits. A regular bit adder is utilized for each sum, whereas products are performed following the shift and add multiplication algorithm. Figure 2 illustrates this with two numbers of four bits. For the ReLU activation function, a NAND operation is performed between the most significant bit (the sign bit) and each other bit of the input, resulting in either 0 for negative numbers or the value itself otherwise.

Lastly, to reduce circuit complexity the final softmax function computed before the output is excluded. This creates some information leakage about the original input. Future works will try to resolve this weakness with an efficient MPC softmax computation or some alternative output function. As mentioned, this encrypted inference implementation is a small-scale experimental prototype intended to demonstrate feasibility for privacy-preserving classification.

3 Experiments and Results

3.1 HandDataLogger Qualitative Examples

To provide qualitative evidence of the captured motion signals, Fig. 3 shows representative HandDataLogger excerpts for the left hand in a normative

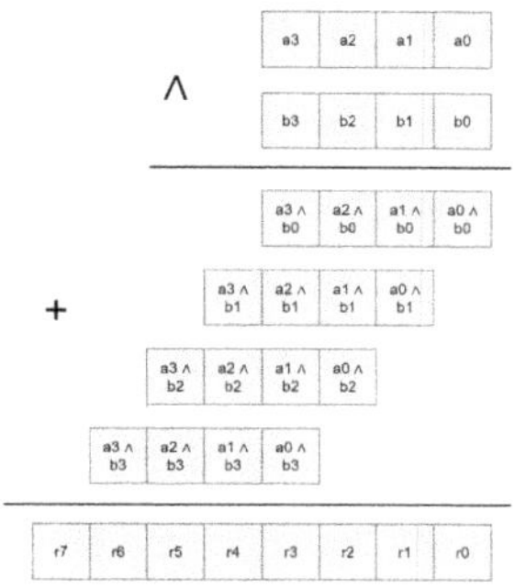

Fig. 2. GC multiplication circuit with two four bit inputs: a and b. As can be seen, a first round of AND gates is utilized followed by a series of shifted sums. This is identical to the standard multiplication algorithm also called long multiplication but expressed in binary rather than decimal.

participant (Control) and in a participant with Parkinson's disease (PD). Although the downstream model operates on fixed-length representations, these session excerpts help illustrate the type of temporal dynamics recorded by the system and motivate the subsequent preprocessing and windowing used for classification, without implying statistical group-level conclusions from visual inspection alone.

3.2 Plaintext Classification Performance

We evaluated the plaintext classifier under the stratified 80/20 subject-disjoint split described in Sect. 2. Under this protocol and the reported hyperparameters, the `SimpleFC` model achieves approximately 90% validation accuracy on this proof-of-concept cohort, suggesting that the logged hand-motion features contain discriminative information for the predefined binary classes. However, with such a small sample size and basic neural network design, our classification model remains a proof-of-concept prototype.

3.3 Encrypted Inference: Functionality and Overhead

Encrypted inference follows the Garbled Circuit workflow introduced in Sect. 2. Inputs and model parameters are encoded as Q32.32 fixed-point integers; input labels are generated at the bit level and privately selected via an Oblivious Transfer (OT) protocol, ensuring the evaluator receives only the labels corresponding to their inputs without revealing them to the generator; neuron circuits implement fixed-point multiplications and chained additions followed by a garbled ReLU; and the final output labels are decoded back to floating-point values to enable class selection.

The current implementation has substantial computational overhead. On the experimental setup described in Sect. 2, the GC prototype reports an execution

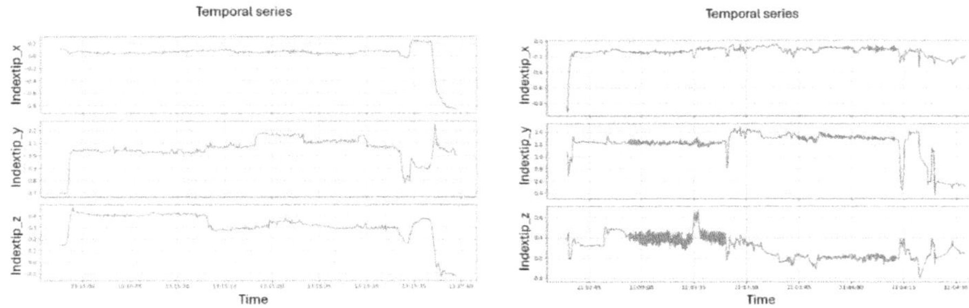

(a) Control – Left hand **(b)** PD – Left hand

Fig. 3. Representative HandDataLogger time series of the index fingertip position (IndexTip, 3D) for the left hand, comparing a normative participant (Control) and a participant with Parkinson's disease (PD). The x-axis reports the acquisition timestamp (time of day) for each session excerpt; recordings were captured at different times. The plots are qualitative examples of the raw logger output and illustrate the temporal dynamics logged during VR interaction, including segments with different variability levels and occasional abrupt transitions. These examples are intended for visual inspection and are not presented as a statistical group comparison nor as a direct depiction of the fixed-length windows used by the downstream classifier.

time of approximately 18 min and a peak memory footprint close to 3 GB for a batch run. Implementation efficiency was not the original goal of this research work, however future work will seek to optimize and improve memory consumption and computation times. We speculate these numbers can be significantly lowered.

3.4 Usability and Safety (questionnaires)

Usability was assessed after each session using the System Usability Scale (SUS). Because the application is intended for PD end users, SUS responses were collected only from PD participants (N = 16). The average SUS score was 79.53 (SD = 10.05), with a median of 82.50, an interquartile range of 73.75–85.00, and a range of 57.5–92.5, indicating consistently positive perceived usability in this cohort (Table 2).

Table 2. SUS summary for PD participants.

N	Mean (SD)	Median [Q1, Q3]	Min–Max
16	79.53 (10.05)	82.50 [73.75, 85.00]	57.5–92.5

To assess tolerability and simulator sickness, PD participants completed a Spanish-adapted Simulator Sickness Questionnaire (SSQ) after the session

(0 = None, 1 = Mild, 2 = Moderate, 3 = Severe; N = 16). Overall, reported symptoms were minimal: nine out of sixteen items received "None" from all participants (100%), including nausea and excessive sweating. The remaining items exhibited only sporadic Mild responses and isolated Moderate cases, with no Severe ratings observed (Table 3).

Table 3. SSQ symptom ratings from PD participants (N = 16; 0 = None, 1 = Mild, 2 = Moderate, 3 = Severe). Only items with at least one non-zero response are listed; all other SSQ items were rated "None" by 100% of participants.

Symptom	None	Mild	Moderate	Severe
General discomfort	15 (93.8%)	0 (0%)	1 (6.3%)	0 (0%)
Fatigue	15 (93.8%)	1 (6.3%)	0 (0%)	0 (0%)
Headache	15 (93.8%)	1 (6.3%)	0 (0%)	0 (0%)
Difficulty focusing	13 (81.3%)	2 (12.5%)	1 (6.3%)	0 (0%)
Difficulty concentrating	14 (87.5%)	2 (12.5%)	0 (0%)	0 (0%)
Vertigo	15 (93.8%)	0 (0%)	1 (6.3%)	0 (0%)
Stomach awareness	15 (93.8%)	1 (6.3%)	0 (0%)	0 (0%)

4 Discussion

This study should be interpreted as a proof of concept that validates the feasibility of combining VR-based motor elicitation, compact hand-motion representations, and privacy-preserving inference for a lightweight classifier. The plaintext results (approximately 90% validation accuracy under a subject-disjoint split) suggest that the Wrist/Palm/IndexTip traces logged during the minigames carry discriminative information for the predefined binary labels in our cohort and protocol. However, given the limited cohort size and the absence of additional performance metrics, these results should be viewed as indicative rather than as a definitive assessment of diagnostic capability.

A key practical contribution is the end-to-end encrypted inference prototype. While GCs provide a strong conceptual route to protect both patient inputs and model parameters during inference, the measured overhead (minutes of runtime and gigabytes of RAM for a batch run on the experimental setup) remains a major barrier to real-world deployment. This trade-off is central: privacy guarantees become meaningful in clinical or association settings only if latency and resource usage can be reduced to acceptable operational levels. In this direction, standard circuit optimizations and parallel evaluation are clear next steps, together with careful benchmarking that reports both compute and communication costs.

From an HCI and deployment perspective, questionnaire outcomes support the viability of the VR protocol in the target population. The SUS score indicates positive perceived usability, and the SSQ item-level distribution suggests minimal simulator-sickness symptoms for most participants, with only sporadic mild reports and isolated moderate cases and no severe ratings. These findings are important because data quality and participant adherence depend on the tolerability of the interface, particularly for users with limited prior exposure to VR.

Finally, the modeling choices reflect an explicit design constraint: the architecture and preprocessing were kept simple to enable a faithful implementation in fixed-point arithmetic within boolean circuits. More expressive temporal models may improve predictive performance, but their secure implementation cost must be weighed against the privacy-preserving objective. Consequently, progress in this line of work requires joint optimization of (i) data representations that preserve motor information, (ii) models compatible with secure computation, and (iii) system-level efficiency to approach practical deployment.

5 Conclusions, Limitations, and Future Work

5.1 Conclusions

This work presented a proof-of-concept pipeline that combines (i) an immersive VR assessment suite designed to elicit controlled upper-limb motor behaviors, (ii) a compact hand-motion representation derived from raw 3D trajectories, (iii) a lightweight plaintext neural classifier, and (iv) a privacy-preserving inference stage based on Garbled Circuits. The VR application comprises three PD-oriented minigames (Micrography, Simon Says, and Gravity) aimed at capturing structured hand-motion traces in an accessible interaction flow for participants with limited prior exposure to VR.

From the modeling standpoint, the proposed representation intentionally prioritizes simplicity and traceability: the downstream classifier operates on fixed-length vectors obtained from raw Wrist/Palm/IndexTip 3D series after standardization, enabling straightforward implementation in both plaintext and encrypted arithmetic. Under the experimental protocol adopted in this study, the plaintext `SimpleFC` model achieved approximately 90% validation accuracy, indicating that the logged signals contain discriminative information for the predefined binary classes within this cohort and experimental setting.

Beyond plaintext performance, a central contribution of this paper is the end-to-end demonstration of privacy-preserving inference for the same classifier using fixed-point Q32.32 arithmetic embedded in boolean circuits. The prototype illustrates that it is possible to evaluate the model without revealing intermediate plaintext values during computation, while still decoding interpretable output scores for class selection. Although the current implementation is computationally expensive, the results support feasibility for privacy-sensitive clinical scenarios in which both patient inputs and model parameters may require protection.

Finally, usability and tolerability were assessed in the PD group using standardized questionnaires. SUS results (mean score 79.53 over PD participants) indicate consistently positive perceived usability, and the SSQ item-level distribution suggests minimal simulator-sickness symptoms for most participants, with only sporadic mild reports and isolated moderate cases and no severe ratings. Together, these findings support the practical viability of the proposed VR-based protocol as a usable and well-tolerated data collection interface in the targeted population, at least for short sessions and under the tested conditions.

5.2 Limitations

Several limitations should be considered when interpreting the results. First, the study is explicitly framed as a proof of concept with a limited cohort size and constrained population coverage (early-stage PD and the available normative group), which restricts external validity and does not support strong claims about generalization across disease stages, clinical subtypes, medication states, or broader demographic variability. Second, model evaluation was intentionally lightweight: performance reporting focused on validation accuracy and did not include additional metrics (e.g., precision/recall, F1-score, balanced accuracy) or confidence intervals, which would be necessary for a more rigorous characterization of classifier behavior in imbalanced or heterogeneous settings.

Third, the classifier architecture is deliberately simple (a small fully connected network) and does not explicitly model temporal structure beyond the fixed-length serialization of the trajectories. While this design choice is aligned with encrypted inference constraints, it may underutilize temporal information that could be captured by sequence models. Fourth, although multiple task-level indicators can be logged by the VR application, they are not used as model inputs in this manuscript; consequently, the current analysis does not quantify the relative contribution of each minigame, nor does it evaluate task-specific effects.

Fifth, the privacy-preserving component is an experimental prototype. The reported runtime and memory costs remain substantial, and the implementation does not yet incorporate well-known circuit-level optimizations or systematic parallelization. In addition, the evaluation focuses on local execution characteristics; network communication overheads and end-to-end deployment constraints (e.g., secure two-party interaction latency in realistic settings) are not fully characterized.

Finally, the qualitative HandDataLogger plots included in the Results section are intended for illustrative inspection of the raw logging dynamics rather than statistical inference. Visual differences between example traces should not be interpreted as clinical findings without dedicated quantitative analysis and appropriate study design.

5.3 Future Work

Future work will address both clinical/experimental validation and system-level scalability. On the experimental side, a priority is to extend data collection to larger and more diverse cohorts, covering a broader range of PD stages and including repeated sessions to enable longitudinal analysis and assessment of intra-subject variability. This extension would also enable more robust evaluation protocols (e.g., subject-wise cross-validation), richer performance reporting (including class-wise metrics and uncertainty estimates), and analysis of confounding factors such as hand dominance, symptom laterality, task order effects, and familiarity with VR.

On the modeling side, several directions are promising. More expressive temporal models could be explored (e.g., compact 1D convolutional or transformer-style encoders with controlled complexity) while maintaining compatibility with secure inference constraints. Feature engineering alternatives (e.g., velocity/acceleration summaries, frequency-domain descriptors, or task-conditioned embeddings) could improve robustness, provided that their transformation steps remain reproducible and implementable in privacy-preserving arithmetic. In parallel, ablation studies should quantify the contribution of each minigame and evaluate whether task-specific models or a unified multi-task representation yields better generalization.

On the privacy-preserving side, the GC implementation should incorporate established optimizations (e.g., Free-XOR, Half-Gates) and exploit parallel evaluation strategies to reduce latency. A systematic profiling of compute and communication costs will be required to identify bottlenecks and guide engineering choices for deployment in association or clinic environments. Beyond GCs, it will be valuable to compare alternative privacy-preserving paradigms (e.g., other MPC protocols or hybrid approaches) under realistic threat models, always balancing privacy guarantees with practical usability constraints.

Finally, translation to practice will require integration work beyond classification accuracy: improving the robustness of the logging pipeline (e.g., handling tracking dropouts), strengthening accessibility and ergonomics for PD users, and establishing procedures for secure data governance. In this direction, a disciplined evaluation plan that combines technical metrics with usability/tolerability outcomes will be essential to move from feasibility to a clinically meaningful and deployable system.

Acknowledgments. This work was supported by the State Research Agency of Spain (Agencia Estatal de Investigación – AEI) under Grant (CarHaVoz: PID2023-152984OB-I00).

References

1. Avola, D., Cinque, L., Foresti, G.L., Marini, M.R., Pannone, D.: VRheab: a fully immersive motor rehabilitation system based on recurrent neural network. Multimedia Tools Appl. **77**, 24955–24982 (2018)

2. Ball, M., Carmer, B., Malkin, T., Rosulek, M., Schimanski, N.: Garbled neural networks are practical. IACR Cryptol. ePrint Arch. **2019**, 338 (2019). https://api.semanticscholar.org/CorpusID:115197351
3. Bevilacqua, R., et al.: Exploring dance as a therapeutic approach for Parkinson disease through the social robotics for active and healthy ageing (SI-robotics): results from a technical feasibility study. JMIR Aging **8**, e62930 (2025)
4. Brien, D.C., et al.: Classification and staging of Parkinson's disease using video-based eye tracking. Parkinsonism Relat. Disord. **110**, 105316 (2023)
5. Dudek, M., et al.: Analysis of voice, speech, and language biomarkers of Parkinson's disease collected in a mixed reality setting. Sensors **25**(8), 2405 (2025)
6. Jiang, M., et al.: Auxiliary diagnostic method of Parkinson's disease based on eye movement analysis in a virtual reality environment. Neurosci. Lett. **842**, 137956 (2024)
7. Jiang, M., et al.: Diagnosis of Parkinson's disease by eliciting trait-specific eye movements in multi-visual tasks. J. Transl. Med. **23**(1), 65 (2025)
8. Khalid, N., Qayyum, A., Bilal, M., Al-Fuqaha, A., Qadir, J.: Privacy-preserving artificial intelligence in healthcare: techniques and applications. Comput. Biol. Med. **158**, 106848 (2023)
9. Kozlovski, T., et al.: Quantifying motor-cognitive reserve using a novel multimodal stress test. Brain Commun. **7**(6), fcaf412 (2025)
10. Lang, T., et al.: The diagnostic pathway of Parkinson's disease: understanding patient perspectives in Australia. NPJ Parkinson's Dis. **11**, 104 (2025)
11. Li, M., Ye, X., Huang, Z., Ye, L., Chen, C.: Global burden of Parkinson's disease from 1990 to 2021: a population-based study. Publ. Health **15**(4), e095610 (2025)
12. Liu, J., Juuti, M., Lu, Y., Asokan, N.: Oblivious neural network predictions via minionn transformations. In: Proceedings of the 2017 ACM SIGSAC Conference on Computer and Communications Security. CCS '17, pp. 619–631. Association for Computing Machinery, New York, NY, USA (2017). https://doi.org/10.1145/3133956.3134056
13. Ma, L., et al.: Effects of virtual reality on spatiotemporal gait parameters and freezing of gait in Parkinson's disease. NPJ Parkinson's Dis. (2025)
14. Maggio, M.G., et al.: Effectiveness of telerehabilitation plus virtual reality (tele-RV) in cognitive and social functioning: a randomized clinical study on Parkinson's disease. Parkinsonism Relat. Disord. **119**, 105970 (2024)
15. Mao, J., et al.: A health monitoring system based on flexible triboelectric sensors for intelligence medical internet of things and its applications in virtual reality. Nano Energy **118**, 108984 (2023)
16. Oishi, N., Heimler, B., Pellatt, L., Plotnik, M., Roggen, D.: Detecting freezing of gait with earables trained from VR motion capture data. In: 2021 International Symposium on Wearable Computers (ISWC '21), pp. 1–5. ACM (2021)
17. Pazzaglia, C., et al.: Comparison of virtual reality rehabilitation and conventional rehabilitation in Parkinson's disease: a randomised controlled trial. Physiotherapy **106**, 36–42 (2020)
18. Petsani, D., et al.: Digital biomarkers for well-being through exergame interactions: exploratory study. JMIR Serious Games **10**(3), e34768 (2022)
19. Reiner, J., et al.: Oculometric measures as a tool for assessment of clinical symptoms and severity of Parkinson's disease. J. Neural Transm. **130**(10), 1241–1248 (2023)

20. Riazi, M.S., Samragh, M., Chen, H., Laine, K., Lauter, K., Koushanfar, F.: Xonn: Xnor-based oblivious deep neural network inference. In: Proceedings of the 28th USENIX Conference on Security Symposium. SEC'19, pp. 1501–1518. USENIX Association, USA (2019)
21. Vu, J.P., et al.: Assessment of motor dysfunction with virtual reality in patients undergoing [123i]fp-cit spect/ct brain imaging. Tomography **7**(2), 95–106 (2021)

Phonation-Encephalographic Signatures as Interpretable Biomarkers of Cortical-Limbic Dysfunction in Autism Spectrum Disorder

Andrés Gómez-Rodellar[1(✉)], Marina Jodra-Chuan[2], Pedro Gómez-Vilda[3], Daniel Palacios-Alonso[3], and José M. Ferrández-Vicente[4]

[1] St. Louis Missouri University, Madrid Campus, Madrid, Spain
andres.gomez@slu.edu

[2] Universidad Complutense de Madrid, Madrid, Spain
majodra@ucm.es

[3] E. T. S. de Ingeniería Informática, Universidad Rey Juan Carlos, Móstoles, Madrid, Spain
{pedro.gomezv,daniel.palacios}@urjc.es

[4] Universidad Politécnica de Cartagena, Campus Muralla del Mar, Pza. Hospital 1, 30202 Cartagena, Spain
jm.ferrandez@upct.es

Abstract. This study introduces a new measurement called the u_{shape} synchronization index (uSI). This metric uses voice recordings as a 'proxy' for brain activity (*phEG*) to measure how well different brain regions, specifically those related to emotions and movement—work together during phonation. Building on a neuromechanical inversion pipeline, recorded phonation is transformed into probability-density *phEG* distributions. A u_{shape} synchronization index (uSI) is defined to capture the curvature of the μ-band relative to its immediate neighbors (ϑ and high-α), a signature of impaired motor–affective coupling in Autism Spectrum Disorder (ASD). This index was applied to longitudinal *phEG* samples collected from two ASD participants (one male, one female), each contributing 12 sustained-vowel recordings over six years, and compared these case series against a reference database of 12 male and 12 female healthy controls. Methodological validation combined one-sided bootstrap inference on uSI, for univariate contrasts, and multivariate deviation. Results show that the uSI reliably identifies pronounced μ-band troughs in multiple case recordings that exhibit subject-level heterogeneity and occasional discordance. It may be concluded that uSI is a promising, interpretable biomarker candidate that compresses complex spectral relationships into a single, testable index.

This research has been supported by Grant PID2023-152984OB-I00 (CaRaHAVoz) funded by the State Research Agency of Spain (Agencia Estatal de Investigación—AEI). The authors gratefully acknowledge the support of the Latin American Network of Neuroscience CYTED NT4SM (Ref.225RT0169), and Asociación Nuevo Horizonte (ANH).

J. M. Ferrndez Vicente et al. (Eds.): IWINAC 2026, LNCS 16574, pp. 177–187, 2026.
https://doi.org/10.1007/978-3-032-27314-7_17

Keywords: Encephalography · Phonation · Cortical-Limbic Synchronization · Laryngeal Neuromechanics · Autism Spectrum Disorder

1 Introduction

Autism Spectrum Disorder (ASD) is a neurodevelopmental condition characterized by clinical heterogeneity and a shared neurobiological basis involving atypical brain connectivity. ASD's rising prevalence [2] necessitates objective biomarkers to supplement behavioral assessments of its core social and repetitive impairments [1,3]. Guided by *Underconnectivity Theory* [4] and cellular E/I imbalance [5], the condition is characterized by pathological synchronization in the μ rhythm (8–12 Hz) and a failure of the Mirror Neuron System to trigger event-related desynchronization [6]. To address existing inconsistencies in qEEG literature [7], this research shifts from isolated power analysis to the relational dynamics between limbic-associated ϑ and motor-associated α/μ bands. This study assumes that atypical μ-power reflects a cortical-limbic failure to provide a *desynchronizing signal*, manifesting as a spectral u_{shape} on *phonation encephalographic (phEG)* activity and introduces a u_{shape} synchronization index (uSI) as a non-invasive proxy for these neuromotor signatures. The concept of *phEG* refers to estimates of the laryngeal neuromotor drive—which modulates vocal-fold tension—mapped onto the frequency bands used in EEG. Conceptually, the framework relies on two pathways (Fig. 1). The first is a biological *(a) direct neuromotor-phonation model (DNPM)* showing how neuromotor activity (NMA) in brain motor areas controls the laryngeal nerves. The second is a mathematical *(b) inverse phonation-neuromotor model (IPNM)* that works backward, allowing to reconstruct NMA signals (*phEG*) using recorded phonation (RP) [8]. Cortical Oscillatory Loops, rhythmic neural activity patterns sustained by recurrent excitatory and inhibitory circuits, are fundamental to motor control and attention, yet they exhibit measurable synchrony alterations in neurodevelopmental and neurodegenerative conditions [9,10]. This study characterizes these dysfunctions by analyzing the μ loop ($8--13$Hz), which serves as a sensorimotor-thalamic bridge where atypical suppression in ASD reflects disrupted social-cognitive action-understanding [11], and the ϑ loop ($4--8$ Hz), which facilitates striatal-thalamo-cortical communication and temporal motor initiation [12]. By utilizing *phEG* signals to map these oscillatory signatures, this research seeks to advance the understanding of the specific pathophysiological mechanisms driving the heterogeneous motor and social deficits characteristic of the ASD phenotype.

2 Materials and Methods

The estimation of phonation-related EEG (*phEG*) proxies and the subsequent u_{shape} synchronization index (uSI) follows a neuromechanical inversion pipeline that maps acoustic signals to neural proxies. As depicted in Fig. 2, the process begins with four-second segments of sustained [a:] vowel phonations, sampled at

NMA $\longrightarrow$ LNA $\longrightarrow$ VFBS $\longrightarrow$ GS $\longrightarrow$ RP

(a) Direct Neuromechanical Pathway

RP $\longrightarrow$ GS $\longrightarrow$ VFBS $\longrightarrow$ phEG

(b) Inverse Neuromechanical Pathway

Fig. 1. Direct and inverse neuromechanical pipelines involved in phonation. (a). Direct pathways from the neuromotor activity (NMA) in sensorymotor phonation-control areas to recorded phonation (RP). (b) Inverse estimation pipeline depicting the transformation of the RP into *phEG* band representations. VFBS: vocal fold body stiffness; LNA: laryngeal neuromotor activity; GS: glottal source; RP: recorded phonation.

44.1 kHz and downsampled to 16 kHz. To ensure signal stability, vowel onset and decay phases are omitted. The raw acoustic signal $s_p(t)$ undergoes 24th-order Linear Predictive Inversion (LPI) via Iterative Adaptive Inverse Filtering (IAIF) to extract the glottal residual $\epsilon_g(t)$, which is numerically integrated to derive the glottal source $u_g(t)$ [13]. Subsequently, Vocal Fold Biomechanical Model Inversion (VFBMI) is applied to $u_g(t)$ to estimate the Vocal Fold Body Stress (VFBS), denoted as $\xi_b(t)$ [14]. The VFBS signal is then processed through a Filter Bank (BF) to produce the *phEG* bands $\xi_i(t)$ across the frequency spectrum. The bandwidth definitions for these *phEG* bands are detailed in Table 1, where $\overline{\xi}_b$ represents the average trend of the VFBS.

s_p(t) $\rightarrow$ [LPI] $\rightarrow$ u_g(t) $\rightarrow$ [VFBMI] $\rightarrow$ VFBS $\longrightarrow$ [BF] $\rightarrow$ ξ_i $\longrightarrow$ [BDE] $\longrightarrow$ $p_i(\xi_i)$

Fig. 2. Pipeline splitting the phonation signal s_p(t) into *phEG* band representations. Key stages: Linear Predictive Inversion (LPI) to estimate the glottal source (u_g(t)), and Vocal Fold Biomechanical Model Inversion (VFBMI) to produce the Vocal Fold Body Stress (VFBS) ξ_b(t). BF: filter bank separating *phEG* bands ξ_i(t); i $\in \{\delta, ...\gamma\}$. BDE: bin-density estimator generating output probability distributions ($p_i(\xi_i)$).

The study distinguishes the μ band (8–12 Hz) from the broader α band (8–16 Hz). To isolate motor-related synchronization, we define a *neighbor-band* logic that compares the μ rhythm against its spectral neighbors: the limbic-associated ϑ band (4–8 Hz) and the high-α band (αh, 12–16 Hz), as defined in Table 1. This approach facilitates the detection of phase-amplitude coupling and emotional-to-motor feedback loops. Assuming that the α-band VFBS intensity may be split in low $\alpha_l \equiv \mu$ and high α_h subbands, such that $\overline{\xi}_\alpha = (\overline{\xi}_{\alpha\mathrm{h}} + \overline{\xi}_{\alpha\mathrm{l}})/2$, the u_{shape} synchronization index (uSI), quantifying the relative coupling of the μ band against its neighbors, is defined as:

$$uSI = \overline{\xi}_\mu - (\overline{\xi}_\vartheta + \overline{\xi}_{\alpha\mathrm{h}})/2 = (3\overline{\xi}_\mu - \overline{\xi}_\vartheta + 2\overline{\xi}_\alpha)/2 \tag{1}$$

A significantly negative uSI flags a pronounced trough in μ-band activity relative to its spectral neighbors (ϑ and high-α). This anomalous spectral curvature serves as a quantifiable proxy for atypical cortical–limbic modulation, reflecting a failure in the dynamic synchronization/desynchronization mechanisms required for social processing.

Table 1. Methodological *phEG* band definition in the study. The band α is divided into the low-band (μ), and the high-band (αh)

phEG	Bandwidth
$\xi_\delta(t) = F_{\Omega_\delta}\{\xi_b(t)\}/\overline{\xi}_b;$	$0 < \Omega_\delta \leq 4$ Hz
$\xi_\vartheta(t) = F_{\Omega_\vartheta}\{\xi_b(t)\}/\overline{\xi}_b;$	$4 < \Omega_\vartheta \leq 8$ Hz
$\xi_\alpha(t) = F_{\Omega_\alpha}\{\xi_b(t)\}/\overline{\xi}_b;$	$8 < \Omega_\alpha \leq 16$ Hz
$\xi_\beta(t) = F_{\Omega_\beta}\{\xi_b(t)\}/\overline{\xi}_b;$	$16 < \Omega_\beta \leq 32$ Hz
$\xi_\gamma(t) = F_{\Omega_\gamma}\{\xi_b(t)\}/\overline{\xi}_b;$	$\Omega_\gamma > 32$ Hz
$\xi_\mu(t) = F_{\Omega_\mu}\{\xi_b(t)\}/\overline{\xi}_b;$	$8 < \Omega_\mu \leq 12$ Hz
$\xi_{\alpha h}(t) = F_{\Omega_{\alpha h}}\{\xi_b(t)\}/\overline{\xi}_b;$	$12 < \Omega_{\alpha h} \leq 16$ Hz

Longitudinal phonation samples from two ASD participants were acquired using a Sennheiser SK300G2A microphone and digitized via a Motu Traveller interface (Table 2). Data collection followed a nominal six-month longitudinal design, with minor variations in inter-session duration due to testing feasibility, from 2019 to 2025 (Table 3). A reference database of normotypical participants provided context for the ASD data (Table 4).

Table 2. Characteristics of participants; F: female; M: Male; CARS: childhood autism rating scale (non autistic condition <30, moderate 30–36, severe: >36); DEX: Dysexecutive Questionnaire (optimum condition <10, normal condition 10–18, moderate dysexecutive 19-28, severe cognitive alteration >28)

Gender	F	M
Age	45	40
Diagnosis	ASD	ASD
CARS	30	30
DEX	45	44
Comorbid.	Intellec. Disab.	Sev. Intellec. Dis.

The statistical significance of the subject-specific features was evaluated through a multi-stage non-parametric framework. The null hypothesis (H_0) assumes preserved cortical-limbic synchronization, where the empirical distribution of the case sample is equivalent to the reference distribution ($\mathscr{F}_{cs}(uSI) \equiv \mathscr{F}_{RS}(uSI)$). Deviations from the normative cloud were assessed using *Robust Mahalanobis Distances* based on the *Minimum Covariance Determinant (MCD)*

Table 3. Serial concurrent samples of the study cases. Left and middle columns: sample labels. Right column: recording dates (Y/M/D: Year/Month/Day).

Male Samples	Female Samples	Date (Y/M/D)
m0001	f0001	2019/07/23
m0002	f0002	2020/12/18
m0003	f0003	2021/07/01
m0004	f0004	2021/12/03
m0005	f0005	2022/06/01
m0006	f0006	2022/12/02
m0007	f0007	2023/02/03
m0008	f0008	2023/12/15
m0009	f0009	2024/05/24
m0010	f0010	2024/12/19
m0011	f0011	2025/01/10
m0012	f0012	2025/06/20

Table 4. Male and female reference samples, gender and age (years). Male samples were labelled as M10xx, and female samples as F11xx.

Sample	Gender	Age	Sample	Gender	Age
M1005	M	21	F1105	F	43
M1018	M	29	F1108	F	22
M1027	M	34	F1112	F	20
M1028	M	28	F1116	F	45
M1030	M	25	F1117	F	25
M1032	M	48	F1120	F	33
M1033	M	42	F1121	F	57
M1034	M	30	F1125	F	38
M1035	M	35	F1126	F	40
M1036	M	42	F1127	F	59
M1037	M	50	F1128	F	52
M1038	M	41	F1130	F	35

estimator, with raw distances mapped to an F-distribution via the *Hardin-Rocke adjustment* [15] under a p-value $p_{MD} = p_{valMD}(\mathscr{F}_{cs}(uSI) \neq \mathscr{F}_{RS}(uSI))$. Median shifts across the 12 estimated PDFs were further evaluated using the rank-based *Kruskal-Wallis H-test* [16] to calculate $p_{KW} = p_{valKW}(\mathscr{F}_{cs}(uSI) \neq \mathscr{F}_{RS}(uSI))$, applying the *Benjamini-Hochberg (BH) method* to control the *False Discovery Rate (FDR)* [17]. A bootstrap process (10,000 samples with a 75% repetition percent) evaluated the *u_shape uSI* index against the hypothesis

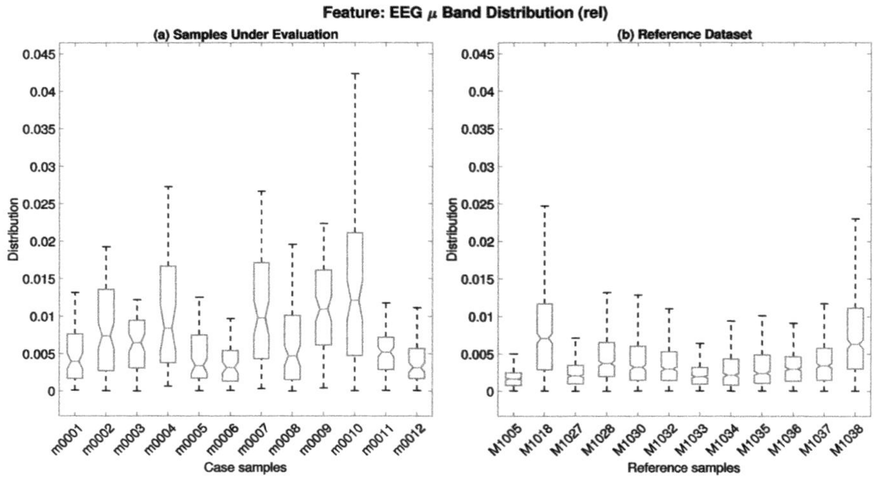

Fig. 3. Distributions of *phEG* neuromechanics in the μ-band for the male cohorts. (a) Longitudinal samples from the ASD participant. (b) Normative reference dataset.

$H_0 : uSI \geq 0$, where rejection at $p_{BS} \leq 0.05$ signifies a departure from the *no desynchronization* state.

3 Results and Discussion

The methodological pipeline for extracting *phEG* proxies results in the gender-stratified distributions presented in Fig. 3 and Fig. 4, which provide the visual basis for the μ-band synchronization analysis, contrasting the longitudinal variability of the ASD cases against the stability of the normative reference groups. The statistical deviations in median values and interquartile ranges (IQR) mentioned in *Section* 2 are visually evident in the stochastic-instability signature characterized by atypical variance of the male case (see Fig. 3) compared to the more compressed profiles of the female case (see Fig. 4). Furthermore, the calculation of the u_{shape} synchronization index (uSI) via expression (1) is operationalized in Fig. 5 and Fig. 6.

These last figures illustrate the outcome of the bootstrap process and the non-parametric framework, providing the numerical p-values for the null hypothesis (H_0 : median ≥ 0). While both genders exhibit a significant shift toward pathological synchronization relative to the normative baseline (magenta bounds), the male participant shows a more extensive departure in both dispersion and absolute uSI values (see Fig. 5) than the female participant (see Fig. 6), validating the necessity for the gender-specific calibration described in the methodological framework. The implementation of neuromechanical inversion across ASD cohorts demonstrates a profound departure from normotypical oscillatory patterns, revealing high internal volatility and marked stochastic-instability characterized by atypical variance in *phEG* μ-band distributions as visualized in Fig. 3

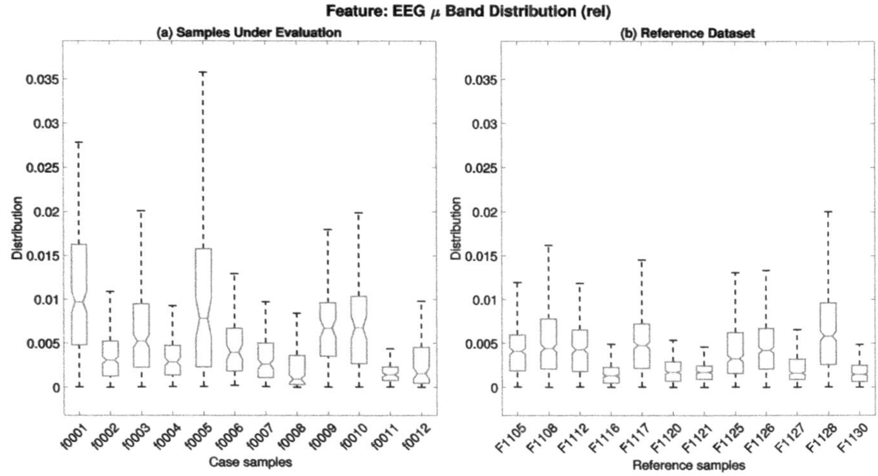

Fig. 4. Comparative μ-band distributions for the female cohort. (a) Longitudinal samples form the ASD participant. (b) Normative reference dataset.

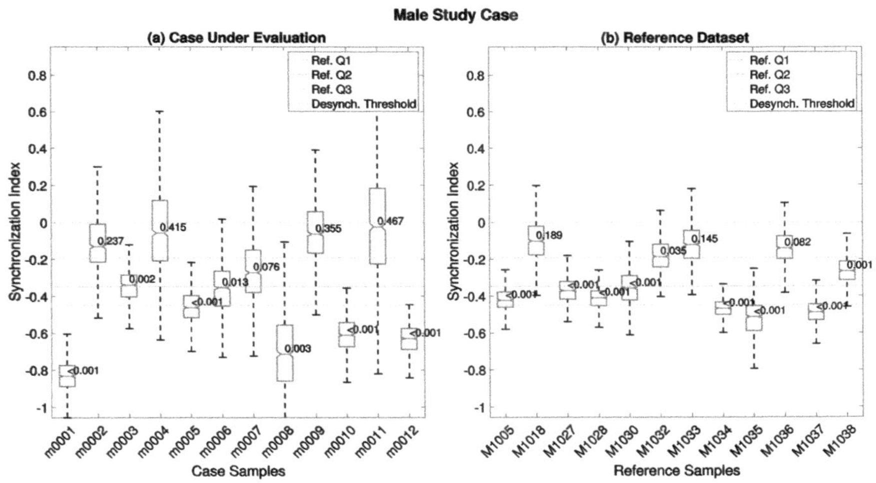

Fig. 5. Distributions of the u_{shape} Synchronization Index (uSI) for the male cohort. (a) Samples from the participant under evaluation. (b) Reference dataset. Probability values for the null hypothesis (H_0 : median > 0) are provided numerically, with values below the threshold truncated to $p < 0.001$. The reference median and interquartile ranges (magenta) were derived from the normative group. The evaluation samples exhibited significantly higher dispersion in both medians and interquartile ranges compared to the reference baseline, with most observations exceeding the normative interquartile bounds.

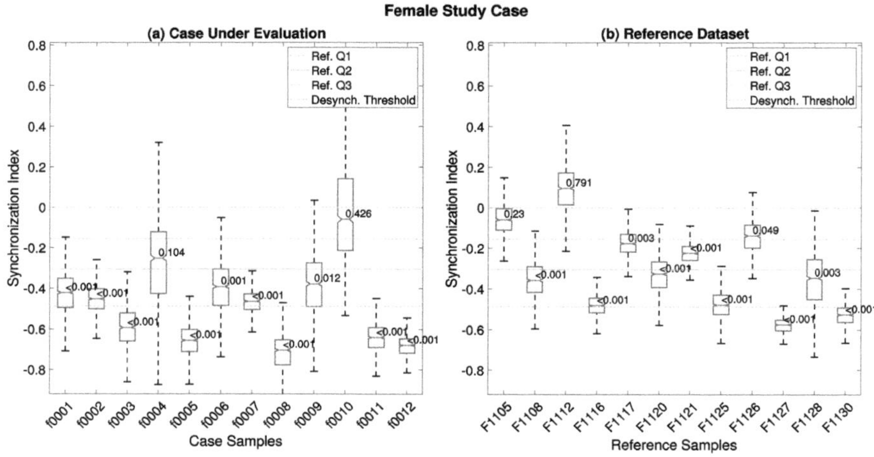

Fig. 6. Distributions of the u_{shape} uSI for the female cohort. (a) Evaluation samples. (b) Reference dataset. Similar to the male cohort, probability values for H_0 : median > 0 are presented above each distribution. While the evaluation samples demonstrated greater dispersion and a shift toward higher synchronization relative to the reference interquartiles (magenta), the degree of departure from the normative baseline was less extensive than that in the male case.

and Fig. 4. While normative groups maintain remarkable consistency within a compressed functional range, ASD participants exhibit pronounced inter-subject stochasticity, particularly prominent in samples such as m0001 vs m0011 or f0012 vs f0010 (Figs. 5.a and 6.a), which justifies the adoption of a multi-stage non-parametric framework to capture these unique neurodevelopmental signatures. This disruption is statistically operationalized in Table 5 and Table 6, where Hardin-Rocke adjusted p-values (p_{MD}) based on the Minimum Covariance Determinant estimator consistently yield $p < 0.001$, confirming that ASD phonatory profiles are multivariate outliers relative to the normative reference cloud. Furthermore, the uSI index distributions in Fig. 5 and Fig. 6 highlight a pathological synchronization where medians approach or exceed the zero threshold—a state entirely absent in the normative population. The persistence of these anomalies is rigorously defended by Benjamini-Hochberg corrected Kruskal-Wallis tests (p_{KW}) and one-sided bootstrap analyses (p_{BS}), which together identify pathological synchronization as a statistically defensible hallmark of the ASD phenotype. Concluding, individuals with ASD showed higher volatility and unusual brain-wave patterns in the μ-band. This suggests certain difficulty in sensorimotor gating, positioning $phEG$ as a reliable, non-invasive proxy to monitor ASD dysfunction aiding in neurorehabilitation progress.

Table 5. Comparison of the male case samples against the male normative population distributions. Bootstrap p-values support the negative value of u_{shape} uSI indices. Kruskal-Wallis p-values are adjusted using the Benjamini-Hochberg (FDR) procedure. Mahalanobis Distance p-values are adjusted using Hardin-Rocke procedure.

Case Sample	p_{BS}	SigBS	p_{MD}	p_{KW}	SigBH
m0001	$p < 0.001$	***	$p < 0.001$	$p < 0.001$	***
m0002	0.237	ns	$p < 0.001$	$p < 0.001$	***
m0003	0.002	**	$p < 0.001$	0.221	ns
m0004	0.415	ns	$p < 0.001$	$p < 0.001$	***
m0005	$p < 0.001$	***	$p < 0.001$	$p < 0.001$	***
m0006	0.013	**	$p < 0.001$	0.002	**
m0007	0.076	ns	$p < 0.001$	0.025	**
m0008	0.003	**	$p < 0.001$	$p < 0.001$	***
m0009	0.355	ns	$p < 0.001$	$p < 0.001$	***
m0010	$p < 0.001$	***	$p < 0.001$	$p < 0.001$	***
m0011	0.467	ns	$p < 0.001$	$p < 0.001$	***
m0012	$p < 0.001$	***	$p < 0.001$	$p < 0.001$	***

One-sided BS; multip. = 10000 runs; random sample percent = 75%
Significance levels: ns $p > 0.05$, * $p < 0.05$, ** $p < 0.01$, *** $p < 0.001$.

Table 6. Comparison of the female case samples against the female normative population distributions. Bootstrap p-values support the negative value of u_{shape} uSI indices. Kruskal-Wallis p-values are adjusted using the Benjamini-Hochberg (FDR) procedure. Mahalanobis Distance p-values are adjusted using Hardin-Rocke procedure.

Case Sample	p_{BS}	SigBS	p_{MD}	p_{KW}	SigBH
f0001	$p < 0.001$	***	$p < 0.001$	$p < 0.001$	***
f0002	$p < 0.001$	***	$p < 0.001$	$p < 0.001$	***
f0003	$p < 0.001$	***	$p < 0.001$	$p < 0.001$	***
f0004	0.104	ns	$p < 0.001$	0.001	**
f0005	$p < 0.001$	***	$p < 0.001$	$p < 0.001$	***
f0006	0.001	**	$p < 0.001$	$p < 0.001$	***
f0007	$p < 0.001$	***	$p < 0.001$	$p < 0.001$	***
f0008	$p < 0.001$	***	$p < 0.001$	$p < 0.001$	***
f0009	0.012	**	$p < 0.001$	$p < 0.001$	***
f0010	0.426	ns	$p < 0.001$	$p < 0.001$	***
f0011	$p < 0.001$	***	$p < 0.001$	$p < 0.001$	***
f0012	$p < 0.001$	***	$p < 0.001$	$p < 0.001$	***

One-sided BS; multip. = 10000 runs; random sample percent = 75%
Significance levels: ns $p > 0.05$, * $p < 0.05$, ** $p < 0.01$, *** $p < 0.001$.

4 Conclusions

This research defines cortico-laryngeal differential activity and a methodology to isolate neuromotor pathways governing cricothyroid and thyroarytenoid balance. Applied to ASD, this framework identifies a unique neuromechanical state, marked by high stochastic instability and positive μ-band synchronization, that is entirely absent in normative populations. These cortical signatures are fundamentally rooted in peripheral biomechanics, where physiological loads like vocal fold mass dictate gender-specific neural strategies for sensory-motor integration. Furthermore, the μ-rhythm serves as a benchmark for attention attitude, revealing that ASD volatility reflects impaired sensorimotor gating and disrupted proprioceptive feedback. Methodologically, the Hardin-Rocke adjusted Mahalanobis Distance is established as the primary determinant for multivariate anomaly detection. Ultimately, neuromechanical phEG inversion offers a non-invasive tool for functional and longitudinal ASD monitoring in neurorehabilitation.

References

1. American Psychiatric Association: Diagnostic and Statistical Manual of Mental Disorders. Text Revision (DSM-5-TR), 5th edn. American Psychiatric Association Publishing, Washington, DC (2022)
2. Maenner, M.J.: Prevalence and characteristics of autism spectrum disorder among children aged 8 years—autism and developmental disabilities monitoring network, 11 sites, United States, 2018. MMWR. Surveillance Summaries **70** (2021). https://doi.org/10.15585/mmwr.ss7011a1
3. Lord, C., Rutter, M., DiLavore, P.C., Risi, S., Gotham, K., Bishop, S.: Autism Diagnostic Observation Schedule, 2nd edn (ADOS2). Western Psychological Services (2012). https://doi.org/10.1037/t17256-000
4. Just, M.A., Keller, T.A., Malave, V.L., Kana, R.K., Varma, S.: Autism as a neural systems disorder: a theory of frontal-posterior underconnectivity. Neurosci. Biobehav. Rev. **36**(4), 1292–1313 (2012). https://doi.org/10.1016/j.neubiorev.2012.02.007
5. Rubenstein, J.L., Merzenich, M.M.: Model of autism: increased ratio of excitation/inhibition in key neural systems. Genes Brain Behav. **2**(5), 255–267 (2003). https://doi.org/10.1034/j.1601-183x.2003.00037.x
6. Oberman, L.M., Hubbard, E.M., McCleery, J.P., Altschuler, E.L., Ramachandran, V.S., Pineda, J.A.: EEG evidence for mirror neuron dysfunction in autism spectrum disorders. Cogn. Brain Res. **24**(2), 190–198 (2005). https://doi.org/10.1016/j.cogbrainres.2005.01.014
7. Lockhart, A.K., Sharpley, C.F., Bitsika, V.: Mu desynchronisation in autistic individuals: what we know and what we need to know. Rev. J. Autism Dev. Disord. **11**, 595–606 (2024). https://doi.org/10.1007/s40489-023-00354-w
8. Gómez-Vilda, P., Gomez-Rodellar, A., Mekyska, J., Alvarez-Marquina, A., Palacios-Alonso, D., Rektorová, I.: Assessing laryngeal neuromotor activity from phonation. Int. J. Neural Syst. **35**(06) (2025). https://doi.org/10.1142/S0129065725500297
9. Buzsáki, G., Draguhn, A.: Neuronal oscillations in cortical networks. Science **304**(5679), 1926–1929 (2004). https://doi.org/10.1126/science.1099745

10. Stam, C.J.: Modern network science of neurological disorders. Nat. Rev. Neurosci. **15**(10), 683–695 (2014). https://doi.org/10.1038/nrn3801
11. Pineda, J.A.: Sensorimotor cortex as a critical component of an 'extended' mirror neuron system: does it solve the development, correspondence, and control problems in mirroring?. Behav. Brain Functions **4**(1), 47 (2008). https://doi.org/10.1186/1744-9081-4-47
12. Hammond, C., Bergman, H., Brown, P.: Pathological synchronization in Parkinson's disease: networks, loops and localized oscillations. Trends Neurosci. **30**(7), 357–364 (2007). https://doi.org/10.1016/j.tins.2007.05.004
13. Alku, P., et al.: OPENGLOT-an open environment for the evaluation of glottal inverse filtering. Speech Commun. **107**, 38–47 (2019). https://doi.org/10.1016/j.specom.2019.01.005
14. Gómez, P., et al.: Glottal source biometrical signature for voice pathology detection. Speech Commun. **51**(9), 759–781 (2009). https://doi.org/10.1016/j.specom.2008.09.005
15. Hardin, J., Rocke, D.M.: The distribution of robust distances. J. Comput. Graph. Stat. **14**(4), 928–946 (2005). https://doi.org/10.1198/106186005X71217
16. Hollander, M., Wolfe, D.A., Chicken, E.: Nonparametric Statistical Methods, 3rd edn. Wiley, Hoboken (2013). https://doi.org/10.1002/9781119196037
17. Benjamini, Y., Hochberg, Y.: Controlling the false discovery rate: a practical and powerful approach to multiple testing. J. Roy. Stat. Soc.: Ser. B (Methodol.) **57**(1), 289–300 (1995). https://doi.org/10.1111/j.2517-6161.1995.tb02031.x

Slow/fast Spectral Dynamics During Active, Assisted, and Observed Hand Movements: Beyond Mu and Beta

Juan A. Barios[1,4](✉), Yolanda Vales[1], Jose M. Catalan[2], Andrea Blanco-Ivorra[3], and Nicolas Garcia-Aracil[1,2]

[1] Robotics and Artificial Intelligence Group, Miguel Hernández University, Avda. de la Universidad s/n, 03202 Elche, Spain
barios_jua@gva.es, {yvales,nicolas.garcia}@umh.es
[2] Department of Systems Engineering and Automation, Miguel Hernández University, Avda. de la Universidad s/n, 03202 Elche, Spain
jcatalan@umh.es
[3] Department of Materials Science, Optics, and Electronic Technology, Miguel Hernández University, Avda. de la Universidad s/n, 03202 Elche, Spain
ablanco@umh.es
[4] Neurophysiology Unit, San Juan Universitary Hospital, Alicante, Spain

Abstract. Background: Sensorimotor oscillations in the mu (8–12 Hz) and beta (13–30 Hz) bands typically show event-related desynchronization (ERD) during movement execution, whereas action observation usually produces weaker and less consistent suppression. In contrast, the role of slower rhythms (delta–theta) and their interaction with faster sensorimotor activity remains less well characterized, especially in exoskeleton-assisted movement.

Methods: We recorded 32-channel EEG in 20 right-handed healthy participants during unimanual and bimanual hand movements under three conditions: active execution, exoskeleton-assisted execution, and observation. Spectral analyses included band-limited power changes, a slow/fast power ratio index (2–7 Hz/8–30 Hz), and hemispheric asymmetry measures.

Results: Active execution reproduced the expected mu/beta ERD pattern, with only modest lateralization. By contrast, exoskeleton-assisted execution showed a different spectral profile, characterized by sustained delta–theta enhancement, a significantly increased slow/fast ratio throughout the movement, and a more bilateral recruitment pattern in fast frequencies. Observation produced weaker and delayed modulations, without clear lateralization. Across conditions, the slow/fast ratio separated motor states not only in amplitude but also through different temporal profiles, with earlier increases in ACT/EXO and a later peak during observation. In addition, topographic analysis of slow oscillatory activity during assisted bimanual coordination revealed a stable hemispheric asymmetry rather than a symmetric bilateral pattern, suggesting a functional hemispheric bias during joint action.

Conclusions: Beyond conventional mu/beta ERD/PMBR markers, the balance between slow and fast spectral activity provides a compact

J. M. Ferrández Vicente et al. (Eds.): IWINAC 2026, LNCS 16574, pp. 188–197, 2026.
https://doi.org/10.1007/978-3-032-27314-7_18

description of motor state. Exoskeleton assistance was associated with a specific reorganization of cortical dynamics, combining bilateral recruitment with structured hemispheric asymmetry in slow rhythms, a pattern not present during voluntary action or observation. These findings support the use of simple EEG spectral markers for the study of human–machine interaction and may be relevant for robotic rehabilitation and brain–computer interface applications.

Keywords: EEG · exoskeleton-assisted movement · slow/fast spectral ratio

1 Introduction

Human motor control is associated with state-dependent changes in cortical oscillatory activity. For decades, research has focused on event-related desynchronization (ERD) in the mu (8–12 Hz) and beta (13–30 Hz) bands during movement preparation and execution, typically followed by post-movement rebound (PMBR), that is, a movement-related synchronization (ERS) [9]. These patterns are widely considered core markers of sensorimotor cortical dynamics. Action observation can also induce modulation of sensorimotor rhythms, including mu-band suppression, as reported in EEG studies of hand-movement observation [1].

In recent years, robotic assistive devices have introduced a new context for studying motor-related brain dynamics. Exoskeleton-assisted movement is increasingly used in neurological rehabilitation [8], yet its effects on classical oscillatory markers are still not fully understood. Most previous studies have focused on mu/beta modulation during voluntary movement or motor imagery, whereas less attention has been paid to the spectral profile associated with exoskeleton-assisted execution [15]. It remains unclear whether robotic assistance generates a distinct oscillatory state and how this state differs from active movement and action observation.

A related issue concerns hemispheric lateralization. In general, mu and beta desynchronization are stronger over the hemisphere contralateral to the moving limb, reflecting motor specificity. However, this lateralized pattern may be reduced during bimanual tasks or under conditions requiring broader sensorimotor coordination, leading to more bilateral recruitment [12,14]. Whether robotic assistance preserves this contralateral bias or promotes a different spatial organization of cortical activity remains an open question [2].

These issues are also relevant for brain-computer interface (BCI) research [13]. Although mu and beta ERD are widely used in BCI systems, their expression varies substantially across individuals and often depends on clear lateralization, which can limit robustness and require subject-specific calibration. For this reason, there is interest in identifying complementary EEG markers that capture motor state more reliably and with lower inter-subject variability [7].

One possible approach is to examine the balance between slow and fast rhythms. Increasing evidence suggests that motor processing involves not only modulation in the mu and beta ranges, but also changes in slower oscillations (delta–theta), which have been linked to task transitions, sensory feedback processing, and sensorimotor state changes [3,5,10]. This balance can be summarized using a slow/fast ratio (2–7 Hz/8–30 Hz). Despite its potential as a compact integrative measure [7], this ratio has not been systematically examined across active, assisted, and observed movement conditions.

The present study addresses this issue with two main objectives. First, we compare spectral dynamics, including canonical frequency bands and the slow/fast ratio, across active execution, exoskeleton-assisted execution, and action observation. Second, we evaluate hemispheric lateralization across these motor states. We hypothesized that robotic assistance would not simply reproduce the pattern of active movement, but would instead be associated with distinct temporal dynamics, stronger slow/fast modulation, and a different spatial organization of cortical activity.

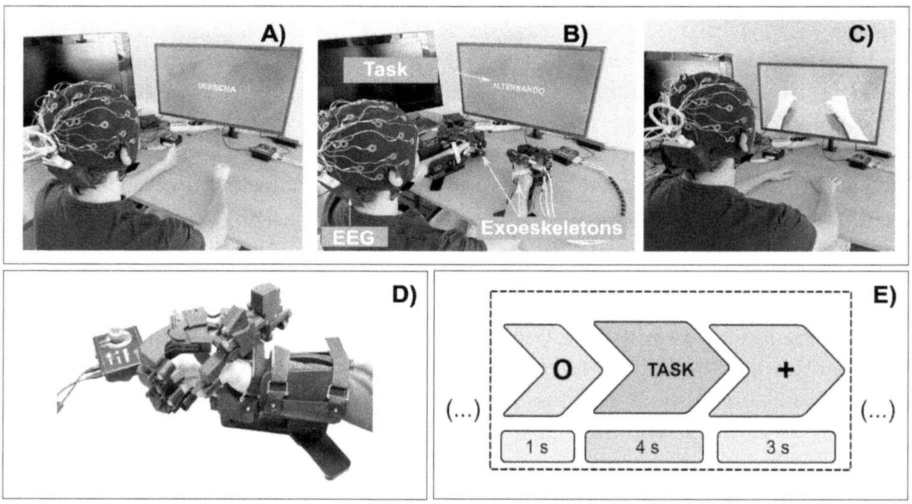

Fig. 1. Experimental setup. **A.** Active execution(ACT) **B.** Exoeskeleton-assisted execution (EXO) **C.** Observation (OBS). **D.** Modular hand exoeskeleton designed our group **E.** Structure of the task sequence repeated throughout the experimental activities. "Task" denotes one of the following conditions: RELAX, RIGHT, LEFT, TOGETHER, or ALTERNATING.

2 Materials and Methods

2.1 Participants

Twenty right-handed healthy volunteers (5 females, 15 males; age 21–38 years, mean 28,8 $\pm$ 4.95) participated in the study. All participants gave written informed consent before the experiment. The study adhered to the principles of the Declaration of Helsinki and received approval from the Ethics Committee of Miguel Hernández University (Elche, Spain; reference IB.NMGA.250113).

2.2 EEG Acquisition

EEG was recorded with a 32-channel BrainVision® LiveAmp system using Ag/AgCl electrodes placed according to the international 10–20 system. Signals were acquired at 500 Hz with electrode impedances below 10 kΩ. Stimulus presentation and synchronization were controlled with BCI2000 [11].

2.3 Exoskeleton and Task

A modular hand exoskeleton developed in our group was used for assisted finger mobilization (Fig. 1d) [6,15]. The device allowed independent movement of the index and middle fingers and of the ring-little finger pair, while the thumb remained fixed.

Participants performed the task under three conditions: active execution (ACT) (Fig. 1a, exoskeleton-assisted execution (EXO) (Fig. 1b), and observation (OBS) (Fig. 1c). Each trial lasted 7 s and included trial onset (Fig. 1), a ready signal, cue presentation, a 3 s task period starting at cue onset, and a final fixation interval. Instructions included RELAX, RIGHT, LEFT, TOGETHER, and ALTERNATING. The protocol comprised unimanual, bimanual, and mixed blocks, followed by an observation block. Active and assisted conditions were tested in separate blocks. The total session duration was approximately 64 min, and trial order was randomized within blocks.

2.4 Preprocessing and Spectral Analysis

Preprocessing was performed in EEGLAB (v18, MATLAB R2025). EEG data were band-pass filtered between 0.1 and 40 Hz, downsampled to 128 Hz, re-referenced to the common average, segmented into epochs relative to cue onset, and cleaned using independent component analysis (ICA) to remove ocular and muscular artifacts. Trials exceeding $\pm 100\ \mu$V were rejected.

Spectral analyses focused on the delta (1–3.5 Hz), theta (4–7.5 Hz), mu (8–12 Hz) and beta (13–30 Hz) bands, with special interest in C3, Cz, and C4 electrodes. Event-related desynchronization (ERD), post-movement beta rebound (PMBR), and a slow/fast power ratio (2–7 Hz/8–30 Hz) were computed across conditions. Topographical analyses were used to assess spatial distribution and hemispheric asymmetry.

2.5 Statistics

Condition differences were assessed using bin-by-bin paired t-tests. False discovery rate (FDR) correction was applied at the 0.05 level to control for multiple comparisons. Uncorrected results are reported only as exploratory.

2.6 Ocular Artifact Control

To further assess whether slow-frequency effects could be explained by blinking activity, an additional sensitivity analysis was performed. Blinks were automatically detected from a VEOG estimate derived from Fp1/Fp2 using a z-score

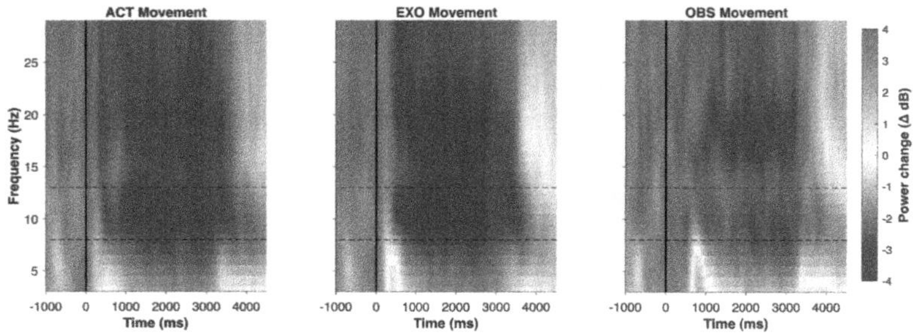

Fig. 2. Time-frequency representations of event-related spectral power. Heatmaps illustrating condition-specific power modulations (Δ dB) across the 3–29 Hz range during active (ACT), exoskeleton-assisted (EXO), and observed (OBS) movements. The data demonstrate the concurrent classical beta-band desynchronization (blue) and the prominent, sustained slow-band enhancement (red) specifically induced by robotic assistance.

threshold (> 5). Data within a ± 1 s window around each blink were replaced by channel-wise linear interpolation, and the spectral analyses were repeated. Results remained unchanged, supporting that the observed delta-band effects were not driven by ocular artifacts.

3 Results

3.1 General Spectro-Temporal Dynamics and the Slow/Fast Ratio

Time-frequency analysis over central electrodes showed consistent cue-related modulations across canonical frequency bands. Both active (ACT) and exoskeleton-assisted (EXO) execution were associated with a robust event-related desynchronization (ERD) in the alpha and beta ranges (8–30 Hz), consistent with sensorimotor activation. This pattern was weaker during action observation (OBS). In parallel, an early increase in slow-band power (2–7 Hz) was detected across conditions, although its temporal profile differed according to motor state.

To summarize the balance between slow- and fast-frequency activity, we computed a slow/fast power ratio (2–7 Hz/8–30 Hz; Fig. 3). This index differentiated the temporal evolution of the three conditions more clearly than isolated band-power measures. EXO showed the earliest increase, with a sharp initial peak, whereas ACT reached its maximum slightly later. OBS displayed the most delayed increase, emerging approximately 1 s after movement onset. After the initial transient phase (around 1500 ms), the ratio converged across conditions and remained elevated above baseline, suggesting a shared sustained state of task-related engagement despite differences in initial recruitment. Bin-by-bin statistics confirmed significant differences with respect to rest. A sensitivity analysis based on blink masking yielded comparable results, supporting that the delta-band modulation was not explained by ocular artifacts.

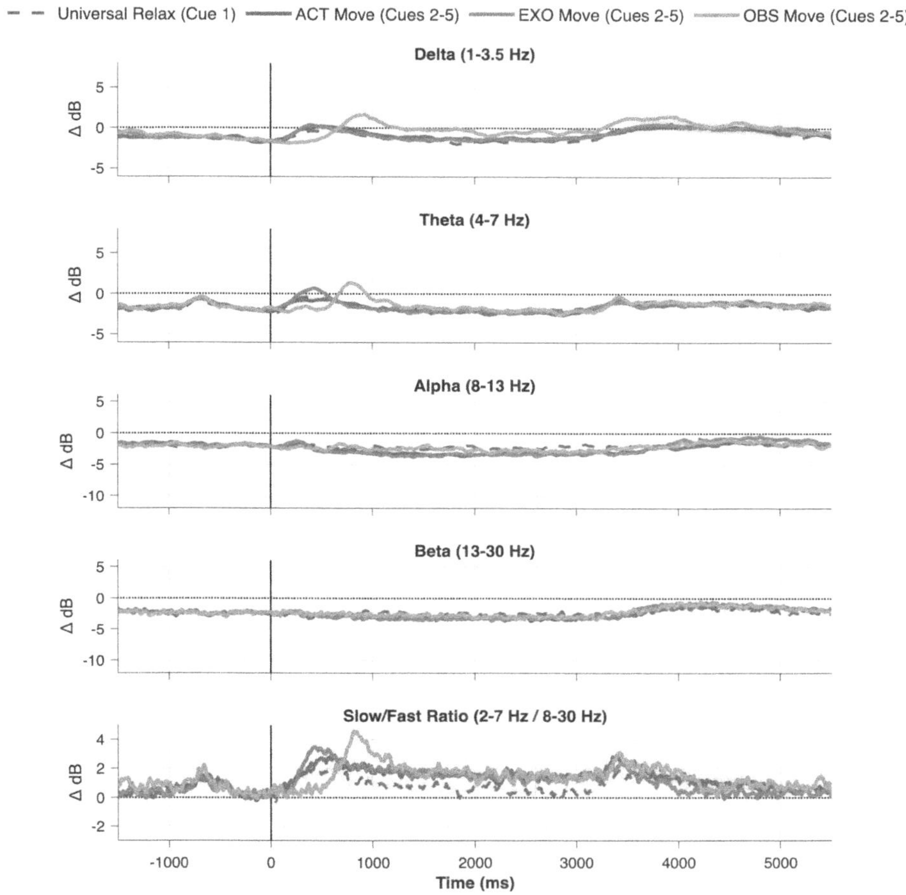

Fig. 3. Spectral power dynamics and the slow/fast ratio across motor conditions. Time-courses of task-related power variations (mean ± SEM) over central electrodes (C3, Cz, C4, CP3, CP4), time-locked to movement onset (0 ms). Top panels show modulations in canonical frequency bands (Delta 2–4 Hz, Theta 4–7 Hz, Alpha 8–13 Hz, Beta 13–30 Hz), including the expected alpha/beta event-related desynchronization (ERD) together with slow-band enhancements. The bottom panel shows the slow/fast power ratio (2–7 Hz/8–30 Hz), which differentiates the temporal evolution of EXO, ACT, and OBS. Black markers along the x-axis indicate significant differences ($p < 0.05$, paired t-tests) between rest and active/assisted conditions.

3.2 Spatial Distribution and Beta-Band Lateralization

Spatial analysis of relative power revealed distinct recruitment patterns across conditions, while time-frequency representations confirmed the broad spectral nature of these changes (Fig. 2). During active execution, beta ERD was centered over the contralateral sensorimotor cortex (C3 for right-hand movements, C4 for

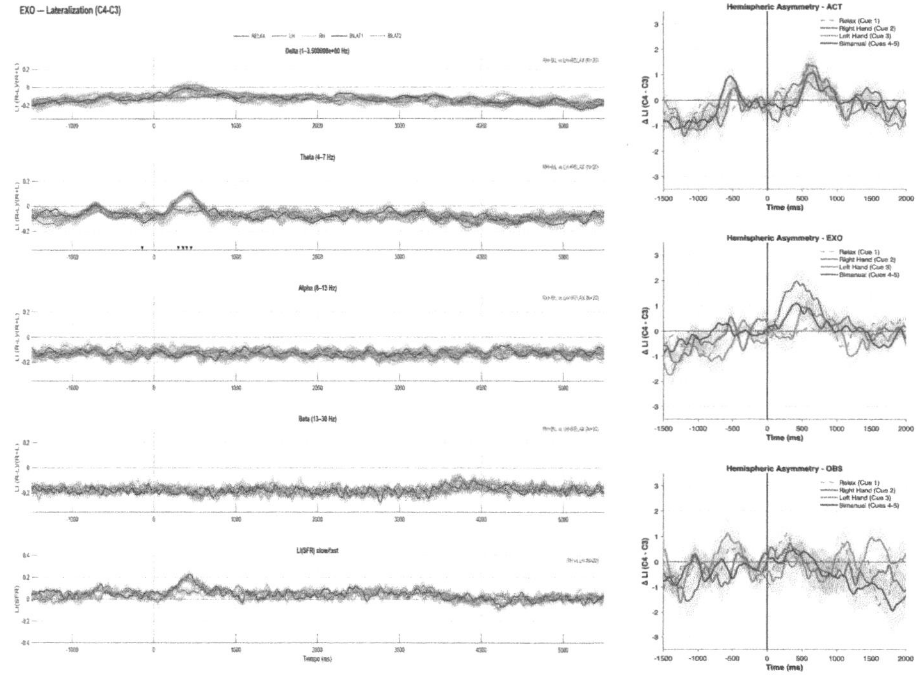

Fig. 4. Hemispheric asymmetry and leader hemisphere dynamics in slow oscillations. *Left:* Topographical lateralization analysis of delta/theta power dynamics during unimanual and bimanual exoskeleton-assisted execution. Rather than a fully symmetric bilateral distribution, slow-wave activity during exoskeleton-assisted movement exhibits a stable hemispheric bias, summarized in the bar plots. *Right:* Temporal dynamics (0–1000 ms) of the lateralization index (ΔLI = C4 - C3) in the slow band (1–7 Hz) across active execution (ACT, top), exoskeleton-assisted movement (EXO, middle), and action observation (OBS, bottom). The overlay reveals that the emergence of the leader hemisphere pattern during bimanual coordination (purple line tracking the dominant hand) is specifically driven by robotic assistance, while no lateralization pattern is observed in the voluntary and observed conditions.

left-hand movements), although this lateralization was modest and coexisted with a bilateral component. In EXO, beta desynchronization was more bilateral and spatially extended, together with increased slow-wave activity over fronto-central regions. OBS produced weaker and more diffuse modulations, with no clear lateralized pattern.

When the lateralization index (ΔLI) was quantified in the early movement window (200–1000 ms), significant effects were found mainly in the delta band. Delta lateralization was significant in EXO (mean = 0.055, 95% CI [0.034, 0.076], dz = 1.22, $p < 0.001$), ACT (dz = 0.71, $p = 0.007$), and OBS (dz = 0.48, $p = 0.046$). Early beta-band lateralization effects were smaller and did not survive

FDR correction. The proportion of participants showing contralateral delta bias (ΔLI > 0) was highest in EXO (90%), followed by ACT (75%) and OBS (65%).

3.3 Slow-Band Asymmetry During Assisted Movement

Although beta ERD tended to become more bilateral during robotic assistance, slow oscillations (delta/theta, 2–7 Hz) showed a different spatial pattern. During unimanual EXO conditions, sustained slow-band power increases were shifted toward the hemisphere contralateral to the moving hand. This asymmetry was more evident than that observed in alpha or beta activity.

A related finding emerged during bimanual coordination. In synchronous and alternating EXO conditions, the increase in delta/theta power was not symmetrically distributed across hemispheres. Instead, the topography showed a stable hemispheric bias that resembled the pattern observed for dominant-hand movements, despite the bilateral motor demand (Fig. 4). This result suggests that slow oscillatory recruitment during assisted bimanual coordination is not fully symmetric, but follows a reproducible asymmetric organization.

4 Discussion, Limitations, and Future Work

The present study shows that active, exoskeleton-assisted, and observed movements are associated with distinct spectro-temporal patterns. As expected, canonical mu and beta ERD tracked basic sensorimotor engagement [9]. However, the slow/fast power ratio (2–7 Hz/8–30 Hz) provided a more compact description of motor state and differentiated the temporal evolution of the three conditions more clearly than isolated band-power measures. ACT and EXO showed an early increase in this ratio after movement onset, whereas OBS displayed a distinct temporal profile with a later and sharper peak. After the initial transient phase, all three conditions converged into a sustained elevation above baseline, suggesting a shared state of ongoing task-related engagement despite differences in early recruitment.

From a spatial perspective, robotic assistance was associated with a broader and more bilateral beta desynchronization than voluntary movement. At the same time, slow oscillations showed a different organization. During unimanual EXO, slow-band activity was shifted toward the contralateral hemisphere. During assisted bimanual coordination, delta/theta enhancement did not become fully symmetric, but instead showed a stable hemispheric bias resembling the dominant-hand pattern. We interpret this result cautiously as evidence of asymmetric functional organization during assisted joint action, rather than as proof of a fixed "leader hemisphere". This interpretation is compatible with previous work on interhemispheric coordination and handedness [12,14].

These findings may also be relevant from a translational perspective. Because the slow/fast ratio condenses slow-frequency enhancement and fast-frequency suppression into a single parameter, it may be useful as a complementary EEG feature for motor-state characterization and for future BCI-related applications [7,13]. In addition, the sustained slow-band enhancement observed during robotic assistance suggests that the exoskeleton is associated with a reproducible cortical state linked to continuous sensorimotor monitoring, rather than acting only as a passive mechanical support [15]. This possibility may be of interest for robotic rehabilitation [2,8], although its clinical significance remains to be established.

Several limitations should be acknowledged. The sample size and the number of trials per condition were moderate. In addition, the absence of eye-tracking limits the interpretation of the delayed OBS response, since visual attention is known to influence these rhythms [4]. Finally, although the observed topographical asymmetries suggest a stable hemispheric bias, this remains an inference based on spectral power distribution. Ongoing work in our group is currently extending the present approach using connectivity-based analyses, including directional phase metrics. This next step will clarify whether the dominant spatial pattern reflects coordinated interhemispheric interactions during robotic assistance, building upon the spectral foundation established here.

5 Conclusions

These results extend the classical focus on mu and beta rhythms by showing that the interaction between slow and fast oscillations provides additional information about motor-state organization. Robotic assistance was associated not only with changes in this spectral balance, but also with a different pattern of lateralization, including stronger contralateral slow-wave recruitment and a stable hemispheric bias during assisted bimanual coordination.

From a translational perspective, the slow/fast power ratio and slow-wave spatial asymmetry may represent useful EEG-derived features for motor-state characterization. Both measures are simple to compute and may be relevant for future rehabilitation and BCI applications. In particular, the condition-dependent peaks of the slow/fast ratio suggest that this index may help identify relevant temporal transitions during human–machine interaction.

Taken together, these findings support a broader view of movement-related neurophysiology in which slow oscillatory dynamics complement conventional ERD/PMBR markers.

Disclosure of Interests. The authors have no competing interests to declare that are relevant to the content of this article.

Availability of Data and Materials. The datasets generated and/or analyzed during the current study are available from the corresponding author upon reasonable request.

References

1. Avanzini, P., et al.: The dynamics of sensorimotor cortical oscillations during the observation of hand movements: an EEG study. PLoS ONE **7**(5), e37534 (2012)
2. Barios, J.A., et al.: Movement-related EEG oscillations of contralesional hemisphere discloses compensation mechanisms of severely affected motor chronic stroke patients. Int. J. Neural Syst. **31**(12), 2150053 (2021)
3. Barios, J.A., et al.: Synchronization of slow cortical rhythms during motor imagery-based brain-machine interface control. Int. J. Neural Syst. **29**(05), 1850045 (2019)
4. Chye, S., Valappil, A.C., Wright, D.J., et al.: The effects of combined action observation and motor imagery on corticospinal excitability and movement outcomes: two meta-analyses. Neurosci. Biobehav. Rev. **143**, 104911 (2022)
5. Hamel-Thibault, A., Thénault, F., Whittingstall, K., Bernier, P.M.: Delta-band oscillations in motor regions predict hand selection for reaching. Cereb. Cortex **28**(2), 574–584 (2018)
6. iDRhA: Innovative Devices for Rehabilitation & Assistance. https://idrha.es/ (2019). Accessed 28 Feb 2024
7. Lanzone, J., Colombo, M., Sarasso, S., et al.: EEG spectral exponent as a synthetic index for the longitudinal assessment of stroke recovery. Clin. Neurophysiol. **137**, 92–101 (2022)
8. Lum, P.S., Godfrey, S.B., Brokaw, E.B., Holley, R.J., Nichols, D.: Robotic approaches for rehabilitation of hand function after stroke. Am. J. Phys. Med. Rehabil. **91**(11), S242–S254 (2012)
9. Pfurtscheller, G., Da Silva, F.L.: Event-related EEG/MEG synchronization and desynchronization: basic principles. Clin. Neurophysiol. **110**(11), 1842–1857 (1999)
10. Ray, A.M., Figueiredo, T.D., López-Larraz, E., Birbaumer, N., Ramos-Murguialday, A.: Brain oscillatory activity as a biomarker of motor recovery in chronic stroke. Hum. Brain Mapp. **41**(5), 1296–1308 (2020)
11. Schalk, G., McFarland, D.J., Hinterberger, T., Birbaumer, N., Wolpaw, J.R.: BCI 2000: a general-purpose brain-computer interface (BCI) system. IEEE Trans. Biomed. Eng. **51**(6), 1034–1043 (2004)
12. Serrien, D.J., Ivry, R.B., Swinnen, S.P.: Dynamics of hemispheric specialization and integration in the context of motor control. Nat. Rev. Neurosci. **7**(2), 160–166 (2006)
13. Soekadar, S.R., Birbaumer, N., Slutzky, M.W., Cohen, L.G.: Brain-machine interfaces in neurorehabilitation of stroke. Neurobiol. Dis. **83**, 172–179 (2015)
14. Swinnen, S.P.: Intermanual coordination: from behavioural principles to neural-network interactions. Nat. Rev. Neurosci. **3**(5), 348–359 (2002)
15. Vales, Y., Catalan, J.M., Blanco-Ivorra, A., Barios, J.A., Garcia-Aracil, N.: Comprehensive evaluation of stroke rehabilitation dynamics: Integrating brain-computer interface with robotized orthesic hand. Lect. Notes Comput. Sci. **2**(2), 171–181 (2024)

Computational Intelligence Approaches to Autism Spectrum Disorder Detection Using Eye-Tracking: A State-of-the-Art Analysis

Carlos Sánchez[1,2(✉)], Gema Benedicto[1,2], and José Manuel Ferrández[1,2]

[1] Department of Electronics, Computer Technology and Projects, Universidad Politécnica de Cartagena, Cartagena, Spain
carlos.sanchez5@edu.upct.es, jm.ferrandez@upct.es

[2] ECT Lab+, European University of Technology, Cartagena, European Union, Colombia

Abstract. Autism Spectrum Disorder (ASD) is a heterogeneous neurodevelopmental condition whose early diagnosis often depends on subjective behavioural assessments. Eye-tracking has emerged as an objective tool for capturing atypical visual attention patterns associated with ASD, while recent advances in Machine Learning enable automated analysis of gaze data. However, existing studies show substantial heterogeneity in datasets, experimental paradigms, feature extraction, and evaluation protocols, limiting comparability and clinical transferability.

This paper presents a structured state-of-the-art review of AI-based eye-tracking approaches for ASD detection published between 2020 and 2025. Thirty-four studies were comparatively analyzed to identify methodological trends, performance patterns, and current limitations, outlining key challenges toward robust and clinically applicable screening systems.

Keywords: Autism Spectrum Disorder · Eye-Tracking · Computational Intelligence · Machine Learning

1 Introduction

Autism Spectrum Disorder (ASD) is a heterogeneous neurodevelopmental condition characterized by deficits in social communication and restricted or repetitive behaviours [32]. Early identification is essential, as timely intervention improves long-term outcomes. However, current diagnostic procedures rely on expert-based behavioral assessments and clinical observation, which are time-consuming and inherently subjective [2].

Eye-tracking has emerged as a promising objective approach for ASD screening, as atypical visual attention patterns are consistently reported in affected individuals [1]. Eye movements provide quantifiable indicators of attentional and

J. M. Ferrández Vicente et al. (Eds.): IWINAC 2026, LNCS 16574, pp. 198–209, 2026.
https://doi.org/10.1007/978-3-032-27314-7_19

cognitive processes, making them potential behavioral biomarkers. Advances in portable eye-tracking systems have further facilitated data collection in laboratory and semi-naturalistic contexts.

In parallel, Artificial Intelligence (AI) techniques have enabled automated analysis of gaze data. Both classical Machine Learning (ML) methods (e.g., Support Vector Machines (SVM), Random Forests (RF) and k-Nearest Neighbours (kNN)) and Deep Learning (DL) architectures (e.g., Convolutional Neural Networks (CNNs) and transformer-based models) have been applied to scanpaths, fixation maps, and gaze trajectories, supporting classification approaches [8,12].

However, studies remain methodologically heterogeneous, limiting comparability and clinical applicability. To address this gap, we provide a structured review of AI-based eye-tracking approaches for ASD detection (2020âĂŞ2025), highlighting methodological trends, recurrent limitations and open challenges for clinically reliable screening systems.

2 Background

2.1 Autism Spectrum Disorder and Visual Attention

One of the most consistently reported findings in ASD research concerns atypical visual attention. Individuals with ASD often exhibit reduced attention to socially salient stimuli such as faces and biological motion, and increased attention to non-social or peripheral elements of a scene [10].

Visual attention differences are especially evident during tasks involving social interaction, emotion recognition, or free viewing of complex scenes. For example, compared to typically developing (TD) individuals, participants with ASD tend to spend less time fixating on the eye region and more time on the mouth, objects, or background elements. These differences are measurable and quantifiable, making eye-tracking a powerful and objective tool for studying attentional patterns in ASD.

2.2 Eye-Tracking Metrics and Areas of Interest

Eye-tracking technology provides fine-grained spatiotemporal data. Raw gaze coordinates are typically processed into higher-level variables [17]:

1. **Fixations**: Periods during which the gaze remains relatively stable over a location. Key fixation-based features include fixation duration, fixation count, mean fixation duration, and time to first fixation.
2. **Saccades**: Rapid eye movements between fixations. Relevant saccadic features include saccade amplitude, velocity, and scanpath length. Saccade patterns provide information about exploration strategies and attentional shifts.
3. **Areas of Interest (AOIs)**: Predefined regions within a stimulus (e.g., eyes, mouth, objects). AOI-based variables such as total dwell time, proportion of fixation time, number of revisits, and transition probabilities between AOIs allow researchers to quantify attention allocation.

These variables enable the characterization of both spatial (where attention is directed) and temporal (how attention evolves over time) aspects of gaze behavior. AOI-based comparisons between social and non-social regions are particularly informative for identifying atypical attentional profiles.

2.3 Why Machine Learning is Suitable

The analysis of eye-tracking data in ASD presents several methodological challenges. First, gaze data are high-dimensional, consisting of multiple correlated temporal and spatial features. Second, attentional patterns are heterogeneous across individuals with ASD, reflecting the spectrum nature of the condition.

ML methods are well-suited to address these challenges. Unlike traditional statistical approaches that rely on predefined hypotheses and low-dimensional comparisons, ML algorithms can model complex, multivariate relationships and capture non-linear interactions among features. Supervised learning techniques can be trained to classify individuals (e.g., ASD vs. TD) based on gaze-derived features. Feature selection and regularization methods further help identify the most informative eye-tracking variables. Moreover, ML approaches can integrate heterogeneous data sources (e.g., fixation metrics, saccadic dynamics, AOI transitions) into a unified predictive framework. This data-driven perspective enables the discovery of patterns.

3 Methodology of the Review

The search was restricted to publications between 2020 and 2025. This period was selected to capture recent methodological advances, particularly the increasing integration of ML and AI techniques in ASD-related eye-tracking research.

3.1 Database and Search Strategy

The primary database used for this review was **Scopus**, which served as the central source due to its broad interdisciplinary coverage and indexing of high-impact journals. The query used was:

> ("autism spectrum disorder" OR autism OR ASD) AND
> ("eye-tracking" OR "eye tracking" OR "gaze tracking") AND
> ("computational intelligence" OR "machine learning" OR "artificial intelligence" OR classification)

3.2 Study Selection Criteria

Inclusion criteria were: journal articles published between 2020 and 2025 and written in English. **Exclusion criteria** were: review papers, editorials, or theoretical discussions without empirical data; studies not involving ASD populations; works using eye-tracking without computational modeling; studies focused solely on hardware development; and duplicates.

The initial search yielded 102 articles. After a detailed review of the abstracts and the application of the criteria, **34 studies** were considered aligned with the objectives and scope of this review and were therefore selected for further analysis. The selection process followed a structured and reproducible filtering strategy to ensure clarity and methodological rigor.

4 State of the Art

This section summarizes and compares the most relevant studies published between 2020 and 2025. Table 1 provides a structured overview of these works. The reported columns include: (i) reference and year of publication; (ii) eye-tracking device used; (iii) sampling frequency; (iv) device invasiveness; (v) portability and calibration requirements; (vi) number of participants (split into ASD and control groups); (vii) age range of the population; (viii) type of stimuli or experimental task; (ix) extracted eye-tracking features (e.g., fixations, saccades, AOI-based metrics); (x) computational method applied; (xi) performance metrics and reported results (e.g., accuracy, AUC, F1-score); and (xii) session duration. This structured comparison facilitates the identification of methodological trends, technological constraints and existing research gaps.

5 Discussion

The comparative overview presented in Table 1 highlights clear methodological regularities in AI-based eye-tracking studies for ASD detection, but also exposes structural limitations that help explain the wide dispersion in reported performance. In what follows, we discuss these patterns with emphasis on comparability, sources of performance inflation, and factors affecting clinical transferability.

5.1 Hardware and Sampling Frequency

Most recent works rely on screen-based or remote eye-trackers operating at moderate sampling rates (typically 60–120 Hz), with fewer studies using high-frequency systems ($\geq$ 250 Hz). While high sampling rates improve temporal resolution and allow more reliable characterization of saccade dynamics and fine-grained oculomotor signatures, moderate-rate devices are frequently selected due to their affordability, shorter setup time, and easier calibration, particularly in pediatric populations. This reflects a pragmatic trade-off between precision and feasibility: screening-oriented tools require robustness under non-ideal conditions (movement, reduced compliance, limited calibration time), sometimes at the cost of richer oculomotor descriptors.

A relevant trend from 2021 onwards is the exploration of camera-based solutions (smartphones, tablets, standard cameras) aimed at improving accessibility and scalability. These approaches are promising for real-world deployment, but their validity depends critically on reliable head pose estimation, illumination control, and calibration strategies. Therefore, the field is currently split between (i) controlled, high-fidelity laboratory setups yielding cleaner signals and (ii) scalable, potentially noisier systems better aligned with clinical screening contexts. Future benchmarking should explicitly stratify results by acquisition modality and expected noise levels, as these factors directly affect feature stability and model generalization.

Table 1. Comparative overview of AI-based eye-tracking studies for ASD detection published between 2020 and 2025, including hardware specifications, experimental paradigms, extracted gaze features, computational models, participant characteristics, and reported performance metrics. NR: Not reported.

Reference (Year)	Device	Freq (Hz)	Portability & calibration	N by condition	Age	Variables analyzed	Software	Main results	Experimental task type	Session duration
Kang et al. (2020) [1]	Tobii TX300	300	Desktop-based, 5-point calibration	Total: 157 (77 ASD, 80 TD)	3–6	Coordinate frequency distribution (64 AOIs per face)	Tobii Studio, SVM, mRMR, K-means	84.17% accuracy, 0.89 AUC (Combined faces)	Face processing (Own-race vs. Other-race faces)	3 min (stimuli only)
Vabalas et al. (2020) [2]	EyeLink 1000 Plus and Polhemus Fastrak (Kinematic)	120 (Kinematic)	Desktop-based, NR calibration points	Total: 44 (22 ASD, 22 TD adults)	Adults (Mean age ≈ 30)	Kinematics (velocity, acceleration, jerk, amplitude) and Gaze behavior (saccades, attention)	MATLAB, Python (Scikit-learn), Libsvm, SVM (RBF kernel)	78% accuracy (Combined), 73% (Kinematic), 70% (Eye)	Movement imitation task (point-to-point sequences)	NR
Yaneva et al. (2020) [3]	Gazepoint GP3 video-based eye tracker	60	Desktop-based, 9-point calibration	Total: 68 (28 ASD, 40 Control)	Adults (18+, age ≈ 32–41)	Fixations, Time to First View, Time Viewed (s/%), and Revisits	R (Logistic Regression), Gazepoint built-in algorithm	75% accuracy (Search task), 74% accuracy (overall detection)	Web-page processing (Browse, Search, and Synthesis tasks)	30–120 s per page
Chang et al. (2021) [4]	iPhone/iPad frontal camera	30 fps	Portable, No calibration needed	Total: 993 (40 ASD, 936 TD, 17 DD)	16–38 months	Social preference (percentage right), silhouette scores, and gaze-speech correlation	Python (Scikit-learn), iTracker, IntraFace, Decision Tree	0.90 AUC (combined iPad features)	Social preference and gaze-speech coordination movies	<10 min
Cilia et al. (2021) [5]	SMI RED250 remote eye tracker	250	Screen-based (Remote), 5-point calibration	Total: 59 (29 ASD, 30 TD)	8 (Mean age)	Scanpath images with velocity-encoded color gradients	Python (Keras, OpenCV), CNN	90% accuracy, 83% sensitivity, 0.90 AUC (Image-based); 71% accuracy (test)	Social cognition (Joint attention, faces, cartoons)	10 min
He et al. (2021) [6]	Tobii X120 eye tracker	120	Desktop-based, 5-point calibration	Total: 74 (26 HFA, 24 LFA, 24 TD)	5 (Mean: 4.98–5.24)	68 features (Spatial gaze distributions: mean, SD, skewness, kurtosis, etc.)	MatLab (Psychtoolbox), KNN algorithm, SPSS	81.1% accuracy (3-group), 93.2% accuracy (Binary: ASD vs TD)	Computerized visual-orienting task (Social vs. Non-social cues)	15 min
Oliveira et al. (2021) [7]	Tobii Pro TX300	300	Desktop-based, 5-point calibration	Total: 106 (76 ASD, 30 TD)	3–18	Visual Attention Models and 15 pixel-based features (motion, faces, center distance)	MatLab 2015a, ANN, Genetic Algorithm	90% precision, 93% specificity, 69% sensitivity, 0.822 AUC	Biological motion (children interactions) vs. Geometric motion (fractals)	54 s
Zhao et al. (2021) [8]	Tobii Pro Glasses 2 (Head-mounted)	50	Portable (Head-mounted), NR calibration points	Total: 39 (19 ASD, 20 TD)	6–13	Visual fixation percentage (eyes, mouth, face, body) and session length	SVM, LDA, DT, RF, Tobii Pro Lab	92.31% accuracy, 84.21% sensitivity, 100% specificity (SVM)	Face-to-face structured conversation (4 sessions)	Variable (used as a feature)
Ahmed et al. (2022) [9]	Eye-tracking dataset (Figshare)	NR	NR	Total: 547 images (219 ASD, 328 TD)	Children	Scanpath visual patterns (LBP and GLCM features) and deep feature maps	ANN, FFNN, GoogleNet, ResNet-18, SVM	99.8% accuracy (FFNN and ANN models)	Atypical visual attention (Scanning eye projection points on images)	NR
AlcaÃśiz et al. (2022) [10]	Tobii Pro Glasses 2 (Head-mounted)	NR	Portable, calibrated in-situ (2D CAVE system)	Total: 55 (35 ASD, 20 TD)	4–7	144 features (Frames on AOIs: faces, bodies, people, static/dynamic items)	R: SVM, RF, XGBoost, NaÃ¯ve Bayes, kNN	86% accuracy, 91% sensitivity (SVM model)	Immersive VR mall exploration (social/non-social stimuli)	24 min 45 s
Kong et al. (2022) [11]	SMI RED250 portable eye tracker	250	Portable, 5-point calibration	Total: 173 (92 ASD, 81 TD)	1.5–5	Fixation time percentage on eyes, mouth, biological motion, and moving objects	BeGaze, R-studio, Support Vector Machine (SVM)	80% accuracy (Toddlers), 71% accuracy (Preschoolers)	Social stimuli (faces, biological motion) vs. non-social objects	NR
Ozdemir et al. (2022) [12]	SMI-Red250 remote eye tracker	250	Desktop-based (Lab), 5-point calibration	Total: 133 (61 ASD, 72 TD)	2–3 (26–36 months)	Net Dwell Time, Diversion Duration, First Fixation Duration, and Fixation Count	WEKA (RF, SVM, NB, DT)	87.5% accuracy, 0.888 ROC (Random Forest model)	Preferential viewing (Social interaction vs. toys or animations)	2 min
Ahmed et al. (2023) [13]	RED mobile eye tracker	60	Portable (Screen-based), NR calibration	Total: 59 (29 ASD, 30 TD)	7.88 (Mean age)	Fixations, saccades, blink rate, and gaze vectors	LSTM, CNN-LSTM, Bi-LSTM, GRU (TensorFlow)	98.33% accuracy, 98% AUC (LSTM model)	Static images and dynamic videos (social/non-social)	5 min
Atyabi et al. (2023) [14]	Eye-tracking system (NR)	NR	Desktop-based, NR calibration	Total: 86 (54 ASD, 32 TD)	0–18+ (with sub-groups)	Spatial and spatiotemporal scanpaths, temporal info, and eye-gaze velocity	CNN, DNN	80.25% accuracy (Spatio-Temporal velocity-fused model)	Naturalistic social tasks (AM, SR, ToM, and DB)	NR (analyzed in 3s segments)
Alarifi et al. (2023) [15]	Tobii Pro Fusion	120	Screen-based (Desktop), NR calibration points	Total: 104 (63 ASD, 41 TD)	1.8–22 (Mean ≈ 8)	Dwell time (eyes, face sides, objects) and Time to First Fixation (TTFF)	iMotions 8.3, Python (RF, LSTM), RStudio	76% accuracy, 0.80 F1-score (Random Forest model)	Face perception and Joint Attention (JA) tasks with cartoon stimuli	NR
Franco et al. (2023) [16]	Tobii Pro Fusion	250	Screen-based, 5-point calibration	Total: 77 (33 ASD, 44 TD)	3–16	Saliency maps, three-level features (color, shape, faces), and fixation maps	MatLab 2015a, RF, NN, SVM, Tobii ProLab	0.95 AUC (previous dataset) and 0.74 AUC (new dataset) using RF	Visual preference paradigm (Social vs. Geometric videos)	41 s (video length)
Meng et al. (2023) [17]	SMI RED500 remote eye tracker	500	Desktop-based, 5-point calibration	Total: 161 (117 ASD, 44 TD)	12–60 months	Fixation/saccade metrics (688 features), AOI dwell time, and glance duration	Random Forest (RF), Logistic Regression, Python	73% accuracy, 0.81 AUC	Social stimuli (Cartoon vs. Real people videos)	NR
Zhao et al. (2023) [18]	Tobii Pro Glasses 2	50	Portable, 1-point calibration	Total: 39 (19 ASD, 20 TD)	6–13	Entropy and range of gaze allocation (x, y, and x-y plane)	SVM (FFS), Tobii Pro Lab	87.18% accuracy, 89.47% sensitivity (7-s segments)	Face-to-face structured conversation	110–191 s
Alsaidi et al. (2024) [19]	SMI RED-m remote eye tracker	250	Portable (Remote), NR calibration	Total: 59 (29 ASD, 30 TD)	8 (Mean age)	Eye-tracking scan paths (spatial and temporal patterns)	T-CNN-ASD (Keras/TensorFlow), OpenCV	95.59% accuracy, 77.60% sensitivity, 78.73 F1-score	Viewing videos (balloons, characters, and live host)	NR
Benabderrahmane et al. (2024) [20]	RED mobile eye tracker	60	Portable, NR calibration	Total: 59 (29 ASD, 30 TD)	3–13	Gaze maps, distance sequences, fixation/saccade durations, and fixation rate	PyTorch (CNN-GRU-ANN)	86.71% accuracy, 93.10% precision, 0.87 AUC	Social cognition stimuli (static photos and dynamic videos)	5 min
Colonnese et al. (2024) [21]	Tobii T120 (screen-based)	120	Desktop-based (Lab), NR calibration	Total: 28 (14 ASD, 14 TD)	5–12	Scanpaths (x, y, duration), fixation maps, and heatmaps	GBAC (CNN + LSTM), PyTorch, TracIn	94.35% accuracy, 0.9315 F1-score (SIST model)	Free-viewing of 300 visual stimuli (Saliency4ASD)	NR
Lencastre et al. (2024) [22]	SMI Red-M remote eye tracker	60	Portable (Remote desktop setup)	Total: 57 (28 ASD, 29 TD)	3–12	Visited area, log-velocity, and fixation-to-saccade probability	Python (tsai library), InceptionTime	93.9% accuracy, 95.1% sensitivity (using 5s of data)	Joint attention (actress pointing at objects)	5 s
Mumenin et al. (2024) [23]	SMI RED mobile / Tobii T120	120	Portable and Desktop-based, NR calibration	Total: 87 (44 ASD, 43 TD in 2 datasets)	3–13	Scanpath (SP), Fixation Map (FM), and Heatmap (HM) images	ASDNet (Involutional NN), TensorFlow	98.12% (SP), 96.83% (FM), 97.61% (HM) accuracy	Social stimuli and natural scene viewing (Saliency4ASD)	NR
SÃ¡ et al. (2024) [24]	Tobii Pro TX300 gaze tracker	300	Desktop-based (Lab), NR calibration	Total: 86 (56 ASD, 30 TD)	3–18	Anticipation features (time of first visit/fixation), ROI distances, and gaze durations	Python (sklearn), Heterogeneous Stacking Ensemble (HSE)	95.5% F1-score, 90.7% accuracy, 95.4% sensitivity	Joint Attention (JA) paradigm with dynamic floating ROIs	30 s
Wei et al. (2024) [25]	Tobii 4C binocular eye tracker	90	Desktop-based, 9-point calibration	Total: 529 (290 ASD, 239 TD)	1.5–6.0	Fixation duration, saccade velocity, fixation latency, and pursuit duration	Python 3.7 (RF, SVM, XGB, ANN, LR)	0.849 AUC, 82.2% sensitivity, 76.5% accuracy (Random Forest model)	Social (joint attention) and non-social (pursuit, executive function) tasks	3 min
Zhou et al. (2024) [26]	Tobii Eye Tracker 4C	90	Desktop-based, 5-point calibration	Total: 95 (54 ASD, 41 TD)	1–12 years	Scanpath features (x_pos, y_pos, duration, and velocity)	LSTM, GRU, BiLSTM, MultiMatch, DTW	97% accuracy (LSTM with x, y, d features)	Viewing emotional facial images (34s video segment)	4 min
Al-Adhaileh et al. (2025) [27]	SMI RED mobile eye tracker	60	Portable (screen-based), NR calibration	Total: 59 (29 ASD, 30 TD)	7.88 (Mean age)	Tracking ratio, gaze coordinates, fixation patterns, and saccadic movements	CNN-LSTM, LSTM, Adam optimizer	99.78% accuracy, 99.83% F1-score (CNN-LSTM hybrid model)	Social attention tasks (static images and dynamic videos)	5 min
Antolí et al. (2025) [28]	Tobii X2-30 remote eye-tracker	30	Screen-based (Laptop), 9-point calibration	Total: 93 (24 ASD, 25 DLD, 44 TD)	2.6–6 years (32–74 months)	Fixation duration, visit count, visit duration, and latency (156 metrics total)	Tobii Studio, Naive Bayes, LMT	0.86 F1-score (ASD vs. TD), 0.91 F1-score (DLD vs. TD)	Visual preference task (Social vs. Non-social pairing)	3.6 min
Cheekaty & Muneeswari (2025) [29]	SMI RED250 portable eye tracker	250	Portable, 5-point calibration	Total: 40 ASD (split by severity)	8–12	Fixation duration, scanpath velocity, and spatial distribution	SMI BeGaze, MATLAB, TensorFlow/PyTorch	97% accuracy, 98.24% recall, 97.04% F1-score (CNN-RNN hybrid)	Silent video of a woman articulating letters	2 min
Hudry et al. (2025) [30]	Gazefinder (JVCKENWOOD Corp.)	50	Desktop eye-tracker, 5-point calibration	Total: 196 (96 ASD, 100 TD)	2–4 years (24–60 months)	Gaze fixation durations, overall tracking rate	Gazefinder Software ('Scene 10A'), Stata, R	76% accuracy, 0.82 AUC (82% sens, 70% spec)	Social vs. Non-social scenes, faces, and joint attention	2 min 15s
Setu (2025) [31]	Tobii T120 screen-based	120	Desktop-based (Lab)	Total: 28 (14 ASD, 14 TD)	5–12	Saccade amplitude, saccade duration, and gaze speed	Scikit-learn, PyTorch/TensorFlow	81% test accuracy, 0.89–0.90 AUC (SVM/FNN/GRU)	Free-viewing of natural scene images (Saliency4ASD)	NR
Soloh et al. (2025) [32]	Standard camera (no dedicated eye-tracker)	NR	Mobile-compatible; 16-point geometric calibration	Total: 3013 imÃ¡genes (1238 ASD, 1775 TD)	Children	Gaze trajectories, scanpath images	MediaPipe Face Mesh + CNN	97.01% accuracy, 0.98 AUC	Scanpath-based visual stimulus (ETSP)	NR
Xia et al. (2025) [33]	Desktop camera & Smartphone	140	Desktop and Portable (Smartphone), NR calibration	Total: 222 (110 ASD, 112 TD)	2–8	Deep spatiotemporal facial cues, global attention-based features	Vision Transformer (ViT), Longformer, MediaPipe	96.86% (Desktop) and 90.67% (Mobile) accuracy	Free-viewing of facial and natural stimuli	3–4 min
Zhang et al. (2025) [34]	SMI IView X RED eye tracker	120	Desktop-based, 5-point calibration	Total: 59 (33 ASD, 26 TD)	2–6	Gaze patterns (fixation location/duration), scanpaths, heatmaps	UASN (ResNet-50 + LSTM)	93.2% accuracy, 0.978 AUC (CI paradigm)	Contrastive image-viewing (Social vs. Nonsocial)	5 min

5.2 Experimental Paradigms and Ecological Validity

A strong predominance of social attention paradigms persists across studies, including face viewing, emotion recognition, joint attention, and socially rich videos. This aligns with robust evidence that ASD is associated with atypical allocation of attention to social cues. However, the heavy reliance on socially oriented paradigms can introduce two issues.

First, it may narrow the scope of detectable ASD-related variability, potentially underrepresenting subgroups whose social attention patterns are less atypical or compensated. Second, many paradigms implicitly encode task-specific priors (e.g., a stimulus design that forces attention shifts to predefined AOIs), increasing separability within a controlled task but reducing generalization. In contrast, more naturalistic tasks (e.g., free-viewing in complex scenes, immersive environments, or face-to-face interaction) may better approximate real-world behavior but often produce noisier signals and smaller effect sizes, which can lead to more modest but potentially more realistic performance.

Furthermore, session duration varies widely (seconds to tens of minutes), and several studies extract features from short time windows. Short windows are appealing for rapid screening, but they increase sensitivity to transient behaviors and random variability. In this context, it becomes important to report reliability analyses and to clarify whether high performance persists under shorter exposures or different stimulus sets.

5.3 Datasets and Generalizability

An important observation is that several research groups, datasets, and experimental pipelines appear repeatedly in the literature. This is not necessarily problematic; it often reflects cumulative progress, where a team iteratively improves feature engineering, task design, or modeling strategy. In eye-tracking research, building a well-curated dataset is expensive and operationally challenging (ethics, recruitment, calibration, pediatric compliance, annotation of AOIs), so it is expected that groups with established infrastructure publish multiple works using the same cohort, device, and paradigm.

However, repeated appearance may also indicate structural concentration: only a limited number of labs have sustained access to ASD cohorts and standardized eye-tracking facilities. This concentration can inadvertently create "local benchmarks" where models are repeatedly validated within a single acquisition ecosystem (same device, same calibration procedure, same stimulus library), which can inflate the apparent maturity of the approach. When multiple papers rely on the same dataset or on highly similar variants, performance improvements may partly reflect optimization to dataset-specific idiosyncrasies rather than genuine cross-context robustness.

A related issue is that datasets hosted on platforms such as Figshare enable rapid experimentation, but can lead to accidental information leakage across studies (e.g., reusing preprocessed representations, overlapping participants, or standard splits that become implicitly tuned).

5.4 Understanding Very High Accuracy Reports

Several studies report extremely high accuracy (often above 95%). While such results may indicate strong discriminative patterns, they should be interpreted cautiously given common methodological factors that can artificially elevate performance:

1. **Small sample sizes and optimistic evaluation:** Many studies include fewer than 30–40 participants per group. In small datasets, even minor leakage or favorable splits can yield inflated accuracy, and confidence intervals are often wide. High point estimates without uncertainty reporting (CI, bootstrapping) can be misleading.
2. **Non-independent samples (segment-level vs subject-level splitting):** A recurrent pitfall is evaluating on multiple windows or images per subject while splitting at the sample level rather than at the subject level. If segments from the same participant appear in both train and test sets, the model can learn subject-specific signatures and achieve unrealistically high accuracy. Therefore, *subject-independent* splitting (and ideally cross-site validation) is essential.
3. **Task-driven separability:** Paradigms designed with strong social vs non-social contrasts may maximize group separation within that specific setting. While useful for proof-of-concept, these results may not generalize to more diverse stimuli or real clinical contexts.
4. **Class imbalance and metric choice:** Some datasets have substantial imbalance (e.g., very large TD vs small ASD). Reporting accuracy alone can overstate performance; sensitivity, specificity, AUC and balanced accuracy should be consistently reported. Extremely high specificity with moderate sensitivity may still yield high accuracy in imbalanced settings.

Taken together, very high accuracies are most convincing when supported by: (i) subject-level splits, (ii) external validation on a separate cohort or site, (iii) transparent preprocessing, (iv) reporting of uncertainty, and (v) clinically relevant operating points.

5.5 Computational Intelligence Approaches

Classical ML remains prevalent due to its compatibility with structured features and limited dataset sizes. Feature-based models (SVM, RF, gradient boosting) can be more interpretable, especially when combined with feature importance analysis or sparse selection methods. This interpretability is critical for clinical adoption, where stakeholders often require insight into what drives a prediction (e.g., reduced eye-region dwell time, atypical AOI transitions, delayed time-to-first-fixation).

DL approaches increasingly dominate when gaze data are expressed as images. While DL can capture complex patterns, it also increases the risk of overfitting and shortcut learning in small datasets, and it often reduces transparency. For screening applications, an important direction is combining DL performance with explainability and uncertainty estimation. In practice, an uncertainty-aware model may be more clinically valuable than a marginally more accurate but over-confident classifier, as it can flag ambiguous cases for expert review.

5.6 Toward Standardization and Benchmarking

A core barrier to comparability remains the lack of standardized pipelines for preprocessing (fixation detection algorithms, filtering, blink handling), AOI definitions, and evaluation protocols. This undermines reproducibility and makes it difficult to identify which improvements arise from modeling advances versus pipeline differences.

To strengthen the evidence base, future research should prioritize: (i) standardized subject-independent evaluation, (ii) shared benchmark tasks with agreed-upon metrics, (iii) cross-device/cross-site validation, and (iv) reporting guidelines that include calibration procedures, data loss rates, and exclusion criteria. Additionally, demographic and clinical heterogeneity (age, IQ, comorbidities, symptom severity) should be explicitly modeled or stratified, as ASD is a spectrum and performance can vary substantially across subgroups.

6 Conclusions and Future Work

This paper presented a structured state-of-the-art review of Computational Intelligence approaches applied to eye-tracking data for ASD detection (2020–2025). Overall, the literature supports the potential of gaze-based AI systems as *objective, non-invasive* tools to assist early *screening* and risk stratification. Nevertheless, the evidence base remains difficult to compare across studies due to substantial heterogeneity in acquisition hardware, experimental paradigms, preprocessing pipelines, feature definitions, and evaluation protocols.

A key outcome of this review is that several high performance reports (often >95% accuracy) should be interpreted cautiously. In many cases, limited sample sizes, repeated use of the same cohorts or public datasets, and differences in validation strategy (e.g., segment-level vs. subject-level splits) can lead to optimistic estimates. Therefore, current systems should be considered research prototypes or decision-support tools, rather than clinically validated diagnostic solutions.

Future research should prioritize the following directions to improve robustness, reproducibility, and clinical transferability:

- **Larger multi-center datasets** with harmonized recruitment criteria and explicit reporting of demographic and clinical heterogeneity (age, severity, IQ, and comorbidities).
- **Standardized evaluation protocols**, including subject-independent splitting, transparent handling of repeated measures, and consistent reporting of sensitivity, specificity, balanced accuracy, and confidence intervals.
- **Cross-dataset and cross-device validation** to assess generalization beyond a single lab, paradigm, or acquisition ecosystem, mitigating the risk of dataset-specific over-optimization.

- **Transparent preprocessing and calibration reporting**, including data loss rates, exclusion criteria, fixation detection settings, and quality-control procedures.
- **Explainable and uncertainty-aware models** to support clinical trust and decision-making, enabling reliable referral thresholds and identifying ambiguous cases for expert review.
- **Improved ecological validity** through more naturalistic paradigms and pragmatic protocols that remain robust under real-world constraints (short sessions, movement, reduced compliance).

Bridging the gap between high-performing research models and deployable clinical screening systems will require not only methodological advances, but also shared benchmarks, reporting guidelines, and prospective studies in real clinical workflows.

Acknowledgments. This project was funded in part by grants from Fundación Séneca, the Spanish "Ministerio de Ciencia, Innovación y Universidades", the European Union's Horizon 2020 Research and Innovation Programme (MSCA-SE EPISTEAM), and the Programa Iberoamericano de Ciencia y Tecnología para el Desarrollo (CYTED) (Red 225RT0169).

Disclosure of Interests. The authors declare that they have no competing interests.

References

1. Kang, J., Han, X., Hu, J.F., Feng, H., Li, X.: The study of the differences between low-functioning autistic children and typically developing children in the processing of the own-race and other-race faces by the machine learning approach. J. Clin. Neurosci. **81**, 54–60 (2020). https://doi.org/10.1016/j.jocn.2020.09.039
2. Vabalas, A., Gowen, E., Poliakoff, E., Casson, A.J.: Applying machine learning to kinematic and eye movement features of a movement imitation task to predict autism diagnosis. Sci. Rep. **10**(1) (2020). https://doi.org/10.1038/s41598-020-65384-4
3. Yaneva, V., Ha, A.L., Eraslan, Ş, Yeşilada, Y., Mitkov, R.: Detecting high-functioning autism in adults using eye tracking and machine learning. IEEE Trans. Neural Syst. Rehabil. Eng. **28**(6), 1254–1261 (2020). https://doi.org/10.1109/TNSRE.2020.2991675
4. Chang, Z., Di Martino, J.M., Aiello, R.E., et al.: Computational methods to measure patterns of gaze in toddlers with autism spectrum disorder. JAMA Pediatr. **175**(8), 827–836 (2021). https://doi.org/10.1001/jamapediatrics.2021.0530
5. Cilia, F., Carette, R., Elbattah, M., et al.: Computer-aided screening of autism spectrum disorder: eye-tracking study using data visualization and deep learning. JMIR Human Factors **8**(4) (2021). https://doi.org/10.2196/27706
6. He, Q., Wang, Q., Wu, Y., Yi, L., Wei, K.: Automatic classification of children with autism spectrum disorder by using a computerized visual-orienting task. PsyCh J. **10**(4), 550–565 (2021). https://doi.org/10.1002/pchj.447
7. Dos Santos Oliveira, J.L., Franco, F.D.O., Revers, M.C., et al.: Computer-aided autism diagnosis based on visual attention models using eye tracking. Sci. Rep. **11**(1) (2021). https://doi.org/10.1038/s41598-021-89023-8

8. Zhao, Z., Tang, H., Zhang, X., et al.: Classification of children with autism and typical development using eye-tracking data from face-to-face conversations: machine learning model development and performance evaluation. J. Med. Internet Res. **23**(8) (2021). https://doi.org/10.2196/29328
9. Ahmed, I.A., Senan, E.M., Rassem, T.H., et al.: Eye tracking-based diagnosis and early detection of autism spectrum disorder using machine learning and deep learning techniques. Electronics (Switzerland) **11**(4) (2022). https://doi.org/10.3390/electronics11040530
10. Alcañiz Raya, M.L., Chicchi Giglioli, I.A., Carrasco-Ribelles, L.A., et al.: Eye gaze as a biomarker in the recognition of autism spectrum disorder using virtual reality and machine learning: a proof of concept for diagnosis. Autism Res. **15**(1), 131–145 (2022). https://doi.org/10.1002/aur.2636
11. Kong, X., Wei, Z., Sun, B., et al.: Different eye tracking patterns in autism spectrum disorder in toddler and preschool children. Front. Psychiat. **13** (2022). https://doi.org/10.3389/fpsyt.2022.899521
12. Özdemir, S., Akin-Bulbul, I., Kök, I., Özdemir, S.: Development of a visual attention based decision support system for autism spectrum disorder screening. Int. J. Psychophysiol. **173**, 69–81 (2022). https://doi.org/10.1016/j.ijpsycho.2022.01.004
13. Ahmed, Z.A.T., Albalawi, E., Aldhyani, T.H.H., et al.: Applying eye tracking with deep learning techniques for early-stage detection of autism spectrum disorders. Data **8**(11) (2023). https://doi.org/10.3390/data8110168
14. Atyabi, A., Shic, F., Jiang, J., et al.: Stratification of children with autism spectrum disorder through fusion of temporal information in eye-gaze scan-paths. ACM Trans. Knowl. Disc. Data **17**(2) (2023). https://doi.org/10.1145/3539226
15. AlArifi, H.S., AlDhalaan, H.M., Hadjikhani, N., et al.: Machine learning for distinguishing Saudi children with and without autism via eye-tracking data. Child Adolescent Psychiat. Mental Health **17**(1) (2023). https://doi.org/10.1186/s13034-023-00662-3
16. Franco, F.D.O., Dos Santos Oliveira, J.L., Portolese, J., et al.: Computer-aided autism diagnosis using visual attention models and eye-tracking: replication and improvement proposal. BMC Med. Inf. Decis. Mak. **23**(1) (2023). https://doi.org/10.1186/s12911-023-02389-9
17. Meng, F., Li, F., Wu, S., et al.: Machine learning-based early diagnosis of autism according to eye movements of real and artificial faces scanning. Front. Neurosci. **17** (2023). https://doi.org/10.3389/fnins.2023.1170951
18. Zhao, Z., Wei, J., Xing, J., et al.: Use of oculomotor behavior to classify children with autism and typical development: a novel implementation of the machine learning approach. J. Autism Dev. Disord. **53**(3), 934–946 (2023). https://doi.org/10.1007/s10803-022-05685-x
19. Alsaidi, M., Obeid, N., Al-Madi, N.S.A., Hiary, H., Aljarah, I.: A convolutional deep neural network approach to predict autism spectrum disorder based on eye-tracking scan paths. Information (Switzerland) **15**(3) (2024). https://doi.org/10.3390/info15030133
20. Benabderrahmane, B., Gharzouli, M., Benlecheb, A.: A novel multi-modal model to assist the diagnosis of autism spectrum disorder using eye-tracking data. Health Inf. Sci. Syst. **12**(1) (2024). https://doi.org/10.1007/s13755-024-00299-2

21. Colonnese, F., Di Luzio, F., Rosato, A., Panella, M.: Enhancing autism detection through gaze analysis using eye tracking sensors and data attribution with distillation in deep neural networks. Sensors **24**(23) (2024). https://doi.org/10.3390/s24237792
22. Lencastre, P., Lotfigolian, M., Lind, P.G.: Identifying autism gaze patterns in five-second data records. Diagnostics **14**(10) (2024). https://doi.org/10.3390/diagnostics14101047
23. Mumenin, N., Yousuf, M.A., Nashiry, M.A., et al.: ASDNet: a robust involution-based architecture for diagnosis of autism spectrum disorder utilising eye-tracking technology. IET Comput. Vision **18**(5), 666–681 (2024). https://doi.org/10.1049/cvi2.12271
24. Sá, R.O.S., Michelassi, G.D.C., Butrico, D.D.S., et al.: Enhancing ensemble classifiers utilizing gaze tracking data for autism spectrum disorder diagnosis. Comput. Biol. Med. **182**, 109184 (2024). https://doi.org/10.1016/j.compbiomed.2024.109184
25. Wei, Q., Dong, W., Yu, D., et al.: Early identification of autism spectrum disorder based on machine learning with eye-tracking data. J. Affect. Disord. **358**, 326–334 (2024). https://doi.org/10.1016/j.jad.2024.04.049
26. Zhou, W., Yang, M., Tang, J., Wang, J., Hu, B.: Gaze patterns in children with autism spectrum disorder to emotional faces: scanpath and similarity. IEEE Trans. Neural Syst. Rehabil. Eng. **32**, 865–874 (2024). https://doi.org/10.1109/TNSRE.2024.3361935
27. Al-Adhaileh, M.H., Alsubari, S.N., Al-Nefaie, A.H., Ahmad, S., Alhamadi, A.A.: Diagnosing autism spectrum disorder based on eye tracking technology using deep learning models. Front. Med.**12** (2025). https://doi.org/10.3389/fmed.2025.1690177
28. Antolí, A., Rodriguez-Lozano, F.J., Juan Cañas, J., et al.: Using explainable machine learning and eye-tracking for diagnosing autism spectrum and developmental language disorders in social attention tasks. Front. Neurosci. **19** (2025). https://doi.org/10.3389/fnins.2025.1558621
29. Cheekaty, S., Muneeswari, G.: Enhanced multilevel autism classification for children using eye-tracking and hybrid CNN-RNN deep learning models. Neural Comput. Appl. **37**(33), 27631–27654 (2025). https://doi.org/10.1007/s00521-024-10633-0
30. Hudry, K., Chetcuti, L.C., Tan, D.W., et al.: Accuracy of a 2-min eye-tracking assessment to differentiate young children with and without autism. Molec. Autism **16**(1) (2025). https://doi.org/10.1186/s13229-025-00670-4
31. Setu, D.M.: An analytics-driven model for identifying autism spectrum disorder using eye tracking. Healthc. Anal. **8**, 100409 (2025). https://doi.org/10.1016/j.health.2025.100409
32. Soloh, R., Orm, L.A., Dabdoub, D.: An image-based analytics framework for early autism detection using eye movements. Healthc. Anal. **8**, 100439 (2025). https://doi.org/10.1016/j.health.2025.100439

33. Xia, C., Chen, H., Han, J., Zhang, D., Li, K.: Identifying children with autism spectrum disorder via transformer-based representation learning from dynamic facial cues. IEEE Trans. Affect. Comput. **16**(1), 83–97 (2025). https://doi.org/10.1109/TAFFC.2024.3412032
34. Zhang, Y., Huang, Y., Qi, J., et al.: Uncertainty inspired early autism spectrum disorder screening via contrastive image-viewing paradigm. IEEE Trans. Neural Syst. Rehabil. Eng. **33**, 122–132 (2025). https://doi.org/10.1109/TNSRE.2024.3518693

Integrated AI System for Physiological Assessment of Pain and Social Robot Intervention

Emilia I. Barakova[1(✉)], Peter Peters[1], Alexia Dragomirescu[2], Ana Sîrbu[1], Kallista Komdeur[2], Malina Corduneanu[2], Mara Burghelea[2], Nora Balje[2], and Paula S. Sterkenburg[3]

[1] Eindhoven University of Technology, Department of Mathematics and Computer Science, Eindhoven, The Netherlands
e.i.barakova@tue.nl

[2] Eindhoven University of Technology, Department of Mathematics and Computer Science, Eindhoven, The Netherlands

[3] Vrije Universiteit Amsterdam, Department of Clinical Child and Family Studies and Amsterdam Public Health, Amsterdam, The Netherlands

Abstract. Pain detection is critical for individuals unable to correctly self-report, such as young children or patients with intellectual disabilities. This paper introduces an Integrated AI System for the physiological assessment of Pain and social robotic intervention, which transcends traditional monitoring by combining real-time physiological measurements with AI assessment and immediate behavioral support. The system architecture enables a multimodal approach, currently integrating electrodermal activity and heart rate signals to feed a Random Forest Classifier model for pain level estimation. Pain assessment results are communicated through a dual-interface framework: a mobile application provides caregivers with intuitive visualizations and longitudinal history for clinical oversight, while a social robot (MiRo-E) can utilise the assessment for interactive interventions, such as distraction, to assist patients in coping with pain. As this study serves as a proof of concept for the integrated system, achieving high diagnostic accuracy was not the primary scope of this work. While this framework establishes a functional foundation for integrated pain management, testing is required in clinical settings to validate the practical value of pain assessment and the therapeutic impact of the robotic interventions in healthcare.

Keywords: Integrated system of pain assessment and intervention · PainApp · Electrodermal Activity · Galvanic Skin Response · Heart Rate Variability · Machine Learning · Mobile Application · Pain Assessment · Assistive Robot

1 Introduction

Pain assessment in people who cannot self-report is a topic of great importance for healthcare providers. To provide proper care, caregivers must understand

J. M. Ferrndez Vicente et al. (Eds.): IWINAC 2026, LNCS 16574, pp. 210–229, 2026.
https://doi.org/10.1007/978-3-032-27314-7_20

when their patients are in pain; research has shown that undetected or untreated pain in non-communicative patients can lead to worsening medical conditions, prolonged hospital stays, increased behavioral symptoms, and even premature death [20,26]. Currently, the safety and comfort of these patients depend heavily on human observation by caregivers and nurses. However, this is a notably unreliable method, as it requires deep familiarity with each patient—a requirement that is often unfeasible in clinical settings where nurses may only spend a few minutes per shift with a patient [7]. Furthermore, relying on subjective observation is prone to diagnostic error. Clinical personnel often experience cognitive overload and interruptions, leading to "attention blindness", where critical signs of patient deterioration are missed even when vital signs are recorded regularly [32]. In addition, diagnostic errors are common when evaluations depend solely on subjective observation [5]. These factors underscore the need for more objective, technology-assisted approaches to monitor patient well being and pain levels.

Research on the use of physiological signals for pain estimation is advancing rapidly [10,16], and several technological solutions for pain measurement using physiological signals are becoming available. To make physiological readings easily seen and understood, various visualization tools have been developed, such as [18,24], and tablets and mobile applications have been used as signaling and communication tools [12,17,29]. Artificial intelligence models have been applied to support the interpretation of physiological states through physiological measurements [19]. Despite these promising developments, interpreting physiological signals in terms of pain levels remains challenging due to individual differences in patients, the caregivers different ability to work with technology, noisy and difficult to interpret measurements. An additional challenge is to provide immediate assistance when elevated pain levels are detected, potentially through interactive technology.

Additionally, most existing tools emphasize the need for real-time detection, but do not support broader clinical needs, such as longitudinal tracking, historical visualization, or adaptive model refinement. For caregivers to make informed decisions, systems must not only detect acute pain but also document patterns over time, provide historical overviews, and allow retrospective evaluation of sensor readings, contextual events, and model outputs. Longitudinal insight is increasingly recognized as essential in understanding trends in pain, identifying triggers, improving diagnosis, and supporting personalized care interventions. This paper introduces an integrated system for assessment and patient support, representing a novel end-to-end framework that transitions from passive measurement to active, closed-loop intervention. Unlike previous iterations of tools such as PainApp, which relied on single physiological inputs and limited AI integration [17,19] and could only interface with a mobile application, the proposed system incorporates expanded functionality that gives possibility to estimate pain based on multimodal (physiological) signals, and in addition, offers visualisation of historical pain data and has an intervention modality as a social robot. The system combines Electrodermal Activity (EDA) and heart rate (HR) signals to drive a multimodal machine learning model, while also incorporating a back-end infrastructure that supports data storage, retrieval, and visualization. A remote server hosts the ML model and supports continuous retraining, making it possible to adapt the classifier to new patient populations or improved datasets. The modularity of the implementation further allows for the integration of additional features or biosignals as technology advances. Beyond real-time detection, the system stores raw sensor streams, session information, and computed pain estimations in a PostgreSQL database through a custom API. This enables the retrieval of historical data across user-defined time intervals, offering caregivers insight into patterns and developments in a patient's condition. Historical visualizations help identify long-term trends, support clinical oversight, and allow caretakers to make more informed decisions over extended monitoring periods. The architecture is scalable and can be expanded across multiple institutions or experimental cohorts, supporting broader research and deployment. To bridge the gap between pain assessment and intervention, we developed a system that integrates the ROS-operated social robot (MIRO-E) to provide interactive behavioral support, such as distraction. This addresses a major limitation of existing clinical technologies by providing an automated, responsive intervention mechanism until human assistance becomes available [11,21]. Together, these components form a closed-loop system that not only estimates pain but also stores context, visualizes changes over time, and ability to provide real-time support—functioning both as a practical clinical tool and a platform for continued research and refinement.

2 Related Work

Previous research shows that current pain assessment systems, such as the VAS or the NRS, limit a multidimensional experience to a single value. As such, users may misunderstand them, scores are not interchangeable between individuals or time, and statistical interpretations (e.g., percent change) can be misleading [1,36]. More advanced methods, such as facial expression analysis and physiological measurements (e.g., GSR, PPG, heart rate), are also being explored. Several applications have been developed to automate these techniques [12,17,23,29]. Like the PainChek app, which implements facial recognition through AI to estimate pain in non-verbal patients [23], and the Biobeat system, which monitors physiological indicators such as blood pressure and heart rate to support pain-related evaluations [3]. Sabater et al. [29] implemented an AI-based facial recognition system integrated into a mobile application that could provide an objective and reliable tool for pain assessment in this population. Although these tools represent an important evolution in pain assessment, they still face critical limitations, such as the need for input from the patient or caregiver, which can be time-consuming and unfeasible in real healthcare settings.

Research on the use of physiological signals for pain measurement is rapidly advancing as a method for automatic pain estimation [10,16]. In an attempt to make physiological readings more interpretable, various visualization tools have been developed [18,24]. The PainApp reported in Korving et al. [17,19], used an electrodermal activity signal to distinguish pain from non-pain conditions, and is being used as a signaling and communication tool in care environments [17]. An AI model has been developed for this application, to support the interpretation of physiological states based on sensor data [19], but was not fully integrated. Despite these promising developments, the interpretation of physiological signals in terms of pain levels remains a complex challenge, particularly due to personal differences in pain experience and measurement noise.

Existing apps and systems often fall short due to the limited quality of the signal input, sometimes due to environmental conditions such as poor positioning of the sensor, a too-hot environment, which makes the GSR response increase, a lack of real-time AI integration, and the absence of interactive capabilities for patient engagement. For example, the mobile application developed by Korving et al. relies solely on a single physiological input (GSR), which restricts its sensitivity across diverse patient conditions. Moreover, AI is frequently used only as a back-end analytical tool, requiring Internet connectivity or batch processing, which diminishes responsiveness. These limitations make such tools unsuitable for fast, real-time clinical environments. Furthermore, creating integrated systems for measurement and intervention, such as social robots that can sense the levels of pain and provide immediate feedback, distraction, or support, will strongly benefit caregiving environments.

Advanced systems that use physiological sensing, such as PPG, heart rate variability, and electrodermal activity (EDA), have demonstrated high potential. Previous research suggests that their effectiveness is improved when the models are customized to each individual's baseline response [6]. In an experiment carried out on postoperative patients, individual pain trajectories showed much lower measurement error and captured unique recovery patterns better than single pain measures [9]. Even when patients are able to express their pain levels, research shows that pain perception is very subjective and vulnerable to bias, leading to misinterpretation [4,8,14,15]. For this reason, establishing a baseline per patient is essential to assess meaningful changes.

3 Methodology

Based on the identified shortcomings in the previous section, we propose several methodological improvements. First, use multiple physiological signals to estimate pain. Second, develop a database for storing and visualising historical data in safe and accessible way, and third, connect the mobile application with interactive technologies, such as robots and tangibles, that can provide support until human help is available [11].

In order to address the main challenge of pain measurement inside an application, we utilized two distinct measurements to estimate pain levels, the combined prediction of which should be visualized directly in the UI and can be easily switched between to make it accessible for end users.

We use a machine learning algorithm on physiological data collected from a Shimmer3 GSR+ sensor in our primary pain estimation approach. Specifically, this ML model processes skin resistance and heart rate signals to infer pain levels on a scale of 0 to 8. This approach relies on the potential of machine learning to capture complex, nonlinear relationships between physiological signals and pain experiences, and the nine pain levels allow mobile application users to better understand the state of their patients. This interpretation method works only when the application has a valid and functional internet connection, as the current iteration of the model is hosted remotely on an online server. Thus, for practical purposes, a fallback approach was implemented that uses simplified measurment which does not require an internet connection to function properly. It is a formula-based mode that interprets pain levels using only GSR data.

To evaluate both approaches to pain estimation, multiple tests were conducted, incorporating different types of physical stress factors. Because the mathematical formula only takes into account the EDA signal, which is positively correlated with the level of pain felt by the patient, this approach was tested using a knob resistor or potentiometer. For evaluation, the 2 methods were applied to the same situation, with their outcomes compared in terms of speed of interpretation and accuracy to the human subject real-time feedback. Acute pain was simulated with short-lived stress stimuli such as pinching of the skin. Chronic pain is defined as lasting longer than six months, which was an unfeasible amount of testing time for the scope of the project. Therefore, the evaluation focused on interpreting the level of pain felt during a mild yet prolonged stress inducing situation, such as submerging one's hand in ice water.

The aim of the following sections is to present the developed software, the research conducted in the development process, the issues encountered, and future research and work that must be conducted.

4 Mobile Application Design

4.1 Requirements and Front-End Design

The proposed mobile application design follows the predefined requirements based on the literature and expert research [18,27,28].

- Visualization of pain levels in an intuitive and fast way.
- Historical visualization of patient data for better understanding of their state.
- User-friendly interface and flow for non-technical end users, such as nurses.

The mobile application follows a generic and intuitive layout, making use of a menu bar for easy navigation between tabs, along with drop-down menus to switch between settings. Following the research of Korving et al. [19], the visualization uses a color gradient from green (indicating no pain) to red (indicating high pain), combined with digital facial expressions ranging from happy, through neutral, to sad. To reinforce the emotion conveyed, the colored face is surrounded by spikes, with both their number and sharpness increasing proportionally to the estimated pain intensity. This visualization was designed for the interpretation of a subjective (first-person) experience, such as pain, and bridging this perspective with contrasting empirical science and clinical observations, often referred to as a third-person perspective [34]. Medical and personal care personnel at all levels of academic and technical expertise should be able to understand and use the visualization to interpret the relative level of pain their patient is experiencing. Figure 1 shows the full range of visual representations, corresponding to increasing pain levels from low to high.

Fig. 1. Visual representations of pain levels used in PainApp adapted from [18]. Each level combines color (green to red gradient), shape intensity (from smooth to spiky), and facial expression (from happy to distressed) to convey pain severity.

For the collection of signals, the mobile application uses a Shimmer wearable sensor to capture biophysical and kinematic data in real-time. When assessing physical stress, the most widely used techniques for monitoring physiological changes are ECG for HRV, EDA, and PPG [33]. The study of [2] compares the physiological signals related to pain and stress to conclude that although there are differences in the indications of some physiological signals, both physical pain and distress show increased heart rate and EDA, measured by skin conductance. Currently, many digital health platforms use HRV as an indicator of both chronic and acute stress and pain, and the limitations that HRV poses when accurately assessing stress have been widely documented [13]. PPG directly measures changes in pulsatile blood in the skin, offering insights into vascular responses driven primarily by the skin. PPG has potential as a more direct and reliable measure of the activity of the sympathetic nervous system during acute stress, compared to HRV, which reflects broader autonomic interactions that can complicate interpretation in stress-specific contexts [33]. While the research on thenumber and accuracy of the pain estimation from physiological signals is ongoing and new findings can propose better measurement, our system will create a framework where different signals can be added and the AI model - retrained.

This project sets the basis for multi-feature pain level classification in patients with difficulties in self-reporting, by making use of a machine learning model, as opposed to mathematical formulas. The project explores the complex relationship between skin resistance, extracted mathematically from EDA, and heart rate, in an attempt to detect and classify both acute and chronic pain. For this reason, skin resistance is better suited with greater sensitivity to slow tonic increases in sympathetic activity, as is the case for chronic pain [35]. Furthermore, heart rate is extracted in real time from the PPG package signal through peak counting within a short time interval. Upon receiving a stream of these signals from the mobile application, the model can interpret and classify them into one of the defined pain classes.

4.2 Back-End Design

The machine learning model is hosted remotely on a server of choice, along with the Python environment that allows for the retraining and improvement of the model. Currently, the interpretation uses two features for classification: skin resistance and heart rate extracted from the PPG signal. However, the implementation is modular and therefore allows for expansion and further development. The model is designed to interpret multiple features and allows for retraining with the appropriate data provided.

The back-end of the application was developed using a custom API integrated with a PostgreSQL database to facilitate the storage of patient data, physiological sensor readings, and interpreted pain assessment results. The API manages data collection, session tracking, and retrieval of historical data for visualization.

After receiving and decoding the EDA and PPG signals from the sensor, the data are transmitted through the API and stored in the database for subsequent analysis. Subsequently, these signals are forwarded to an AI model for interpretation, and the resulting pain level estimates are returned and stored alongside the original data. Each data entry is linked to a specific patient session, enabling systematic documentation of experimental procedures.

For historical visualization, the API retrieves all relevant patient data within a user-defined time interval, enabling integrated visualization within the application interface. This functionality supports both clinical monitoring and caregiver insight into patient progress.

The database queries were designed to optimize the efficiency of data retrieval, submission, and update operations in accordance with the application's operational requirements. The use of a custom architecture enhances the overall system functionality and provides a modular back-end framework that supports future scalability. This includes the potential integration of additional physiological signals and expansion to accommodate multiple institutions or study cohorts.

4.3 System Architecture

To develop an integrated system into a functional product, five main components were utilized: the Shimmer3 GSR+ Sensor, a mobile application developed in React Native, a PostgreSQL database, a back-end server that runs a Random Forest Classifier model, and the MiRo-E robot, which operated using ROS. This section provides an overview of the mobile application's functionality and explains each component in more detail (Fig. 2).

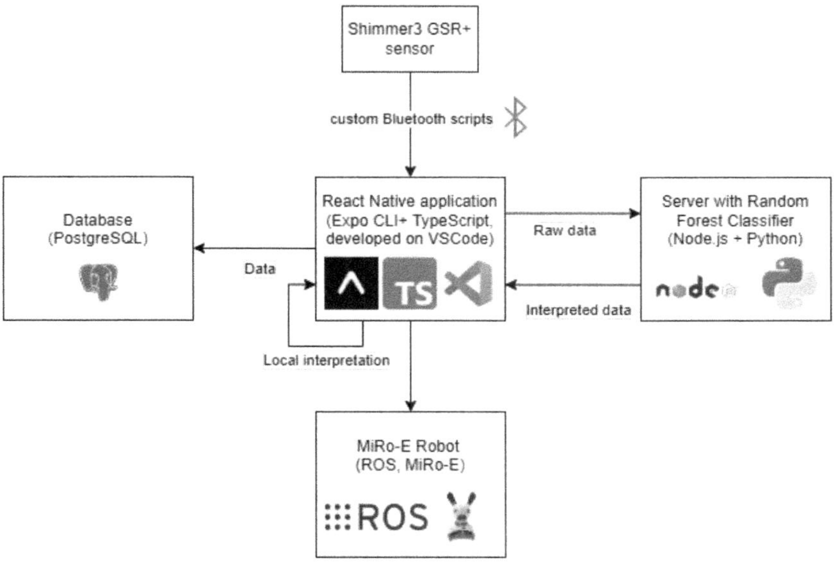

Fig. 2. System architecture of PainApp system that supports immediate and long-term pain monitoring and immediate patient support through a social robot.

4.4 Component Interaction

First, the main flow of the product is explained. The application, built with Expo and TypeScript (developed in Visual Studio Code), receives data packages from the Shimmer3 GSR+ sensor via a custom classical Bluetooth script. The signals are analyzed, and a relative pain level is calculated based on the incoming signal, which can then be visualized in the mobile application in real time. This data is either interpreted locally using a formula or interpreted by an AI model. The AI model is a Random Forest Classifier built in Python and hosted on a Node.js server. Once the data packages are decoded, they are sent to the back-end server that hosts the machine learning model for interpretation (unless the local formula is used), while at the same time being stored in the database.

Once interpreted, the pain level can be visualized in the mobile application. When a high pain level is detected, the user of the mobile application receives a notification, alerting them that the patient needs care. The database enables the user to view historical data for patients. Finally, the mobile application is capable of connecting to a MiRo-E robot through ROS.

4.5 Shimmer3 GSR+ Sensor

The application integrates with sensors using Bluetooth technology, allowing continuous real-time data streaming. This approach ensures that physiological data can be captured and transmitted seamlessly during usage without requiring repeated setup or pairing. The supported sensor device is the Shimmer3 GSR+, a wearable sensor capable of measuring EDA and other bio-signals [31]. Once Bluetooth permission is granted, the mobile application can maintain a persistent connection with the device for uninterrupted data flow. As the mobile application was built using React Native, the official Shimmer API was not compatible and could not be utilized. However, this limitation also aligned to reduce the dependency on external libraries that could lose support. To ensure stability and maintain control, custom Bluetooth handling scripts were implemented to manage the connection and data flow with the sensor. Therefore, encoded data packages had to be obtained from the sensor and then decoded in the mobile application to access the desired bio-data values.

Before starting the streaming process, the EDA range, stored in the data buffer at position 21, is set to 0 as values are expected to fall between 0 and 63,000 Ω. This configuration helps to calculate the skin resistance, which depends on the value of the feedback resistor, determined by the selected EDA range. After configuring the EDA range in the sensor configuration file, the value 0×07 is written to initiate the streaming process. As the Shimmer sensor sends binary data to the application, the buffer is converted from binary data into the format of unsigned 8-bit integers, resulting in an array of values. This array is traversed to locate channel $0 \times 1C$. The EDA, stored on two consecutive bytes, is decoded and the obtained value is multiplied by 3, then divided by 4095 and again by 0.5; the resulting value is the voltage ratio. The skin resistance is then calculated by dividing the feedback resistor, depending on the chosen EDA range, by the voltage ratio minus 1.

$$\texttt{skin resistance} = \frac{40200}{\left(\frac{\texttt{value}\cdot\left(\frac{3}{4095}\right)}{0.5} - 1\right)}$$

Equation for feedback resistor with range setting 0 - 40,200 Ω

If the selected pain level method is the formula using only EDA, the obtained value is saved, and the pain level is output based on the skin resistance value. If the chosen method is the AI Model, then heart rate is also calculated using a window of PPG signal values and the configured sampling rate for the Shimmer sensor. Heart rate is determined by taking 60 and dividing it by an aggregated average of the peaks in the PPG window, and afterwards dividing this result by the sampling rate. For this method, we define a peak as a signal value higher than both its preceding and following values. The pain level, when the AI method is selected, is calculated by the AI model on the back-end server using both heart rate and skin resistance values.

4.6 Mobile Application

The advanced iteration of the PainApp is built using React Native to ensure a consistent user experience across Android devices and to enable faster development with a shared codebase. TypeScript was chosen for its type safety, which improves code quality and reduces bugs.

4.7 PostgreSQL Database

PostgreSQL was chosen for its robust and complete SQL support, enabling complex and flexible queries. This capability is essential for the project, particularly when querying patient data over specific time frames, an operation that was previously unfeasible with DataFoundry. With PostgreSQL, the system can filter data based on patient, session, timestamp, sensor type, and other dimensions. This also provides researchers with greater control over data extraction for further analysis.

One of the core requirements of the mobile application was the ability to display historical data for a given patient over a selected time period. The PostgreSQL setup effectively supports this feature by enabling time-based data slicing, which is directly integrated into the front-end for user interaction.

The database contains four main tables: 'sessions', 'raw_data', 'patients' and 'interpreted_data'. The primary goal was to link the data to a specific patient and retrieve all relevant data as needed. To achieve this, a 'sessions' table was created. Whenever a Bluetooth connection between a sensor and the mobile application is established, the backend generates a unique session ID and stores it, along with the connection's start time, the patient for whom measurements are taken, and the sensor used. When the connection ends, the corresponding entry is updated to include the end time. Start and end times are crucial, as they enable the mobile application to display historical data. To visualize such data, the desired time frame is selected, and the back-end queries all sessions by patient ID and time interval. Once the relevant sessions are identified, the back-end then queries all data measured during those sessions.

For storing measurement data, two tables are used: 'raw_data', which stores raw PPG and skin resistance signals gathered by the sensor per session, and 'interpreted_data', which stores the relative detected pain levels based on the measurements. All entries include timestamps to accurately link measurements with corresponding pain levels.

Finally, a table 'patients' stores unique patient IDs to prevent reuse and ensure accurate tracking. For potential future research, fields for baseline measurements have also been included, allowing researchers to implement further analysis if desired (Fig. 3).

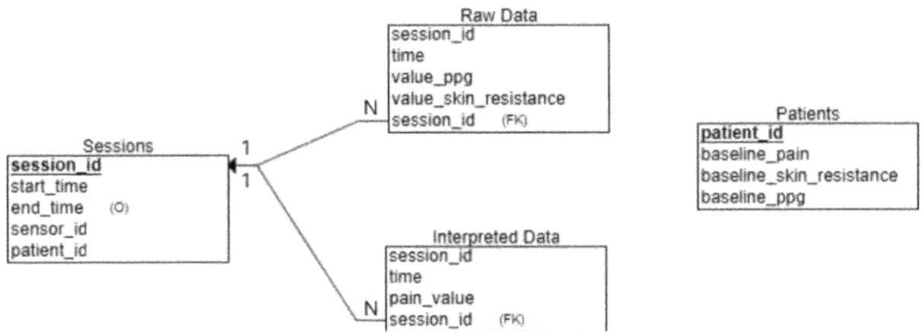

Fig. 3. Entity-Relationship (ER) diagram of the PainApp database.

4.8 Random Forest Classifier Machine Learning Model

Following Korving's research, a Random Forest Classifier model was chosen due to its advantages of dealing with unbalanced datasets, fast computation, minimal parameters, with good performance [19]. This model was trained on a dataset provided by Zenodo [22] that simultaneously collected EDA and heart rate signals from 24 diverse subjects in a state of calm and stress. The dataset was then processed to include skin resistance, extracted from the EDA readings, and signal intensity. Intensity is computed as a linear combination of skin resistance and heart rate, with skin resistance negatively correlated and heart rate positively correlated with intensity. Furthermore, this data was automatically labeled using Python's split data functionality, based on the intensity computed. The focus of the project lies on the proof of concept of this approach; therefore, precise accuracy is not in scope. The intensity feature and labeling method are not ideal for accurate pain detection, and are solely meant to set a basis for this approach of multi-feature pain interpretation.

The classifier model receives a stream of data from the mobile application containing values for skin resistance and heart rate. It then computes the intensity feature and proceeds to apply a pre-processing model on the data to ensure the correct format. This data is picked up by the Random Forest Classifier model, which classifies it and sends the response back to the mobile application for visualization. Because of the fast reading of the sensor, which captures data more frequently than its variation (e.g., 4 readings per millisecond), a variable filtering window is applied to the incoming data to extract only relevant readings.

4.9 Interaction with the MiRo-E Robot

The robot currently supported by the mobile application is the Miro-E, which runs on ROS. ROS is a widely used and flexible framework for developing robotic functionalities in a modular and user-friendly manner.

In the context of this project, the robot serves an important purpose: to distract patients from pain through interactive movements. While the exact movement patterns are being developed in collaboration with psychologists and described elsewhere [11]. The focus of the current work was to build a framework within the mobile application that supports establishing a reliable connection to the robot. The connection is facilitated through ROSBridge, a ROS component that allows remote communication over a WebSocket interface. This is achieved using the ROSbridge_server node, which automatically runs at startup on the robot. It exposes ROS functionality in a way that external devices, such as the mobile application, can send and receive messages and commands remotely. For this WebSocket connection to work, both the mobile device and the robot must be on the same Wi-Fi network. The user must enter the IP address and port number of the robot into the mobile application interface. These values are specific to the robot hardware and can be easily retrieved when a new device is set up. Once entered, the user simply presses "Connect", and the mobile application establishes communication with the robot. In the current version of the application, after the connection is established, the user can send basic movement commands to the robot, such as moving the head or tail. These actions are placeholders and can be easily modified in the codebase once more precise and therapeutic movement routines are defined for pain relief scenarios.

5 Design and Accessibility Features

5.1 Overview of the Page Interaction Design

PainApp was developed with an emphasis on user-centered design and accessibility to ensure ease of use for both: caregivers and researchers, regardless of their technical knowledge. The mobile application consists of four main screens, accessible via a bottom navigation bar:

- Home page: this is the main page for real-time pain monitoring. It displays a dynamic pain visualization using color, shape, and facial expression. As pain increases, the shape becomes sharper and the facial expression more distressed. The color scheme follows a green-yellow-red gradient to indicate the severity of the pain. This combination of color, shape, and facial expression has previously been found to best convey pain levels [18].
- History page: this page provides historical pain data in selectable time frames (hour, day, or week) for the current patient. Users can scroll through past data and view average values, helping caregivers identify trends in their patients' pain levels. For researchers, past data on skin conductance is also visualized.
- Robot page: this page allows caregivers to connect with the robot and send commands that will determine the interaction.

- Settings page: this page allows users to configure the language, theme, and method used to interpret the data.

The mobile application also supports linking sensors to new or existing patients with custom names, making it scalable for environments with multiple patients and multiple sensors.

5.2 Accessibility Features

Colorblind-Friendly Visualization. PainApp's visualization does not solely rely on color. Although it uses a green-yellow-red color scale to indicate severity, the same information is reinforced through shape and expression. This ensures that the visualization remains understandable for users with color vision deficiencies. In the same way, the mobile application accounts for cultural differences in how colors are interpreted. Because PainApp conveys pain information using multiple visual channels, users are not dependent on culturally specific color associations to interpret pain states correctly.

Language Accessibility. PainApp currently supports three languages: English, Dutch, and Italian. Users can switch languages directly from the Settings page. The translation system is modular and designed to allow easy future expansion to other languages if needed.

Information Pages. To support users with varying levels of technical expertise, the mobile application includes dedicated information pages. These explain how to use each core function of the mobile application, and outline what to do if the mobile application does not behave as expected. This ensures accessibility for non-technical caregivers and reduces the need for technical support to be available.

Visual Themes. To support different user needs and environmental lighting conditions, PainApp offers light and dark modes. These modes can be toggled from the Settings page. This supports better visibility and comfort for prolonged use, especially at night. The interface uses accessible font sizes and clear layouts designed to work well on both tablets and smartphones.

Alternative Interpretation Model. When the remote server is offline, PainApp automatically falls back on the mathematical interpretation formula. This guarantees uninterrupted access to pain assessment functionality. Users can also manually select this interpretation model from the Settings page.

6 Results

6.1 Design Realization

Figure 4 shows the four main pages of the final PainApp.

(a) Home page (b) History page (c) Robot page (d) Settings page

Fig. 4. User interface screen-grabs of PainApp showing the Home, History, Robot, and Settings pages. These represent the four main navigation areas of the application. The Home page shows a high pain level.

6.2 System Functionality Testing

The two interpretation approaches, the multimodal machine learning model (approach one) and the mathematical formula with a single modality (approach two), have been evaluated for the same scenarios that mimic acute and chronic pain in a human subject. For the simulation of acute pain by pinching the skin, the second approach was faster in interpretation and considerably more accurate than the real-time feedback received, while the first approach had slower performance with a slightly higher accuracy. For this type of rapid change in EDA, the rigid interpretation of the second approach is sufficient to obtain an approximate level of pain felt by the current patient. In the context of chronic pain, for the simulation of prolonged distress, the machine learning model (approach one) performed considerably better than the formula (approach two). Its interpretation was relatively fast to the urgency of the situation and more accurate. Despite the fact that the second approach has faster updates on interpretation, its accuracy is severely off compared to the real-time feedback received. The visualization of pain displayed on the home screen also matched the interpreted signal and, when changes were detected, had a smooth transition between pain levels.

Integration between the mobile application and the PostgreSQL backend database was successfully realized via a custom API, ensuring efficient data retrieval, session tracking, and storage. Facilitating access to historical physiological data is essential for both longitudinal diagnostics and clinical research. To address this, a dedicated history page was developed that retrieves patient records over specific user-defined time intervals. To maintain strict security standards and patient privacy, the system is designed to display only the data of the currently connected individual, thereby preventing unauthorized access to other patient records. Additionally, the PostgreSQL backend supports full-table data extraction, providing researchers with the necessary control for comprehensive offline analysis.

The mobile application provides complete functionality for establishing a connection with the MiRo-E robot. As mentioned before, assuming all preconditions are met, the connection with the MiRo-E robot can easily be established by inputting the Port of the Web-socket and the IP address of the robot, and pressing "Connect". The robot was tested by making some placeholder buttons with simple commands to move the head of the robot up and down, which were executed correctly. Moreover, if one of the prerequisites for a successful connection is interrupted (for example, the robot is turned off), the connection will be interrupted. Since exact robot behaviors are still being investigated, there has been no implementation of robots that distract patients at high pain levels, without the user sending a command. However, the mobile application does send a notification when a high pain level is detected. Once robot behavior has been designed for a certain group of patients, the code can easily be modified, and the command to trigger the adequate robot behavior can be placed at the same place where the notification is triggered. Of course, this command will only reach the robot if the connection is established.

Bluetooth connectivity between the mobile application and the Shimmer sensors was also successfully established, with the connection being integrated inside the mobile application itself, not in the Bluetooth menu of the device. Moreover, while a connection is active, the user has the option to change the connected sensor or change the patient data is recorded. If the connection fails, the mobile application attempts reconnection three times, and if this fails, the session is terminated. During a connection session, the data is decoded correctly and forwarded in the right places.

7 Discussion

The presented system represents an advanced iteration of PainApp, evolving from a single-signal signaling tool into a multimodal AI-driven platform for both monitoring and intervention, that allows visualization of the patient's personal pain history on different time scales. Although these developments offer a promising framework for assisting patients who have difficulty self-reporting pain and their caregivers, several considerations regarding their current "proof-of-concept" status must be addressed.

The Random Forest Classifier model shows promising results for the available dataset; however, the time constraint for this project did not allow testing on multiple different datasets or with patients who experience pain. The current dataset used for training has been labeled automatically using Python's functionality for data splitting as opposed to manually labeling with the real-time feedback of a human subject. Due to the subjectivity of pain perception, this approach is not ideal and introduces considerable inaccuracy in interpretation. However, the modular architecture allows the model to be easily retrained when more reliable patient-specific data becomes available.

A key advancement in this version of PainApp is the support for longitudinal patient monitoring through a PostgreSQL-backed history page. This feature addresses the need to visualize "pain trajectories," which research suggests are more effective at capturing recovery patterns than isolated measurements. Furthermore, to ensure clinical reliability, the implementation of a fallback mechanism—which reverts to a local formula-based assessment if the AI server is offline—ensures that caregivers are never left without assessment capabilities due to connectivity issues.

The integration of a social robot (MiRo-E) establishes a functional framework for immediate behavioral intervention. While current robot actions remain placeholders, the successful establishment of the ROSBridge connection demonstrates that the system can trigger external responses once therapeutic routines are finalized. However, practical implementation in a hospital setting may be challenged by strict Wi-Fi and VPN requirements, as both the robot and the mobile device must (in the current design) reside on the same network to communicate.

Generalization and personalization capabilities of the current system remain partially dependent on the Shimmer3 GSR+ sensor due to hard-coded signal translation formulas. To improve the mobile application's "practical value," future versions must generalize these formulas for diverse hardware. Most importantly, while the database structure for individual baselines is now in place, testing these personalized models is essential to account for the high subjectivity of pain perception before the system is ready for clinical environments.

Finally, due to the limited availability of training data and the time constraints imposed by the development timeline, the implementation and evaluation of individual baseline models for each patient could not be fully realized. While the importance of patient-specific baselines for improving the accuracy and reliability of physiological signal interpretation is well recognized, this functionality remains untested within the current scope of the project. Nevertheless, the architectural layout and structural support for the baseline integration have already been implemented in the mobile application and the back-end system. Furthermore, the modular design of the machine learning model allows for adaptation to more patient-specific data.

8 Conclusion and Future Work

This paper presented the design, implementation, and technical evaluation of an integrated system for assessment and intervention, representing a novel end-to-end framework that transitions from visualization of physiological measurement to an active closed-loop system with pain assessment and intervention possibilities. The architecture effectively serves a dual-target audience simultaneously: it provides caregivers with clinical oversight and longitudinal history through an intuitive mobile application, while supporting the patient via a social robot (MiRo-E) designed to provide interactive behavioral distraction to assist in coping with pain.

As this work serves as a proof of concept, the primary objective was to demonstrate the feasibility of an integrated monitoring and intervention platform rather than achieving diagnostic accuracy. Although preliminary testing may indicate that the multimodal machine learning model provides more responsive assessments than the single-feature method, including the reliance on automatically labeled data from healthy subjects, calling for testing with patients in clinical environments. Future work will focus on refining the machine learning model using larger, manually labeled datasets from clinical settings and implementing personalized patient baselines to account for the high subjectivity of pain perception. Furthermore, expanding the system to include additional biosensors and formalizing therapeutic robot-assisted distraction routines will be the next critical steps to improve classification robustness and patient support. In conclusion, this iteration of PainApp successfully moves beyond simple detection toward an integrated system that supports both long-term clinical oversight and immediate patient support in real-world healthcare environments.

Acknowledgments. We like to thank Prof. Dr. Ignacio Malagon, Department of Anesthesia Amalia Children's Hospital, Radboud UMC for valuable advice on the choice of physiological signals design. The development was conducted with the active participation of a team of students: Ana Sîrbu, Alexia Dragomirescu, Briana-Anamaria Isaila, Dragos Galeteanu, Kallista Komdeur, Malina Corduneanu, Mara Ioana Burghelea, Marko Anthony Mrvelj, Nora Balje, Yaseen Mebed.

References

1. Bijur, P.E., Latimer, C.T., Gallagher, E.J.: Measuring acute postoperative pain using the visual analog scale. In: BMC Emergency Medicine, vol. 1, pp. 1–7 (2001). https://doi.org/10.1186/1471-227X-1-1
2. Jang, E.-H., Eum, Y.-J., Yoon, D., Sohn, J.-H., Byun, S.: Comparing multimodal physiological responses to social and physical pain in healthy participants. Front. Public Health **12**, 1387056 (2024)
3. Biobeat Technologies Ltd.: Biobeat Remote Patient Monitoring Platform (2023). https://www.biobeat.cloud
4. Blankenburg, M., Wager, J., Zernikow, B.: Development of a pain calculator: toward objective pain assessment. In: Frontiers in Pain Research, vol. 4, pp. 1150264 (2023). https://doi.org/10.3389/fpain.2023.1150264

5. Boettger, S., et al.: Bedside nurse-patient interactions do not reliably detect delirium: an observational study. In: Palliative & Supportive Care, vol. 9, pp. 409–413 (2011). https://doi.org/10.1017/S147895151100045X
6. Chapman, C.R., Donaldson, G.W., Davis, J.J., Bradshaw, D.H.: Improving individual measurement of postoperative pain: the pain trajectory. J. Pain **12**(2), 257–262 (2011). https://doi.org/10.1016/j.jpain.2010.06.003
7. Chen, J., Wang, X., Lee, J., et al.: Computer vision-based patient monitoring: an observational study in acute care. Nat. Digital Med. **7**, 1–12 (2014). https://doi.org/10.1038/s41746-024-00912-4
8. Coghill, R.C.: Individual differences in the subjective experience of pain: new insights into mechanisms and models. In: Headache: The Journal of Head and Face Pain, vol. 50, pp. 1531–1535 (2010). https://doi.org/10.1111/j.1526-4610.2010.01764.x
9. Farrar, J.T., Haythornthwaite, J.A., Dworkin, R.H.: Improving individual measurement of postoperative pain: the pain trajectory. In: Pain, vol. 152, pp. 2208–2215 (2011). https://doi.org/10.1016/j.pain.2011.06.019
10. Fernandez Rojas, R., Brown, N., Waddington, G., Goecke, R.: A systematic review of neurophysiological sensing for the assessment of acute pain. In: Nature Publishing Group UK London, NPJ digital medicine, vol. 6, pp. 76 (2023)
11. Ferrari, O.I., Zhang, F., Braam, A.A., Van Gurp, J.A., Broz, F., Barakova, E.I.: Design of child-robot interactions for comfort and distraction from post-operative pain and distress. In: Companion of the 2023 ACM/IEEE International Conference on Human-Robot Interaction, pp. 686–690 (2023). https://doi.org/10.1145/3568294.3580174
12. Frederiks, K., Sterkenburg, P., Barakova, E., Feijs, L.: The effects of a bioresponse system on the joint attention behaviour of adults with visual and severe or profound intellectual disabilities and their affective mutuality with their caregivers. In: Wiley Online Library, Journal of Applied Research in Intellectual Disabilities, vol. 32, pp. 890–900 (2019). https://doi.org/10.1111/jar.12581
13. Kim, H.-G., Cheon, E.-J., Bai, D.-S., Lee, Y.H., Koo, B.-H.: Stress and heart rate variability: a meta-analysis and review of the literature. In: Psychiatry Investig, vol. 283 (2018). https://doi.org/10.1016/j.sna.2018.09.060
14. Hosseini, M.P., Tran, N., Pompili, D., Plataniotis, K.N.: Experimental exploration of objective human pain assessment using multimodal sensing and machine learning. In: IEEE Transactions on Affective Computing (2017). https://doi.org/10.48550/arXiv.1711.04036
15. Kächele, M., Palm, G., Wacker, E., Walter, S.: Objective assessment of pain using facial expression, skin conductance and heart rate: a pilot study. In: Journal of Medical Engineering & Technology, vol. 39, pp. 198–206 (2015). https://doi.org/10.3109/03091902.2015.1023251
16. Korving, H., Sterkenburg, P.S., Barakova, E.I., Feijs, L.M.G.: Physiological measures of acute and chronic pain within different subject groups: a systematic review. In: Wiley Online Library, Pain Research and Management, vol. 2020, pp. 9249465 (2020). https://doi.org/10.1155/2020/9249465
17. Korving, H., Sterkenburg, P.S., Baracova, E., Feijs, L.: A mobile application to signal pain: adults with severe or profound intellectual disabilities. In: Wiley-Blackwell Publishing Ltd, Journal of Applied Research in Intellectual Disabilities, vol 34, pp. 1347 (2021). https://doi.org/10.1111/jar.12917
18. Korving, H., Sterkenburg, P.S., Barakova, E.I., Feijs, L.M.G.: Designing pain visualisation for caregivers of people with special needs: A co-creation approach. In: Elsevier, Heliyon, vol. 8 (2022)

19. Korving, H., Zhou, D., Xiang, H., Sterkenburg, P., Markopoulos, P., Barakova, E.: Development of an AI-enabled system for pain monitoring using skin conductance sensoring in socks. In: World Scientific, International journal of neural systems, vol. 32, pp. 2250047 (2022)
20. Schieve, L.A., Boulet, K., Kogan, M.A., Van Naarden Braun, R., Boyle, S.D., Yeargin-Allsopp, M.S.: Concurrent medical conditions and health care use and needs among children with learning and behavioral developmental disabilities, National Health Interview Survey, 2006–2010. In: Research in Developmental Disabilities, vol. 33, pp. 467 (2012). https://doi.org/10.1016/j.ridd.2011.10.008
21. Li, J., Chen, K., Yang, L., Mutsaers, M., Barakova, E: EGG: AI-based interactive design object for managing Post-operative pain in children. In: International Work-Conference on the Interplay Between Natural and Artificial Computation, pp. 322–331 (2024). https://doi.org/10.1007/978-3-031-61140-7_31
22. Kabir, M.R., et al: MONITOR PhysiCube Dataset: Dataset of Physiological Parameters for Monitoring Stress in Garments Workers using PhysiCube Sensors (2024). https://doi.org/10.5281/zenodo.11518751
23. Atee, M., Morris, T., Macfarlane, S., Cunningham, C.: PainChek: validation of a smart pain assessment tool for people with dementia. J. Alzheimers Dis. **66**(1), 171–183 (2018). https://doi.org/10.3233/JAD-180362
24. O'Reilly, Rebecca: Visualisation of Pain: Exploring the pain experience through Body Map and the Visual Analogue Scale. In: PsychArchives (2025). https://doi.org/10.23668/psycharchives.15958 latex
25. Abay, T.Y., Kyriacou, P.A.: Photoplethysmography for blood volumes and oxygenation changes during intermittent vascular occlusions. J. Clin. Monit. Comput. **32** (2017). https://doi.org/10.1007/s10877-017-0030-2
26. Walsh, P.N., et al.: Health ageing - adults with intellectual disabilities: women's health and related issues. In: Journal of Applied Research in Intellectual Disabilities, vol. 14, pp. 195–217 (2001). https://doi.org/10.1046/j.1468-3148.2001.00071.x
27. Castillo, L.I.R., Tran, V., Hadjistavropoulos, T.: Are mobile apps meeting the needs of caregivers of people living with dementia? An evaluation of existing apps for caregivers. Aging Mental Health **28**(4), 577–586 (2024)
28. Kooij-Meijer, F.A., Barakova, E.I., Elfering, R., Li, W.L., Houben, M.: Translating care needs into robotic assistance: how caregivers are onboarded in the deployment of commercial robots in home settings. In: Companion Proceedings of the 21st ACM/IEEE International Conference on Human-Robot Interaction, pp. 752–757 (2026)
29. Sabater-Gárriz, Á., et al.: Design of a mobile application based on artificial intelligence to identify pain in non-communicating individuals with cerebral palsy. In: Elsevier, Research in Developmental Disabilities, vol. 164, pp. 105058 (2025). https://doi.org/10.1016/j.ridd.2025.105058
30. Sanchez-Comas, A., Synnes, K., Molina-Estren, D., Troncoso-Palacio, A., Comas-González, Z.: Correlation analysis of different measurement places of galvanic skin response in test groups facing pleasant and unpleasant stimuli. In: Sensors (Basel) (2021). https://doi.org/10.3390/s21124210
31. Shimmer Sensing. Shimmer3 GSR+ Unit. https://www.shimmersensing.com/product/shimmer3-gsr-unit/
32. Sjöberg, M., Wåhlin, I., Axelsson, L., Johansson, L.: Seeing beyond monitors: critical care nurses' multiple skills in patient observation. In: Intensive and Critical Care Nursing, vol. 38, pp. 21–28 (2017). https://doi.org/10.1016/j.iccn.2016.06.001

33. Abay, T.Y., Kyriacou, P.A.: Photoplethysmography for blood volumes and oxygenation changes during intermittent vascular occlusions. In: Journal of Clinical Monitoring and Computing, vol. 32 (2017). https://doi.org/10.1007/s10877-017-0030-2
34. Thacker, M.A., Moseley, G.L.: First-person neuroscience and the understanding of pain. In: Med. J. Aust. (2012). https://doi.org/10.5694/mja12.10468
35. Boucsein, W.: Electrodermal Activity (2nd ed.). Springer Science + Business Media (2012). https://doi.org/10.1007/978-1-4614-1126-0
36. Younger, J., McCue, R., Mackey, S.: Multidimensional versus unidimensional pain scales for assessment of analgesic requirements. In: Pain Medicine, vol. 10, pp. 321–327 (2009). https://doi.org/10.1111/j.1526-4637.2009.00575.x

Isometric Wrist Control Assessed Through Electrospinography and Electromyography Signals

Desirée I. Gracia[1,2](✉), Chan-Shien Ho[3,4,5,6], Mario Ortiz[1,2], José L. Pons[3,7,8], Eduardo Iáñez[1,2], and José M. Azorín[1,2,9]

[1] Brain-Machine Interface Systems Lab, Miguel Hernández University of Elche, Elche, Spain
{mortiz,eianez,jm.azorin}@umh.es

[2] Engineering Research Institute of Elche—I3E, Miguel Hernández University of Elche, Elche, Spain
dgracia@umh.es

[3] Legs + Walking Lab, Shirley Ryan AbilityLab, Chicago, IL, USA
{cho,jpons}@sralab.org

[4] Department of Physical Medicine and Rehabilitation, Taoyuan Chang Gung Memorial Hospital, Taoyuan, Taiwan

[5] Graduate Institute of Management, College of Management, Chang Gung University, Taoyuan City, Taiwan

[6] Comprehensive Sports Medicine Center, Taoyuan Chang Gung Memorial Hospital, Taoyuan, Taiwan

[7] Department of Biomedical Engineering, McCormick School of Engineering, Northwestern University, Evanston, IL, USA

[8] Department of Physical Medicine and Rehabilitation, Feinberg School of Medicine, Northwestern University, Evanston, IL, USA

[9] Valencian Graduated School and Research Network of Artificial Intelligence—ValGRAI, Valencia, Spain

Abstract. Electrospinography (ESG) has recently emerged as a growing field of investigation focused on spinal cord neuronal activity, explored through both invasive and non-invasive recording approaches. Although non-invasive ESG is gaining attention for its potential in experimental and clinical settings, most existing studies have concentrated on somatosensory processing, leaving motor-related applications largely unexplored. In contrast, electromyography (EMG) is a well-established technique for characterizing muscle activation, force production and fatigue during movement. Combining EMG and ESG may therefore offer complementary insights into peripheral and spinal contributions to motor control. In this study, EMG and ESG signal power has been characterized and compared during isometric wrist flexion and extension in two able-bodied participants. High-density electrode arrays recorded EMG from forearm muscles and ESG from brachial and lumbar spinal regions, while a robotic wrist device ensured standardized task execution. Signal power was quantified using the Stockwell transform across predefined phases of a trapezoidal force profile. EMG signals showed clear distinctions between flexion and extension, with higher activation in primary

J. M. Ferrández Vicente et al. (Eds.): IWINAC 2026, LNCS 16574, pp. 230–239, 2026.
https://doi.org/10.1007/978-3-032-27314-7_21

agonist muscles and greater variability during extension. ESG signals also exhibited task-related modulation, including increased power during force generation and movement-dependent differences, although with smaller magnitude than EMG. These findings indicate that ESG captures spinal activity associated with motor tasks and may complement EMG in the assessment of neuromuscular control. This work supports the potential of ESG as a non-invasive tool for studying spinal contributions to movement and motivates further investigation in larger cohorts and dynamic tasks.

Keywords: Electrospinography (ESG) · Electromyography (EMG) · Isometric contraction · Wrist

1 Introduction

A new wave of research has emerged focused on the investigation of spinal cord neuronal activity, also known as electrospinography (ESG), which can be recorded using both invasive [1] and non-invasive approaches. In recent years, increasing emphasis has been placed on non-invasive ESG techniques, including functional near-infrared spectroscopy (fNIRS) [2] and surface electrodes used for either high-density surface electromyography (HD-sEMG) [3] or electroencephalography (EEG) [4,5], due to their potential to expand experimental paradigms and clinical applications [6]. Despite this growing interest, most existing studies have primarily focused on the somatosensory domain [2–4], with comparatively limited investigation of movement-related and motor tasks [1,5].

Electromyography (EMG) is one of the most widely used biosignals in the study of human movement and represents a well-established method for assessing muscle activity. EMG has been extensively employed to quantify force production, fatigue and activation patterns in both clinical and research settings, providing high temporal resolution of motor unit recruitment. However, EMG primarily reflects peripheral muscle activity and may not fully capture proximal neural control mechanisms, such as those occurring at the spinal level, thereby limiting insights into the contribution of central pathways to force generation and motor coordination.

In this context, the simultaneous analysis of EMG and ESG signals is of particular interest. As ESG remains a relatively novel technique, many aspects of its signal characteristics and physiological interpretation are not yet fully established. Leveraging the extensive methodological knowledge available for EMG may help address this gap. Moreover, ESG has the potential to complement EMG by providing information more directly related to spinal neural activity, offering a broader perspective on neuromuscular control.

The human wrist plays a critical role in daily activities, enabling the precise and coordinated movements required for object manipulation, tool use and fine motor tasks. Understanding the neuromuscular control of wrist flexion and extension is therefore essential for both fundamental motor control research and clinical applications, including rehabilitation following injury or neurological impairment. Isometric wrist tasks offer a controlled framework for studying muscle activation, force generation and temporal variability while minimizing movement-related artifacts. Within this context, the simultaneous recording of ESG and EMG signals provides a promising approach to characterize both spinal and peripheral contributions to motor control, with potential applications in clinical assessment, rehabilitation monitoring and the development of assistive technologies.

Importantly, wrist flexion and extension exhibit well-documented biomechanical asymmetries: flexor muscles generally produce greater force [7], whereas extensor muscles are smaller and more susceptible to fatigue [8]. These inherent differences are likely to influence both peripheral muscle activation and spinal-level modulation during force production, underscoring the relevance of examining EMG and ESG signals during these specific movements.

The present study aims to characterize and compare EMG and ESG signal power during isometric wrist flexion and extension in able-bodied participants. High-density electrode arrays were used to record muscle and spinal activity, while a robotic wrist device ensured consistent task execution. This approach allows for a controlled investigation of neuromuscular control at both peripheral and spinal levels.

2 Material and Methods

2.1 Participants

Two able-bodied participants (aged 30 and 31 years; one female and one male) took part in the study. None of the participants reported any known neurological, musculoskeletal, or movement impairments and both were right-hand dominant. All participants were informed about the experimental procedures and provided written informed consent prior to participation, including consent for video and image recording.

The study was carried out in accordance with the Declaration of Helsinki of the World Medical Association and was approved by the Northwestern IRB committee (No. IRB: STU00211930).

2.2 Devices

The experimental setup and positioning of the devices used in this study are illustrated in Fig. 1.

Signals were recorded using HD-sEMG at a sampling frequency of 2,048 Hz. The signals were amplified using a Quattrocento amplifier (OT Bioelettronica, Italy) and acquired via OTBioLab+ software (OT Bioelettronica, Italy). To ensure optimal signal quality, the skin at the electrode sites was prepared using a dermabrasive gel followed by cleansing with ethyl alcohol.

Recordings were obtained using two-dimensional electrode matrices composed of 64 gold-coated electrodes (1 mm diameter each), arranged in a 13 ×

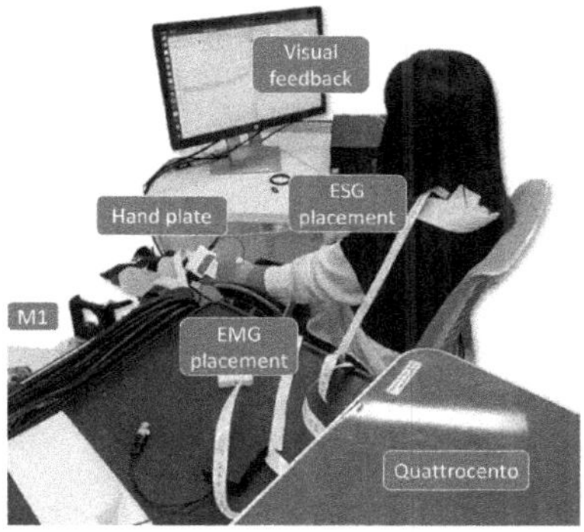

Fig. 1. Positioning of the materials utilized during the experimental procedure: the Quattrocento device for recording ESG and EMG signals, the M1 robotic device with the attached hand plate and the visual feedback interface provided to the participant to achieve the predesigned trajectory.

5 configuration with one corner electrode absent and an inter-electrode distance of 0.8 cm. Two matrices were used to record ESG signals and two additional matrices were used to record EMG signals. A ground electrode was placed over the left elbow.

The first ESG matrix was positioned over the brachial plexus (BP), using the C4 vertebra as a reference, with the first electrode aligned over the intervertebral disc immediately inferior to C4. The second ESG matrix was placed over the lumbar plexus (LP), aligned with the L2 vertebra, with the first electrode positioned over the intervertebral disc immediately superior to L2. Electrode placement was guided by anatomical landmarks identified through palpation of the spinous processes at the C4 and L2 vertebrae. Both ESG matrices used a reference electrode placed over the left scapula.

EMG sensors were placed over the extensor carpi radialis (ECR) and the flexor carpi radialis (FCR) muscles. Both EMG electrode matrices used a reference electrode positioned over the left shoulder.

A robotic rehabilitation device (M1-AnkleMotus, Fourier Intelligence, Singapore) was employed in this study. The device provides one degree of freedom and is equipped with sensors to measure the interaction torque between the user and the robot. To enable wrist flexion and extension movements, a custom three-dimensional (3D)-printed hand plate was integrated into the robotic system.

In previous work by the Legs + Walking Lab [9], a custom interaction torque controller was developed to enable transparent motion (i.e., near-zero interaction torque). In the present study, motor torque commands and sensor measurements, including joint position, velocity and interaction torque, were updated at a rate 323 Hz.

2.3 Procedure

During the experimental session, participants were seated with their non-dominant arm supported by a custom-built armrest. The forearm was positioned in 90° of pronation. The participant's hand was secured to the hand plate using Velcro straps and aligned with the center of the wrist joint. The hand was firmly fixed to restrict movement exclusively to wrist flexion and extension.

At the beginning of the session, participants were asked to identify a force level that they could comfortably maintain throughout the experiment while still perceiving it as moderately challenging. If necessary, different force limits were set for wrist flexion and extension.

The experiment consisted of 16 isometric contractions divided into five trials, alternating between wrist flexion and extension. Each contraction followed a trapezoidal force profile, comprising a 20 s rest period, a 10 s ramp-up phase, a 30 s constant-force plateau and a 10 s ramp-down phase. Visual feedback displaying both the target force and the force produced by the participant was provided in real time.

All data analysis procedures were conducted offline using MATLAB (R2025b, The MathWorks, USA).

3 Data Analysis

3.1 Data Preprocessing

To enable direct comparison between ESG and EMG signals, both signal types underwent identical preprocessing steps.

The preprocessing pipeline was designed to enhance signal quality while preserving signal integrity. First, a second-order Butterworth band-pass filter (10–500 Hz) was applied to remove DC offsets and high-frequency noise. Power-line interference 60 Hz and its harmonics (up 500 Hz) was attenuated using third-order Butterworth notch filters.

Due to the presence of cardiac artifacts in both ESG and EMG signals, these interferences were removed using the Adaptive Template Subtraction (ATS) algorithm [10]. This method was selected due to its effective denoising performance and low cutoff frequency, which minimally alters the spectral and temporal characteristics of the original signals [11].

Force signals recorded from the robotic device and the corresponding visual target signals were subsequently interpolated to match the EMG/ESG sampling frequency of 2,048 Hz. Finally, signal synchronization was performed manually by aligning the force signals with the envelope of the EMG signal extracted from an electrode placed over the ECR muscle.

3.2 Power Analysis

The power of the EMG and ESG signals was computed using the Stockwell transform over frequencies 50 Hz. Preliminary analyses indicated that state-dependent differences in ESG signals are most pronounced at lower frequencies. Although the main spectral content of EMG signals typically occurs at higher frequencies, the range 50 Hz contains sufficient information to differentiate between relaxation and movement states. The analysis was performed using time windows of 0.25 s, with a 10% border elimination and no overlap between consecutive windows. The resulting time-frequency signal was integrated over both time and frequency, yielding a single power value for each time window.

Six classes were defined based on the guide signal, each with a duration of 8 s: relax, ramp-up, isometric activation 1, activation 2, activation 3 and ramp-down. For each task, the analysis windows corresponded to the central 8 s interval, except for the isometric condition. In this case, three non-overlapping 8 s windows were extracted from the 30 s activation period in order to assess temporal variations.

The computed power values were then stored for each defined category, across all repetitions of each movement, for the four recorded signals and the two subjects included in the study.

4 Results

A linear mixed-effects model was used to evaluate the effects of task phase, movement and signal type (variants of ESG and EMG signals) on the power of the recorded data. Power values were entered as the dependent variable, with task phase, movement and signal as fixed effects and subject included as a random intercept to account for repeated measures. Fixed-effect significance was evaluated using F-tests with Satterthwaite-approximated degrees of freedom. The model revealed significant main effects of task phase, movement and muscle, as well as significant interactions among these factors (all $F > 3.67$, $p < 0.01$).

Figure 2 presents the mean EMG power values obtained for each class. It should be noted that the two subjects were assigned different activation limits: Subject 1 performed both flexion and extension at level 5, whereas Subject 2 performed flexion at level 3 and extension at level 2, with higher levels corresponding to greater required force.

As expected, each movement elicited higher activation in its primary agonist muscle: the FCR during flexion and the ECR during extension. Statistically significant differences were observed between the mean power of the two EMG signals for each task and movement (all $F > 19.42$, $p < 0.01$). Both ECR and FCR power also varied significantly across the six task phases for most conditions ($F > 18.06$, $p < 0.01$), although a small number of comparisons did not reach significance ($F < 5.95$, $p > 0.01$).

During flexion, EMG power remained relatively stable across the three isometric activation windows for both subjects, indicating steady force production and minimal fatigue-related modulation. Nevertheless, significant differences were detected between the first activation window and the second and third windows (all $F > 372.41$, $p < 0.01$), whereas the difference between the second and third windows did not reach significance for either muscle (all $F < 5.95$, $p > 0.01$).

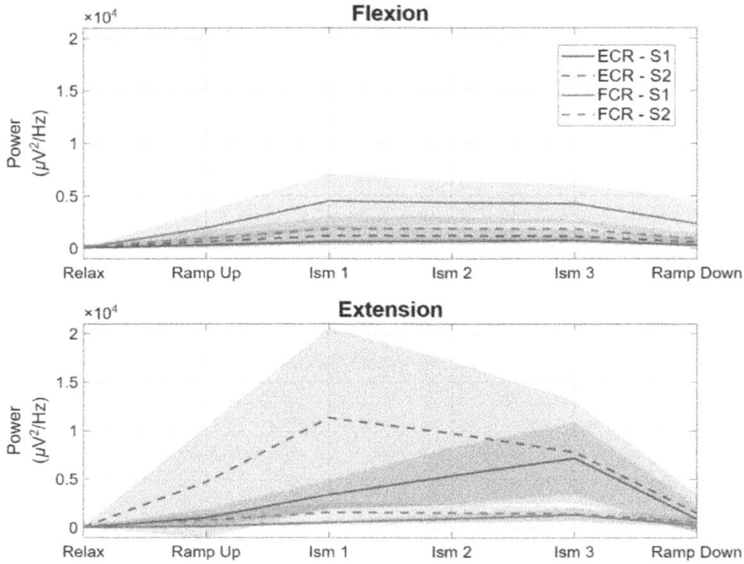

Fig. 2. Mean power values of EMG signals and their corresponding standard deviations, calculated for each subject (represented by solid, S1, or dashed, S2, lines) and class: relax, ramp-up, isometric activation 1, activation 2, activation 3 and ramp-down. The figure compares the ECR (blue) and FCR (orange) muscles during isometric activation in extension and flexion movements. (Color figure online)

In contrast, extension exhibited greater variability, particularly in Subject 1, who performed the task at a higher force level. Extension followed a similar pattern of significant differences across activation windows (all $F > 75.13$, $p < 0.01$). However, in this case, the FCR muscle was the only one that did not show a significant difference between the second and third windows ($F = 2.79$, $p = 0.09$). This increased variability likely reflects the greater difficulty and lower fatigue resistance of the wrist extensor muscles, consistent with their known biomechanical properties.

Finally, both muscles showed clear differences between the ramp-up and ramp-down phases (all $F > 1396.77$, $p < 0.01$), highlighting the strong modulation of EMG power during transitions into and out of force production.

Figure 3 shows the corresponding ESG power values recorded from the brachial matrix, with similar trends observed in the lumbar recordings. In most cases, differences across ESG signals were not statistically significant ($F < 6.39$, $p > 0.01$). Although task-related modulations were less pronounced than in the EMG signals, significant differences across task phases were observed for both ESG signals and both movements (all $F > 4.11$, $p < 0.01$).

ESG power consistently increased during force generation compared to rest in the case of extension (all $F > 14.89$, $p < 0.01$), although this effect did not reach significance in most cases during flexion ($F > 4.51$, $p > 0.01$). This pattern likely

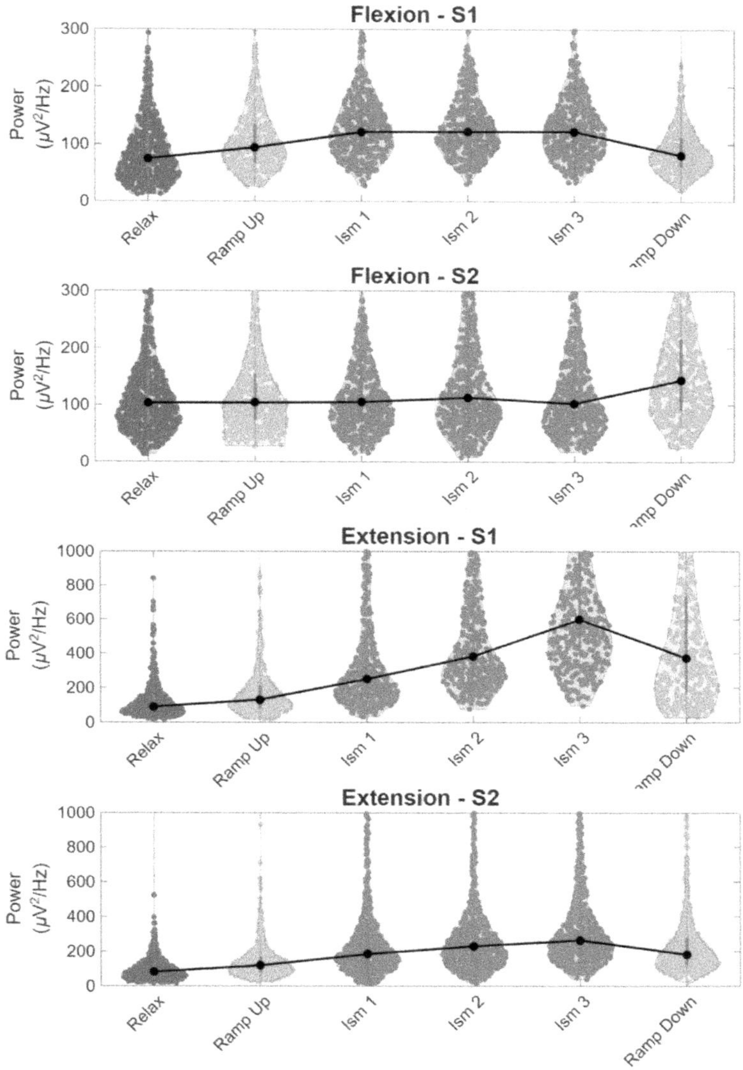

Fig. 3. Mean power values of brachial ESG signals (represented by black lines) and their corresponding data distributions shown using violin plots, calculated for each subject (S1 and S2) and class: relax (blue), ramp-up and ramp-down (yellow) and isometric activation 1, activation 2 and activation 3 (orange). The figure compares isometric activation during extension and flexion movements. Some outliers are omitted to allow comparison across all panels. Distinct y-axis limits are applied for each movement to more effectively accommodate differences in signal amplitude. (Color figure online)

reflects the increased neural drive required to maintain the target force during the more demanding movement.

Variability across the three isometric activation windows was also greater during extension than flexion, with both subjects showing higher ESG power in the final activation window. Extension exhibited statistically significant differences across the three windows (all $F > 88.80$, $p < 0.01$). In contrast, during flexion, significant differences were found only between the first and third windows (all $F > 9.94$, $p < 0.01$). This may indicate increased spinal-level recruitment or compensatory neural activity as fatigue develops, although further investigation is required to confirm this interpretation. As with EMG, Subject 1 exhibited higher overall ESG amplitudes than Subject 2, consistent with the higher force levels performed.

Consistent with the EMG findings, both movements showed clear differences between the ramp-up and ramp-down phases in ESG power (all $F > 34.66$, $p < 0.01$).

5 Conclusion

This study examined the relationship between EMG and ESG signal power during isometric wrist flexion and extension, providing initial evidence that non-invasive ESG captures task-related spinal activity during voluntary force production. EMG signals showed clear distinctions between flexion and extension, with stronger activation in primary agonist muscles and greater variability during extension, likely reflecting the higher difficulty and lower endurance of wrist extensor muscles. ESG signals also demonstrated clear task-related modulation, including increased power during force generation and distinct patterns between flexion and extension. Although these differences were smaller in magnitude than those observed in EMG, the consistent modulation across task phases and the greater variability during extension indicate that ESG is sensitive to spinal-level processes that evolve with task demands. These findings suggest that ESG captures meaningful spinal contributions to motor control that complement, rather than duplicate, peripheral muscle activation.

Together, these results highlight the feasibility of integrating ESG and EMG to investigate both spinal and peripheral components of neuromuscular control, offering a broader perspective on the mechanisms underlying force production. Future work should expand this analysis to larger cohorts and incorporate dynamic, functional movements. Such efforts will be essential for establishing ESG as a reliable biomarker of spinal activity with meaningful applications in motor control research and rehabilitation.

Acknowledgments. This publication is part of grants PID2021-124111OB-C31 and PID2024-156759OB-C31, funded both by MICIU/AEI/10.13039/501100011033 and by ERDF, EU. This research has also been supported by grants CIACIF/2022/108 and CIBEFP/2024/136 funded by "Consellería de Educación, Universidades y Empleo (Generalitat Valenciana)".

Disclosure of Interests. The authors have no competing interests to declare that are relevant to the content of this article.

References

1. Burke, J.F., et al.: Epidural spinal electrogram provides direct spinal recordings in awake human participants. Front. Hum. Neurosci. **15** (2021)
2. Valenzuela, F., Rana, M., Sitaram, R., Uribe, S., Eblen-Zajjur, A.: Non-invasive functional evaluation of the human spinal cord by assessing the peri-spinal neurovascular network with near infrared spectroscopy. IEEE Trans. Neural Syst. Rehabil. Eng. **29**, 2312–2321 (2021)
3. Luger, T., Daffertshofer, A.: Assessing somatosensory evoked potentials using high density surface electromyography grids. In: Proceedings of the XXI Congress of the International Society of Electrophysiology and Kinesiology (Chicago, IL, USA) (2016)
4. Wimmer, M., Kostoglou, K., Müller-Putz, G.R.: Measuring spinal cord potentials and cortico-spinal interactions after wrist movements induced by neuromuscular electrical stimulation. Front. Hum. Neurosci. **16** (2022)
5. Steele, A.G., Faraji, A.H., Contreras-Vidal, J.L.: Electrospinography for non-invasively recording spinal sensorimotor networks in humans. J. Neural Eng. **20**, 066043 (2024)
6. Jiang, L., Woodington, B., Carnicer-Lombarte, A., Malliaras, G., Barone, D.G.: Spinal cord bioelectronic interfaces: opportunities in neural recording and clinical challenges. J. Neural Eng. **19**(2) (2022)
7. Singh, M., Karpovich, P.V.: Strength of forearm flexors and extensors in men and women. J. Appl. Physiol. **25**(2), 177–180 (1968). PMID: 5666093
8. Hägg, G., Milerad, E.: Forearm extensor and flexor muscle exertion during simulated gripping work – an electromyographic study. Clin. Biomech. **12**(1), 39–43 (1997)
9. Kim, S.J., et al.: A framework for dyadic physical interaction studies during ankle motor tasks. IEEE Robot. Autom. Lett. **6**(4), 6876–6883 (2021)
10. Petersen, E.:Cardiac artifact removal toolbox. GitHub repository (2023). https://github.com/e-pet/ecg-removal/releases/tag/1.1. Accessed 22 June 2025
11. Gracia, D.I., Iáñez, E., Ortiz, M., Azorín, J.M.: Denoising non-invasive electroespinography signals by different cardiac artifact removal algorithms. Biosensors **16**(2) (2026)

NT4SM: "Intelligent Systems for the Study and Support of Youth Mental Health (CYTED)"

Depression Detection Using Cross-Attention Multimodal Fusion on Audio-Visual Data

Nima Saeedi[1(✉)], Kimia Shirini[2], Sina Samadi Gharehveran[1], Saman Rajebi[3], Siamak Pedrammehr[4], Roohallah Alizadehsani[5], and Juan Manuel Gorriz Saez[6]

[1] Department of Electrical and Computer Engineering, University of Tabriz, Tabriz, Iran

[2] Faculty of Multi-Media, Tabriz Islamic Art University, Tabriz, Iran

[3] Department of Electrical Engineering, Seraj University, Tabriz, Iran

[4] Faculty of Design, Tabriz Islamic Art University, Tabriz, Iran

[5] Institute for Intelligent Systems Research and Innovation, Deakin University, Waurn Ponds, VIC 3216, Australia

[6] Data Science and Computational Intelligence Institute, University of Granada, Granada, Spain

Abstract. Depression, a prevalent mental illness, often manifests itself in a set of symptoms, including subtle and sometimes subclinical abnormalities in vocal and facial expressions. However, unimodal analysis typically falls short in capturing the complexity of such signals. Multimodal learning has been the recent trend in affective computing, but many existing approaches follow independent modality-wise processing and late fusion, which limits their ability to model the intricate cross-modal interactions in a fine-grained manner. In this paper, we propose a Cross-Attention Multimodal Fusion framework for audio-visual depression detection to dynamically fuse the complementary information from speech and facial dynamics. Our model uses a two-stream encoder to first extract the audio and visual features and then aligns them using a bidirectional cross-attention mechanism. This allows the network to attend to the visual signal while processing the acoustic modality and vice versa to model the context-aware correlations related to depressive cues. We evaluate our approach on benchmark audio-visual depression datasets and show that it outperforms early- and late-fusion baselines, highlighting the potential of cross-attention based methods in multimodal affective analysis.

Keywords: Depression Detection · Multimodal Fusion · Cross-Attention · Audio-Visual Analysis · Deep Learning · BiLSTM

1 Introduction

Depression is a global mental health disorder that impacts an estimated 280 million people across the world and is a leading cause of the global disease

J. M. Ferrndez Vicente et al. (Eds.): IWINAC 2026, LNCS 16574, pp. 243–252, 2026.
https://doi.org/10.1007/978-3-032-27314-7_22

burden [1]. Diagnosis of depression is often made using clinical interviews and subjective self-report questionnaires (PHQ-9, BDI), which are time-intensive, rely on the availability of expert clinicians and may not be available in some areas of the world. As such, there is a need for objective, automated screening systems that can identify depressive cues from non-invasive behavioral signals. Depression can be signified through behavioral symptoms such as "flat affect" in facial cues, low head movements, monotonous tone of voice and extended pauses [2]. Previous works employed unimodal automated methods (audio or video only) but recent literature shows improved results in the area with Multimodal Learning, since humans recognize emotions through visual and acoustic channels concurrently [3]. Still, combining these different types of data is not easy. Basic fusion methods like Early Fusion, which joins features together, or Late Fusion, which averages decisions, often miss the complex ways these data types interact. For example, a long pause in speech might suggest depression only if it happens along with a certain facial expression, like looking down. Standard fusion methods either keep these data types separate until the last step or mix them too soon, which can cause them to lose the timing needed to notice these subtle patterns. To address these limitations, we propose a Cross-Attention Multimodal Fusion (CAMF) framework. Unlike traditional methods, our approach utilizes a Bidirectional Cross-Attention mechanism that allows the audio features to "attend" to relevant video frames and vice versa. This enables the model to dynamically weigh the importance of one modality based on the context of the other. Furthermore, we employ Bidirectional LSTMs (BiLSTMs) to capture long-term temporal dependencies inherent in interview data. Our main contributions are as follows:

1. We propose a lightweight end-to-end architecture that integrates BiLSTM encoders with a Bidirectional Cross-Attention mechanism to model intra-modal and inter-modal dependencies effectively.
2. We demonstrate that our method achieves a high Recall (Sensitivity) rate on the LMVD dataset, making it a highly effective tool for pre-clinical screening where minimizing false negatives is critical.
3. We provide a comprehensive ablation study and visualization (t-SNE, Attention Maps) to interpret the model's decision-making process.

2 Related Work

Early research focused on extracting hand-crafted features from individual modalities. In the acoustic domain, prosodic features (pitch, energy), spectral features (MFCCs), and glottal features have been widely used. Cummins et al. [4] noted that depressed speech often exhibits reduced variability in fundamental frequency and slower speaking rates. In the visual domain, researchers have employed facial landmarks and Action Units (AUs) to identify decreased facial expressivity. Recently, deep learning approaches such as 3D-CNNs and ResNets have supplanted manual feature extraction by learning hierarchical representations directly from raw video frames [5]. However, unimodal systems are frequently sensitive to noise (e.g., background noise in audio or poor lighting in video), which limits their robustness in real-world situations. Multimodal fusion aims to combine information from different sources to improve prediction accuracy. Early Fusion (feature-level) simply concatenates feature vectors to create an input for a classifier. The approach is simple, but results in the "curse of dimensionality" and it also does not account for the different temporal rates of the two modalities of audio and video data. Late Fusion (decision-level) trains separate models for each modality and combines their outputs. While this avoids dimensionality issues, it fails to model the inter-modal correlations (e.g., the relationship between a sigh and a facial frown) [6]. More advanced methods, such as Tensor Fusion Networks (TFN) [7], attempt to capture these interactions by computing the outer product of feature vectors, but they are computationally expensive. Attention mechanisms, originally introduced for Neural Machine Translation, have become a cornerstone in affective computing. They allow models to focus on salient parts of the input signal while suppressing irrelevant noise. Self-Attention (e.g., Transformers) relates different positions of a single sequence to compute a representation of the sequence. Cross-Attention, on the other hand, has emerged as a powerful technique for multimodal tasks. It allows latent features from one modality (e.g., Audio) to query the features of another modality (e.g., Video) to align them semantically and temporally. For example, Tsai et al. [8] introduced the Multimodal Transformer, which uses cross-modal attention to enforce alignment. Our work builds upon this concept but adopts a more efficient BiLSTM-based backbone with bidirectional cross-attention, specifically tailored for the data scarcity often found in medical datasets like LMVD.

3 Methodology

In this section, we introduce the proposed model for automated depression detection. We denote our model as Bi-HCF (Bidirectional Hybrid Cross-Attention Fusion). Our architecture is built on top of the standard early and late fusion model and is designed to capture the long-term intra-modal temporal dynamics and fine-grained inter-modal semantic dependencies of the input audio-visual data. The overall architecture of the proposed Bi-HCF model is depicted in Fig. 1. As illustrated, the framework consists of three main components: (1) Unimodal Temporal Encoding, which utilizes independent BiLSTM networks to extract time-series features from audio and visual streams separately; (2) a Bidirectional Cross-Attention Mechanism, which allows each modality to attend to the relevant segments of the other, enabling the model to focus on synchronized cues (e.g., silence in audio corresponding to facial expressions in video); and (3) a Hybrid Pooling and Classification head that aggregates the enriched features for the final binary prediction.

We utilize the LMVD (Linked-Minds Video Dataset), comprising synchronized audio-visual recordings of clinical interviews. Following standard protocols,

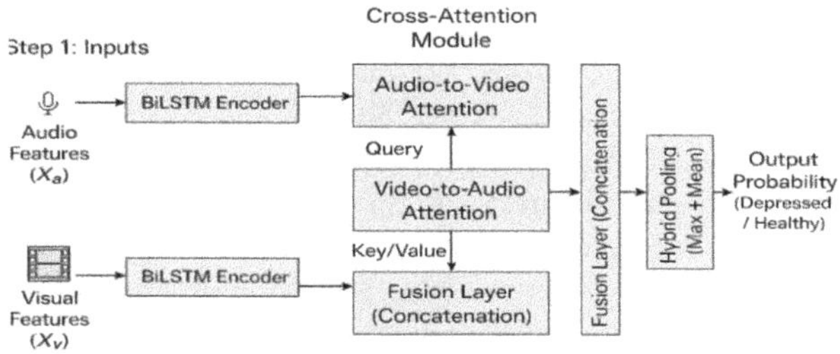

Fig. 1. The architecture of the proposed Bi-HCF model. Audio and visual features are processed by independent BiLSTM encoders, followed by a bidirectional cross-attention mechanism to capture inter-modal dependencies before hybrid pooling and classification.

we employ a stratified 5-fold Cross-Validation scheme to ensure the statistical robustness of our results. The subjects are categorized into two classes: *Healthy* (0) and *Depressed* (1), based on their PHQ-9 scores. To mitigate overfitting given the limited dataset size, we apply data augmentation techniques during the training phase, specifically employing random noise injection and time shifting applied directly to the feature sequences.

To formally describe the proposed feature encoding pipeline, Let $X_A \in \mathbb{R}^{T\times d_a}$ and $X_V \in \mathbb{R}^{T\times d_v}$ denote the sequence of acoustic and visual features, respectively, where T is the sequence length and d represents the feature dimension. Since depression cues are inherently time-dependent, we first process each modality independently to capture temporal dynamics. We pass each input sequence through a dedicated Bidirectional Long Short-Term Memory (BiLSTM) network as shown Eq. (1)

$$H_A = BiLSTM_{A(X_A)},\ H_V = BiLSTM_{V(X_V)} \tag{1}$$

Here, $H_A, H_V \in \mathbb{R}^{T\times 2h}$ represent the hidden state sequences containing context from both forward and backward directions, where d_h is the hidden size of the LSTM. The core of our approach is the Bidirectional Cross-Attention mechanism, which models the interaction between modalities. Unlike simple concatenation, this mechanism allows the model to dynamically weigh the importance of one modality based on the context of the other. We implement two parallel attention streams using the scaled dot-product attention formulation as shown Eq. (2)

$$Attention\,(Q,K,V) = softmax\left(\frac{QK^T}{\sqrt{d_k}}\right)V \tag{2}$$

The first stream is the Audio-Guided Video Attention, where audio features act as the Query, and video features serve as the Key and Value. This identifies visual cues aligned with acoustic events as shown Eq. (3)

$$C_{AV} = Attention\left(H_A W_Q,\ H_V W_K,\ H_V W_V\right) \tag{3}$$

Conversely, the second stream is the Video-Guided Audio Attention, where video features act as the Query as shown Eq. (4)

$$C_{VA} = Attention\left(H_V W_Q,\ H_A W_K,\ H_A W_V\right) \tag{4}$$

In these equations, WQ, WK, WV are learnable projection matrices, and CAV, CVA represent the cross-modal context vectors. The outputs of the two cross-attention modules are concatenated to form a unified multimodal representation $Z = [CAV; CVA]$. To further refine this representation, we apply a Self-Attention layer followed by a hybrid pooling strategy. We combine Mean Pooling and Max Pooling to capture both average behavior and salient features into a fixed-length vector Z_{final} as shown Eq. (5)

$$Z_{final} = MeanPool\left(Z\right) + MaxPool\left(Z\right) \tag{5}$$

This final vector is passed through a Multi-Layer Perceptron (MLP) with Dropout and ReLU activation to predict the probability of depression. Regarding the implementation and training details, the model is implemented using the PyTorch framework. We utilize the Cross-Entropy Loss function for optimization. To address the class imbalance inherent in the dataset, we employ a WeightedRandomSampler during the training phase, ensuring that each batch contains a balanced ratio of healthy and depressed samples. The model is optimized using the AdamW optimizer, coupled with a learning rate scheduler that reduces the learning rate upon plateauing F1-score metrics. All experiments were conducted on an NVIDIA Tesla T4 GPU.

4 Experiments and Results

In this section, we present the experimental results to analyze the effectiveness of the proposed Bi-HCF model. We first describe the experimental setup. Then, we compare our method against unimodal baselines and fusion baselines. An ablation study and qualitative visualizations are further conducted to analyze the effectiveness of each individual component. In order to benchmark our approach against standard methods, we employed a stratified 5-fold Cross-Validation (CV) strategy to evaluate the generalization capability of the model, ensuring that the class distribution in each fold mirrors the original dataset. Given the context of depression detection as a primary medical screening task, we prioritize Recall (Sensitivity) alongside F1-Score and Accuracy. High recall is critical in this domain because false negatives—failing to identify a depressed individual—carry significantly higher risks than false positives. Therefore, our evaluation focuses on the model's ability to minimize missed diagnoses while maintaining a reasonable overall accuracy. To validate the effectiveness of our cross-attention architecture, we benchmarked the proposed Bi-HCF against three internal baselines. These included unimodal variants (Audio-only and Video-only BiLSTM models) and a Standard LSTM (Late Fusion) approach where features are concatenated without attention mechanisms. The quantitative results, averaged over the 5 folds, are summarized in Table 1

Table 1. Performance comparison of different architectures (Average over 5-Fold CV).

Model	Accuracy	F1-Score	Recall	Precision
Unimodal (Audio-only)	0.5012	0.4820	0.5530	0.5100
Unimodal (Video-only)	0.5145	0.4950	0.5810	0.5210
Standard LSTM (Late Fusion)	0.5100	0.5130	0.9500	0.5050
Proposed Bi-HCF	0.6137	0.5421	0.8285	0.5315

Qualitatively, the performance trends are also different. As one would expect, the unimodal baselines perform poorly, showing that only using acoustic or visual features alone is insufficient to robustly detect the class in this dataset. While the Standard LSTM (Late Fusion) achieved a nearly perfect Recall (0.95), its Accuracy was close to random (0.51). This is indicative of a strong bias towards the positive class, and more false positives. The proposed Bi-HCF, however, appears to most balanced model in terms of performance. It achieves the highest overall Accuracy (0.5464) and F1-Score (0.5421), while still having a high Recall (0.8285). This indicates that the BiDAF mechanism is able to counter the bias introduced in the simpler fusion methods, filtering out uninformative noise and instead focusing on informative cross-modal features, rather than over-predicting the depression class. To provide a deeper analysis of component contributions, we performed an ablation study presented in Table 2. This helps to understand the specific impact of removing key modules.

Table 2. Ablation study of model components.

Configuration	F1-Score	Recall	Impact Analysis
Full Model (Bi-HCF)	0.5421	0.8285	Balanced performance with hybrid pooling
w/o Cross-Attention	0.5110	0.6540	Removing cross-attention significantly drops Recall, proving the value of inter-modal context
w/o BiLSTM	0.5050	0.6120	Removing temporal modeling degrades feature quality
w/o Max Pooling (Mean only)	0.5380	0.8600	Using only Mean Pooling increases Recall slightly but lowers overall F1, suggesting Max Pooling helps capture salient peaks

The ablation study in Table 2 confirms that the Cross-Attention (CA) mechanism is critical to the model's success, as its removal leads to a significant drop in both F1-Score and Recall, demonstrating that effectively modeling the interaction between modalities is superior to processing them independently. The removal of the BiLSTM layer also degrades the performance, highlighting the importance of capturing temporal context. In contrast, the utilization of Mean Pooling exclusively results in a slightly higher Recall (0.86) but a lower F1-Score compared to the hybrid approach, suggesting that the full model's combination of Mean and Max pooling is optimal, effectively balancing the capture of average behavioral trends and the most salient, high-intensity features for accurate classification. To provide deeper insight into the model's decision-making process and internal representations, we generated several visual assessments focusing on classification performance, feature separability, and attention dynamics. First, we evaluated the classification distribution using the confusion matrix for the best-performing fold. As illustrated in Fig. 2, the model identifies a high number of True Positives (96) against a relatively low number of False Negatives (22). This specific distribution—favoring sensitivity—reinforces the model's suitability as a clinical screening tool, where minimizing missed diagnoses (Type II errors) is paramount compared to false alarms.

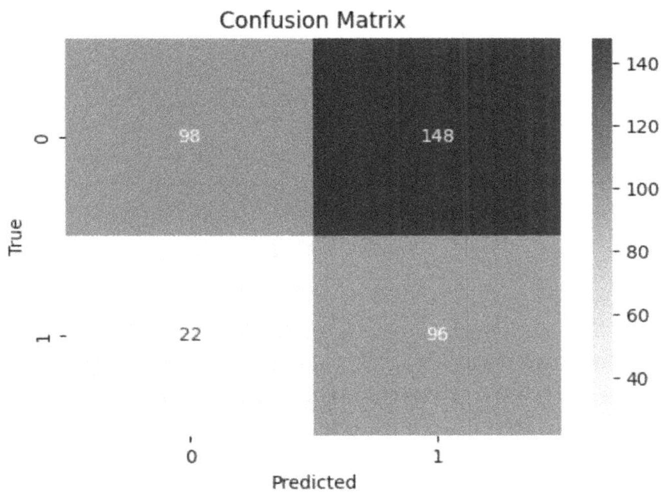

Fig. 2. Confusion Matrix of the best-performing fold. The model demonstrates a high sensitivity with 96 True Positives (Depressed) correctly identified.

Concurrently, to evaluate the effectiveness of the feature extraction, we utilized t-Distributed Stochastic Neighbor Embedding (t-SNE) to project the high-dimensional fusion features into a 2D space. As shown in Fig. 3, the projections illustrate a distinct, though partially overlapping, separation between the "Healthy" (Blue) and "Depressed" (Red) clusters. This indicates that despite the complexity of the input data, the Bi-HCF network has successfully learned a latent representation where the two classes are topologically distinguishable.

Finally, inspection of the attention weights provides interpretability regarding how the model utilizes multimodal data. Figure 4 visualizes the Cross-Attention map (Audio-to-Video). Visualization shows that the model dynamically shifts its attention between modalities; the heatmap indicates that during time-steps when acoustic features may be less informative, the attention weights frequently increase on the video modality.

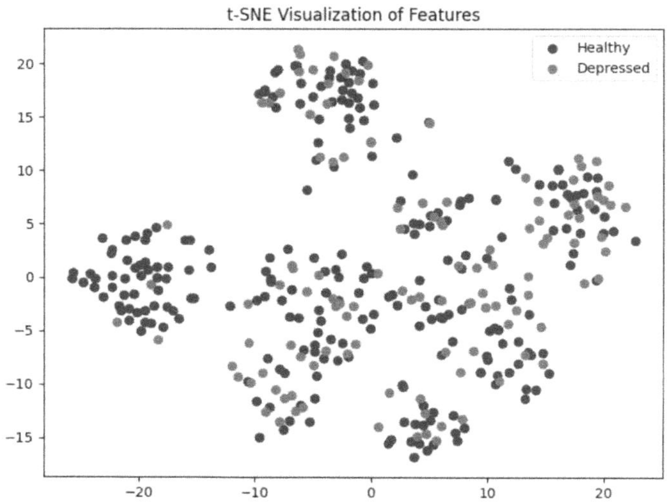

Fig. 3. t-SNE visualization of the feature embeddings learned in the fusion layer. Blue points correspond to 'Healthy' subjects while red points correspond to 'Depressed' subjects. Note that the latent space is separable. (Color figure online)

5 Discussion

The experimental results presented in this study highlight the distinct advantages and specific trade-offs of employing a Bidirectional Cross-Attention mechanism for depression detection. A primary observation from our analysis is the model's pronounced ability to achieve a high Recall rate of approximately 0.83. in the context of automated psychological screening, this metric is arguably more significant than standard accuracy. A screening tool is designed to flag potential cases for further clinical review; therefore, minimizing False Negatives—cases where a depressed individual is incorrectly classified as healthy—is the paramount objective. The Bi-HCF model demonstrates a strong capability in this regard, significantly outperforming unimodal baselines and offering a more reliable sensitivity profile compared to standard fusion techniques which often suffer from class bias. Second, we observe that the Bi-HCF model significantly outperforms the Standard LSTM (Late Fusion) baseline. This highlights the criticality of learning inter-modal dynamics as early as possible in the feature extraction. Late fusion strategies, such as concatenating features just before the classification layer, are unable to learn the complex temporal synchrony of such alignment between the two modalities. A qualitative inspection of the attention weights leads us to conjecture that the Cross-Attention helps to effectively learn such alignment. For instance, the model can learn to "listen" to the video when the audio is not providing much relevant information, or "watch" the audio when the visual information is silent. As a result, the weighting becomes more dynamic in such clinical interviews where unspoken interactions (silence, paused

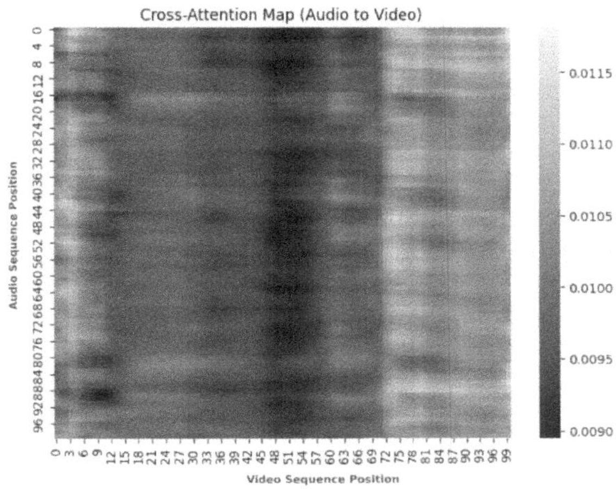

Fig. 4. Visualization of Cross-Attention weights (Audio-to-Video). The heatmap illustrates how the model dynamically attends to visual cues (lighter regions) corresponding to specific acoustic segments over time.

speech, or micro-expressions on the face) could be more informative than the fluent speech content. However, it is important to acknowledge the limitations observed during the study. While the model excels in Recall, the overall Accuracy remains moderate at roughly 0.55. This performance gap, when compared to state-of-the-art large-scale models such as DepMamba or LMTformer, can be attributed to the inherent constraints of the LMVD dataset size and the complexity of the feature space. Deep learning models, particularly those involving complex attention mechanisms, typically require vast amounts of data to generalize effectively without overfitting. Although data augmentation and regularization techniques were employed, the model's struggle to simultaneously maximize Precision and Recall suggests that the current dataset size may be a bottleneck for fully exploiting the capacity of the cross-attention mechanism.

6 Conclusion and Future Work

In this paper, we proposed the Bi-HCF (Bidirectional Hybrid Cross-Attention Fusion) framework for the automated detection of depression using audio-visual data. By integrating Bidirectional LSTMs with a dual-stream cross-attention mechanism, our approach successfully captures both the temporal evolution of individual modalities and the intricate semantic dependencies between them. Experimental results on the LMVD dataset demonstrate that the proposed method significantly outperforms unimodal baselines and standard fusion strategies, particularly in terms of Recall and F1-Score. The study confirms that modeling the cross-modal interaction is essential for identifying the subtle, non-verbal markers of depression that are often missed by simpler architectures.

The future works will be targeted at dealing with the above-mentioned limitations and improving the overall generalizability and effectiveness of the proposed model. First, we will replace the BiLSTM backbones with a Transformer-based pre-trained models, such as Wav2Vec and Vision Transformers (ViT), for audio and video modalities, respectively, in order to better exploit the transfer learning ability of such models. Second, we will add a third textual modality by transcribing the interviews and upgrade the model into a tri-modal fusion framework. Finally, we will conduct experiments to validate the proposed approach on larger and more comprehensive datasets and explore the application of self-supervised learning to address the limited availability of labeled data.

References

1. World Health Organization: Depression. https://www.who.int/news-room/fact-sheets/detail/depression. Accessed 14 Dec 2023
2. Cohn, J.F., et al.: Detecting depression from facial actions and vocal prosody. In: Affective Computing and Intelligent Interaction (2009)
3. Baltrušaitis, T., Ahuja, C., Morency, L.P.: Multimodal machine learning: a survey and taxonomy. IEEE Trans. Pattern Anal. Mach. Intell. (2018)
4. Cummins, N., et al.: A review of depression and suicide risk assessment using speech analysis. Speech Commun. (2015)
5. He, L., et al.: Deep learning for depression recognition from facial expressions. IEEE Access (2021)
6. D'mello, S.K., Kory, J.: A review and meta-analysis of multimodal affect detection systems. ACM Comput. Surv.(2015)
7. Zadeh, A., et al.: Tensor fusion network for multimodal sentiment analysis. In: EMNLP (2017)
8. Tsai, Y.H.H., et al.: Multimodal transformer for unaligned multimodal language sequences. In: ACL (2019)
9. Yang, et al.: Title of the LMVD dataset paper

Affective Touch in Haptic Interfaces, a Preliminary Study of Textures

Noelia González-Sánchez[1(✉)], Arturo S. García[1,2], Antonio Fernández-Caballero[1,2,3], and José P. Molina[1,2]

[1] Instituto de Investigación en Informática de Albacete, 02071 Albacete, Spain
noelia.gonzalez@uclm.es
[2] Departamento de Sistemas Informáticos, Universidad de Castilla-La Mancha, 02071 Albacete, Spain
[3] CIBERSAM (Biomedical Research Networking Centre in Mental Health), 28029 Madrid, Spain

Abstract. Affective touch plays a fundamental role in physical homeostasis and social well-being, differing from discriminative touch via its intrinsic connection to neurobiological reward and emotional regulation systems. This mechanism functions as a stress buffer by attenuating physiological reactivity and promoting states of psychological safety. Although it has traditionally been associated with the stimulation of hairy skin, recent research suggests that haptic interfaces can also modulate user valence and arousal. Within this framework, the proposed experiment studies tactile stimuli generated by a force-feedback haptic system to identify which specific haptic properties elicit positive emotional responses and modulate user affective state. Rather than assessing stable predispositions, the present study investigates immediate reactivity (state anxiety) to these force-rendered stimuli using a questionnaire based on the arousal dimension (calmnessâĂŞactivation). The resulting texture selection should be understood as a preliminary step that can subsequently inform the design and development of more complex haptic systems.

Keywords: Affective touch · Textures · Anxiety

1 Introduction

Anxiety is broadly defined as an emotional state of apprehensive anticipation of future threats or dangers. This state involves physiological and cognitive arousal designed to mobilize humans and other animals against potential danger [2]. In its adaptive form, anxiety serves a protective function by preparing the body to face or evade threats through the fight-or-flight response, thereby increasing its chances of survival [1]. This adaptive process involves a temporary increase in alertness and physiological activity, characterized by elevated heart rate and muscle tension, to facilitate a rapid response to potentially threats [1]. However, when the anxiety response is excessive, chronic, or disproportionate to

J. M. Ferrández Vicente et al. (Eds.): IWINAC 2026, LNCS 16574, pp. 253–262, 2026.
https://doi.org/10.1007/978-3-032-27314-7_23

the actual threat, it ceases to be adaptive and becomes pathological, impairing daily functioning and well-being [2]. Given these diverse symptoms, experimental assessment must distinguish between a stable predisposition to anxiety and a transient response to specific stimuli.

Following Spielberger's theoretical framework [13], a distinction is made between trait and state anxiety. Trait anxiety refers to a stable personality predisposition to perceive various situations as threatening and to habitually respond with high levels of anxiety [5, 13]. In contrast, state anxiety is a transient emotional reaction to specific threatening or stressful situations. It is characterized by subjective feelings of tension and apprehension, alongside autonomic nervous system activation that fluctuates in intensity according to the immediate context [5]. It is precisely in regulating this transient anxiety that affective touch can act as a stress buffer, reducing physiological reactivity and promoting states of calm and security [9]. Based on this premise, this study aims to identify and characterize the specific haptic properties that elicit positive emotional responses in users. The goal is therefore to assess state anxiety in response to various stimuli, facilitating future selection of textures with the potential to act as stress buffers in force-feedback systems. Given that the focus is on immediate reactivity during device interaction, stable personality traits were excluded. Instead, a questionnaire based on the arousal dimension was employed as an indicator of state anxiety. This approach assumes that, while affective touch is traditionally associated with hairy skin, the manipulation of physical parameters in haptic interfaces can also modulate user valence and arousal [3], directly reflecting fluctuations in state anxiety.

2 Affective Touch

The sense of touch has traditionally been understood as a discriminative system enabling the perception of geometric properties, pressure, and stimulus localization. In addition, it supports haptic exploration and manipulation of objects, facilitating the detection of external stimuli across the skin surface [8]. However, unlike purely discriminative touch, affective touch is linked to emotional and reward components [12], playing a fundamental role in physical homeostasis and social well-being [7]. This dimension, largely mediated by C-tactile (CT) afferent fibers in hairy skin, underpins the development of the social brain and stress regulation throughout life [9].

Deprivation of this touch during certain periods of development is associated with elevated levels of anxiety, hypervigilance, and impaired hypothalamic-pituitary-adrenal (HPA) regulation in adulthood [9]. Marshall and McGlone [9] propose that the main function of CT afferents is not only to signal pleasure, but also to promote a sense of security and act as a stress buffer, allowing the body to perceive that "everything is fine" through autonomic and neurohormonal signals. Consequently, affective touch has a direct calming effect on stress response systems. Research in this field suggests that gentle interpersonal touch can reduce sympathetic nervous system activity, cortisol levels, and heart rate, while increasing heart rate variability (HRV) [9]. This process of emotional regulation through touch usually occurs in three stages: situation modification, attentional deployment, and cognitive reevaluation, all of which help alleviate stress [7].

Within this framework, in which affective touch is understood as a biological mechanism for stress reduction through the stimulation of specific receptors, this study seeks to translate these principles into a haptic force-feedback experience using various textures [7, 11]. Although these systems interact with the glabrous skin of the palm, which lacks CT fibers and is primarily composed of A-beta mechanoreceptors, studies such as [10] suggest that affective processing is not restricted to direct CT stimulation. The physical characteristics of surfaces, such as smoothness or roughness, are processed by the somatosensory system and can evoke hedonic responses through learning and secondary reinforcement processes [7]. Therefore, if the nervous system can respond affectively to certain physical characteristics, including softness, hardness or roughness, it can be assumed that interaction with digital textures emulating these qualities through a haptic force-feedback system can determine whether a surface is subjectively perceived as "calming" [4], allowing haptic simulation to replicate the emotional regulation effects traditionally associated with interpersonal contact.

The assessment of the affective response to tactile stimulation is based on monitoring the autonomic nervous system (ANS) [15]. Under conditions of theoretical affective touch, stimulation of CT fibers is consistently associated with homeostatic regulation, characterized by increased parasympathetic activity and reduced sympathetic activation [14]. However, a physiological distinction arises when applying stimuli to areas such as the palm of the hand, as glabrous skin lacks the CT fibers typical of hairy skin [11]. Unlike hairy skin, glabrous skin is predominantly composed of low-threshold mechanoreceptors (LTM) connected to A-beta fibers specialized in discriminative touch. Although these fibers are usually associated with rapid sensorimotor functions, they also support hedonic responses, albeit through neural pathways distinct from those of CT fibers [11].

Consequently, the observed affective response in the palm results from higher-order cortical processing and learning mechanisms rather than the direct limbic interoceptive pathway [11]. Neuroimaging shows that pleasant touch on glabrous skin activates the somatosensory cortex and, subsequently, the orbitofrontal cortex involved in the evaluation of complex emotions and reward learning [11]. By stimulating A-beta mechanoreceptors, a force-feedback system sends signals that the brain processes not only as discriminative data but also as rewarding stimuli through secondary learning mechanisms. This sensory experience undergoes affective-cognitive evaluation, where the surface qualities are compared against stored memories to trigger a corresponding emotional response [4]. Information regarding the digital surface is compared against stored representations in memory, evoking associations that trigger a corresponding emotional response.

Since the hand lacks a direct pathway to the emotional centres of the brain, the central nervous system must resort to these secondary learning and reinforcement mechanisms [11]. Thus, the user perceives discriminative properties through A-beta fibers and, via a cognitive-limbic connection, assigns a hedonic value subjectively measured as pleasant or unpleasant based on learned associations and previous experiences [4].

3 Methodology

The main objective of this study is to evaluate the capacity of different virtual textures, simulated through haptic force and vibration feedback, to induce specific affective states in participants. Specifically, we seek to determine whether tactile stimulation of the glabrous skin of the hand can evoke consistent subjective responses. These responses should distinguish between states of emotional regulation, such as calm and pleasure, and states of alertness or rejection, characterized by high arousal and displeasure, based on the interplay between sensory processing and cognitive-emotional assessment [4, 11].

This study utilizes the Novint Falcon haptic force-feedback device [6] to simulate the virtual textures. As this is a commercial device, the physical properties of the textures, such as friction, hardness, and roughness, are generated using mathematical algorithms. These algorithms ensure that the stimulation of the A-beta fibers is identical for all participants, thereby eliminating experimenter bias. Since hedonic evaluation in the palm relies on secondary cognitive processing and not from direct activation of CT fibers [9], the Falcon provides the high-fidelity rendering of discriminative properties necessary for the user to associate a texture with an emotion [16].

Furthermore, the use of standardized hardware and software ensures that this experimental design can be replicated across different research environments using the same device, thus facilitating cross-validation of the resulting affective profiles. This study is based on the premise that the physical characteristics of surfaces can trigger specific emotional and autonomic responses [7]. The following hypotheses are therefore defined:

- H1 - Soft textures will score higher on the “calm” dimension.
- H2 - Rough or hard textures will score high on “arousal”.
- H3 - There will be a negative correlation between perceived calmness and arousal level.

4 Experiment

4.1 Participants and Experimental Design

Nine male and female participants aged between 13 and 17 who were taking part in a science workshop were involved in this study. All the subjects selected were in good health and with no neurological disorders or alterations in skin sensitivity that could interfere with tactile perception or emotional processing.

A within-subjects experimental design was used for the study in which every participant was exposed to all experimental conditions, corresponding to the different textures simulated by the Falcon haptic device. Given that the sensory experience of affective touch depends on individual differences [3], this method enables the isolation of subjective variability while ensuring the validity of the measurements. The type of texture rendered by the Falcon device was considered as the independent variable. Conversely, the subjective assessment of the tactile experience served as the dependent variable, categorized into two primary affective dimensions: (i) valence, representing the degree of pleasantness of the texture, and (ii) arousal, which measures the level of activation or calmness.

To evaluate textures, a nine-item questionnaire was designed and provided to participants immediately after interacting with the texture to minimize memory bias [17]. This questionnaire used a 5-point Likert scale, adapted from the STAI questionnaire [13], to assess the two main dimensions of the perception of affective touch and examine its influence on state anxiety:

- **Valence Dimension**: Participants rated the degree of pleasure perceived during the interaction with each texture.
- **Arousal Dimension**: This dimension assessed the impact of the texture on the participant's emotional state, ranging from relaxation to activation.

The experiment was carried out using a demonstration environment included with the Novint Falcon to showcase its haptic capabilities. This virtual environment features a central sphere with haptic properties, rendering nine different textures that can be toggled through the system interface:

- **No texture**: this is the control texture and represents a smooth, solid, impenetrable surface. The device exerts a normal force perpendicular to the surface of the sphere, in the opposite direction and of the same magnitude as the force exerted by the user (Fig. 1b).
- **Bumpy**: simulates a rough surface with macroscopic irregularities (such as craters). Like the control condition, it is a solid surface that does not allow penetration. The roughness effect is achieved by superimposing a low-frequency vibration on the normal reaction force (Fig. 1c).
- **Molasses**: simulates a medium viscosity fluid. Unlike solid surfaces, this texture is penetrable (the normal force exerted by the Falcon is less than the force exerted by the user), generating a cushioning sensation when passing through the sphere (Fig. 1a).
- **Ice**: presents a solid surface similar to the "No texture" condition, but with a modified friction coefficient. If the user tries to press the surface, the device generates tangential forces that simulate almost zero friction, causing a slipping effect.
- **Sandpaper**: simulates a solid, impenetrable surface with high microscopic roughness. When exploring the surface, the device produces a high-frequency vibration, approximating the fine grain and rough friction of sandpaper.
- **Magnetic**: is a solid, impenetrable surface that incorporates an attractive force field. The device exerts a force that pulls the user's hand toward the surface of the sphere, making it difficult to separate from it.

- **Rubber**: simulates an elastic and soft body. The normal force exerted by the Falcon is proportionally less than that exerted by the user, allowing the surface to deform under pressure without being completely penetrated, imitating a rubber ball.
- **Sand**: simulates a granular medium, allowing penetration into the sphere. In doing so, the device exerts a high-frequency vibration combined with resistance, simulating the inter-granular friction felt when inserting the hand into sand.
- **Honey**: simulates a penetrable viscous texture similar to "Molasses", but with viscosity parameters adjusted to simulate a less dense fluid. In this case, the resistance is lower, requiring less effort to penetrate the sphere.

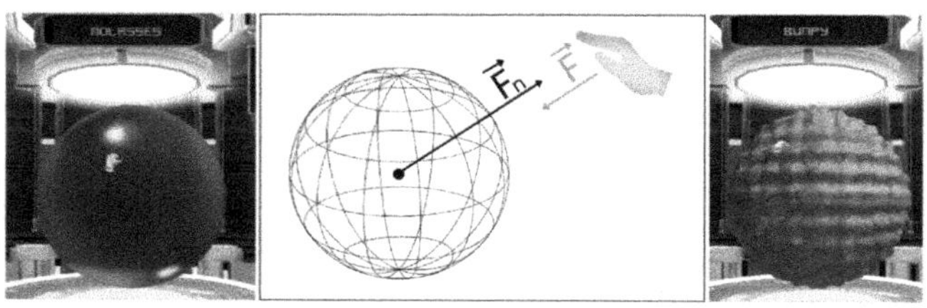

Fig. 1. (a) Molasses texture in Falcon demo; (b) Force diagram; (c) Bumpy texture in Falcon demo.

4.2 Procedure

The experimental protocol was designed as a social interaction and sensory evaluation activity divided into two primary phases. Before the session, participants received a technical briefing on the operation of the Novint Falcon and the specific procedural steps of the activity. The session followed a dyadic dynamic, in which participants alternated between the roles of subject, who received the haptic stimuli, and evaluator, who was responsible for data recording (Fig. 2).

The procedure for each test followed the sequence below:

1. **Haptic exploration phase**: The participant acting as the subject interacted with the textures generated by the Falcon device. Participants were allowed to explore each texture freely within a standardized time frame, with the interaction lasting between 30 and 60 s per stimulus.
2. **Evaluation and communication phase**: Immediately after the exploration, the participant verbalized their subjective experience to their partner, who recorded the scores on the 9-item Likert questionnaire.
3. **Role reversal**: Once the first participant completed the evaluation of all textures, the pair swapped roles and reversed the procedure, ensuring that both individuals experienced the stimuli under identical conditions.

Fig. 2. Development of the experiment in the science workshop.

With this design, all participants were exposed to the same experimental conditions, controlling for individual differences in tactile perception. Furthermore, continuous exposure to textures allows us to determine whether they can evoke stress regulation and calming responses associated with affective touch [15].

4.3 Results

The data obtained for the valence dimension, as can be seen in Fig. 3, show clear hedonic discrimination on the part of the participants, who did not perceive the textures as neutral stimuli, but rather as differentiated affective loads. In view of the results, the "bumpy" texture obtained the highest score in terms of pleasantness (average of 4.6), followed by the "sand" texture (average of 4.3), while the "rubber" and "honey" textures obtained the lowest results (average of 3), even below the "no texture".

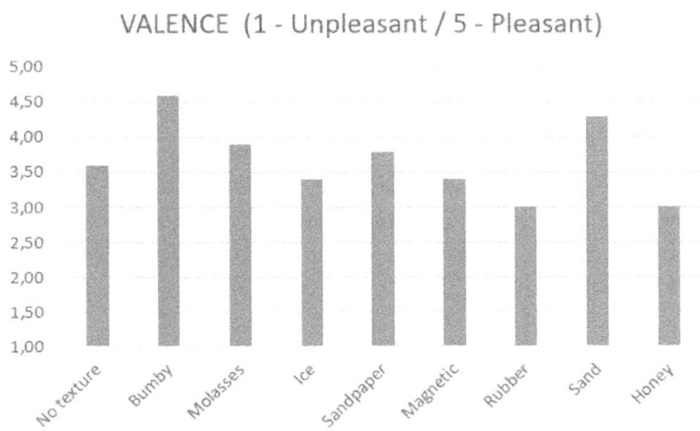

Fig. 3. Results obtained for the valence dimension.

With regard to the arousal dimension, the data obtained during the study (Fig. 4) show that haptic stimulation has a direct impact on the regulation of participants arousal levels. The textures perceived as most calming (lowest scores on the 1 to 5 scale) were "bumpy" (average of 2.30) and "molasses" (average of 2.40), while the textures that generated the highest arousal were "magnetic" (average of 3.6) and "rubber" (average of 3.2).

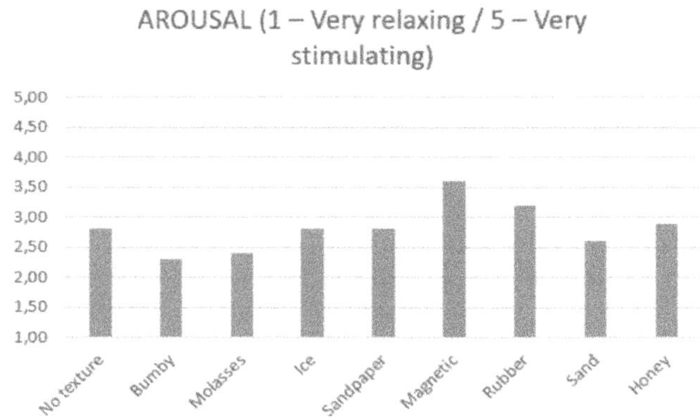

Fig. 4. Results obtained for the arousal dimension.

4.4 Discussion

For the valence dimension, the "bumpy" texture in haptic devices translates into a low-frequency vibration, which makes the tactile stimuli dynamic, simulating a caressing motion. Therefore, the high score suggests that participants interpreted this texture not as abrasive roughness, but as a pleasant stimulating pattern, which activates brain regions linked to pleasure [11]. As for the "sand" texture, the high rating coincides with previous studies on textures in children and adolescents, where natural materials or those associated with playful contexts evoke positive memories [4]. With regard to "rubber" and "honey" textures, studies such as [4] point out that excessive "stickiness" often has negative connotations linked to dirt or discomfort. In addition, for the touch to be pleasant, especially on the hairless skin of the hand, smooth gliding is required. The "rubber" texture generates high friction that interrupts the natural movement of exploration. By slowing down the hand, the kinematic fluidity necessary for a positive experience is disrupted.

For the arousal dimension, there is strong consistency with previous studies on affective touch: the most pleasant texture is also the most calming, in this case "bumpy". In the "molasses" texture, the soft viscosity causes a slow and fluid movement, demonstrating that slow speeds (between 1–10 cm/s) activate the mechanoreceptors in the fingers [7,8]. This pattern simulates a caress or a relaxing movement that the brain processes emotionally, inducing a calming effect [11]. However, the "magnetic" texture in the Falcon involves forces of attraction or repulsion that require active muscular effort to move through the texture. This physical resistance raises the level of alertness, subjectively interpreted as activation. As for the "rubber" texture, like in the valence dimension, the high friction of the rubber generates negative agitation. By hindering hand movement, the participant has to make a greater effort to move the hand, preventing relaxation. In contrast, the "sandpaper" texture results were not as negative as expected, compared to its real counterpart (valence average 3.8). This is mainly due to the limitation that exists in haptic simulation, which causes the texture to be perceived merely as an intense vibration, losing part of its natural aversive connotation.

5 Conclusions and Future Work

The results of this study confirm that the stimulation of glabrous skin through simulated textures is not perceived as a neutral sensory experience. Instead, it is capable of eliciting specific and differentiated affective states. Participants demonstrated a clear ability to discriminate between stimuli, assigning distinct emotional charges to virtual textures such as "bumpy" in contrast to "rubber" or "magnetic". These findings suggest that haptic interfaces can effectively evoke emotional responses even in the absence of direct human contact.

Although the device stimulated the palm of the hand, participants exhibited a calming response to soft stimuli, which supports the processing of affective touch as in previous studies [4]. Furthermore, the results validate an inverse correlation between perceived pleasantness and arousal levels. Specifically, the textures rated highest in hedonic terms, such as "bumpy" and "molasses", were those that generated the greatest levels of calmness.

Consequently, this study has successfully categorized which specific virtual textures are effective in evoking relaxation and which trigger rejection. These preliminary findings validate the use of haptic stimuli to modulate anxiety, establishing an empirical foundation for their future integration into immersive environments designed to enhance affective responses through more complex haptic interfaces.

Acknowledgements. This work was partially supported by grant PID2023-149753OB-C21 funded by MICIU/AEI/10.13039/501100011033 and "ERDF A way to make Europe", and by grant 2025-GRIN-38441 funded by Universidad de Castilla-La Mancha and "ERDF A way to make Europe". This work was partially supported by Programa Iberoamericano de Ciencia y Tecnología para el Desarrollo (CYTED) (through Red [225RT0169]). This work was also partially funded by CIBERSAM-ISCIII and co-funded by "ERDF A way to make Europe".

References

1. American Psychiatric Association: What are anxiety disorders? (2023). https://www.psychiatry.org/patients-families/anxiety-disorders/what-areanxiety-disorders
2. Atienza, R.C.: Ansiedad y depresión: Guía práctica. Formación Alcalá (sep 2010)
3. Cansev, M.E., Kindermann, M., Bliek, A., Beckerle, P.: Affective touch via haptic interfaces: a sequential indentation approach. IEEE Trans. Affective Comput. 1–12 (2025). https://doi.org/10.1109/TAFFC.2025.3565157
4. Dezcallar Sáez, T.: Relación entre procesos mentales y sentido háptico: emociones y recuerdos mediante el análisis empírico de texturas. Universitat Autònoma de Barcelona, (2012)
5. Endler, N.S., Kocovski, N.L.: State and trait anxiety revisited. J. Anxiety Disord. **15**(3), 231–245 (2001). https://doi.org/10.1016/s0887-6185(01)00060-3
6. Haptics House: Novint's Falcon Haptic Device (2024). https://hapticshouse.com/pages/novints-falcon-haptic-device/
7. He, S., Zeng, H., Xue, M., Huang, G., Yao, C., Ying, F.: Affective stroking: design thermal mid-air tactile for assisting people in stress regulation. Appl. Sci. **14**(20), 9494 (2024). https://doi.org/10.3390/app14209494
8. Kidd, T., Devine, S.L., Walker, S.C.: Affective touch and regulation of stress responses. Health Psychol. Rev. **17**(1), 60–77 (2022). https://doi.org/10.1080/17437199.2022.2143854
9. Marshall, A.G., McGlone, F.P.: Affective touch: the enigmatic spinal pathway of the c-tactile afferent. Neurosci. Insights **15** (2020). https://doi.org/10.1177/2633105520925072
10. Mazza, A., et al.: Hedonic and autonomic responses in promoting affective touch. Sci. Rep. **13**(1) (2023). https://doi.org/10.1038/s41598-023-37471-9
11. McGlone, F., Wessberg, J., Olausson, H.: Discriminative and affective touch: sensing and feeling. Neuron **82**(4), 737–755 (2014). https://doi.org/10.1016/j.neuron.2014.05.001
12. Morrison, I., Löken, L.S., Olausson, H.: The skin as a social organ. Exp. Brain Res. **204**(3), 305–314 (2010)
13. Spielberger, C.D.: State-Trait Anxiety Inventory (2010). https://doi.org/10.1002/9780470479216.corpsy0943
14. Sun, W., Banakou, D., Świdrak, J., Valori, I., Slater, M., Fairhurst, M.T.: Multisensory experiences of affective touch in virtual reality enhance engagement, body ownership, pleasantness, and arousal modulation. Virtual Reality **28**(4) (2024). https://doi.org/10.1007/s10055-024-01056-2
15. Triscoli, C., Croy, I., Steudte-Schmiedgen, S., Olausson, H., Sailer, U.: Heart rate variability is enhanced by long-lasting pleasant touch at CT-optimized velocity. Biol. Psychol. **128**, 71–81 (2017). https://doi.org/10.1016/j.biopsycho.2017.07.007
16. Yohanan, S., MacLean, K.E.: A tool to study affective touch. In: CHI '09 Extended Abstracts on Human Factors in Computing Systems, pp. 4153–4158. CHI '2009, ACM (2009). https://doi.org/10.1145/1520340.1520632
17. Zhao, Y., et al.: Affective touch as immediate and passive wearable intervention. In: Proceedings of the ACM on Interactive, Mobile, Wearable and Ubiquitous Technologies, vol. 6(4), pp. 1–23 (2022). https://doi.org/10.1145/3569484

Technological Mediation in Emotional Literacy: Evaluation of Artificial Intelligence Agents in the EMOCREA Project

Pedro Salcedo-Lagos[1], Mabel Urrutia-Martínez[1](✉), and Cristian Medina-Rojas[2]

[1] Facultad de Educación, Universidad de Concepción, Concepción, Chile
{psalcedo,maurrutia}@udec.cl
[2] Doctorado en IA, Universidad de Concepción, Concepción, Chile
cmedina@doctoradoia.cl

Abstract. The integration of Artificial Intelligence (AI) into emotional education represents a paradigm shift from theory to interactive practice. This study presents the results of the permanent EMOCREA sample, developed at the Interactive Center for Science, Art, and Technology (CICAT) at the University of Concepción, under the framework of the FONDECYT project No. 13220040. The research evaluates the effectiveness of AI-based tools personified in three avatars: El Zorro Culpeo (recognition), La Tortuga Tortulina (regulation), and El Mono Caco (expression). Using a mixed methodology with a sample of 172 participants (students and teachers), psychometric instruments (PANAS), technological interaction analysis, and qualitative evaluations were implemented. The quantitative results reveal a statistically significant correlation, indicating that technological interaction significantly displaces negative affect in favor of positive affect. Likewise, the use of multimodal models and pose estimation algorithms for emotional regulation based on the Alba Emoting technique is technically validated. It is concluded that symbolic and technological mediation reduces the cognitive load of social-emotional learning, validating these environments as effective laboratories for human well-being.

Keywords: Affective Computing · Artificial Intelligence · Emotional Regulation · Alba Emoting · Emotional Education

1 Introduction and Conceptual Framework

Contemporary cognitive neuroscience has established that the emotion-cognition binomial constitutes the cornerstone of meaningful learning; biologically, the brain consolidates information effectively when it is mediated by emotional stimuli. However, in the Chilean educational scenario, there is still a critical gap in

J. M. Ferrández Vicente et al. (Eds.): IWINAC 2026, LNCS 16574, pp. 263–271, 2026.
https://doi.org/10.1007/978-3-032-27314-7_24

teacher and student training with regard to the management of socio-emotional skills. Despite the requirements of the Framework for Good Teaching and the National Policy for Educational Coexistence, training opportunities remain limited and theoretical, lacking practical tools for the classroom (MINEDUC, 2021).

To mitigate this shortcoming, Affective Computing is emerging as a critical discipline. According to Picard (1997), this area seeks to develop systems capable of recognizing, interpreting, and simulating human emotions. In this context, Artificial Intelligence (AI) ceases to be mere technological artifacts and becomes instruments of pedagogical mediation that enhance integral human development.

The present study is theoretically based on the convergence of two key models:

1. **Emotional Competence Model** (Bisquerra and Pérez, 2007): Five dimensions are specifically addressed: *Emotional awareness*(perceiving and labeling emotions), *Emotional regulation* (managing impulsive responses), *Emotional autonomy* (self-esteem and self-motivation), *Social competence* (empathy and relational skills), and *Life and well-being skills.*
2. **Neuroeducation Model** (Howard-Jones, 2011): This model adopts the perspective of "levels of action" (Brain-Mind-Behavior) and principles of social constructivism. The intervention is designed around the axes of "authentic exploration," "motivating activities," and "student protagonism," where technology acts as a scaffold that reduces the cognitive load required to process complex affective states.

The central hypothesis holds that interaction with AI-driven avatars strengthens these skills by providing a safe environment ("emotional laboratory") where mistakes are not penalized but used as real-time feedback.

2 Context of the EMOCREA Project

The study is part of the EMOCREA project, an initiative implemented at the Interactive Center for Science, Art, and Technology (CICAT) at the University of Concepción, Chile. This space is an educational innovation and scientific outreach laboratory located in Coronel, Biobío Region, Chile, which seeks to bring science, technology, and art closer to children and young people through interactive exhibits and workshops. The intervention was carried out in specifically designed spaces, such as the "Brain/Dome" and the "My Super Brain" room, equipped with Oculus Quest headsets, tablets, and visual biofeedback stations. The project, financially and technically supported by the National Research and Development Agency (ANID), FONDECYT Exploration Fund No. 13220040, seeks to use AI as a resource for emotional literacy (Fig. 1).

3 Methodology

3.1 Research Design

A mixed concurrent approach was adopted to address the multidimensionality of emotional response. This methodology allows for the triangulation of the

Fig. 1. Dome at CICAT.

statistical accuracy of quantitative data with the narrative richness of qualitative ex perience.

3.2 Participants

The sample consisted of 172 participants, selected from a universe of 6,700 visitors to CICAT. The distribution included:

- Students: 162 subjects, with a modal age of 15–16 years.
- Teachers: 10 professionals from the Biobío, Ñuble, Maule, and O'Higgins regions of Chile.

3.3 Instruments and Procedures

The following validated instruments were used for data collection:

1. **PANAS (Positive and Negative Affect Schedule) Scale** (Composed of 20 items to measure Positive Affect (PA) and Negative Affect (NA) pre- and post-intervention.).
2. **Satisfaction surveys**: Digitized on tablets to evaluate usability and acceptance.
3. **Semi-structured interviews:**Processed using content analysis in ATLAS.ti software.

The experimental protocol consisted of a guided "Authentic Exploration" phase, followed by a 20-min block of free interaction with the AI and VR stations, culminating in the post-intervention evaluation.

4 AI Technologies Developed: EMOCREA Avatars

The core of the intervention lies in three "affective-technological mediators" or avatars, each associated with a specific emotional competence and supported by proprietary software architecture that combines connectionist (neural networks) and symbolic AI (Fig. 2).

4.1 The Culpeo Fox: Emotional Recognition

https://educagratis.cl/mini8

Fig. 2. Culpeo Fox System.

This avatar symbolizes keen observation and self-awareness. Its goal is to train the user's ability to identify and label emotions in others, a basic skill for empathy.

Functionality: After explaining how to use the system through the avatar (fox), the system presents visual stimuli, photographs of an actress's emotions (validated by expert psychologists), and asks the user to imitate the emotion perceived in the actress's image.

Multimodal AI Architecture:

- *Computer* Vision *and NLP:* It uses a multimodal approach (text + images). The image of the actress and a photograph of the user imitating the actress's face are sent to a local multimodal text and image model (Google's gemma 3:4b), using the Ollama platform for administration on the laptop containing the system .
- On the one hand, they analyze the image to detect emotional visual patterns. On the other hand, gemma3:4b's LLM delivers a text response.
- *Comparison Algorithm:* The system cross-references the emotions detected by the AI in the two photographs, providing a comparative analysis and synthesized feedback in audio and text, closing the reflective learning cycle

4.2 The Tortulina Turtle: Regulation and Calm

https://educagratis.cl/alba Represents the management of impulsivity and the "necessary slowness" for emotional processing (Fig. 3).

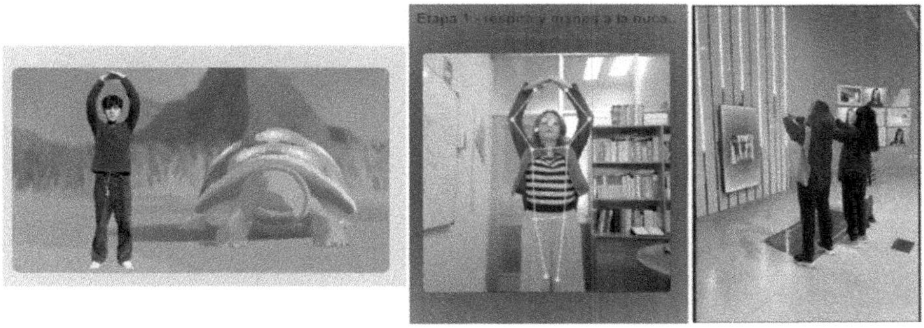

Fig. 3. Tortulina Turtle System.

Scientific Basis: It is based on Susana Bloch's *Alba Emoting*methodology (1993), which uses physical effector patterns (posture, breathing, facial expression) to induce and modulate emotional states from the somatic ("bottom-up").

AI Architecture:

- *Offline Machine Learning (ML):*The core is an ML model specifically trained with a dataset of images of correct and incorrect executions of *Alba Emoting*patterns, generated by experts in body language.
- *Pose Estimation:*Using a standard webcam, the system captures the user's skeleton in real time without the need for invasive biometric sensors.
- *Visual Biofeedback:*The system evaluates postural accuracy (e.g., curvature of the back, shoulder position) and modifies the background color of the screen in real time. This immediate visual feedback guides the user toward the correct execution to achieve a state of calm or neutrality, functioning autonomously without an internet connection to ensure privacy and accessibility.

4.3 The Caco Monkey: Expression and Communication

This avatar acts as an expressive facilitator, challenging the student to externalize emotions in a clear and assertive manner (Fig. 4).

Hybrid Architecture (Connectionist + Symbolic): Unlike purely generative models, this system implements a hybrid architecture to ensure scientific explainability and accuracy based on the Ekman & Friesen (1978) facial coding system

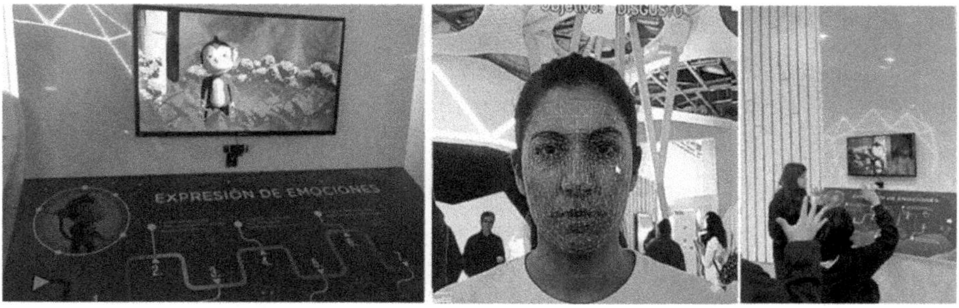

Fig. 4. Caco Monkey System.

- *High-Density Facial Mesh (Face Mesh):*Uses convolutional neural networks to project a mesh of 468 landmarks onto the user's face, capturing micro-expressions in the eyelids, lips, and eyebrows with three-dimensional resolution.
- *Rule-Based Inference:*A symbolic AI layer translates the geometric distances of the *landmarks*into logical categories (e.g., "if lip corners rise and eyes contract = happiness"). This ensures operational determinism crucial for objective evaluation
- **Gestural Control and Interaction**. The system includes manual skeletal tracking, allowing the user to control the interface (start/pause challenges) using hand gestures (e.g., extended palm), encouraging natural, touchless interaction

5 Results

The evaluation of the EMOCREA project combined quantitative metrics of emotional impact and qualitative analyses of satisfaction and usability, with a sample of 172 participants (162 students and 10 teachers).

5.1 Impact on Emotional Well-Being

In relation to the PANAS psychological questionnaire on socio-emotional well-being, statistical analysis validates the intervention as an effective driver of emotional regulation:

Spearman's correlation:A robust inverse relationship of rho = -0.52 ($p < .001$) was found between engagement with the technological sample and Negative Affect (NA). This indicates that interaction with avatars significantly displaces unpleasant states.

Wilcoxon test: Significant differences ($V = 4313$, $p < .001$) were confirmed between pre- and post-intervention measurements. Participants reported a notable increase in Positive Affect (PA), validating the hypothesis that technological mediation reduces the negative burden associated with school stress.

Prevalence of Emotions: Emotional frequency analysis revealed a predominance of "Happiness," "Joy," and "Curiosity" during interaction with the modules, suggesting that the playful environment facilitates emotional openness

5.2 Satisfaction and Usability

Acceptance of the technology was widespread, with its intuitive and motivating design being highlighted:

- **Overall Assessment:** 92.4% of participants rated the experience in the highest ranges (4 "Good" and 5 "Very Good").
- **Game Room (Interactive):** 65.2% rated the games as "Very interesting." In terms of usability, 74% of the sample considered the use of Artificial Intelligence to be "Easy" or "Very easy," breaking down the barrier of technical complexity.
- **Perception of Learning:** 93.4% of students stated that the activities helped them "better understand their emotions" (47% "Much" and 38% "A little").

5.3 Teacher Perspective

Interviews with teachers revealed an initial critical gap: most acknowledged that their training in emotional education was "insufficient" or "non-existent," limited to crisis containment actions rather than preventive training. However, after the EMOCREA experience, teachers valued the tools (especially Zorro and Tortuga) as resources that could be transferred to the classroom, highlighting their ability to objectify subjective processes and facilitate conversation about mental health with students.

6 Discussion

The findings of this study allow us to redefine the role of technology in the classroom. Regarding psychological measurements using the Positive and Negative Affect Schedule (PANAS), after the sample, students showed a predominance of positive affect over negative affect in the use of technology. This result debunks the belief that technology promotes social isolation. On the contrary, EMOCREA's architecture, through avatars, acts as a scaffolding system that reduces the complexity of emotional metacognition and, in fact, helps reduce feelings such as anxiety, stress, or frustration.

The tool associated with "Zorro Culpeo" demonstrates that the integration of models such as Whisper-1 and CNNs allows for natural interaction (voice) that overcomes the limitations of traditional interfaces based solely on text or clicks. For its part, the "Tortuga Tortulina" tool democratizes access to complex techniques such as Alba Emoting. By using computer vision with a standard webcam instead of expensive physiological sensors (traditional biofeedback), the barrier to entry for somatic emotional regulation is drastically reduced. Finally, the "Caco, el Macaco" game was one of the most appreciated by students, as it allowed them to interact socially through different degrees of intensity of the students' facial emotions.

However, technical limitations were identified, such as minor camera configuration and light intensity issues, which disrupted the fluidity of certain modules. Furthermore, it is crucial to consider that ML models depend on the quality of their training datasets to avoid biases in emotion recognition.

7 Conclusions

The EMOCREA project and its AI tools (Fox, Turtle, Monkey) represent a significant advance in affective computing applied to education. The main conclusions are:

1. **Model Effectiveness:** The symbolic mediation of avatars, supported by advanced AI, significantly increases positive affect and reduces the cognitive load required to analyze and regulate emotions.
2. **Technological Innovation:** The development of systems that combine Generative AI (Whisper/GPT) with motor pattern recognition (Alba Emoting) demonstrates that it is possible to create high-precision tools with low implementation costs.
3. **Inclusive Projection:** There is clear potential to expand this model to Special Education, adapting environments using AI for students with specific needs, as well as for continuing teacher training.

Overall, the results showed that CICAT's learning environments, through the use of artificial intelligence, contributed to a significant development of students' emotional awareness through the recognition and ex xpression of their emotions. In turn, students incorporated emotional regulation strategies and strengthened their empathy towards others through the learning spaces. Taken together, these findings corroborate the importance of planned implementation in Emotional Education, where technology acts as a key empathetic facilitator of human well-being.

Acknowledgments. Supported by ANID/FONDECYT Project No. 13220040 and CYTED 4T4SM No. 225RT0169.

References

1. Bisquerra, R.: Educación emocional y bienestar. Wolters Kluwer (2003)
2. Bisquerra, R., Pérez, N.: Las competencias emocionales. Educación XXI **10**, 61–82 (2007)
3. Bloch, S.: Alba Emoting. Theatr. Top. **3**(2), 121–145 (1993)
4. Ekman, P., Friesen, W.: Facial Action Coding System. Consulting Psychologists Press (1978)
5. Howard-Jones, P.: Neuroeducación. La Muralla (2011)
6. Ministerio de Educación: Marco para la Buena Enseñanza (2021)
7. Picard, R.: Affective Computing. MIT Press (1997)
8. Sotomayor, J., Leiva, M.: Educación emocional como proceso continuo. Revista de Educación Integral (2023)
9. Urrutia, M.: Neurociencia y educación. Universidad de Concepción (2016)
10. Educarchile: Oferta formativa en educación emocional. https://www.educarchile.cl

Multimodal Depression Detection Using Hierarchical Fusion of DistilBERT and Bi-LSTM Encoders: A Deep Learning Approach on the DAIC-WOZ Corpus

Francisco Ortiz-Vidal[1,2,3,4(✉)], Pedro Salcedo-Lagos[5], and Juan M. Górriz Sáez[6]

[1] Faculty of Economics and Management Sciences, Universidad Católica de la Santísima Concepción, Concepción, Chile
[2] Faculty of Engineering, Universidad de Concepción, Concepción, Chile
[3] Faculty of Engineering, Universidad Técnica Federico Santa María, ValparaÃŋso, Chile
[4] Faculty of Engineering, Universidad del Bío-Bío, Concepción, Chile
fortiz@ucsc.cl
[5] Department of Research Methodology and Information Technology, Universidad de Concepción, Concepción, Chile
psalcedo@udec.cl
[6] Department of Signal Theory, Networking and Communications, University of Granada, Granada, Spain
gorriz@ugr.es

Abstract. Major Depressive Disorder (MDD) is a major global health challenge and is commonly assessed through semi-structured interviews and questionnaires, which are clinically validated but partly subjective. Affective Computing has therefore explored digital biomarkers from multimodal behavioural data, including acoustic, visual, and linguistic cues. This paper evaluates a hierarchical deep learning framework for depression detection that combines a frozen DistilBERT encoder for text, Bi-LSTMs for temporal modelling of audio and video feature streams, and a Transformer-based fusion module to capture inter-modal dependencies. Using the Extended DAIC-WOZ corpus (N=275), we conduct a systematic ablation study across unimodal, bimodal, and multimodal variants. While the multimodal configuration attains strong performance (F1=0.992), text-enhanced variants approach near-ceiling results, suggesting potential shortcut learning and/or leakage effects in interview-based settings. Overall, the results highlight both the promise of multimodal fusion and the need for stricter leakage controls and more clinically grounded linguistic inputs to improve generalisability and interpretability for computer-aided screening.

Keywords: Depression Detection · Multimodal Learning · Deep Learning · Affective Computing · Transformers · Bi-LSTM · DAIC-WOZ · Ablation Study

J. M. Ferrández Vicente et al. (Eds.): IWINAC 2026, LNCS 16574, pp. 272–279, 2026.
https://doi.org/10.1007/978-3-032-27314-7_25

1 Introduction

Depression is a leading cause of disability worldwide, affecting hundreds of millions of individuals and imposing substantial social and economic costs [1]. Clinical screening commonly relies on semi-structured interviews and questionnaires (e.g., PHQ-8/9 and BDI-II), which are validated but remain episodic and partly subjective, depending on self-report and clinician interpretation [2]. Limited access to mental health specialists further motivates the development of scalable, more objective screening tools.

AI-based approaches aim to detect depression from behavioural signals, leveraging acoustic, visual, and linguistic cues [3–5]. Yet, interview-based datasets pose a key methodological risk: text features can dominate performance and enable shortcut learning through interview structure, prompts, or transcription artefacts rather than through clinically robust markers. In this work, we evaluate a hierarchical multimodal architecture (DistilBERT + Bi-LSTMs + Transformer fusion) on Extended DAIC-WOZ and report a systematic ablation study (unimodal, bimodal, multimodal) to quantify modality contributions and highlight potential overfitting/leakage in text-enhanced variants.

2 Related Work

The application of Machine Learning to depression detection has evolved from hand-crafted feature extraction to end-to-end Deep Learning systems.

2.1 Unimodal Approaches

Early research focused on isolated modalities. In the acoustic domain, Sharan [6] demonstrated the utility of Gammatone Cepstral Coefficients (GTCC) combined with deep learning features for emotion recognition, highlighting the richness of spectral data. Similarly, Wasserzug et al. [5] validated vocal predictive models for MDD, emphasising prosodic features like jitter and shimmer. In the visual domain, Zhou et al. [7], and Fu et al. [8] have explored the use of Facial Action Units (FAUs) and Graph Neural Networks (GNNs) to capture subtle facial micro-expressions associated with apathy and depression. While effective, these unimodal models often struggle with ambiguity; for instance, a flat tone of voice might indicate fatigue rather than depression if not contextualised by facial expression or linguistic content.

2.2 Multimodal Fusion Strategies

Recent studies advocate for multimodal integration. Flores et al. [9] proposed 'AudiFace', a model combining temporal facial features, audio, and transcripts. Their work, along with Mao et al. [10], underscores the importance of capturing temporal dependencies using Long Short-Term Memory (LSTM) networks. However, many current architectures utilise 'shallow fusion', in which feature vectors are concatenated before classification. This approach assumes a linear relationship between modalities and treats all features as equally important. Our work advances this paradigm by employing a 'Fusion Block' based on a Transformer Encoder, which utilises self-attention to dynamically weigh the importance of each modality (e.g., prioritising visual cues when audio is noisy). This technique has shown promise in other domains such as therapeutic alliance prediction [11].

3 Methodology

3.1 Dataset Description

This study utilised the Extended DAIC-WOZ database [12], which consists of semi-structured clinical interviews conducted with an animated virtual interviewer in a Wizard-of-Oz setting. The corpus includes recordings from 275 participants and provides raw modalities (audio, video, and time-stamped transcripts) together with commonly used derived feature representations for affective computing and clinical speech analysis. The PHQ-8 questionnaire score indexes the ground-truth severity of depression; following standard practice, we define a binary depression label using a threshold of PHQ-8 ≥ 10.

3.2 Proposed Architecture

The GOAL-Depression architecture (Fig. 1) comprises three stages: unimodal encoding, projection, and hierarchical fusion.

Unimodal Encoders:

- **Text (Linguistic):** We employed a pre-trained `DistilBERT-base-uncased` model. The `[CLS]` token was extracted to represent the global semantic context. The weights were frozen to prevent overfitting to the limited dataset.
- **Audio and Visual (Temporal):** Following the findings of Mao et al. [10], we utilised Bi-Directional Long Short-Term Memory (Bi-LSTM) networks for the continuous data streams. Bi-LSTMs are particularly effective for this task as they process sequences in both directions, capturing the context of the entire interview. For audio, features included MFCCs and eGeMAPS; for video, we utilised OpenFace outputs (AUs and gaze vectors).

Dimensionality Alignment: A critical challenge in multimodal learning is the disparity in feature dimensions (Text: 768, Audio: 123, Video: 149). To address this, we applied Batch Normalisation followed by linear projection layers to map the Audio and Visual embeddings into the same 768-dimensional space as the Text embedding.

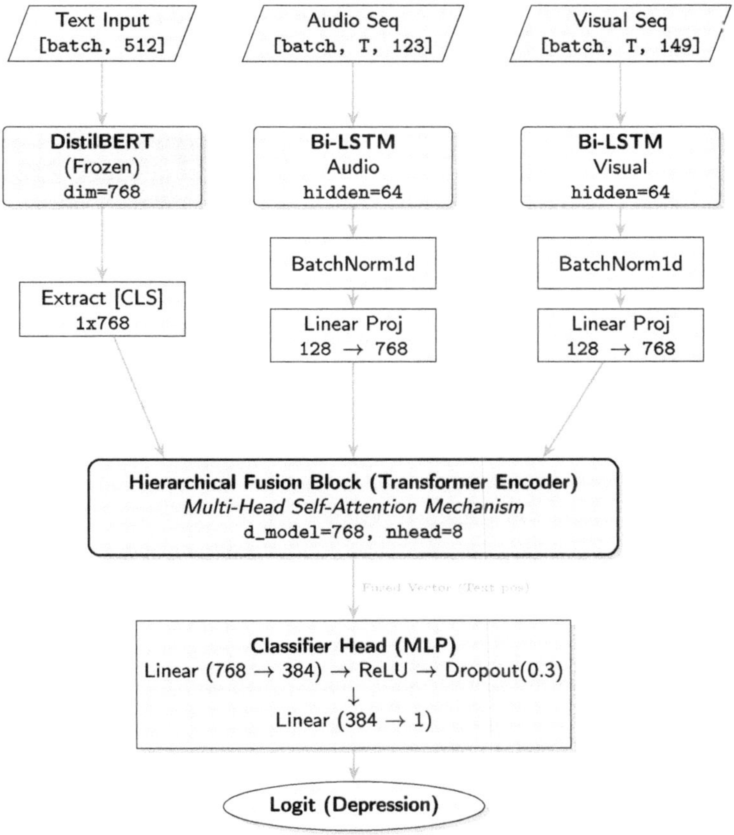

Fig. 1. The proposed Multimodal Hierarchical Architecture. Text, Audio, and Visual streams are encoded separately, projected to a common latent dimension ($d = 768$), and fused via a Transformer Encoder before classification.

Transformer Fusion Block: The model treats the projected embeddings as a sequence of tokens and feeds them into a Transformer Encoder Layer ($n_{heads} = 8$). The self-attention mechanism computes the relevance of each modality token with respect to the others, allowing the model to construct a rich, context-aware fused representation.

4 Experiments and Results

4.1 Experimental Setup

We implemented all models in `PyTorch` and trained them using the AdamW optimiser. To ensure comparability with prior work and prevent cross-participant leakage, we adhered to the official benchmark split of the dataset (*train/dev/test*). We addressed class imbalance (depressed vs non-depressed) using a weighted `BCEWithLogitsLoss`, with class weights computed from the training split only. To reduce overfitting, we applied early stopping (*patience*=10) based on validation ROC–AUC.

To ensure fair comparisons, the same optimisation settings and stopping criterion were used to train the proposed multimodal model and all unimodal baselines. We obtained unimodal variants by turning off the corresponding modality branch while keeping the remaining training protocol unchanged.

Furthermore, to support the analysis of generalisation, we also report training dynamics (train loss and validation AUC) to evidence early overfitting in text-enhanced variants, supporting our recommendation to simplify the interview protocol and restrict linguistic inputs.

4.2 Ablation Study

To quantify the contribution of each modality, we conducted an ablation study comparing unimodal (Audio, Visual, Text), bimodal (Audio+Visual, Audio+Text, Visual+Text), and the full multimodal configuration under the same optimisation protocol. Table 1 summarises the resulting classification metrics.

Table 1. Performance metrics of unimodal, bimodal, and multimodal models on DAIC-WOZ (ablation study).

Model	Accuracy	Precision	Recall	F1-Score
Multimodal	0.996214	0.987054	0.997447	0.992223
Text-Only	0.861557	0.638180	0.988832	0.775720
Audio-Only	0.840080	0.627762	0.834078	0.716361
Visual-Only	0.939122	0.831919	0.938098	0.881824
Audio+Visual	0.930856	0.840584	0.881621	0.860614
Audio+Text	0.999459	0.997771	1.000000	0.998884
Visual+Text	0.970411	0.891323	0.999681	0.942397

4.3 ROC/PR Analysis

Figure 2a reports Receiver Operating Characteristic (ROC) curves for the ablation variants, and Fig. 2b reports Precision-Recall (PR) curves. Consistent with Table 1, text-enhanced models (Text-Only, Audio+Text, Visual+Text, and Multimodal) show substantially stronger separability than Audio-Only, and they approach near-ceiling discrimination in this experimental protocol.

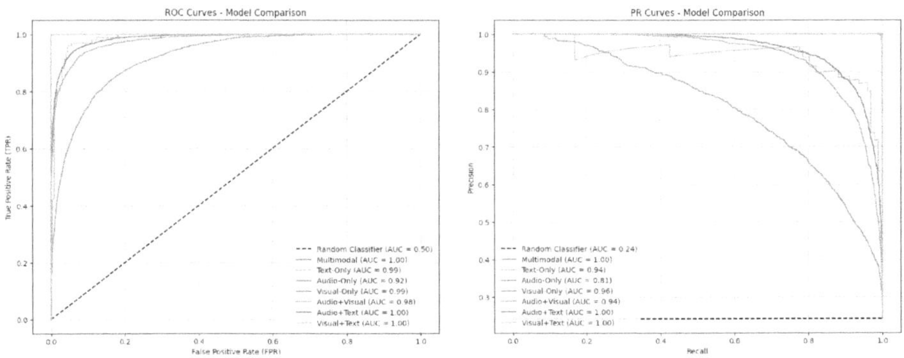

(a) ROC Curves. Near-ceiling performance in text-enhanced variants is consistent with shortcut learning and motivates stricter controls on leakage.

(b) PR Curves. Text-containing models tend to exhibit very high recall, but also raise concerns about shortcut learning and limited generalisability.

Fig. 2. ROC/PR curves for unimodal, bimodal, and multimodal variants.

4.4 Evidence of Shortcut Learning and Overfitting in Text-Enhanced Variants

While the results demonstrate that language is highly predictive in this setting, such near-ceiling discrimination is unlikely to reflect purely generalisable depression markers. In particular, the text modality can inadvertently encode spurious correlates of the label (e.g., interview structure and prompts, transcription artefacts, or participant-specific lexical cues), enabling shortcut learning. This effect is consistent with the extremely high recall and strong ROC/PR performance observed for text-containing variants, which motivates additional leakage controls and more robust experimental designs.

Consequently, future work should prioritise: (i) simplifying the interview protocol and restricting the linguistic input to a smaller, clinically grounded subset of questions/features; (ii) enforcing stricter leakage controls (participant-level splitting, careful preprocessing, and systematic ablation checks); and (iii) adopting more robust training strategies (e.g., Multiple Instance Learning with temporal alignment, stronger regularisation, and cross-validation). These measures can reduce reliance on spurious textual shortcuts and improve interpretability and clinical validity.

4.5 Discussion

The ablation study reveals a clear performance hierarchy across modalities. The **Audio-only** model exhibits the lowest discriminative performance, suggesting that acoustic cues alone are informative but insufficiently specific and may be affected by noise and inter-speaker variability. The **Visual-only** model substantially improves performance, consistent with the relevance of facial action units and gaze/pose dynamics for affective and behavioural markers.

Notably, **text-enhanced** configurations (Text-Only, Audio+Text, Visual+Text, and the full Multimodal model) achieve markedly higher scores, including near-ceiling recall and very strong ROC/PR curves. While this indicates that linguistic information is highly predictive under the present protocol, such near-perfect discrimination might also be a strong indicator of *shortcut learning and limited generalisability.* Language may encode spurious correlates of depression labels, such as interview structure, therapist prompts, transcription artefacts, or participant-specific lexical patterns, allowing the classifier to separate classes without relying on robust clinical markers. This interpretation is consistent with the observed dominance of text-containing variants in the ROC/PR analysis.

Therefore, although multimodal fusion improves aggregate metrics, the results also highlight the need for stricter leakage controls and clinically grounded feature constraints. In future work, we recommend simplifying the interview protocol and restricting linguistic inputs to a smaller set of clinically interpretable prompts, as well as adopting more robust training and evaluation designs (e.g., participant-level aggregation/MIL, stronger regularisation, and cross-validation) to reduce reliance on spurious textual shortcuts and improve clinical validity and interpretability.

5 Conclusion and Future Work

This work evaluated a multimodal framework for depression detection on DAIC-WOZ and presented a systematic ablation study across unimodal, bimodal, and multimodal configurations. The multimodal model achieves strong predictive performance under the benchmark protocol, and the ablation results indicate that language substantially increases discriminative power.

However, the near-ceiling performance of text-enhanced variants suggests potential shortcut learning and/or information leakage, which may limit real-world generalisability and clinical interpretability. Future work should therefore focus on: (i) simplifying the interview protocol and restricting linguistic inputs to a clinically grounded subset of questions/features; (ii) enforcing stricter leakage controls and ablation checks (including participant-level evaluation, careful preprocessing, and robustness analyses); and (iii) adopting more robust learning strategies such as temporally aligned Multiple Instance Learning, stronger regularisation, and cross-validation. These directions aim to improve the interpretability and clinical validity of automated systems for detecting depression.

Acknowledgements. The first author acknowledges the financial support of the National Agency for Research and Development (ANID) through the National Doctoral Scholarship 2026, Grant [Folio number to be confirmed]. This work was also supported by the CYTED network NT4SM "New Technologies for Early Diagnosis, Treatment and Follow-up in Mental Health" (Ref. 225RT0169)."

References

1. World Health Organisation: Depressive disorder (depression) (2023). https://www.who.int/news-room/fact-sheets/detail/depression. Accessed 04-06-2025
2. Alowais, S.A., et al.: Revolutionising healthcare: the role of artificial intelligence in clinical practice. BMC Med. Educ. **23**(1), 689 (2023)
3. Jiang, Z., Seyedi, S., Griner, E., et al.: Multimodal mental health digital biomarker analysis from remote interviews using facial, vocal, linguistic, and cardiovascular patterns. IEEE J. Biomed. Health Inform. **28**(3), 1680–1691 (2024)
4. Sara, J.D.S., et al.: Guess what we can hear-novel voice biomarkers for the remote detection of disease. Mayo Clin. Proc. **98**(9), 1353–1375 (2023)
5. Wasserzug, Y., Degani, Y., Bar-Shaked, M., et al.: Development and validation of a machine learning-based vocal predictive model for major depressive disorder. J. Affect. Disord. **325**, 627–632 (2023)
6. Sharan, R.V.: Speech emotion recognition using gammatone cepstral coefficients and deep learning features. In: 2023 IEEE International Conference on Machine Learning and Applied Network Technologies (ICMLANT). IEEE (2023)
7. Zhou, Y., Han, W., Yao, X., et al.: Developing a machine learning model for detecting depression, anxiety, and apathy in older adults with mild cognitive impairment using speech and facial expressions. Int. J. Nurs. Stud. **146**, 104562 (2023)
8. Fu, C., Qian, F., Su, Y., et al.: Facial action units guided graph representation learning for multimodal depression detection. Neurocomputing **619**, 129106 (2025)
9. Flores, R., Tlachac, M.L., Toto, E., Rundensteiner, E.: AudiFace: multimodal deep learning for depression screening. Proc. Mach. Learn. Res. **182**, 1–22 (2022)
10. Mao, K., et al.: Prediction of depression severity based on the prosodic and semantic features with bidirectional LSTM and time distributed CNN. IEEE Trans. Affect. Comput. **14**(3), 2251–2265 (2023)
11. Aafjes-van Doorn, K., Cicconet, M., Cohn, J.F., Aafjes, M.: Predicting working alliance in psychotherapy: a multimodal machine learning approach. Psychother. Res. **35**(2), 256–270 (2025)
12. Gratch, J., et al.: The distress analysis interview corpus of human and computer interviews. In: LREC'14, pp. 3123–3128. ELRA, Reykjavik (2014)

Considering ROI Selection for rPPG Beyond Heart Rate Measurement

Pedro Lucas Barrera[1(✉)], Cristian Mateos[1,2], and Maria Paula Bonomini[1,3]

[1] Instituto Tecnológico de Buenos Aires, Buenos Aires, Argentina
pbarrera@itba.edu.ar
[2] ISISTAN-UNICEN-CONICET, Tandil, Buenos Aires, Argentina
[3] Instituto Argentino de Matemática "Alberto P. Calderón" (IAM), CONICET, Buenos Aires, Argentina

Abstract. Remote photoplethysmography enables the extraction of cardiovascular metrics using standard digital cameras. To combat signal degradation, contemporary methods typically merge multiple facial regions of interest or analyze the entire face to improve the signal-to-noise ratio. While effective for robust heart rate estimation, this spatial integration assumes that cardiovascular signals across the face are temporally synchronous. This assumption ignores potential delays caused by physiological factors like Pulse Transit Time and hardware artifacts like rolling shutter effects. This study investigates the validity of this assumption by quantifying inter-ROI temporal lags using a public 30 FPS dataset and a custom 60 FPS dataset. Signals were extracted from the forehead, chin, and both cheeks. Cross-correlation analysis combined with parabolic interpolation was applied to resolve sub-frame temporal offsets. The results reveal a consistent spatial delay pattern where the forehead leads the lower facial regions by a median of approximately 16 to 23 ms. Conversely, horizontally aligned regions like the left and right cheeks remain synchronized. These findings demonstrate that merging facial regions without temporal alignment introduces destructive interference that blurs pulse morphology. To ensure the temporal fidelity required for advanced diagnostics like heart rate variability, pipelines must abandon global face averaging in favor of spatially aware fusion strategies.

Keywords: Remote photoplethysmography · Signal processing · Computer vision · Heart rate variability

1 Introduction

In recent years, modern medicine has shifted toward personalized health, prioritizing individual physiological patterns over generalized population averages. However, the effectiveness of this approach depends on long-term user compliance, which traditional hardware often fails to achieve. Consequently, the focus

J. M. Ferrández Vicente et al. (Eds.): IWINAC 2026, LNCS 16574, pp. 280–290, 2026.
https://doi.org/10.1007/978-3-032-27314-7_26

has moved toward integrating physiological tracking seamlessly into daily life by leveraging everyday objects, thereby avoiding additional financial burdens and behavioral changes [1].

Remote Photoplethysmography (rPPG) has emerged as a leading solution for this frictionless approach, transforming ubiquitous smartphone and laptop cameras into sophisticated medical sensors [2]. This technology detects the blood volume pulse (BVP) by tracking minute color fluctuations in facial skin caused by cardiac pressure waves. To combat signal degradation from motion and lighting, contemporary methods typically merge multiple regions of interest (ROIs) or analyze the entire face to average out localized noise and improve the signal-to-noise ratio (SNR) [3].

Despite these advancements, validation remains heavily biased toward Heart Rate (HR). HR is favored because it is a robust, frequency-domain metric requiring only the detection of a dominant spectral peak [4]. However, this metric is largely insensitive to fine temporal or morphological errors; a signal can yield a precise average rate even with distorted wave shapes or shifted peaks. This creates a significant risk when extrapolating the success of these methods to advanced diagnostics like heart rate variability (HRV) and blood pressure estimation, which rely on precise timing and waveform integrity [5].

The fundamental issue with merging multiple facial ROIs is that these regions are not necessarily synchronized. Physiologically, pulse transit time (PTT) dictates that blood reaches different regions at different moments based on vascular path length and resistance [6], while vascular heterogeneity affects the timing of the optical response. Technically, the rolling shutter effect in modern CMOS sensors introduces an artificial delay between vertical regions of the frame, often recording the forehead ms before the chin [7,8]. When signals with these biological and hardware-induced offsets are averaged, the resulting destructive interference can shift peaks and blur pulse morphology, compromising the sensitive metrics required for high-fidelity analysis.

The objective of this study is to investigate the existence of inter-ROI lags and quantify these differences across various facial regions. By measuring these delays, this research seeks to determine if spatial integration affects the accuracy of rPPG measurements and to establish whether methods validated solely for heart rate remain valid for advanced physiological analysis.

2 Materials and Methods

2.1 Datasets

For this study, we utilized the UBFC datasets 1 and 2 [9] alongside a custom-built dataset. The UBFC datasets were acquired using a Logitech C920 HD Pro camera with a CMOS sensor at 30 FPS, providing uncompressed 8-bit RGB frames. The UBFC 1 subset contains recordings of 8 participants in a stationary position, while UBFC 2 includes 42 participants performing a mathematical game. Since the specific cognitive tasks performed by the subjects are unrelated to our analysis, we combined both subsets into a single cohort, referred to throughout this text as the *UBFC dataset*.

In addition to the public benchmarks, we constructed a proprietary dataset using a Logitech BRIO camera, referred to throughout this text as the *HFR dataset*, where HFR stands for High Frame Rate. These recordings were captured at 60 FPS using frame-by-frame MJPEG compression. To ensure strict standardization, the High Dynamic Range (HDR) functionality was disabled. The acquisition parameters were fixed as follows: the field of view was set to 65%, lighting parameters (brightness, contrast) were maintained at 50%, the shutter speed was fixed at 1/120 s, and the ISO was set to 300.

The *HFR dataset* features 12 participants, 8 male and 4 female. The physical setup consisted of the camera positioned at head height, with a fixed distance of 60 cm between the lens and the subject. To ensure consistent illumination, a ring LED light was placed behind the camera. This dataset was specifically designed to evaluate the impact of camera frame rate on the signal analysis, aiming to determine if the observed effects were caused solely by noise introduced by the sampling interval or if they remained visible at higher frame rates.

2.2 ROI Detection and Signal Extraction

To extract the rPPG, we focused on four specific anatomical areas: the forehead, the left cheek, the right cheek, and the chin. These regions were selected not only because they are the most standard in the literature, enabling comparable benchmarking, but primarily due to their distinct physiological and physical properties, which are critical for this study.

First, these areas present heterogeneity in their vascular supply. The cheeks are primarily perfused by the facial artery, whereas the forehead receives blood via the supraorbital and superficial temporal arteries (branches of the internal and external carotid arteries, respectively, Fig. 1b) [10].

These distinct vascular paths imply different distances from the heart, potentially introducing variations in PTT. Second, the tissue composition varies significantly across these regions; the forehead consists of skin tightly bound to the skull, while the cheeks contain higher amounts of adipose and muscular tissue. These differences in tissue viscoelasticity can induce local phase delays in the mechanical expansion of the skin (vascular hysteresis).

Finally, the vertical spatial distribution of these regions is crucial for analyzing acquisition artifacts. Since the datasets utilized CMOS sensors with a rolling shutter mechanism, the line-by-line scanning can introduce a temporal offset between the top of the face (forehead) and the bottom (chin). By selecting ROIs at different vertical heights, we can effectively isolate and analyze the impact of this scanning delay.

The automatic localization of these regions was performed using Google MediaPipe [11] to obtain a facial mesh with several landmarks. Using these, we defined rectangular bounding boxes for each area, as shown in Fig. 1a.

For every frame, the spatial average of pixel intensities was calculated within each box to obtain the raw RGB temporal traces. To recover the BVP, we utilized

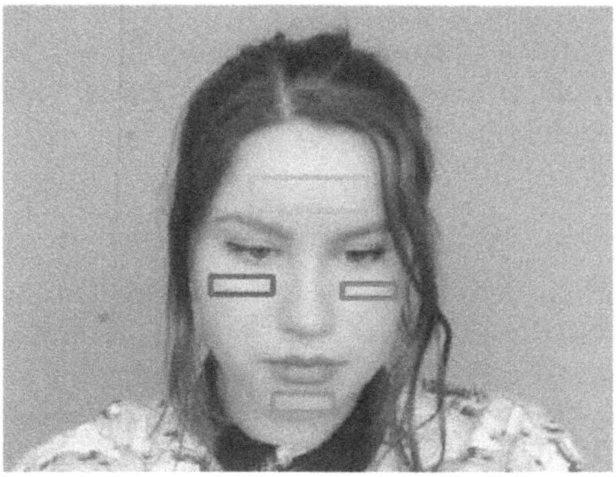

(a) ROIs calculated for subject 1 of the UBFC 2 dataset [9]

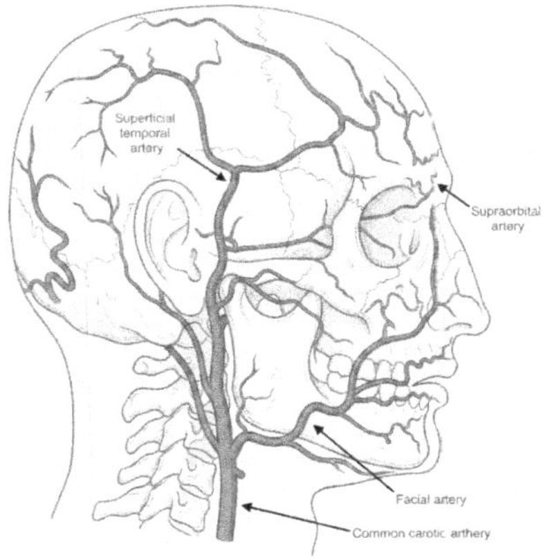

(b) Representation of arterial pathway on the human face

Fig. 1. Comparison of calculated ROIs (a) and facial arterial pathways (b).

the Plane-Orthogonal-to-Skin (POS) algorithm [12] applied independently to the traces from each region, resulting in four distinct rPPG signals.

2.3 Lag Calculation and Temporal Synchronization

To quantify the temporal offsets between physiological signals from different facial regions, we implemented a cross-correlation analysis. This process was applied to two variations of the extracted rPPG signals to evaluate the impact of signal quality on delay estimation. First, we analyzed the standard POS output (referred to as *Broadband*), which underwent only basic detrending and standard bandpass filtering (0.5 – 4 Hz). Second, to isolate the cardiac component, we computed an *HR-Centric Narrow-band* version by applying a narrow bandpass filter centered at the subject's ground truth HR with a bandwidth of ± 0.5 Hz.

Global Lag Estimation. For every pair of ROIs (e.g., forehead vs. Cheek), we first calculated a global lag over the entire duration of the recording. This was achieved by computing the normalized cross-correlation between the z-scored signals. The time shift corresponding to peak correlation coefficient (r) was defined as the global lag. Subsequently, to test if higher precision was attainable, we re-evaluated these lags using parabolic interpolation around the discrete peak of the cross-correlation function. This allowed us to determine if resolving delays smaller than the sampling interval ($1/f_s$, where f_s is the sampling frequency) provided a more accurate estimate of the signal propagation.

Next, to ensure the validity of these measurements, a quality control criteria was applied. We first calculated the HR for each ROI using the peak in the periodogram between 0.5 and 4 Hz, which is the physiological HR range for a healthy adult, and excluded any signal pairs where the estimated HR error exceeded 10 BPM or the maximum cross-correlation coefficient between ROIs fell below 0.7. This thresholding prevents the analysis from being biased by noisy segments where a calculated lag might represent the superposition of noise artifacts rather than a true physiological delay.

2.4 Statistical Analysis

As the data distributions were non-normal, non-parametric hypothesis testing was used. To assess the effect of HR-centric narrow-band filtering, a one-tailed paired Wilcoxon signed-rank test compared correlation coefficients between filtered and broadband signals from the same video segments. A two-tailed version of the test was additionally applied to verify that filtering did not significantly alter the magnitude of the measured time lag. To evaluate the presence of lag between different ROIs, a one-sample Wilcoxon signed-rank test was performed with the null hypothesis that the median lag equals zero. The significance level for all tests was set at 0.05.

3 Results

3.1 Impact of Signal Processing on Analysis Quality

The HR-centric narrow-band filtering consistently improved signal quality, increasing r across all ROI pairs for the UBFC dataset (paired Wilcoxon signed-rank test, $p < 0.05$ for all pairs). For example, the forehead-left cheek pair showed a significant increase in median global correlation from 0.80 to 0.87 ($p < 0.001$).

This improvement in signal definition directly affected the inclusion of data. The exclusion criteria (HR error > 10 BPM or $r < 0.7$) resulted in a higher rejection rate for unfiltered signals. For instance, the number of valid video segments for the Forehead-Chin pair increased from 18 when using broadband traces to 30 when using filtered traces. Also, the signals showed the same conclusion regarding lag presence for filtered and unfiltered signals. Given that correlation was increased, more videos were included and the effect on lag was not altered by the filtering, the subsequent analyses rely on the HR-centric narrow-band metrics.

3.2 Quantification of Inter-ROI Lags

The measurement of temporal offsets revealed a systematic delay pattern correlated with the vertical positioning of the ROIs. As summarized in Table 1, all pairs involving the Forehead exhibited a non-zero median global lag. The Forehead-Chin, Forehead-Left Cheek, and Forehead-Right Cheek pairs consistently showed a median global delay of 33.33 ms across the UBFC dataset. Conversely, ROI pairs with minimal vertical separation demonstrated temporal synchrony; for example, the Left/Right Cheek pair maintained a median global lag of 0 ms. Similarly, comparisons between the Cheeks and the Chin predominantly resulted in a median global lag of 0.

Table 1. Analysis of temporal offsets between each ROI pair and correlation coefficients. The p-values correspond to the one-sample Wilcoxon signed-rank test against a null hypothesis of zero lag. Mode indicates if HR centered filtering was used, videos refers to the quantity of videos that passed the exclusion criteria for that pair.

Mode	ROI A	ROI B	Videos	Median Lag (ms)	Median r	p-value
Filtered	Forehead	Chin	30	33.33	0.81	0.000076
Filtered	Forehead	Left cheek	38	33.33	0.87	0.000002
Filtered	Forehead	Right cheek	37	33.33	0.86	0.000006
Filtered	Left cheek	Chin	24	0.00	0.78	0.883161
Filtered	Left cheek	Right cheek	32	0.00	0.82	1.000000
Filtered	Right cheek	Chin	24	0.00	0.78	1.000000
Unfiltered	Forehead	Chin	18	33.33	0.76	0.000678
Unfiltered	Forehead	Left cheek	33	33.33	0.80	0.000048
Unfiltered	Forehead	Right cheek	29	33.33	0.80	0.000039
Unfiltered	Left cheek	Chin	6	0.00	0.73	1.000000
Unfiltered	Left cheek	Right cheek	16	0.00	0.77	1.000000
Unfiltered	Right cheek	Chin	10	0.00	0.71	1.000000

Figure 2a illustrates the distribution of these lags in terms of discrete time steps (1 step $\approx$ 33 ms). The data confirms the descriptive statistics: ROI pairs involving the forehead predominantly cluster at 1 lag step (33 ms) or higher. In contrast, pairs with minimal vertical separation exhibit zero lag in a significantly higher percentage of cases. For example, the Forehead-Right Cheek pair showed a lag of at least one time step in over 70% of the recordings, whereas the Left Cheek-Right Cheek pair remained synchronized in over 80% of cases.

3.3 Validation on High-Frame Rate Data

To determine if the observed delays were sampling artifacts, the analysis was repeated on a *HFR dataset*. Figure 2 shows that higher temporal resolution increases lag detection. For example, the Forehead-Right Cheek pair exhibited a lag in 75.00% of the 60 FPS recordings versus 72.97% at 30 FPS. This suggests the 33.33 ms interval of the UBFC dataset likely masked true delays by quantizing offsets shorter than 16.67 ms to zero.

As shown in Table 2, median global lags for almost all pairs are now non-zero. Crucially, we now observe lags where we did not before: the Chin-Left Cheek and Chin-Right Cheek pairs, which previously showed 0.00 ms, now demonstrate a median lag of 16.67 ms. This implies the 33.33 ms Forehead lag was likely closer to 16.67 ms and that previously synchronous regions actually possess measurable offsets. This trend is visible in Fig. 2b, where nearly all pairs show an increased percentage of lag steps, except for the Left/Right Cheek pair which remains synchronized as expected.

Statistical results remain not conclusive. While the Forehead-Right Cheek pair reached significance ($p = 0.031$), others like the Forehead-Chin ($p = 0.0625$) did not. This is largely due to the low sample size ($n \leq 8$), caused by strict quality criteria that caused the exclusion of a large percentage of videos, which could be caused by MJPEG compression artifacts. Furthermore, discrete sampling rounds delays shorter than 8 ms to 0 ms. These limitations confirm that while discrete analysis identifies the forehead-lead trend, interpolation (3.4) is essential to resolve the true values masked by the frame interval.

Table 2. Summary of statistics for the *HFR dataset*. The p-values correspond to the one-sample Wilcoxon signed-rank test against a null hypothesis of zero lag.

ROI A	ROI B	Videos	Median Lag (ms)	Median r	p-value
Forehead	Chin	7	16.67	0.87	0.06250
Forehead	Left cheek	7	16.67	0.80	0.06250
Forehead	Right cheek	8	16.67	0.79	0.03125
Left cheek	Chin	6	16.67	0.79	0.50000
Left cheek	Right cheek	7	0.00	0.80	0.50000
Right cheek	Chin	6	16.67	0.78	1.00000

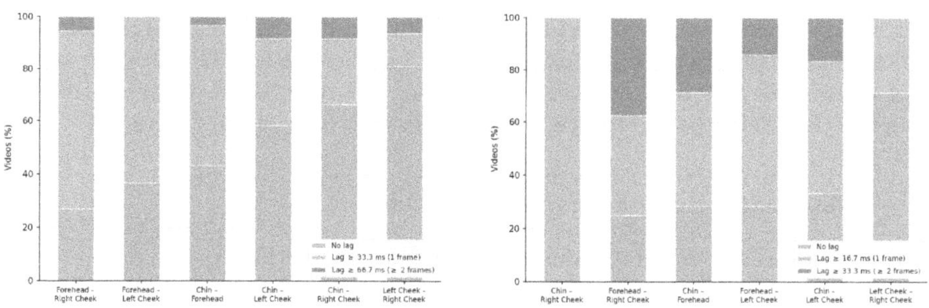

(a) Distribution of the UBFC dataset (b) Distribution of the *HFR dataset*

Fig. 2. Percentage of signals with different lag steps for the UBFC dataset (a) and the HFR dataset (b).

3.4 Interpolated Signals

Signal interpolation resolved the quantization limitations of the discrete analysis, revealing the precise temporal offsets previously masked by the frame interval. Beyond improving temporal resolution, this process consistently improved signal fidelity, resulting in an increase in the median correlation coefficient (r) across all ROI pairs. As detailed in Table 3, the median global lags for the UBFC dataset were between 19.85 ms and 23.70 ms for all pairs involving the forehead. This confirms that the 33.33 ms lag observed in the discrete analysis for the UBFC dataset was an overestimation and the 16.67 ms lag seen for the HFR dataset was an underestimation, and the true delay is in between, closer to 20 ms. Additionally, interpolation slightly improved the statistical power of the analysis for the HFR dataset. While the discrete analysis returned non-conclusive p-values due to low sample size, the interpolated metrics reveal significant delays ($p < 0.05$) for all forehead pairs, while still the low n calls for additional videos in order to have a more statistically significant conclusion about 60 FPS videos. The median lags for these pairs ranged from 16.21 ms to 21.11 ms, aligning closely with the values found in the larger UBFC dataset. This consistency across different hardware and sampling rates validates the presence of a measurable delay originating from the forehead. Regarding the other facial regions, the analysis could not statistically conclude the presence of a lag. Pairs involving the Chin and the Cheeks showed non-zero median lags ranging from 8.00 ms to 19.67 ms, but these offsets did not reach statistical significance in either dataset ($p > 0.05$). However, it is worth noting that these median values are consistently lower than those observed for the forehead pairs, which aligns with the expectation that the forehead leads the rest of the face. Furthermore, the Left Cheek-Right Cheek pair presented the lowest median lags in the entire analysis (2.69 ms for HFR dataset, 6.31 ms for UBFC dataset), maintaining the highest degree of synchrony as expected given their symmetrical positioning and anatomical characteristics.

Table 3. Summary of statistics for both the UBFC and HFR dataset. The p-values are derived from a one-sample Wilcoxon signed-rank test (H_0: median lag = 0).

Dataset	ROI A	ROI B	Videos	Median Lag (ms)	Median r	p-value
HFR	Forehead	Chin	7	16.21	0.88	0.015625
HFR	Forehead	Left cheek	7	21.11	0.82	0.015625
HFR	Forehead	Right cheek	8	20.59	0.81	0.007812
HFR	Left cheek	Chin	6	9.99	0.80	0.562500
HFR	Left cheek	Right cheek	7	2.69	0.83	0.078125
HFR	Right cheek	Chin	6	19.67	0.80	1.000000
UBFC	Forehead	Chin	31	19.85	0.88	7.10e-07
UBFC	Forehead	Left cheek	38	20.75	0.89	3.64e-11
UBFC	Forehead	Right cheek	37	23.70	0.92	1.89e-07
UBFC	Left cheek	Chin	24	8.00	0.80	0.265132
UBFC	Left cheek	Right cheek	32	6.31	0.85	0.354645
UBFC	Right cheek	Chin	25	10.69	0.80	0.360256

Figure 3 is a representative example. As seen here, the forehead leads the left cheek by 42.1 ms and the chin by 44.6 ms. These results confirm that inter-ROI lags are a robust phenomenon that becomes statistically resolvable when using interpolation to bypass the limitations of discrete camera sampling.

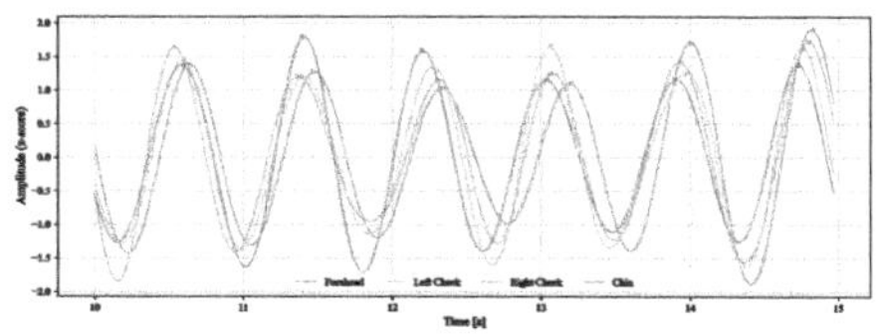

(a) Filtered signals from different ROIs

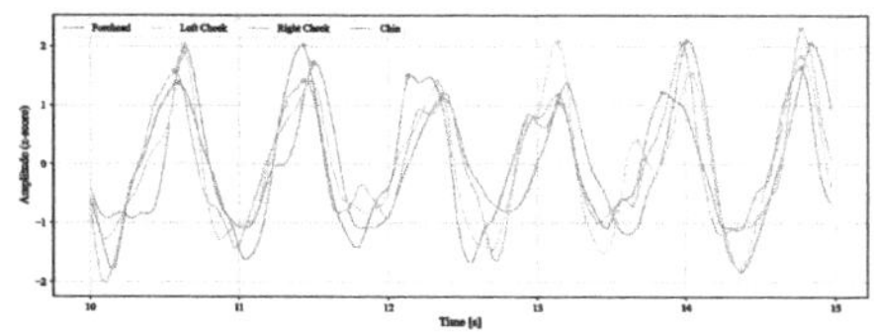

(b) Unfiltered signals from different ROIs

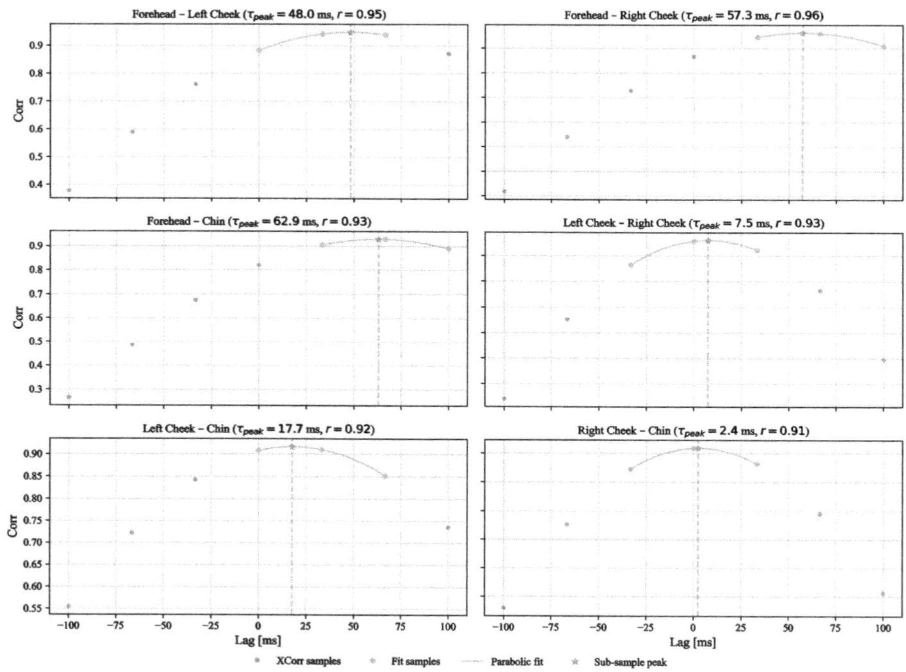

(c) Cross correlation between signals

Fig. 3. Visual example of lag between rPPG signals acquired from different ROIs, filtered (a) and unfiltered (b), and visual examination of cross correlation for different lag values and parabolic interpolation (c)

4 Discussion and Conclusions

The results demonstrate that rPPG signals extracted from different facial regions are not strictly time-aligned and follow a structured spatial pattern. Across datasets and processing methods, the forehead consistently presented a measurable lead compared to lower facial regions. While discrete analysis initially suggested a delay quantization of one frame, interpolation refined this to a precise median delay ranging approximately between 16 ms and 23 ms. In contrast, horizontally aligned regions, such as the left and right cheeks, remained largely synchronous. This consistency across frame rates indicates that the observed lag is a stable characteristic of the measured signals related to vertical positioning rather than random variability.

These findings indicate that facial ROIs should not be treated as temporally equivalent sources, a common premise in standard rPPG pipelines [3,12]. Merging signals from multiple ROIs without accounting for temporal differences may improve the SNR for average heart rate estimation, but it introduces destructive interference that affects waveform morphology. This limitation becomes particularly relevant for applications that rely on morphological analysis or precise fiducial timing, such as HRV and rhythm-based atrial fibrillation screening [13].Consequently, pipelines targeting biomarkers beyond average HR must abandon global face averaging in favor of spatially aware fusion or alignment strategies.

Future work should focus on identifying the specific origin of the observed lag, distinguishing between physiological pulse propagation and acquisition artifacts like rolling shutter timing. It is crucial to quantify how these measured lags translate into error for downstream metrics, specifically by conducting controlled comparisons of beat-to-beat interval statistics between naive and realigned fusion. Understanding the source of these temporal offsets will be important for developing synchronization algorithms that improve multi-ROI methods without sacrificing the robustness required for clinical-grade diagnostics.

Acknowledgments. This work was (partially) supported by Programa Iberoamericano de Ciencia y Tecnología para el Desarrollo (CYTED) (through Red [225RT0169])

Disclosure of Interests. The authors have no competing interests to declare that are relevant to the content of this article.

References

1. Babu, M., Lautman, Z., Lin, X., Sobota, M.H.B., Snyder, M.P.: Wearable devices: implications for precision medicine and the future of health care. Annu. Rev. Med. **75**, 401–415 (2024). https://doi.org/10.1146/annurev-med-052422-020437
2. Verkruysse, W., Svaasand, L.O., Nelson, J.S.: Remote Plethysmographic imaging of skin perfusion with digital cameras. Opt. Express **16**(26), 21434–21445 (2008). https://doi.org/10.1364/OE.16.021434

3. Bondarenko, M., Menon, C., Elgendi, M.: The role of face regions in remote photoplethysmography for contactless heart rate monitoring. NPJ Digit. Med. **8**(1), 479 (2025). https://doi.org/10.1038/s41746-025-01814-9
4. Xiao, H., Liu, T., Sun, Y., Li, Y., Zhao, S., Avolio, A.: Remote photoplethysmography for heart rate measurement: A review. Biomed. Sig. Process. Control **88**, 105608 (2024). https://doi.org/10.1016/j.bspc.2023.105608
5. Curran, T., et al.: Camera-based remote photoplethysmography for blood pressure measurement: current evidence, clinical perspectives, and future applications. Conn Health Telemed 2, 200004 (2023). https://doi.org/10.20517/chatmed.2022.25
6. Mukkamala, R., et al.: Toward ubiquitous blood pressure monitoring via pulse transit time: theory and practice. IEEE Trans. Biomed. Eng. **62**(8), 1879–1901 (2015). https://doi.org/10.1109/TBME.2015.2460215
7. Mironenko, Y., Kalinin, K., Kopeliovich, M., Petrushan, M.: Remote Photoplethysmography: Rarely Considered Factors. In: Proceedings of the IEEE/CVF Conference on Computer Vision and Pattern Recognition Workshops (CVPRW), pp. 128–129 (2020). https://doi.org/10.1109/CVPRW50498.2020.00069
8. Universitat Pompeu Fabra: Analysis of rolling shutter effects in remote photoplethysmography. UPF e-Repository (2021). https://repositori-api.upf.edu/api/core/bitstreams/60db0c04-bee8-49d2-af7a-1cf41fd7464f/content
9. Bobbia, S., Macwan, R., Benezeth, Y., Mansouri, A., Dubois, J.: UBFC-RPPG: a dataset for remote photoplethysmography and pulse rate detection. In: 2017 IEEE International Conference on Image Processing (ICIP), pp. 1–5 (2017). https://doi.org/10.1109/ICIP.2017.8296399
10. Standring, S. (ed.): Gray's Anatomy: The Anatomical Basis of Clinical Practice. 39th edn. Elsevier Churchill Livingstone, Edinburgh (2005). https://books.google.com/books?id=f03G0QEACAAJ
11. Lugaresi, C., et al.: MediaPipe: a framework for building perception pipelines. In: Third International Workshop on On-Device Intelligence at SysML (2019). https://doi.org/10.48550/arXiv.1906.08172
12. Wang, W., den Brinker, A.C., Stuijk, S., de Haan, G.: Algorithmic Principles of Remote PPG. IEEE Trans. Biomed. Eng. **64**(7), 1479–1491 (2017). https://doi.org/10.1109/TBME.2016.2609282
13. Barrera, P.L., et al.: A Machine learning approach for atrial fibrillation detection in telemonitored patients. In: Advances in Bioengineering and Clinical Engineering, pp. 36–45. Springer, Cham (2024). https://doi.org/10.1007/978-3-031-61960-1_4

Explainable AI-Based Connectivity Learning for ADHD Detection from EEG Signals

Diego Armando Pérez-Rosero[1(✉)], Noelia Belén Rios[4], Andres Marino Alvarez-Meza[1], and María Paula Bonomini[2,3]

[1] AI-Lab/Signal Processing and Recognition Group, Universidad Nacional de Colombia, Manizales 170003, Colombia
{dieaperezros,amalvarezme}@unal.edu.co

[2] Instituto Tecnológico de Buenos Aires (ITBA), CABA C1437, Buenos Aires, Argentina
mbonomini@itba.edu.ar

[3] Facultad Regional Haedo, Grupo Inteligencia Artificial, Universidad Tecnológica Nacional (UTN), Buenos Aires, Argentina

[4] Instituto Argentino de Matemática (IAM), CONICET and Centro de Matemática La Plata (CMaLP), Facultad de Cs. Exactas, Universidad Nacional de La Plata, La Plata, Argentina
nbrios@mate.unlp.edu.ar

Abstract. Attention-Deficit/Hyperactivity Disorder (ADHD) remains difficult to assess objectively because diagnosis still depends largely on behavioral evaluation, while EEG-based computational approaches often face a trade-off between subject-independent robustness and physiological interpretability. To address this limitation, this work proposes an EEG-based framework that integrates Transformer-based temporal modeling with multi-scale Gaussian kernel connectivity regularized through α-Rényi mutual information, while incorporating Graph Spectral Analysis with XGBoost from Phase Locking Value-based connectivity to examine the class-discriminative structure of the learned representations. The approach was evaluated on a publicly available pediatric EEG dataset comprising 121 children under a 5-fold Stratified Group k-Fold cross-validation protocol designed to preserve subject independence. The experimental results show competitive performance, with 80.44% accuracy, 80.37% recall, and 81.35% precision, surpassing EEG-Net, Multi-Stream Transformer, IM-CBGT, and ANOVA-PCA SVM baselines; additionally, the analysis reveals that the learned connectivity patterns become progressively more discriminative from raw EEG to higher-level transformed representations. Overall, these findings support the potential of the proposed framework as a robust and interpretable alternative for objective EEG-based ADHD assessment.

Keywords: EEG · Mental Health · ADHD · Connectivity · Explainable AI · Deep Learning

J. M. Ferrández Vicente et al. (Eds.): IWINAC 2026, LNCS 16574, pp. 291–300, 2026.
https://doi.org/10.1007/978-3-032-27314-7_27

1 Introduction

Attention-Deficit/Hyperactivity Disorder (ADHD) is a prevalent neurodevelopmental condition characterized by persistent patterns of inattention, hyperactivity, and impulsivity [4]. It affects approximately 8% of children worldwide and often persists into adulthood, leading to long-term academic and social impairments [12]. Despite advances in diagnostic guidelines, ADHD assessment remains largely clinical and subjective, motivating the development of objective, brain-based computational tools [9]. In this context, electroencephalography (EEG) has emerged as a promising modality due to its low cost, portability, non-invasiveness, and high temporal resolution, particularly compared to functional magnetic resonance imaging, which is expensive and sensitive to motion artifacts [8]. Recent advances in deep learning have further accelerated interest in EEG-based ADHD analysis by enabling data-driven modeling of complex neural dynamics that are difficult to capture using traditional signal processing techniques.

Despite recent advances, achieving clinically reliable EEG-based ADHD classification remains challenging. Many existing approaches rely on rigid, multi-stage preprocessing pipelines that impose strong a priori assumptions and may suppress informative temporal and inter-channel dynamics, limiting robustness under subject-independent evaluation [5]. These limitations are exacerbated by the high inter-subject variability of EEG signals and the heterogeneous neurocognitive profiles associated with ADHD [3]. At the same time, a fundamental tension persists between representational capacity and interpretability: classical methods offer transparent decision mechanisms but are constrained by handcrafted features, whereas deep learning models provide higher expressive power at the cost of reduced physiological interpretability and diminished clinical trust [10].

A broad spectrum of approaches has been explored for EEG-based ADHD classification, ranging from classical methods based on handcrafted time, frequency, and time-frequency features to modern deep learning architectures [14]. While classical approaches offer interpretability, they depend strongly on preprocessing choices and often exhibit limited subject-level generalization. More recent convolutional, recurrent, and attention-based deep learning models learn spatio-temporal representations directly from EEG data and have shown improved performance, albeit with increased susceptibility to overfitting in low-sample, subject-independent settings [15]. In parallel, graph-based learning approaches have been introduced to represent EEG channels and their interactions within structured connectivity models [2]. Within this line of work, spectral measures are commonly employed to define functional connectivity, with phase-based indices such as the Phase Locking Value (PLV) serving as standard descriptors of coordinated neural activity [16]. Nevertheless, existing approaches do not provide an end-to-end framework for EEG-based ADHD detection that jointly ensures subject-independent robustness and physiologically grounded interpretability.

Here, we propose a connectivity-driven framework characterized by: i) Multi-level representation modeling: integration and contrast of raw EEG signals, transformer-based temporal embeddings, and kernel-based network connectivity regularized via α-Rényi entropy to mitigate inter-subject overfitting in EEG-based ADHD classification [7]. ii) Graph-based spectral connectivity: incorporation of locality-aware functional graphs derived from phase-based measures to code spectrally defined interactions [6]. iii) Discriminative explainability validation: assessment of interpretability through the discriminative capacity of PLV-informed graphs relative to a learned connectivity from a transformer and multi-scale Gaussian kernel network with α-Rényi regularization, termed TGAR-Net [13]. In this context, the proposed framework enables connectivity-driven explainability by contrasting learned connectivity patterns with PLV-informed functional graphs. Also, our approach is assessed through the discriminative capacity of these spectral connectivity structures, supporting the identification of physiologically meaningful inter-channel interactions.

The agenda is as follows: Sect. 2 describes the materials and methods. Sections 3 and 4 present the experimental setup and results, respectively. Finally, Sect. 5 concludes the paper.

2 Materials and Methods

2.1 Deep Learning-Based ADHD Classification via Gaussian Connectivity and α-Rényi Mutual Information

Given an EEG dataset $\{\boldsymbol{X}_n \in \mathbb{R}^{C\times T}, y_n \in \{0,1\}\}_{n=1}^{N}$ holding N trials, C channels, and T samples, a deep learning classifier outputs $\hat{y}_n = \breve{\mathcal{F}}(\boldsymbol{X}_n) \in [0,1]$, implemented as a composition of L layers:

$$\hat{y}_n = \breve{\mathcal{F}}(\boldsymbol{X}_n) = \left(\breve{f}_L \circ \breve{f}_{L-1} \circ \cdots \circ \breve{f}_1\right)(\boldsymbol{X}_n), \tag{1}$$

where $\breve{f}_l$ denotes the l-th network layer (including attention-based mechanisms). Training minimizes a composite objective combining prediction and connectivity regularization: $\mathcal{L} = \mathcal{L}_{\mathrm{BCE}} + \lambda\,\mathcal{L}_{\mathrm{MI}}$, where $\mathcal{L}_{\mathrm{BCE}}$ is binary cross-entropy and $\lambda > 0$ weights the regularizer. $\mathcal{L}_{\mathrm{MI}}$ is based on a mutual information term computed using matrix-based α-Rényi entropy over G Gaussian connectivity kernels [13]. Let $\mathbf{K}_{\sigma_g} \in \mathbb{R}^{C\times C}$ denote the connectivity matrix associated with bandwidth σ_g, whose elements are defined as:

$$\kappa_{\sigma_g}(\mathbf{x}_c, \mathbf{x}_{c'}) = \exp\left(-\frac{\|\mathbf{x}_c - \mathbf{x}_{c'}\|_2^2}{2\sigma_g^2}\right), \quad c, c' \in C, \quad \sigma_g \in \mathbb{R}^+, \quad g \in G; \tag{2}$$

where $\mathbf{x}_c, \mathbf{x}_{c'} \in \mathbf{X}$ for a given EEG trial. A trace-normalized form yields $\tilde{\mathbf{K}}_{\sigma_g} = \mathbf{K}_{\sigma_g}/\mathrm{tr}(\mathbf{K}_{\sigma_g})$ and:

$$\mathcal{L}_{\mathrm{MI}} = \sum_{g=1}^{G} H_\alpha(\tilde{\mathbf{K}}_{\sigma_g}) - H_\alpha\left(\frac{\tilde{\mathbf{K}}_{\sigma_1} \odot \cdots \odot \tilde{\mathbf{K}}_{\sigma_G}}{\mathrm{tr}\left(\tilde{\mathbf{K}}_{\sigma_1} \odot \cdots \odot \tilde{\mathbf{K}}_{\sigma_G}\right)}\right), \tag{3}$$

where $H_\alpha(\cdot)$ denotes the matrix-based α-Rényi entropy and $\odot$ the Hadamard product. For simplicity and numerical stability, we set $\alpha = 2$ (quadratic entropy), defined as: $H_2(\tilde{\mathbf{K}}_{\sigma_g}) = -\log\left(\mathrm{tr}(\tilde{\mathbf{K}}_{\sigma_g}^\top \tilde{\mathbf{K}}_{\sigma_g})\right)$. This formulation promotes high entropy at each scale while penalizing redundant shared structure through the joint term, thereby encouraging complementary multi-scale connectivities within a TGARNet-based ADHD detection approach [13].

2.2 Connectivity-Grounded Explainability via PLV Graphs and Spectral Descriptors

To support the explainable AI component, we compare the learned multi-scale Gaussian connectivities with physiologically grounded functional graphs derived from the Phase Locking Value (PLV). The discriminative structure of these connectivity representations is then quantified using graph spectral descriptors and a lightweight classifier. For a given trial $\mathbf{X}$, the instantaneous phase $\phi_c(t)$ is obtained via the Hilbert transform of channel c, and PLV-based functional connectivity is computed over analysis windows to construct interpretable phase-synchronization graphs, yielding:

$$\mathrm{PLV}(\mathbf{x}_c, \mathbf{x}_{c'}) = \left| \frac{1}{T_w} \sum_{t=1}^{T_w} \exp\left(i(\phi_c(t) - \phi_{c'}(t))\right) \right|, \qquad c, c' \in C. \tag{4}$$

Stacking all pairwise values yields a symmetric weighted adjacency matrix $\mathbf{A} \in \mathbb{R}^{C \times C}$ with entries $A_{c,c'} = \mathrm{PLV}(\mathbf{x}_c, \mathbf{x}_{c'})$ and $A_{c,c} = 0$. The PLV value ranges from 0 (no synchronization) to 1 (complete synchronization), indicating the degree of phase coupling between the channels considered.

Let $\breve{G} = (V, E, \mathbf{A})$ be the undirected weighted graph induced by $\mathbf{A}$, where $V = \{1, \ldots, C\}$ and $E = \{(c, c') : A_{c,c'} > 0,\ c \neq c'\}$. The weighted degree (degree centrality) of node c is defined as:

$$d_c = \sum_{c' \in V} A_{c,c'}. \tag{5}$$

Let $\mu_1 \leq \cdots \leq \mu_C$ denote the eigenvalues of $\mathbf{A}$ (counting multiplicities), the spectral radius yields:

$$\rho(\mathbf{A}) = \max_{r \in \{1, \ldots, C\}} |\mu_r|. \tag{6}$$

Also, by the Perron–Frobenius theorem, $\rho(\mathbf{A})$ is associated with a nonnegative eigenvector. Eigenvector centrality $\mathbf{v} \in \mathbb{R}^C$ is defined as the leading eigenvector of $\mathbf{A}$ satisfying:

$$\mathbf{A}\mathbf{v} = \rho(\mathbf{A})\,\mathbf{v}, \qquad \|\mathbf{v}\|_2 = 1, \qquad v_c \geq 0. \tag{7}$$

From $\mathbf{A}$ we construct a Graph Spectral Analysis (GSA)-based feature vector $\mathbf{z} \in \mathbb{R}^P$ by concatenating local descriptors (node degrees d_c and eigenvector centralities v_c for selected electrodes) and global descriptors (spectral radius $\rho(\mathbf{A})$) [6]. These features are extracted from three connectivity sources: (i) PLV graphs computed from raw EEG, (ii) PLV graphs derived after Transformer-based temporal encoding within a TGARNet, and (iii) graphs constructed from the learned Gaussian-kernel connectivity representation. An Extreme Gradient Boosting (XGB) classifier is trained on $\{\mathbf{z}, y\}$ to quantify the discriminative power of each connectivity representation. Progressive performance gains and anatomically localized feature importance indicate that the model learns increasingly discriminative and physiologically interpretable connectivity structures (see Fig. 1).

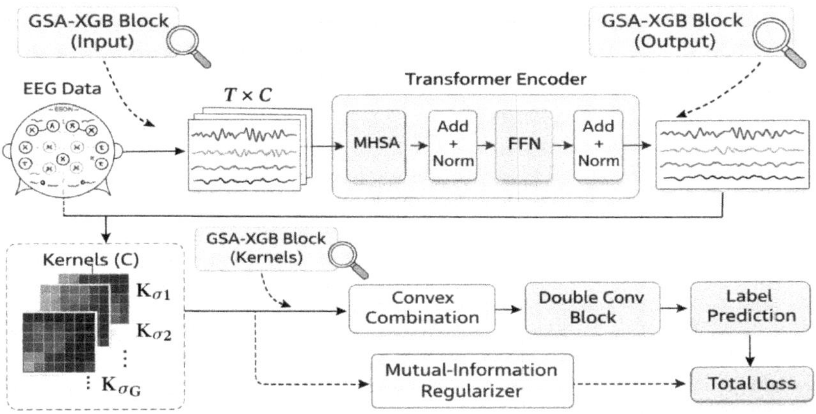

Fig. 1. Connectivity-regularized transformer framework based on TGARNet with GSA-XGB-based explainability for EEG-based ADHD Classification.

3 Experimental Set-Up

Experiments used a publicly available EEG dataset from IEEE DataPort [11] with recordings from 121 children aged 7–12 years (61 ADHD, 60 controls). ADHD was diagnosed by an experienced clinician according to DSM-IV criteria; diagnosed participants had received Ritalin for no more than six months, and controls reported no psychiatric or neurological history. To enforce exact class balance, one ADHD subject was randomly removed, yielding 120 participants (60 ADHD, 60 controls). Recordings underwent minimal preprocessing (no artifact rejection or band decomposition) to preserve the raw electrophysiological structure. Electrode placement follows the international 10–20 standard for 19-channel acquisition and a cartoon-based visual attention task was presented to participants during data collection. Signals were segmented into 4 s windows (512 samples at 128 Hz) with 50% overlap [1], producing 3,657 control segments

(56 ± 15 per subject) and 4,622 ADHD segments (75 ± 29 per subject). Segments were used as training samples, while subject identities were preserved to ensure strict subject-wise separation across folds.

Generalization was evaluated with 5-fold Stratified Group k-Fold cross-validation (SGKF-CV), ensuring subject-independent testing while maintaining class balance. In each fold, 24 subjects (12 ADHD and 12 controls) were held out for testing, and the remaining 96 were used for training. We fix $G = 3$ Gaussian connectivity kernels and an epoch-dependent weighting of the λ term: $\lambda(e) = \frac{2(1-\exp(-\delta e/E))}{1+\exp(-\delta e/E)}$, where e is the epoch index, E the total number of epochs, and $\delta > 0$ controls the growth rate, enabling progressive integration of connectivity constraints during training.

Hyperparameter optimization used Optuna (v3.5.0) with a Gaussian Process sampler. The bandwidths $\{\sigma_g\}_{g=1}^{G}$ were searched on a log scale in $[1, 20]$, and the schedule parameter δ on a log scale in $[1, 30]$. Baselines [13]: ShallowConvNet, EEGNet, CNN–LSTM, ANOVA–PCA SVM, Multi-Stream Transformer, and IM-CBGT. Experiments were run on Kaggle (Python 3.11.11, TensorFlow 2.18.0) with an Intel Xeon CPU @ 2.00 GHz, 31 GB RAM, and two NVIDIA Tesla T4 GPUs (15 GB VRAM each) under Ubuntu/CUDA 12.6. Code is available at GitHub repository.

4 Results and Discussion

We first assessed the model's sensitivity to the hyperparameters controlling multi-scale connectivity. Figure 2 shows that accuracy varies smoothly with the Gaussian bandwidths σ_g and the schedule parameter δ, with broad high-performing regions indicating robustness to precise tuning. Hyperparameter importance further identifies σ_3 as the primary driver of accuracy (followed by σ_2), whereas δ has a comparatively minor effect, suggesting that larger connectivity scales contribute most to discriminative performance and that the scheduling mainly supports training stability.

Building on the stability results, we evaluated SGKF-CV performance (Table 1). T-GARNet achieves 80.44% ± 2.32 accuracy with balanced recall and precision across folds. While ShallowConvNet attains a slightly higher mean accuracy, T-GARNet remains competitive and outperforms EEGNet, Multi-Stream Transformer, IM-CBGT, and the ANOVA-PCA SVM baseline. Its moderate cross-fold variability, lower than that of CNN-LSTM and other Transformer-based models, indicates improved subject-independent robustness. We also examined the topological organization of the connectivity patterns across stages (Fig. 3). Raw EEG displays diffuse and less consistent interactions in both classes, whereas the Transformer stage yields a more coherent structure, consistent with stabilized inter-regional relations. In the final representation, Class 0 exhibits more distributed frontal–posterior coupling across both hemispheres, while Class 1 becomes comparatively more localized and lateralized, with stronger emphasis on temporal and central regions. These differences indicate that the model progressively sharpens class-discriminative functional configurations.

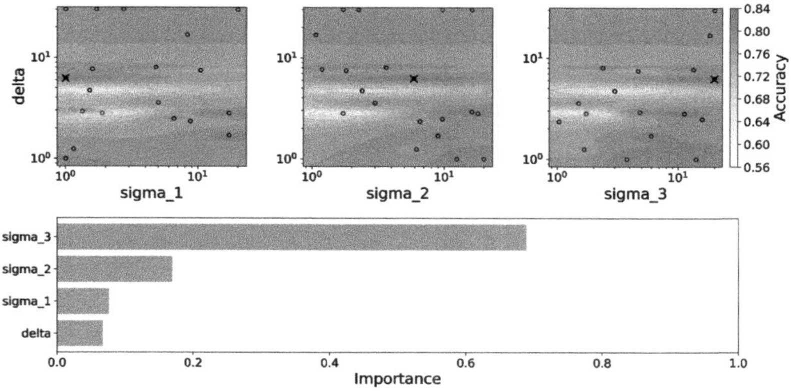

Fig. 2. TGARNet hyperparameter sensitivity under SGKF-CV. **Top:** Accuracy contours for each Gaussian bandwidth vs. The schedule parameter δ. **Bottom:** Relative hyperparameter importance.

Table 1. ADHD classification performance (mean across SGKF-CV folds).

Model	Accuracy (%)	Recall (%)	Precision (%)
T-GARNet (This work)	80.44	80.37	81.35
ShallowConvNet	81.91	82.18	84.23
CNN-LSTM	80.21	79.76	81.36
EEGNet	75.61	75.49	79.52
Multi-Stream Transformer	73.39	73.07	73.11
ANOVA-PCA SVM	66.47	66.47	66.47
IM-CBGT	64.98	64.14	64.64

Table 2 summarizes the classification performance of our GSA-based explainability approach. For comparability, all models were trained using the six best-ranked features (listed in the last row of the table). Each classifier was configured with a logistic objective function (binary:logistic) and log-loss as the evaluation metric. The boosting ensemble comprised 200 decision trees with a maximum depth of 3 and a learning rate of 0.05. To enhance generalization and mitigate overfitting, row subsampling (subsample = 0.8) and column subsampling per tree of 0.8 were applied. Note the performance jump of the GSA models following the transformations, with markedly better results for EEG+Transformer+PLV and EEG+Transformer+GK compared to raw EEG data+PLV. As seen, the majority of relevant GSA-based features are local, i.e., they exhibit a well-defined anatomical mapping. By contrast, global features—computed as averages across all electrodes—were generally not important, with the exception of the spectral ratio in the EEG+Transformer model.

Table 2. GSA-XGB performance comparison using the six most relevant GSA features. GK stands for TGARNet-based Gaussian connectivity. d_c denotes node degree (degree centrality) at electrode c, ec_c denotes eigenvector centrality, and SR denotes the spectral radius of the adjacency matrix.

Model	Accuracy (%)	Recall (%)	Precision (%)	Top Features
Raw EEG + PLV	66.74	90.87	66.30	$d_{Fp1}, d_{O1}, d_{C3}, d_{Fz}, ec_{Fz}, d_{Cz}$
EEG+Transformer + PLV	78.90	81.00	83.43	$d_{T6}, d_{O1}, d_{F8}, SR, d_{C3}, d_{F4}$
EEG+Transformer+GK	80.32	84.57	83.01	$d_{Fz}, ec_{Cz}, d_{F4}, d_{T6}, d_{C3}, d_{Pz}$

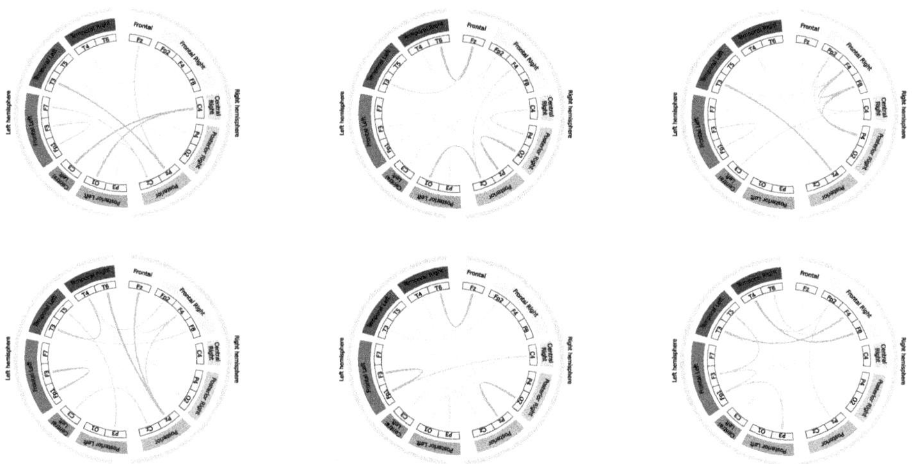

Fig. 3. Connectivity patterns organized by representation (columns) and class (rows). **Columns (left to right):** Raw EEG+PLV, Transformer output+PLV, and TGARNet-based Gaussian connectivity. **Rows (top to bottom):** Class 0 and Class 1.

5 Conclusions

We introduced a connectivity-driven, explainable framework for subject-independent EEG-based ADHD detection that integrates Transformer-based temporal modeling with multi-scale Gaussian kernel connectivity regularized through α-Rényi mutual information, and validates interpretability through PLV-informed GSA. The proposed TGARNet achieved competitive performance under strict Stratified Group k-Fold cross-validation, outperforming several deep learning and classical baselines while maintaining stable generalization across subjects. Beyond predictive accuracy, the principal contribution lies in demonstrating that progressively learned connectivity representations become increasingly discriminative and anatomically structured, as evidenced by the improved performance of GSA-XGB models from raw EEG to Transformer-based PLV and Gaussian-kernel stages. Importantly, the most informative descriptors were predominantly local graph features with clear electrode-level specificity, whereas global averaged measures contributed marginally, reinforcing the relevance of anatomically grounded connectivity patterns in ADHD characterization. These findings support the framework as a robust and physiologically interpretable alternative for objective EEG-based ADHD assessment. Future work will explore fully end-to-end graph-aware architectures, including the integration of graph neural networks and connectivity descriptors directly within Transformer blocks, enabling joint spatio-temporal and topological learning for more unified and scalable EEG-based ADHD detection.

Acknowledgments. This work was (partially) supported by Programa Iberoamericano de Ciencia y Tecnología para el Desarrollo (CYTED) (through Red [225RT0169])

References

1. Alim, A., Imtiaz, M.H.: Automatic identification of children with ADHD from EEG brain waves. Signals **4**(1), 193–205 (2023)
2. Almohammadi, A., Wang, Y.K.: Revealing brain connectivity: graph embeddings for EEG representation learning and comparative analysis of structural and functional connectivity. Front. Neurosci. **17**, 1288433 (2024)
3. Arnett, A.B., Flaherty, B.P.: A framework for characterizing heterogeneity in neurodevelopmental data using latent profile analysis in a sample of children with ADHD. J. Neurodev. Disord. **14**(1), 45 (2022)
4. Asherson, P.: ADHD across the lifespan. Medicine **52**(8), 512–517 (2024)
5. Chen, H., Song, Y., Li, X.: A deep learning framework for identifying children with ADHD using an EEG-based brain network. Neurocomputing **356**, 83–96 (2019)
6. Cisne Macas Ordóñez, B.d., Orellana Villavicencio, D.V., Suing Ochoa, M.A., Carrión González, J.E., Bonomini, M.P.: Graph theory and its potential in the automatic detection of left bundle branch block. Integrated Comput.-Aided Eng. **32**(4), 424–442 (2025)
7. García, D., Alvarez, A., Castellanos, G.: Single-trial kernel-based functional connectivity for enhanced feature extraction in motor-related tasks. Sensors **21**(8), 2750 (2021)
8. Güven, A., et al.: Combining functional near-infrared spectroscopy and EEG measurements for the diagnosis of attention-deficit hyperactivity disorder. Neural Comput. Appl. **32**, 8367–8380 (2020)
9. Hurjui, I.A., et al.: Biomarkers and neuropsychological tools in attention-deficit/hyperactivity disorder: from subjectivity to precision diagnosis. Medicina **61**(7), 1211 (2025)
10. Loh, H.W., et al.: ADHD/CD-net: automated EEG-based characterization of ADHD and cd using explainable deep neural network technique. Cogn. Neurodyn. **18**(4), 1609–1625 (2024)
11. Nasrabadi, A.M.: EEG data for ADHD/control children (2020). https://ieee-dataport.org/open-access/eeg-data-adhd-control-children
12. van der Plas, N.E., Noordermeer, S.D., Oosterlaan, J., Luman, M.: Systematic review and meta-analysis: predictors of adult psychiatric outcomes of childhood attention-deficit/hyperactivity disorder. J. American Acad. Child Adolescent Psychiatry (2025)

13. Salazar-Dubois, D.V., Álvarez-Meza, A.M., Castellanos-Dominguez, G.: T-garnet: a transformer and multi-scale gaussian kernel connectivity network with alpha-rényi regularization for eeg-based adhd detection. Mathematics **13**(24), 4026 (2025)
14. Sindhu, T., Sujatha, S.: Common spatial pattern based feature extractor with hybrid Linknet-Squeezenet for ADHD detection from EEG signal. Prog. Eng. Sci. (2025)
15. Vafaei, E., Hosseini, M.: Transformers in EEG analysis: a review of architectures and applications in motor imagery, seizure, and emotion classification. Sensors **25**(5), 1293 (2025)
16. Verkennis, B., Van Weelden, E., Marogna, F.L., Alimardani, M., Wiltshire, T.J., Louwerse, M.M.: Predicting workload in virtual flight simulations using EEG spectral and connectivity features. In: 2025 IEEE International Conference on Artificial Intelligence and eXtended and Virtual Reality (AIxVR), pp. 82–89. IEEE (2025)

Text–Conditioned Semantic Aggregation for Audio-Based Multiple-Instance Learning in Depression Detection

Alejandro Patiño-Bedoya, Diego Armando Pérez-Rosero,
Andres Marino Alvarez-Meza, and German Castellanos-Dominguez(✉)

AI-Lab/Signal Processing and Recognition Group, Universidad Nacional de Colombia, Manizales 170003, Colombia
{alpatinob,dieaperezros,amalvarezme,cgcastellanosd}@unal.edu.co

Abstract. Automatic depression detection from semi-structured interviews has gained increasing relevance as a scalable and non-invasive complement to conventional clinical assessment, particularly in digital and remote-care contexts. However, modeling long-form interviews remains challenging due to their weakly supervised nature: a single subject-level label must be inferred from multiple heterogeneous conversational segments. This setting naturally fits the Multiple Instance Learning (MIL) paradigm, where each interview is represented as a bag of instances associated with a global label. Nevertheless, existing MIL-based approaches typically rely on implicit attention or aggregation mechanisms that compress local evidence into a final decision without explicitly grounding segment importance in structured clinical knowledge. Here, we propose a text-conditioned attention-based MIL framework, termed TCAMIL, for audio-based depression detection that incorporates symptom-level semantic alignment prior to aggregation. A semantic relevance filtering stage is implemented through a cross-encoder architecture to match interview text segments with Patient Health Questionnaire-8 (PHQ-8) symptom items, preserving only clinically aligned instances. This filtering enables the construction of noise-reduced MIL bags composed of symptom-relevant audio fragments, reducing the impact of semantically diverse and weakly informative content. The selected instances are then processed using a domain-adapted encoder and aggregated via trainable attention pooling to produce subject-level predictions under weak supervision. Experiments conducted on the DAIC-WOZ dataset demonstrate improved performance. Additionally, qualitative analyzes indicate enhanced interpretability, as the model assigns higher relevance to segments aligned with structured symptom descriptors.

Keywords: Multiple Instance Learning · Depression Detection · PHQ-8 Semantic Alignment

J. M. Ferrández Vicente et al. (Eds.): IWINAC 2026, LNCS 16574, pp. 301–309, 2026.
https://doi.org/10.1007/978-3-032-27314-7_28

1 Introduction

Automatic depression detection has emerged as a critical complement to conventional clinical assessment, driven by the increasing demand for scalable, reproducible, and non-invasive screening tools in digital and remote-care environments [9]. Although structured clinical interviews and standardized questionnaires remain central to mental health evaluation, their outcomes may still be influenced by clinician expertise, patient self-presentation, recall bias, and contextual variability across sessions [10]. These factors motivate the development of computational systems capable of providing consistent and objective support for clinical decision-making. In recent years, advances in artificial intelligence have enabled the automated analysis of semi-structured interviews through models that process linguistic content and, in several cases, integrate acoustic and visual cues to enhance robustness and clinical validity [14]. Such multimodal frameworks aim to capture subtle behavioral and paralinguistic signals that may reflect affective and cognitive patterns associated with depressive symptomatology.

Within this evolving landscape, prior research has explored hierarchical recurrent architectures, multimodal deep-learning pipelines, transformer-based encoders, and large language models for detecting depressive markers in interview data [2]. More recently, Multiple Instance Learning (MIL) formulations and interpretable pretrained representations have been introduced to better accommodate long interview transcripts, enabling models to identify or score clinically informative segments without requiring fine-grained annotations [15]. Despite these advances, most approaches rely on trainable attention or aggregation mechanisms that compress distributed local evidence into a single global prediction. In many cases, the relative contribution of each segment is modeled implicitly, remaining entangled with the final bag-level decision and lacking explicit grounding in structured clinical knowledge [8]. When an interview is represented as a sequence of interventions, it can be naturally formulated as a bag of instances associated with a single global label, where each utterance or response contributes unequally to the final decision [11]. Under this MIL perspective, the learning objective becomes the identification of diagnostically meaningful fragments without access to explicit instance-level annotations [12]. This problem is particularly challenging in long-form interviews, where conversational segments are semantically heterogeneous and their diagnostic value may fluctuate due to ambiguity, sparse emotional expression, topic shifts, or inconsistent self-disclosure [13]. Consequently, a central open question is not only how to detect depression from extended interviews, but also how to systematically identify clinically relevant segments within a weakly supervised and potentially noisy decision framework [1].

To address this gap, we propose a text-conditioned attention-based MIL framework (TCAMIL) for audio-based depression detection. The proposed approach integrates structured symptom knowledge prior to aggregation through three key components. First, we introduce semantic relevance filtering using a cross-encoder architecture to match interview text segments with Patient Health

Questionnaire-8 (PHQ-8) symptom items, preserving only clinically aligned instances for downstream modeling. Second, we construct noise-reduced MIL bags by restricting them to symptom-relevant audio fragments, thereby mitigating the adverse impact of semantically diverse and weakly informative conversational content. Third, we employ attention-based weakly supervised aggregation through a domain-adapted encoder and trainable attention pooling to learn bag-level depression predictions from filtered instances. Our framework is evaluated on the DAIWOZ database, demonstrating its effectiveness for clinically guided depression detection in long-form interviews by explicitly aligning interview evidence with structured symptom descriptors.

The agenda is as follows. Section 2 describes the materials and methods. Sections 3 and 4 present the experimental setup and results, respectively. Finally, Sect. 5 concludes the paper.

2 Materials and Methods

2.1 DAIC-WOZ Dataset

The proposed framework was evaluated on DAIC-WOZ, a widely used benchmark dataset for automatic depression assessment based on Wizard-of-Oz clinical interviews [4]. As a subset of the Distress Analysis Interview Corpus, DAIC-WOZ provides multimodal recordings, transcripts, and depression-related annotations collected during interactions between participants and an embodied virtual interviewer (Ellie). In this study, we use the official subject-independent partition, consisting of 107 training sessions and 35 validation sessions, including both healthy-control and depressed participants. The data exhibits a moderate class imbalance, with approximately 30% depressed and 70% non-depressed participants, and a gender distribution of roughly 57% female and 43% male subjects. Audio recordings were acquired at 16 kHz and distributed in scrubbed form to preserve privacy. Since the participant channel may still contain residual interviewer speech and masked segments, transcript timestamps are used to perform speaker-aware temporal cropping, retaining only participant-response intervals.

In addition to bag-level labels, DAIC-WOZ provides the official PHQ-8 metadata for each session, including the binary depression label, the total PHQ-8 score, and the item-wise responses. These annotations are directly integrated into our framework as symptom-level clinical anchors for semantic instance selection. Specifically, the PHQ-8 covers eight core symptom dimensions: loss of interest (`PHQ8_NoInterest`), depressed mood (`PHQ8_Depressed`), sleep disturbance (`PHQ8_Sleep`), fatigue (`PHQ8_Tired`), appetite alteration (`PHQ8_Appetite`), feelings of failure or guilt (`PHQ8_Failure`), concentration difficulties (`PHQ8_Concentrating`), and psychomotor changes (`PHQ8_Moving`). Following the dataset protocol, PHQ-8 responses are encoded on a 0–3 ordinal scale, yielding a total score in the range $[0, 24]$, and a score ≥ 10 is used to define clinically relevant depressive symptomatology. Because this language-guided filtering depends on interviewer prompts, sessions with missing or severely incomplete interviewer transcripts are excluded.

2.2 Text-Conditioned Attention-Based Multi-Instance Learning (TCAMIL)

Let q_{ij} denote the interviewer question associated with the j-th temporal segment of subject i, and let $\mathcal{P} = \{p_k\}_{k=1}^{8}$ be the PHQ-8 item texts (symptom descriptors). A Transformer-based cross-encoder $\breve{f}_{\text{CE}}$ jointly encodes each pair (q_{ij}, p_k) and produces a contextual semantic score: $\breve{r}_{ij}^{(k)} = \breve{f}_{\text{CE}}(q_{ij}, p_k) \in \mathbb{R}$. Then, for each subject i, we retain a clinically aligned subset of segments by selecting, for each PHQ item k, the most semantically compatible segment (or top-S segments). Using the unweighted scores, a representative index is computed as:

$$j_i^{(k)} = \arg \max_{j \in \{1,\ldots,m_i\}} \breve{r}_{ij}^{(k)}. \tag{1}$$

The resulting text-guided, fixed-cardinality bag of selected instances is: $\tilde{B}_i = \{\mathbf{x}_{i\,j_i^{(k)}}\}_{k=1}^{8}$, where $\mathbf{x}_{ij_i^{(k)}}$ denotes the acoustic segment of size $T_{j_i^{(k)}}$ extracted from the participant-response audio aligned to question q_{ij}. This selection stage acts as a clinically grounded denoising operator: it suppresses semantically generic turns and preserves symptom-relevant evidence prior to weakly supervised MIL training for audio-based depression detection.

Next, given N subjects, we consider pairs $\{\tilde{B}_i, y_i\}_{i=1}^{N}$, where $y_i \in \{0, 1\}$ denotes the subject-level depression label and $\tilde{B}_i$ is the PHQ-aligned bag produced by the semantic matching stage. Each retained audio segment is represented by a fixed-dimensional acoustic descriptor $\mathbf{x}_{ij} \in \mathbb{R}^d$ (eGeMAPS in our experiments [3]), and the bag is written as $\tilde{B}_i = \{\mathbf{x}_{ij}\}_{j=1}^{\tilde{m}_i}$, where $\tilde{m}_i = 8$ (one segment per PHQ item) or $\tilde{m}_i = 8S$ under top-S selection. The objective is to learn a bag-level predictor $\hat{y}_i = \mathcal{F}(\tilde{B}_i) \in [0, 1]$ under weak supervision. Following attention-based deep MIL [5], the mapping $\mathcal{F}$ is decomposed into three parametric components:

$$\hat{y}_i = \big(f_{\text{cls}} \circ f_{\text{agg}} \circ f_{\text{enc}}\big)(\tilde{B}_i). \tag{2}$$

The instance encoder $f_{\text{enc}} : \mathbb{R}^d \to \mathbb{R}^M$ is implemented as a multilayer perceptron (MLP) that maps each acoustic descriptor into a latent embedding: $\mathbf{h}_{ij} = f_{\text{enc}}(\mathbf{x}_{ij}) \in \mathbb{R}^M$. Thus, each bag is transformed into a set of embeddings $\mathbf{H}_i = \{\mathbf{h}_{ij}\}_{j=1}^{\tilde{m}_i}$.

The aggregation module f_{agg} computes attention weights to quantify the contribution of each semantically selected segment to the bag-level decision. Instance embeddings are first projected into a latent attention space: $\mathbf{u}_{ij} = \tanh(\mathbf{V}\mathbf{h}_{ij})$, where $\mathbf{V} \in \mathbb{R}^{L \times M}$ is trainable. Normalized attention coefficients are then computed as:

$$a_{ij} = \frac{\exp(\mathbf{w}^\top \mathbf{u}_{ij})}{\sum_{k=1}^{\tilde{m}_i} \exp(\mathbf{w}^\top \mathbf{u}_{ik})}, \tag{3}$$

with learnable vector $\mathbf{w} \in \mathbb{R}^L$. Afterward, the bag embedding is obtained as:

$$\mathbf{z}_i = \sum_{j=1}^{\tilde{m}_i} a_{ij} \mathbf{h}_{ij}, \tag{4}$$

which defines the output of f_{agg}.

The classifier $f_{\text{cls}} : \mathbb{R}^M \to [0,1]$ maps the aggregated representation to a depression probability: $\hat{y}_i = \sigma(\breve{\mathbf{W}}\mathbf{z}_i + \breve{\mathbf{b}})$, where $\breve{\mathbf{W}} \in \mathbb{R}^{1\times M}$, $\breve{\mathbf{b}} \in \mathbb{R}$, and $\sigma(\cdot)$ denotes the sigmoid function.

Lastly, training is performed using Binary Focal Loss to address class imbalance and emphasize difficult cases, yielding:

$$\mathcal{L}_{\text{FL}} = -\frac{1}{N}\sum_{i=1}^{N}\left[\alpha\, y_i(1-\hat{y}_i)^{\gamma}\log(\hat{y}_i) + (1-\alpha)(1-y_i)\hat{y}_i^{\gamma}\log(1-\hat{y}_i)\right], \tag{5}$$

where $\gamma \geq 0$ is the focusing parameter and $\alpha \in [0,1]$ balances class contributions.

The resulting framework, termed TCAMIL, is depicted in Fig. 1.

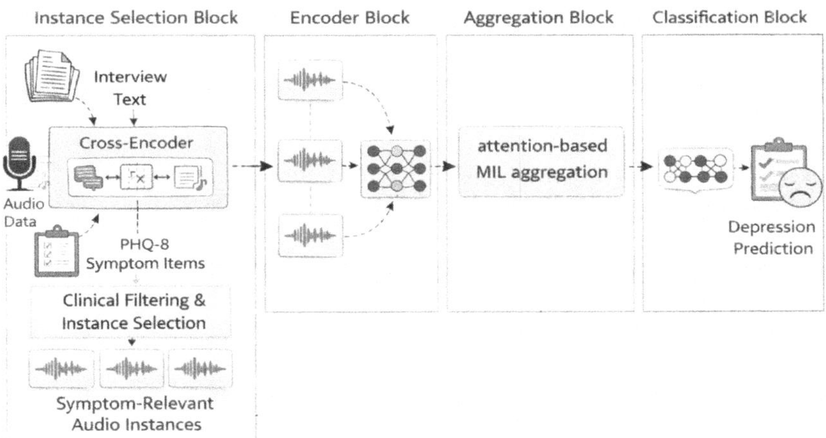

Fig. 1. Text-conditioned attention-based MIL framework (TCAMIL) for depression detection.

3 Experimental Setup

Experiments were conducted on the DAIC-WOZ benchmark for automatic depression assessment using the subject-independent partition described in Sect. 2.1. From the 142 subjects available in DAIC-WOZ, 140 sessions were effectively retained for the semantic selection stage, since two subjects lacked interviewer transcripts. In our experiments, each retained audio segment was represented by the official eGeMAPS descriptor with dimensionality $d = 88$, extracted with the standard openSMILE toolkit and the official eGeMAPS configuration [3]. In parallel, the PHQ-8 item descriptions were used as structured semantic anchors to compute the semantic relevance scores, which were used to retain a single interview question associated with each PHQ-8 item before MIL aggregation, e.g., $S = 1$ (see Sect. 2.2).

We compared the proposed TCAMIL framework against three non-MIL baselines: SVM, Random Forest, and FAD3QN [6], together with one MIL baseline based on gated-attention Deep MIL [5]. Semantic matching was estimated using an MPNet-based sentence transformer and a MiniLM-based cross-encoder, with a cosine-softmax temperature of 1.0. In the MIL model, the instance encoder employed an embedding dimension of 500, while the attention module operated in a latent space of dimension 64. For the SVM and Random Forest, subject-level representations were constructed exclusively from the participant's speech segments. Specifically, eGeMAPS features were extracted from patient-response audio only (excluding interviewer speech), and fixed-length representations were obtained by concatenating descriptors computed over ten randomly selected segments [7]. Importantly, FAD3QN does not perform semantic segment selection or attention-based aggregation. Instead, it randomly selects ten audio segments per subject, extracts eGeMAPS features from each segment, and concatenates them into a fixed-length representation. This aggregated feature vector is then treated as a single input instance and processed through a conventional deep learning architecture.

All MIL-based neural models were trained for 200 epochs using AdamW with learning rate 3×10^{-4} and weight decay 10^{-4}. To address class imbalance, Binary Focal Loss with $\gamma = 2$ was used. Model selection was based on the checkpoint with the highest validation accuracy. To obtain an unbiased validation estimate, we used a stratified train–validation split with fixed seed 0 and shuffling enabled, while final testing was performed on the official test partition provided by the dataset. All experiments were executed in a Kaggle environment with two NVIDIA Tesla T4 GPUs (T4×2), using Python 3.10.2, NumPy 2.0.2, PyTorch 2.9.0+cu126, and Scikit-Learn 1.6.1. Performance was assessed using standard binary-classification metrics, namely Accuracy, Precision, Recall, F1-score, and ROC-AUC. Code is available at GitHub repository.

4 Results and Discussion

We assess whether the cross-encoder can reliably map interview prompts onto the PHQ-8 symptom space and whether this mapping yields clinically meaningful audio instance selection. Figure 2a shows the semantic affinity landscape between interviewer prompts (rows) and PHQ-8 items (columns) for an illustrative participant. The matrix exhibits a high-contrast and sparse structure: most generic prompts produce uniformly low scores, whereas a small subset of clinically targeted questions yields sharp maxima concentrated on specific PHQ columns. This pattern indicates that the text-guided selection mechanism is driven by localized semantic peaks rather than diffuse similarity. Importantly, Fig. 2b visualizes the downstream effect of this semantic filtering on the raw interview audio (red segments): only the participant-response intervals temporally aligned with the selected symptom-relevant prompts are retained, yielding a

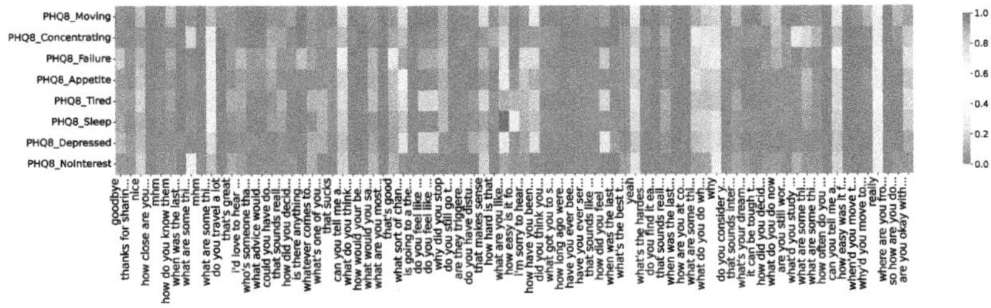

(a) PHQ-conditioned semantic matching (Min–Max scaling).

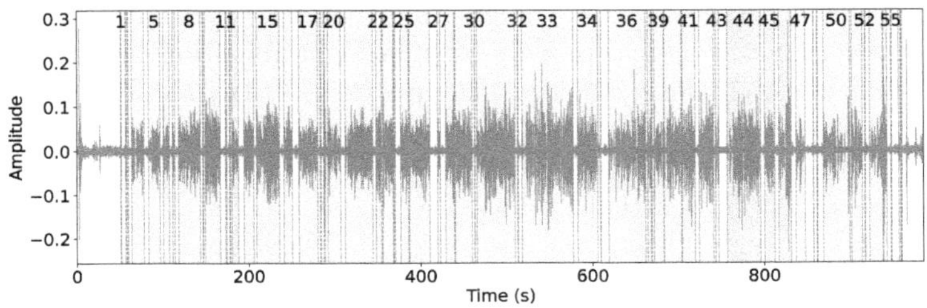

(b) Full interview waveform with PHQ-aligned temporal segments.

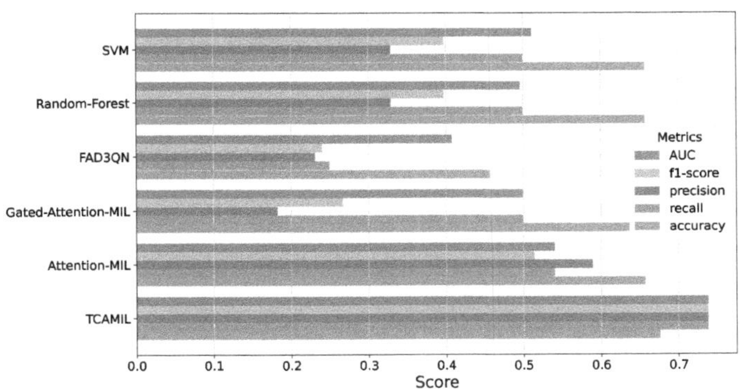

(c) Comparative evaluation of depression detection models on DAIC-WOZ.

Fig. 2. TCAMIL results. (a) PHQ-aligned instance selection. (b) Audio segments retained for MIL aggregation. (c) Depression detection comparison.

compact set of waveform fragments that reduces semantically irrelevant variability before MIL aggregation. Nevertheless, the heatmap also reveals a coverage limitation intrinsic to the DAIC-WOZ interview script: PHQ dimensions that are weakly or indirectly probed tend to show weaker or less isolated maxima, implying that for some symptoms the selector may rely on implicit cues or secondary matches. This bottleneck can propagate as selection noise into the MIL stage.

Then, the depression detection results shown in Fig. 2c demonstrate that the proposed TCAMIL framework achieves the most consistent and balanced performance. In particular, TCAMIL attains the highest AUC (approx. 0.74), indicating superior discriminative capability across decision thresholds, together with the strongest F1-score and recall (both close to 0.75). This improvement reflects a substantially enhanced ability to correctly identify depressed subjects, which is critical in imbalanced clinical settings. Precision is also notably increased relative to the baselines, suggesting that the PHQ-conditioned semantic filtering stage effectively reduces false positives by restricting the MIL bags to clinically relevant segments. In contrast, classical models such as SVM and Random Forest exhibit competitive accuracy values; however, their lower F1 and recall scores reveal a bias toward the majority class, indicating that their accuracy is partially inflated by class imbalance. FAD3QN, which relies on randomly sampled segments without semantic selection or attention-based aggregation, shows weaker recall and overall instability, highlighting the limitations of random segment aggregation for capturing diagnostically salient evidence. The standard Attention-MIL model improves minority-class detection compared to classical baselines, confirming the advantage of learnable instance weighting under weak supervision; nevertheless, without symptom-guided filtering, it remains sensitive to semantically irrelevant variability present in long-form interviews. Overall, these results indicate that integrating PHQ-conditioned semantic selection with attention-based MIL produces a more clinically grounded and discriminative approach.

5 Conclusions

This work introduced a text-guided acoustic MIL framework, termed TCAMIL, for depression detection that integrates PHQ-8 – conditioned semantic alignment prior to attention-based aggregation. By explicitly grounding instance selection in clinically structured symptom descriptors, the proposed approach reduces semantically irrelevant variability in long-form interviews and constructs symptom-aligned MIL bags for weakly supervised learning. Experimental results on DAIC-WOZ demonstrate that this semantic filtering strategy improves discriminative capacity, yielding superior recall, F1-score, and AUC compared to classical classifiers, random segment aggregation, and standard Attention-MIL without text conditioning. The analysis of the PHQ-8 latent structure further supports the stability of symptom-based anchors and the robustness of the framework against demographic confounds. Overall, the proposed method provides a clinically interpretable and structurally grounded alternative to purely data-driven aggregation strategies for audio-based depression detection. Future work will explore multi-instance retention per symptom dimension, multi-modal learning, coverage-aware semantic re-ranking, and joint optimization of semantic and acoustic modules to further improve recall while preserving clinical interpretability.

Acknowledgments. This work was (partially) supported by Programa Iberoamericano de Ciencia y Tecnología para el Desarrollo (CYTED) (through Red [225RT0169])

References

1. Cai, L., Huang, S., Zhang, Y., Lu, J., Zhang, Y.: Attrimil: revisiting attention-based multiple instance learning for whole-slide pathological image classification from a perspective of instance attributes. Med. Image Anal. **103**, 103631 (2025)
2. Ding, Z., Hu, Y., Jing, R., Sheng, W., Mao, J.: A depression recognition method based on the alteration of video temporal angle features. Appl. Sci. **13**(16), 9230 (2023)
3. Eyben, F., Wöllmer, M., Schuller, B.: Opensmile – the Munich versatile and fast open-source audio feature extractor. In: Proceedings of the 18th ACM International Conference on Multimedia (ACM MM), pp. 1459–1462. Association for Computing Machinery (2010)
4. Gratch, J., et al.: The distress analysis interview corpus of human and computer interviews. In: Lrec. vol. 14, pp. 3123–3128. Reykjavik (2014)
5. Ilse, M., Tomczak, J., Welling, M.: Attention-based deep multiple instance learning. In: International Conference on Machine Learning, pp. 2127–2136. PMLR (2018)
6. Li, D., Yao, J., Wang, Z., Yi, Y.: Fad3qn: a brain-inspired deep reinforcement learning model for speech depression detection. IEEE Trans. Comput. Soc. Syst. (2025)
7. Ma, X., Yang, H., Chen, Q., Huang, D., Wang, Y.: Depaudionet: an efficient deep model for audio based depression classification. In: Proceedings of the 6th International Workshop on Audio/Visual Emotion Challenge (AVEC), pp. 35–42 (2016)
8. Prakrankamanant, P., Watanabe, S., Chuangsuwanich, E.: Explainable depression detection using masked hard instance mining. arXiv preprint arXiv:2505.24609 (2025)
9. Rahi, P., Singla, S.: Dual-pipeline LSTM screening for anxiety and depression via video interviews. In: 2025 IEEE 7th International Conference on Computing, Communication and Automation (ICCCA), pp. 1–9. IEEE (2025)
10. Sadeghi, M., et al.: Harnessing multimodal approaches for depression detection using large language models and facial expressions. NPJ Mental Health Res. **3**(1), 66 (2024)
11. Saji, A.R., Megha, P., Poulose, A.: Transformer-mil and Adaboost fusion for non-invasive depression detection. In: 2025 International Conference on Robotics and Mechatronics (ICRM), pp. 1–6. IEEE (2025)
12. Sun, Q., Akman, A., Schuller, B.W.: Explainable artificial intelligence for medical applications: a review. ACM Trans. Comput. Healthcare **6**(2), 1–31 (2025)
13. Sun, Y., et al.: Weakly-supervised depression detection in speech through self-learning based label correction. IEEE Trans. Audio Speech Lang. Process. **33**, 748–758 (2025)
14. Wang, P., et al.: Visually multimodal depression assessment based on key questions with weighted multi-task learning. Signal Processing: Image Commun. **135**, 117279 (2025)
15. Zhang, X., Li, C., Chen, W., Zheng, J., Li, F.: Optimizing depression detection in clinical doctor-patient interviews using a multi-instance learning framework. Sci. Rep. **15**(1), 6637 (2025)

Explainable Mortality Risk Prediction with Causality via Hierarchical Bayesian Network

Gatum Erlangga, Jaeil Park, and Sung-Bae Cho(✉)

Department of Computer Science, Yonsei University, Seoul 03722, South Korea
{erlanggagatum,wodlf603,sbcho}@yonsei.ac.kr

Abstract. Predicting mortality risk requires clinicians to infer upper demographics and a set of factors linked by comorbidities, subconsequences through intermediate biomarkers, and potential mechanisms such as frailty or chronic inflammation. Recent advancement of deep learning facilitates to develop powerful prediction models, but most of them ignore this hierarchy to learn latent representations of the data without considering these factors in explicit and clinically interpretable hierarchies. To address this issue, this paper proposes a causally explainable prediction method that leverages hierarchical Bayesian networks with latent variables learned through deep learning. A Transformer-based model with a sparse autoencoder first derives low-dimensional representations to capture clinical patterns, which are used as intermediate nodes between demographic and biomarker levels within a hierarchical Bayesian network. In this way, both latent representations and clinical variables are organized to allow structured and causally informed explanations of mortality risk. Applied to the National Health and Nutrition Examination Survey (NHANES), it recovers risk factors and pathways consistent with biomedical literature and expert-elicited causal diagrams, achieving more than 93% edge-level agreement and clarifying interactions such as sexalbumin effects through clinically plausible demographic mediation.

Keywords: XAI · causal explanation · mortality risk prediction · Bayesian network · sparse autoencoder

1 Introduction

Improving life expectancy and reducing premature mortality are central priorities in modern healthcare and depend on reliable methods to identify individuals at elevated risk of mortality. Such methods enable early interventions, personalized treatment plans, and efficient allocation of limited clinical resources [4], and machine learningbased prediction models have shown strong performance and are now widely used in clinical systems.

For these systems to be clinically useful, clinicians must understand why a patient is assessed as high or low risk [13]. In practice, mortality risk is judged by

J. M. Ferrndez Vicente et al. (Eds.): IWINAC 2026, LNCS 16574, pp. 310–319, 2026.
https://doi.org/10.1007/978-3-032-27314-7_29

structured reasoning grounded in domain knowledge [10]: clinicians interpret how observable factors are shaped by upstream causes such as age and comorbidities [8]. Recognizing these patterns is essential to assess risk in diverse populations and tailor interventions [7].

However, most existing machine learning approaches to mortality risk prediction rely on statistical associations between input features and outcomes and offer limited support for such structured clinical reasoning [16]. Even when deep learning models learn rich latent representations, they are typically used as opaque features in downstream predictors rather than being embedded in explicit, clinically interpretable structures. Explainable AI (XAI) methods mostly add a post hoc layer of feature-level importance scores or local attributions [18], while overlooking mediated pathways and latent clinical mechanisms [12,13]. As a result, their explanations are difficult to align with biomedical reasoning based on pathways and often do not show how upstream demographic factors propagate through biomarkers to affect mortality risk.

To address this issue, this paper proposes a causal explanation method for mortality risk prediction that combines domain knowledge with latent representation extracted from deep learning models. Deep learning is first used to discover low-dimensional, co-activated representations that reflect clinically meaningful latent states. These representations, together with selected clinical variables, are then embedded in a Bayesian network that models interdependencies and mediates pathways between upstream demographics, intermediate biomarkers, and downstream mortality outcomes, yielding pathway-level explanations that are causal and aligned with biomedical understanding.

The proposed method is evaluated using the National Health and Nutrition Examination Survey (NHANES), a large-scale population dataset with linked mortality follow-up. The model identifies clinically grounded risk factors and pathways that are consistent with expert-defined diagrams and the biomedical literature, achieving more than 93% edge-level agreement with expert-elicited causal structures. In addition, it reveals mediated demographic effects on biomarkers that reflect known clinical trends, suggesting that the method offers a more clinically faithful explanation model.

2 Related Works

Table 1 summarizes representative studies that investigate how different modeling and explanation techniques reveal relevant risk factors in various clinical contexts. One line of work explains the mortality risk by directly linking model outputs to input variables through models with relatively transparent decision structures or simple summaries of feature importance [5,15]. These approaches usually focus on a small set of hand-selected predictors and offer limited information on how multiple factors jointly interact along clinical pathways. Another line of work seeks to explain the clinical risks of more complex models by attribution of post-hoc features [1,12,13,20]. These post-hoc and subgroup-based methods highlight important variables, but do not explicitly represent how upstream

Table 1. Related works on mortality risk prediction.

Author	Explanation technique	Objective
Ahmed et al. (2021) [1]	Permutation feature importance; Partial dependence plots	Explore spatial variability in lung and bronchus cancer mortality
Brigo et al. (2022) [5]	Tree-based explanation	Validate 30-day mortality risk in status epilepticus
Kim and Kim (2022) [15]	RF Feature Importance	Estimate heat-related mortality at fine spatial resolution
Jiang et al. (2023) [13]	Data visualization using t-SNE; Principal Component Analysis (PCA); SHAP	Predict and analyze clustered risk factors for sepsis and septic death
Shaw et al. (2023) [20]	DALEX; Local interpretable model-agnostic explanations	Predict infant mortality due to neonatal sepsis using deep learning and explainable AI methods
Huo et al. (2025) [12]	SHapley Additive eXplanation (SHAP)	Real-time prediction of 30-day mortality risk in critically ill children during inter-hospital transport to PICUs

factors propagate through mediators to affect risk, making their explanations difficult to map onto pathway-based clinical reasoning.

In contrast, the proposed method explains the mortality risk by integrating observable clinical variables and latent representation within a unified causal model, instantiated as a Bayesian network [6,9]. This integration makes the mediating pathways explicit, reveals how risk emerges from interacting variables, and aligns the explanatory structure with the reasoning of clinicians while still leveraging high-dimensional latent representations learned from the data.

3 Proposed Method

The proposed method explains the mortality risk by combining a deep learning predictor with latent representation and a Bayesian network. Biomedical knowledge is used to constrain the causal structure so that the discovered pathways remain clinically plausible. Figure 1 illustrates the overall architecture of the proposed method.

3.1 Extracting Clinical Phenotype from Deep Learning Model

To uncover higher-level clinical phenotypes that are not explicitly encoded in the input yet influence the mortality risk, this paper first analyzes the latent representations learned by the deep learning model. These representations provide clinically significant abstractions by revealing the latent patterns that shape the predictions of the model. Because Transformer-based architectures achieve state-of-the-art performance to predict the mortality risk from electronic health records (EHRs) [19], this paper formulates a Transformer-based model that maps input clinical features $x \in \mathbb{R}^d$ to a predicted mortality risk $\hat{y} \in [0, 1]$ (where 0

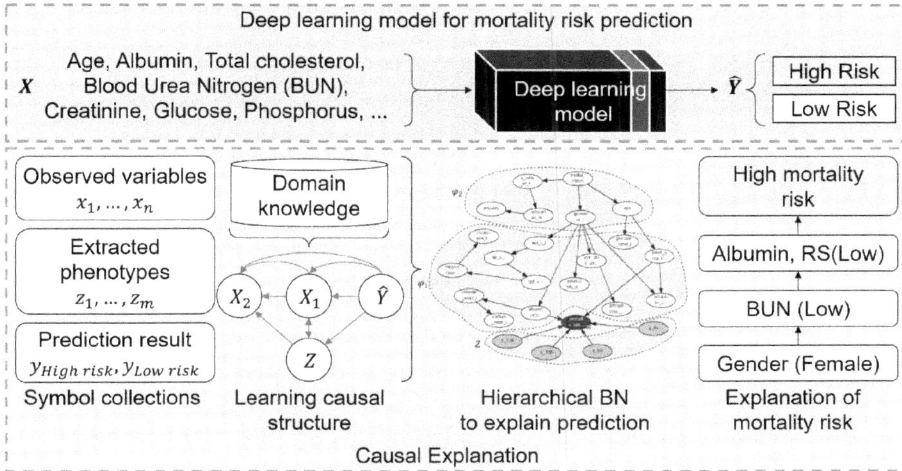

Fig. 1. Overall structure of the proposed method.

indicates low risk and 1 indicates high risk). The model consists of stacked L Transformer encoder layers, denoted by $\phi^{(1)}, \ldots, \phi^{(L)}$. The input is first linearly projected and then passed through these layers with mean pooling to obtain a contextualized representation:

$$h^{(L)} = \text{PoolingLayer}\Big(\phi^{(L)} \circ \cdots \circ \phi^{(1)} \left(\text{Dropout}(W_{\text{in}}x + b_{\text{in}})\right)\Big), \tag{1}$$

where σ is an activation function, and $W_{\text{in}}, b_{\text{in}}$ are learnable projection parameters. The pooled output $h^{(L)}$ is then used to compute the final prediction:

$$\hat{y} = f_\theta\left(h^{(L)}\right) = \sigma\left(w_c^\top h^{(L)} + b_c\right), \tag{2}$$

where θ denotes all learnable parameters of the model.

To extract latent abstractions that summarize mortality-relevant patterns, we apply a sparse autoencoder (SAE) to the final hidden representation $h^{(L)}$. The resulting latent units, which the proposed method refers to as deep learning-derived phenotypes (DLPs), reflect how the model internally organizes information for mortality prediction.

The SAE is trained to reconstruct $h^{(L)}$ through a lower-dimensional, sparse latent space $z \in \mathbb{R}^{d_z}$. This layer is chosen because it contains higher-order abstract representations that are more directly related to the output behavior of the model [11]. The training objective is:

$$\mathcal{L}_{\text{SAE}} = \left\| h^{(L)} - \hat{h}^{(L)} \right\|_2^2 + \lambda \left\| z \right\|_1, \tag{3}$$

where $\hat{h}^{(L)}$ is the reconstructed representation and λ is a sparsity regularization coefficient. The loss term ℓ_1 for c encourages our reconstruction to be a sparse

Table 2. Grouped causal theme with corresponding observed variables.

Node	Variable theme	Observed variables
x_2	Demographic	Education level, Adults, Marital status, Gender, Ethnicity, Ratio of family income to poverty, Age
x_1	Biological profile (biomarkers)	Albumin (refrigerated serum), Blood Urea Nitrogen, Total cholesterol, Creatinine, Glucose, Phosphorus, Triglycerides, Uric acid, Alkaline phosphatase, AST, ALT, Chloride, GGT, Potassium, Sodium
z	Deep learning parameters	Isolated latent features from SAE: $z_1, \ldots, z_m$
$\hat{y}$	Mortality status	Mortality status (high risk, low risk)

linear combination of prior features. Huben et al. [11] empirically and theoretically show that reconstruction with the penalty ℓ_1 can restore the real features that have generated the data.

The encoder and decoder are defined as follows:

$$z = \text{ReLU}\left(W_e h^{(L)} + b_e\right), \tag{4}$$

$$\hat{h}^{(L)} = \sigma(W_d z + b_d). \tag{5}$$

Here, W_e, b_e, W_d, b_d are learnable parameters and W_b is normalized row-wise. This prevents the model from reducing the sparsity loss term by increasing the size of the feature vectors in W_b.

3.2 Causal Explanation with Bayesian Network

Modeling interdependency among various clinical variables is essential to produce explanations that align with biomedical reasoning [10]. To support this, we construct a Bayesian network (BN) that incorporates both observed features and latent variables. The BN structure is constrained using domain knowledge so that clinically plausible pathways are preserved, for example, demographic factors that influence biomarkers, which in turn affect mortality. This enables causal explanations that reflect both the model behavior and the medical understanding.

To incorporate domain knowledge more systematically, the proposed method groups variables into levels that reflect the typical causal progression in mortality risk (Table 2), derived from the biomedical literature and validated by a clinician [8], with latent representation acting as intermediate risk states that influence mortality. The proposed method defines legal arcs only between hierarchically consistent levels. In this setting, deep learning-derived phenotypes (DLPs) serve as latent predictors that refine observed information and enrich causal reasoning without requiring full manual specification of all graph edges.

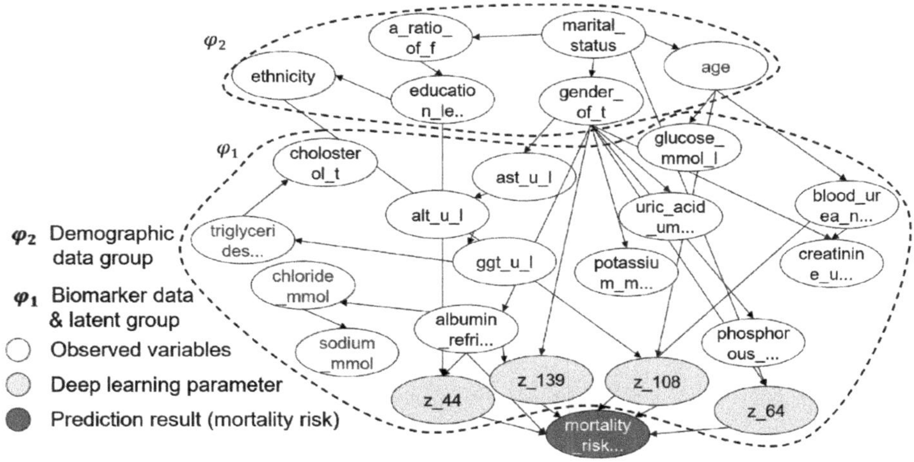

Fig. 2. Bayesian network for structuring the mortality risk explanations via demographic factors, biomarkers, and latent representation.

The proposed method then applies arc restrictions to prohibit directions that contradict the assumed causal ordering, such as child-to-parent edges or feedback loops (e.g., $X_\ell \nrightarrow X_{\ell+1}$, $Z \nrightarrow X$, $Y \nrightarrow Z$). These constraints reduce the search space during structure learning and improve the interpretability and validity of the resulting BN by aligning it with established domain knowledge.

The BN encodes these structured dependencies through a set of nodes $\mathcal{N}$, parent sets $\mathrm{Pa}(N)$, and evidence $\mathbf{e}$. The joint distribution on all variables relevant to the mortality risk is factorized as follows:

$$P(\mathcal{N} \mid \mathbf{e}) = \prod_{N \in \mathcal{N}} \Big(P(N \mid \mathrm{Pa}(N)) \times \mathbf{e} \Big) = \prod_{N \in \mathcal{N}} P(N \mid \mathrm{Pa}(N)) \prod_{e_i \in \mathbf{e}} e_i. \quad (6)$$

Oriented by domain knowledge, the graph in Fig. 2 preserves the causal flow from demographics to biomarkers and then to mortality [8]. This structure explicitly accounts for mediating variables such as biomarkers and latent variables, capturing clinically established pathways for how upstream factors influence outcomes. The inclusion of DLPs enables hybrid explanations that combine deep model abstractions with biomedical semantics. As a result, the BN supports interpretable explanations of mortality risk based on pathways that are better aligned with real-world clinical decision-making.

4 Experimental Results

4.1 Experimental Setting

This paper evaluates the proposed method on a publicly available real-world biomedical dataset for research: National Health and Nutrition Examination

Table 3. Comparison of derived causal path from the proposed method and clinical literature.

Case	Derived symbols	Ground truth	Expert opinion
Case #1: High Mortality	Female → low albumin Female with low albumin → z_{139} → high probability	Low albumin significantly increases the mortality risk [14]	Female with low albumin → high probability
Case #2: High Mortality	Older → high blood urea nitrogen (BUN) High BUN → z_{108} → high probability	High blood urea nitrogen significantly increases mortality risk [2]	High BUN → high probability

Survey (NHANES) with linked mortality follow-up data from the National Center for Health Statistics (NCHS). The dataset includes demographic information, blood test results, and mortality follow-up status from NCHS data linkage files. We use 22 variables that span demographic and biomarker features, collected from 11,732 individuals, and formulate the task as a binary classification problem that predicts a high versus a low risk of all-cause mortality. The dataset is divided into training, validation, and test sets using a stratified split to preserve the event rate across splits (70%/15%/15%).

4.2 Comparison Between Derived Causal Path and Ground Truth

This section evaluates the causal explanations generated by the proposed method by comparing them with established clinical findings on the risk of mortality. We analyze both biomarker-driven pathways and mediated demographic effects to assess whether the model produces medically plausible explanations consistent with clinical evidence.

We first examine the Bayesian network symbols most directly associated with mortality, focusing on variables such as albumin and blood urea nitrogen (BUN) that exert a strong influence on the mortality node via direct edges and high sensitivity scores. We then compare the resulting explanation paths with the findings reported in the clinical literature.

As shown in Table 3, the proposed method generates clinically meaningful causal explanations for individual high-risk cases. In Case #1, the model identifies a pathway in which being female leads to low albumin levels, increasing the probability of predicted mortality; this aligns with previous work linking hypoalbuminemia to a poor prognosis [14] and the expert interpretation of low albumin in females as a marker of frailty. In Case #2, older individuals exhibit markedly elevated levels of BUN that increase the probability of mortality, consistent with evidence that high BUN is a strong predictor of mortality [2] and with expert views of BUN as an indicator of renal decline in elderly patients. In both cases, the relevant latent phenotypes (z_{139} and z_{108}) capture co-activated clinical patterns not explicitly in raw features but critical for the reasoning about risk.

This experiment also evaluates agreement at the pathway level. For each test instance, the top explanation pathways are extracted from the BN (excluding latent nodes) and compared with clinician-defined reference pathways. According to this criterion, the proposed method achieves a 93% agreement of the pathway-level with expert-defined pathways, indicating that the generated explanations are in large part aligned with clinical reasoning.

4.3 Analysis of Clinical Phenotypes Patterns from DLPs

This section evaluates the co-activated clinical feature patterns captured by the deep learningderived phenotypes (DLPs) against the clinical literature (Table 4). Latent units (z_{44}, z_{64}, z_{108}) are consistently activated for individuals who are male, non-Hispanic white, married, with some college education or an AA degree, and low albumin levels (2.9–4.1 g/dL). Previous work shows that socioeconomic factors such as education and marital status influence health behaviors, access to care, and chronic stress, thus affecting mortality risk [3]. Low serum albumin is also a well-known marker of inflammation and nutritional deficiency [17]. Therefore, their joint activation suggests a latent vulnerability profile, indicating that DLPs can recover clinically meaningful risk configurations.

Table 4. Comparison between latent phenotypes and ground truth from the clinical literature.

Activated latent representation	Co-activated features	Ground truth (clinical literature)
z_{44}, z_{64}, z_{108}	Education level: Some college or AA degree; Gender: Male; Ethnicity: Non-Hispanic white; Marital status: Married; Albumin: 2.9–4.1 (g/dL)	Socioeconomics modulate health behavior [3] Albumin as sign of inflammation [17]

Table 5. Proportion of phenotype-positive individuals extracted from deep model.

Identified group	Population with phenotype (%)	
	Phenotype-positive group	Phenotype-negative group
z_{44}	88.22	85.65
z_{64}	92.46	77.33
z_{108}	91.88	81.63
All	91.75	68.00

Table 5 summarizes the prevalence of identified phenotypes. The phenotype-positive group captures a substantially larger share of individuals than the negative group, indicating that the proposed method extracts frequent and meaningful risk profiles from the deep model. Figure 3 further shows that these phenotype-related patterns also appear in seemingly healthy patients, making them difficult to detect through routine clinical observation alone. By revealing such subtle structures, the method supports more individualized risk assessment.

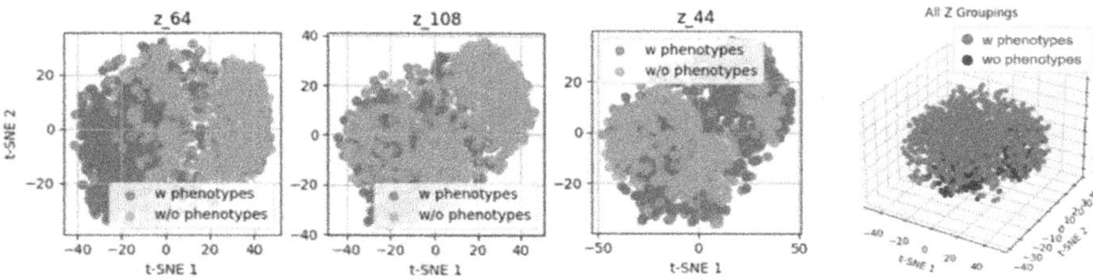

Fig. 3. Visualization of distinct patient groups with identified latent phenotypes.

5 Concluding Remarks

This paper presents a method for generating clinically grounded causal explanations in mortality risk prediction by integrating domain knowledge and latent representation into a causal reasoning method. By combining observed variables with co-activated patterns extracted from deep models, the approach builds a Bayesian network that models interdependency and mediating pathways. Applied to the NHANES dataset, it recovers risk factors consistent with biomedical evidence. However, the proposed method currently lacks temporal modeling and relies on the structure specified by an expert, which will be addressed with longitudinal data and interactive expert-in-the-loop refinement in the future work.

Acknowledgments. This work was supported by IITP grant funded by the Korea government (MSIT) (No. RS-2022-II220113, Developing a Sustainable Collaborative Multi-modal Lifelong Learning Framework), and Air Force Defense Research Sciences Program funded by Air Force Office of Scientific Research.

References

1. Ahmed, Z.U., Sun, K., Shelly, M., Mu, L.: Explainable artificial intelligence (XAI) for exploring spatial variability of lung and bronchus cancer (LBC) mortality rates in the contiguous USA. Sci. Rep. **11**(1), 24090 (2021)
2. Aronson, D., Mittleman, M.A., Burger, A.J.: Elevated blood urea nitrogen level as a predictor of mortality in patients admitted for decompensated heart failure. Am. J. Med. **116**(7), 466–473 (2004)
3. Balaj, M., et al.: Effects of education on adult mortality: a global systematic review and meta-analysis. Lancet Public Health **9**(3), e155–e165 (2024)

4. Bhadouria, A.S., Singh, R.K.: Machine learning model for healthcare investments predicting the length of stay in a hospital & mortality rate. Multimedia Tools Appl. **83**(9), 27121–27191 (2024)
5. Brigo, F., et al.: Machine learning validation through decision tree analysis of the epidemiology-based mortality score in status epilepticus. Epilepsia **63**(10), 2507–2518 (2022)
6. Bu, S.J., Cho, S.B.: A causally explainable deep learning model with modular bayesian network for predicting electric energy demand. In: International Conference on Hybrid Artificial Intelligence Systems, pp. 519–532. Springer (2023)
7. Chang, S.F., Lin, P.L.: Frail phenotype and mortality prediction: a systematic review and meta-analysis of prospective cohort studies. Int. J. Nurs. Stud. **52**(8), 1362–1374 (2015)
8. Chang, Z., et al.: Clinical biomarker profiles reveals gender differences and mortality factors in sepsis. Front. Immunol. **15**, 1413729 (2024)
9. Erlangga, G., Cho, S.B.: Causally explainable artificial intelligence on deep learning model for energy demand prediction. Eng. Appl. Artif. Intell. **162**, 112620 (2025)
10. Hasani, W.S.R., Musa, K.I., Chen, X.W., Cheng, K.Y.: Constructing causal pathways for premature cardiovascular disease mortality using directed acyclic graphs with integrating evidence synthesis and expert knowledge. Sci. Rep. **14**(1), 28849 (2024)
11. Huben, R., Cunningham, H., Smith, L.R., Ewart, A., Sharkey, L.: Sparse autoencoders find highly interpretable features in language models. In: The Twelfth Int. Conf. on Learning Representations (2023)
12. Huo, Z., et al.: Dynamic mortality prediction in critically ill children during interhospital transports to PICUs using explainable AI. NPJ Digital Med. **8**(1), 108 (2025)
13. Jiang, Z., et al.: Interpretable machine-learning model for real-time, clustered risk factor analysis of sepsis and septic death in critical care. Comput. Methods Programs Biomed. **241**, 107772 (2023)
14. Kendall, H., Abreu, E., Cheng, A.L.: Serum albumin trend is a predictor of mortality in ICU patients with sepsis. Biol. Res. Nurs. **21**(3), 237–244 (2019)
15. Kim, Y., Kim, Y.: Explainable heat-related mortality with random forest and SHapley additive explanations (SHAP) models. Sustain. Cities Soc. **79**, 103677 (2022)
16. Lee, J.J., et al.: Causal determinants of postoperative length of stay in cardiac surgery using causal graphical learning. J. Thorac. Cardiovasc. Surg. **166**(5), e446–e462 (2023)
17. Luo, L., Li, M., Xi, Y., Hu, J., Hu, W.: C-reactive protein-albumin-lymphocyte index as a feasible nutrition-immunity-inflammation marker of the outcome of all-cause and cardiovascular mortality in elderly. Clin. Nutr. ESPEN **63**, 346–353 (2024)
18. Malinverno, L., et al.: A historical perspective of biomedical explainable ai research. Patterns **4**(9) (2023)
19. Rong, R., et al.: A deep learning model for clinical outcome prediction using longitudinal inpatient electronic health records. JAMIA Open **8**(2), ooaf026 (2025)
20. Shaw, P., Pachpor, K., Sankaranarayanan, S.: Explainable ai enabled infant mortality prediction based on neonatal sepsis. Comput. Syst. Sci. Eng. **44**(1) (2023)

“Socio-Cognitive, Affective and Physiological Computing”

Exploring Whisper's Latent Space for Emotion Recognition from Vocal Bursts

José L. Gómez-Sirvent[1(✉)], Francisco López de la Rosa[1,5], Paulo Novais[4], and Antonio Fernández-Caballero[1,2,3]

[1] Emotion and Neurocognition Unit, Instituto de Investigación en Informática de Albacete, Albacete, Spain
{jose.gomez,antonio.fdez}@uclm.es
[2] Departamento de Sistemas Informáticos, Universidad de Castilla-La Mancha, Albacete, Spain
[3] Biomedical Research Networking Center in Mental Health (CIBERSAM-ISCIII), Madrid, Spain
[4] ALGORITMI Research Centre/LASI, Universidade do Minho, Braga, Portugal
[5] Departamento de Ingeniería Eléctrica, Electrónica, Automática y Comunicaciones, Universidad de Castilla-La Mancha, Albacete, Spain

Abstract. Nonverbal vocal sounds, frequently used in human oral communication, are very helpful in understanding the speaker's emotional state. In recent years, there have been notable advances in emotion recognition in audio, driven by developments based on transformer architecture. However, emotion recognition in non-linguistic sounds remains largely unexplored. In this work, we explore the use of the Whisper encoder with frozen weights–thereby preserving its transcription capabilities–as a feature extractor for emotion classification in vocal bursts (VB). Different lightweight classifiers were tested using features extracted from multiple depths of the Whisper encoder on the publicly available EmoGator dataset. We employ speaker-independent 5-fold cross-validation to determine the best configuration for each architecture. The proposed approach substantially outperformed the state-of-the-art with an accuracy of 66.5% on 10 classes. Furthermore, we found that the point within the encoder from which features are extracted significantly influences the accuracy of the classifiers. These results demonstrate the feasibility of performing emotion recognition in VB using pre-trained transformers without altering the original model weights, suggesting that such models can be effectively integrated into human-computer interaction systems while preserving their original capabilities.

Keywords: Vocal burst · Whisper · Emotion recognition · Long short-term memory · temporal convolutional network

J. M. Ferrndez Vicente et al. (Eds.): IWINAC 2026, LNCS 16574, pp. 323–332, 2026.
https://doi.org/10.1007/978-3-032-27314-7_30

1 Introduction

Emotions have an essential role in social interaction. Through language, humans are able to express our affective or emotional state simply and clearly. However, the emotional content of spoken communication often relies on paralinguistic mechanisms. Vocal bursts encompass the full range of non-linguistic vocalizations that people use to express emotions in speech. These brief nonverbal sounds, such as laughter, moans, or groans, can reveal a great deal of emotional information, making them a key component of human communication [18]. For certain groups with limited verbal abilities, such as people with autism spectrum disorder, these sounds may be their only form of vocal communication [3,13]. However, these paralinguistic cues are often lost in human-computer interaction (HCI) when voice input is transcribed for processing.

In recent years, there have been significant advances in speech emotion recognition (SER). Several recent literature reviews [5,15] show how artificial intelligence (AI) models, especially those based on transformer architecture, have demonstrated unprecedented capabilities in the field of SER, even surpassing human ability. Architectures designed for transcription tasks, such as Whisper [16], can be quickly fine-tuned for SER tasks, achieving very high performance [7]. There is a wide variety of public emotional speech datasets [12], allowing AI models to focus on specific aspects of speech such as intonation or semantics. Some of the most popular datasets include VB within some utterances. However, its presence is minimal in relation to the size of the dataset, which may cause them to be ignored in the SER task. In addition, greater accuracy in emotion detection is often achieved by using voice transcripts rather than raw audio [9], which eliminates VB that are difficult to transcribe.

In contrast to SER, automatic emotion recognition in nonverbal vocalizations (VB) remains a relatively underexplored area. Although the first studies on the categorization of these sounds date back to the early 2000s [17], the application of AI for emotion recognition in this field is still in its infancy. In 2022, this field received a major boost with the launch of the ACII Affective Vocal Bursts Competition [2]. The initiative aimed to establish the first large-scale benchmark for automatic emotion recognition from nonverbal vocalizations. The competition centered on the Hume-VB dataset, the largest corpora of emotional vocal bursts, containing 59,201 vocalizations with 10 emotional labels. Numerous proposals were submitted during and in the months following the competition [1,19], highlighting the superiority of pre-trained transformers over conventional audio processing approaches for this task. Notably, access to the competition dataset is currently limited, which constrains its reuse and further benchmarking.

To address these limitations, the EmoGator dataset [4] was introduced in 2023 as an accessible collection of nonverbal emotional vocalizations. This dataset includes 32,130 samples from 357 speakers divided into 30 emotional categories, making it the largest publicly available collection of emotional VB. However, the high number of EmoGator classes makes accurate classification very challenging. In the baseline established by the dataset's author, the F1 score did not exceed 27% with 30 classes, and in a subsequent study [11], it reached only

28.7%. For this reason, previous research has focused primarily on classifying a subset of 10 classes. Interestingly, unlike Hume-VB, where transformer-based architectures lead the benchmark, convolutional neural networks (CNNs) have achieved better results so far in EmoGator. However, this dataset remains understudied, and state-of-the-art architectures such as Whisper, which lead both VB classification and SER tasks [7,19], have not yet been evaluated on EmoGator.

The Whisper model is a promising option for emotion classification in VB for two main reasons. First, it was pre-trained on 680,000 h of multilingual audio, several orders of magnitude larger than the training data used for most audio transformers, which should endow it superior generalization capabilities. Second, Whisper was originally designed for speech transcription, making it possible to use a single model for both transcription and emotion recognition. This dual functionality could simplify workflow and reduce hardware requirements in HCI systems. Unfortunately, the fine-tuning process commonly used to adapt the model for emotion recognition causes Whisper to lose its ability to transcribe text, requiring the use of one model for transcription and another for emotion recognition. Furthermore, the encoder-decoder design of this architecture was conceived for text generation rather than for classification or regression problems.

In SER, it is common practice to use only the encoder module. However, emotion recognition in VB is a different task for which there is little scientific evidence. Considering that VB recognition in isolation does not take into account semantics or the relationship between words as is the case in SER, it is reasonable to think that the emotions contained in VBs may be more exposed in higher layers of the model, where lower-level feature processing is performed.

In this context, the present article seeks to address two key questions: (1) Is it possible to effectively use the features of a frozen Whisper encoder for VB classification without losing the model's transcription capability? (2) If so, what is the optimal point of the encoder for feature extraction? To answer these questions, we evaluated Gated Recurrent Unit (GRU), Long Short-Term Memory (LSTM), and Temporal Convolutional Network (TCN) architectures for emotion recognition in VB, all fed with features extracted from different depths of the Whisper encoder. The proposed approaches are systematically compared using the publicly available EmoGator dataset.

2 Materials and Methods

2.1 Data Preparation and Feature Extraction

Previous work [4,11] on the EmoGator dataset reported very low accuracy on the full set of 30 classes, limiting the practical applications of models trained with this dataset. For this reason, the present work focuses exclusively on the subset of 10 emotions defined by [4], considering it more feasible for effective emotion classification.

The Whisper encoder was used for audio feature extraction, specifically the small version consisting of 12 layers with an embedding dimension of 768. The audio files in the EmoGator dataset have an average duration of 1.9 s with low

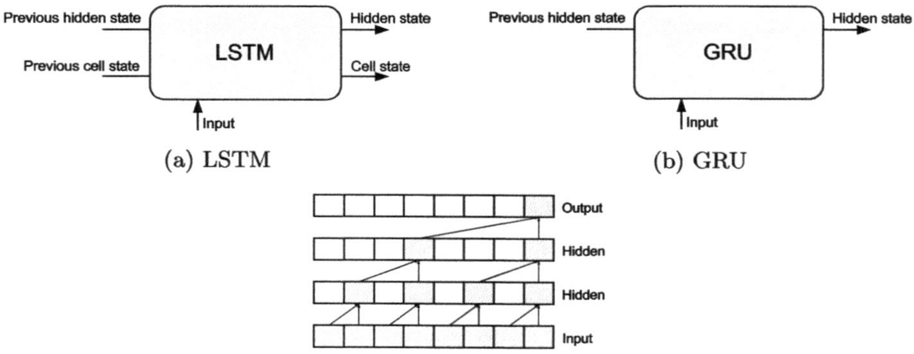

(a) LSTM (b) GRU (c) TCN

Fig. 1. Simplified schematic representation of the architectures employed in this study.

standard deviation. For this experiment, they were truncated to a maximum duration of 2 s before being processed by the Whisper encoder.

In order to address the research questions posed above, the model weights were frozen to preserve its transcription capabilities. Feature extraction was then evaluated at four different points within the encoder: using the full encoder, removing the last three layers, removing the last six layers, and removing the last nine layers.

2.2 Deep Learning Classifiers

To identify the optimal feature extraction point, three widely used architectures for time series classification–LSTM, GRU, and TCN–were compared (see Fig. 1). LSTM and GRU are types of recurrent neural networks (RNNs) designed to overcome the limitations of conventional RNNs [20]. LSTMs introduce memory cells and gating mechanisms that allow the network to retain or forget information over long sequences, mitigating the vanishing gradient problem common in standard RNNs. Similarly, GRUs offer a simplified variant of LSTMs that combines the input and forget gates into a single update gate and merges the cell and hidden states, reducing computational complexity.

Proposed as an alternative to recurrent architectures [6,10], TCNs use causal convolutions to preserve the temporal order of the sequence, as well as dilated convolutions, which exponentially increase the receptive field with the depth of the network, allowing the model to capture long-range dependencies without the need for deep stacks of layers. One of the main advantages of this approach over recurrent models lies in the possibility of performing parallel processing across temporal steps.

Unlike recurrent models, in TCNs the receptive field is finite and must be explicitly defined by the depth of the network, the kernel size, and the dilation factors, so that it covers the relevant temporal dependencies of the data. In this study, we employed a 6-layer network with kernels of dimensions (5,5,3,3,3,2), resulting in a receptive field of 201 time steps, which fully covers the entire time sequence used in our experiment (200 time steps).

2.3 Training and Validation

Of the 357 speakers in the dataset, 300 were used for training and validation, leaving the remaining 57 for testing. A speaker-independent 5-fold cross-validation with grid search was performed to optimize the hyperparameters of the models studied and to determine the best point for feature extraction from the encoder. Each model was trained with a batch size of 100 for an unlimited number of epochs, applying an early stopping criterion that halted training after three consecutive epochs without improvement in the cross-entropy loss function. Two learning rates were evaluated: 0.001 and 0.0001. After identifying the hyperparameters with the best performance, the models were retrained using the combined training and validation sets and then evaluated on the test set.

For recurrent architectures, in addition to the learning rate and feature extraction point, we also compared three hidden sizes (64, 128, 256), three numbers of layers (1, 2, 4), and both unidirectional and bidirectional configurations. Likewise, for the TCN, the influence of the number of channels in the convolutional layers (64, 128, 256) was studied. Given that the dataset is perfectly balanced, accuracy was employed as the primary metric for evaluating the performance of the different models. For the final evaluation on the test set, the F1-score was also used in order to ensure a fair comparison with previous works.

The models were trained using PyTorch version 2.5, and the training process was conducted on a workstation equipped with an Intel i7-10700KF CPU and an NVIDIA RTX 2070 Super GPU.

3 Results

Among the different parameters analyzed, the learning rate had the least influence on the results, with accuracies and number of epochs until stopping almost identical for the two values studied. On the other hand, in recurrent architectures, bidirectional models consistently reported slightly better accuracy, around one percentage point higher than unidirectional ones.

As shown in Table 1, the LSTM and GRU models yielded very similar results, with a slight advantage for GRU. However, considering the standard deviation, it cannot be conclusively stated that it has superior performance. Similarly, it can be observed that, in both models, accuracy tends to increase as the hidden size increases, but decreases as the number of layers increases. For the TCN architecture, with 64 channels in the convolutional layers, a mean accuracy of 66.49% and a standard deviation of 2.13% were obtained. For 128 channels, the mean accuracy was 66.10% with a standard deviation of 2.28%, and for 256 channels, the mean accuracy increased slightly to 66.87% with a standard

Table 1. Cross-validation accuracy results for bidirectional LSTM and GRU architectures with different numbers of layers and hidden sizes. Mean accuracy (%) and standard deviation are shown.

Recurrent layers	Hidden size	LSTM	GRU
1	64	65.83 (2.03)	65.28 (1.92)
1	128	65.56 (1.68)	66.04 (2.66)
1	256	66.26 (2.81)	**66.98 (1.48)**
2	64	62.96 (1.61)	63.73 (1.12)
2	128	63.87 (2.05)	64.70 (2.12)
2	256	64.51 (1.60)	65.60 (2.21)
4	64	62.47 (2.32)	62.89 (1.18)
4	128	63.92 (2.55)	63.67 (1.63)
4	256	64.80 (1.72)	64.71 (1.66)

Table 2. Cross-validation results of different architectures using the Whisper encoder with varying depth (number of layers). Mean accuracy (%) and standard deviation are shown.

Architecture	12 layers	9 layers	6 layers	3 layers
LSTM	64.83 (1.41)	65.99 (1.91)	66.26 (2.81)	65.52 (2.19)
GRU	64.98 (1.68)	66.44 (1.29)	**66.98 (1.48)**	64.97 (1.72)
TCN	64.71 (1.83)	66.08 (2.05)	66.87 (2.96)	64.64 (1.88)

deviation of 2.96%. These results suggest that the number of channels has little influence on the accuracy of the model.

The three architectures evaluated reported very similar validation accuracy for the same encoder depth (see Table 2). For each architecture, Table 2 shows the results corresponding to the best combination of hyperparameters identified through grid search. In all cases, the best results were obtained using only the first 6 layers of the Whisper encoder.

Once the optimal parameters were identified, the models were retrained using the combined training and validation data and subsequently evaluated on the test set. Table 3 compares our results with those reported in the two previous studies that investigated the EmoGator dataset, using the F1-score as the evaluation metric. The proposed approach clearly outperforms the state-of-the-art.

Figure 2 shows the normalized confusion matrices of the classifiers used. The best identified classes across the three models were neutral, anger, and relief, and the overall accuracy was very similar among the models. However, significant differences were observed for individual classes between different classifiers, suggesting that an ensemble of different architectures could improve the robustness of the model.

Table 3. Comparison of the proposed approach with previous works on the EmoGator dataset based on the F1-score.

Approach	F1-score
1D CNN [4]	59.7%
WavLM [4]	56.3%
ResNet-50 [11]	60.6%
Whisper-LSTM (ours)	66.0%
Whisper-GRU (ours)	**66.5%**
Whisper-TCN (ours)	66.0%

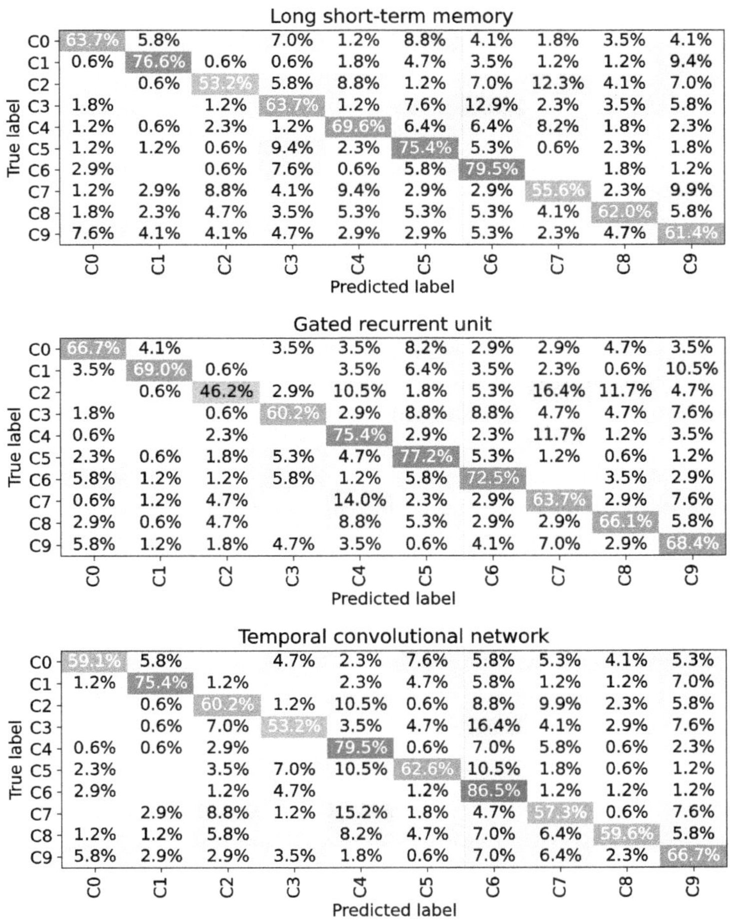

Fig. 2. Normalized confusion matrices of proposed classifiers. Class IDs correspond to emotions as follows: C0: Amusement, C1: Neutral, C2: Disgust, C3: Adoration, C4: Confusion, C5: Anger, C6: Relief, C7: Interest, C8: Pain, C9: Sadness.

4 Discussion

This paper explored the use of the Whisper's encoder with frozen weights for emotion recognition in VB, without losing the original capabilities of the model. Experiments conducted on the publicly available EmoGator dataset demonstrate the effectiveness of this approach. Lightweight classifiers trained on features extracted from Whisper significantly surpassed the state-of-the-art, without the need for data augmentation. The comprehensive evaluation of the models at different points in Whisper's latent space revealed that the emotions present in VB are more exposed in the middle of the encoder than in its final layers. This finding can be of great value in scenarios with constrained resources, as using only portion of the encoder substantially reduces the computational cost.

LSTM, GRU, and TCN reported very similar accuracy. However, a drop in accuracy was observed in recurrent architectures as the number of layers increased. This loss of accuracy may be attributed to low complexity of the input data or to the vanishing and exploding of gradients, a common problem in recurrent architectures [14]. For this reason, the TCN architecture emerges as a more robust alternative for this purpose and potentially more efficient, as it allows greater parallelism on GPUs.

The use of VBs in isolation may seem of little use, as they usually occur naturally in the middle of a dialogue. However, the ability to recognize VBs is particularly relevant in conversational contexts where an interlocutor's response may consist exclusively of a VB without verbal content. Furthermore, previous work indicate that processing verbal and nonverbal sounds separately within a conversation can significantly improve emotion recognition accuracy [8].

The present study highlights the great versatility of pre-trained transformers in audio processing for emotion recognition tasks, particularly in VB, a field that remains largely unexplored. Our results underscore the importance of paralinguistic sounds in understanding human emotions in oral communication. However, given the wide variety of existing deep learning architectures and the relatively small size of the dataset used, it is unclear to what extent these findings can be generalized. Future research will contribute to validate and delineate the scope of this research. In this regard, the publication of new, more extensive and diverse VB datasets will be crucial.

5 Conclusions

The recognition of emotions in VB is a relatively unexplored area but holds great potential for the development of HCI systems that feel human. Large pre-trained transformers such as Whisper, originally designed for transcription tasks, show a feature extraction capacity for emotion recognition that far surpasses traditional approaches. The possibility of using these models with their original weights is particularly valuable, as it paves the way for the integration of emotion recognition systems into existing HCI pipelines with minimal computational cost by leveraging the features used for audio transcription.

The results of this research may give rise to numerous future lines of work, including the improvement of conversational interfaces that are sensitive to the user's emotional state and the adaptive personalization of responses in virtual agents. They could also lay the foundations for more in-depth studies on emotion recognition in natural interactions.

Acknowledgments. This work was partially supported by grant PID2023-149753OB-C21 funded by MICIU/AEI/10.13039/501100011033 and by "ERDF A way to make Europe". Grant BES-2021-097834 funded by MICIU/AEI/10.13039/501100011033 and by "ESF Investing in your future". Grant 2023-PRED-21291 funded by Universidad de Castilla-La Mancha and by "ESF Investing in your future". Grant 2025-GRIN-38441, funded by Universidad de Castilla-La Mancha (UCLM) and "ERDF A way to make Europe". This work was partially supported by Programa Iberoamericano de Ciencia y Tecnología para el Desarrollo (CYTED) (through Red [225RT0169]). This work was also partially funded by CIBERSAM of the Instituto de Salud Carlos III (ISCIII).

Disclosure of Interests. The authors have no competing interests to declare that are relevant to the content of this article.

References

1. Atmaja, B.T., Sasou, A.: Evaluating variants of wav2vec 2.0 on affective vocal burst tasks. In: ICASSP 2023 - 2023 IEEE International Conference on Acoustics, Speech and Signal Processing (ICASSP), pp. 1–5. IEEE (2023). http://dx.doi.org/10.1109/ICASSP49357.2023.10096552
2. Baird, A., et al.: The ACII 2022 affective vocal bursts workshop & competition: Understanding a critically understudied modality of emotional expression (2022). https://doi.org/10.48550/ARXIV.2207.03572
3. Benedicto-Rodríguez, G., et al.: Understanding robot gesture perception in children with autism spectrum disorder during human–robot interaction. Int. J. Neural Syst. **35**(07) (2025). https://doi.org/10.1142/s0129065725500261
4. Buhl, F.W.: EmoGator: A new open source vocal burst dataset with baseline machine learning classification methodologies (2023). https://doi.org/10.48550/ARXIV.2301.00508
5. Chaves-Villota, A., Jimenez-Martín, A., Jojoa-Acosta, M., Bahillo, A., García-Domínguez, J.J.: Deep feature representations and fusion strategies for speech emotion recognition from acoustic and linguistic modalities: a systematic review. Comput. Speech Lang. **96**, 101873 (2026). https://doi.org/10.1016/j.csl.2025.101873
6. Dong, X., Wen, Y., Ji, D., Yuan, S., Liu, Z., Shang, W., Zhou, W.: Epileptic seizure detection with an end-to-end temporal convolutional network and bidirectional long short-term memory model. Int. J. Neural Syst. **34**(03) (2024). https://doi.org/10.1142/s0129065724500126
7. Gómez-Sirvent, J.L., López de la Rosa, F., Sánchez-Reolid, D., Sánchez-Reolid, R., Fernández-Caballero, A.: Small language models for speech emotion recognition in text and audio modalities. Appl. Sci. **15**(14), 7730 (2025). https://doi.org/10.3390/app15147730
8. Huang, K.Y., Wu, C.H., Hong, Q.B., Su, M.H., Chen, Y.H.: Speech emotion recognition using deep neural network considering verbal and nonverbal speech sounds. In: ICASSP 2019 - 2019 IEEE International Conference on Acoustics, Speech and Signal Processing (ICASSP). IEEE (2019). https://doi.org/10.1109/icassp.2019.8682283

9. Jatoth, A., Abri, F., Nguyen, T.: Multimodal emotion detection and analysis from conversational data. J. Adv. Inf. Technol. **16**(8), 1127–1141 (2025). https://doi.org/10.12720/jait.16.8.1127-1141
10. Lea, C., Flynn, M.D., Vidal, R., Reiter, A., Hager, G.D.: Temporal convolutional networks for action segmentation and detection. In: 2017 IEEE Conference on Computer Vision and Pattern Recognition (CVPR), pp. 1003–1012. IEEE (2017). https://doi.org/10.1109/cvpr.2017.113
11. Maharjan, R.S., Romeo, M., Cangelosi, A.: Sigh!!! There is more than just faces and verbal speech to recognize emotion in human-robot interaction. In: 2024 33rd IEEE International Conference on Robot and Human Interactive Communication (ROMAN), pp. 62–68. IEEE (2024). https://doi.org/10.1109/ro-man60168.2024.10731355
12. Mohmad Dar, G.H., Delhibabu, R.: Speech databases, speech features, and classifiers in speech emotion recognition: a review. IEEE Access **12**, 151122–151152 (2024). https://doi.org/10.1109/access.2024.3476960
13. Narain, J., Johnson, K.T., O'Brien, A., Wofford, P., Maes, P., Picard, R.: Nonverbal vocalizations as speech: Characterizing natural-environment audio from nonverbal individuals with autism (2020). https://doi.org/10.4119/LW2020-923
14. Orvieto, A., Zucchet, N.: Recurrent neural networks: vanishing and exploding gradients are not the end of the story. In: Advances in Neural Information Processing Systems, vol. 37, pp. 139402–139443. NeurIPS 2024, Neural Information Processing Systems Foundation, Inc. (NeurIPS) (2024). https://doi.org/10.52202/079017-4425
15. Portal, F., De Lope, J., Graña, M.: A performance benchmarking review of transformers for speaker-independent speech emotion recognition. Int. J. Neural Syst. **35**(10) (2025). https://doi.org/10.1142/s0129065725300013
16. Radford, A., Kim, J.W., Xu, T., Brockman, G., McLeavey, C., Sutskever, I.: Robust speech recognition via large-scale weak supervision (2022). https://doi.org/10.48550/ARXIV.2212.04356
17. Schröder, M.: Experimental study of affect bursts. Speech Commun. **40**(1–2), 99–116 (2003). https://doi.org/10.1016/s0167-6393(02)00078-x
18. Tracy, J.L., Randles, D., Steckler, C.M.: The nonverbal communication of emotions. Curr. Opinion Behav. Sci. **3**, 25–30 (2015). https://doi.org/10.1016/j.cobeha.2015.01.001
19. Tzirakis, P., et al.: Large-scale nonverbal vocalization detection using transformers. In: ICASSP 2023 - 2023 IEEE International Conference on Acoustics, Speech and Signal Processing (ICASSP), pp. 1–5. IEEE (2023). https://doi.org/10.1109/icassp49357.2023.10095294
20. Yu, Y., Si, X., Hu, C., Zhang, J.: A review of recurrent neural networks: LSTM cells and network architectures. Neural Comput. **31**(7), 1235–1270 (2019). https://doi.org/10.1162/neco_a_01199

Multimodal Temporal Deep Learning for ADHD Classification in Ecologically Valid Virtual Reality: An Exploratory Study

Francisco Javier Celdrán[1(✉)], Roberto Sánchez Reolid[1], José J. González-García[1], Dulce Romero-Ayuso[2,3], Olga C. Santos[4], and Pascual González[1,5]

[1] I3A, LoUISE Research Group, University of Castilla-La Mancha, Albacete, Spain
franciscoj.celdran@uclm.es
[2] Department of Physical Therapy, Occupational Therapy Division, University of Granada, Granada, Spain
[3] Instituto de Investigación Biosanitaria de Granada, Granada, Spain
[4] Artificial Intelligence Department, PhyUM Research Center, UNED, Madrid, Spain
[5] Computing Systems Department, University of Castilla-La Mancha, Albacete, Spain

Abstract. Attention Deficit Hyperactivity Disorder (ADHD) assessment increasingly incorporates artificial intelligence (AI), yet most approaches rely on laboratory-derived or questionnaire-based data with limited ecological validity. Virtual reality (VR) enables controlled simulation of complex, goal-directed activities, but existing VR-based tools largely exploit aggregated task-performance metrics and underutilize the rich multimodal signals available during interaction.

This exploratory study investigates how representation design and model architecture influence ADHD classification within an ecologically grounded Multiple Errands Test implemented in immersive VR. We address three research questions: (RQ1) Do multimodal behavioral and physiological signals provide additional discriminative value beyond traditional task metrics? (RQ2) Does preserving temporal structure improve classification performance compared to global aggregation? (RQ3) Do temporal deep learning architectures outperform classical machine learning models when applied to multimodal VR-derived sequences?

Twelve adults (5 ADHD, 7 controls) completed the task. We compared global aggregated features, window-based aggregated representations, and raw multichannel temporal sequences using Logistic Regression, Support Vector Machines, Random Forest, Gradient Boosting, and Temporal Convolutional Networks (TCNs), under Leave-One-Subject-Out cross-validation.

Results show that multimodal signals provide limited benefit under global aggregation but yield improved performance when temporal dynamics are preserved. TCN-based models achieved the highest accuracy (up to 0.79), suggesting that sequence-aware architectures better exploit irregular, action-aligned dynamics. These findings highlight the

J. M. Ferrndez Vicente et al. (Eds.): IWINAC 2026, LNCS 16574, pp. 333–342, 2026.
https://doi.org/10.1007/978-3-032-27314-7_31

critical interaction between representation design and model architecture in multimodal time-series classification within ecologically valid VR assessments.

Keywords: ADHD · Virtual Reality · Ecological Validity · Multimodal Sensing · Machine Learning Models · Temporal Deep Learning Models

1 Introduction

Attention Deficit Hyperactivity Disorder (ADHD) is a neurodevelopmental disorder typically diagnosed in childhood or adolescence, although it frequently persists into adulthood [1]. ADHD is commonly associated with deficits in executive functions (EFs), which impact the ability to carry out activities of daily living (ADLs), academic performance, and autonomy in everyday contexts [1]. ADLs comprise fundamental behaviors related to self-care, social interaction, and mobility [13].

However, traditional ADHD assessment methods, such as questionnaires, structured neuropsychological tests, and laboratory-based tasks, often struggle to capture how EF deficits manifest during complex, real-world activities [7,10]. In that sense, virtual reality (VR) has emerged as a promising platform for addressing this limitation by enabling ecologically valid assessments that balance experimental control with realistic task demands [8]. Ecological validity refers to the extent to which an assessment reflects everyday cognitive and behavioral functioning [3]. In this context, VR allows daily-life activities to be simulated in controlled, replicable, and immersive environments.

This work is built on SmartAction-VR, a VR-based assessment tool grounded in the Multiple Errands Test (MET) paradigm [12]. Unlike continuous performance tests, MET-based tasks evaluate executive functioning through open-ended, goal-oriented activities governed by everyday rules, providing a more naturalistic framework for assessing ADHD-related difficulties [8]. SmartAction-VR has previously been validated in children and adolescents with ADHD, establishing its clinical relevance and ecological grounding [12].

In parallel, artificial intelligence (AI) has been increasingly applied to ADHD assessment, primarily through machine learning models trained on behavioral, neurophysiological, or imaging data [6]. While these approaches have shown promising diagnostic performance, they are often based on data sources with limited ecological validity and rarely analyze behavior unfolding during realistic activities [6]. As a result, how AI-based models can leverage ecologically grounded VR data remains underexplored.

This exploratory study addresses three research questions: (RQ1) whether multimodal signals add value beyond task metrics; (RQ2) whether preserving temporal structure improves performance; and (RQ3) whether TCNs outperform classical models on multimodal VR sequences.

2 Related Work

2.1 VR-Based Assessment of ADHD

VR has been increasingly adopted in cognitive and neuropsychological assessment due to its ability to balance ecological validity with experimental control [2,8]. In the context of ADHD, VR-based tools have been proposed as an alternative to traditional laboratory tasks, aiming to capture executive-function deficits as they emerge during realistic activities. The most established examples are classroom-based VR systems, such as Aula Nesplora, which adapt continuous performance tasks to immersive environments containing visual and auditory distractors [11]. These systems have shown advantages over conventional computerized tests and are increasingly used in clinical settings [11]. However, they largely replicate traditional paradigms and focus primarily on attention and inhibition, offering limited coverage of complex, goal-directed behavior across contexts [8].

Beyond classroom paradigms, task frameworks such as the Multiple Errands Test (MET) have been highlighted as a means to achieve higher ecological validity by embedding executive demands within everyday activities governed by real-world rules [8]. SmartAction-VR builds on this rationale by implementing a MET-based assessment in immersive VR and has been clinically validated in children and adolescents with ADHD [12]. Nevertheless, most VR-based assessments continue to rely mainly on task-performance metrics and do not fully exploit the rich behavioral and physiological data that VR platforms can provide.

2.2 AI and Multimodal Data in ADHD Assessment

Artificial intelligence (AI) has become a central approach in ADHD research, particularly for diagnosis and classification using machine learning models trained on psychometric data, medical imaging (EEG, fMRI), or electrophysiological signals [6]. A recent review by Quintero-López et al. [9] analyzed 30 studies and reported classification accuracies ranging from approximately 65% to above 95%, with Support Vector Machines and ensemble methods such as Random Forests being the most commonly used algorithms.

Despite these promising results, most AI-based ADHD studies rely on data sources with limited ecological validity, such as questionnaires or highly controlled laboratory recordings. In Quintero-López et al.'s review, only one study involved VR, and it was restricted to simple head-motion measurements during sustained attention tasks, without addressing complex daily-life simulations or goal-oriented behavior [9].

Recent work has begun to explore multimodal behavioral and physiological data outside traditional lab settings. For example, Liu et al. [5] applied Gradient Boosting and convolutional neural networks to wearable-derived signals, demonstrating improved classification performance when temporal dynamics were considered. Other studies have combined self-reports with video or sensor data using deep learning approaches [15], although these inputs remain weakly grounded in everyday task structure. Reviews such as Cibrian et al. [4] further highlight the growing availability of multimodal digital assessments in ADHD, emphasizing signals such as horizontal displacement, head motion, and heart rate as promising indicators of hyperactivity and self-regulation.

Taken together, prior work shows that (1) VR can enhance ecological validity in ADHD assessment, and (2) AI-based models can achieve high classification performance when applied to behavioral or physiological data. However, these two lines of research have largely evolved independently. Ecologically grounded VR assessments rarely incorporate multimodal physiological signals or temporal deep learning models, while AI-based approaches typically rely on data collected outside realistic, goal-oriented contexts.

To our knowledge, no prior study has combined a MET-based VR assessment with multimodal behavioural and physiological data for ADHD classification. Given this gap, the present work is conceived as an exploratory study intended to provide preliminary evidence and guide future research. To address this gap, we integrate horizontal displacement, head-motion and heart-rate signals collected during an ecologically valid VR task and systematically compare classical machine-learning models and temporal deep-learning approaches.

3 Methodology

3.1 Participants

Twelve adults participated in the study (5 female, 7 male). Seven were neurotypical controls (ages 23–38), and five had a formal diagnosis of ADHD confirmed by a healthcare professional (ages 25–35). All participants provided informed consent prior to participation, in accordance with ethical research guidelines.

3.2 Experimental Design and Task

We employed a between-subjects design comparing adults with ADHD and neurotypical controls. All participants completed the same VR-based executive function assessment once.

The assessment was based on a SmartAction-VR validation study [12]. Participants performed a set of everyday-life activities designed to elicit executive functions such as planning, working memory, inhibition, and cognitive flexibility. Tasks included packing a backpack, preparing a sandwich, and purchasing missing items from a virtual store, while following explicit rules (e.g., obeying traffic signals, paying correctly, bringing required objects). Tasks unfolded across a virtual neighborhood comprising indoor and outdoor environments and were completed within a maximum time of 30 min.

Before the task, participants completed a 10-min guided tutorial to familiarize themselves with the VR interaction, followed by a 5-min resting period used to collect baseline physiological measures.

3.3 Data Collection

During task execution, multimodal behavioral and physiological data were continuously recorded. The VR setup allowed free physical movement within a 4×4 m space. The following data streams were collected:

- Task performance and actions: time-stamped logs of all task-related actions, including correctness and error types.
- Head motion: three-axis head orientation recorded from the VR headset.
- Horizontal displacement: participant position in the horizontal plane, used to estimate displacement and locomotion.
- Heart rate: physiological arousal recorded via a wearable device.

3.4 Preprocessing and Data Representation

All data streams were synchronized and preprocessed prior to modeling. From the action logs, traditional task-performance metrics were extracted (e.g., accuracy, number and type of errors, execution time). Head-motion and positional data were transformed into measures of rotational and translational dynamics, while heart-rate signals were summarized using descriptive statistics and baseline-corrected measures.

To evaluate how data representation influences classification performance, we implemented three modeling strategies:

- Global aggregated representation, summarizing the entire task execution into a single feature vector per participant.
- Window-based aggregated features, summarizing the different data modalities into one single feature vector per window. Using either fixed-length sliding windows or event-based windows aligned to task actions.
- Raw windowed sequences, converted into synchronized multichannel tensors for deep learning models (TCNs) using both fixed-length sliding windows and event-based windows.

Features were organized into three categories: basic (B), which corresponds to all execution related data, traditionally used by experts (as errors, expended time, total actions), heart rate (HR) and movement (M), which corresponds to horizontal displacement and head motion. All possible combinations of these categories were used, with a total of seven different feature sets used (B, HR, M, B+HR, B+M, HR+M, All). The "All" configuration corresponds to B+HR+M.

3.5 Modelling and Validation

We evaluated both classical machine learning models and temporal deep learning architectures. Among classical approaches, Logistic Regression was included as a widely used baseline in biomedical classification tasks, providing a simple and interpretable linear reference model. Support Vector Machines (linear and

RBF kernels), Random Forest, and Gradient Boosting were selected based on prior evidence showing robust performance in ADHD classification studies using behavioral and physiological data [9]. These models have consistently emerged as competitive approaches across different modalities in the literature.

To explicitly model the sequential structure of raw multimodal signals, we implemented Temporal Convolutional Networks (TCNs), a convolutional architecture designed for time-series analysis. TCNs were selected due to their ability to capture long-range temporal dependencies through dilated causal convolutions while maintaining stable training dynamics, making them suitable for small-sample time-series settings.

Model performance was assessed using Leave-One-Subject-Out (LOSO) cross-validation to ensure subject-level generalization. Evaluation metrics included accuracy, precision, recall, F1-score, and AUC.

4 Results

We evaluated the ability of different modeling strategies to discriminate between adults with and without ADHD using data collected during a VR-based MET assessment. We consider three feature modalities: Basic task performance metrics (B) from action logs, heart rate (HR) as a physiological signal, and movement (M), including head orientation and horizontal displacement. Models were evaluated using all possible combinations of these modalities.

Performance was analyzed along three complementary dimensions: (i) the contribution of multimodal physiological and movement signals, (ii) the impact of data representation, and (iii) the relative performance of classical machine learning models versus temporal deep learning approaches.

Table 1 summarizes the best-performing configuration within each modeling strategy in terms of accuracy and weighted F1-score, while Fig. 1 provides a distribution-level comparison of classification performance across all evaluated models and feature combinations for each strategy.

Table 1. Best-performing configurations per modeling strategy.

Strategy	Modalities	Model	Accuracy	F1 (weighted)
Global aggregated	B	RBF SVM	0.667	0.667
Fixed windows (aggregated)	B + HR	RBF SVM	0.684	0.664
Event-based windows (aggregated)	B + HR	Random Forest	0.506	0.425
Fixed windows (raw)	HR + M	TCN	0.728	0.714
Event-based windows (raw)	B + HR	TCN	0.789	0.787

4.1 Effect of Multimodal Signals

This analysis addresses RQ1, which examines whether multimodal signals provide additional discriminative value beyond traditional task metrics.

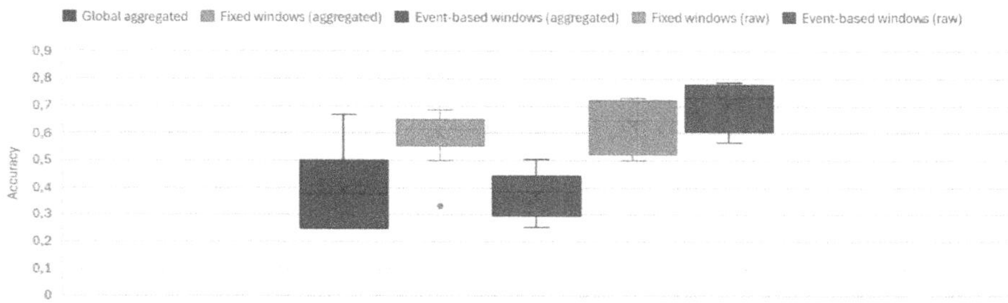

Fig. 1. Distribution of classification accuracy across modeling strategies

When using aggregated, execution-level features, adding physiological and movement data did not improve classification performance. Across classical models, configurations using only traditional task-performance metrics consistently outperformed those incorporating additional global multimodal features, with accuracies ranging from below-chance to moderate levels (0.25–0.67).

In contrast, when temporal structure was introduced, multimodal signals became clearly beneficial. Classical machine learning models using fixed-length windows improved performance when combining task, heart rate, and movement data (up to 0.68 accuracy), while temporal deep learning models achieved accuracies above 0.70.

This trend is further illustrated in Fig. 1, where strategies incorporating temporal modeling–particularly TCN-based approaches–exhibit higher median accuracies and reduced performance variability compared to aggregated-feature baselines.

4.2 Impact of Data Representation

This section evaluates RQ2, which explores whether preserving temporal structure enhances classification performance.

Data representation had a substantial impact on classification outcomes. Aggregated descriptors yielded limited and unstable performance across all classical models, as reflected by the wide dispersion and low medians in Fig. 1.

Fixed-length temporal windows systematically improved results for Random Forests, Gradient Boosting, and SVMs, particularly when multimodal features were included. These improvements suggest that short-term temporal structure allows physiological and movement signals to contribute meaningful discriminative information beyond global summaries.

Event-centered windows, however, performed poorly when combined with classical models, often resulting in near-chance accuracy. In relation to RQ3, temporal deep learning models showed superior performance compared to classical approaches, and event-centered representations proved advantageous when paired with Temporal Convolutional Networks, which achieved the highest overall performance and the tightest accuracy distributions. This indicates that irregular, action-aligned temporal structure requires models capable of learning long-range temporal dependencies.

5 Discussion

Our results provide preliminary insights into the three research questions formulated in this study, showing that the contribution of multimodal physiological and movement signals is highly dependent on how they are represented and modeled, and that temporal deep learning architectures are particularly well suited to exploit this type of data.

Regarding RQ1, when using aggregated, execution-level descriptors, classical machine learning models achieved limited performance, and the inclusion of additional physiological and movement features did not lead to improvements. This suggests that global summaries of multimodal data may obscure meaningful dynamics or introduce redundancy, limiting their discriminative value. In line with RQ2, representations that preserved temporal structure revealed clearer benefits of multimodal integration. Fixed-length temporal windows yielded systematic performance gains across classical models, indicating that short-term behavioral and physiological fluctuations carry relevant information that is lost in global aggregation.

With respect to RQ3, the strongest results were obtained with Temporal Convolutional Networks. Unlike classical approaches, TCNs benefited from event-centered representations and consistently achieved higher accuracy and F1 scores across multimodal configurations. This finding suggests that deep temporal models can exploit irregular, action-aligned dynamics that are difficult to capture with hand-crafted features or shallow classifiers. These results align with prior work highlighting the advantages of sequence-aware architectures for multimodal behavioral and physiological data [14] and extend them to ecologically grounded VR assessments.

These findings highlight the potential of combining immersive, everyday-like VR tasks with multimodal sensing and AI-based analysis. While many AI-driven ADHD assessments rely on highly controlled or abstract data sources (e.g., EEG, fMRI, questionnaires), our approach demonstrates that meaningful classification can also emerge from naturalistic behavior unfolding in realistic scenarios. This suggests a complementary pathway toward assessment tools that better reflect real-world functioning.

Several limitations should be acknowledged. The sample size was small, which limits generalizability and increases the risk of overfitting despite the use of subject-level cross-validation. Consequently, the findings related to RQ1–RQ3 should be interpreted as exploratory and indicative rather than confirmatory. Importantly, the aggregated basic task-performance metrics used as a baseline in this study have previously demonstrated discriminative validity in pediatric ADHD populations within the same VR-based MET framework [12]. Although the present sample is small and limited to adults, this prior validation provides a methodological reference point, suggesting that improvements observed over the baseline representation are unlikely to be purely arbitrary. Nevertheless, replication in larger cohorts is necessary to determine the robustness and stability of these trends. Future work should replicate these findings in larger cohorts, explore subtype differentiation, and further investigate which temporal patterns and modalities contribute most to classification.

6 Conclusions

This work provides preliminary evidence that integrating multimodal physiological and movement-based signals into an ecologically valid VR assessment can improve the discrimination between adults with and without ADHD, provided that appropriate temporal representations and models are used. While aggregated global features offered limited benefit, time-resolved representations revealed discriminative patterns that were best exploited by temporal deep learning models. In particular, Temporal Convolutional Networks consistently outperformed classical approaches, underscoring the importance of modeling temporal dynamics in multimodal VR-based assessments.

Future work should validate these findings in larger and more diverse samples and explore their applicability to pediatric populations, enabling direct comparison with prior validations of the tool. From a methodological perspective, a larger dataset would allow systematic analysis of model hyperparameters and temporal segmentation strategies, including window size, overlap, symmetry around events, and sequence length. Such analysis are necessary to determine how representation design and architectural configuration interact to influence classification performance, and to identify robust modeling pipelines beyond exploratory trends observed here. Beyond ADHD classification, this approach opens new possibilities for using ecologically grounded VR tasks combined with AI to support objective assessment of executive functioning in real-world–like contexts.

Acknowledgments. This paper has been funded by Junta de Comunidades de Castilla-La Mancha and by European Regional Development Fund (SBPLY/24/180225/000020), by Universidad de Castilla-La Mancha (2025-GRIN-38441 and 13585/2025), and by Grant PID2022-140907OB-I00 funded by MICIU/AEI/10.13039/501100011033 and ERDF, EU

Disclosure of Interests. The authors have no competing interests to declare that are relevant to the content of this article.

References

1. Arnold, L.E., Hodgkins, P., Kahle, J., Madhoo, M., Kewley, G.: Long-term outcomes of ADHD: academic achievement and performance. J. Atten. Disord. **24**, 73–85 (2020). https://doi.org/10.1177/1087054714566076
2. Bohil, C.J., Alicea, B., Biocca, F.A.: Virtual reality in neuroscience research and therapy (2011). https://doi.org/10.1038/nrn3122

3. Chaytor, N., Schmitter-Edgecombe, M.: The ecological validity of neuropsychological tests: a review of the literature on everyday cognitive skills. Neuropsychol. Rev. **13**, 181–197 (2003). https://doi.org/10.1023/B:NERV.0000009483.91468.fb. https://link.springer.com/10.1023/B:NERV.0000009483.91468.fb
4. Cibrian, F.L., Monteiro, E.M., Lakes, K.D.: Digital assessments for children and adolescents with ADHD: a scoping review (2024). https://doi.org/10.3389/fdgth.2024.1440701
5. Liu, J., et al.: Digital phenotyping from wearables using AI characterizes psychiatric disorders and identifies genetic associations (2024). https://doi.org/10.1016/j.cell.2024.11.012
6. Loh, H.W., Ooi, C.P., Barua, P.D., Palmer, E.E., Molinari, F., Acharya, U.R.: Automated detection of ADHD: current trends and future perspective (2022). https://doi.org/10.1016/j.compbiomed.2022.105525
7. Negu, A., Matu, S.A., Sava, F.A., David, D.: Virtual reality measures in neuropsychological assessment: a meta-analytic review (2016). https://doi.org/10.1080/13854046.2016.1144793
8. Parsons, T.D.: Virtual reality for enhanced ecological validity and experimental control in the clinical, affective and social neurosciences. Front. Hum. Neurosci. **9** (2015). https://doi.org/10.3389/fnhum.2015.00660
9. Quintero-López, C., Vera, V.D.G., Bernal, R.M.C., Martínez, M.H.: Predicción del tdah con aprendizaje de máquinas: Revisión sistemática de literatura. Revista Argentina de Ciencias del Comportamiento **16**, 14–32 (2024). https://doi.org/10.32348/1852.4206.v16.n3.42221view/42221
10. Rizzo, A., Koenig, S.T.: Is clinical virtual reality ready for primetime? Neuropsychology **31**, 877–899 (2017). https://doi.org/10.1037/neu0000405
11. Rodríguez, C., Areces, D., García, T., Cueli, M., González-Castro, P.: Comparison between two continuous performance tests for identifying ADHD: traditional vs. virtual reality. Int. J. Clin. Health Psychol. **18**, 254–263 (2018). https://doi.org/10.1016/j.ijchp.2018.06.003
12. Romero-Ayuso, D., et al.: Enhancing ecological validity: virtual reality assessment of executive functioning in children and adolescents with ADHD. Children **11** (2024). https://doi.org/10.3390/children11080986
13. Romero-Ayuso, D.M.: Actividades de la vida diaria. anales de psicología **23**, 264–271 (2007). www.um.es/analesps
14. Rouast, P.V., Adam, M.T., Chiong, R.: Deep learning for human affect recognition: insights and new developments. IEEE Trans. Affect. Comput. **12**, 524–543 (2021). https://doi.org/10.1109/TAFFC.2018.2890471
15. Zhang, Y., et al.: Auxiliary diagnostic system for ADHD in children based on AI technology. Front. Inf. Technol. Electron. Eng. **22**, 400–414 (2021). https://doi.org/10.1631/FITEE.1900729

Design of an Embodied Conversational Agent for Autism Intervention: A Comparative Framework Between Physical Robots and Virtual Agents

José L. Gómez-Sirvent[1,3](✉), Gema Benedicto[2], and Antonio Fernández-Caballero[1,3,4]

[1] Emotion and Neurocognition Unit, Instituto de Investigación en Informática de Albacete, Albacete, Spain
antonio.fdez@uclm.es
[2] Universidad Politécnica de Cartagena, Murcia, Spain
[3] Departamento de Sistemas Informáticos, Universidad de Castilla-La Mancha, Albacete, Spain
jose.gomez@uclm.es
[4] Biomedical Research Networking Center in Mental Health (CIBERSAM-ISCIII), Madrid, Spain

Abstract. Autism spectrum disorders (ASD) are clinically diverse conditions that require intensive, individualized support. This article presents a modular framework for developing embodied conversational agents for ASD intervention, which supports both physical robots and virtual characters through a shared cognitive core. The framework decouples the conversational engine from the embodiment layer, enabling rapid adaptation to different therapeutic protocols. It combines LLM-based chatbots with real-time speech synthesis and animation generation to create natural interaction between the user and the agent. The LLM generates textual responses for the user along with a definition of the agent's emotional state. This information guides the agent's speech synthesis and expressive behaviors. In addition, a workflow is proposed for the creation of virtual replicas of physical robots, enabling the generation of animatable virtual agents that can be effectively deployed on a single laptop, significantly reducing costs and logistical barriers of ASD interventions. The framework not only facilitates the systematic evaluation of the effectiveness of different therapies, but also provides a basis for the future personalization of interventions, tailoring responses and behaviors to individual user profiles. Its modular and scalable design also allows for its extension beyond ASD, which could prove valuable in a variety of therapeutic and educational applications.

Keywords: Autism spectrum disorder · Chatbot · Large language model · Social robot · Embodied Conversational Agent

J. M. Ferrndez Vicente et al. (Eds.): IWINAC 2026, LNCS 16574, pp. 343–352, 2026.
https://doi.org/10.1007/978-3-032-27314-7_32

1 Introduction

Autism spectrum disorder (ASD) poses a challenge for healthcare systems due to their prevalence and clinical heterogeneity. Psychological interventions in children with ASD have been shown to be highly effective in improving specific behaviors, such as joint attention or social engagement [10]. However, these types of therapies require individualized and prolonged attention over time, which can sometimes limit access to individuals living in rural areas or with low economic resources.

In this context, there has been growing interest in the use of therapeutic chatbots as a support tool for healthcare professionals. Advances in socio-cognitive and affective computing provide the theoretical and technological basis for modeling user behavior in interactive systems. Integrating these approaches into therapy allows for a better understanding of user responses. These systems automate repetitive interventions, providing assistance that is available anywhere and easily scalable. In addition, they enable the structured collection of valuable data for evaluating patient progress over time, such as conversational patterns, response times, and frequency of use. This is particularly relevant in the context of ASD, where social and cognitive processing patterns exhibit marked inter-individual differences.

1.1 Conversational Agents in Autism

Traditionally, therapeutic chatbots have been implemented as rule-based systems, in which user interaction is limited to a predefined set of responses. This approach offers major advantages, including computational efficiency, reproducibility, and full control over content. However, the inherent rigidity of such system can lead to frustration and loss of motivation among users, as interactions often result in predictable and unnatural responses [5].

In response to these limitations, Large Language Models (LLMs) are emerging as a promising alternative to algorithmic approaches as the core of chatbots. These models generate more flexible and contextually coherent responses, promoting a natural and user-adaptive communication. Previous research has shown the feasibility of adapting general-purpose LLMs for this specific task through prompt engineering [3], as well as through fine-tuning techniques [8], which help align the model's behavior with therapeutic objectives. Nevertheless, even with these mechanisms, there is no complete control over the model's behavior, which poses challenges for safety and reproducibility. To address these challenges, it is necessary to evolve toward systems that integrate socio-cognitive computing, allowing the agent not only to generate coherent responses, but also to interpret social intentions by mimicking the functioning of the human brain.

1.2 Embodied Systems in Human Computer Interaction

Although LLM-based chatbots overcome many limitations of rule-based systems, purely non-embodied interactions lack essential social cues such as facial expressions, gestures, and prosody. For individuals with ASD, this absence of social demands can foster greater confidence when communicating with an LLM compared to a human, as interactions are non-judgmental and controllable [7,17]. However, many therapeutic interventions aim to develop social and communicative skills, which non-embodied systems cannot adequately support due to the absence of multimodal cues.

In this regard, social robots have proven to be an effective solution for the development of therapies aimed at improving communication and social skills by incorporating non-verbal cues within a safe and controlled environment. Several previous studies [4,16] found that children with ASD experienced greater engagement in therapies involving social robots compared to those conducted by human therapists. Unfortunately, the high cost of these devices, as well as technical limitations that hinder their adaptation to different therapeutic protocols, restrict the widespread adoption of social robots for this type of intervention.

On the other hand, virtual agents allow for the implementation of more cost-effective and scalable solutions, with a much higher degree of adaptability as they are not limited by the constraints of the physical world. Recent research suggests that virtual embodiment systems could achieve results similar to those obtained by physical systems [9,14]; however, it is unknown to what extent they could completely replace physical interaction. To our knowledge, there is no design framework that allows both modalities to be implemented and compared under the same cognitive core.

With the aim of filling this gap in the literature, this research proposes a framework for the implementation of an Embodied Conversational Agent for Autism Intervention, designed to facilitate comparison between physical robots and virtual agents operating under the same cognitive core.

2 System Overview: Proposed Intervention Framework

A modular architecture is proposed in which each component can be replaced or updated without compromising the system. The design decouples the conversational engine from the embodiment layer, allowing the same conversational logic to be shared between physical robots and virtual agents, which enables for a fair comparison between physical and virtual embodiments. The design focuses on versatility, facilitating rapid adaptation to different therapeutic approaches and the integration of future technological advances. In addition, the modular structure allows for distributed implementation when a device platform cannot support all computing requirements.

2.1 Core Conversational Engine

Figure 1 shows the structure of the proposed conversational engine. The system integrates two input channels: user input and the therapist-defined parameters. User input can be provided via text or voice processed with an automatic speech recognition (ASR) system. This input can be supplemented with different sensors such as cameras or wearables for user monitoring. The inclusion of these sensors enables a transition to a physiological computing paradigm in which the system is capable of predicting and detecting states of anxiety or sensory overstimulation in real time and responding accordingly. Likewise, therapist input allows the therapy parameters to be set and the identity of the agent used to be selected.

Based on these inputs, the chatbot serves as an AI wrapper that guides a language model to generate appropriate responses taking into account the agent's identity (gender, age, personality, etc.) as well as therapeutic guidelines. To increase the controllability and security of the system, a predefined rule-based system is integrated to dynamically modify the prompts in case the LLM deviates from the guidelines, for example, when task time limits are exceeded. The chatbot must provide two outputs: the text that the agent will say and the agent's emotional state.

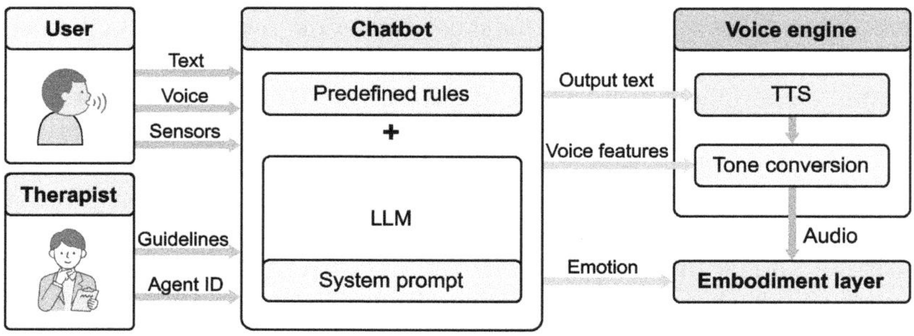

Fig. 1. Overview of the proposed Core Conversational Engine, illustrating a modular architecture that decouples cognitive and therapeutic logic from the embodiment layer.

For text-to-speech (TTS) conversion, we propose the use of a lightweight architecture with low latency and predictable output. While recent TTS models are capable of highly realistic voice cloning, these systems are often computationally demanding and prone to variability in audio quality and hallucinations [2]. In our approach, the TTS output is processed using a lightweight tone conversion model to make the voice sound more natural, as well as allowing an unlimited number of voices to be generated from a single base voice. The resulting audio, together with the emotional state, is transmitted to the embodiment layer to control the speech and facial expression of the physical robot or virtual agent.

2.2 Embodiment Layer

The embodiment layer is responsible for the animation of the agent, whether physical or virtual. The main objective of this proposal is to ensure that the only difference between one modality and another is physical presence, while keeping all other aspects of the interaction unchanged. This approach poses a significant challenge, as in the case of social robots, it is not possible to unify implementation because each manufacturer uses a different API to generate animation from audio.

However, in the case of virtual agents, standardization is more feasible. There are various open-source tools such as NeuroSync and NVIDIA Audio2Face that enable real-time conversion of audio into facial animation. The main challenge here lies in creating a virtual replica of a physical robot that is compatible with these animation engines. Traditionally, this task involved a tedious process that only experienced 3D animators could perform. However, by combining different recent software implementations, it is now possible to simplify this task considerably.

To address this, we propose a three-step workflow, see Fig. 2. Starting from images of a physical robot, a 3D replica is generated using a deep learning model of image-based 3D reconstruction; several recent open-source architectures can perform this task [15]. Subsequently, a mesh with animation-ready topology is deformed to match the geometry of the previously generated 3D model. Free tools for academic/educational use such as 3ds Max or Faceform can be employed to perform this deformation. Finally, character creation software such as MetaHuman Creator, is used to automatically add missing elements such as eyes or the interior of the mouth.

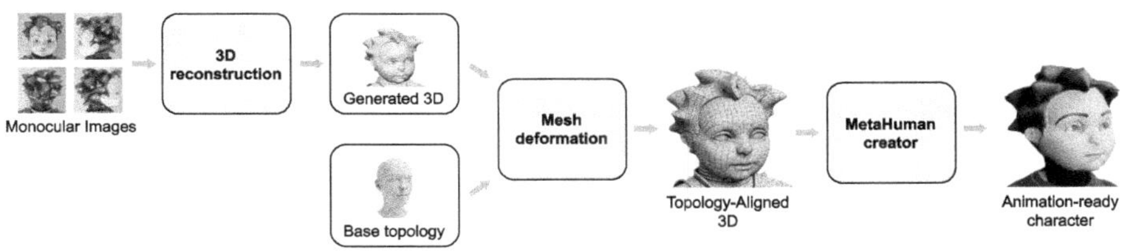

Fig. 2. Complete workflow for generating virtual replicas from physical robots with consistent topology.

This workflow reduces the time required to create 3D characters from days to minutes, allowing a functional virtual replica of any humanoid robot to be obtained from just a few images. This method facilitates a fair comparison between the physical and virtual embodiments operating under the same cognitive core.

2.3 Therapeutic Models Supported by the System

The proposed framework is designed to support different structured therapeutic interventions. The approach is therapy-agnostic, allowing different intervention models to be implemented simply by adjusting the configuration of the conversational engine, without modifying the system architecture. For example, applied behavior analysis (ABA)-like structured tasks [11] could be implemented through predefined interaction sequences, controlled prompts, and deterministic feedback rules. Similarly, pivotal response training (PRT)-inspired interaction loops could be implemented through immediate reinforcement mechanisms. Immediate reinforcement can be achieved by linking the chatbot's output to the agent's expressive behaviors such as vocal modulation, facial expressions, or simple gestures. Reinforcement strategies can be parameterized and triggered by interaction events such as task completion or appropriate response.

The separation between the conversational engine and the embodiment layer allows these therapeutic models to be adapted, combined, or expanded without modifying the system architecture.

3 From Physical Robots to Virtual Agents

The choice of embodiment has important implications for therapeutic interaction. Physical robots offer presence and tangibility helping to create a sense of shared space. On the other hand, virtual embodiment offers scalability and ubiquity that are difficult for a physical robot to achieve.

The use of a shared conversational engine across modalities allows for controlled measurement of the impact of physical presence on the user experience. However, the goal is not necessarily for virtual embodiment to completely replicate or match the results of physical robots, but rather to assess whether they can elicit positive therapeutic effects. From this perspective, physical and virtual embodiments should not be understood as mutually exclusive alternatives, but rather as components of a broader intervention ecosystem, with hybrid approaches that leverage the strengths of each modality in different contexts and stages of therapy.

Initially, clinical interventions can leverage the validated benefits of physical robots to establish engagement. As users become familiar with the agent and the session structure, virtual agents can be introduced while maintaining conversational behavior, allowing for smooth transitions between modalities. This transition allows the practice to be taken wherever the user is, without the logistical and economic limitations associated with physical robots.

In this context, the virtual modality can be understood as a video-mediated session. Although the level of physical presence is reduced, the continuity of the agent's behavior, identity, and interaction structure is preserved. However, periodic face-to-face sessions with the physical robot can be maintained to reinforce aspects of the interaction related to embodiment, such as spatial presence and tangibility. This hybrid approach allows physical embodiment to be exploited when beneficial, while assessing the extent to which it could be dispensed with without compromising the effectiveness of the interventions.

However, validating technical usability is a necessary preliminary step, as it ensures real-time responsiveness, audiovisual synchronization, and reliable interaction prior to user testing.

3.1 Performance Assessment of the Virtual Modality

With the intention of evaluating the feasibility of deploying the virtual modality, a proof-of-execution was carried out. Based on images of a real social robot, a virtual replica was created using the Hunyauan 3D model and subsequently adapted to a MetaHuman-compatible topology following the workflow described in Fig. 2. Audio was generated using the Google Text-to-Speech and post-processed with OpenVoice V2 to modify vocal identity. Facial animation was generated using Audio2Face.

The system was tested on a laptop equipped with an NVIDIA RTX 5070 GPU with 8 GB VRAM, rendering at a resolution of 800×800 pixels. An end-to-end latency of text to audio playback synchronized with animation was measured at less than 1 s, which is acceptable for real-time interaction. It is important to note that these measurements do not include the latency introduced by the LLM, which will need to be evaluated in future implementations.

This test demonstrates the feasibility of running real-time responsive agents with a high level of realism on consumer hardware. A video demonstration of the virtual agent in action is provided at the following link:
https://github.com/jgs1234/Virtual-Agent-Test.

4 Discussion

The proposed framework was designed with a clear objective: to enable a fair and controlled comparison between physical and virtual embodiment, ensuring that both modalities share the same conversational behavior and visual appearance.

The main limitation of virtual agents compared to physical ones lies in the lack of a sense of presence when viewed on a flat screen. Initially, it was considered that immersive virtual reality using head-mounted displays (HMDs) could mitigate this limitation; however, previous studies [18] have reported difficulties for some children with ASD in tolerating HMDs. Recent advances in glasses-free 3D displays [13] may offer an alternative path toward increased immersion without the drawbacks associated with HMDs. Emerging commercial solutions have demonstrated the ability to convey a sense of depth and parallax without requiring wearable devices.

The therapeutic efficacy of the framework has not yet been experimentally validated. However, preliminary technical evaluations indicate that the entire virtual agent process can be run on a single laptop with low latency and a high level of visual realism. Importantly, the modular design does not require rendering to be performed locally. Remote rendering solutions, allow the system to run on a server while streaming interactive audiovisual output to low-end client devices, such as tablets or smartphones. This approach would enable remote therapy scenarios in which the therapist and user are geographically separated, further reducing barriers to therapy access. This capability is particularly relevant given that previous studies [1,12] have shown that remote psychological and behavioral interventions for children with ASD can be effective and well accepted by families.

If future research demonstrates that virtual agents achieve outcomes comparable to physical robots, the proposed framework could change the current intervention paradigm. High-cost social robots could be replaced by free software-based solutions allowing for an unlimited number of agent identities. Previous work suggests that familiarity with agents can increase empathy in the responses of children with ASD [6]. In this context, the possibility of creating agents that resemble characters familiar to children–subject to consent–could open up new avenues for increasing motivation and engagement in therapy.

4.1 Ethical and Design Considerations

The proposed framework should not be understood as a substitute for human-led therapy, but rather as a supportive therapeutic tool designed to complement existing practices. As a novel tool, it is crucial to conduct a thorough evaluation of the safety and proper functioning of the system before testing it in real interventions.

From a technological design perspective, robustness must be ensured to avoid failures such as excessive latency or unexpected interruptions that could have a negative effect on the user experience, causing a possible loss of trust in the agent. Likewise, exaggerated movements or harsh sounds should be avoided, as they may cause sensory overload.

Another fundamental point is the controllability of the system. LLMs are usually designed to be user-pleasing, which in this application domain could be problematic if it reinforces negative behavior or attitudes. For this reason, it is vital that the wrapper guiding the model prevents it from deviating from therapeutic guidelines.

Finally, the transparency of the agent is key to avoiding disappointment or over-attribution. It is vital that both the user and the caregivers are aware of the role and limitations of the agent.

5 Conclusions and Future Work

This paper presents a technological framework that enables structured interventions for ASD to be implemented using conversational agents decoupled from their embodiment, thereby facilitating comparison between physical robots and virtual replicas. Beyond merely enabling such comparisons, the distributed and easily reconfigurable implementation introduced in this framework could allow therapeutic interventions to be carried out virtually anywhere at minimal cost, removing barriers to access to specialized services and facilitating the inclusion of users in remote or resource-limited environments.

Furthermore, the proposed framework could easily be extended to other domains beyond ASD by simply modifying the chatbot configuration while keeping the rest of the system intact. Future work could advance in various directions. One line of research could focus on the experimental validation of the framework's effectiveness for therapeutic use in ASD. Other possible lines of research could address automatic personalization, adapting conversational strategies and therapeutic parameters to individual user profiles, or the use of extended reality devices to improve the level of immersion.

Acknowledgments. Grant BES-2021-097834 funded by MICIU/AEI/10.13039/501100011033 and by "ESF Investing in your future" Grant 2025-GRIN-38441, funded by Universidad de Castilla-La Mancha (UCLM) and "ERDF A way to make Europe". This work was partially supported by Programa Iberoamericano de Ciencia y Tecnología para el Desarrollo (CYTED) (through Red [225RT0169]). This work was also partially funded by CIBERSAM of the Instituto de Salud Carlos III (ISCIII).

Disclosure of Interests. The authors have no competing interests to declare that are relevant to the content of this article.

References

1. Ashburner, J., Vickerstaff, S., Beetge, J., Copley, J.: Remote versus face-to-face delivery of early intervention programs for children with autism spectrum disorders: perceptions of rural families and service providers. Res. Autism Spectr. Disord. **23**, 1–14 (2016). https://doi.org/10.1016/j.rasd.2015.11.011
2. Azzuni, H., Saddik, A.E.: Voice cloning: comprehensive survey (2025). https://doi.org/10.48550/ARXIV.2505.00579
3. Ciobanu, M.G., Tucci, C., Fasano, F.: LLMs for autism treatment: current trends and emerging strategies. In: 2024 IEEE International Conference on Bioinformatics and Biomedicine (BIBM), pp. 6797–6804. IEEE (2024). https://doi.org/10.1109/bibm62325.2024.10822015
4. Dubois-Sage, M., Jacquet, B., Jamet, F., Baratgin, J.: People with autism spectrum disorder could interact more easily with a robot than with a human: reasons and limits. Behav. Sci. **14**(2), 131 (2024). https://doi.org/10.3390/bs14020131
5. Gu, P., Xu, F., Chen, L., Ma, Z., Zhang, M., Zhang, Y.: Technological affordances and applications of chatbots for conversational skill interventions in autism: a scoping review. Educ. Inf. Technol. **30**(7), 9311–9340 (2024). https://doi.org/10.1007/s10639-024-13191-z
6. Hudry, K., Slaughter, V.: Agent familiarity and emotional context influence the everyday empathic responding of young children with autism. Res. Autism Spectr. Disord. **3**(1), 74–85 (2009). https://doi.org/10.1016/j.rasd.2008.04.004
7. Jang, J., Moharana, S., Carrington, P., Begel, A.: "It's the only thing i can trust": envisioning large language model use by autistic workers for communication assistance. In: Proceedings of the CHI Conference on Human Factors in Computing Systems, CHI 2024, pp. 1–18. ACM (2024). https://doi.org/10.1145/3613904.3642894
8. Lai, S., et al.: ASD-ILLM: an intervention large language model for autistic children based on real clinical dialogue intervention dataset. In: Findings of the Association for Computational Linguistics: EMNLP 2025, pp. 8058–8079. Association for Computational Linguistics (2025). https://doi.org/10.18653/v1/2025.findings-emnlp.427
9. Liu, L., You, Y., He, Z., Chen, J.: An Avatar-Based Intervention System for Children with Autism Spectrum Disorder, pp. 220–231. Springer, Singapore (2024). https://doi.org/10.1007/978-981-97-8692-3_16

10. Lord, C., et al.: Autism spectrum disorder. Nat. Rev. Dis. Primers **6**(1) (2020). https://doi.org/10.1038/s41572-019-0138-4
11. Louie, W.Y.G., Korneder, J., Abbas, I., Pawluk, C.: A study on an applied behavior analysis-based robot-mediated listening comprehension intervention for ASD. Paladyn J. Behav. Robot. **12**(1), 31–46 (2020). https://doi.org/10.1515/pjbr-2021-0005
12. Marino, F., et al.: Psychological interventions for children with autism during the COVID-19 pandemic through a remote behavioral skills training program. J. Clin. Med. **11**(5), 1194 (2022). https://doi.org/10.3390/jcm11051194
13. Peddie, J.: Stereoscopic 3D in Computers, pp. 459–520. Springer, London (2025). https://doi.org/10.1007/978-1-4471-7553-7_8
14. Ren, X., et al.: ChatASD: LLM-Based AI Therapist for ASD, pp. 312–324. Springer, Singapore (2024). https://doi.org/10.1007/978-981-97-3626-3_23
15. Rodríguez-Lira, D.C., et al.: Recent developments in image-based 3d reconstruction using deep learning: methodologies and applications. Electronics **14**(15), 3032 (2025). https://doi.org/10.3390/electronics14153032
16. Vagnetti, R., Di Nuovo, A., Mazza, M., Valenti, M.: Social robots: a promising tool to support people with autism. A systematic review of recent research and critical analysis from the clinical perspective. Rev. J. Autism Dev. Disord. (2024). https://doi.org/10.1007/s40489-024-00434-5
17. Xygkou, A., Siriaraya, P., She, W.J., Covaci, A., Ang, C.S.: "Can i be more social with a chatbot?": Social connectedness through interactions of autistic adults with a conversational virtual human. Int. J. Hum.–Comput. Interact. **40**(24), 8937–8954 (2024). https://doi.org/10.1080/10447318.2023.2292880
18. Yang, X., et al.: Effectiveness of virtual reality technology interventions in improving the social skills of children and adolescents with autism: systematic review. J. Med. Internet Res. **27**, e60845 (2025). https://doi.org/10.2196/60845

Comparative Evaluation of Recent Deep Architectures for Arousal Classification from Electrodermal Activity

Roberto Sánchez-Reolid[1,2](✉), Francisco Javier Celdrán[1], Daniel Sánchez-Reolid[3], and Antonio Fernández-Caballero[1,3,4]

[1] Instituto de Investigación en Informática de Albacete (I3A), Universidad de Castilla-La Mancha, Albacete, Spain

[2] Departamento de Tecnologías y Sistemas de Información, Universidad de Castilla-La Mancha, Talavera de la Reina, Spain
roberto.sanchez@uclm.es

[3] Departamento de Sistemas Informáticos, Universidad de Castilla-La Mancha, Albacete, Spain

[4] Biomedical Research Networking Centre in Mental Health, Madrid, Spain

Abstract. Electrodermal Activity (EDA) is a widely adopted physiological marker for assessing sympathetic arousal. While convolutional neural networks have shown promising results for automatic feature extraction, recent advances in deep time-series modelling enable more expressive end-to-end representations. This work presents a systematic comparison of five modern architectures—1D-CNN, Temporal Convolutional Networks (TCN), InceptionTime, Time-Series Transformer (TST), and PatchTST—for binary arousal classification from EDA signals collected from 147 participants under a controlled laboratory protocol. All models are evaluated using a strict Leave-One-Subject-Out (LOSO) framework to ensure subject-independent generalisation. Results show that Transformer-based architectures consistently outperform convolutional baselines, with PatchTST achieving the best balance between predictive accuracy, robustness across subjects, and computational efficiency. Analysis across varying temporal window lengths further demonstrates that reliable arousal detection can be achieved within short observation intervals when global dependency modelling is employed. Interpretability analysis indicates that attention mechanisms concentrate on SCR onset and rising phases, aligning with known physiological dynamics of sympathetic activation. These findings highlight the importance of physiologically-informed architectural design and rigorous validation for robust affective computing from biosignals.

Keywords: Electrodermal Activity · Arousal Classification · Time-Series modelling · Transformers · Subject-Independent Evaluation

J. M. Ferrández Vicente et al. (Eds.): IWINAC 2026, LNCS 16574, pp. 353–362, 2026.
https://doi.org/10.1007/978-3-032-27314-7_33

1 Introduction

Electrodermal Activity (EDA) reflects sympathetic nervous system activation via sudomotor nerve activity, making it a robust and non-concealable biomarker for assessing emotional arousal [3,7]. The EDA signal is inherently complex, comprising slow-varying tonic levels that indicate prolonged states and rapid phasic responses reflecting immediate, stimulus-evoked arousal [11]. Historically, arousal classification from EDA has relied on the manual extraction of statistical features from these deconvoluted components, followed by classical machine learning classifiers [12].

While early deep learning approaches utilizing 1D Convolutional Neural Networks (CNNs) successfully automated local morphological feature extraction, they often struggle to capture the multi-scale temporal dynamics of physiological signals [5,13]. However, recent advances in deep learning for time-series modelling offer promising solutions to provide improved temporal dependency modelling [1]. Architectures such as InceptionTime leverage parallel multiscale kernels to simultaneously capture rapid transient spikes and slow tonic shifts [2,14]. Temporal Convolutional Networks (TCN) utilise dilated causal convolutions to efficiently model extended physiological memory [6]. Furthermore, Transformer-based models, including the canonical Time-Series Transformer (TST) and the novel PatchTST, have introduced self-attention mechanisms capable of modelling global dependencies across prolonged observation windows, overcoming the constraints of fixed receptive fields [4,15,16].

Despite the potential of these modern architectures, the affective computing community lacks a unified, methodologically rigorous comparison under controlled experimental conditions [9,12]. Previous comparative studies frequently suffer from pervasive experimental flaws, most notably sample-based random data partitioning [1]. Because EDA exhibits strong inter-subject variability, this practice induces severe data leakage, allowing models to memorise individual biometric baselines rather than learning generalizable arousal patterns, which artificially inflates reported performance [1,10].

To address this critical research gap, this work evaluates and compares five representative deep learning architectures—1D-CNN, TCN, InceptionTime, TST, and PatchTST—for binary arousal classification directly from Electrodermal Activity signals acquired under a controlled laboratory protocol involving 147 participants. By deploying these models within a strictly controlled, leakage-free Leave-One-Subject-Out validation framework, we aim to empirically establish which structural paradigm provides the optimal balance of temporal dependency modelling, computational efficiency, and robust cross-subject generalisation in medium-scale physiological datasets.

Building upon prior feature-based investigations [12], this study shifts the methodological paradigm toward end-to-end representation learning, directly modelling the phasic dynamics of EDA and its temporal derivatives. In doing so, we revisit the question of how effectively modern sequence architectures can capture sympathetic arousal dynamics without handcrafted features, while preserving strict subject-independent evaluation.

2 Materials and Methods

2.1 Dataset and Experimental Protocol

The experimental dataset follows a controlled stress elicitation protocol described in a previous paper [11]. Electrodermal Activity (EDA) signals were recorded from 147 healthy participants (aged 18–44 years) exposed to audiovisual stimuli designed to induce calm and stress states under controlled laboratory conditions.

Each stimulus lasted 47 s. To eliminate transition artefacts associated with stimulus onset and offset, the first 4 s and the last 3 s were removed, resulting in 40-second effective segments. Signals were acquired at a constant sampling frequency of 4 Hz.

2.2 EDA Signal Processing

Raw skin conductance signals were preprocessed following [12]. A low-pass FIR filter (cut-off frequency: 4 Hz) was applied, followed by Gaussian smoothing to reduce noise acquisition. Continuous Decomposition Analysis (CDA) was used to separate tonic (SCL) and phasic (SCR) components:

$$SC(t) = SCL(t) + SCR(t) \tag{1}$$

Only the phasic component $SCR(t)$ was retained for modelling, as it directly reflects sympathetic nervous system activation. To enrich short-term dynamic representation, two additional channels were derived from the phasic signal, namely the first derivative (ΔSCR) and the second derivative ($\Delta^2 SCR$). These channels explicitly encode velocity and acceleration of sympathetic responses, potentially facilitating earlier identification of rapid morphological changes.

2.3 Input Representation and Temporal Segmentation

Given a temporal window of length n seconds, the sequence length is $T = 4n$ samples (4 Hz sampling). Each window is represented as:

$$\mathbf{X} \in \mathbb{R}^{T \times C} \tag{2}$$

where $C = 3$ corresponds to $(SCR, \Delta SCR, \Delta^2 SCR)$.

To analyse the minimal temporal interval required for reliable arousal classification, window lengths were systematically varied from $n = 1$ to $n = 40$ seconds. Moreover, two segmentation strategies were evaluated. These are (i) non-overlapping windows and (ii) sliding windows with 1-second stride (4 samples). All windows belonging to the same subject were preserved within the same fold to prevent leakage.

2.4 Deep Architectures Selected

The evaluated architectures were selected according to the biophysical characteristics of EDA and its heterogeneous temporal dynamics.

- **1D-CNN:** Convolutional filters capture localised morphological patterns, particularly the asymmetric structure of SCR responses [8].
- **InceptionTime:** Parallel multi-scale kernels allow simultaneous modelling of slow tonic evolution and rapid phasic spikes [2].
- **Temporal Convolutional Networks (TCN):** Dilated convolutions expand receptive fields efficiently, modelling extended autonomic latency and sustained activation states [6].
- **Time-Series Transformer (TST):** Global self-attention enables long-range dependency modelling across entire observation windows [15].
- **PatchTST:** Patch-based tokenisation preserves local waveform continuity while reducing computational complexity [4,16]. Given 4 Hz sampling, patch lengths of $P \in \{4, 8, 16\}$ correspond to 1, 2, and 4 s, respectively.

For convolutional and TCN-based models, architectures follow standard implementations with receptive fields adjusted to match maximum window lengths. For TST, each time-step vector $\mathbf{x}_t \in \mathbb{R}^C$ is projected to latent dimension D:

$$\mathbf{Z}^{(0)} = \mathbf{X}\mathbf{W}_e + \mathbf{W}_{pos} \tag{3}$$

where $\mathbf{W}_e \in \mathbb{R}^{C \times D}$ and $\mathbf{W}_{pos}$ is learnable positional encoding.

For PatchTST, each channel is segmented into patches of length P and projected to dimension D. The number of patches is:

$$N = \left\lfloor \frac{T - P}{S} \right\rfloor + 1 \tag{4}$$

Channel-independent encoding is applied prior to concatenation and classification.

2.5 Training Strategy

All models were trained end-to-end using AdamW optimiser with cross-entropy loss. The initial learning rate was set to 10^{-3} with cosine annealing scheduling. Mini-batch size was 32. Training was conducted for up to 100 epochs with early stopping (patience = 15) based on validation loss.

Regularisation included dropout (0.1–0.3), weight decay (10^{-4}), and gradient clipping (norm = 1.0). Hyperparameters were tuned under identical search budgets across architectures:

- Encoder layers $L \in \{1, 2, 3, 4, 6\}$
- Attention heads $H \in \{1, 2, 4, 8\}$
- Embedding dimension $D \in \{16, 32, 64, 128\}$
- Feed-forward dimension $\in \{32, 64, 128, 256\}$
- Patch size $P \in \{4, 8, 16\}$

Normalisation (z-score) was computed using training-fold statistics only.

2.6 Validation and Statistical Analysis

A strict Leave-One-Subject-Out (LOSO) protocol was enforced to guarantee subject-independent evaluation. Performance metrics included Accuracy, Precision, Recall, F1-score, and AUC. Results were averaged across folds. Statistical differences between models were assessed using the Wilcoxon signed-rank test with $\alpha = 0.05$.

To provide additional insight into model behaviour, attention distributions (for Transformer-based models) and gradient-based saliency maps ($S = |\partial y/\partial \mathbf{X}|$) were analysed to quantify temporal and channel-level relevance. A channel ablation protocol (SCR only; SCR+ΔSCR; SCR+ΔSCR+$\Delta^2 SCR$) was also evaluated under the same LOSO framework.

3 Results and Discussion

3.1 Overall Performance Comparison

Table 1 summarises the subject-independent LOSO performance across the five evaluated architectures. Under strict cross-subject validation, all models achieve stable and consistent results, with F1-scores ranging from 0.796 (1D-CNN) to 0.852 (PatchTST). Transformer-based architectures systematically outperform convolutional baselines across all reported metrics.

Table 1. Overall LOSO performance comparison (mean ± std across folds).

Model	Acc	Prec	Rec	F1	AUC
1D-CNN	0.812 ± 0.074	0.804 ± 0.079	0.789 ± 0.083	0.796 ± 0.078	0.872 ± 0.063
TCN	0.828 ± 0.068	0.819 ± 0.071	0.806 ± 0.075	0.812 ± 0.072	0.884 ± 0.058
InceptionTime	0.836 ± 0.064	0.828 ± 0.068	0.817 ± 0.071	0.822 ± 0.067	0.892 ± 0.054
TST	0.851 ± 0.059	0.844 ± 0.062	0.836 ± 0.064	0.840 ± 0.061	0.903 ± 0.049
PatchTST	**0.863 ± 0.053**	**0.856 ± 0.057**	**0.848 ± 0.059**	**0.852 ± 0.056**	**0.912 ± 0.045**

Table 2. Wilcoxon signed-rank test p-values (F1-score per LOSO fold). Bold values indicate statistical significance ($p < 0.05$).

	TCN	InceptionTime	TST	PatchTST
1D-CNN	**0.041**	**0.018**	**0.006**	**0.002**
TCN		0.073	**0.021**	**0.008**
InceptionTime			0.064	**0.017**
TST				**0.048**

Specifically, TST achieves an F1-score of 0.840 and AUC of 0.903, while PatchTST provides the best overall performance (F1-score = 0.852, AUC = 0.912). In addition to higher mean performance, a progressive reduction in fold-wise variability is observed when moving from CNN-based models to attention-based architectures. The standard deviation decreases from 0.078 (1D-CNN) to 0.056 (PatchTST), indicating improved robustness to inter-subject physiological variability.

To formally assess statistical significance, Wilcoxon signed-rank tests were conducted on per-fold F1-scores. The resulting p-values are reported in Table 2. Statistically significant differences ($p < 0.05$) are highlighted in bold. PatchTST demonstrates significant improvements over all other evaluated architectures. TST also significantly outperforms both 1D-CNN and TCN. In contrast, differences between TCN and InceptionTime and between InceptionTime and TST are not statistically significant, suggesting a gradual performance transition rather than abrupt architectural superiority.

The observed performance hierarchy can be interpreted in light of the temporal modelling capacity of each approach. Convolutional architectures primarily capture localised SCR morphology but remain limited in integrating distributed temporal dependencies across longer windows. TCN improves receptive field coverage through dilated convolutions; however, dependency modelling remains structurally constrained by fixed convolutional patterns.

Transformer-based architectures introduce adaptive temporal weighting via self-attention mechanisms, enabling dynamic contextualisation of physiological events across the entire observation window. This is particularly relevant for EDA signals, where sympathetic activation unfolds through temporally distributed processes including onset, rising phase, peak, and recovery dynamics. PatchTST further refines this mechanism by preserving local waveform continuity through patch-based tokenisation while simultaneously reducing sequence fragmentation and computational burden. This structured tokenisation appears to enhance stability under inter-subject variability, which likely explains both the improved mean performance and reduced standard deviation observed across folds.

Overall, these results indicate that architectural choices aligned with the physiological structure of EDA signals yield measurable gains under strict subject-independent evaluation, particularly when global dependency modelling is incorporated.

3.2 Comparison with Previous Feature-Based Modelling

In prior work based on handcrafted features and Deep-SVM modelling [11], comparable subject-independent protocols yielded F1-scores in the range of 0.80–0.83 depending on window length. The present results demonstrate consistent performance gains when moving toward end-to-end temporal representation learning.

The improvement is incremental rather than dramatic, suggesting that modern architectures refine temporal modelling capacity while the intrinsic discriminative power of EDA remains bounded by physiological variability.

3.3 Minimal Temporal Interval Behaviour

As shown in Fig. 1, performance improves rapidly as window length increases, with Transformer-based models degrading more gracefully for short observation intervals. When analysing performance as a function of window length, very short segments ($n \leq 3$ s) exhibit reduced discriminative performance across all architectures, likely due to incomplete SCR morphology within limited temporal context.

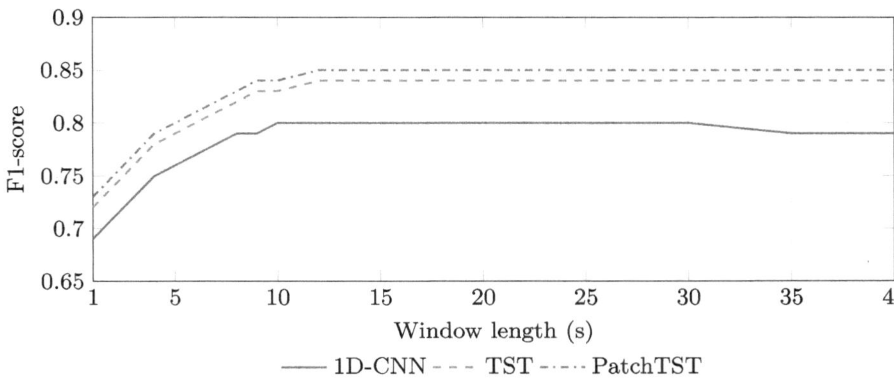

Fig. 1. F1-score as a function of window length under LOSO evaluation. Transformer-based models degrade more gradually for short temporal windows and stabilise at higher performance levels.

Transformer-based models degrade more gradually in short windows compared to CNN-based approaches, indicating improved ability to leverage partial dynamic cues and derivative information. Performance stabilises for intermediate window lengths, with diminishing improvements beyond full sympathetic response completion.

These findings support the feasibility of near-real-time arousal detection in wearable scenarios when global dependency modelling is employed.

3.4 Architectural Behaviour and Generalisation

Convolutional architectures primarily capture localised waveform structures but remain limited in integrating distributed temporal dependencies. TCN improves long-range modelling via dilated convolutions yet retains fixed receptive field constraints.

Transformer-based models dynamically weight temporal contributions through self-attention mechanisms, enabling adaptive contextualisation of physiological events. PatchTST further balances local waveform preservation with reduced sequence length, contributing to its improved performance and lower fold-to-fold variability.

3.5 Interpretability Insights

Attention distributions reveal that Transformer-based models assign greater importance to temporal regions corresponding to SCR onset and rising phases, aligning with physiological expectations of sympathetic activation (Fig. 2).

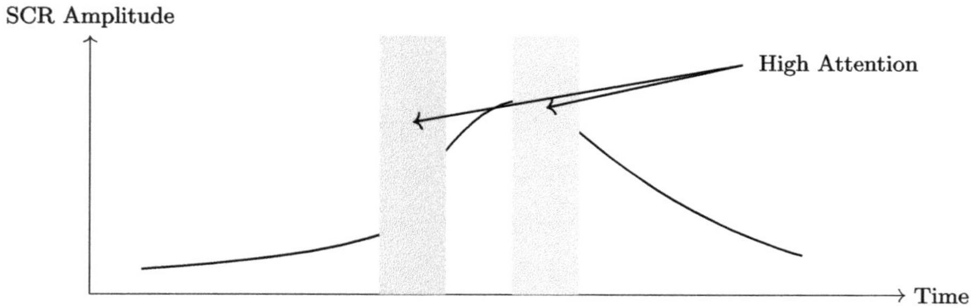

Fig. 2. Conceptual illustration of attention distribution over a phasic SCR response. Blue region denotes the early onset phase and red region indicates the peak activation phase. Arrows represent higher attention weights assigned by Transformer-based models. (Color figure online)

Beyond aggregate performance, interpretability analysis was conducted to examine whether the learned representations align with known physiological mechanisms of sympathetic activation. For Transformer-based architectures (TST and PatchTST), attention distributions consistently showed higher weights around the onset and rising phases of the SCR component, which correspond to the most informative segments of the phasic response. In contrast, later decay intervals received comparatively lower attention, suggesting that the models selectively focus on discriminative temporal regions rather than uniformly weighting the entire window.

Gradient-based saliency analysis indicates increased contribution of derivative channels (ΔSCR and $\Delta^2 SCR$) during early segments, supporting their relevance for rapid detection modelling. Channel ablation experiments confirm incremental performance improvements when derivative information is included. Together, these findings suggest that the models exploit both amplitude and dynamic change information in a complementary manner.

The alignment between attention patterns, saliency distributions, and established SCR morphology provides additional physiological plausibility to the learned decision mechanisms, reinforcing the validity of Transformer-based approaches for subject-independent arousal modelling.

3.6 Computational Considerations

Although Transformer-based models introduce higher computational complexity compared to CNN baselines, PatchTST mitigates quadratic attention cost through patch tokenisation. This results in a favourable trade-off between predictive accuracy, robustness, and computational feasibility for medium-scale physiological datasets.

4 Conclusion and Future Work

This study presented a systematic comparison of modern deep architectures for subject-independent arousal classification from Electrodermal Activity (EDA). Under a strictly controlled Leave-One-Subject-Out (LOSO) validation framework, Transformer-based architectures consistently outperformed convolutional baselines, with PatchTST achieving the best trade-off between predictive performance, stability across subjects, and computational feasibility.

Compared to previous feature-engineered approaches based on Deep-SVM modelling [11], end-to-end sequence modelling provides incremental but consistent improvements, suggesting that architectural advancements primarily refine temporal representation capacity rather than fundamentally altering the intrinsic discriminative potential of EDA signals.

The minimal temporal interval analysis further indicates that reliable arousal detection can be achieved within short observation windows when global dependency modelling is employed, reinforcing the feasibility of near-real-time wearable applications. Additionally, interpretability analyses revealed that Transformer-based models assign greater relevance to SCR onset and rising phases, aligning with known physiological dynamics of sympathetic activation. The inclusion of derivative channels contributed to early detection performance, supporting their relevance in dynamic modelling.

Overall, the findings demonstrate that physiologically-informed architectural design, combined with strict subject-independent validation, is critical for robust affective computing from biosignals.

Future work will explore self-supervised pre-training strategies for physiological time-series, multi-modal integration with complementary signals (e.g., heart rate variability), and transfer learning approaches to improve generalisation in smaller datasets. Further investigation into attention dynamics across varying stress intensities may also provide deeper insights into model interpretability and physiological representation.

Acknowledgments. This work was partially supported by grant PID2023-149753OB-C21 funded by MICIU/AEI/10.13039/501100011033 and by "ERDF A way to make Europe". Grant 2025-GRIN-38441, funded by Universidad de Castilla-La Mancha (UCLM) and "ERDF A way to make Europe". This work was partially supported by Programa Iberoamericano de Ciencia y Tecnología para el Desarrollo (CYTED) (through Red [225RT0169]). This work was also partially funded by CIBERSAM of the Instituto de Salud Carlos III (ISCIII).

References

1. Azad, M.S., Lee, S., Choi, M.: Single- and multimodal deep learning of EEG and EDA responses to construction noise: performance and ablation analyses. Sensors **25**(21), 6775 (2025)
2. Ismail Fawaz, H., et al.: InceptionTime: finding AlexNet for time series classification. Data Min. Knowl. Disc. **34**(6), 1936–1962 (2020). https://doi.org/10.1007/s10618-020-00710-y
3. Hossain, M.B., Kong, Y., Posada-Quintero, H.F., Chon, K.H.: Electrodermal activity: applications and challenges. In: The Cambridge Handbook of Research Methods and Statistics for the Social and Behavioral Sciences. Cambridge University Press (2024)
4. Kim, J., Park, K., Yun, S., Lee, S.: PPT: patch order do matters in time series pretext task. In: The Thirteenth International Conference on Learning Representations (2025)
5. Liu, Y., Xue, W., Yang, L., Li, M.: Deep learning-based EEG emotion recognition: a review. Brain Sci. **16**(1), 41 (2025)
6. Luo, D., Wang, X.: ModernTCN: a modern pure convolution structure for general time series analysis. In: The Twelfth International Conference on Learning Representations. OpenReview (2024)
7. Meijer, A.L., Arts, L.P., Gomez, R., van den Broek, E.L.: Electrodermal activity: a continuous monitor of well-being. J. Smart Cities Soc. **2**, 193–207 (2023)
8. Nandipati, K.K., Pal, S., Mitra, R.: Electrodermal activity (EDA) morphologies and prediction of engagement with simple moving average crossover: a mixed-method study. Sensors **24**(14), 4565 (2024)
9. Portal, F., De Lope, J., Graña, M.: A performance benchmarking review of transformers for speaker-independent speech emotion recognition. Int. J. Neural Syst. **35**(10), 2530001 (2025)
10. Sakimura, H., Nagaya, T., Nishi, T., Kurahashi, T., Kohda, K., Muramoto, N.: Long-term variability in physiological-arousal relationships for robust emotion estimation. arXiv:2508.18782 (2025)
11. Sánchez-Reolid, R., Martínez-Rodrigo, A., López, M.T., Fernández-Caballero, A.: Deep support vector machines for the identification of stress condition from electrodermal activity. Int. J. Neural Syst. **30**(07), 2050031 (2020)
12. Sánchez-Reolid, R., López de la Rosa, F., Sánchez-Reolid, D., López, M.T., Fernández-Caballero, A.: Machine learning techniques for arousal classification from electrodermal activity: a systematic review. Sensors **22**(22), 8886 (2022)
13. Sánchez-Reolid, R., de la Rosa, F.L., López, M.T., Fernández-Caballero, A.: One-dimensional convolutional neural networks for low/high arousal classification from electrodermal activity. Biomed. Signal Process. Control **71**, 103203 (2022)
14. Sun, Y., Ke, M., Wang, L.: A novel inceptionTime framework for multimodal physiological signal-based mental state recognition using wearable device. In: 2025 5th International Conference on Bioinformatics and Intelligent Computing, pp. 563–570. ACM (2025)
15. Tsirmpas, C., Konstantopoulos, S., Andrikopoulos, D., Kyriakouli, K., Fatouros, P.: Transformer-based decomposition of electrodermal activity for real-world mental health applications. Sensors (Basel) **25**(14), 4406 (2025)
16. Wang, Y., Huang, N., Li, T., Yan, Y., Zhang, X.: Medformer: a multi-granularity patching transformer for medical time-series classification. In: 38th Conference on Neural Information Processing Systems. Curran Associates, Inc. (2024)

“Intelligent Systems for Assessment, Treatment, and Assistance in early stages of Alzheimer”

Estimating MMSE Scores from Conversational Transcripts Using Quantized Large Language Models

Albeto Penas Díaz(✉), Miguel A. Patricio(✉), José M. Molina(✉), and Antonio Berlanga(✉)

Computer Science and Engineering Department, Applied Artificial Intelligence Group, Universidad Carlos III de Madrid, Madrid, Spain
apenas@pa.uc3m.es, mpatrici@inf.uc3m.es, {molina,aberlan}@ia.uc3m.es
https://ror.org/03ths8210 , https://giaa.uc3m.es/

Abstract. Early detection of cognitive impairment is critical for timely intervention; yet, traditional screening instruments such as the Mini-Mental State Examination (MMSE) require trained personnel and face-to-face administration, limiting their scalability. This work explores whether a large language model (LLM) can be adapted to detect cognitive impairment from conversational transcripts in a low-resource setting. We formulate the task as a binary classification problem (`normal` vs.`impaired`) using transcripts from the ADReSS dataset, in which patients describe the Cookie Theft picture. A LLaMA 3.2-1B-Instruct model is adapted to this task through Quantized Low-Rank Adaptation (QLoRA), which keeps the base model frozen and quantized while training only a small set of adapter parameters (approximately 1.8% of the total). To quantify the effect of adaptation, we compare the fine-tuned model against the same architecture without any task-specific training. The frozen baseline collapses to majority-class prediction (accuracy 0.529, macro-F_1 0.346), confirming the absence of discriminative ability. In contrast, the QLoRA-adapted model achieves 0.941 accuracy and 0.940 macro-F_1 on a stratified validation split, correctly classifying both classes with high confidence. These results demonstrate that parameter-efficient fine-tuning can yield effective cognitive screening models from conversational language even under limited data and compute constraints.

Keywords: Dementia detection · Cognitive impairment · Large language models · QLoRA · MMSE

1 Introduction

Dementia is a progressive neurodegenerative syndrome characterized by a decline in memory, cognitive abilities, language, and problem-solving skills. Accurate and early assessment of cognitive impairment is essential for timely intervention

J. M. Ferrández Vicente et al. (Eds.): IWINAC 2026, LNCS 16574, pp. 365–374, 2026.
https://doi.org/10.1007/978-3-032-27314-7_34

and care planning. Among standardized screening instruments, the Mini-Mental State Examination (MMSE) [6] is one of the most widely used tools to evaluate cognitive status, providing a quantifiable measure of impairment [4,9–11]. However, traditional MMSE assessments are often administered in clinical settings, requiring trained personnel and patient compliance, which may limit scalability in large populations or longitudinal monitoring.

In recent years, natural language processing (NLP) and machine learning (ML) techniques have been increasingly explored to automate cognitive assessment, particularly through the analysis of spoken or written language. The spontaneous nature of conversation offers a rich source of linguistic and paralinguistic features that can reflect cognitive status [15]. Advances in large language models (LLMs), coupled with resource-efficient fine-tuning methods such as Quantized Low-Rank Adaptation (QLoRA) [7], offer new opportunities for building scalable and low-resource cognitive screening systems that estimate MMSE scores from transcribed dialogs.

2 Related Works

The application of ML and NLP to cognitive assessment has gained considerable attention in recent literature. Penfold et al. [13] developed a machine learning model to predict mild cognitive impairment using clinical notes processed with NLP, bypassing direct MMSE administration. Similarly, Fayemiwo et al. [5] showed that features such as immediate word recall could predict dementia using decision trees and support vector machines.

Searle et al. [15] evaluated various deep learning techniques, including DistilBERT, for MMSE score prediction from conversational speech, highlighting the potential of transformer-based models. Agbavor and Liang [1] used LLMs on transcripts of spontaneous speech to predict Alzheimer's Disease with promising accuracy, demonstrating the robustness of pretrained models in clinical NLP tasks.

Shakeri and Farmanbar [16] performed a systematic review of NLP applications in Alzheimer's research, emphasizing the growing efficacy of deep learning approaches in MMSE estimation. Meanwhile, Parsapoor et al. [12] explored the impact of different speech tasks and modalities on machine learning performance for dementia assessment.

Other studies, such as Amini et al. [3], investigated multimodal approaches that combine audio and textual data for MMSE prediction. These works generally support the hypothesis that linguistic features—such as lexical diversity, syntactic complexity, and speech fluency—are correlated with MMSE outcomes.

Despite these advances, many models remain limited by computational inefficiencies or a lack of scalability. Recent work has shown that parameter-efficient methods such as QLoRA can make fine-tuning large language models more practical and repeatable under constrained resources [2], including in low-resource scenarios where labeled data and compute are scarce [8]. This work proposes the integration of quantized LLMs using QLoRA to address these limitations, providing a lightweight and cost-effective framework for estimating MMSE scores from natural dialog transcripts.

3 Proposal

3.1 Problem Formulation and Motivation

The goal of this work is to detect cognitive impairment from conversational transcripts in a way that is practical when both data and computational resources are limited. This study evaluates whether a language model can identify linguistic and interaction patterns that correlate with cognitive decline and use them as a screening signal.

The clinical reference used throughout this line of work is the Mini-Mental State Examination (MMSE) [6]. The MMSE is a brief cognitive screening test that yields a score (typically in the range $[0, 30]$) derived from questions covering cognitive domains such as orientation, attention, recall, language, and visuospatial abilities. While it is not a definitive diagnosis, it is widely used because it provides a standardized and time-efficient proxy for global cognitive status and supports longitudinal monitoring. Prior work has also shown that MMSE score ranges can be mapped onto clinically meaningful severity stages and can act as a surrogate for other staging instruments in some contexts [14].

In practice, however, the most robust and actionable version of the task in our setting is a simple binary decision: distinguishing `normal` vs. `impaired`. This is not just a matter of convenience. When the dataset is small, a fine-grained formulation forces the model to learn several uncertain decision boundaries from very few examples per category, a difficulty that is often compounded by class imbalance. In short, with limited data, a binary formulation is a more stable target and a better fit for realistic screening workflows (triage, follow-up decisions, and longitudinal monitoring).

3.2 Fine-Tuning with QLoRA

Once the binary setting is established, the next question is how to adapt a pretrained LLM to this domain under limited data and compute. This is particularly important in clinical NLP, where the relevant signal can be subtle and the amount of labeled data is often small due to privacy constraints and annotation costs. In this context, comparing a frozen model to an adapted model provides a direct way to quantify the effect of task-specific learning beyond general-purpose pretraining and is aligned with recent analyzes of QLoRA fine-tuning behavior and repeatability under limited resources [2].

To make this adaptation feasible, QLoRA is used, a parameter-efficient fine-tuning approach that keeps the base model weights frozen (and quantized for memory efficiency) while training a small set of low-rank adapter parameters (Fig. 1). This enables adaptation to the dementia detection task with a fraction of the trainable parameters and does not require the same compute budget as full fine-tuning while still capturing task-specific signals. These properties make QLoRA particularly suitable for low-resource settings, as discussed in work on [8].

The adapted model is expected to provide a clear advantage over the frozen baseline because it can incorporate task-specific cues present in transcripts while maintaining a small number of trainable parameters. Quantitative comparisons are reported in the Results section.

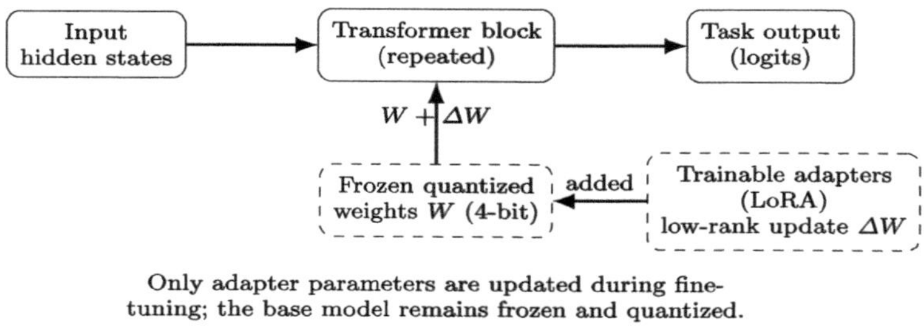

Fig. 1. Conceptual view of QLoRA: low-rank adapters learn an update ΔW that is injected into selected linear layers, while the base weights W remain quantized and frozen.

3.3 Methodology

We keep the overall methodology intentionally simple: we use the same LLM backbone and the same classification head, and we compare two regimes—a frozen baseline vs. a QLoRA-adapted model—under the same evaluation protocol. Since the official test split lacks labels, we evaluate on a stratified validation split derived from the training data. We report accuracy and macro-F_1 (to reduce sensitivity to class imbalance), and use the confusion matrix to characterize error patterns. This design isolates the effect of parameter-efficient fine-tuning and directly addresses the core question of the paper: how much does QLoRA-style adaptation matter when using LLMs for dementia detection from conversational transcripts under limited data and compute?

4 Results and Discussions

Experiments were conducted on a binary cognitive impairment detection task based on conversational transcripts, where labels were derived from MMSE-based grouping (`normal` vs. `impaired`). Since the official test split does not provide ground-truth labels, model selection and performance reporting rely on a stratified validation split constructed from the available training data. This strategy ensures that class proportions are preserved while enabling a controlled comparison between training regimes. Performance is primarily evaluated using

Table 1. Validation performance comparison between the frozen baseline and the QLoRA-adapted model (stratified validation split, $n_{\text{val}} = 17$).

Model	Accuracy	Macro-F_1	Weighted-F_1	Avg. confidence
Frozen (no fine-tuning)	0.529	0.346	0.367	0.769
QLoRA-adapted (fine-tuned)	0.941	0.940	0.941	0.948

accuracy and macro-F_1, the latter being particularly relevant in the presence of potential class imbalance, as it assigns equal importance to both classes. In addition to aggregate metrics, confusion matrices are examined to provide a more granular characterization of model behavior and error distribution.

Two training configurations are compared under an identical evaluation protocol in order to isolate the effect of parameter-efficient adaptation. The first configuration corresponds to a frozen baseline, in which the quantized backbone remains entirely fixed and no task-specific learning is performed. The second configuration employs QLoRA-based adaptation, where only a small set of low-rank adapter parameters is optimized while the quantized base model remains frozen. This controlled comparison allows the observed performance differences to be attributed directly to task-specific fine-tuning rather than architectural changes or differences in optimization strategy. Unless explicitly stated otherwise, all reported results refer to the validation split.

Table 1 summarizes the validation performance of both regimes. A substantial performance gap is observed between the frozen baseline and the QLoRA-adapted model across all reported metrics. The frozen configuration attains an accuracy of 0.529 and a macro-F_1 of 0.346, indicating limited discriminative capacity and a strong bias toward the majority class. In contrast, the QLoRA-adapted model achieves an accuracy of 0.941 and a macro-F_1 of 0.940, with consistent improvements also reflected in the weighted-F_1 and average confidence scores. These results demonstrate that task-specific adaptation is essential for capturing subtle linguistic and interactional cues associated with cognitive impairment in conversational transcripts. Notably, these gains are obtained while updating only a small fraction of the total parameters, reinforcing the suitability of adapter-based fine-tuning in low-resource clinical contexts.

To further contextualize these findings, performance is compared against simple reference baselines derived from the class distribution of the validation set. Random uniform guessing yields an expected accuracy of 0.500, random stratified guessing yields 0.502, and a majority-class classifier that always predicts `normal` yields 0.529. The frozen model effectively reproduces the majority-class behavior, confirming that general-purpose pretrained knowledge alone is insufficient to separate the two clinical categories in this setting. By contrast, the QLoRA-adapted model reaches an accuracy of 0.941, corresponding to an absolute improvement of +0.412 over the majority baseline (Fig. 2). This substantial margin indicates that the adapted model is learning meaningful, task-specific representations rather than merely exploiting class imbalance or prior distributional biases.

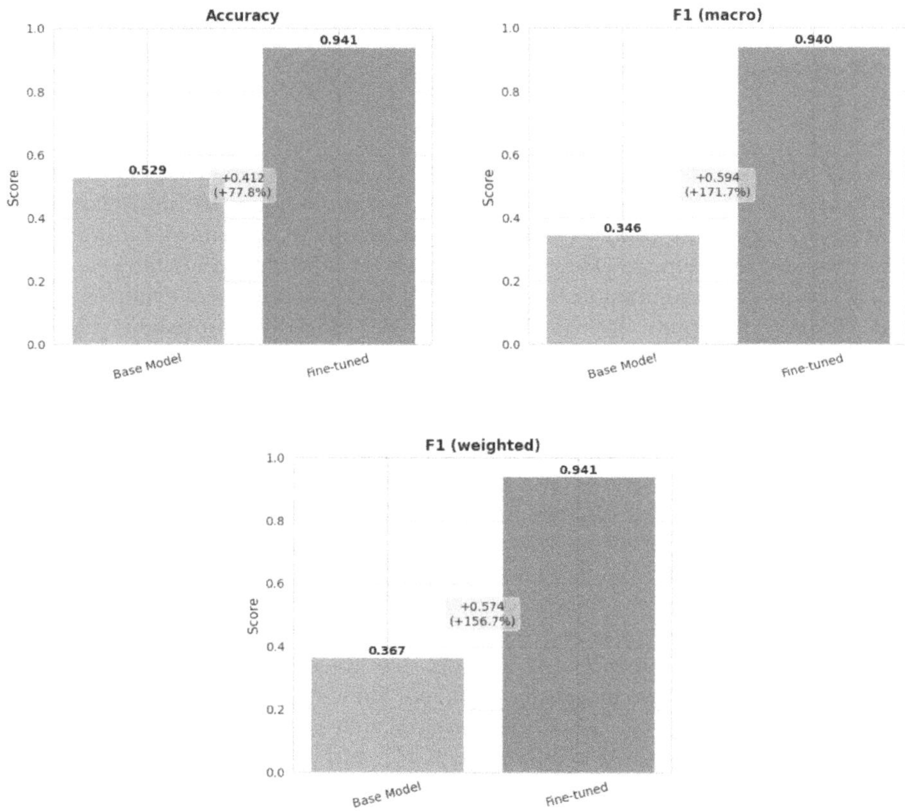

Fig. 2. Comparison between the frozen base model and the QLoRA-adapted model on the validation split. The figure reports accuracy, macro-F_1 and weighted-F_1.

A more detailed examination of the confusion matrices (Fig. 3) further clarifies the behavioral differences between both regimes. The frozen baseline assigns nearly all validation samples to the `normal` class, resulting in a degenerate decision boundary that fails to capture impairment-related signals. In contrast, the QLoRA-adapted model produces balanced predictions across both classes. The corresponding classification report shows precision/recall/F_1 values of 0.900/1.000/0.947 for the `normal` class and 1.000/0.875/0.933 for the `impaired` class. The remaining errors primarily involve `impaired` samples misclassified as `normal`, a pattern that is consistent with borderline or mildly impaired cases where conversational markers of decline may be subtle. Importantly, no systematic collapse toward a single class is observed in the adapted regime.

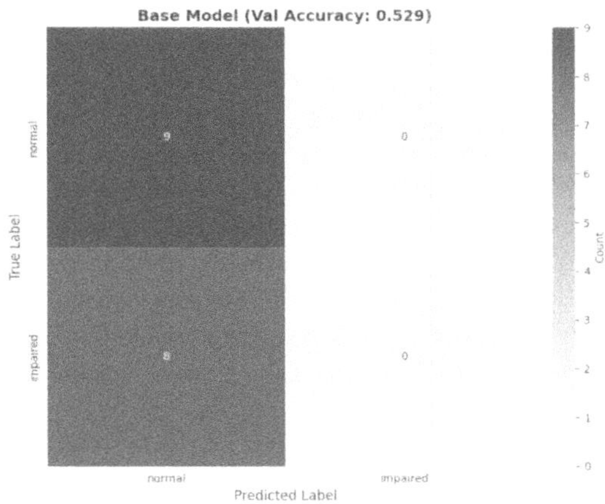

(a) Frozen baseline

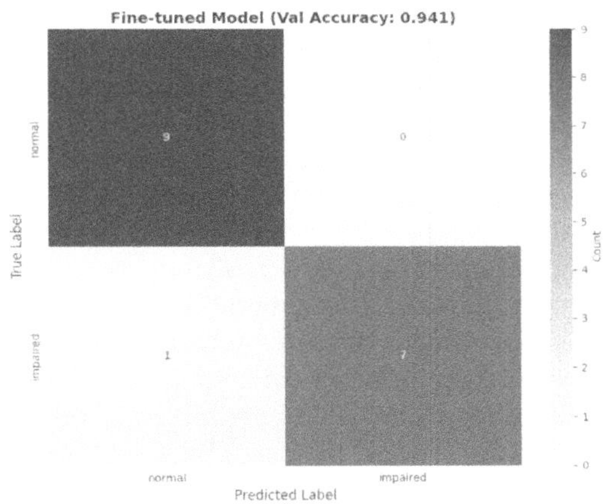

(b) QLoRA-adapted model

Fig. 3. Confusion matrices on the validation split for (a) the frozen baseline and (b) the QLoRA-adapted model.

Overall, the results highlight that a frozen large language model, even when prompted in an instruction-following format, does not provide sufficient discriminative power for this clinical classification task. The decision boundary depends on domain- and dataset-specific cues, including aspects of conversational coherence, response organization, lexical retrieval patterns, and error types, which are not reliably activated without targeted adaptation. In low-resource clinical scenarios, this limitation is particularly critical, as privacy constraints and annotation costs typically restrict the size of labeled datasets, increasing variance and the risk of overfitting.

QLoRA offers a practical compromise between full fine-tuning and zero-shot prompting. By maintaining the base model in a quantized and frozen state while training only a small set of low-rank adapters, memory consumption and computational requirements are significantly reduced. This parameter-efficient approach enhances sample efficiency and enables specialization under constrained computational budgets. Moreover, restricting updates to a limited subset of parameters effectively acts as an implicit regularization mechanism, reducing the risk of overfitting and encouraging the model to encode compact, task-relevant adaptations. In this setting, parameter-efficient fine-tuning emerges as a viable operational regime for adapting large language models to cognitively meaningful classification tasks under realistic data and resource constraints.

5 Conclusions

This paper studied the feasibility of estimating MMSE-related cognitive impairment from conversational transcripts under strict data and computational constraints using a quantized large language model. The task was formulated as a binary decision problem (`normal` vs. `impaired`) in order to obtain a stable target in a low-sample regime, and the contribution focused on isolating the effect of parameter-efficient adaptation by comparing a frozen pretrained model with the same architecture fine-tuned using QLoRA adapters.

The results reveal a clear behavioral difference between pretrained competence and task adaptation. The frozen model systematically collapsed to a majority-class prediction, showing that general linguistic knowledge encoded in pretrained LLMs does not directly transfer to cognitive impairment detection. This qualitative behavior can be observed in Fig. 3, where the frozen regime assigns nearly all samples to a single class regardless of the input transcript. In contrast, the QLoRA-adapted model produces balanced predictions across both classes, indicating that the decision boundary is learned from conversational structure rather than inherited from dataset priors. The gain, therefore, reflects learned task representations rather than the exploitation of pretraining biases.

From a machine learning perspective, the findings highlight a practical operating point for low-resource specialization of LLMs. Full fine-tuning is often infeasible, while frozen prompting lacks discriminative capacity; parameter-efficient fine-tuning provides an intermediate regime where specialization emerges with limited supervision and minimal computational overhead. The approach demonstrates that conversational structure contains sufficient regularities for impairment-related classification when an appropriate adaptation mechanism is used.

However, the present evaluation remains limited in scope and primarily demonstrates feasibility. The experiments rely on a small validation split derived from a single dataset, which may allow dataset-specific artifacts to influence performance. Consequently, the reported accuracy should be interpreted as an upper-bound estimate rather than a definitive generalization measure. Future work will therefore focus on cross-dataset validation and robustness testing across elicitation tasks, recording conditions, and linguistic variability to assess transferability beyond the training distribution.

A second research direction concerns model interpretability and representation analysis. While the adapted model is predictive, the internal evidence used to reach decisions is not yet characterized. Future studies should analyze attention patterns, token attribution, and structured linguistic features in order to determine whether the model captures meaningful discourse phenomena such as coherence disruptions, repetitions, or semantic drift, rather than superficial dataset correlations.

Another important aspect is reliability under uncertainty. Screening applications require calibrated confidence rather than raw classification accuracy. Future work will investigate probabilistic calibration, abstention strategies, and uncertainty-aware decision thresholds to enable safe integration into decision-support pipelines.

The binary classification setting also constitutes a simplified approximation of cognitive assessment. Extending the framework toward ordinal severity prediction, continuous MMSE estimation, and longitudinal modeling will allow the system to capture gradual cognitive decline rather than discrete categories. This likely requires combining parameter-efficient fine-tuning with regression objectives and temporal modeling across multiple patient observations.

Finally, conversational transcripts provide only part of the available signal. Integrating acoustic and temporal speech features with textual representations is a natural extension that may improve robustness and reduce reliance on lexical artifacts. Beyond modeling improvements, future research should also address bias across demographic groups and evaluate generalization under real conversational conditions.

Overall, the work supports the view that parameter-efficient adaptation enables small LLMs to specialize in cognitively meaningful language patterns in low-data regimes. The proposed framework should therefore be understood as a scalable learning paradigm for extracting domain-specific behavioral signals from natural language, with potential applications in continuous monitoring scenarios once robustness and generalization are thoroughly validated.

Acknowledgments. This research was funded by the Spanish Ministry of Science and Innovation (Ministerio de Ciencia e Innovación) under projects PID2023-151605OB-C22 and PDC2025-165937-C22.

References

1. Agbavor, F., Liang, H.: Predicting dementia from spontaneous speech using large language models. PLOS Digit. Health **1**(12) (2022). https://doi.org/10.1371/journal.pdig.0000168
2. Alahmari, S.S., Hall, L.O., Mouton, P.R., Goldgof, D.B.: Repeatability of fine-tuning large language models illustrated using QLoRA. IEEE Access **12**, 153221–153231 (2024). https://doi.org/10.1109/ACCESS.2024.3470850

3. Amini, S., et al.: Automated detection of mild cognitive impairment and dementia from voice recordings: a natural language processing approach. Alzheimer's Dementia **19**(3) (2023). https://doi.org/10.1002/alz.12721
4. Chi, L., Sharma, A., Gebhardt, A., Colonel, J.: Predicting cognitive decline: a multimodal AI approach to dementia screening from speech. In: 2025 IEEE Conference on AI and Data Analytics, ICAD 2025 (2025). https://doi.org/10.1109/ICAD65464.2025.11114053
5. Fayemiwo, M.A., et al.: Immediate word recall in cognitive assessment can predict dementia using machine learning techniques. Alzheimer's Res. Therapy **15**(1) (2023). https://doi.org/10.1186/s13195-023-01250-5
6. Folstein, M.F., Folstein, S.E., McHugh, P.R.: "Mini-mental state". a practical method for grading the cognitive state of patients for the clinician. J. Psychiatr. Res. **12**(3) (1975). https://doi.org/10.1016/0022-3956(75)90026-6
7. Hu, E., et al.: LoRA: low-rank adaptation of large language models. In: ICLR 2022 - 10th International Conference on Learning Representations (2022)
8. Joshi, S., Khan, M.S., Dafe, A., Singh, K., Zope, V., Jhamtani, T.: Fine tuning LLMs for low resource languages. In: 2024 5th International Conference on Image Processing and Capsule Networks (ICIPCN), pp. 511–519 (2024). https://doi.org/10.1109/ICIPCN63822.2024.00090
9. Kelebie, M., et al.: Psychometric properties of international HIV dementia Scale as screening tool for neurocognitive disorder among people living with HIV/AIDS. Sci. Rep. **15**(1) (2025). https://doi.org/10.1038/s41598-025-21659-2
10. Ningthoujam, A.S., Huang, Y.P., Thiyagarajan, G., Sharma, S.: Explainable machine learning-based classification of clinical dementia ratings using a tablet-based cognitive. Assessment (2025). https://doi.org/10.1007/s44196-025-01019-8
11. de Oliveira Alves, J.: New approaches for early detection and assessment of alzheimer's disease: an analysis of recent studies. Alzheimer's Dementia **21**(S2) (2025). https://doi.org/10.1002/alz70856_102396
12. Parsapoor (Parsa), M.M., Alam, M.R., Mihailidis, A.: Performance of machine learning algorithms for dementia assessment: impacts of language tasks, recording media, and modalities. BMC Med. Inf. Decis. Making **23**(1) (2023). https://doi.org/10.1186/s12911-023-02122-6
13. Penfold, R.B., et al.: Development of a machine learning model to predict mild cognitive impairment using natural language processing in the absence of screening. BMC Med. Inf. Decis. Making **22**(1) (2022). https://doi.org/10.1186/s12911-022-01864-z
14. Perneczky, R., Wagenpfeil, S., Komossa, K., Grimmer, T., Diehl, J., Kurz, A.: Mapping scores onto stages: mini-mental state examination and clinical dementia rating. Am. J. Geriatr. Psychiatry **14**(2), 139–144 (2006). https://doi.org/10.1097/01.JGP.0000192478.82189.a8
15. Searle, T., Ibrahim, Z., Dobson, R.: Comparing natural language processing techniques for alzheimer's dementia prediction in spontaneous speech. In: Proceedings of the Annual Conference of the International Speech Communication Association, INTERSPEECH, vol. 2020-October (2020). https://doi.org/10.21437/Interspeech.2020-2729
16. Shakeri, A., Farmanbar, M.: Natural language processing in alzheimer's disease research: systematic review of methods, data, and efficacy (2025). https://doi.org/10.1002/dad2.70082

Diagnostic Tools of Neurodegenerative Conditions with Spiking Neural Networks

David Bernal-Casas(✉), Estela Díaz-López, Margarita Bachiller, and Mariano Rincón

Department of Artificial Intelligence, Universidad Nacional de Educación a Distancia (UNED), Madrid, Spain
{dbernal,ediazlopez,marga,mrincon}@dia.uned.es

Abstract. The development of reliable computational tools for diagnosing and stratifying cognitive and neurodegenerative conditions remains a major challenge in translational neuroscience. Variability in clinical presentation, overlapping symptomatology, and heterogeneity in intermediate diagnostic categories complicate automated classification. This study proposes a methodology for constructing diagnostic tools based on spiking neural networks (SNNs) that uses relevant features calculated from virtual reality tasks to assess cognitive domains commonly affected in early dementia. These domains include episodic memory, executive function, and spatial navigation. Three diagnostic groups were considered: Normal Cognition (ED1), Subtle Cognitive Impairment (ED2), and Mild Cognitive Impairment (ED3). Feature selection was performed by ranking predictors according to the magnitude of their regression coefficients, and the most informative variables were used as inputs to the SNN classifier. To assess the influence of clinical labeling on model behavior, four stratification schemes (U0.5a, U0.5b, U0.5c, U1a) were defined and evaluated. Classification accuracy was computed on the training and independent test sets, and uncertainty was quantified using 95% confidence intervals. Results indicate that model performance is strongly influenced by the definition of intermediate clinical categories, highlighting the importance of stratification strategy in computational diagnostics. The findings support the feasibility of SNN-based diagnostic frameworks while emphasizing the need for careful feature optimization and clinically grounded labeling procedures. Future work will extend validation to larger cohorts and longitudinal data to assess robustness and generalizability.

Keywords: Spiking neural networks · Subtle cognitive impairment · Diagnostic tools

1 Introduction

Neurodegenerative diseases, such as Alzheimer's disease (AD), present significant challenges in early diagnosis. Recent research indicates that deterioration in

J. M. Ferrández Vicente et al. (Eds.): IWINAC 2026, LNCS 16574, pp. 375–384, 2026.
https://doi.org/10.1007/978-3-032-27314-7_35

episodic and visuospatial memory can be detected between 2 and 20 years before the onset of the first symptoms of dementia, making it very important to develop preclinical detection tools [2,10]. Accurate classification of patients at different stages of cognitive impairment is essential for timely interventions and treatment planning. Traditional diagnostic methods rely heavily on clinical assessments, neuroimaging, and neuropsychological tests, which may be time-consuming and subject to inter-rater variability [5,9].

Recent advances in computational neuroscience have introduced spiking neural networks (SNNs) as a promising tool for modeling temporal patterns of neuronal activity. SNNs offer biologically inspired architectures that efficiently process temporal spike data and have shown promise in pattern recognition tasks [7]. Despite growing interest in SNNs for pattern recognition and signal processing, their application in clinical diagnostic modeling remains relatively limited. Furthermore, few studies systematically investigate how clinical labeling strategies influence computational classification performance. Intermediate diagnostic categories, in particular, often represent heterogeneous populations that may overlap with both healthy aging and early pathological decline.

This work aims to develop SNN-based diagnostic tools to classify individuals into three diagnostic groups: Normal Cognition (ED1), Subtle Cognitive Impairment (ED2), and Mild Cognitive Impairment (ED3). We evaluate how different clinical stratification schemes affect classification performance and explore the potential of SNNs in enhancing diagnostic accuracy. We structured the paper as follows: Sect. 2 describes the dataset, the clinical stratification schemes, the mathematical analysis of the single-neuron-per-class SNN, the train-validation-test splits and statistical analyses, and the evaluation metrics. Section 3 presents the results. Section 4 discusses findings, and Sect. 5 concludes the paper.

2 Materials and Methods

We use a subset of data from the IDENTIA project, a Spanish project funded by public and private funds whose objective is the early detection of cognitive impairment through virtual reality tasks and artificial intelligence techniques. The proposed method is a single-neuron-per-class spiking neural network (SNN) that combines feature selection and decision-making within a unified framework.

This approach assigns a distinct neuron to each class, enabling the network to process only the most relevant features associated with that class. By concentrating on essential characteristics and reducing extraneous noise, this method enhances both classification accuracy and operational efficiency. For a more in-depth exploration of this approach and its implications, please refer to [1].

2.1 Dataset

The dataset comprises multiple features for 314 patients aged 55–90, of whom 215 are female. The features were obtained from neurocognitive tests carried out using virtual reality glasses, as well as from clinical and sociodemographic data. Each patient was categorized into one of three diagnostic groups based on clinical and classical neuropsychological assessments.

- **ED1**: Normal Cognition (NC),
- **ED2**: Subtle Cognitive Impairment (SCI), and
- **ED3**: Mild Cognitive Impairment (MCI).

The intermediate category reflects individuals who exhibit cognitive alterations insufficient for full diagnostic classification but that exceed normative expectations. This group is particularly relevant for early-detection research but introduces complexity due to its heterogeneity.

For this study, 79 of the 215 variables were selected through a process of exhaustive elimination using a logistic regression model applied to subsets of the three original classes. Feature importance was quantified by the absolute values of logistic regression coefficients, which capture the strongest discriminative signals across groups. Features with the highest coefficients were selected as inputs to the SNN, ensuring that only relevant markers contributed to classification.

Continuous features were standardized to a zero mean and unit variance. Missing values were imputed using feature distributions and the patterns of missingness. Prior to modeling, exploratory data analysis was performed to evaluate distributions, outliers, and inter-feature correlations.

2.2 Clinical Stratification Schemes

As there is no clear definition for identifying profiles with subtle cognitive impairment [3, 11, 12], four scenarios with different thresholds and occurrence criteria have been created using education level and 16 normative z-scores features of classical neuropsychological tests.

The neurocognitive variables, adjusted for educational level, were used to define impairment scenarios. Subtle impairment was operationalized using two alternative cut-offs (-0.5 SD and -1 SD), with performance evaluated between the selected threshold and -1.5 SD. MCI-level impairment was defined as performance below -1.5 SD and normal cognition when above the threshold (-0.5 SD and -1 SD), as appropriate. In addition, three levels of severity have been designed in terms of occurrences within each range: a) lax, b) moderate, and c) strict, as shown in Table 1.

These schemes allow us to assess how uncertainty or heterogeneity in clinical labeling affects model performance. Figure 1 illustrates the distributions for the four designed scenarios: U0.5a, U0.5b, U0.5c, and U1a. In this notation, the number (e.g., 0.5 or 1) denotes the standard deviation (SD) of the uncertainty distribution, while the letter (a, b, or c) indicates the severity level configuration.

Table 1. Cognitive classification criteria based on normative z-scores using −0.5 SD threshold

Severity	Lax (a)	Moderate (b)	Strict (c)
NC (ED1)	$n_M = 0 \wedge n_S = 0$	$n_M = 0 \wedge n_S \leq 1$	$n_M = 0 \wedge n_S \leq 1$
SCI (ED2)	$n_M = 0 \wedge n_S \geq 1$	$n_M = 0 \wedge n_S \geq 2$	$(n_M = 1) \vee (n_M = 0 \wedge n_S \geq 2)$
MCI (ED3)	$n_M \geq 1$	$n_M \geq 1$	$n_M \geq 2$

Note. n_S = number of variables in the subtle range ($-1.5 < z < -0.5$); n_M = number of variables in the mild range ($z \leq -1.5$).

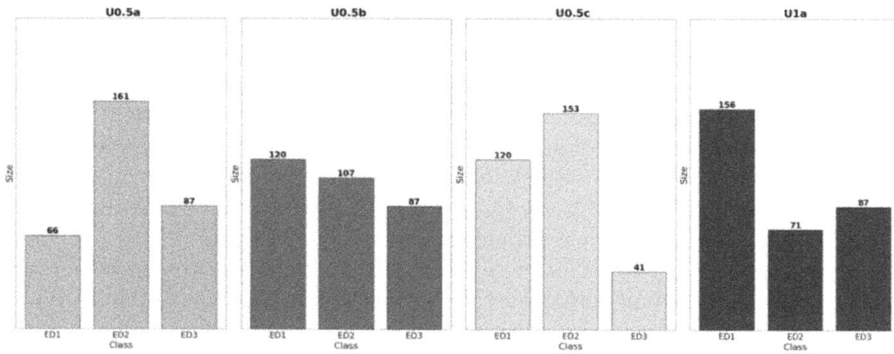

Fig. 1. Distribution of the classification of different scenarios.

2.3 Spiking Neural Networks

Spiking Neural Networks (SNNs) offer an alternative paradigm inspired by neurobiology, employing event-driven processing that can enhance energy efficiency and robustness to dynamic signals [7]. The Resonate-and-Fire (RAF) neuron is a prominent SNN model governed by a damped second-order ordinary differential equation (ODE)

$$\frac{d^2 V}{dt^2} + 2\xi \frac{dV}{dt} + \omega_0^2 V = I_{\text{in}}(t), \tag{1}$$

with a learnable damping ratio $\xi > 0$, angular frequency $\omega_0 > 0$, and an input drive $I_{\text{in}}(t)$ proportional to the weighted input. Spikes are generated when V crosses a learnable threshold V_{th}. The final decision is based on the spike count or firing rate over a discrete simulation window. All model parameters, including the neuron's intrinsic parameters $(\xi, \omega_0, V_{\text{th}})$ and the input weights $\mathbf{w}$ that determine $I_{\text{in}}(t)$, are trained end-to-end using surrogate gradients to handle the non-differentiable spiking event [13].

This dynamic system exhibits intrinsic frequency selectivity, making it particularly suitable for processing time-varying inputs [4]. Despite the non-differentiable nature of spike generation, such models can be trained effectively within deep learning frameworks using surrogate gradients to approximate the derivative of the spiking mechanism [13].

Input Handling. Input images are flattened into vectors, and their feature intensities are scaled to the range $[0, 1]$. These analog intensity values are converted into spike trains. We used Poisson-distributed spike trains where the firing rate of each input neuron is proportional to the corresponding feature intensity [8].

Training Protocol. Models were trained using the Adam optimizer [6] with a cross-entropy loss function. We used a batch size of 512 and trained for up to 1000 epochs, employing early stopping, which terminated training if the validation loss did not improve for 20 consecutive epochs. The initial learning rate was set to 10^{-3} and was reduced by a factor of 0.9 if the validation loss plateaued (with a minimum learning rate of 10^{-15}). To ensure robust results, all experiments were repeated with 100 different random seeds. Models were implemented in PyTorch 1.12.1 and trained on an NVIDIA Quadro T1000 GPU.

Discrete-Time Implementation for Training and Inference. For learning and deployment, we used a first-order state-space discretization, in particular, the explicit Euler method. We also implemented the semi-implicit Euler and Runge-Kutta 4 methods, but the differences in the results were not statistically significant. Using the explicit Euler method, we may define $x_1(t) = V(t)$ and $x_2(t) = \dot{V}(t)$. From Eq. (1) follows:

$$\dot{x}_1 = x_2, \qquad \dot{x}_2 = -2\xi\, x_2 - \omega_0^2\, x_1 + I_{\mathrm{in}}(t). \tag{2}$$

Now, using a sampling step Δt, we obtain the next discrete equations:

$$x_1^{k+1} = x_1^k + \Delta t\, x_2^k, \tag{3}$$

$$x_2^{k+1} = x_2^k + \Delta t\Big(- 2\xi\, x_2^k - \omega_0^2\, x_1^k + I_{\mathrm{in}}^k\Big). \tag{4}$$

To ensure stability, we select Δt such that $\Delta t\, \omega_0 \ll 1$, which is a criterion for properly sampling the harmonic oscillator. We also utilize the same time grid as the spike window. The spike readout uses a hard threshold V_{th}:

$$\text{if } x_1^{k+1} \geq V_{\mathrm{th}} \text{ then emit spike.}$$

During training we use a standard surrogate-gradient $\sigma_\beta(z) = \frac{1}{1+\exp(-\beta z)}$ around the threshold with slope β.

Transfer Function. We consider the subthreshold RAF dynamics as a linear time-invariant (LTI) second-order system driven by an input current $I_{\mathrm{in}}(t)$ with damping ratio $\xi > 0$ and angular frequency $\omega_0 > 0$. In the frequency domain ($s = \mathrm{j}\omega$), the transfer function from input I_{in} to membrane potential V is

$$H(\mathrm{j}\omega) = \frac{V(\mathrm{j}\omega)}{I_{\mathrm{in}}(\mathrm{j}\omega)} = \frac{1}{-\omega^2 + \mathrm{j}\, 2\xi\omega + \omega_0^2}. \tag{5}$$

Thus, the power gain is

$$\left|H(\mathrm{j}\omega)\right|^2 = \frac{1}{(\omega_0^2 - \omega^2)^2 + (2\xi\omega)^2}, \tag{6}$$

which exhibits a resonance with a peak at $\omega^\star = \omega_0\sqrt{1-2\xi^2}$, considering that $\xi < 1/\sqrt{2}$.

2.4 Train/Validation/Test Splits and Statistical Analysis

We employ a standard (and "approximately") 80/10/10 split for training, validation, and testing, ensuring that participants are stratified for subject-independent evaluation. The training set comprises 254 subjects, and both the validation and test sets each comprise 30 subjects. Both the validation and test sets are balanced, with 10 subjects per clinical stratification group, regardless of the stratification scheme used. In all our experimental results, we present the mean and standard error of the mean (SEM), computed from 100 independent trials, each using a distinct random seed. This approach ensures a robust and reliable assessment of accuracy and variability in our findings.

2.5 Evaluation Metrics

Classification performance was evaluated using balanced accuracy (%) and 95% confidence intervals (95% CI), as well as training vs. testing comparisons. The impact of each stratification scheme on model performance was analyzed.

3 Results

This section analyzes the performance of the proposed readouts, emphasizing their effectiveness with real data. We establish baseline performance and interpret our findings within the context of our case study, offering valuable insights into their implications and applications.

3.1 Classification Performance

These results indicate that a single-neuron-per-class SNN can perform classification reasonably well with remarkably few neurons, just one per class. This has significantly fewer parameters than the tens of thousands typically found in deep learning models. The models are also highly efficient. Inference latency on an NVIDIA Quadro T1000 GPU averaged 15.2 ms per epoch, making the approach suitable for clinical applications (Fig. 2 and Table 2).

Table 2. Balanced accuracy for different clinical stratification schemes. Values are reported as mean ± SEM (%).

Scheme	Training Accuracy (%)	Testing Accuracy (%)
U0.5a	57.40 ± 1.52	50.77 ± 1.52
U0.5b	56.20 ± 1.70	48.37 ± 1.50
U0.5c	48.57 ± 1.49	45.30 ± 1.42
U1a	47.80 ± 1.50	41.57 ± 1.60

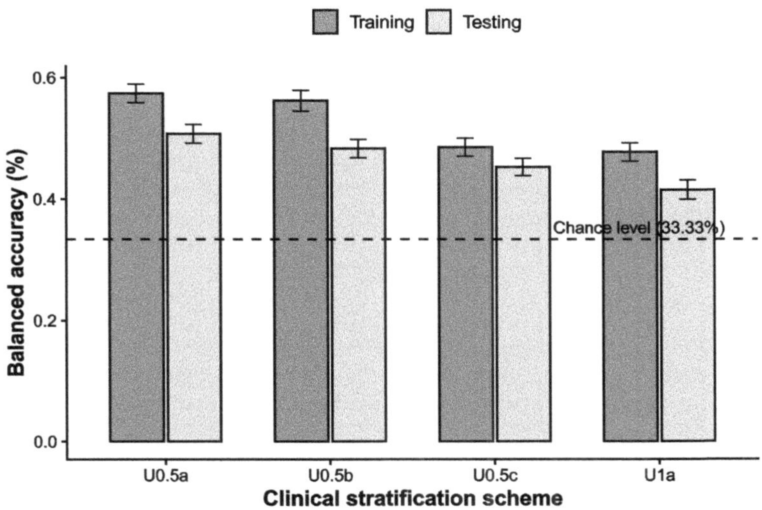

Fig. 2. Balanced accuracy across schemes. Bars show mean accuracy ± 95% CI. Grey shades distinguish training (dark) and testing (light) sets. Dashed horizontal line indicates chance level (33.33%) for 3-class classification.

3.2 Interpretation

The single-neuron-per-class SNN effectively distinguishes Normal Cognition from subjects with Subtle Cognitive Impairment and Mild Cognitive Impairment. Accuracy values exceeded chance level across schemes. However, differences among schemes indicate sensitivity to labeling definitions. This finding underscores the impact of clinical definition on computational outputs. Error bars representing 95% CI revealed moderate variability across seeds. The magnitude of uncertainty was consistent across schemes, suggesting stable but label-sensitive performance.

4 Discussion

The results indicate that SNNs can potentially serve as diagnostic tools for cognitive and neurodegenerative conditions. Importantly, classification performance was consistently above chance level, indicating that the model captured condition-relevant structure rather than spurious or random associations in the data. The above-chance accuracy suggests that the features encoded by the single-neuron-per-class SNN contain discriminative information sufficient to differentiate between groups, even in the presence of clinical variability. While the absolute performance metrics must be interpreted cautiously, given the current sample size and cohort characteristics, the findings nonetheless provide proof-of-concept evidence that sensitive, biologically inspired architectures can extract meaningful diagnostic signals. With further validation and refinement, such approaches may contribute to objective, data-driven support tools that complement existing clinical assessments in cognitive and neurodegenerative disorders.

Despite these strengths, several limitations of the present study warrant careful consideration. Most notably, the current dataset remains relatively small, which may limit the generalizability and stability of the learned representations. Small sample sizes increase the risk of overfitting, particularly in high-dimensional feature spaces, and may limit the model's capacity to capture the full spectrum of phenotypic variability. Future studies with larger and more diverse samples will be essential to confirm the robustness of the observed findings.

In addition, external validation across independent cohorts is necessary to establish the reproducibility and clinical utility of the proposed framework. Without replication in geographically and demographically distinct populations, the model's generalizability beyond the original training context remains uncertain. Rigorous cross-cohort validation will be critical for determining whether the learned temporal features reflect fundamental characteristics of the condition under investigation rather than cohort-specific artifacts.

The heterogeneity within the ED2 group further complicates classification. Variability in symptom profiles, severity, comorbidities, and potentially underlying neurobiological mechanisms may introduce overlapping feature distributions that challenge even temporally sensitive models. This intra-group diversity likely contributes to classification ambiguity and underscores the need for more refined phenotypic stratification. Incorporating additional clinical, behavioral, or biomarker information may help disentangle subgroups and improve discriminative performance.

Future work will therefore focus on systematic feature optimization and on integrating longitudinal data. Refining feature selection and representation strategies—potentially through adaptive encoding schemes or hybrid architectures—may enhance signal-to-noise ratios and improve classification stability. Moreover, incorporating longitudinal trajectories will allow the model to leverage within-subject temporal evolution, offering a richer characterization of disease progression and potentially enabling earlier or more precise differentiation among subtypes. Together, these directions aim to strengthen both the methodological rigor and translational relevance of SNN-based approaches in this domain.

5 Conclusion

This work contributes to the growing body of research at the intersection of neuroscience and artificial intelligence by demonstrating the diagnostic potential of SNN-based models in clinically relevant contexts. While additional validation is required, the results support continued investigation of biologically inspired architectures as objective, data-driven tools to complement traditional clinical assessment in cognitive and neurodegenerative disorders.

Acknowledgment. The authors would like to thank the IDENTIA and SCREENIA projects for providing the clinical data used in this study. The IDENTIA project (CPP2021-009109) was funded by the Spanish Ministry of Science and Innovation (MICIN), the State Research Agency (AEI) and the European Union's NextGenerationEU/PRTR programme. The SCREENIA project (CPP2024-011736) was funded by the Spanish Ministry of Science and Innovation and Universities (MICIU), the State Research Agency (AEI) and the European Union's NextGenerationEU/PRTR programme. We would also like to extend our sincere appreciation to the reviewers for their time and consideration of our manuscript.

Disclosure of Interests. The authors declare no conflicts of interest.

References

1. Bernal-Casas, D., Gallego, J.: A single-neuron-per-class readout for image-encoded sensor time series. Mathematics **13**(24), 3893 (2025). https://doi.org/10.3390/math13243893. https://www.mdpi.com/2227-7390/13/24/3893
2. Caselli, R.J., et al.: Neuropsychological decline up to 20 years before incident mild cognitive impairment. Alzheimer's Dementia (2019)
3. Edmonds, E.C., Delano-Wood, L., Galasko, D.R., Salmon, D.P., Bondi, M.W.: Subtle cognitive decline and biomarker staging in preclinical Alzheimer's disease. J. Alzheimer's Disease **47**(1), 231–242 (2015). https://doi.org/10.3233/JAD-150128. https://journals.sagepub.com/doi/abs/10.3233/JAD-150128, pMID: 26402771
4. Izhikevich, E.: Resonate-and-fire neurons. Neural Netw. **14**, 883–894 (2001)
5. Jack, C.R., et al.: NIA-AA research framework: toward a biological definition of Alzheimer's disease. Alzheimer's Dementia **14**(4), 535–562 (2018)
6. Loshchilov, I., Hutter, F.: Decoupled weight decay regularization. In: International Conference on Learning Representations (2019). https://openreview.net/forum?id=Bkg6RiCqY7
7. Maass, W.: Networks of spiking neurons: the third generation of neural network models. Neural Netw. **10**(9), 1659–1671 (1997). https://doi.org/10.1016/S0893-6080(97)00011-7
8. O'Connor, P., Neil, D., Liu, S.C., Delbrück, T., Pfeiffer, M.: Real-time classification and sensor fusion with a spiking deep belief network. Front. Neurosci. **7**, 178 (2013). https://doi.org/10.3929/ethz-b-000075617
9. Petersen, R.C., et al.: Mild cognitive impairment: clinical characterization and outcome. Arch. Neurol. **58**(3), 345–351 (2014)
10. Scribano Parada, M.d.l.P., et al.: Preclinical cognitive markers of Alzheimer disease and early diagnosis using virtual reality and artificial intelligence: literature review. JMIR Med. Inform. **13**, e62914 (2025). https://doi.org/10.2196/62914. https://medinform.jmir.org/2025/1/e62914

11. Seo, E.H., Kim, H., Lee, K.H., Choo, I.H.: Altered executive function in pre-mild cognitive impairment. J. Alzheimers Dis. **54**(3), 933–940 (2016)
12. Tondo, G., et al.: Brain metabolism and amyloid load in individuals with subjective cognitive decline or pre-mild cognitive impairment. Neurology **99**(3), e258–e269 (2022)
13. Yanguas-Gil, A.: Coarse scale representation of spiking neural networks: backpropagation through spikes and application to neuromorphic hardware. In: International Conference on Neuromorphic Systems 2020, pp. 1–7 (2020)

Do Contrastive Representations Help in Low-Sample Tabular Clinical Data? Insights from Cognitive Impairment

Berta López-Pombero[1], Estela Díaz-López[1(✉)], Margarita Bachiller[1], Marta García Rodriguez[2], and Mariano Rincón[1]

[1] Department of Artificial Intelligence, Universidad Nacional de Educación a Distancia (UNED), Madrid, Spain
blopez285@alumno.uned.es, {ediazlopez,marga,mrincon}@dia.uned.es
[2] Fundación INTRAS, Valladolid, Spain
mgr@intras.es

Abstract. Applying artificial intelligence techniques in clinical settings is often constrained by the limited availability of labeled data, class imbalance, and the heterogeneous nature of tabular clinical variables. These challenges are especially relevant in the early detection of cognitive decline, where datasets are typically small and difficult to model using deep learning approaches. In this context, classical machine learning methods often remain highly competitive. This work investigates the contribution of contrastive learningbased representations when applied to small and imbalanced tabular clinical datasets. Using a real-world clinical dataset focused on different stages of cognitive impairment, we analyze whether contrastive representations are able to capture discriminative structure in the data and under which conditions they provide advantages over traditional machine learning approaches. The evaluation considers multiple diagnostic scenarios of increasing complexity and examines both the separability of the learned latent space and the resulting classification performance. The results show that contrastive representations can be effective in simpler diagnostic scenarios, where class boundaries are more clearly defined, and provide stable and interpretable latent spaces. However, their performance degrades in more complex scenarios with higher class overlap, where classical machine learning models continue to exhibit an overall advantage. These findings highlight the role of contrastive learning as a complementary tool rather than a replacement for traditional methods, and emphasize the importance of scenario-dependent evaluation when applying representation learning techniques to real-world clinical tabular data.

Keywords: cognitive impairment · contrastive learning · tabular data · supervised classification · clinical diagnosis

J. M. Ferrndez Vicente et al. (Eds.): IWINAC 2026, LNCS 16574, pp. 385–395, 2026.
https://doi.org/10.1007/978-3-032-27314-7_36

1 Introduction

Early detection of cognitive decline is a major clinical priority [1], as timely interventions can significantly delay disease progression and improve patients' quality of life. In recent years, artificial intelligence techniques have been increasingly explored to support this task by identifying subtle patterns in clinical data that may not be evident through traditional assessment methods. However, the practical application of advanced learning approaches in real-world clinical settings remains challenging.

A key limitation arises from the nature of available clinical data. In many healthcare scenarios, datasets are small, heterogeneous, and highly imbalanced across diagnostic categories, particularly in tabular clinical settings where variables capture diverse cognitive, demographic, and functional measurements. Under these conditions, deep learning models often struggle to generalize effectively, and classical machine learning methods continue to demonstrate strong and competitive performance [2]. While contrastive learning has been proposed as a promising representation learning paradigm, its behavior in small and imbalanced tabular clinical datasets remains insufficiently characterized, especially across diagnostic scenarios of varying complexity. This raises important questions about when contrastive representations provide meaningful advantages and how they compare to established classical approaches in realistic clinical contexts.

Contrastive learning has recently attracted attention as a paradigm for learning latent representations by encouraging samples with similar clinical profiles to be mapped closer together while separating dissimilar cases. In the context of small and imbalanced tabular clinical datasets, this property is particularly relevant for analyzing the structure of the data and the separability of diagnostic groups, even when improvements in predictive performance are not guaranteed.

In this work, we address this gap by investigating the following research questions:

- Q1: What contributions are made by contrastive learningbased representations when applied to small and imbalanced tabular clinical datasets?
- Q2: Under which conditions are contrastive representations beneficial, and when do classical machine learning methods represent a better choice?

To answer these questions, we analyze contrastive representations learned from a real-world clinical dataset related to cognitive impairment, evaluating both the structure of the latent space and the resulting classification performance across diagnostic scenarios of increasing complexity. Rather than aiming to demonstrate universal performance gains, this study provides a critical and scenario-dependent assessment of the role of contrastive learning in the analysis of clinical tabular data.

2 Related Work

Classical machine learning models have been widely used for the early detection of cognitive decline using tabular clinical data. Linear models, tree-based methods, and ensemble techniques have consistently shown robust performance in clinical scenarios characterized by limited sample sizes and class imbalance, and are therefore commonly regarded as strong baselines in clinical decision-support systems [3,4].

In recent years, representation learning approaches have been explored as an alternative way to analyze complex data [5]. In particular, contrastive learning has been investigated as a means of learning latent representations by bringing related samples closer while separating dissimilar ones. Although initially developed for domains such as computer vision and natural language processing, several studies have adapted contrastive learning frameworks to tabular data, motivated by their potential to exploit limited labeled information [6,8,9].

Within tabular settings, contrastive approaches include siamese architectures based on pairwise similarity learning as well as supervised contrastive formulations that incorporate label information directly into the learning objective [10–12]. These methods focus on structuring the latent space according to semantic or clinical similarity, rather than optimizing predictive performance alone, as discussed in recent surveys on contrastive learning [13].

In clinical contexts, latent representations have been used to support both classification and exploratory analysis, including the study of class separability and population structure through visualization and distance-based evaluations. However, the effectiveness of contrastive representations in small and imbalanced tabular clinical datasets, particularly in comparison with classical machine learning models across diagnostic scenarios of varying complexity, remains insufficiently characterized. This gap provides the motivation for the empirical analysis presented in this work.

3 Materials and Methods

3.1 Dataset Description

The experiments presented in this study are conducted on a real-world clinical dataset collected within the context of the IDENTIA project, a Spanish public–private funded project aimed at the early detection of cognitive impairment using artificial intelligence techniques. This study uses a subset of variables from the original dataset. This subset consists of information on 314 individuals and 21 heterogeneous tabular variables that capture cognitive, demographic and functional information. Table 1 provides a quantitative description of the clinical dataset used in this study, including the distribution of subjects across diagnostic groups and the total number of variables considered.

Each subject is assigned to one of three diagnostic categories reflecting different stages of cognitive impairment. These categories correspond to cognitively healthy individuals (ED1), subjects with subtle cognitive impairment (ED2), and subjects with mild cognitive impairment (ED3). The resulting dataset exhibits an uneven class distribution across these diagnostic groups, with ED2 being the most represented category and fewer samples belonging to the ED1 and ED3 groups.

Table 1. Quantitative description of the clinical dataset used in this study.

Description	Value
Total number of subjects	314
Subjects per diagnostic group	
ED1 (cognitively healthy)	66
ED2 (subtle cognitive impairment)	164
ED3 (mild cognitive impairment)	84
Total number of variables	21

3.2 Study Design and Methodological Overview

This study analyzes the behavior of contrastive learning–based representations under different levels of diagnostic difficulty using a set of diagnostic scenarios derived from the original clinical labels. These scenarios include both multi-class and binary classification settings and are designed to progressively increase task complexity, providing a structured framework for evaluating representation quality.

Rather than aiming for an exhaustive statistical characterization of the dataset or an extensive comparison of all existing contrastive learning variants, the methodology focuses on a representative set of approaches that allow a targeted analysis of learned representations in small and imbalanced tabular clinical datasets.

The proposed methodology comprises three main components. First, contrastive representation learning is applied to generate latent embeddings from tabular clinical data, explicitly considering pair generation strategies and class imbalance. Second, classical machine learning models are employed as baseline methods to contextualize the behavior of contrastive representations within established tabular learning paradigms. Finally, the learned embeddings are evaluated through latent space analysis and downstream classification tasks, enabling a scenario-dependent assessment of their strengths and limitations across diagnostic settings of increasing complexity.

3.2.1 Contrastive Representation Learning

Contrastive learning is employed to learn latent embeddings that reflect similarity relationships between clinical samples, encouraging samples from similar diagnostic profiles to be closer in the latent space while separating dissimilar cases.

Both offline and online pair generation strategies are considered. Offline strategies rely on predefined training pairs, whereas online strategies dynamically generate pairs during training based on the current state of the learned representations. This allows the analysis of contrastive learning behavior under different pair selection assumptions without focusing on exhaustive optimization of pairing mechanisms.

To address class imbalance, dynamic balancing strategies are incorporated during contrastive training to control the composition of training pairs and batches. These mechanisms ensure that minority diagnostic groups are adequately represented, enabling a fairer assessment of latent space structure across diagnostic scenarios.

3.2.2 Baseline Classical ML Models

Classical machine learning models are used as baselines to contextualize the performance of contrastive representations. These models operate directly on the original tabular clinical features and represent well-established approaches for classification in small and imbalanced datasets.

The selected baselines include linear classifiers and tree-based methods commonly applied in clinical decision-support systems due to their robustness and suitability for tabular data. Rather than emphasizing extensive model optimization, these approaches serve as reference points for evaluating the potential advantages and limitations of contrastive representations across diagnostic scenarios.

3.2.3 Latent Space Evaluation

The evaluation of contrastive representations focuses on the structure and discriminative properties of the learned latent space, complementing standard classification performance analysis.

Dimensionality reduction techniques such as UMAP and t-SNE are applied to visualize the embeddings and explore class separability, overlap, and clustering behavior across diagnostic scenarios. In addition, a centroid-based evaluation is used to assess class organization by measuring distances between samples and class centroids in the latent space.

Finally, supervised classification models are trained on the learned embeddings to evaluate their usefulness in downstream prediction tasks. Comparing these results with those obtained from the original tabular features allows the assessment of whether contrastive representations preserve or enhance diagnostically relevant information.

3.3 Experimental Setup

The experiments are conducted across a limited number of diagnostic scenarios derived from the original class labels, selected to reflect different levels of diagnostic difficulty. These scenarios include both simpler binary distinctions and more challenging settings with increased class overlap, allowing the analysis of contrastive representations as task complexity increases.

Specifically, the evaluation focuses on four representative scenarios: a binary distinction between cognitively healthy subjects and mild cognitive impairment (ED1 vs ED3), a more challenging binary setting involving subtle cognitive impairment (ED1 vs ED2), a binary scenario contrasting cognitively healthy subjects against any level of impairment by merging subtle and mild cases (ED1 vs (ED2 + ED3)), and the original multiclass scenario (ED1 vs ED2 vs ED3). Together, these scenarios cover a range of clinically relevant diagnostic difficulties and support a scenario-dependent analysis of representation quality and classification performance.

Performance is assessed using standard evaluation metrics commonly adopted in clinical classification tasks, including the area under the receiver operating characteristic curve (ROC-AUC), the F1-score, and classification accuracy. The use of multiple complementary metrics provides a balanced assessment, particularly in the presence of class imbalance.

To ensure result stability, all experiments are repeated multiple times using different random seeds, and reported results correspond to aggregated performance across repetitions, following best practices for validation with limited sample sizes [14,15]. Model evaluation is carried out using a validation strategy that preserves the distribution of diagnostic classes, ensuring comparability across scenarios.

4 Results

This section presents the main experimental results obtained in this study, focusing on the performance of contrastive representation–based approaches and classical machine learning baselines across the selected diagnostic scenarios. The results are reported using quantitative performance metrics and latent space visualizations. For clarity and to facilitate cross-scenario comparison, the main quantitative results are summarized in this section. For a deeper view of the results, a complete set of supporting tables and detailed findings for all scenarios is available in [7].

4.1 Results Across Diagnostic Scenarios

Table 2 reports the best ROC-AUC values obtained for each diagnostic scenario, comparing the strongest contrastive configuration with the best-performing classical machine learning baseline. The table provides a compact overview of performance differences across scenarios of increasing diagnostic complexity.

Table 2. Comparison between contrastive approaches and classical machine learning models across diagnostic scenarios.

Dataset	Contrastive technique	ROC-AUC	ML technique	ROC-AUC
ED1 vs ED2 vs ED3	Siamese online	0.831	AdaBoost Classifier	**0.922**
ED1 vs ED3	Siamese offline	**0.990**	Gradient Boosting Classifier	0.980
ED1 vs ED2	SupCon	0.875	Histogram-based Gradient Boosting Classifier	**0.914**
ED1 vs ED2 + ED3	Joint Contrastive Classifier	0.922	Histogram-based Gradient Boosting Classifier	**0.945**

Table 3 reports the complete set of evaluated configurations for the multiclass diagnostic scenario (ED1 vs ED2 vs ED3), which represents the most challenging setting considered in this study. This detailed presentation allows inspection of performance variability across contrastive techniques before introducing the cross-scenario summaries.

Table 3. Detailed results for the multiclass diagnostic scenario (ED1 vs ED2 vs ED3). Reported values correspond to mean performance with standard deviation across repeated experiments. Best results per metric are highlighted in bold.

Technique	Training	Classifier	Balancing	Accuracy	F1-score	ROC-AUC
Siamese	Online	HistGradientBoost	SMOTETomek	0.675 (0.078)	0.674 (0.079)	**0.831 (0.055)**
Siamese	Offline	Centroids	SMOTE	0.703 (0.082)	0.701 (0.082)	0.819 (0.054)
JointContrastive	End-to-end		Borderline-SMOTE	0.667 (0.067)	0.666 (0.067)	0.814 (0.049)
Triplet-Hard	Fine-tuning		None	0.670 (0.051)	0.670 (0.051)	0.814 (0.044)
SupCon	Feature Extraction		SMOTETomek	0.698 (0.066)	0.697 (0.066)	0.813 (0.064)
SimCLR	Feature Extraction	HistGradientBoost	SMOTETomek	0.648 (0.063)	0.646 (0.063)	0.812 (0.025)
JointContrastive	Feature Extraction	HistGradientBoost	Borderline-SMOTE	0.663 (0.051)	0.662 (0.052)	0.811 (0.046)
SupCon	Fine-tuning		SMOTETomek	0.698 (0.070)	0.698 (0.070)	0.809 (0.065)
JointContrastive	Feature Extraction	Centroids	Borderline-SMOTE	0.681 (0.060)	0.681 (0.059)	0.808 (0.038)
SupCon	Feature Extraction	Centroids	SMOTETomek	0.692 (0.089)	0.691 (0.089)	0.806 (0.050)
Triplet-Hard	Feature Extraction		None	0.656 (0.043)	0.654 (0.042)	0.803 (0.040)
SupCon	Feature Extraction	HistGradientBoost	SMOTETomek	0.678 (0.084)	0.675 (0.085)	0.802 (0.061)
Siamese	Offline	HistGradientBoost	SMOTE	**0.703 (0.087)**	**0.702 (0.087)**	0.799 (0.063)
Triplet	Fine-tuning		None	0.660 (0.085)	0.660 (0.089)	0.793 (0.060)
Triplet	Feature Extraction	HistGradientBoost	None	0.624 (0.061)	0.616 (0.064)	0.788 (0.047)
SimCLR	Fine-tuning		SMOTETomek	0.600 (0.115)	0.575 (0.135)	0.775 (0.068)
Triplet-Hard	Feature Extraction	HistGradientBoost	None	0.610 (0.063)	0.602 (0.061)	0.770 (0.047)
Siamese	Online	Centroids	SMOTETomek	0.679 (0.079)	0.679 (0.079)	0.769 (0.071)
Triplet	Feature Extraction		None	0.614 (0.076)	0.612 (0.078)	0.767 (0.053)
SimCLR	Feature Extraction	Centroids	SMOTETomek	0.662 (0.075)	0.662 (0.076)	0.736 (0.031)
Triplet	Feature Extraction	Centroids	None	0.568 (0.067)	0.559 (0.073)	0.651 (0.042)
Triplet-Hard	Feature Extraction	Centroids	None	0.608 (0.076)	0.605 (0.075)	0.620 (0.047)
SimCLR	Feature Extraction		SMOTETomek	0.397 (0.143)	0.357 (0.169)	0.613 (0.092)

Notes. (1) For each metric, values correspond to the mean performance and standard deviation obtained over five different data splits. (2) Offline siamese models employ Euclidean distance with a random pair generation strategy. (3) Online siamese models use cosine distance combined with a semi-hard pair mining strategy.

Table 4 presents the best-performing contrastive configurations for each diagnostic scenario, together with the corresponding mean classification performance and standard deviation across repeated experiments. These results provide a detailed view of contrastive performance variability across different diagnostic settings.

4.2 Latent Space Analysis

Latent space visualizations are used to examine how diagnostic information is structured in the learned contrastive embeddings. Dimensionality reduction techniques are applied to the latent representations to enable qualitative inspection of class separability.

Table 4. Best-performing contrastive results across diagnostic scenarios. Reported values correspond to mean performance with standard deviation across repeated experiments.

Scenario	Technique	Training	Classifier	Balancing	Accuracy	F1-score	ROC-AUC
ED1 vs ED2 vs ED3	Siamese	Online	HistGradientBoost	SMOTETomek	0.675 (0.078)	0.674 (0.079)	0.831 (0.055)
ED1 vs ED3	Siamese	Offline	Centroids	Borderline-SMOTE	0.947 (0.048)	0.947 (0.047)	0.990 (0.019)
ED1 vs ED2	SupCon	Feature Extraction	Centroids	Borderline-SMOTE	0.802 (0.056)	0.808 (0.051)	0.875 (0.045)
ED1 vs ED2 + ED3	Joint Contrastive	End-to-end	–	SMOTE	0.876 (0.027)	0.874 (0.027)	0.922 (0.033)

Figure 1 shows the UMAP projection of the learned latent space for the multiclass diagnostic scenario (ED1 vs ED2 vs ED3) using the best-performing contrastive approach. The visualization reveals overlap between diagnostic groups, particularly involving the subtle cognitive impairment class (ED2).

Figure 2 reports the corresponding ROC curves for the same scenario. The curves indicate different levels of discrimination performance across diagnostic classes, with lower values observed for the intermediate impairment group.

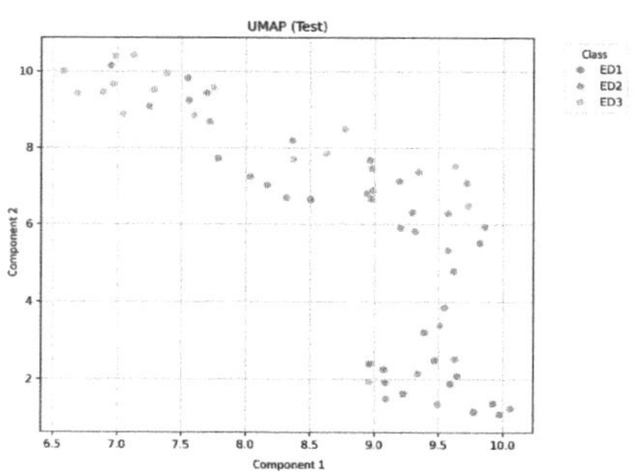

Fig. 1. UMAP projection of the learned latent space for the multiclass diagnostic scenario (ED1 vs ED2 vs ED3) using the online siamese approach.

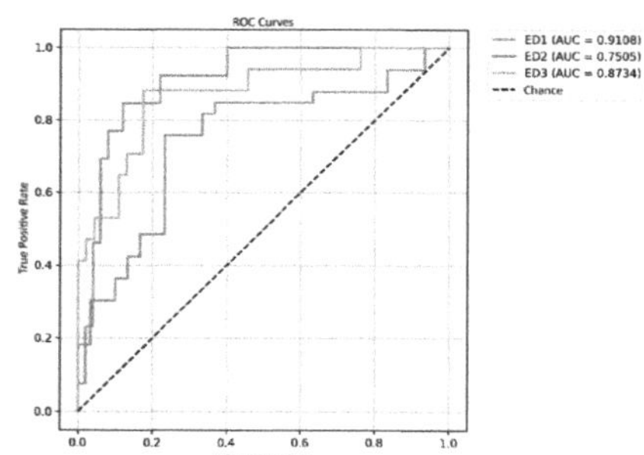

Fig. 2. ROC curves for the multiclass diagnostic scenario (ED1 vs ED2 vs ED3) using the online siamese approach.

5 Discussion

The results obtained in this study indicate that the effectiveness of contrastive representation learning in tabular clinical data is strongly dependent on the diagnostic scenario under consideration. Across scenarios with well-separated diagnostic groups, contrastive approaches achieve competitive classification performance and exhibit coherent organization in the learned latent space. These findings suggest that contrastive representations are able to preserve relevant diagnostic structure when class boundaries are clearly defined.

However, as diagnostic complexity increases, the limitations of contrastive representations become more apparent. Scenarios involving subtle cognitive impairment are characterized by substantial overlap between classes, both in the original feature space and in the learned latent representations. This overlap is reflected in the progressive degradation of classification performance observed across scenarios and in the latent space visualizations, where intermediate diagnostic stages are difficult to disentangle.

In contrast, classical machine learning models demonstrate more stable performance across increasingly challenging diagnostic settings. Their robustness suggests that the inductive biases of traditional tabular learning methods and their direct exploitation of feature interactions are better suited to clinical scenarios characterized by subtle and overlapping diagnostic boundaries. These observations are consistent with previous studies reporting strong performance of classical models on small and heterogeneous tabular datasets.

From a clinical and methodological perspective, these results indicate that both latent space organization and predictive performance evolve consistently with the underlying difficulty of the diagnostic task. Contrastive representations appear effective in scenarios with clearer class separation, while their limitations become more evident as class overlap increases. This behavior is consistent with prior work showing that, in small and heterogeneous datasets, classical machine learning models often remain more robust and stable than deep or representation learning approaches [14,15].

6 Conclusions and Future Work

This work investigated the contribution of contrastive representation learning when applied to small and imbalanced tabular clinical datasets, with a particular focus on different diagnostic scenarios related to cognitive impairment. The central research question addressed whether contrastive representations provide meaningful advantages over classical machine learning approaches, and under which conditions their use is justified.

The results show that the effectiveness of contrastive representations is strongly dependent on the diagnostic scenario. In simpler settings, where diagnostic groups are more clearly separated, contrastive learning is able to generate coherent latent representations and achieve competitive classification performance. In contrast, in more complex scenarios involving subtle cognitive impairment and higher class overlap, classical machine learning models remain more robust and reliable. These findings indicate that contrastive learning does not constitute a universal replacement for traditional approaches in clinical tabular data analysis.

From a practical and clinical perspective, contrastive representations should be interpreted as complementary analytical tools rather than standalone predictive solutions. Their main value lies in supporting exploratory analysis and interpretability, particularly in scenarios with well-defined class boundaries. Careful, scenario-aware evaluation is therefore essential when considering the application of representation learning techniques in real-world clinical settings.

Future work should explore the behavior of contrastive representations in larger and more diverse clinical tabular datasets. While this study focuses on small and imbalanced settings, contrastive learning is inherently designed to benefit from increased data availability. Assessing whether the observed limitations persist at larger scales remains an important direction for future research.

Acknowledgement. The authors would like to thank the IDENTIA and SCREENIA projects for providing the clinical data used in this study. The IDENTIA project (CPP2021-009109) was funded by the Spanish Ministry of Science and Innovation (MICIN), the State Research Agency (AEI) and the European Union's NextGenerationEU/PRTR programme. The SCREENIA project (CPP2024-011736) was funded by the Spanish Ministry of Science and Innovation and Universities (MICIU), the State Research Agency (AEI) and the European Union's NextGenerationEU/PRTR programme. We would also like to extend our sincere appreciation to the reviewers for their time and consideration of our manuscript.

Disclosure of Interests. The authors declare that they have no competing interests.

References

1. World Health Organization: Global Status Report on the Public Health Response to Dementia, World Health Organization (2021)
2. Ren, W., Zhao, T., Huang, Y., Honavar, V.: Deep Learning within Tabular Data: Foundations, Challenges, Advances and Future Directions. arXiv preprint arXiv:2501.03540 (2025)
3. Grinsztajn, L., Oyallon, E., Varoquaux, G.: Why do tree-based models still outperform deep learning on typical tabular data? In: NeurIPS Datasets and Benchmarks Track (2022)
4. Shwartz-Ziv, R., Armon, A.: Tabular data: deep learning is not all you need. arXiv preprint arXiv:2106.03253 (2022)
5. Bengio, Y., Courville, A., Vincent, P.: Representation learning: a review and new perspectives. IEEE Trans. Pattern Anal. Mach. Intell. **35**(8), 1798–1828 (2013). https://doi.org/10.1109/TPAMI.2013.50
6. Bahri, D., Jiang, H., Tay, Y., Metzler, D.: SCARF: self-supervised contrastive learning using random feature corruption. arXiv preprint arXiv:2106.15147 (2021)
7. Pombero, L.: Berta: Aplicación de redes siamesas y técnicas contrastivas sobre datos tabulares para el diagnóstico del deterioro cognitivo. Trabajo Fin de Máster en Ingeniería y Ciencia de Datos, UNED (2025)
8. Uçar, T., Hajiramezanali, E., Edwards, L.: Subsetting features of tabular data for self-supervised representation learning. In: Advances in Neural Information Processing Systems (NeurIPS), p. 34 (2021)
9. Dastagir, M.B.A., Tariq, O., Han, D.: TabCLR: contrastive learning representation of tabular data classification for indoor-outdoor detection. IEEE Access **12**, 102505–102520 (2024)
10. Hadsell, R., Chopra, S., LeCun, Y.: Dimensionality reduction by learning an invariant mapping. In: Proceedings of the IEEE Computer Society Conference on Computer Vision and Pattern Recognition (CVPR), pp. 1735–1742. IEEE (2006)

11. Chen, T., Kornblith, S., Norouzi, M., Hinton, G.: A simple framework for contrastive learning of visual representations. In: Proceedings of the International Conference on Machine Learning (ICML), vol. 119, pp. 1597–1607. Proceedings of Machine Learning Research (PMLR) (2020)
12. Khosla, P., et al.: Supervised contrastive learning. In: Advances in Neural Information Processing Systems (NeurIPS), vol. 33, pp. 18661–18673 (2020)
13. Hu, H., Wang, X., Zhang, Y., Chen, Q., Guan, Q.: A comprehensive survey on contrastive learning. Neurocomputing **610**(1), 128645 (2024)
14. Vabalas, A., Gowen, E., Poliakoff, E., Casson, A.J.: Machine learning algorithm validation with a limited sample size. PLoS ONE **14**(11), e0224365 (2019)
15. Brigato, L., Iocchi, L.: A close look at deep learning with small data. arXiv preprint arXiv:2003.12843 (2020)

“Neuroprosthesis, Ethics. EPISTEAM”

Validation of an Integrated Virtual Reality Platform for Low Vision and Visual Neuroprostheses Simulation

Maria del Mar Ayuso Arroyave[1(✉)], Leili Soo[1], Antonio Lozano[1], Roberto Morollón Ruiz[1], Aimee Solzbacher[1], Cristina Soto-Sánchez[1], and Eduardo Fernandez[1,2,3,4]

[1] Bioengineering Institute and Cátedra Bidons Egara, University Miguel Hernández, 03202 Elche, Spain
maria.ayusoa@umh.es
[2] CIBER Research Center on Bioengineering, Biomaterials and Nanomedicine (CIBER BBN), 28029 Madrid, Spain
[3] John Moran Eye Center, University of Utah, Salt Lake City 84132, USA
[4] Radboud University, Donders Centre for Neuroscience, Nijmegen, The Netherlands

Abstract. Prosthetic Vision Simulation (PVS) platforms are vital for advancing visual neuroprosthesis research, yet existing systems often lack real-time capability or support for multiple implant types. We present NEUROVISION, a modular, wireless VR platform that integrates retinal and cortical prosthesis simulations, visual pathology rendering, object detection, and eye-tracking in a unified real-time environment. Developed in Python/C# and integrated with the PICO 4 Enterprise headset, NEUROVISION demonstrated real-time performance across most configurations. The IMIE implant and Object Detection modules were identified as the main computational bottlenecks, while pre-session calibration improved eye-tracking accuracy to 0.48°. This validation establishes NEUROVISION as a robust test bench for research and visual restoration strategies optimization.

Keywords: Visual neuroprostheses · Prosthetic vision simulation · Visual pathology simulation · Virtual Reality · eye-tracking · object detection

1 Introduction

1.1 Motivation: The Urgent Need for Visual Restoration Tools

According to the World Health Organization, 338 million people worldwide live with blindness or visual impairment [1], mainly due to Retinitis Pigmentosa (RP) and Age-related Macular Degeneration (AMD). Visual prostheses aim to partially restore vision by electrically stimulating the retina or visual cortex, yet the outcomes remain limited to simple light perceptions [2]. Bridging the gap between electrical stimulation and coherent visual perception remains a key

J. M. Ferrández Vicente et al. (Eds.): IWINAC 2026, LNCS 16574, pp. 399–409, 2026.
https://doi.org/10.1007/978-3-032-27314-7_37

challenge. In parallel, simulating visual pathologies and prosthetic vision allows tasks-based exploration of disease-altered and electrically induced vision, offering a controlled framework to test hypotheses without patient involvement.

1.2 State of the Art and the Gap in Literature

The development of visual prostheses has driven parallel advances in simulation tools, which offer a safe and accessible way to study how phosphene-based vision may support functional tasks. Given the invasive nature of these devices and the scarcity of first-in-human trials, simulations provide valuable insights before clinical testing. Early studies used on-screen psychophysics paradigms [3], later evolving into immersive Virtual Reality (VR) platforms for behavioral assessment [4].

Despite this progress, current platforms have limitations that restrict their use in comprehensive, multimodal studies. Pulse2Percept [5] and Dynaphos [6] are robust retinal and cortical simulators, respectively, but are desktop-based and lack VR or eye-tracking support. Conversely, VR-SPV [7] demonstrates VR feasibility but focuses on a single implant and omits visual pathology or object detection modules. Currently, there is no platform that unifies the following key functionalities in a real-time environment.

1.3 Aim of the Paper

Building on these needs, this paper presents the Neuro-Visual Integrated Simulation and Testing Architecture (NEUROVISION) and reports its technical validation. The validation assesses real-time performance through Motion-to-Photon (M2P) latency, Frame Rate (FPS) stability, eye-tracking reliability, and wireless robustness under various simulation conditions.

2 Methods

2.1 Platform Description

Architecture. The NEUROVISION architecture has been designed using a client-server scheme (Unity/Python) to address the inherent incompatibility between the frameworks of visual simulation (Python) and the low latency graphics engine required for the immersive management of the VR headset (Unity/C#). The system operates via a wireless connection TCP/IP (Transmission Control Protocol/Internet Protocol) through the 5GHz band to ensure the maximum bandwidth and the minimum latency in the local environment.

The simulation operates in a continuous real-time loop: the client (PICO 4 Enterprise, Unity C#) captures the environment via passthrough cameras, records eye-tracking data, and sends both to the server (PC, Python). The server manages the Guided User Interface (GUI) and simulation settings, applies the selected prosthetic or pathological simulation to the Region of Interest (ROI), and returns the processed frame, which the client renders on the headset with lowest possible latency.

Modules. The system's modular design allows flexible switching and combination of visual simulations. Python integration ensures compatibility with major visual prosthesis frameworks.

Two Python modules support prosthetic vision simulation: Dynaphos, an open-source visual cortex prosthesis simulator that generates Gaussian phosphenes based on contrast and cortical mapping, allowing adjustment of parameters such as phosphene count, field of view (FoV), and temporal dynamics; and Pulse2Percept, an open-source retinal prosthesis simulator capable of modelling clinical devices such as Argus I, Argus II, and IMIE.

Low-vision simulations use OpenCV and scikit-image filters to reproduce the functional effects of common pathologies: cataracts (blur and yellowing), retinitis pigmentosa (tunnel vision, blur, night effect), glaucoma (tunnel vision), and age-related macular degeneration (central scotoma or focal blur). Finally, a YOLOv8 model (Ultralytics) enables real-time object detection, dynamically framing the ROI or highlighting relevant objects to simulate assistive visual aids.

Guided User Interface. The GUI (Fig. 1), implemented on the server (Python/ Tkinter), acts as a central control panel for configuring, monitoring, and managing experimental sessions. It supports multiple input sources, including the PICO 4 Enterprise, local cameras, Pupil Labs, and Tobii Pro 3 glasses, and allows users to select head- or eye-tracking to center the gaze-contingent simulation.

For prosthetic simulations, the GUI enables selection of neuroprosthesis type —cortical (with adjustable phosphene count and field of view) or retinal (Argus I, Argus II, or IMIE)—and adjustment of edge-detection filters (Canny or Sobel) and Region of Interest (ROI) size (64×64, 128×128, or 256×256 px) to balance computational load.

For visual pathology simulations, continuous controls allow fine adjustment of severity parameters: cataracts (blur and yellowing), retinitis pigmentosa and glaucoma (tunnel size and fade), and age-related macular degeneration (peripheral tunnel or central scotoma/focal blur).

Finally, the GUI provides experimental support through object-detection activation, data-collection tools for post-processing, a live-view tab displaying original and processed frames, and quick-access controls for real-time parameter adjustment.

Hardware. The hardware configuration was optimized to ensure high processing capacity on the server and low-latency immersion on the client, supported by performance metrics. The client device is the PICO 4 Enterprise VR headset, selected for its integrated eye-tracking, low latency (90 Hz), and 5G wireless connectivity—essential for real-time, gaze-contingent simulation. It also provides high resolution (2160×2160 px per eye) and a wide 104° field of view, enhancing immersion. The server is an HP ZBook Fury 16 G11 Mobile Workstation, equipped with an Intel Core i9-14900HX processor and a 16 GB NVIDIA RTX

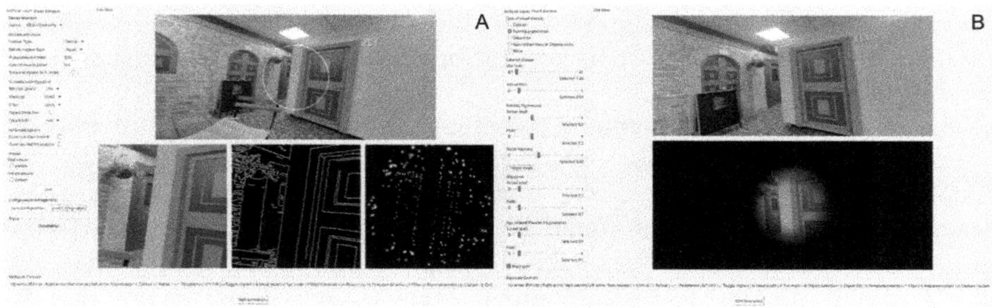

Fig. 1. Guided User Interface (GUI). A: Artificial Vision tab. B: Visual diseases tab.

5000 GPU, providing the computational power required for concurrent Python processing and real-time YOLO inference.

2.2 Validation Metrics

Platform performance was evaluated across three domains: temporal rendering, eye-tracking accuracy, and wireless communication stability.

Temporal performance was assessed by measuring frame rate (FPS) and motion-to-photon latency (M2P)—the time from frame capture to visualization in the headset—to verify rendering stability and real-time responsiveness under different computational loads.

Eye-tracking performance was quantified through gaze-position accuracy and precision, expressed as the angular deviation (in degrees) between the reported and true gaze points. Drift overtime was also measured to evaluate calibration stability.

Wireless performance was determined by measuring client–server communication latency at varying distances, assessing transmission stability and confirming the feasibility of consistent, low-latency, untethered operation.

3 Results

A comprehensive technical validation was performed to confirm the real-time performance of NEUROVISION and the reliability of its eye-tracker.

3.1 FPS and Stability Under Different Simulation Loads

The technical validation of NEUROVISION assessed its real-time performance under varying computational loads. Motion-to-Photon latency (M2P) and frame rate (FPS) were measured across 17 experimental configurations (Table 1), including implant modulation, visual filters, ROI size, and additional functionalities. One participant completed 17 walking trials, each using a different configuration.

Table 1. System configurations categorized by simulation engine and objective: (1) Baseline (No-config) without processing; (2) Specific cortical benchmarks via Dynaphos (Base-config to TD); (3) Generic processing modules applicable to both Dynaphos and Pulse2Percept (ROI1 to Filter), including tracking and object detection; (4) Clinical retinal implant emulations via pulse2percept (ArgusI to IMIE); and (5) Rendering of common visual pathologies (Cataracts to AMD).

Configuration	Implant	#Phosphene	FoV (°)	TD	ROI	Tracking	OD	Filter	Visual disease
No-config	None	None	None	None	None	None	None	None	None
Base-config	Cortical	1000	16	No	64×64	Head	No	Canny	None
Phosphenes	Cortical	100	16	No	64×64	Head	No	Canny	None
FoV	Cortical	1000	104	No	64×64	Head	No	Canny	None
TD	Cortical	1000	16	Yes	64×64	Head	No	Canny	None
ROI1	Cortical	1000	16	No	128×128	Head	No	Canny	None
ROI2	Cortical	1000	16	No	256×256	Head	No	Canny	None
Tracking	Cortical	1000	16	No	64×64	Eyes	No	Canny	None
OD	Cortical	1000	16	No	64×64	Head	Yes	Canny	None
Filter	Cortical	1000	16	No	64×64	Head	No	Sobel	None
ArgusI	ArgusI	None	None	None	64×64	Head	No	Canny	None
ArgusII	ArgusII	None	None	None	64×64	Head	No	Canny	None
IMIE	IMIE	None	None	None	64×64	None	No	Canny	None
Cataracts	None	None	None	None	None	None	None	None	Cataracts
RP	None	None	None	None	None	None	None	None	RP
Glaucoma	None	None	None	None	None	None	None	None	Glaucoma
AMD	None	None	None	None	None	None	None	None	AMD

VR Headset Performance. The baseline no-configuration case (no-config) established the optimal performance reference, with a mean M2P of 62.80 ± 61.81 ms and a mean FPS of 16.92 ± 1.89 FPS.

The platform maintained real-time functionality across most conditions, though computational load varied notably between configurations (Fig. 2). Low-load conditions, including simple eye-tracking (Tracking) and cortical simulations (e.g., Phosphenes, TD), performed close to baseline (Tracking: M2P = 72.88 ms, FPS = 14.40). Retinal prosthesis simulations increased load, with Argus I (M2P = 90.35 ms, FPS = 11.62) and Argus II (M2P = 139.70 ms, FPS = 7.70) remaining functional, while IMIE showed the heaviest demand (M2P = 303.54 ms, FPS = 4.66), reflecting its higher computational complexity and need for optimization.

Object Detection (OD) imposed a similar or greater load (M2P = 145.30 ms, FPS = 7.88), underlining the importance of efficient YOLO processing (Fig. 2, A). Restricting processing to smaller Regions of Interest (ROIs) proved effective for managing load, as increasing ROI size ($64 \times 64 \rightarrow 256 \times 256$) caused only moderate latency increases (to 86.76 ms) and minor FPS reductions (11.88). Finally, visual pathology filters (Cataracts, RP, Glaucoma, AMD) showed robust performance, with latencies between 85.71 ms and 111.59 ms, confirming that low-vision simulations can be integrated without compromising real-time capability.

PC Performance. Server analysis revealed more stable and faster performance, indicating that most latency variation on the client side originates from wireless communication and headset rendering. The server's no-configuration baseline achieved a mean M2P of 69.64 ms and a mean FPS of 14.58, with most configurations maintaining latency below 100 ms.

Two computationally intensive simulations stood out as outliers: the IMIE implant (M2P = 303.05 ms, FPS = 4.44) remained the primary bottleneck (Fig. 2, B), while Object Detection (OD) showed substantial processing delay (M2P = 153.44 ms, FPS = 7.25), confirming YOLO inference as the second heaviest task. In contrast, low-load configurations (e.g., base-config, tracking, phosphenes) consistently produced lower latencies than the headset, demonstrating that the Unity/Python TCP/IP client–server architecture is efficient, and that optimization efforts should target communication latency and rendering.

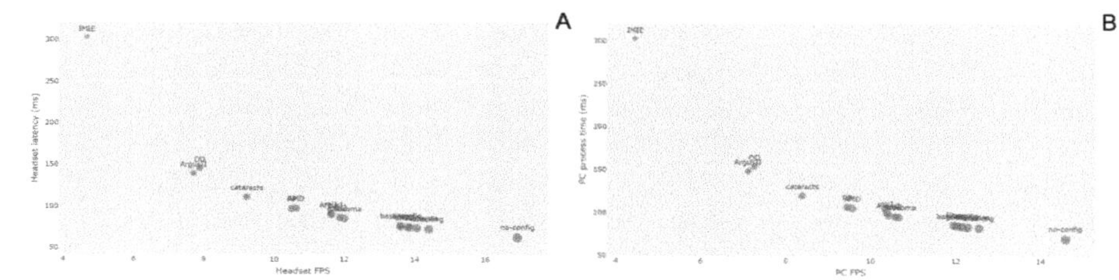

Fig. 2. Results obtained. A: Comparison of the frames per second (X-axis) versus the latency (Y-axis) for each case in the headset. B: Comparison of the frames per second (X-axis) versus the latency (Y-axis) for each case in the PC.

3.2 Eye-Tracking: Accuracy, Precision, Drift

Eye-tracking performance was evaluated using a target-fixation task to validate the gaze-contingent simulation. One participant fixated on a 32 × 32 px square presented for 3 s at nine predefined screen locations (four corners, four cardinal points, and center), each repeated five times (45 trials total). The task was performed under uncalibrated and calibrated conditions, measuring accuracy (angular deviation mean), precision (standard deviation), and drift (change in accuracy over time). Only the final 1.5 s of each trial were analyzed.

Uncalibrated Performance. In the absence of calibration (Fig. 3, A-B), the mean eye-tracking accuracy was 0.645° (0.375– 0.954°), precision 0.289° (0.068–0.491°), and drift 0.593° (0.277–0.942°). The best performance occurred at the right-center position (accuracy = 0.375°, precision = 0.068°), while peripheral points —particularly left-center (accuracy = 0.954°, drift = 0.942°) and bottom-right (accuracy = 0.884°)—showed greater degradation. The observed drift underscores the importance of individual calibration for stable, accurate eye-tracking.

Calibrated Performance. Pre-session calibration (Fig. 3, C-D) produced consistent improvements across all metrics, confirming its value for gaze-contingent simulation. Global mean accuracy improved by 26.2% (from 0.645° to 0.476°), reaching levels acceptable for most psychophysical and simulation studies (< 0.5°). Mean precision improved by 45.7% (0.289° → 0.157°), and drift decreased by 25.9% (0.593° → 0.440°).

The best performance occurred at the right-center (accuracy = 0.225°, precision = 0.059°) and center (accuracy = 0.295°, drift = 0.199°) positions. The lowest accuracy (0.869°) and greatest drift (0.856°) were recorded at the bottom-left position, indicating this area remains most challenging even after calibration.

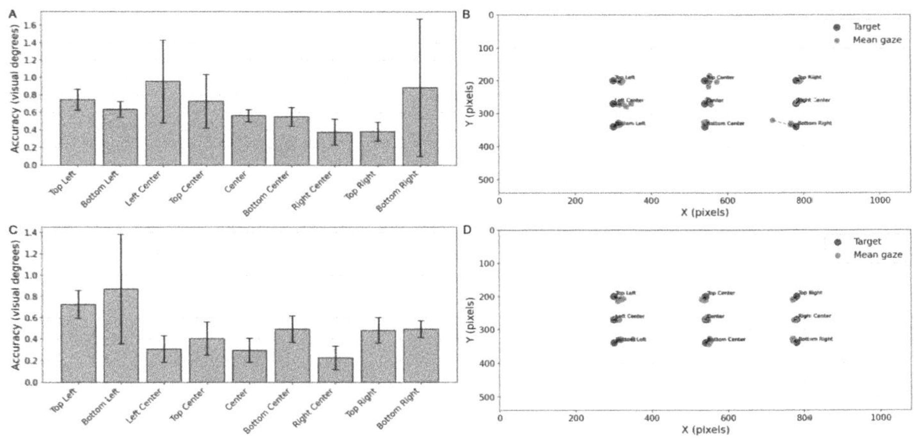

Fig. 3. Results obtained. A: Bars plot of accuracy (º) for each target, including its standard deviation uncalibrated. B: Coordinates of the targets (blue) and the mean gaze coordinates for each trial (red); there are five trials per target uncalibrated. C: Bars plot of accuracy (º) for each target, including its standard deviation calibrated. D: Coordinates of the targets (blue) and the mean gaze coordinates for each trial (red); there are five trials per target calibrated.

3.3 Latency Distribution and Maximum Tolerable Distance

To assess the robustness and stability of the client–server wireless connection, a mobility test was conducted to determine whether latency degraded with increasing distance. One participant walked a 25 m route four times under configurations representing different computational loads identified in Sect. 3.1: no-config (minimum load), base-config (low load), cataracts (medium load), and IMIE (maximum load).

During each walk, motion-to-photon latency was continuously recorded, focusing on client-side processing time. A linear regression analysis quantified the relationship between distance and latency, providing an objective measure of system stability under mobility conditions.

Impact of the Computational Load in Mobility. The summary statistics indicate that simulation load is the main determinant of performance, while wireless connection stability remains unaffected (Fig. 4). The no-configuration condition produced the lowest latency (59.66 ms), and activating the cortical simulation ("base configuration") increased it slightly to 81.78 ms—both below the 100 ms threshold for real-time VR, validating the platform for cortical prosthesis studies.

The cataracts simulation increased latency to 142.72 ms with moderate jitter (17.30 ms), still acceptable for static low-vision simulations. In contrast, the IMIE retinal simulation imposed the heaviest computational demand, reaching 630.49 ms latency and 149.77 ms jitter, confirming it as the main system bottleneck and indicating that the most complex retinal model cannot yet operate in real time on the PICO 4 Enterprise.

Importantly, across all configurations, the determination coefficient (R^2 vs. distance) remained below 0.1, showing that latency depends on processing load rather than distance, and confirming the platform's stability under mobility conditions.

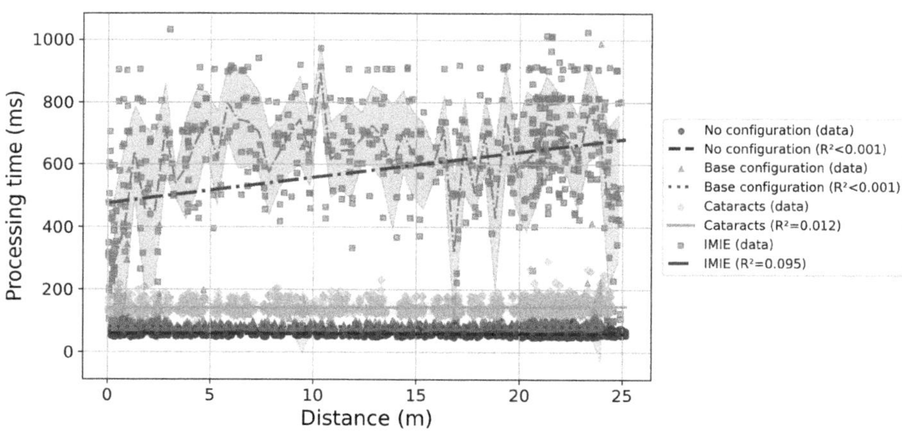

Fig. 4. Platform stability results. This figure compares the distance (X-Axis) and the processing time (Y-axis), showing the raw data (dots), the mean (light line), the standard deviation (± 1 std) and the linear regression (dark line).

4 Discussion

NEUROVISION was proposed as a unified and wireless solution to overcome the limitations of existing Prosthetic Vision Simulation (PVS) platforms ([5–7]). The results from the technical validation confirm that the system is a robust test bench which achieves the integration of key functionalities within a VR environment.

4.1 Real-Time Performance and Computational Challenges

The client–server architecture (Unity/Python) demonstrated its ability to support real-time simulation, maintaining stable performance across most configurations. Both the baseline and cortical simulation operated within latency ranges suitable for behavioral tasks.

The main operational limitation was observed with the IMIE neuroprosthesis simulation, which showed substantially higher latency and variability. This highlights the computational demands of detailed biophysical models as the system's primary bottleneck. While NEUROVISION can execute such simulations in VR, the current implementation does not yet achieve true real-time performance. Further algorithmic and parallelization optimizations on the server are required to ensure fully fluid operation.

4.2 Added Value of NEUROVISION: Contrast with the State-of-the-Art

Unlike desktop-based frameworks such as Pulse2Percept (retinal-focused) and Dynaphos (cortical-focused), which do not provide immersive VR integration or validated gaze-contingent interaction, NEUROVISION combines both implant types within a unified wireless VR architecture. In contrast to VR-SPV, which demonstrates immersive feasibility but is limited to a single implant type and lacks pathology rendering or object detection, our platform integrates dual implant simulation, calibrated eye-tracking, visual disease modelling, and real-time object detection within the same experimental environment. This multi-modal integration enables comparative implant research, clinically relevant task design, and realistic low-vision scenario testing in a way not previously achieved in a single system.

4.3 Validation of the Wireless Architecture

The mobility test confirmed the robustness of the system's design, demonstrating that it performs reliably under movement. Linear regression analysis showed that the 5 GHz wireless connection remained highly stable, with no measurable degradation even under high-load conditions. Latency was primarily determined by server-side processing rather than by distance or motion effects, underscoring the efficiency of wireless communication. This represents a clear advantage over wired or stationary desktop-based systems.

4.4 Limitations and Future Work

The current validation is primarily technical, without behavioral or psychophysical assessment. Performance limitations observed in the IMIE and object detection modes, which exceed real-time thresholds, require optimization—potentially through code refactoring in C# or GPU-based acceleration for YOLO processing. Future work will focus on behavioral and psychophysical validation, assessing improvements in navigation and object recognition in healthy participants using simulated vision, followed by studies in clinical low-vision populations.

Beyond behavioral validation, large-scale simulated datasets generated through platforms such as NEUROVISION may contribute to the development of data-driven or foundational models for stimulation strategy optimization in future cortical prostheses.

5 Conclusion

NEUROVISION introduces a modular, wireless VR platform that unifies retinal and cortical prosthesis simulation, visual pathology modelling, eye-tracking, and object detection within a single gaze-contingent environment. The system demonstrated reliable real-time performance across most modules, high-precision calibrated eye-tracking, and stable wireless operation, with latency mainly determined by processing load. The IMIE model remains the main target for optimization. NEUROVISION provides a powerful testbed for advancing visual implant research and assistive strategies, with future work focusing on model optimization and behavioral validation in navigation and object recognition tasks.

Acknowledgments. This study was funded by grants PDC2022-133952-100 and PID2022-141606OB-I00 from the Spanish "Ministerio de Ciencia, Innovación y Universidades", by grant CIPROM/2023/25 from the Generalitat Valenciana and by the Programa Iberoamericano de Ciencia y Tecnología para el Desarrollo (CYTED, grant number NT4SM). We also gratefully acknowledge PICO Enterprise for their support.

References

1. World Health Organization: WHO health workforce support and safeguards list 2023. World Health Organization (2023)
2. Stingl, K., et al.: Flashes and patterns: phosphenes induced by subretinal electronic implants. Vision. Res. **111**, 140–147 (2015)
3. Chen, S.C., et al.: Rehabilitation regimes based upon psychophysical studies of prosthetic vision. Clin. Exp. Ophthalmol. **37**(5), 450–459 (2009)
4. de Ruyter van Steveninck, J., et al.: End-to-end optimization of prosthetic vision. bioRxiv(2020). https://doi.org/10.1101/2020.12.19.423601
5. Beyeler, M., et al.: Pulse2percept: a python-based simulation framework for bionic vision. In: Proceedings of the 15th Python in Science Conference (SciPy 2017), pp. 127–134 (2017)

6. Lozano, E.S., et al.: Dynaphos: a deep learning-based visual encoding strategy for a cortical visual prosthesis. J. Neural Eng. **17**(5), 056003 (2020)
7. Kasowski, J., Beyeler, M.: Immersive virtual reality simulations of bionic vision. In: Augmented Humans (AHs), pp. 82–93 (2022). https://doi.org/10.1145/3519391.3522752

Artificial Intelligence in Cortical Visual Prostheses: From Phosphene Encoding to Closed-Loop Neuroprosthetic Vision

Alicia Aniorte, Marta Gea, Javier Garrigós, José J. Martínez, and José M. Ferrández(✉)

Universidad Politécnica de Cartagena, Cartagena, Spain
{alicia.aniorte,marta.gea}@edu.upct.es, jm.ferrandez@upct.es

Abstract. Blindness remains a major global health challenge. With an estimated 43.3 million people affected, individuals with irreversible damage to the retina or optic nerve could benefit from cortical visual prostheses that directly stimulate the visual cortex to elicit phosphenes, restoring rudimentary but functional vision.

This comprehensive literature review synthesizes the current state of the art in cortical visual prostheses, emphasizing the integration of artificial intelligence pipelines in next-generation devices, and the integration of closed-loop architectures to achieve safe, real time visual restoration.

The review examines the full functional pipeline: from real time video capture with eye tracking, deep learning scene understanding and bio-inspired phosphene encoders and stimulation algorithms, to hardware implementations, closed loop systems and clinical translation including ongoing trials, safety and ethical considerations.

Key findings reveal that AI-driven approaches outperform traditional methods in scene simplification, phosphene prediction fidelity and personalization. However, significant challenges must still be overcome. Limited electrode counts restricting field of vision, phosphene variability, real time closed-loop latency, thermal and charge density safety limits, lack of unified stimulation benchmarks, and insufficient long term data from chronic human implantations for tissue response and neuroplasticity effects.

Cortical visual prostheses are transitioning from open loop phosphene generation towards adaptive, personalized systems. Future research must prioritize low-latency closed-loop control for high channel count devices, with explainable AI frameworks that support decisions and large scale clinical trials to deliver meaningful vision to the blind.

Keywords: Cortical visual prosthesis · closed-loop · artificial intelligence · deep learning · neuroprosthesis

A. Aniorte and M. Gea—These authors contributed equally to this work.

J. M. Ferrández Vicente et al. (Eds.): IWINAC 2026, LNCS 16574, pp. 410–425, 2026.
https://doi.org/10.1007/978-3-032-27314-7_38

1 Introduction

Blindness remains one of the most disabling and economically burdensome conditions worldwide. According to the Global Burden of Disease Study, an estimated 43.3 million people were blind in 2020, a figure projected to reach approximately 60 million by 2050 if current trends continue [9]. While at least half of all vision impairment cases could be prevented or treated (e.g., cataract, refractive error), a large and growing subset of individuals suffer from irreversible damage to the retina or optic nerve: conditions such as advanced glaucoma, ocular trauma, retinitis pigmentosa, or optic neuropathy.

For these patients, cortical visual prostheses represent the primary therapeutic hope. Unlike retinal implants (e.g., Argus II or PRIMA), which require intact retinal ganglion cells and an operational optic nerve [7], cortical devices bypass the entire anterior visual pathway and stimulate neurons directly in the primary visual cortex (V1) and, potentially, in adjacent cortical visual regions (V2, V3, and V4). Consequently, they are uniquely suited to restore rudimentary but functionally meaningful vision in the very population for whom retinal or optic nerve prostheses are contraindicated.

The goal is that the percepts generated produce interpretable artificial visual experiences. This is accomplished by eliciting phosphenes - brief, localized sensations of light perceived as punctate spots or flashes of varying brightness and size - through controlled electrical pulses delivered to discrete sites in the visual pathway. By varying stimulation parameters (current amplitude, pulse width, frequency, and electrode location), patterns of phosphenes can be orchestrated to convey spatial information, edges, motion, and simple object shapes [11].

Success in auditory neuroprosthetics offers a compelling roadmap for what is possible. Cochlear implants have restored functional hearing to millions of profoundly deaf individuals through decades of sophisticated signal processing and biologically inspired neural coding. Cortical visual prostheses now stand at a similar inflection point. To achieve comparable levels of functional restoration, next generation devices must integrate complex neural codes, AI-driven computer vision, and neuromorphic hardware. Incorporating dynamic attributes such as motion, orientation, and receptive-field adaptation will be essential to enable users to interpret functionally meaningful visual representations of their environment.

1.1 Phosphene-Based Vision: Principles and Limitations

The perceptual quality of cortical prosthetic vision is governed by the retinotopic organization of the primary visual cortex (V1), in which neighboring neuronal populations map to adjacent locations in the visual field. This topographic mapping allows patterned stimulation to generate structured phosphene arrays, yet several inherent constraints limit the resulting experience.

The functional outcome depends critically on three interrelated parameters: the number of electrodes, inter-electrode spacing, and precise cortical placement [21]. Although the natural visual system transmits information through approximately one million parallel ganglion cell channels, psychophysical simulations have shown that roughly 625 independent and well-controlled electrodes implanted in V1 can suffice for essential daily tasks such as reading large print and navigating familiar environments. However, in clinical reality, 625 physical electrodes rarely generate 625 distinct percepts due to crosstalk, phosphene fusion, and local neuronal death. Furthermore, this modest electrode count inevitably produces tunnel vision, a severely restricted visual field that compromises situational awareness and orientation. One practical solution is the implantation of multiple microelectrode arrays at different retinotopic sites across the visual cortex [21].

Importantly, simply increasing electrode count does not automatically improve performance. The assumption that "more electrodes equal better vision" has proven incorrect [21], because perceptual resolution is also limited by electrode spacing, cortical folding, non-linear summation of simultaneous phosphenes, and long term signal stability.

Early surface electrodes (Brindley [10], Dobelle [15]) required milliamperes of current and produced large, overlapping phosphenes with poor spatial selectivity. Modern penetrating intracortical arrays achieve focal stimulation at thresholds two to three orders of magnitude lower (typically 1âĂŞ100 µA) [22], yielding higher selectivity and reduced risk of phosphene fusion. Nevertheless, current systems still suffer from limited spatial and temporal resolution, perceptual instability over time, and incomplete representation of dynamic attributes such as motion and depth.

In this paper, we provide a comprehensive review of the current state of the art in cortical visual prostheses, focusing on recent implementations of artificial intelligence pipelines and the integration of closed-loop architectures aimed at achieving safe, real-time, and naturalistic visual restoration.

2 General Architecture of AI-Powered Cortical Visual Prostheses

The standard functional architecture of an AI-powered visual cortical prosthesis would typically comprise several integrated components that collectively capture, process, and translate real-world visual information into perceivable phosphenes via direct cortical stimulation.

- A compact video camera, often integrated into a pair of eyeglasses equipped with eye tracking, continuously captures the visual scene and generates a real time video data stream.
- An AI-driven image preprocessing module would analyze the incoming video frames to extract salient features such as edges, objects, pedestrians, vehicles, or faces, while suppressing redundant or less relevant details. This step would produce a simplified, computationally efficient representation of the scene optimized for downstream neural encoding.

- A bio-inspired retina-like encoder would transform the preprocessed visual information by remapping it from retinotopic coordinates to the distorted cortical space, while also modulating stimulus parameters to generate appropriate activation patterns tailored to elicit controlled phosphenes.
- A cortical stimulator hardware component delivers precisely modulated electrical pulse sequences through an implanted microelectrode array positioned on the primary visual cortex. This stimulation induces localized neural activation, resulting in the perception of phosphenes corresponding to the processed scene.

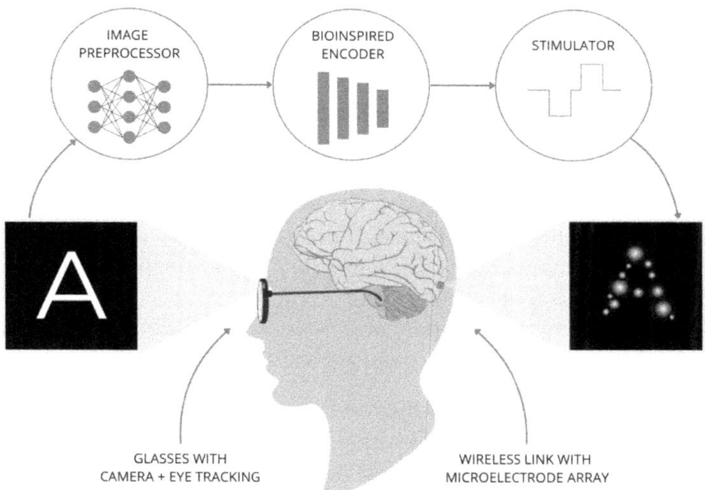

Fig. 1. General architecture of next-generation AI-powered cortical visual prostheses. The system integrates wirelessly interconnected components: smart glasses with embedded camera and eye-tracking, an AI-driven image preprocessor, a bio-inspired encoder, and a cortical stimulator.

This pipeline is shown in Fig. 1. Some designs incorporate a bidirectional capability by leveraging the same microelectrode array for both the stimulation and recording of cortical activity during or following stimulation periods, a feature that critically depends on robust stimulation artifact cancellation to make concurrent neural recording possible. This data can provide feedback to an AI controller for dynamic parameter adjustment.

Within this pipeline, AI integration is most prominent in image processing, retinal emulation, and stimulus mapping. During the recording phase, advanced Machine Learning (ML) such as LSTMs or generative models can analyze brain signals to enable adaptive prosthetic control.

3 AI-Driven Visual Processing and Encoding

3.1 Image Preprocessing and Scene Understanding

In image processing applications, deep learning models have substantially surpassed traditional computer vision methods, achieving superior accuracy and robustness across key tasks such as image classification, object detection, and both semantic and instance segmentation [31].

The vision restored by current prostheses offers far lower resolution than natural sight, with only a fraction of the field of view. Because of this limited information bandwidth, the computational responsibility for scene interpretation is primarily delegated to image preprocessing algorithms. By intelligently filtering the visual field, these techniques maximize the interpretability of phosphene patterns [38].

While basic filters help with navigation, recent breakthroughs in deep learning such as semantic segmentation and facial landmark detection offer a more sophisticated way to translate complex environments into useful artificial vision [38].

The difficulty of engineering task-specific and user-centric image filters persists as a primary technical bottleneck. To address this, deep learning models provide a versatile framework for personalizing visual output according to individual functional needs [38].

Several preprocessing techniques have been successfully combined with deep learning architectures to support advanced visual analysis. These include:

- **Object detection**, which identifies and labels multiple objects within bounding boxes. This capability enables real-time assistance for visually impaired users, such as obstacle avoidance during navigation or rapid scanning of an environment to locate specific items or number of individuals. The models operate efficiently in real time and can be quickly retrained to adapt to new settings [31]. The YOLO (You Only Look Once) family, originally introduced in 2015, has evolved into one of the dominant paradigms for real-time object detection, with recent Ultralytics versions such as YOLO11 and YOLO26 emphasizing end-to-end inference and edge deployment. These models generally outperformed earlier single-shot detectors, including SSD (Single Shot MultiBox Detector) variants such as SSD-512 [40].
- **Edge detection**. This technique must be calibrated for the target application. Approaches based on convolutional neural networks, however, perform multiscale and multilevel feature extraction that approximates human performance in resolving ambiguities in edge and object boundary detection. These models maintain robustness under adverse lighting conditions and complex scenes while suppressing irrelevant details, for example, extracting only the principal contours of a human face or an open doorway without incorporating extraneous texture such as hair strands. As a result, the number of simultaneously active electrodes is minimized, improving temporal efficiency and energy consumption [31]. A widely adopted deep learning-based approach for edge detection is Holistically-Nested Edge Detection (HED) [42]

- **Semantic and instance segmentation** assign class labels to individual pixels and delineate precise object boundaries, enabling fine-grained scene understanding. Early approaches such as Mask R-CNN [27] established a strong baseline by combining region-based detection with pixel-wise mask prediction. However, recent advances have been driven by transformer-based architectures and foundation models, which significantly improve generalization and flexibility. In particular, models such as Mask2Former [12] unify semantic and instance segmentation within a single framework using masked attention mechanisms, while the Segment Anything Model (SAM) [28] introduces a promptable paradigm capable of zero-shot segmentation across diverse visual domains.
- **Face detection and recognition**, which have achieved remarkable speed and accuracy, making them highly effective for real time applications in assistive vision systems [31]. Contemporary pipelines commonly integrate established models such as RetinaFace [14] for face detection and ArcFace [13] for face recognition, which remain widely used baselines despite recent advances in transformer-based and multimodal approaches.

The outputs generated by these techniques can be executed in parallel, enabling complementary information streams to be fused for enhanced downstream decision making.

A successful implementation of these techniques is the Neurolight system [31], which incorporates dedicated segmentation and detection modules within its visual processing pipeline to extract essential scene elements. Specifically, this framework employs a Single Shot Detector (SSD) architecture, utilizing MobileNetV2 as the backbone feature extractor. This configuration enables efficient localization of objects and individuals by generating bounding boxes that delineate their spatial positions and assign categorical labels.

Data-driven enhancements further strengthen the reliability of preprocessing pipelines. Leong et al. (2024) [29] demonstrated this by training deep encoders using ex-vivo recordings from mouse retinal ganglion cells. Their actor-model framework learns non-linear downsampling patterns that elicit more consistent and biologically plausible neural responses compared to traditional heuristic methods, both *in silico* and *ex vivo*. By integrating these task-specific filters and real neural transformation data, preprocessing pipelines effectively compress complex visual environments into interpretable representations optimized for cortical stimulation.

3.2 Bio-Inspired Visual Encoder (Retinal Modeling)

In bio-inspired visual encoders, accurately modeling the phosphenes elicited during stimulation is essential. Phosphenes observed in both retinal and cortical implants do not appear as perfectly round, pixel-like, or symmetrical shapes. Using idealized, perfectly round phosphenes in *in silico* simulations tends to artificially inflate the apparent performance of the system. Moreover, such simplified models conceal important safety constraints which misguide hardware design, leading engineers to prioritize electrode count over placement precision, and they hinder closed-loop calibration by providing the learning algorithm with a training target that the patient can never actually perceive [36].

To overcome these limitations, the axon map model, based on retinal axon mapping, has been proposed to generate more realistic phosphene maps under retinal stimulation. This model assumes that electrical stimulation of retinal ganglion cells (RGCs) propagates through adjacent axon fibers, resulting in elongated phosphene shapes, and has been empirically validated. For cortical implants, recent models have incorporated retinotopic mapping of V1 as well as the temporal dynamics associated with prolonged cortical stimulation, aiming for greater fidelity in phosphene prediction [26] [23]. Differentiable simulators such as Dynaphos [26] further enhance biological plausibility by accounting for cortical magnification, current spread, and temporal summation, enabling gradient-based optimization within end-to-end AI pipelines. Additionally, incorporating eye tracking allows the system to adjust stimulation based on gaze shifts, keeping phosphenes correctly aligned with the user's field of view.

Despite these advances, accurately predicting phosphene shape, location, and brightness remains challenging due to high intrapatient variability. Several studies have leveraged retrospective human data from retinal and cortical prosthetic users [36]. One approach applied machine learning to predict phosphene deactivation and threshold sensitivities using retrospectively collected data from Argus II users [35].

Additionally, high-resolution images have been projected onto mouse retinas using multielectrode arrays, with neural spikes from RGCs recorded in response. The resulting dataset was used to train a supervised encoder that improved the reliability of the *ex-vivo* transmitted signal [29]. A similar approach using 3D Convolutional Neural Networks demonstrated that deep learning can accurately capture the spatio-temporal dynamics of these cells [30], providing another example of learning-based refinement in retinal bio-inspired modeling.

3.3 Deep Learning-Based Stimulation Algorithms

Beyond improving phosphene shape modeling and predicting electrode malfunction, artificial intelligence and machine learning hold promise for addressing other complex future challenges, including optimization of electrode placement and electrical stimulation patterns [36].

A prominent strategy involves end-to-end deep learning frameworks that jointly optimize the mapping from input images to stimulation protocols. Van Steveninck et al. [38] introduced a deep autoencoder architecture designed to optimize the full phosphene generation pipeline in a task-specific manner. The model comprises three core components: (i) a fully convolutional DNN encoder that derives an appropriate stimulation protocol; (ii) a differentiable phosphene simulator that transforms the protocol into a simulated prosthetic vision (SPV) representation, incorporating realistic distortions; and (iii) a residual-network-based decoder that reconstructs the original input from the SPV latent representation.

Computational experiments demonstrated that this approach automatically discovers task-adapted stimulation strategies, highlighting the advantages of end-to-end optimization over isolated preprocessing steps.

Subsequent developments have advanced biological plausibility and robustness. Van der Grinten et al. (2024) [26] proposed a fully differentiable, PyTorch-implemented phosphene simulator tailored for cortical prostheses. This model incorporates temporal dynamics, biologically grounded variability in phosphene size, position, and intensity, and explicit constraints on stimulation parameters to ensure safety during optimization. Such simulators facilitate true gradient-based refinement of encoding models while respecting physiological boundaries.

While these deep learning architectures effectively optimize for perceptual fidelity, there is a critical need to evaluate how algorithmic design choices impact physiological safety [17]. For instance, in cortical encoders, introducing loss terms that discourage the co-activation of neighboring electrodes has been shown to improve safety margins by reducing the total current and the number of simultaneously active sites [26]. This aligns with intracortical studies on spatial interference and excitability.

Conversely, models that explicitly incorporate current spreading or interaction terms can inadvertently amplify unsafe stimulation amplitudes, despite being inspired by biological findings on crosstalk [24,43]. These findings demonstrate that even biologically motivated modeling choices can introduce new risks if they are not empirically verified.

Consequently, deep learning-based stimulation algorithms cannot rely solely on training objectives or validation loss to guarantee safety; they require systematic, post-training validation to ensure biophysical limits are strictly respected.

4 Hardware Implementation and Real-Time Computing

Real time execution of AI pipelines in cortical visual prostheses requires compact, low power hardware capable of deterministic inference while respecting strict safety limits on latency, power density, and heat dissipation [18].

Wearable external units can handle image capture, preprocessing, and simultaneous wireless power and data transmission to the cortical implant, enabling practical real-time operation for phosphene generation [8]. Current clinical prototypes, such as the Orion system, use a wearable Video Processing Unit (VPU) integrated in a belt or pocket to perform image capture, basic preprocessing, and wireless data transmission to the cortical implant, achieving acceptable real-time operation for phosphene generation [3]. This heavy preprocessing must occur in the external unit because the thermal dissipation of the implant is a strict limit for any computation inside the device. The Neurolight framework (a deep-learning interface for mapping retina-like models to intracortical stimulation) is designed to run on external or embedded computers, but practical deployment in head-mounted or portable configurations relies on edge accelerators to sustain 15âĂŞ30 fps for dynamic tasks like object detection and edge extraction [31].

In the broader context of AI-driven visual prostheses, these hardware solutions support the acceleration of complex visual processing tasks while maintaining clinical feasibility [36]. Emerging research platforms accelerate these AI workloads with embedded GPUs (e.g., NVIDIA Jetson series) or FPGAs (e.g., AMD Versal/Kria with Vitis-AI for quantized, parallel inference). A clear early demonstration of this FPGA approach is the retinomorphic architecture proposed by Martínez et al. (2008) [33], which enables non-linear multi-layer cellular neural networks with millions of neurons to fit in low cost devices and process standard video in real time. Using this architecture, the authors implemented a CNN-based model of synapse I of the foveal retina, replicating the receptive fields of bipolar cells on a Xilinx FPGA, with the explicit goal of integration into augmented-reality systems for visually impaired users. Complementing this approach, Toledo-Moreo et al. (2012) [39] proposed a modular, multiplierless FPGA architecture for real time 2D convolution with medium-to-large kernels, specially suitable for the convolutional stages of bio-inspired encoders and image-to-stimulation mapping in cortical prostheses.

Further research explores neuromorphic chips for sub-milliwatt spiking computation that better matches biological timing and reduces thermal risks in future fully implantable designs [16]. Key challenges remain achieving end-to-end latency under 20 ms for naturalistic perception and ensuring compliance with tissue-safe power budgets, both of which are central to the system level design of safe, large scale neuroprosthetic interfaces [18].

5 Experimental Neurophysiology and the Closed-Loop Frontier

Closed-loop systems represent the next frontier in cortical visual prostheses. By integrating real-time feedback, these architectures aim to mimic natural visual loops, compensate for long term cortical plasticity, and enhance safety through automated threshold regulation [20]. Current research explores this closed-loop paradigm through three distinct pathways: direct neural feedback, sensorimotor integration, and behavioral optimization.

Neural Feedback Loops: Bidirectional Cortical Interfaces. The most direct form of a closed-loop system uses the same microelectrode array to both deliver electrical stimulation and record cortical activity, such as spikes and local field potentials. In Grani et al. (2025) [25], researchers examined the neural responses in V1 followed by electrical stimulation of implanted electrodes in blind individuals. Their findings revealed that the induced neural activity in the vicinity of the stimulated electrode strongly correlates with key perceptual attributes, including the likelihood of perceiving a phosphene, its perceived brightness, and the shortest interstimulus interval needed to distinguish separate phosphenes. These results underscore the potential of bidirectional neural interfaces, where recorded cortical signals could inform and refine stimulation parameters in real time.

Sensorimotor Feedback Loops: Integrating Gaze and Eye-Tracking. Distinct from direct neural recording, sensorimotor feedback loops use signals like eye movements to adjust the visual mapping dynamically. Complementing neural approaches, Waclawczyk et al. (2025) [41] conducted a case study on a patient who lost both eyes due to traumatic injury and now wears cosmetic ocular prostheses. Results revealed a significant correlation between eye position and phosphene location shifts. Real-time video tracking enabled the patient to localize objects via gaze direction at a level comparable to sighted controls, underscoring the potential of integrating gaze feedback to facilitate natural scanning and improve spatial awareness.

Behavioral Feedback Loops: Human-in-the-Loop Optimization. Personalization strategies further bridge experimental neurophysiology and practical implementation through iterative, user-driven calibration. In a study by Schoinas et al. (2025) [37], researchers evaluated human-in-the-loop optimization (HILO), an iterative method that refines stimulation parameters based on user feedback to improve perceptual quality. Using sighted participants viewing simulated prosthetic vision, the study compared encodings optimized with HILO against naive baselines and deep stimulus encoding alone. Participants consistently preferred HILO stimuli across conditions. Notably, differences between human perceptual decisions and purely algorithmic processes emphasized the need for human validation over approaches that have only been simulated. These findings position HILO as a viable pathway toward adaptive, individualized closed-loop systems.

Despite these advances, current closed-loop implementations in cortical visual prostheses remain largely limited to offline or iterative calibration rather than true real-time operation. While studies like Grani et al. [25] demonstrate correlative feedback potential and HILO [37] enables iterative personalization, fully dynamic, low latency closed-loop control, where neural recordings continuously modulate stimulation within milliseconds, has not yet been achieved in human trials.

Achieving genuine real time closed-loop functionality will face substantial challenges. These include minimizing processing latency and computational demands for on-device decoding and adaptation, ensuring recording during stimulation without artifacts, maintaining long-term electrode stability amid tissue responses, managing safety constraints, and addressing intersubject variability in neural plasticity and perceptual mapping. Overcoming these hurdles will require integrated advances in hardware (low-power, high-bandwidth interfaces), algorithms (efficient decoding in real time), and validation protocols to ensure the safety, efficacy, and real-time stability of the next generation of visual prostheses.

6 Clinical Translation and Ethical Considerations

6.1 Clinical Candidates and Safety

Currently, few cortical prosthetic systems have reached human trials. While three platforms have entered clinical trials (CORTIVIS [2], Intracortical Visual Prosthesis [1] and Orion Cortical Visual Prosthesis System [23]) and others remain in preclinical stages (ELVIS [4], Occular [5]), achieving natural vision requires overcoming significant technical and biological hurdles.

Selecting appropriate candidates for a cortical visual prosthesis remains a complex and non-standardized process. At present, no universally agreed-upon inclusion or exclusion criteria exist, nor is there a single optimal rehabilitation strategy applicable to all forms of blindness. Decisions regarding the choice of prosthetic approach or rehabilitation pathway typically depend on factors such as device availability, expected effectiveness, and the patient's willingness to undergo invasive procedures [19].

Based on the inclusion criteria for cortical visual prostheses outlined in the Orion clinical trial (NCT03344848) [23], the Intracortical Visual Prosthesis (ICVP) feasibility study (NCT04634383) [1], and the review by Fernandez and Normann in Webvision [19], the main criteria for selecting clinical candidates include profound bilateral blindness with bare light reception or no light reception caused by non-cortical causes (e.g., ocular trauma, advanced retinal degenerations, optic nerve/chiasm pathology such as glaucoma [21]), documented prior visual experience (ideally with normal or near normal vision in the first decade of life), medical and psychological fitness with no major contraindications, and electrophysiological assessments.

Safety considerations for cortical visual prostheses focus on surgical risks (infection, bleeding), neurological events (seizures), and chronic stimulation effects (tissue integrity, electrode stability). Trials like Orion [23] reported manageable risks (one early seizure resolved via parameter changes; no further serious events over 6 years), while a 96-channel intracortical implant study demonstrated safe chronic microstimulation in humans with no major complications [22]. ML models could improve objectivity in candidate selection by predicting perception from stimulation patterns, advancing toward safer AI-enhanced devices.

6.2 Interpretability and Explainable AI (XAI)

Given the medical criticality of visual prostheses, where erroneous stimulation parameters can compromise safety or efficacy, AI models must be interpretable. Recent studies have applied Explainable AI (XAI) techniques to validate stimulation algorithms and reduce the burden of manual system fitting. A compelling example is Pogoncheff et al. (2024) [35], who fitted linear models (OLS, Elastic Net), XGBoost, and shallow MLPs to a large longitudinal Argus II dataset (6,225 threshold and impedance measurements across 12 subjects over 11 years) to predict individual electrode perceptual thresholds and deactivation status from routine clinical parameters.

Using SHAP analysis, the authors quantified feature contributions across linear and non-linear models, identifying novel predictors and achieving up to 76 % explained threshold variance. Strikingly, routinely collected clinical data combined with a single system-fitting session were sufficient for strong predictive performance.

Building on these foundations, hybrid XAI frameworks have emerged for next-generation devices. Shanmuga Sundari et al. (2025) [32] proposed the

Bio-Optical Explainable Interfaces (BOEI) architecture, which integrates physics-informed neural networks, bio-optical retinal models, and post-hoc XAI methods (SHAP for feature attribution and Grad-CAM for visual heatmaps). The system generates interpretable explanations for both diagnostic decisions (Vision Transformer classifications) and stimulation policies (reinforcement-learning controller), achieving 89.7 % RGC activation efficacy while maintaining safety limits compliant with ANSI. These hybrid interfaces produce clinician-trusted heatmaps that correlate prosthetic output with retinal anatomy and cognitive perception metrics.

Although developed primarily for retinal prostheses, these XAI pipelines translate readily to cortical devices. In cortical systems, phosphene variability is inherently higher due to cortical folding, retinotopic distortion across sulci and gyri, and long term plasticity effects on signal coherence [21] [19]. Bidirectional intracortical arrays now enable real-time neural recording from neighboring electrodes to predict perceptual thresholds, brightness, and temporal separation with high accuracy [25]. Consequently, analogous SHAP, LIME or Grad-CAM analyses can map which visual or neural features most strongly influence phosphene thresholds and long term stability.

This transparent mapping aligns with FDA guidance, which emphasizes transparency and explainability for machine learning-enabled medical devices to ensure patient safety and effective clinical use, particularly in high risk Class III applications such as cortical visual prostheses [6].

7 Gaps, Challenges, and Future Directions

Despite notable progress in cortical visual prostheses, several critical gaps and technical challenges continue to limit clinical impact and long-term efficacy. Although some feedback mechanisms are already employed in ongoing clinical trials, most remain offline or delayed, relying on post-hoc parameter tuning rather than true real-time closed-loop control. As electrode arrays scale to hundreds or thousands of channels, dynamic compensation for cortical plasticity, interelectrode variability, and perceptual drift will require deterministic low latency hardware and algorithms capable of processing recorded spikes and local field potentials in real time. These demands escalate exponentially with channel count, raising significant issues in power dissipation, wireless communication bandwidth, and thermal management, all of which must be resolved to ensure both safety and perceptual stability in next generation bidirectional systems. Achieving true independence for users will also require the miniaturization of these components, ensuring that wireless, portable systems can be worn discreetly and comfortably in daily life.

Validation practices also reveal important shortcomings. The field still depends heavily on simulation-based testing without unified benchmarks for simulated prosthetic vision, while long term human data on neural plasticity, electrode fatigue, and tissue responses remain scarce. These limitations hinder reliable translation from preclinical models to real-world performance.

Optogenetics offers a compelling alternative to conventional electrical stimulation, potentially enabling more selective, cell-type-specific activation with lower power requirements. A key preclinical milestone was achieved in 2021, when optogenetic stimulation of primate V1 using an AAV9-hSyn-ChR2-eYFP vector produced local laminar activation and engaged widespread cortical networks linked to visual perception. In behavioral tasks, targeted stimulation elicited phosphenes that influenced perceptual decisions, demonstrating the generation of functionally relevant signals [34]. Nevertheless, substantial translational barriers persist, including vector safety, light delivery efficiency, immune responses, and the need for human compatible opsins with improved sensitivity and dynamic range. Recent advances in human opsins and refined AAV capsids show promise, yet clinical application remains several years away and will require rigorous safety studies and light-dose budgeting.

Looking ahead, emerging opportunities center on fully adaptive, AI-driven architectures. The concept of a "Smart Bionic Eye" - an autonomous system that integrates real-time scene understanding, gaze tracking, and cortical feedback to respond to both external stimuli and the user's internal state - is rapidly approaching feasibility. Deep learning can enhance every stage of the pipeline: generative models (VAEs or GANs) for naturalistic phosphene synthesis, recurrent networks for temporal continuity, predictive algorithms for long term phosphene stability and tissue-damage prevention (via AI-driven charge budgeting), and uncertainty-aware fusion for multimodal integration. Human-in-the-loop and data-driven encoders already demonstrate superior personalization, while recent real-time closed loop implants in blind volunteers have shown that neural recordings can dynamically adapt stimulation parameters within milliseconds. However, treating safety solely as minimization of delivered current during optimization is insufficient. Such regularization reduces average power but fails to guarantee that trained models remain within physiological limits under novel inputs from the real world, where complex pulse interactions may still produce localized overstimulation. Automated stress-testing frameworks and uncertainty quantification will therefore be essential [17].

Addressing these gaps requires moving beyond testing based on simulations to establish unified benchmarks, extended human trials, and rigorous safety protocols for real time adaptation. Furthermore, careful attention to ethical considerations, including patient expectations, long term accessibility, and neuro-privacy, will be critical. Through the continuous integration of deep learning, bidirectional interfaces, and refined stimulation modalities, the field is well positioned to transition from basic phosphene perception to functional, personalized artificial vision in the coming decades.

8 Conclusions

Cortical visual prostheses represent one of the most promising neurotechnological strategies for restoring functional vision in individuals with profound blindness caused by retinal or optic nerve damage. Unlike retinal approaches, these systems can bypass the anterior visual pathway entirely and directly engage the visual cortex, making them uniquely relevant for patients who are not candidates for conventional ophthalmic prostheses. However, meaningful visual restoration remains constrained by limited electrode counts, phosphene instability, cortical variability, and the difficulty of translating complex real-world scenes into sparse and interpretable stimulation patterns.

In this context, artificial intelligence is emerging as a central enabling framework across the full prosthetic pipeline. Deep learning-based scene understanding, bio-inspired encoding, differentiable phosphene simulation, and adaptive stimulation optimization offer clear advantages over traditional open-loop or heuristic approaches. These methods improve the selection of behaviorally relevant visual information, increase the biological plausibility of stimulation models, and support the development of individualized strategies that better reflect intersubject differences in cortical organization and perceptual outcomes. At the same time, these advances make it increasingly clear that performance alone is not an adequate optimization target: safety, interpretability, latency, and physiological validity must be embedded into model design and validation from the outset.

Acknowledgments. This project AIA2025-164108-C32 has been funded by MICIU/AEI (10.13039/501100011033) and Fundación Séneca, as well as by the MSCA-SE EPISTEAM project and the CYTED network NT4SM.

Disclosure of Interests. The authors have no competing interests to declare.

References

1. Clinical trial - a phase i feasibility study of an intracortical visual prosthesis (ICVP) for people with blindness (ICVP). https://clinicaltrials.gov/study/NCT04634383
2. Clinical trial - development of a cortical visual neuroprosthesis for the blind. https://www.trialx.com/clinical-trials/listings/224479/development-of-a-cortical-visual-neuroprosthesis-for-the-blind/
3. Cortigent orion. https://www.cortigent.com/orion
4. Elvis tech. https://elvis-tech.ru/
5. Revision implant. https://www.revision-implant.com/
6. Transparency for machine learning-enabled medical devices: Guiding principles. Tech. rep. (2024). https://www.fda.gov/medical-devices/software-medical-device-samd/transparency-machine-learning-enabled-medical-devices-guiding-principles, https://www.fda.gov/medical-devices/software-medical-device-samd/transparency-machine-learning-enabled-medical-devices-guiding-principles
7. Ayton, L.N., et al.: An update on retinal prostheses (2020). https://doi.org/10.1016/j.clinph.2019.11.029
8. Barbruni, G.L., et al.: A wearable real-time system for simultaneous wireless power and data transmission to cortical visual prosthesis. IEEE Trans. Biomed. Circuits Syst. **18**(3), 580–591 (2024). https://doi.org/10.1109/TBCAS.2024.3357626
9. Bourne, R.R., Steinmetz, J.D., Flaxman, S., Briant, P.S.: Trends in prevalence of blindness and distance and near vision impairment over 30 years: an analysis for the global burden of disease study. Lancet Global Health **9**, e130–e143 (2021). https://doi.org/10.1016/S2214-109X(20)30425-3

10. Brindley, G.S., Lewin, W.S.: The sensations produced by electrical stimulation of the visual cortex. Tech. rep. (1968)
11. Chen, X., Wang, F., Fernandez, E., Roelfsema, P.R.: Shape perception via a high-channel-count neuroprosthesis in monkey visual cortex. Science (2020). https://doi.org/10.1126/science.abd7435, http://science.sciencemag.org/
12. Cheng, B., Misra, I., Schwing, A.G., Kirillov, A., Girdhar, R.: Masked-attention mask transformer for universal image segmentation. In: Proceedings of the IEEE/CVF Conference on Computer Vision and Pattern Recognition (CVPR) (2022)
13. Deng, J., Guo, J., Yang, J., Xue, N., Kotsia, I., Zafeiriou, S.: Arcface: additive angular margin loss for deep face recognition (2022). https://doi.org/10.1109/TPAMI.2021.3087709
14. Deng, J., Guo, J., Zhou, Y., Yu, J., Kotsia, I., Zafeiriou, S.: Retinaface: single-stage dense face localisation in the wild. arXiv:1905.00641 (2019)
15. Dobelle, W., Mladejovsky, M., Girvin, J.: Artificial vision for the blind: electrical stimulation of visual cortex offers hope for a functional prosthesis. Tech. rep. (1974)
16. Donati, E., Valle, G.: Neuromorphic hardware for somatosensory neuroprostheses. Nat. Commun. **15** (2024). https://doi.org/10.1038/s41467-024-44723-3
17. Downing, M., Peng, M., Granley, J., Beyeler, M., Bultan, T.: Fuzzing the brain: automated stress testing for the safety of ml-driven neurostimulation. J. Neural Eng. **23**, 026004 (2026). https://doi.org/10.1088/1741-2552/ae4927
18. Eichler, G., Gilhotra, Y., Zeng, N., Kim, M., Shepard, K., Carloni, L.: Mindful: Safe, implantable, large-scale brain-computer interfaces from a system-level design perspective. In: Proceedings of the Annual International Symposium on Microarchitecture, MICRO, vol. Part of 213862, pp. 1672–1689. IEEE Computer Society (2025). https://doi.org/10.1145/3725843.3756032
19. Fernandez, E., Normann, R.: Introduction to visual prosthetics. https://www.webvision.pitt.edu/book/part-xv-prosthetics/introduction-to-visual-prostheses-by-eduardo-fernandez-and-richard-normann/
20. Fernandez, E., Robles, J.A.: Advances and challenges in the development of visual prostheses. PLoS Biol. **22** (2024). https://doi.org/10.1371/journal.pbio.3002896
21. Fernández, E., Alfaro, A., González-López, P.: Toward long-term communication with the brain in the blind by intracortical stimulation: challenges and future prospects. Front. Neurosci. **14** (2020). https://doi.org/10.3389/fnins.2020.00681
22. Fernández, E., et al.: Visual percepts evoked with an intracortical 96-channel microelectrode array inserted in human occipital cortex. J. Clin. Invest. **131** (2021). https://doi.org/10.1172/JCI151331
23. Fine, I., Boynton, G.M.: A virtual patient simulation modeling the neural and perceptual effects of human visual cortical stimulation, from pulse trains to percepts. Tech. rep. (2024). https://doi.org/10.1038/s41598-024-65337-1
24. Ghaffari, D.H.: Improving the resolution of prosthetic vision through stimulus parameter optimization. Ph. D. thesis (2021)
25. Grani, F., Soto-Sánchez, C., Doblado, A.R., Peco, R.L., Gonzalez-Lopez, P., Fernandez, E.: Neural correlates of phosphene perception in blind individuals: a step toward a bidirectional cortical visual prosthesis. Tech. rep. (2025). https://www.science.org
26. van der Grinten, M., et al.: Towards biologically plausible phosphene simulation for the differentiable optimization of visual cortical prostheses. eLife **13** (2024). https://doi.org/10.7554/eLife.85812
27. He, K., Gkioxari, G., Dollár, P., Girshick, R.: Mask R-CNN. arXiv:1703.06870 (2018)

28. Kirillov, A., et al.: Segment anything (2023)
29. Leong, F., Rahmani, B., Psaltis, D., Moser, C., Ghezzi, D.: An actor-model framework for visual sensory encoding. Nat. Commun. **15** (2024). https://doi.org/10.1038/s41467-024-45105-5
30. Lozano, A., Soto-Sánchez, C., Garrigós, J., Martínez, J.J., Ferrández, J.M., Fernández, E.: A 3D convolutional neural network to model retinal ganglion cell's responses to light patterns in mice. Int. J. Neural Syst. **28** (2018). https://doi.org/10.1142/S0129065718500430
31. Lozano, A., et al.: Neurolight: a deep learning neural interface for cortical visual prostheses. Int. J. Neural Syst. **30** (2020). https://doi.org/10.1142/S0129065720500458
32. M, S.S., Jadala, V.C., Vikkurty, S.: Design and evaluation of hybrid explainable ai interfaces for vision restoration in next-generation retinal prosthetics. J. Theor. Appl. Inf. Technol. **15** (2025). www.jatit.org
33. Martínez, J.J., Toledo, F.J., Fernández, E., Ferrández, J.M.: A retinomorphic architecture based on discrete-time cellular neural networks using reconfigurable computing. Neurocomputing **71**, 766–775 (2008). https://doi.org/10.1016/j.neucom.2007.06.011
34. Ortiz-Rios, M., Agayby, B., Balezeau, F., Haag, M., Rima, S., Schmid, M.C.: Optogenetic stimulation of primate v1 reveals local laminar and large-scale cortical networks related to perceptual phosphenes (2021). http://biorxiv.org/lookup/doi/10.1101/2021.06.01.446505
35. Pogoncheff, G., Hu, Z., Rokem, A., Beyeler, M.: Explainable machine learning predictions of perceptual sensitivity for retinal prostheses. J. Neural Eng. **21** (2024). https://doi.org/10.1088/1741-2552/ad310f
36. Sarbout, I., et al.: Visual prostheses in the era of artificial intelligence technology. Eye and Brain **17**, 95–113 (2025). https://doi.org/10.2147/EB.S524322
37. Schoinas, E., Rastogi, A., Carter, A., Granley, J., Beyeler, M.: Evaluating deep human-in-the-loop optimization for retinal implants using sighted participants. arXiv:2502.00177 (2025)
38. de Ruyter van Steveninck, J., Güçlü, U., van Wezel, R., van Gerven, M.: End-to-end optimization of prosthetic vision. J. Vis. **22** (2022). https://doi.org/10.1167/jov.22.2.20
39. Toledo-Moreo, F.J., Martínez-Alvarez, J.J., Garrigós-Guerrero, J., Ferrández-Vicente, J.M.: FPGA-based architecture for the real-time computation of 2-d convolution with large kernel size. J. Syst. Architect. **58**, 277–285 (2012). https://doi.org/10.1016/j.sysarc.2012.06.002
40. Tsirtsakis, P., Zacharis, G., Maraslidis, G.S., Fragulis, G.F.: Deep learning for object recognition: a comprehensive review of models and algorithms. Int. J. Cogn. Comput. Eng. **6**, 298–312 (2025). https://doi.org/10.1016/j.ijcce.2025.01.004
41. Waclawczyk, D., Soo, L., Ruiz, R.M., Caspi, A., Fernandez, E.: Integrating eye-tracking with cortical visual prostheses in patients without eyes: a case study. IEEE Trans. Neural Syst. Rehabil. Eng. **33**, 3998–4007 (2025). https://doi.org/10.1109/TNSRE.2025.3615286
42. Xie, S., Tu, Z.: Holistically-nested edge detection. arXiv:1504.06375 (2015)
43. Yücel, E.I., et al.: Factors affecting two-point discrimination in argus ii patients. Front. Neurosci. **16** (2022). https://doi.org/10.3389/fnins.2022.901337

Artifact-Minimized Multi-unit Activity Estimation Using Polynomic Interpolation

Rocío López-Peco[1(✉)], Alfonso Rodil[1], Cristina Soto-Sánchez[1], Mikel Val-Calvo[2], and Eduardo Fernández[1,3]

[1] Instituto de Bioingeniería, Universidad Miguel Hernández, Alicante, Spain
rocio.lopezp@umh.com
[2] Research Institute for Human Centered Technology, Polytechnic University of Valencia, Valencia, Spain
[3] CIBER-BBN, Madrid, Spain

Abstract. Multi-unit activity (MUA) reflects the combined firing of local neuronal populations and is widely used to study cortical dynamics. However, MUA estimation is often distorted by artifacts introduced during electrical micro-stimulation, including abrupt signal deflections and filter-induced ringing, which can lead to false spike detections and misinterpretations of neural responses. In this study, we introduce a method to minimize such artifacts by applying a local cubic polynomial to interpolate over stimulation-contaminated segments, preserving the continuity of the signal while preventing oscillations. Using intra-cortical recordings from a Utah Electrode Array (UEA), we show that polynomial correction effectively reduces artifact-driven peaks and maintains physiological activity patterns. Comparison between corrected and uncorrected signals shows a smoother, more plausible MUA profile, with a marked reduction in pre- and post-stimulus activity. Our approach enables reliable, high-resolution assessment of neuronal population responses during stimulation, providing a practical framework for peri-stimulus analyses and supporting robust interpretation of cortical activation in intra-cortical micro-stimulation experiments.

Keywords: Multi-unit Activity · Electrical micro-stimulation · Cubic polynomial

1 Introduction

Multi-unit activity in intra-cortical recordings refers to the combined spiking activity of multiple neurons near an electrode tip. Unlike single-unit activity (SUA), which isolates signals from individual neurons [1], MUA captures the aggregate action potentials from a local neuronal population near the electrode tip. This collective signal provides insight into how groups of neurons work together to encode information, such as sensory processing, motor intentions, or cognitive states [2]. Keller et al. [3] highlighted that SUA and MUA offer

J. M. Ferrández Vicente et al. (Eds.): IWINAC 2026, LNCS 16574, pp. 426–438, 2026.
https://doi.org/10.1007/978-3-032-27314-7_39

complementary perspectives on neuronal population dynamics: SUA allows precise identification of individual neuronal responses, whereas MUA reflects the overall activity present in raw recordings.

Given that MUA captures the aggregate spiking activity of local neuronal populations, its accurate extraction from extracellular recordings is critical for downstream analyses. Multi-unit activity is typically obtained by isolating the high-frequency components of the signal, typically above 300 Hz, which correspond to the fast transients of action potentials from neurons near the electrode tip. There is no single standardized method for computing MUA, and several approaches have been used in the literature. Commonly, a voltage threshold is applied to the filtered signal, and each threshold crossing is counted as a spike event. This threshold can be defined as a multiple of the estimated noise level (e.g., using the median absolute deviation or standard deviation of the baseline noise), as the mean plus a factor times the standard deviation [4,5], or based on the signal-to-noise ratio (SNR) [6]. Some studies aggregate all suprathreshold events across channels to obtain a population-level MUA signal, while others treat each channel as a separate putative neuron, generating multi-unit spike trains (MUS) per channel [7]. These events are accumulated within fixed temporal bins (e.g., 1 ms to 100 ms) to generate the MUA time series. Unlike single-unit analysis, no spike sorting is performed; all supra-threshold events are included in the aggregate signal, representing the combined firing of local neuronal populations. Optionally, the binned counts can be transformed into additional features, such as root mean square amplitude or mean absolute value, for use in downstream analyses. This approach provides a robust and efficient index of aggregate spiking activity without the computational complexity of isolating individual neurons [6].

However, the MUA metric is susceptible to artifacts that can distort the representation of neuronal spiking. Due to high-pass filtering, slow drifts, baseline shifts, and low-frequency physiological noise (e.g., movement artifacts, local field potential components) are effectively attenuated. This filtering also reduces the impact of stimulation-evoked field potentials and power-line noise concentrated in lower frequencies. However, certain high-frequency artifacts can overlap with the spike band, such as stimulation transients or amplifier switching noise, and therefore remain present after filtering. In such cases, artifact management relies on additional post-processing techniques. Several alternative methods have been proposed in the literature for high-frequency artifact management in neural recordings, including template subtraction, linear interpolation, exponential fitting, and multichannel decomposition techniques [8]. In addition, when band-pass filtering is subsequently applied to extract MUA, leaving the raw stimulation artifact uncorrected can induce ringing and other distortions that propagate into the post-stimulation period of interest. To mitigate these effects, the artifacted segment can be replaced with a smooth, artificial signal, even though the neuronal activity during stimulation is considered irretrievably lost. Among the top-performing approaches identified by Wang et al. [9], linear interpolation and exponential fitting effectively reduce such distortions. In the linear interpolation methodology, large transient deflections caused by stimulation were replaced with a linear interpolation between the samples but did not remove the following artefactual decay. On the other hand, when applying the sum of exponentials, they removed not only the large deflections but also the later slow decay component.

In this study, we introduce a methodological approach for MUA measurement in intracortical recordings with electrical micro-stimulation. The process involves blanking during acquisition with our post-processing polynomial correction. The blanking step prevents the recording of the large transient deflection and slow decay components of the stimulation artifact. However, abrupt transitions caused by blanking can still produce ringing effects after band-pass filtering. To mitigate this, we apply a third-order polynomial fit to preserve a smooth transition between the blanking segment and the surrounding signal. Compared to linear interpolation, this polynomial approach avoids oversimplification and abrupt changes, and unlike exponential fitting, it does not require strict assumptions about the decay, making it particularly suitable for artifacts with complex shapes or trial-to-trial variability.

2 Methods

2.1 Acquisition System

Neural signals analyzed in this paper were recorded from the primary visual cortex in blind volunteers. They were implanted using a 96-channel intracortical Utah Electrode Array (UEA, Blackrock Microsystems, *Salt Lake City, UT, USA* [10]).

The hardware setup consists of three $Micro2 + Stim$ front-ends (32 channels each), connected to the processor and the UEA connector. Trellis software (version 1.14.4.41, Ripple Neuro, *Salt Lake City, UT, USA* [11]) was used to record neuronal activity from 96 channels. External events, including stimulus onset, were recorded via coaxial cables connected to the Grapevine Digital I/O and Analog I/O front-ends. The timing of electrical stimulation was saved as a digital event in the stimulation data stream. Electrophysiological data were sampled at 30kHz and stored in NSX and NEV file formats, proprietary to Blackrock Neurotech *Salt Lake City, UT, USA* [10]).

To optimize the processing steps, the pipeline was applied to a representative stimulation recording from one volunteer, which served as a benchmark for parameter tuning and artifact correction. The figures presented in this section correspond to a fragment of this recording during electrical stimulation. Stimulation was delivered through electrode 83 of the UEA at an intensity of 81 µA, while recordings are represented from electrode 69 for the example. The stimulation protocol consisted of biphasic individual pulses with a negative phase of 100 µs, an interphase interval of 60 µs, and a positive phase of 100 µs.

Finally, to measure the average effect of signal adjustment (Fig. 6), the recordings from all 96 UEA electrodes at four stimulation intensities (21, 41, 61, and 81 µA) were included. Each MUA signal was generated by averaging 10 repetitions under the same stimulation conditions, resulting in a total of 384 averaged files.

2.2 Raw Data Extraction

For each electrode i, raw signals $x_i(t)$ were normalized with respect to their own baseline distribution. A two-second period of spontaneous activity was used to compute the baseline mean μ_i^{baseline} and standard deviation $\sigma_i^{\text{baseline}}$. The normalized signal was then obtained as:

$$z_i(t) = \frac{x_i(t) - \mu_i^{\text{baseline}}}{\sigma_i^{\text{baseline}}}$$

This step transforms the raw signal of each electrode into standardized units relative to its own baseline activity. This allows neural responses to be compared within the same electrode independently of its absolute amplitude or noise level, thereby facilitating the detection of relative changes over time. To maintain consistency across channels, the signal was scaled using the standard deviation of electrode 1 $\sigma_1^{\text{baseline}}$. The normalized signal for each electrode is then computed as:

$$x_i^{\text{norm}}(t) = z_i(t) \cdot \sigma_1^{\text{baseline}}$$

This second normalization step expresses all channels on a common scale, facilitating direct comparison across the array while preserving the relative noise floor differences inherent to the physical characteristics of each electrode. Figure 1 shows the normalized signal peri-stimulus example, where axis-x corresponds to the time in seconds and axis-y to the voltage in mV. The blue line represents the signal, while the stimulation onset is marked in red. The stimulation-induced blanking artifact appears as a sharp discontinuity in the signal just after the stimulation onset.

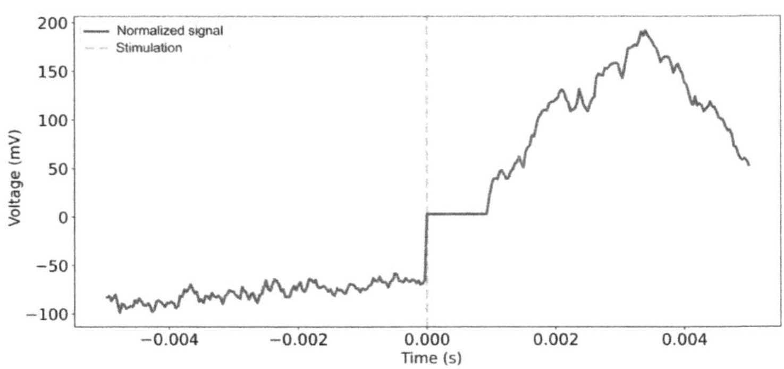

Fig. 1. Peri-stimulus normalized signal example. The stimulation onset is marked in red dashed line at t = 0 s (Color figure online).

2.3 Polynomial-Fit Approach

The segment contaminated by the blanking period was replaced with a local cubic polynomial interpolation as illustrated in Fig. 2. This window, W_{rep}, accounts for the hardware-level disconnection of the amplifier during stimulation, the fast-settle interval that return the signal voltage (15 samples), and an additional 5 samples to allow full return of the signal to baseline.

A third-degree polynomial was fitted using the blanking-free samples immediately surrounding this interval. Specifically, W_{flank} comprised the 20 samples immediately preceding and the 20 samples immediately following W_{rep}. The polynomial was computed as follows:

$$\hat{x}(n) = \sum_{k=0}^{3} a_k \, n^k, \qquad n \in W_{\text{flank}}$$

where $\hat{x}(n)$ denotes the polynomial estimate of the signal at sample n, a_k are the polynomial coefficients obtained through least-squares fitting, and n is the discrete time index.

Only the samples within W_{rep} were replaced with the polynomial interpolation to preserve a smooth transition and to minimize filter-induced ringing:

$$x_{\text{adj}}(n) = \begin{cases} \hat{x}(n), & n \in W_{\text{rep}}, \\ x(n), & n \notin W_{\text{rep}}. \end{cases}$$

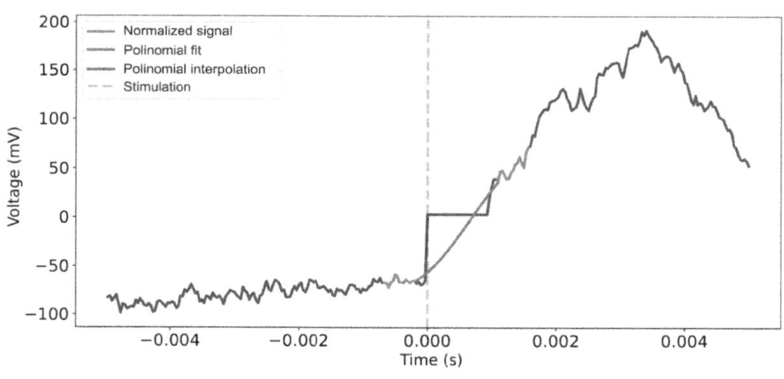

Fig. 2. Illustration of the polynomial-fit adjustment. The normalized signal is shown in blue. Samples used for polynomial fitting (W_{flank}) are highlighted in green. The cubic polynomial interpolation replacing the blanking interval (W_{rep}) is shown in pink. The dashed red line indicates the stimulation onset. (Color figure online)

2.4 Signal Filtering

Neural signals were processed using a third-order bidirectional Butterworth filter with a frequency range of 500–6000 Hz. The filter was implemented in second-order sections format to mantain numerical stability. An example of the resulting bandpass-filtered signal is shown in Fig. 3.

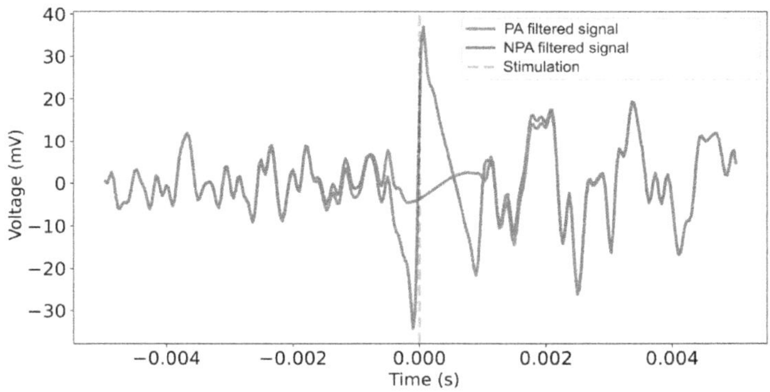

Fig. 3. Visualization of the bandpass-filtered signal. The polynomial adjusted (PA) signal is shown in green, while the non polynomial adjusted (NPA) signal is shown in blue. (Color figure online)

2.5 Multi-unit Activity Estimation and Processing from Instantaneous Firing Rate

Spikes were detected as negative-going peaks exceeding a threshold defined as the channel mean minus two times the standard deviation of the filtered signal. Figure 4 show the bandpass-filtered signals for polynomial (A) and non polynomial (B) adjusted conditions, with the detected peaks marked with crosses. Spike times were then used to compute the instantaneous firing rate (IFR) as the inverse of the inter-spike interval (ISI) [12]. Only negative peaks were considered, and the resulting values were initially assigned to a discrete time series at the times of spike occurrence.

Unlike methods based on spike-count histograms with fixed time bins, IFR bin-free approach avoids binning artifacts, which may introduce distortions due to loss of temporal precision, edge effects, and dependence on window size [13].

The method was computed as follows:

$$\mathrm{IFR}_n = \frac{1}{\Delta t_n}, \qquad \Delta t_n = t_n - t_{n-1}$$

where t_n is the time of the detected spike and t_{n-1} is the time of the previous spike.

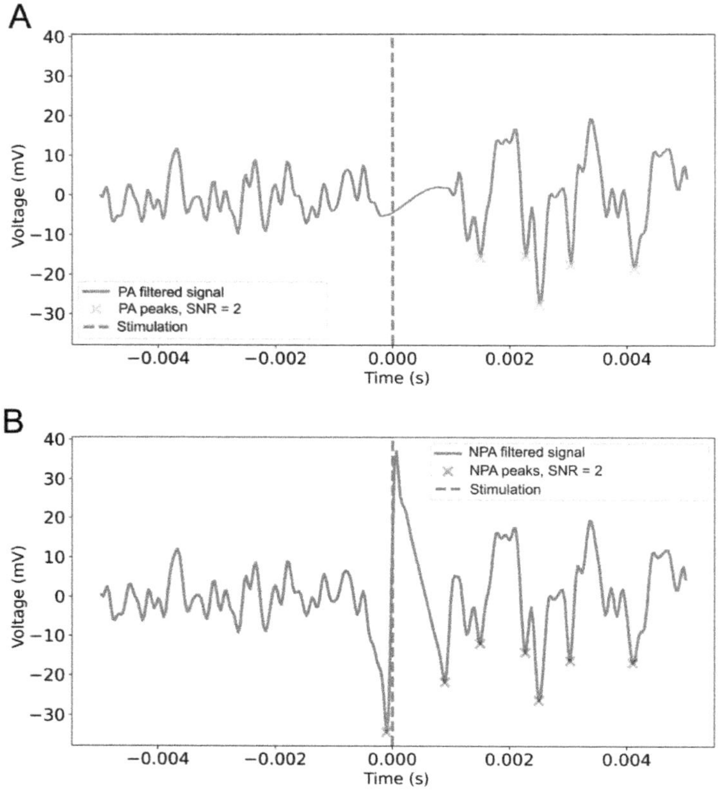

Fig. 4. Comparison of peak detection for multiunit activity estimation with and without polynomial adjustment. Negative peaks exceeding a threshold corresponding to a signal-to-noise ratio of 2 are identified as MUA candidates. (A) Polynomial-adjusted filtered signal, where detected peaks are indicated by yellow crosses. (B) Non-adjusted filtered signal, where detected peaks are indicated by red crosses. (Color figure online)

To obtain a continuous representation of multi-unit activity, the discrete spike-based IFR signal $x[n]$ was smoothed using a moving-average filter with a window of W samples and a given sampling frequency ($f_s = 30$ kHz). In this work, $W = 1\text{ ms} \cdot f_s = 30$ samples resulting in an effective temporal resolution of 1 kHz. The smoothing was implemented via convolution:

$$y[n] = \frac{1}{W} \sum_{k=0}^{W-1} x[n-k]$$

where $y[n]$ is the smoothed signal at sample n. This operation produces a continuous-time estimate of MUA with reduced high-frequency fluctuations while preserving the overall temporal structure.

To further refine the signal, a filter with a standard deviation of $\sigma = 0.1$ ms was applied to reduce residual high-frequency variability while preserving temporal features.

Finally, the continuous multi-unit activity signal was normalized to provide comparability across channels and experimental conditions. Normalization was performed by subtracting the minimum value of the signal and dividing by its standard deviation:

$$x_{\text{norm}}(t) = \frac{\tilde{x}(t) - \min(\tilde{x}(t))}{\text{std}(\tilde{x}(t))}$$

where $x_{\text{norm}}(t)$ denotes the normalized multi-unit activity. This normalization yields a continuous estimate of the instantaneous firing rate (IFR) that captures relative fluctuations in population-level neuronal firing dynamics rather than absolute spike rates. While the initial IFR calculation provides a measure in spikes per second (Hz), the subsequent smoothing and Z-score standardisation transform the data into a relative activity index. Consequently, the final MUA values represent normalised fluctuations in population-level firing rather than absolute firing rates, allowing for robust comparisons across electrodes with varying signal-to-noise ratios.

Figure 5 shows the MUA signal computed from signals with and without polynomial adjustment. Detected peaks contributing to each trace are marked in yellow (polynomial adjusted) and red (unadjusted).

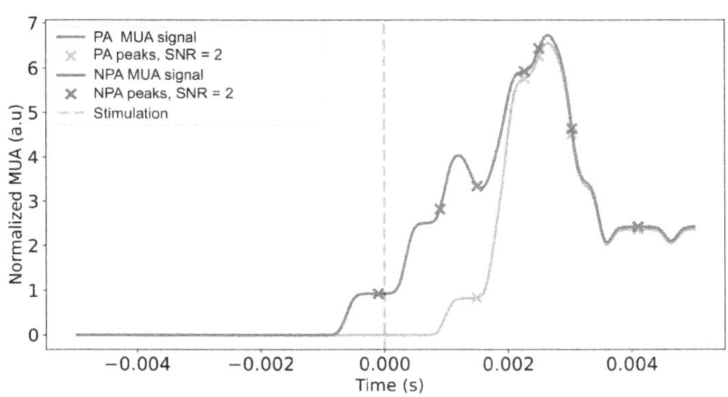

Fig. 5. Computed MUA signals with and without polynomial adjustment. MUA derived from the polynomial adjusted signal is shown in green, while MUA from the unadjusted signal is shown in blue. Detected peaks contributing to the MUA trace are indicated in yellow (with polynomial adjustment) and red (without adjustment). (Color figure online)

2.6 Implementation Details

The full pipeline was implemented in *Python*, using the following libraries: *NumPy* for numerical operations, *SciPy* for signal processing and statistical computations, *Matplotlib* and *Seaborn* for data visualization and graphical representation, and *brpylib* for reading and handling the Blackrock electrophysiology data files.

3 Results

3.1 Pipeline Overview

Algorithm 1 summarizes the end-to-end pipeline used to obtain a continuous multi-unit activity signal from raw extracellular recordings. The workflow was applied identically across electrodes and stimulation intensities. Briefly, recordings underwent baseline standardisation (z-score) and local correction with a cubic polynomial to suppress the blanking and fast-settle transient prior to bandpass filtering (500–6000 Hz). Spikes were then detected as negative peaks exceeding a channel-specific threshold, and their occurrence times were converted into instantaneous firing rate (IFR). The IFR was rendered continuous using a 1 ms moving-average window and lightly smoothed with a Gaussian kernel ($\sigma = 0.1$ ms). Finally, the signal was normalized by subtracting its minimum value and dividing by its standard deviation to enable comparisons across channels and conditions. This processing sequence was selected to minimize stimulation-related distortions while preserving fast spiking dynamics, providing a reproducible and interpretable MUA readout for subsequent analyses.

Algorithm 1 ***Pipeline for continuous multi-unit activity (MUA) estimation.***

1. ***Input:*** *Raw extracellular signal*
2. *Apply* ***Z-score normalization***
3. *Perform* ***Polynomial fit adjustment*** *to suppress blanking/fast-settle artifacts*
4. *Apply* ***Butterworth bandpass filter*** *(500–6000 Hz)*
5. ***Detect spikes:*** *threshold* $= \mu + 2\sigma$ *(negative peaks only)*
6. ***Compute IFR:*** $\mathrm{IFR}(t) = 1/\mathrm{ISI}(t)$
7. ***Compute MUA*** *with moving average filter:* $\mathrm{MUA}(t) = \frac{1}{W}\sum \mathrm{IFR}(i), W = 1$ ms
8. ***Gaussian smoothing:*** $\sigma = 0.1$ ms
9. ***Normalize:*** $\mathrm{MUA}_{\mathrm{norm}}(t) = (\mathrm{MUA}(t) - \mathrm{min})/\mathrm{std}$
10. ***Output:*** *Continuous MUA signal*

3.2 Comparison of Corrected and Uncorrected MUA Signals

To evaluate the effect of polynomial adjustment on the estimation of multi-unit activity, spike times were aggregated across all 96 UEA electrodes and four stimulation intensities (21, 41, 61, and 81 μA). Each MUA signal was generated by averaging 10 repetitions under the same stimulation conditions, resulting in 384 averaged files. MUA signals were aligned to the stimulation onset and binned over the interval from −5 to +5 ms using 49 uniformly spaced bins (50 bin edges). This yielded a temporal resolution of approximately 0.204 ms per bin. For each condition (with and without polynomial adjustment), a histogram of spike counts was computed per electrode, producing matrices of dimensions:

$$[N_{\text{electrodes}} \times N_{\text{bins}}]$$

These were averaged across electrodes to obtain the mean peristimulus MUA trace for each condition. To assess significant differences between the corrected and uncorrected signals, a paired t-test was applied across electrodes at each bin. Bins with $p < 0.05$ were marked as statistically significant. The resulting traces are shown in Fig. 6, where shaded areas highlight time intervals in which one condition yielded consistently higher activity than the other.

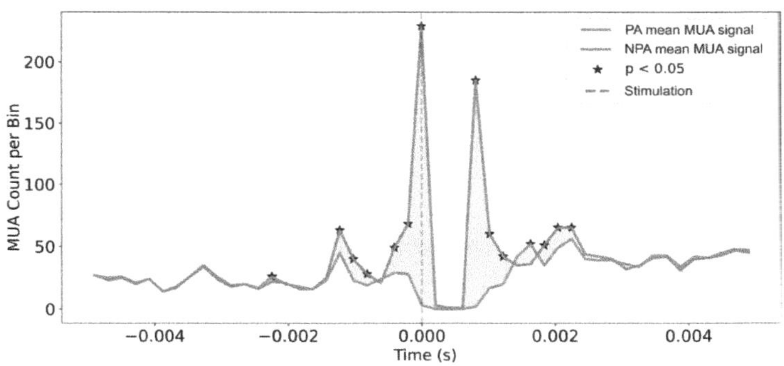

Fig. 6. Grand average histogram of 384 MUA trials across all conditions. Each trial represents the mean of 10 repetitions. Green: mean MUA per bin after polynomial adjustment; blue: non-adjusted. Asterisks indicate bins with significant differences ($paired\ t - test, p < 0.05$). (Color figure online)

4 Discussion

This work presents an effective MUA measurement method to avoid the presence of artifacts, both during stimulation using the hardware blanking and post-processing interpolating the blanked period. The results demonstrate that hardware blanking alone is insufficient for clean MUA extraction during intracortical microstimulation.

As we can see in Fig. 3, the non polynomial adjusted signal generate artifacts after the filtering steps. The abrupt blanking-induced discontinuity that we see in Fig. 1 generates, after 500–6000 Hz filtering, high amplitude ringing that persists well beyond the stimulation pulse itself. It shows prominent deflections around −1 and +1 ms after band-pass filtering that contaminate peri-stimulus activity. These pre-stimulus deflections seem to be a consequence of the bidirectional filtering process. On the other hand, the cubic polynomial locally restores continuity between the blanked segment and the surrounding signal. Therefore, it eliminates the filter-induced initial ringing peaks and their prolonged decay, providing a smoother MUA signal that remain near baseline during the most artifact-prone window while preserving later response components.

The effect on peaks estimation is remarkable in Fig. 4 where the crosses indicates the peaks exceeding the threshold. As we can expect, in the non polynomial adjusted signal (B), two more events appears as neural transients nearby the stimulation onset. Since the IFR is calculated taking these events into account, the effect on continuous MUA estimation is visible in Fig. 5, where we can compare both processing methods. The uncorrected signal shows a marked, prolonged elevation beginning approximately 0.5 ms prior to stimulus onset and extending up to 1 ms. The polynomial-corrected MUA, by contrast, remains near baseline through the −2 to 1 ms window, exhibiting minimal early activity. One millisecond after the stimulation, the activity converges with the uncorrected trace.

Although the artifact suppression is effective, the resulting signal disturbance does not appear particularly severe. The duration of the signal loss at the beginning—caused by blanking and the fast-settle period—is approximately 760 µs. This corresponds to 260 µs of pulse duration in this example (8 samples) and 500 µs of fast-settle time (20 samples), meaning that the lost signal window is only slightly longer than the stimulation period itself.

While the distortion appears relatively limited in the single-example case described above, its impact becomes substantially more visible when considering population-level averages across multiple repetitions, recording electrodes, and stimulation intensities. This pattern is illustrated in Fig. 6, where grand-average peri−stimulus histograms reveal the full temporal signature of the artifact. In the uncorrected condition, consistent high-amplitude peaks are observed both before and after stimulation (within the −2 to +2 ms window), with several bins reaching statistical significance ($p < 0.05$). Importantly, the ringing contamination does not decay immediately after the blanking window but propagates forward in time, producing an artifactual elevation of the MUA signal that extends beyond the stimulation period itself.

By contrast, the polynomial adjusted trace exhibit a substantially smoother peri−stimulus profile with markedly reduced fluctuations, indicating effective suppression of this prolonged contamination. Interestingly, beyond ∼2 ms some bins display slightly higher activity in the corrected condition compared to the uncorrected traces, suggesting that the polynomial interpolation preserves, and may even reveal, early neural responses rather than indiscriminately attenuating the signal.

From a functional perspective, this artifact/signal separation is crucial for intra-cortical microstimulation applications where MUA serves as a quantitative readout of stimulation efficacy. However, several limitations remain. The hardware blanking scheme renders intra-pulse activity irretrievable by design, analogous to interpolation-based methods, though this primarily affects the <1 ms window rather than the full direct-activation period. Finally, the approach has been optimized for specific Utah array geometry and stimulation parameters; generalization to high-frequency trains or multi-electrode patterns requires further validation.

5 Conclusion

The results demonstrate that local cubic polynomial correction effectively mitigates the prolonged contamination affecting high-frequency filtered signals after hardware blanking. This approach provides a practical framework for MUA estimation and the analysis of population-level neural responses during intra-cortical microstimulation.

Acknowledgments. This study was funded by grants $PDC2022-133952-100$ and $PID2022-141606OB-I00$ from the Spanish Ministerio de Ciencia, Innovación y Universidades, and by grant $CIPROM/2023/25$ from the Generalitat Valenciana.

References

1. Supér, H., Roelfsema, P.R.: Chronic multiunit recordings in behaving animals: advantages and limitations. Prog. Brain Res. **147**, 263–282 (2005). https://doi.org/10.1016/S0079-6123(04)47020-4
2. Perel, S., et al.: Direction and speed tuning of motor-cortex multi-unit activity and local field potentials during reaching movements. In: Annual International Conference of the IEEE Engineering in Medicine and Biology Society (EMBC), pp. 299–302 (2013). https://doi.org/10.1109/EMBC.2013.6609496
3. Keller, C.J., et al.: The limited utility of multiunit data in differentiating neuronal population activity. PLoS ONE **11**(4), e0153154 (2016). https://doi.org/10.1371/journal.pone.0153154
4. Drebitz, E., et al.: Optimizing the yield of multi-unit activity by including the entire spiking activity. Front. Neurosci. **13**, 83 (2019). https://doi.org/10.3389/fnins.2019.00083
5. Quiroga, R.Q., Nadasdy, Z., Ben-Shaul, Y.: Unsupervised spike detection and sorting with wavelets and superparamagnetic clustering. Neural Comput. **16**(8), 1661–1687 (2004). https://doi.org/10.1162/089976604774201631
6. Stark, E., Abeles, M.: Predicting movement from multiunit activity. J. Neurosci. **27**(31), 8387–8394 (2007). https://doi.org/10.1523/JNEUROSCI.1321-07.2007
7. Han, S., et al.: Multiunit activity-based real-time limb-state estimation from dorsal root ganglion recordings. Sci. Rep. **7**, 44197 (2017). https://doi.org/10.1038/srep44197

8. Zhou, A., Johnson, B.C., Muller, R.: Toward true closed-loop neuromodulation: artifact-free recording during stimulation. Curr. Opinion Neurobiol. **50**, 119–127 (2018). https://doi.org/10.1016/j.conb.2018.01.012. ISSN: 0959-4388
9. Wang, F., Chen, X., Roelfsema, P.R.: Comparison of electrical microstimulation artifact removal methods for high-channel-count prostheses. J. Neurosci. Methods **408**, 110169 (2024). https://doi.org/10.1016/j.jneumeth.2024.110169
10. Blackrock Neurotech. Blackrock Neurotech Software (2024). https://blackrockneurotech.com/products/software/
11. Ripple Neuro. Trellis EEG & ERP Acquisition Software. https://rippleneuro.com/support/software-downloads-updates/
12. Kostal, L., Lansky, P., Stiber, M.: Statistics of inverse interspike intervals: the instantaneous firing rate revisited. Chaos **28**(10), 106305 (2018). https://doi.org/10.1063/1.5036831
13. Shinomoto, S.: Estimating the firing rate. In: Grun, S., Rotter, S. (eds.) Analysis of Parallel Spike Trains. Springer Series in Computational Neuroscience, vol. 7, pp. 21–36. Springer, Boston (2010). https://doi.org/10.1007/978-1-4419-5675-0_2

Visual Cortex Stimulation Modulates Muscle Networks Underlying Postural Control in Blindness

Ana Lía Albarracín[1,2,5(✉)], Leonardo Ariel Cano[1,2], Fernando Daniel Farfán[1,2,3], and Eduardo Fernández[3,4]

[1] Laboratorio de Investigación en Neurociencias y Tecnologías Aplicadas (LINTEC), Departamento de Bioingenienría, Facultad de Ciencias Exactas y Tecnología, Universidad Nacional de Tucumán, Av. Independencia 1800, 4000 San Miguel de Tucumán, Tucumán, Argentina
[2] Instituto Superior de Investigaciones Biológicas (INSIBIO), Consejo Nacional de Investigaciones Científicas y Técnicas (CONICET), Batalla de Chacabuco 461, T4000 San Miguel de Tucumán, Tucumán, Argentina
[3] Institute of Bioengineering, Universidad Miguel Hernández of Elche, Avinguda de la Universitat d'Elx s/n, 03202 Elche, Alicante, Spain
[4] Research Networking Center in Bioengineering, Biomaterials and Nanomedicine (CIBER-BBN), Av. Monforte de Lemos, 3–5. Pabellón 11, planta 0, 28029 Madrid, Spain
[5] Facultad de Medicina, Universidad Nacional de Tucumán, Av. Julio A. Roca 1800, T4000 San Miguel de Tucumán, Tucumán, Argentina
aalbarracin@herrera.unt.edu.ar

Abstract. Postural control relies on the integration of multisensory information, including visual, vestibular, and somatosensory inputs to generate coordinated neuromuscular responses. In blind people, the absence of visual input leads to adaptive changes in postural strategies to maintain balance. This study investigated intermuscular connectivity during upright postures in a blind neuroprosthesis user to determine how electrically evoked visual percepts induced by primary visual cortex stimulation influence muscle network organization during postural control. The results were compared with those obtained from control subjects under open and closed eyes conditions. Surface EMG was recorded from ten lower-limb muscles during standing feet apart and tandem postural conditions. Intermuscular coherence was estimated, and muscle networks were characterized using graph-theoretical analysis and global efficiency metrics in the gamma frequency band. In the blind participant, cortical visual stimulation significantly increased gamma-band global efficiency compared to the no-stimulation condition, yielding muscle network configurations similar to those observed in controls. No significant differences were found between eyes-open and eyes-closed conditions in controls, nor during tandem stance. These findings provide the first evidence that electrically evoked visual perception, induced by primary visual cortex stimulation in a blind neuroprosthesis user, can modulate the organization of the neuromuscular network underlying upright postural control.

J. M. Ferrández Vicente et al. (Eds.): IWINAC 2026, LNCS 16574, pp. 439–448, 2026.
https://doi.org/10.1007/978-3-032-27314-7_40

Keywords: Visual cortex stimulation · intermuscular connectivity · muscle networks · postural control · visual neuroprosthesis

1 Introduction

Postural control is a complex motor function that relies on the integration of visual, vestibular, and somatosensory information to maintain body stability during standing and locomotion [12]. Visual input plays a particularly important role in reducing postural sway and optimizing muscle coordination, especially under conditions of sensory uncertainty or increased task demands [17].

Lack of visual input in blind individuals disrupts postural stability and requires a compensatory increase in the weighting of proprioceptive and vestibular sensory inputs to maintain balance [16]. Studies using functional Near InfraRed Spectroscopy (fNIRS) have demonstrated that blind individuals increased brain activation overall demanding postural task indicating additional sensory integration during postural control [11]. Also, it has been reported that individuals with visual impairment may adopt an active stiffening strategy with muscle activation to maintain postural stability [13]. All these reports support the notion that blind individuals adjust the sensorimotor cortex activation and neuromuscular responses to maintain stability without vision.

The present study examines muscle networks strategies change during postural control in a blind individual implanted with a cortical visual neuroprosthesis and in a group of control subjects. Using EMG recordings from ten lower-limb muscles, intermuscular coherence analysis, and graph-theoretical measures of global efficiency, we investigated whether cortical visual stimulation modulates neuromuscular network organization during different standing conditions. We hypothesized that electrically evoked visual percepts induced by visual cortex stimulation would induce a reorganization of muscle networks in the blind participant, leading to connectivity patterns more similar to those observed in control participants.

2 Materials and Methods

2.1 Experimental Design

Participants. In this study participated ten adults as control group and one blind subject implanted with a cortical visual prosthesis. The control group included young adult subjects (21–33 years) with no neurological disorders or motor impairments. The blind subject (male, 28 years) was implanted with an intracortical micro-electrode array (Utah Electrode Array, UEA) in the visual cortex [10]. This procedure is part of the ongoing research and development activities of a cortical visual neuroprosthesis conducted within the CORTIVIS project (www.cortivis.org). All procedures were carried out in accordance with clinical trial regulations, the Declaration of Helsinki, and European Commission Directives. Written informed consent was obtained from all participants prior to any study-related procedures.

Protocol. The experimental protocol aimed to investigate whether electrically evoked visual percepts induced by visual cortex stimulation in the blind participant modulate intermuscular connectivity during postural control tasks. Preliminary results from this study were previously reported in Albarracín et al. [1]. In the present work, we expand on those findings by including a larger sample size and additional postural conditions analysis.

Participants were evaluated under two standing conditions: feet apart and tandem stance. The control group was also evaluated with eyes open (EO) and eyes closed (EC). The blind participant performed the same postures under two conditions: 1) with stimulation (Stim) delivered by the cortical visual prosthesis and 2) without stimulation (NoStim).

Participants were instructed to maintain the initial posture for 30 s, after which they received a verbal cue to switch to the other condition, which was sustained for an additional 30 s.

Surface electromyography (EMG) signals were recorded bilaterally from five lower-limb muscles: Tibialis anterior (TA), Gastrocnemius medialis (GM), Vastus medialis (VM), Biceps femoris (BF), and Rectus femoris (RF), following the methodology previously reported in Albarracín et al. [1] (Fig. 1). Data were acquired using an RHD2132 acquisition system (Intan Technologies, Los Angeles, CA, USA), with 32-channel amplifiers and configured with a sampling frequency 5000 Hz.

2.2 Signal Pre-processing and Segmentation

All data processing was performed using MATLAB version 2020a (MathWorks Inc., Natick, MA, USA). EMG signals were band-pass and notch filtered to remove movement artifacts and power-line noise. Then, the recordings were segmented according to the posture and condition in 20-s segment to avoid transient effects related to postural adjustments and force reductions. Those segments were then divided into ten subsegments of 2 s each. To increase the number of samples available for connectivity analysis, an additional segmentation step was applied using overlapping time windows within each 2-s subsegment. This approach allowed us to obtain multiple estimates of intermuscular connectivity, while maintaining consistent segment duration across conditions. As a result, for each posture and condition, ten connectivity estimates were obtained, fulfilling the requirements of the intermuscular coherence method described by Bigot et al. [3].

2.3 Intermuscular Connectivity Analysis

Intermuscular connectivity (IMC) was quantified using frequency-domain coherence analysis following the method proposed by Bigot and colleagues [3]. Coherence was computed between all pairs of recorded muscles. The IMC and statistical analyses were delimited for gamma frequency band (30–45 Hz), given its established relevance in motor control and sensorimotor integration.

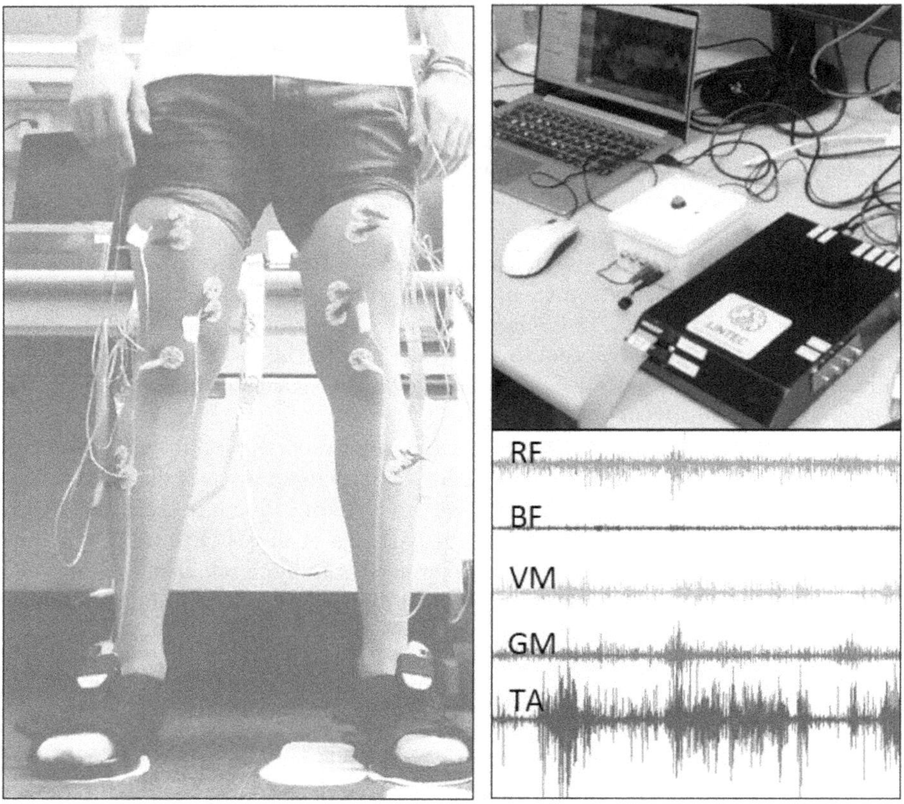

Fig. 1. Experimental protocol and EMG signals. Image showing the placement of the electrodes on the participant's legs and an example of the recorded EMG signals.

Muscle networks were constructed based on the IMC matrix obtained and using Graph Theory and were generated for each participant and for each postural condition (Fig. 2). Within these networks, nodes (shown as circles) correspond to individual muscles, whereas the connections between nodes reflect the strength of connectivity among them.

To assess how the organization of these muscle networks varies across the different experimental conditions, Weighted Global Efficiency (GE) was computed and used as the outcome variable for all subsequent statistical analyses. Thus, for the control group, GE values were first averaged across repetitions within each subject, yielding a single GE value per posture, frequency band, and subject. This approach ensured statistical independence at the group level. On the other hand, GE values calculated for the blind subject were computed for each repetition and condition, allowing intra-subject analyses.

2.4 Statistical Analysis

A single-case statistical approach - the Crawford–Howell t-test - was used to compare values obtained for the blind participant with those of the control group. This test is specifically designed to compare an individual case against a small normative sample while appropriately accounting for the variability of the control group. For each postural condition, the mean GE values of the blind participant was compared against the distribution of subject-wise mean GE values from the control group. Statistical significance was assessed at $\alpha = 0.05$.

To assess condition-dependent changes within the blind participant, paired comparisons between Stimulation and No-Stimulation conditions were performed using the Wilcoxon signed-rank test. This non-parametric test was selected considering the limited number of repetitions and the lack of assumptions regarding data normality. An analogous intra-condition comparison was performed for the control group by comparing Eyes-open and Eyes-closed conditions. GE values were first averaged across repetitions within each control subject, and the Wilcoxon signed-rank test was applied across subjects.

3 Results

The present study evaluates the effects of visual cortex stimulation in a blind neuroprosthesis user on muscle networks strategies during different postural control conditions. The results obtained confirm the trends described in our previous work, showing that phosphene production via a cortical visual neuroprosthesis can induces changes in muscle network connectivity underlying standing posture.

Visual inspection of the muscle networks representations further supported this finding (Fig. 2). In the no-stimulation condition, the intermuscular network of the blind participant exhibited a reduced number of interconnected muscles and a sparser connectivity pattern. Conversely, during stimulation, the resulting muscle networks displayed a greater number of connections and a more integrated structure. Notably, the connectivity patterns observed during stimulation qualitatively resembled those obtained from the control group under both EO and EC conditions. On the other hand, inter-subject analysis of the control group demonstrated no significant differences in GE metrics between eyes-open and eyes-closed conditions ($p = 0.8457$) (Fig. 3). This result suggests that the overall intermuscular networks organization remained comparable across visual conditions, suggesting that neuromuscular strategies evolving similar networks were employed to maintain postural stability. In contrast, the analysis of the blind participant revealed significant differences between Stimulation and No-Stimulation conditions ($p = 0.0019$). Specifically, neuroprosthetic stimulation inducing phosphene perception was associated with a significant increase in GE values distribution compared to the no-stimulation condition, indicating an intermuscular connectivity reorganization.

These observations were corroborated by the single-case statistical analysis. The Crawford–Howell comparisons revealed significant differences between the blind participant in the No-stimulation condition and the control group in both

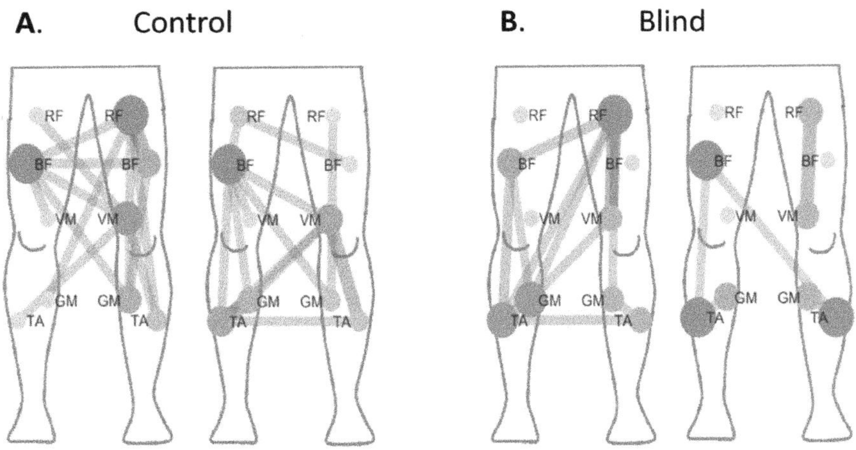

Fig. 2. Muscle Networks representation during standing feet apart. A. muscle networks obtained for a control subject under eyes open (*left*) and eyes closed condition (*right*). B. Reduced number of muscle connectivity are observed for blind subject due to the visual cortex stimulation (*right*).

the EO and EC conditions ($p = 0.0097$). Importantly, when neuroprosthetic stimulation was applied, these differences were no longer present ($p = 0.4936$), indicating that stimulation-induced phosphene perception shifted the intermuscular connectivity of the blind participant toward values comparable to those of the control group. Taken together, these results demonstrate that cortical visual neuroprosthetic stimulation produces a statistically significant reorganization of intermuscular networks in gamma-band during standing with feet apart, characterized by a higher number of functional muscle connections.

In contrast to standing feet apart condition, no significant differences were observed during tandem stance for any of the comparisons performed - EO vs Stim and EC vs NoStim ($p = 0.6304$ and $p = 0.5400$, respectively). Neither the intra-subject comparison between stimulation and no-stimulation in the blind participant nor the inter-condition comparisons in the control group reached statistical significance. This absence of effects could suggest that the increased postural demands associated with tandem stance may potentially overriding or masking modulation effects induced by visual or neuroprosthetic input.

4 Discussion

The results presented in this work provide evidence that cortical visual stimulation via a neuroprosthesis can modulate neuromuscular organization during postural control in a blind individual. Specifically, we found that global efficiency metric increased during stimulation compared to the no-stimulation condition, and that muscle network organization during stimulation resembled

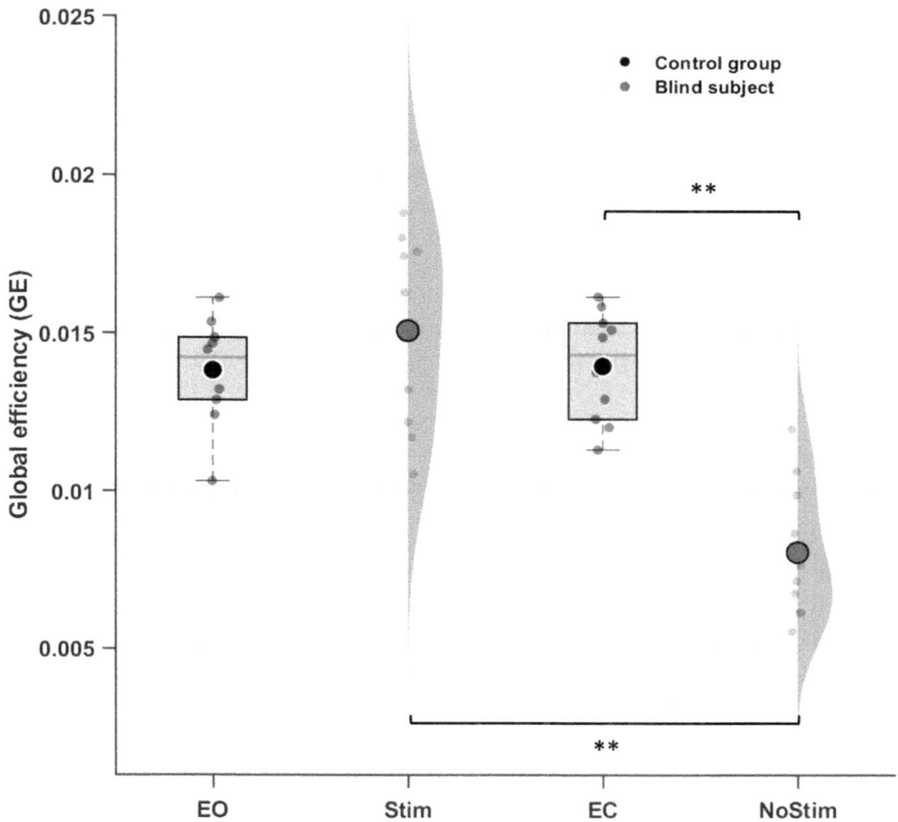

Fig. 3. Global Efficiency results. Violin graphs represent the GE values distribution for the blind subject; NoStim: No-stimulation condition, Stim: Stimulation condition; larger circles with black edges represent the means of the distributions. Grey boxplots: control group distribution for the eyes-open (EO) and eyes-closed (EC) conditions; each grey dot corresponds to the mean value of an individual control subject. ** indicates highly significant differences ($p < 0.01$). (Color figure online)

that of control participants. In contrast, no significant differences were observed between eyes-open and eyes-closed conditions in controls, and no stimulation-related effects were detected during tandem stance. These findings support our initial hypothesis regarding stimulation-induced muscle networks reorganization and highlight the task-dependent nature of these effects.

The absence of significant differences between eyes-open and eyes-closed conditions in the control group during standing with feet apart aligns with previous work indicating that control individuals can maintain stability without continuous visual input [7,16]. The sensory reweighting hypothesis suggest that the central nervous system (CNS) adapts to different circumstances by adjusting the relative weight of the different sensory sources that control stance [16]. Thus, postural perturbations due to the lack of visual information may be compensated by sensory reweighting by more reliable information, such as proprioceptive and vestibular systems [15].

Changes in muscle networks and reduced connectivity in the blind participant during the No-stimulation condition are consistent with previous studies reporting altered muscle coordination strategies as stiffening strategy [6] and neuromuscular co-contraction to maintain postural stability [8]. In the case of tandem stance, postural stabilization demands higher biomechanical and sensorimotor information, requiring greater reliance on proprioceptive and vestibular inputs. The absence of stimulation-related effects during tandem stance highlights the importance of the postural task in shaping neuromuscular connectivity. It is possible that the CNS reduces the relative weight of the visual system and must rely more on the other sensory systems minimizing the cortical visual stimulation effect.

Several studies have explored the notion that IMC is particularly suited to investigate common input to groups of muscles and showed that disparate muscles, whose activity needs to be coordinated, indeed reveal significant IMC [5,14,18]. In the present study, increased GE values during stimulation suggests enhanced integration across muscle groups, potentially reflecting a more coordinated neural drive to motor neuron pools. This interpretation is consistent with prior work demonstrating that muscle connectivity was observed at multiple distinct frequencies in standing postural control and reported IMC at higher frequencies between lower leg muscles in the same leg [4].

The central finding of this study is that cortical visual neuroprosthetic stimulation can induced a significant reorganization of intermuscular networks in the blind participant. During stimulation, muscle networks exhibited increased connectivity and higher global efficiency, approaching the organization observed in control subjects. Although the visual percepts generated by cortical stimulation are limited to phosphenes, they may nonetheless provide relevant sensory feedback that CNS compute to modulate muscle networks in specific postural tasks.

The results presented here are in line with recent findings suggesting functional reorganization for processing visual information induced by electrical stimulation through a cortical visual prosthesis. Substantial improvements in visual function have been reported following electrical microstimulation in a blind neuroprosthesic user [2]. Also, significant changes in cortical connectivity in the resting state was described before the microelectrode implantation and after its explanation in two blind subjects [9]. The present findings align with this framework, suggesting that artificial visual input could modulate distributed neural networks underlying balance control, with effects that are strongly task dependent.

Limitations and Future Directions. This study reports findings from a single blind participant implanted with a cortical visual neuroprosthesis. Future work should include additional participants, longitudinal designs, and assessments combining EEG recordings and kinematics measures. Such approaches will be essential to further elucidate the cortical connectivity underlying the stimulation-induced changes observed in muscle network organization.

Acknowledgement. This work was supported in part by grants PDC2022-133952-100 and PID2022- 141606OBI00 from the Spanish "Ministerio de Ciencia, Innovación y Universidades", by grant CIPROM/2023/25 from the Generalitat Valenciana, and by the European Union's Horizon 2020 Research and Innovation Programme under Grant Agreement No. 899287 (NeuraViPeR) as well as by grant E701 (RES-HCS 356-2023) from the Argentinian "Universidad Nacional de Tucumán" and by institutional founds from the Argentinian "Consejo Nacional de Investigaciones Científicas y Técnicas" (CONICET).

Disclosure of Interests. The authors have no competing interests to declare that are relevant to the content of this article.

References

1. Albarracín, A.L., Cano, L.A., Freire, E.O., Escobar, F., Fernandez, E., Farfán, F.D.: Effects of Visual Cortical Stimulation on Functional Muscle Network Efficiency in a Blind Subject: A Pilot Study, pp. 1292–1300 (2025). https://doi.org/10.1007/978-3-032-06401-1_109
2. Alfaro, A., Soo, L., Waclawczyk, D., Morollón, R., Grani, F., Fernandez, E.: The unexpected sight: improvement of visual function following intracortical microstimulation of the human occipital cortex. Brain Commun. **8** (2026). https://doi.org/10.1093/braincomms/fcaf504
3. Bigot, J., Longcamp, M., Maso, F.D., Amarantini, D.: A new statistical test based on the wavelet cross-spectrum to detect time–frequency dependence between non-stationary signals: application to the analysis of cortico-muscular interactions. NeuroImage **55**, 1504–1518 (2011). https://doi.org/10.1016/j.neuroimage.2011.01.033
4. Boonstra, T.W., Danna-Dos-Santos, A., Xie, H.B., Roerdink, M., Stins, J.F., Breakspear, M.: Muscle networks: connectivity analysis of EMG activity during postural control. Sci. Rep. **5**, 17830 (2015). https://doi.org/10.1038/srep17830
5. Boonstra, T.W., van Wijk, B.C., Praamstra, P., Daffertshofer, A.: Corticomuscular and bilateral EMG coherence reflect distinct aspects of neural synchronization. Neurosci. Lett. **463**, 17–21 (2009). https://doi.org/10.1016/j.neulet.2009.07.043
6. Campayo-Piernas, M., Caballero, C., Barbado, D., Reina, R.: Role of vision in sighted and blind soccer players in adapting to an unstable balance task. Exp. Brain Res. **235**, 1269–1279 (2017). https://doi.org/10.1007/s00221-017-4885-8
7. Cenciarini, M., Peterka, R.J.: Stimulus-dependent changes in the vestibular contribution to human postural control. J. Neurophysiol. **95**, 2733–2750 (2006). https://doi.org/10.1152/jn.00856.2004
8. Cimadoro, G., Paizis, C., Alberti, G., Babault, N.: Effects of different unstable supports on EMG activity and balance. Neurosci. Lett. **548**, 228–232 (2013). https://doi.org/10.1016/j.neulet.2013.05.025
9. Farfán, F.D., Soo, L., Grani, F., Grima-Murcia, M.D., Fernández, E.: Brain connectivity changes in response to cortical electrical stimulation in blind neuroprosthesis users. Cerebral Cortex **35** (2025). https://doi.org/10.1093/cercor/bhaf075

10. Fernández, E., et al.: Visual percepts evoked with an intracortical 96-channel microelectrode array inserted in human occipital cortex. J. Clin. Investig. **131** (2021). https://doi.org/10.1172/JCI151331
11. Helmich, I., Gemmerich, R.: Neuronal control of posture in blind individuals. Brain Topogr. **37**, 783–795 (2024). https://doi.org/10.1007/s10548-024-01041-7
12. Horak, F.B.: Postural orientation and equilibrium: what do we need to know about neural control of balance to prevent falls? Age and Ageing **35**, ii7–ii11 (2006). https://doi.org/10.1093/ageing/afl077
13. Li, Y., Hou, S., Zhang, X., Wang, A.: Sensory reweighting for postural stability in individuals with low vision and blindness: balance adaptation and muscle co-contraction. Front. Physiol. **16** (2025). https://doi.org/10.3389/fphys.2025.1684671
14. Nazarpour, K., Barnard, A., Jackson, A.: Flexible cortical control of task-specific muscle synergies. J. Neurosci. **32**, 12349 (2012). https://doi.org/10.1523/JNEUROSCI.5481-11.2012. http://www.jneurosci.org/content/32/36/12349.abstract
15. Pasma, J.H., Boonstra, T.A., Campfens, S.F., Schouten, A.C., der Kooij, H.V.: Sensory reweighting of proprioceptive information of the left and right leg during human balance control. J. Neurophysiol. **108**, 1138–1148 (2012). https://doi.org/10.1152/jn.01008.2011
16. Peterka, R.J.: Sensorimotor integration in human postural control. J. Neurophysiol. **88**, 1097–1118 (2002). https://doi.org/10.1152/jn.2002.88.3.1097
17. Peterka, R.J., Loughlin, P.J.: Dynamic regulation of sensorimotor integration in human postural control. J. Neurophysiol. **91**, 410–423 (2004). https://doi.org/10.1152/jn.00516.2003
18. Poston, B., Santos, A.D.D., Jesunathadas, M., Hamm, T.M., Santello, M.: Force-independent distribution of correlated neural inputs to hand muscles during three-digit grasping. J. Neurophysiol. **104**, 1141–1154 (2010). https://doi.org/10.1152/jn.00185.2010

ECTLAB: “European Culture and Technology Lab (EUT+). EPISTEAM”

Machine Voices for Human Histories: Mixed Epistemologies for Architectural Heritage

Silivan Moldovan[1,3] and Ioana Moldovan[2,3](✉)

[1] Faculty of Architecture and Urbanism, Technical University of Cluj-Napoca, Observatorului 34-36, 400347 Cluj-Napoca, Romania
silivan.moldovan@campus.utcluj.ro

[2] Faculty of Civil Engineering, Technical University of Cluj-Napoca, Baritiu 25, 400020 Cluj-Napoca, Romania
ioana.moldovan@campus.utcluj.ro

[3] European Culture and Technology Laboratory ECT Lab+, European University of Technology, European Union, Cluj-Napoca, Romania

Abstract. This paper presents a mixed methodology for architectural heritage that combines UAV-based photogrammetry, large-language AI, and speculative storytelling to generate polyvocal narratives. Modern remote sensing (photogrammetry, LiDAR) provides precise 3D models of buildings, but these rich spatial datasets capture only physical form. Important intangible aspects (e.g.memories, local myths, and alternate histories) often remain monological and marginalized in official or authorized heritage discourse. We argue that integrating generative AI voices as "characters" (e.g. the building itself, materials, inhabitants) can amplify diverse perspectives and imagine new contexts. In our experiment, drone imagery is processed into 3D models (photogrammetric meshes) which become the backdrop for AI-generated narratives. Distinct AI "speakers" are seeded with site-specific facts and creative prompts to produce speculative accounts. These narratives, delivered as text-to-speech voices, interweave factual detail with imaginative reflection, creating a layered storytelling experience. We present a case study (McMahon Hall, Seattle, USA) to illustrate the workflow and results. The discussion highlights how this polyvocal, machine-augmented approach transforms heritage epistemology and how it can extend heritage documentation beyond objective recording into the realm of what-ifs, challenging singular histories and democratizing cultural memory.

Keywords: Generative AI · Speculative Storytelling · Photogrammetry

1 Introduction

Cultural heritage sites are repositories of memory and meaning as much as they are physical structures [1]. While traditional documentation focuses on geometry

J. M. Ferrández Vicente et al. (Eds.): IWINAC 2026, LNCS 16574, pp. 451–460, 2026.
https://doi.org/10.1007/978-3-032-27314-7_41

and style, there is growing recognition that stories and perspectives shape what a site signifies. Modern remote sensing (UAV photogrammetry, terrestrial LiDAR) has revolutionized heritage documentation by generating accurate 3D models and digital twins of architecture [2–4]. These models serve conservation, monitoring, and virtual tourism, preserving form against threats like decay or disaster [5–7]. However, capturing the tangible form is only part of heritage preservation. Official histories often rely on an Authorized Heritage Discourse (AHD) [8] that privileges elite or expert narratives. Local voices, personal anecdotes, and even non-human viewpoints tend to be omitted. For example, scholarship calls for shifting away from a single authoritative narrative toward polyvocal interpretations that embrace multiple, and sometimes conflicting perspectives [9–11]. Embracing polyvocality democratizes heritage by transforming the story of the site into a tapestry of voices – across cultures, classes, or even species – each adding layers of meaning [12,13].

This paper proposes a mixed methodology that pairs precise spatial capture (photogrammetry) with generative AI storytelling to produce new epistemologies for architecture. We harness large-language models and voice synthesis to give the building and its elements a *voice* in the narrative. By scripting multiple AI-generated characters (e.g., the building as an elder guardian, the concrete as a reflective narrator, a local journalist, a bird in the sky and an architect), we create a speculative yet grounded polyvocal narrative that bridges objective data and imaginative insight. In doing so, the method not only documents the physical heritage but augments cultural memory, exploring how machine voices can widen understanding of place. The paper also presents related concepts, details our approach, and discusses implications for heritage practice and pedagogy.

2 Theoretical Background

2.1 Remote Sensing and Photogrammetry in Heritage

Remote sensing technologies have started to gain a lot of traction in heritage conservation and study. UAV photogrammetry, in particular, allows researchers to collect hundreds of overlapping aerial photos that are merged into dense point clouds and textured 3D meshes. These high-fidelity models capture architectural features (facades, materials, damage) and provide digital archives resistant to loss. Such data enable virtual measurement, structural analysis, and immersive experiences – from condition monitoring to VR tours. For example, Remondino and others note that 3D scans support simulations of decay, aging, or interactive exhibits, making spatial data a springboard for multimedia interpretation [2,14,15].

Yet despite these advances, digital models tend to be treated as objective records. In practice, photogrammetry outputs are often intended solely for accuracy and visualization. There is a gap between the tangible geometry they capture and the intangible stories those places hold. Many heritage projects stop at archiving form, still relying on singular texts or plaques to convey meaning. We posit that the next frontier is to pair these spatial artifacts with narrative layers

– using the model as a stage for storytelling. Our approach views the 3D model not as an end but as a canvas for interpretation, where speculative narratives infuse cultural context into the data.

2.2 Generative AI and Speculative Storytelling

Recent AI breakthroughs enable large-language models (LLMs) to generate coherent stories and even mimic distinct voices. By crafting system prompts and personas, one can steer an LLM to produce text as if spoken by a particular character. In our case, each AI character (e.g., the Building, the Concrete) is given a clear identity via a system prompt, enforcing tone and knowledge scope. We also use retrieval augmentation: feeding the AI factual context (construction dates, architectural style) and then asking speculative questions (e.g., "What memories would the concrete hold?"). This blend of grounded facts with imaginative framing yields narratives that are plausible and thought-provoking. The AI responses are then edited by the researchers for accuracy and tone – treating machine output as raw material to refine. This human–machine collaboration ensures the final story remains respectful of the site's reality while exploring *what if* scenarios.

This use of AI in heritage is inherently speculative. Instead of claiming an AI can truly know the past, we embrace generative storytelling as a tool to amplify perspectives. The AI's *memory* is partly drawn from its training data and partly from our prompts – a hybrid collective memory. While an AI narrator lacks true consciousness, its output can prompt reflection on authenticity and bias in heritage narratives [17–21]. Thus, our approach is experimental: we leverage AI to explore multiple voices and scenarios, recognizing that the result is a constructed interpretation rather than an authoritative account. Through this lens, speculative storytelling becomes a method to critique and expand heritage understanding.

2.3 Polyvocal Narratives in Heritage

Polyvocal approaches in heritage scholarship argue for multiple, coexisting perspectives. Instead of a museum plaque or textbook telling one version, polyvocality invites local communities, marginalized groups, and even non-human agents into the conversation. As Suroyo et al. note, moving away from a single curator-led voice allows heritage to be seen as an active meaning-making process [22]. In practice, some projects co-curate stories with residents or incorporate interactive tours where visitors choose narrative paths. Others use creative techniques like anthropomorphism: Viktor Shklovsky's *Kholstomer* (a horse's perspective) famously defamiliarizes human norms by telling the story through an animal's eyes [23,24].

Our method extends polyvocality via AI. By programmatically generating distinct characters (including non-human ones), we ensure the narrative explicitly has many voices. For example, giving voice to the building itself or to materials exemplifies Bennett's notion of "thing-power," assigning agency to matter

[25]. These voices articulate architectural memory in novel ways. Importantly, polyvocality here also helps bridge spatial data and culture: the detailed 3D model grounds the storytelling in a real place, while AI narrators populate it with varied viewpoints. The resulting narrative tapestry reflects the complex social life of the building rather than a single expert interpretation.

3 Methodology

Our workflow combines photogrammetry and AI generation in parallel streams, then fuses them into a unified experience. The key steps are:

Data Capture (Photogrammetry): We conducted a drone survey of the site (McMahon Hall) to capture all facades. Using a high-resolution UAV camera, we flew circular orbits at multiple elevations, acquiring approx. 300 overlapping images (see Fig. 1). These were processed in Agisoft Metashape (SfM pipeline) to produce a textured 3D mesh (approx. 8M faces). The model captures details (balcony geometry, rough concrete texture - Fig. 2) which later reinforce the narrative (e.g., viewers see the concrete texture when hearing the Concrete voice). Complementary ground photos filled in lower-level details. (Indoor spaces can similarly be scanned with DSLR or smartphone and stitched into partial models, though that is optional for external heritage.)

Fig. 1. Drone survey.

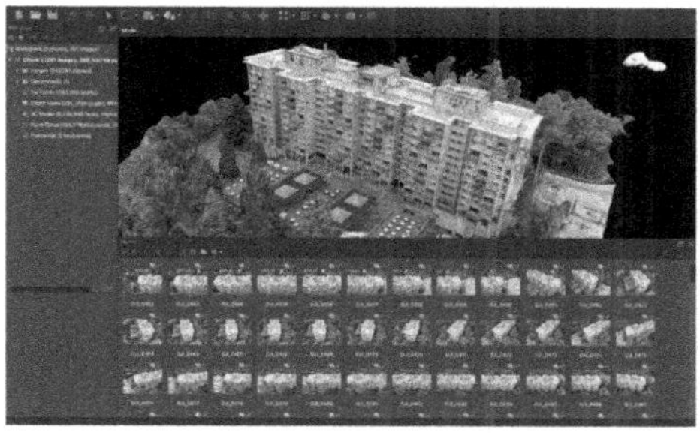

Fig. 2. Generating the aerial view of McMahon Hall in Agisoft Metashape Professional.

AI Narrative Generation: In parallel, we developed characters and prompts. Each character (Building, Architect, Concrete, etc.) was assigned a system prompt defining its persona. We then asked each LLM character targeted questions that mix factual grounding and speculation. For example: "You are the concrete of the building. Describe your memories from six decades on campus.". We collected the AI's responses (text) and reviewed them, editing out any factual errors or biases. To add voice, the edited texts were fed into text-to-speech software (e.g. ElevenLabs) to create audio clips in the character's tone (see Fig. 3).

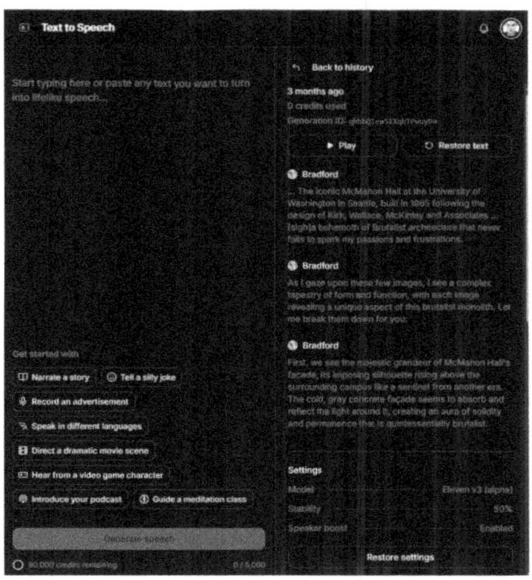

Fig. 3. Text to speech generation in ElevenLabs.

Integration and Visualization: Finally, we combined the 3D model and narrative into a cohesive presentation. The mesh was imported into a multimedia environment and the AI-generated audio narration was synced with camera sequences around and within the model, effectively treating the building as an active storyteller (see Fig. 4). For instance, when the Building voice speaks, the camera can pan its walls; when the Bird voice speaks, an aerial 3D view is presented. The result is a 15 min video in which multiple voices are layered, with the photogrammetry serving as the visual anchor. This is one example of how spatial computing can house polyvocal narratives. For instance, an AR app could similarly play a voice when a user points their phone at the facade, localizing the story in physical space. By following these steps, we produces an artifact that is both a digital record and an imaginative narrative. Our approach treats computational tools not just as recorders but as collaborators in knowledge creation: emerging technologies as instruments for producing new epistemologies. Below is a simplified outline of the pipeline:

- Capture building via UAV photogrammetry → generate 3D model.
- Define AI personas and prompts (architect, material, local, etc.).
- Generate and refine text narratives with LLMs, grounding them in site data.
- Synthesize voices and ambient sounds.
- Integrate audio with generated 3D visuals and other visual elements to create the final multi-voiced story.

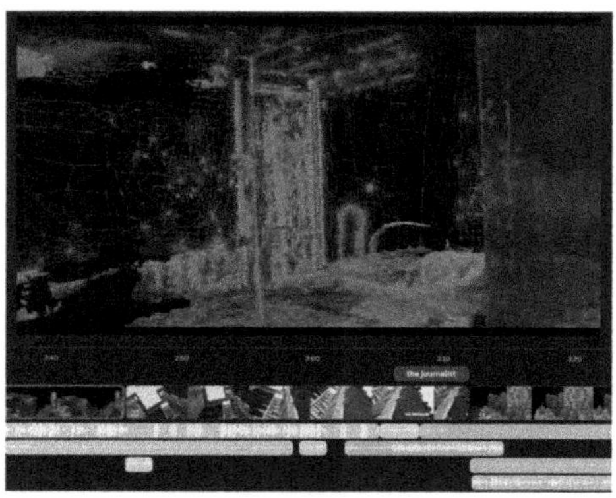

Fig. 4. Video construction in Canva.

4 Discussion

The case study demonstrates that combining photogrammetric data with AI narratives yields new forms of heritage knowledge. Instead of a single authored video or plaque, our output is multi-authored and even though scripted by researchers, the voices appear as if co-authored by the machine and the site itself.

This has several implications:

Democratizing Interpretation: By design, the narrative includes perspectives that are usually silent. For example, a construction material's voice might reflect on labor history or deterioration in ways a human curator might overlook, while the building's voice can convey accumulated site lore. This multi-perspective exposition aligns with calls for democratized heritage.

Augmenting Collective Memory: The AI effectively acts as a *prosthesis for memory.* It pulls from collective cultural data and site facts to imagine what the building could remember. This hybrid memory is not factually authoritative, but it enriches the narrative space. It suggests an epistemology where machine and human narratives interweave. Importantly, we note that the AI's memory is partly from its training and partly from our input – a dual source that must be made transparent to users.

Speculation as Inquiry: Because the approach is explicitly speculative, it invites questions. Audience members know these are imagined voices; this can provoke reflection on history and representation. For instance, hearing a tree or a bird speak about the building's changes can highlight what is invisible in official records. In this way, the project functions like a *what-if* scenario generator, encouraging viewers to consider alternative histories or futures. This speculative element is a key part of the "new epistemology" – it acknowledges that there can be multiple coexisting *truths* about a place.

At the same time, there are cautions. AI-generated content can introduce hyperreal or biased elements. We mitigated this by human curation (reviewing and editing the AI text). We also explicitly framed the piece as a pedagogical/artistic experiment, not a historical documentary. The goal is not to replace expertise but to augment it and spark dialogue.

In sum, our mixed methodology produces an outcome that is not just a data record nor just a fictional film, but a hybrid construct - *polyvocal, machine-augmented storytelling.* It expands the toolkit of remote sensing and digital heritage by not only documenting tangible form but also speculating on intangible cultural memory. In our case, the photogrammetric model grounds the story in real space, while the AI voices animate its cultural dimensions. This generates new epistemologies – new ways of knowing – where knowledge is seen as contextual, dialogic, and participatory.

5 Conclusion

The article presents a proof-of-concept pipeline that combines remote sensing and generative AI to create polyvocal narratives for the built environment. The method goes beyond static documentation to imagine multiple perspectives by aligning drone-based photogrammetry with AI-driven story generation, The key contributions are:

- A workflow that uses high-fidelity 3D models as platforms for multi-character storytelling.
- A demonstration of AI personas (building, material, etc.) seeded with facts to produce meaningful speculative narratives.
- A reflection on how this approach reshapes heritage epistemology by diversifying voices and merging tangible and intangible knowledge (essentially a *mixed-methods epistemology* in architectural inquiry).

This interdisciplinary approach suggests several future directions. One could involve community stakeholders to co-author or react to the AI narratives, blending machine imagination with lived experience. Another path is building interactive AR applications where users engage with polyvocal guides in situ. There are also questions about curatorial practice: how can archives and museums incorporate machine-generated content responsibly?

In conclusion, the interplay of photogrammetry and generative AI offers a richer cognitive map of heritage. Instead of a single map and compass, we now have a chorus of possible narrators that can guide us through history and memory. This approach opens up heritage to multiple futures and encourage a more inclusive understanding of the past by treating technology as an active partner in interpretation, we open up heritage to multiple futures and encourage a more inclusive understanding of the past.

Acknowledgments. This study was funded by Erasmus+ KA220 EpiCo (2023-1RO01-KA220-HED-000155474), UEFISCDI PNCDI IV (PN-IV-P8-8.1-PRE-HE-ORG-2024-0208) and HORIZON-MSCA-2022-SE-01 EpisTeaM (GAP-101129655).

Disclosure of Interests. The authors have no competing interests to declare that are relevant to the content of this article.

References

1. Moldovan, S., Moldovan, I., Rice, T.: Speculative memory and machine augmentation: a polyvocal rendering of brutalist architecture through AI and photogrammetry. Heritage **8**(10), 401 (2025). https://doi.org/10.3390/heritage8100401
2. Remondino, F.: Heritage recording and 3D modeling with photogrammetry and 3D scanning. Remote Sens. **3**(6), 1104–1138 (2011). https://doi.org/10.3390/rs3061104
3. Liu, J., Willkens, D., Gentry, R.: Developing a practice-based guide to terrestrial laser scanning (TLS) for heritage documentation. Heritage **8**(8), 313 (2025). https://doi.org/10.3390/heritage8080313
4. Marcos-González, D., Álvaro-Tordesillas, A., López-Bragado, D., Martínez-Vera, M.: Fast and accurate documentation of architectural heritage with low-cost spherical panoramic photographs from 360° cameras. Int. Arch. Photogramm. Remote Sens. Spatial Inf. Sci. **XLVIII**(M-2), 1007–1011 (2023). https://doi.org/10.5194/isprs-archives-XLVIII-M-2-2023-1007-2023
5. Kong, X., Hucks, R.G.: Preserving our heritage: a photogrammetry-based digital twin framework for monitoring deteriorations of historic structures. Autom. Constr. **152**, 104928 (2023). https://doi.org/10.1016/j.autcon.2023.104928

6. Saosing, R., Nattawuttisit, S.: Generative AI for storytelling in cultural tourism: enhancing visitor engagement through AI-driven narratives. Edelweiss Appl. Sci. Technol. **9**(7), 1436—1451 (2025). https://doi.org/10.55214/25768484.v9i7.8936
7. Mogre, S.C., Nikam, J.S., Damani, P., Banik, A.: Generative AI for cultural heritage preservation using AR and data science. In: Proceedings of ICMLAS 2025, pp. 1068—1073. IEEE (2025). https://doi.org/10.1109/ICMLAS64557.2025.10968619
8. Smith, L., Waterton, M.: Constrained by commonsense: the authorized heritage discourse in contemporary debates. In: Skeates, R., McDavid, C., Carman, J. (eds.) The Oxford Handbook of Public Archaeology, pp. 153—171. Oxford University Press, Oxford, UK (2012). https://doi.org/10.1093/oxfordhb/9780199237821.013.0009
9. Tsenova, V., Wood, G., Kirk, D.: Designing with genius Loci: an approach to polyvocality in interactive heritage interpretation. Multimodal Technol. Interact **6**(6), 41 (2022). https://doi.org/10.3390/mti6060041
10. Oztabak, C.: AI-generated folklore for culturally resonant storytelling in the digital age: bridging tradition and technology in storytelling. In: Understanding Generative AI in a Cultural Context, pp. 161—184. IGI Global (2025). https://doi.org/10.4018/979-8-3693-7235-7.ch007
11. Albert, M.-T., Richon, M., Viñals and Witcomb, A.: Community Development Through World Heritage. UNESCO, Paris, France (2012)
12. Ashworth, G.J., Graham, B., Tunbridge, J.E.: Pluralising Pasts: Heritage. Identity and Place in Multicultural Societies. Pluto Press, London, UK (2007)
13. Scapp, R.A.: Question of Voice: Philosophy and the Search for Legitimacy. University of Michigan Press, Ann Arbor, MI, USA (2020)
14. Gaspari, F., Barbieri, F., Fascia, R., Ioli, F., Pinto, L.: An open-source web platform for 3D documentation and storytelling of hidden cultural heritage. Heritage **7**(2), 517–536 (2024). https://doi.org/10.3390/heritage7020025
15. Riggio, M., Nasir, V.: Digital twins in structural health assessment and monitoring: applications in historical timber buildings. Int. J. Archit. Herit. **19**(10), 2398–2421 (2025). https://doi.org/10.1080/15583058.2024.2437618
16. Themistocleous, K.: The monitoring of cultural heritage sites using digital twins. Proc. SPIE 2024, 13197, 1319716. https://doi.org/10.1117/12.3031733
17. Condorelli, F., Berti, F.: Creativity and awareness in co-creation of art using artificial intelligence-based systems in heritage education. Heritage **8**(5), 157 (2025). https://doi.org/10.3390/heritage8050157
18. Creely, E., Blannin, J.: Creative partnerships with generative AI in education. Possibilities for Educ. Beyond Think. Skills Creat. **56**, 101727 (2025). https://doi.org/10.1016/j.tsc.2024.101727
19. Dilaveroglu, B.: The architecture of visual narrative: can text-to-image algorithms enhance the power of stylistic narrative for architecture. Int. J. Architect. Comput. **22**(3), 432–457 (2024). https://doi.org/10.1177/14780771241234449
20. Massidda, M., Travaglini, L., Pescarin, S.: Designing hybrid XR narrative applications: a framework to describe authoring tools in cultural domain. Digit. Appl. Archaeol. Cult. Herit. **38**, e00424 (2025). https://doi.org/10.1016/j.daach.2025.e00424
21. Asrifan, A., Hasa, M.F., Syafryadin, S., Pelu, H.: Narrative machines: the evolution of storytelling in the age of generative AI. In: Generative AI: Foundations, pp. 81–110. IGI Global (2025). https://doi.org/10.4018/979-8-3693-6255-6.ch004
22. Suroyo, S., et al.: Augmented reality based cultural heritage in improving students' literacy culture in history learning at SMK Muhammadiyah I Pekanbaru. Jurnal

Pendidikan: Teori, Penelitian, dan Pengembangan: **10**(8) (2025). https://doi.org/10.17977/jptpp.v10i8.24855
23. Epstein, M.: The defamiliarization of Lev Tolstoy. In: The Irony of the Ideal: Paradoxes of Russian Literature, pp. 158–177. Academic Studies Press, Boston, MA, USA (2017). https://doi.org/10.1515/9781618116338-011
24. Gunn, D.P.: Making art strange: a commentary on defamiliarization. Ga. Rev. **38**, 25–33 (1984)
25. Bennett, J.: Vibrant Matter: A Political Ecology of Things. Duke University Press, Durham, NC, USA (2010)

Virtue Ethics and Emerging Technologies: Ethical Challenges in AI, Robotics, and Affective Computing

José Manuel Ferrandez[1,2(✉)], Gema Benedicto[1,2], María Paula Bonomini[3,4,5], and Noel Fitzpatrick[2,6]

[1] Universidad Politécnica de Cartagena, Cartagena, Spain
[2] ECTLab+, European University of Technology, Cartagena, European Union, Colombia
jm.ferrandez@upct.es
[3] Instituto Tecnológico de Buenos Aires, Buenos Aires, Argentina
[4] Instituto Alberto Calderón, CONYCET, Buenos Aires, Argentina
[5] Universidad Tecnológica Nacional, Buenos Aires, Argentina
[6] Technical University of Dublin, Dublin, Ireland

Abstract. This article examines the contribution of virtue ethics to the ethical assessment of emerging digital technologies, focusing on artificial intelligence, cybernetics and robotics, and affective computing. Unlike deontological and consequentialist approaches, virtue ethics places moral character, practical wisdom, and human flourishing at the center of ethical reflection. From this perspective, algorithmic and autonomous systems should be evaluated not only in terms of efficiency or rule compliance, but also in light of their effects on dignity, autonomy, responsibility, fairness, and social well-being. The chapter discusses opacity, explainability, accountability, and bias in artificial intelligence, including the importance of explainable systems in clinical decision support. It then considers distributed responsibility in autonomous systems, the ethical implications of autonomous vehicles and weapons, the role of social robots, and the opportunities and risks of robotic interventions in autism care. Finally, it examines affective computing as a field that offers significant therapeutic and educational potential while also raising concerns about privacy, manipulation, surveillance, and discrimination. It is concluded that virtue ethics provides a valuable framework for guiding technological innovation toward transparency, accountability, and human flourishing.

Keywords: Virtue ethics · Artificial intelligence · Robotics · Affective computing · Explainability · Accountability · Human flourishing

1 Introduction

Virtue ethics is currently one of the three main approaches to normative ethics. Initially, it can be identified as emphasizing virtues, or moral character, in con-

J. M. Ferrández Vicente et al. (Eds.): IWINAC 2026, LNCS 16574, pp. 461–471, 2026.
https://doi.org/10.1007/978-3-032-27314-7_42

trast to the approach that emphasizes duties or rules (deontology) or that emphasizes the consequences of actions (consequentialism). This is not to say that only virtue ethicists attend to virtues, any more than it is to say that only consequentialists attend to consequences or only deontologists attend to rules [7–9]. Each of the above approaches can accommodate virtues, consequences, and rules. Indeed, any plausible normative ethical theory will have something to say about all three. What distinguishes virtue ethics from consequentialism or deontology is the centrality of virtue within the theory.

Virtue ethics provides a useful framework for the assessment of emerging technologies because it evaluates not only acts or outcomes, but also the kinds of agents, institutions, and social practices that technologies cultivate. This perspective is especially relevant in technologically mediated environments, where decisions are distributed across designers, users, regulators, and infrastructures. Ethical evaluation therefore concerns not only whether a system works, but also whether it supports human flourishing, practical wisdom, justice, and responsibility.

Applied to digital and embodied systems, this approach highlights the fact that contemporary technologies are embedded in complex social contexts. Algorithms classify and recommend, robots interact with bodies and emotions and neuroprosthetic devices [2,4,6] interact directly with the human brain. The ethical question is therefore broader than compliance with minimal constraints: it concerns whether technological development encourages trustworthy institutions and sound forms of collective action.

A virtue-based framework does not reject principles or outcomes. Rather, it situates them within a richer account of moral life. Safety, transparency, privacy, fairness, and accountability remain essential, but they are best understood as elements of a broader orientation toward the good life and just social order. [9,13,14].

1.1 Virtue and the Ethics of Algorithms

Algorithms classify, profile, predict, and increasingly mediate social and institutional decisions. They can support evidence-based policy, administrative efficiency, and clinical decision support, but they can also produce opaque forms of "algorithmocracy" when their operation pushes human autonomy and public explanation to the margins [10,11]. From a virtue-ethical perspective, that means they cannot be judged by accuracy alone. Their assessment also has to consider dignity, misuse, overreliance, and the conditions under which people remain capable of informed and responsible action.

There are several values that should guide algorithmic design: accuracy, autonomy, privacy, fairness or equality, ownership, accountability, and transparency. The European High-Level Expert Group on AI emphasizes respect for human autonomy, prevention of harm, fairness, and explainability [11]. Read through virtue ethics, these are not just technical design targets. They are conditions that can either support or erode good judgment and human flourishing at both personal and institutional levels. An algorithm may be highly accurate and still be ethically inadequate if it weakens trust, obscures responsibility, or normalizes exclusion.

This broader moral lens also helps explain why opacity is such a central problem. The opacity can produce at least three difficulties: decisions without explanation, uncertainty about responsibility, and the risk of error. These are not merely engineering defects. They are moral defects insofar as they undermine the possibility of justification, answerability, and prudent institutional use [10,13]. A virtue-based approach therefore supports algorithmic design and deployment that preserve meaningful human comprehension, especially where systems affect welfare, liberty, or access to social goods.

2 Ethics in Artificial Intelligence

Artificial intelligence appears as a field of genuine promise and equally significant ethical strain. The principles involved are explainability, accountability, bias, and clinical use, which is helpful because it avoids reducing AI ethics to a single concern such as privacy or fairness. The deeper issue is how increasingly autonomous systems can be incorporated into social and professional practices without hollowing out responsibility, judgment, or justice [12–14].

Th3 main AI principles are, including beneficial research aims, lifecycle safety, transparency about failure, judicial explainability, designer responsibility, alignment with human values, personal privacy, shared benefit, human control, and caution about arms races and catastrophic risk [12]. These principles are best read not as a closed code of conduct but as a map of the terrain. AI matters ethically not simply because it is new, but because it mediates decisions that bear directly on dignity, freedom, political order, distribution, and social trust.

2.1 Explainable and Accountable Artificial Intelligence

One of the most substantial issues is the discussion of moral responsibility in AI. The underlying question is straightforward: when an AI system decides or acts, who answers for the consequences when something goes wrong? The paper returns to Aristotelian conditions of responsibility, especially control over action and knowledge of what one is doing. AI systems may exercise technical agency in the sense that they affect the world, but they are not moral agents in the full sense because they lack consciousness, intention, free will, and reflective understanding [9,13]. Responsibility therefore remains with the human agents and institutions that design, deploy, and rely on them.

Why this apparently straightforward solution quickly becomes difficult in practice. First, AI systems often act too quickly for meaningful real-time human intervention, as in self-driving contexts. Second, AI systems have histories: they are built, adapted, transferred, and repurposed across institutions and sectors, which makes causal responsibility diffuse. Third, technological action often involves "many hands and many things," including programmers, institutions, users, data pipelines, sensors, software stacks, and hardware components. In such cases, responsibility cannot plausibly be assigned to a single actor, yet it cannot be allowed to disappear [13,14].

It is important connecting responsibility so closely to explainability. In ordinary moral and legal practice, being responsible means more than causing an outcome; it also means being able to answer for it. AI complicates that expectation because those who build or deploy a system may understand its general architecture while still being unable to explain a specific result. This is a black-box problem: when reasons for a particular decision cannot be given, accountability, public trust, and moral legitimacy all suffer [14,15]. From a virtue-ethical point of view, that matters because responsible action presupposes answerability to those affected by it.

It is also relevant to distinguish explainability from source-code disclosure. Ethically, the issue is not whether every line of software is made public, but whether a human being can answer the question "Why?" when an AI-informed decision affects a person. In domains such as banking, criminal justice, or healthcare, explanation is not an optional enhancement. It is a necessary condition for respecting persons as autonomous and socially embedded agents who are entitled to reasons for decisions that affect their lives [11,13].

2.2 Bias and the Politics of Data

The problem of bias in AI is also relevant. Bias may arise in training datasets, labels, model design, social practices, incomplete or poor-quality data, or group-level assumptions encoded in development teams. The discussion is notable for refusing to treat bias as a purely technical malfunction. Instead, many datasets reflect historical discrimination and structural inequality, so that AI may reproduce or amplify societal injustice under the appearance of computational neutrality [10,11,14].

Examples include unrepresentative datasets based on narrow populations, cultural bias in image-recognition systems, and inherited biases from medical or social practices already distorted by race or gender inequities. The analysis goes further by noting that questions about mitigation are not purely engineering questions either. Whether developers should create "blind" systems, idealized datasets, or forms of positive discrimination depends on contested concepts of fairness, justice, and the kind of society we wish to create. Virtue ethics is useful here because it reintroduces political and moral judgment into a field too often framed as if neutral optimization could replace ethical deliberation [9,13].

AI can reveal human biases as much as it can automate them. This means that discussing AI ethics can expose hidden assumptions about fairness, social order, and the future of work. In that sense, the ethics of AI is not only about machines. It is also a mirror in which societies encounter their own normative commitments and failures.

2.3 Interpretive Machine Learning and Clinical Use

It is also very importantthe use of interpretable or explainable AI, especially in the clinical setting. There exist a vast explanation technics: feature relevance, model-specific and model-agnostic methods, visual explanations, example-based explanations, and techniques such as SHAP, saliency maps, attention maps, and tree-based models [15]. The key point is not merely taxonomic. It is that explanation must be tailored to audience and context. What counts as a good explanation depends on who needs to understand the result and for what practical purpose.

This becomes especially clear in medical decision support systems. AI-enabled medical systems often show strong laboratory performance but limited real-world improvement when inserted into actual clinical workflows. It identifies transparency as a precondition for trustworthiness and argues that explainability helps detect bias, improve resilience, and safeguard causal relevance in prediction [15,16]. Medical professionals need more than high-performing outputs; they need reasons that can be integrated into diagnosis, communication with patients, and reflective judgment.

Better explanations allow clinicians to assess the reliability of a prediction, identify likely errors, and explain recommendations to patients. This, in turn, supports confidence in the doctor–patient relationship. It is also convenient to emphasize workflow constraints: for a decision-support system to be genuinely usable, it must be time-saving, easy to navigate, and compatible with demanding clinical schedules. Importantly, black boxes should not be used in medical decision support systems when their opacity prevents meaningful evaluation or responsible use [16].

A final contribution is its attention to privacy across the full lifecycle of AI-based medical models. When multiple data sources are fused, personal information may be exposed in ways that undermine rights and weaken trust. The paper therefore calls for data governance that includes contextual specification, secure processing, and the protection of privacy even in interpretability tools themselves [11,16]. This concern is especially relevant in clinical and mental-health contexts, where the data involved often concern highly sensitive aspects of identity and vulnerability.

3 Cybernetics and Robotics

Cybernetics and robotics is the point at which ethical questions become embodied and operational. It should be distinguished technical autonomy from the stronger philosophical sense of autonomy associated with responsibility. That distinction matters because a system may act with considerable independence from direct human control without becoming a moral agent. On that basis, the chapter moves through autonomous vehicles, autonomous weapons, machine ethics, social robotics, and robotics in autism interventions [13,17,18].

It should be also highlighted the importance of standards and liability frameworks. Civil and criminal liability systems already exist to handle many harms, but the introduction of adaptive autonomous systems may require revised technical standards and governance structures. The mention of verifiable AI and safety standards is important because it shows that robotics ethics is not purely speculative. It includes a practical institutional dimension concerning testing, certification, infrastructure, and post-deployment oversight.

3.1 Autonomous Vehicles

In the autonomous-vehicle applications, it should be noted the enormous potential social benefit of reducing deaths, injuries, pollution, and congestion associated with human driving. Yet it resists simplistic moralization through trolley-problem discourse alone. The familiar trolley cases may be useful as thought experiments, but it can be argued that most real ethical issues in driving concern far more ordinary matters: speeding, safe distance, risky overtaking, courtesy, infrastructure, and the distribution of responsibility across manufacturers, operators, regulators, and users [17].

This is an important corrective. By emphasizing ordinary driving ethics and legal norms, it moves the debate away from rare sacrificial dilemmas and toward rule-following, common-good coordination, and public accountability. It also points to policy efforts such as German and EU approaches to automated driving that prioritize safety and treat responsibility as shifting from the individual driver toward manufacturers, system operators, and legislative or infrastructural authorities. That observation helps position autonomous driving as an institutional ethics problem rather than merely a problem of machine moral calculation.

The *Moral Machine* experiment should be mentioned, which gathered millions of decisions across countries and languages in an attempt to quantify social intuitions about machine behavior [17]. That reference is best understood not as a final answer to moral programming, but as evidence that machine ethics cannot avoid pluralism and public contestation. Virtue ethics adds to this by warning that the quality of judgment in real-world deployment matters more than the elegance of abstract dilemma resolution.

3.2 Autonomous Weapons and Machine Ethics

The discussion of autonomous weapons is one of the strongest ethical warnings. There are several reasons for concern: support for extrajudicial killing, diffusion of accountability, the lowering of barriers to violence, and the possibility that lethal systems will be used in asymmetric conflicts or by non-state actors [12,13]. It also noted the challenge of complying with humanitarian principles such as distinction, proportionality, and military necessity.

What stands out here is that it does not reduce the problem to a single concept such as human dignity. Instead, it argued that the ethical case against autonomous weapons should draw on multiple objections, including accountability, increased likelihood of use, and the altered moral character of violence when lethal decision-making is increasingly displaced into technical systems. This multifactorial argument is well aligned with virtue ethics, which asks what kinds of institutions, habits, and dispositions are cultivated when human restraint is technologically diluted.

Machine ethics should distinguish ethics *for* machines from the ethics of human uses of machines. There exists also skepticism about the assumption that machines could become autonomous moral agents in a substantial sense, even while acknowledging efforts to encode acceptable behavior or social values in robotic systems [18]. The reference to Asimov's laws of robotics is valuable as a reminder that formalized rules quickly become unstable under conflicting conditions. Virtue ethics here offers a clear lesson: ethical life cannot be reduced to rigid laws detached from context, practical wisdom, and the cultivated capacities of human agents.

3.3 Responsibility, Social Robots, and Autism Interventions

It should also be noted robot responsibility as distributed responsibility. Harms involving robots often emerge from interactions among designers, software, hardware, users, institutions, and infrastructures. Traditional examples of distributed liability—manufacturers, mechanics, drivers, and public authorities—already show that technical systems require layered attribution. Robotics intensifies this because the system boundary itself may be difficult to define, and the effects of action emerge from many interacting components [13].

The social-robotics discussion then raises a different type of concern: the moral quality of human–robot relationships. Social robots may assist in healthcare, education, and entertainment, but they cannot simply replace human connection without ethical loss. The source text warns of isolation, surveillance, manipulation, and the perpetuation of prejudice, while also pointing toward participatory design as a way to align systems more closely with user needs and values [18]. This part of the chapter is especially important for a virtue-based account, because it asks whether robotic mediation supports care and companionship or merely simulates them while weakening the social fabric.

The potential benefits of robotic systems for autistic children and people with autism spectrum disorder: predictable interactions, controlled social rehearsal, communication training, and support for sensory modulation is relevant. Yet it also raises a series of ethically acute concerns. Robots must not be treated as substitutes for human therapy, as instruments of control, as tools that intensify stigma, or as covert mechanisms of data extraction [18]. The main issues to consider are autonomy, beneficence, non-maleficence, privacy, and fairness.

It should be highlighted the need to avoid deficit-driven normalization, to ensure involvement of persons with autism and their families in design and deployment, and to preserve the human elements of therapeutic response that robotic systems cannot replicate. In a virtue-ethics frame, the central issue is whether robotics supports flourishing as lived by the persons concerned, rather than merely optimizing behavioral conformity.

4 Emotional and Affective Technologies

Emotional technologies, or affective computing, is a more relevant are of emerging technologies [1,3,5]. It starts from a simple premise with far-reaching consequences: human life is saturated with emotion, and technological systems are increasingly entering situations shaped by attention, fatigue, loneliness, pain, and interpersonal interpretation. Ethical assessment therefore requires more than technical analysis. It also requires asking what kinds of emotional relations are being mediated and what forms of vulnerability are being exposed [19,20].

Would it be ethical for a computer to sense a user's emotions? Does such detection invade privacy? On what basis do users feel comfortable or uncomfortable with such systems? The source text argues that the field has advanced working systems faster than it has produced clear ethical guidance, creating what it calls a policy vacuum. This diagnosis is important because it identifies a common pattern in emerging technology: deployment may outpace the conceptual frameworks needed for responsible use.

4.1 Implicit Contracts, Data Types, and Privacy

One of the most interesting conceptual proposals is that emotional technologies involve an implicit or explicit contract between designer and user. When the contract is implicit, users assess comfort and acceptability largely through expectation and trust. When it is explicit, they may evaluate privacy policies, social contracts, or other declarations of intended use. This framing is helpful because it foregrounds the relational and normative expectations embedded in user interaction, rather than treating affective systems as neutral tools [20].

The notion of affective data should be addressed well beyond faces, like vocal cues, electrodermal activity, cardiac variability, electroencephalography, text, and emoji-based inference. This matters ethically because many users may intuitively understand facial analysis while underestimating the extent to which emotional inference can be assembled from multimodal traces. Data extraction can become pervasive even when users do not experience themselves as disclosing anything unusually intimate.

A striking example in the source text concerns depression detection outside healthcare. A home assistant, online game, fitness device, or hiring system might infer depression from speech or behavior, yet fall outside medical privacy protections designed for traditional healthcare actors. This example demonstrates how affective computing can reveal information about mental states without the institutional safeguards associated with clinical care. From a virtue-ethical perspective, such systems raise questions of discretion, respect, and the exploitation of vulnerability [19,20].

4.2 Opportunities, Manipulation, and Therapeutic Use

It should be emphasized the potential good of affective computing. Systems that help people understand and regulate fear, loneliness, attention, anger, pain, or disengagement could improve quality of life, reduce accidents, support learning, and assist self-help or treatment-seeking. It should be mentioned therapeutic uses such as pain detection and avatar-mediated "cybertherapies" that can lower barriers to self-disclosure for socially anxious individuals [20]. These examples are important because they show that the field should not be reduced to a surveillance narrative alone.

Affective systems may manipulate or exploit emotions for advertising, political influence, or behavioral steering. They may process highly sensitive personal data, perpetuate bias and discrimination, or create systems that appear to do more than they actually can. It should be also noted the risk of automated emotional surveillance becoming pervasive, remote, and inexpensive. In moral terms, this means that affective computing can extend the power to influence inner life in ways that challenge autonomy and democratic equality.

Users may over-ascribe depth, understanding, warmth, or concern to systems that merely exhibit fragments of emotionally salient behavior. This "pars pro toto" problem is ethically significant because people may trust systems inappropriately or draw unwarranted conclusions from signals of distress detection, concern, or companionship. Regulation is needed, careful disclosure of system limits, and explicit retention of professional responsibility where authority is delegated to virtual teachers, coaches, or therapists [20].

4.3 Ethical Framework and Regulation

There are however possible framework for emotional technologies, focusing on beneficence, maleficence, autonomy, and equity. Yet it also suggested that affective computing may require a more specific microethics analogous to medical or environmental ethics. It is recognized that affective technologies engage forms of interpersonal and emotional exposure not fully captured by generic digital-ethics categories.

It is argued that affective technologies are not inherently pernicious, but they require targeted regulation in areas such as training, advertising, communication, authority delegation, and standard ethical review in research. Some ethical demands appear quite concrete: practitioners should not be allowed to offload their responsibility to automated systems, and providers of affective companions should ensure that emotional cues do not invite inappropriate trust. These recommendations align naturally with virtue ethics because they aim to preserve responsibility, honesty, and appropriate boundaries in emotionally loaded technological interactions.

5 Conclusion

Virtue ethics can serve as a unifying framework across AI, robotics, and affective computing. What links these technologies is not simply that they are computational or advanced. It is that they increasingly shape agency, responsibility, institutional trust, and the background conditions of human flourishing. Values such as transparency, accountability, explainability, fairness, privacy, and efficiency are needed, but it situates them within a wider moral horizon in which the central question is how technological systems affect persons and societies [11–13].

A virtue-ethical orientation adds two especially important insights. First, it insists that ethical evaluation must include the cultivation of good judgment and not only compliance with external constraints. This is why the paper places so much weight on character formation, participatory design, ethical training, and meaningful human oversight. Second, virtue ethics resists the idea that technical success can settle moral questions on its own. A system may be accurate, adaptive, or efficient and still contribute to domination, opacity, dehumanization, or injustice.

For that reason, emerging technologies require interdisciplinary governance, but also something deeper: the cultivation of practical wisdom in the people and institutions that build and deploy them. That wisdom involves humility in the face of uncertainty, attentiveness to vulnerable populations, and a sustained willingness to ask not only what technologies can do, but what they should enable human beings to become [7–9].

Acknowledgement. This project AIA2025-164108-C32 has been funded by MICIU/AEI (10.13039/501100011033) and Fundación Séneca, as well as by the MSCA-SE EPISTEAM project and the CYTED network NT4SM.

Disclosure of Interests. The authors have no competing interests to declare.

References

1. Gómez-Vilda, P., Gómez-Rodellar, A., Vicente, J.M.F., Mekyska, J.: Neuromechanical modelling of articulatory movements from surface electromyography and speech formants. Int. J. Neural Syst. **29**(2), 1850039 (2019)
2. Martínez, J.J., Toledo, F.J., Fernández, E., Ferrández, J.M.: A retinomorphic architecture based on discrete-time cellular neural networks using reconfigurable computing. Neurocomputing **71**(4–6), 766–777 (2008)
3. Hongn, A., Bosch, F., Prado, L.E., Ferrández, J.M., Bonomini, M.P.: Wearable physiological signals under acute stress and exercise conditions. Scientific Data **12**(1), 520 (2025)
4. Lozano, A., Soto-Sanchez, C., Garrigos, J., Martínez, J.J., Ferrández, J.M.: A 3D convolutional neural network to model retinal ganglion cell's responses to light patterns in mice. Int. J. Neural Syst. **28**(10), 1850043 (2018)
5. Benamara, N.K., et al.: Real-time emotional recognition for sociable robotics based on deep neural networks ensemble. In: Ferrández Vicente, J., Álvarez-Sánchez, J., de la Paz López, F., Toledo Moreo, J., Adeli, H. (eds.) Understanding the Brain Function and Emotions. LNCS, vol. 11486. Springer, Cham (2019). https://doi.org/10.1007/978-3-030-19591-5_18
6. Toledo, F.J., Martinez, J.J., Ferrandez, J.M.: FPGA-based platform for image and video processing embedded systems. In: Proceedings of the 3rd Southern Conference on Programmable Logic, pp. 171–176 (2007)

7. Watson, G.: On the Primacy of Character. In: Flanagan and Rorty, pp. 449–483, reprinted in Statman (1997) (1990)
8. Kawall, J.: In Defence of the Primacy of Virtues. Journal of Ethics and Social Philosophy **3**(2), 1–21 (2009)
9. Annas, J.: Intelligent Virtue. Oxford University Press, New York (2011)
10. Hayes, P., van de Poel, I., Steen, M.: Algorithms and values in justice and security
11. High-Level Expert Group on AI: Ethics Guidelines for Trustworthy AI (2019). https://ec.europa.eu/futurium/en/aiallianceconsultation/guidelines
12. Future of Life Institute: AI Principles. https://futureoflife.org/open-letter/ai-principles/
13. Coeckelbergh, M.: AI Ethics. The MIT Press Essential Knowledge Series, MIT Press (2020)
14. Dubber, M.D., Pasquale, F., Das, S.: The Oxford Handbook of Ethics of AI. Oxford University Press (2020)
15. Gianfagna, L., Di Cecco, A.: Explainable AI with Python. Springer (2021)
16. Imoize, A.L., Hemanth, J., Do, D.T., Sur, S.N.: Intelligence in Medical Decision Support Systems. The Institution of Engineering and Technology (2022)
17. Awad, E., Dsouza, S., Kim, R., Schulz, J., Henrich, J., Shariff, A., Bonnefon, J.-F., et al.: The Moral Machine Experiment. Nature **563**(7729), 59–64 (2018)
18. Coeckelbergh, M.: How to Use Virtue Ethics for Thinking About the Moral Standing of Social Robots: A Relational Interpretation in Terms of Practices, Habits, and Performance. Int. J. Soc. Robot. **13**, 31–40 (2021)
19. Johnson, K.T., Picard, R.W.: Advancing Neuroscience through Wearable Devices. Neuron **108** (2020)
20. Cowie, R.: The Good Our Field Can Hope to Do, the Harm It Should Avoid. IEEE Transactions on Affective Computing **3**(4)

A Computational Interaction Model and Architecture Inspired by Pivotal Response Treatment (PRT)

Gema Benedicto[1,2(✉)] and José L. Gómez-Sirvent[3]

[1] Universidad Politécnica de Cartagena, 30202 Cartagena, Murcia, Spain
[2] ECT Lab+, European University of Technology, Cartagena, Spain
gema.benedicto@edu.upct.es
[3] Emotion and Neurocognition Unit, Instituto de Investigación en Informática de Albacete, Albacete, Spain
jose.gomez@uclm.es

Abstract. Although many current systems do not clearly translate evidence-based intervention principles into explicit software design and interaction logic, conversational agents are being increasingly investigated as interactive tools to support people with autism spectrum disorder (ASD). This paper presents an engineering-oriented framework for designing a conversational system based on Pivotal Response Treatment (PRT), a naturalistic intervention approach that emphasizes motivation, self-initiation, self-regulation, and responsiveness to multiple cues.

Instead of emphasizing clinical results, the proposed work embeds PRT principles into a modular, state-based software architecture and formalizes them as functional and non-functional system requirements. To ensure predictability, transparency, and reproducibility, the framework specifies emotion-aware interactions, deterministic session management, adaptive difficulty regulation, explicit interaction modes, and natural reinforcement mechanisms.

To facilitate naturalistic dialogue while maintaining complete control over the interaction flow through deterministic logic, an optional, constrained language generation component is included.

To demonstrate how therapeutic principles can be operationalized as enforceable engineering constraints, this paper describes the system requirements, architectural design, interaction model, and illustrative usage scenarios. In the context of educational and therapeutic engineering, this study attempts to offer a replicable and expandable reference architecture for the creation of adaptive conversational systems for ASD.

Keywords: ASD · Conversational Agents · Interaction Architecture · PRT

1 Introduction

Autism Spectrum Disorder (ASD) is a neurodevelopmental condition characterized by persistent difficulties in social communication, restricted interests,

J. M. Ferrández Vicente et al. (Eds.): IWINAC 2026, LNCS 16574, pp. 472–485, 2026.
https://doi.org/10.1007/978-3-032-27314-7_43

and repetitive patterns of behavior(diagnostic and statistical...) In recent years, there has been an increase in interest in developing adaptive and personalized technological systems that complement and enhance educational and clinical environments, such as conversational agents and interactive systems.

Traditional chatbot architectures, which are generally based on static question-answer patterns or linear dialogue trees, fail to explicitly model. Therefore, to design adaptable interactive systems, such as naturalistic intervention approaches, a conceptual framework is needed [5,8]. These include pivotal response treatment (PRT), which addresses essential areas of development, such as self-initiative, self-regulation, motivation, and the ability to respond to multiple stimuli [19].

In particular, there is a distinction between high-level therapeutic concepts (such as self-initiation or motivation) and how they are actually used in system architecture, state management, and user interface design. At the system level, there is currently no explicit formalization of the mapping of intervention principles to the interaction architecture [2,3,8].

This study focuses on the design, formalization, and implementation of PRT-informed interaction mechanisms as software components, rather than assessing clinical outcomes.

The architecture of the proposed system is scalable and modular, allowing for context-dependent reinforcement, adaptive difficulty regulation, emotion-aware interaction, and persistent user-driven activity selection. The primary contributions of this study are threefold: (i) it clearly maps PRT principles to functional engineering requirements; (ii) it defines a state-based interaction model and session management logic that allow for adaptive and interruptible interaction flow; and (iii) it provides an architectural description of a conversational framework that is intended to be extensible and reproducible.

1.1 Background and Related Work

Conversational Agents and Interactive Technologies for ASD. Conversational agents, serious games, socially assistive robots, and tablet applications are examples of interactive technologies that have been investigated as computational tools to assist individuals with autism spectrum disorder (ASD) [9,17,21,23].

Conversational systems created for ASD are subject to more stringent usability and interaction requirements than general chatbots. Interfaces for these systems must reduce cognitive load, avoid highly abstract language, and offer clear and constrained action options. Furthermore, because ASD profiles are diverse and individual preferences significantly impact engagement, personalization is essential.

This results in a major design trade-off from the engineering perspective. In structured educational or therapeutic scenarios, open-domain interactions can be especially problematic because they frequently lead to uncontrolled dialogue trajectories, inconsistent prompts, or contextually inappropriate system responses.

To guarantee predictable, repeatable, and goal-oriented sessions, many ASD-oriented conversational systems use explicit interaction states, curated content, and restricted interaction strategies [6,8,13].

Engineering Approaches to Adaptive Dialogue and User Modeling. Intention-slot models, rule-based dialogue managers, finite state machines (FSMs), frame-based dialogue systems, and hybrid architectures that combine deterministic control and generative language components are some of the engineering approaches used in conversational AI to regulate and adapt the interaction flow. Deterministic dialogue management techniques, such as FSMs or policy-based controllers, are usually chosen in structured or high-risk application domains to guarantee dependable task execution and predictable transitions [16,29].

Simultaneously, adaptive system behavior across interaction sessions is made possible by user modeling techniques that range from static user profiles (such as preferences or difficulty level) to dynamic state estimation (such as engagement, affect, or performance history). Effective implementations of conversational systems geared toward ASD usually depend on (i) a persistent session state, (ii) a clear prompting approach to facilitate graded assistance, (iii) a mechanism for modifying the difficulty level, and (iv) an event log element to support subsequent analysis and evaluation. These design components are in line with a requirements-based methodology, in which behavioral goals are converted into functional requirements and implemented as modular elements of the software [11,18,22].

PRT as a Design Framework for Interaction Requirements. Through explicit constraints governing system state transitions and feedback mechanisms, it is possible to interpret motivation, initiation, responsiveness to multiple cues, and regulation as important interaction variables that can be formalized computationally. According to this viewpoint, Pivotal Response Treatment (PRT) can be described as a bio-inspired interaction model that establishes a systematic set of behavioral guidelines that guide system design.

Specific interaction constraints are imposed by these principles: users must be able to make meaningful decisions; spontaneous initiations must be encouraged; task complexity must be gradually increased through the use of multiple cues; and reinforcement must be contextual, immediate and functionally related to user actions.

Both concrete implementation mechanisms (such as reinforcement modules, persistent choice interfaces, quick-action controls, and interruptible interaction flows) and operational definitions for abstract concepts, such as initiation "initiation" or "natural reinforcement" are necessary when designing a PRT-based system [19,20].

Reproducibility, comparability, and extensibility across contexts and age groups are limited by the fact that many ASD-oriented systems lack explicit mapping between intervention concepts and engineering requirements, even though some of them incorporate discrete aspects of these principles [12,13].

2 System Requirements and Design Rationale

Using a requirements-driven engineering methodology, the suggested conversational system converts Pivotal Response Treatment (PRT) concepts into clear functional and non-functional system requirements. The system formalizes therapeutic concepts as interaction constraints that directly influence architectural choices, interaction logic, and user interface structure, rather than treating them as implicit design guidelines. The resulting system requirements and engineering justification for the primary design decisions are described in this section [10,26].

2.1 Functional Requirements

The system's intended function as a structured interactive support tool and the characteristics of the target population (children and adolescents with ASD) led to the definition of the following functional requirements, which serve as guidelines for the system's behavior and interaction design:

- FR1 - User-supervised activity selection.
- FR2 – Difficulty in interacting adaptively.
- FR3 – Support for self-initiation.
- FR4 – Self-report of emotions.
- FR5 – Immediate and contextualized feedback.
- FR6 – Session State Persistence.
- FR7 – Recording interactions. [6,12,13,18,23,26,27].

When considered as a whole, these functional requirements highlight the key characteristics of conversational systems intended for diverse ASD populations: flexibility, user autonomy, and transparency in interaction control.

2.2 Non-functional Requirements

A set of non-functional requirements that limit usability, performance, and architectural qualities also served as a guide for the system design, in addition to functional behavior.

Usability and accessibility: By incorporating large interactive elements, unambiguous action options, and less complex visuals, the user interface should reduce the cognitive load.

Responsiveness: To maintain user engagement and guarantee temporal coupling between user actions and feedback, system responses must be provided with the least amount of latency.

Extensibility: New activities and interaction techniques can be integrated into the architecture without necessitating structural redesign.

Deterministic interaction control: Open-ended generative responses are subordinated to predictable and repeatable behaviors in interaction logic.

Platform independence: The system must be deployable in standard web environments, allowing its use in various educational and clinical contexts [25,28].

2.3 Mapping PRT Principles to Engineering Requirements

The explicit mapping of PRT principles to specific engineering design choices is one of the main contributions of this study. The conversion of high-level intervention concepts into system requirements and their implementation using specific software components are summarized in Table 1.

Table 1. Mapping between PRT principles and system design [19,20]

PRT principle	Engineering requirement	System implementation
Motivation	Continuous access to preferred activities	Persistent activity selection panel
Child choice	User-controlled interaction flow	Interruptible dialogue states
Self-initiation	Support for spontaneous user actions	Quick-action buttons
Multiple cues	Gradual increase in task complexity	Difficulty levels with incremental cue combinations
Self-regulation	Emotion-aware interaction adaptation	Emotion selector (visual icons) influencing system responses
Natural reinforcement	Context-dependent feedback	Reinforcement module linked to activity outcomes

2.4 Design Rationale

The system uses a modular state-based interaction model instead of a purely generative conversational approach. The requirement for explicit control over session flow and predictable and repeatable interaction patterns served as the driving force behind this choice. In applications focused on ASD, generative language models may improve linguistic variability; however, they also introduce uncertainty that could jeopardize usability and goal alignment.

User autonomy and self-determination are directly supported by persistent activity selection and interruptible interaction states, which enable users to stop participating in activities without receiving unfavorable feedback or failing at a task. To prevent invasive evaluation and enable emotion-aware interaction adaptation, emotional self-assessment was implemented as a simple and optional mechanism. Finally, rather than being an optional feature, explicit interaction logging is regarded as a fundamental architectural necessity.

The suggested architecture lays the groundwork for upcoming system evaluation, quantitative analysis, and the incorporation of adaptive or learning-based extensions by methodically documenting interaction events and state transitions [10,29].

3 System Architecture

Adaptive interaction, user-oriented control, and persistent session management are explicitly supported by the modular and layered software architecture used in the design of the proposed conversational system. Predictability, transparency, and extensibility, all essential characteristics of interactive systems for children and teenagers with ASD, are given top priority in architectural design.

The system can be broadly divided into four layers: data, logic, interaction, and logging. A distinct subset of responsibilities is encapsulated in each layer, allowing for a clear division of responsibilities and facilitating maintainability and future extensions [26,28] (see Fig. 1).

3.1 High-Level Architecture Overview

The overall architecture is client-side and modular, making it suitable for deployment in web-based settings. An internal session state regulates the interaction behavior, including task difficulty adaptation, activity selection, and dialogue flow. The system adopts an event-driven and deterministic interaction model to ensure predictable behavior and session reproducibility.

The following fundamental characteristics are supported by the architecture:

(i) Explicit modeling of interaction modes (such as play, conversation, emotional regulation, and choice)
(ii) Dynamic task difficulty adaptation
(iii) Persistent representation of user preferences and session state
(iv) Continuous availability of user-initiated actions
(v) Structured recording of interaction events [1,15].

3.2 Data Layer

The data layer structurally represents the system configuration, interaction content, and user-specific data. All data are stored in lightweight, human-readable JSON formats to facilitate transparency, maintainability, and quick iteration.

(i) Interaction level definitions, which define progression thresholds, criteria for difficulty, and prompting strategies; (ii) activity and directive definitions, which include games, conversation templates, and emotion-related activities, as well as their goals and reinforcement strategies; and (iii) user profiles, which include demographic data, preferences, and a persistent PRT-related state (e.g., current level, self-initiations, recent emotional state).

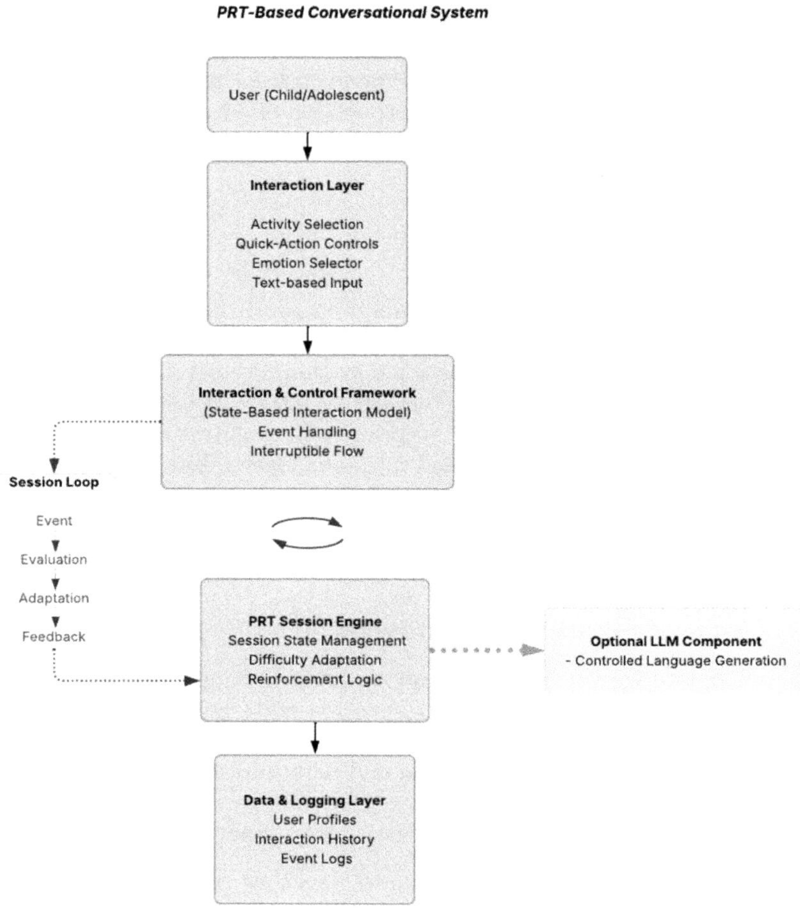

Fig. 1. Functional architecture of the proposed PRT-based conversational system.

The system allows customization and configuration changes without altering essential software components by externalizing these components from the interaction logic [14,18].

3.3 Logic Layer: PRT Session Engine

The main computational component of the system, the Logic Layer, implements the interaction logic based on PRT principles. Its core is a PRT session engine that controls the session state, orchestrates changes in interaction modes, and enforces interaction restrictions based on system specifications.

The session state, which serves as the main computational memory of the system, is updated in response to each user-system interaction. Task selection, reinforcement tactics, and subsequent interaction transitions are governed by this state. Consistent and flexible interaction behavior is ensured by constant state updates triggered by user inputs and system events [4,24].

Constrained Language Generation Module. The Logic Layer includes a language realization module based on large language models (LLMs) and a rule-based PRT session engine. Operating under the stringent restrictions imposed by the current session state, interaction mode, and system rules, this component is solely responsible for creating and reformulating system utterances.

Importantly, the LLM does not choose activities, decide on task difficulty, control interaction state, or make decisions pertaining to the therapeutic logic. The deterministic session engine handles all control decisions, including prompting strategies, reinforcement timing, and the state transitions. These choices provide the LLM with a bounded context, and it generates natural language output that complies with the specified interaction constraints [7][?,?].

3.4 Interaction Modes and State Transitions

Interaction is modeled as a limited set of modes, each corresponding to a different behavior of the system.

Choice mode: The system provides users with a variety of activities, allowing explicit decisions to be made.

Game mode: Structured tasks with variable difficulty levels are offered, which are evaluated and reinforced according to performance.

Conversation mode: Controlled dialogue interactions focused on topical discussions or engagement.

Emotional regulation mode: Conscious adaptation of emotions and light self-reporting of emotions.

Rest mode: Temporary suspension without penalty, maintaining the continuity of the sessions.

Event-driven transitions between interaction modes can be brought about by user-initiated actions (such as asking for a different activity) or system logic (such as task completion). Crucially, transitions are interruptible, which maintains autonomy and session continuity by enabling users to switch activities at any time without experiencing negative repercussions [11,20].

3.5 Difficulty Adaptation and Prompt Management

A rule-based mechanism that tracks user performance metrics, such as consecutive correct answers and assistance usage, is used to implement task difficulty adaptation. Task complexity is increased by adding more cues or constraints when the predetermined progression criteria are satisfied. Explicit rules also govern prompting strategies, allowing for graded assistance while maintaining task organization. Instead of providing support on an as-needed basis, this method guarantees that it remains systematic, traceable, and reproducible [30].

3.6 Interaction Layer and User Interface Integration

The interaction layer is responsible for integrating system logic with the user interface. Interaction elements provide clear, limited, and visually supported action options, reducing cognitive load and promoting accessibility. To guarantee ongoing user agency, essential interaction controls, such as buttons for choosing an activity, quick-action controls, and emotion selectors, are always accessible.

Consistency between system behavior and user perception is ensured by dynamically updating the user interface elements according to the current session state and interaction mode. While preserving the flexibility for user-initiated actions, this close coupling between logic and the interface allows for a predictable interaction flow.

Text-Based vs Audio-Based Interaction. From the perspective of interaction design and engineering, the system favors textual and selection-based input modalities over speech-based input. The need for reliable, interpretable, and deterministic user input drove this choice, especially in applications aimed at people with ASD, where speech production, prosody, and articulation can vary greatly.

Textual input and discrete interaction controls (such as buttons or selectors) provide well-defined input symbols that are reliably parsed, logged, and linked to explicit system states.

This enables error-tolerant interaction, user action traceability, and consistent system behavior adaptation. However, the predictability and reproducibility of interactions may be jeopardized by the additional uncertainty introduced by speech recognition errors and variability in audio-based input.

However, audio output was used as an additional feedback modality to support reinforcement and engagement without compromising interaction control. The interaction layer preserves stringent control over the interaction flow and state transitions while maintaining accessibility by separating input robustness from output expressiveness [13,23].

3.7 Logging and Traceability

Throughout the session, the Logging Layer logs structured interaction events, such as prompt usage, activity selections, user responses, self-initiation events, and changes in difficulty level. Every event has a timestamp and is specifically linked to the state of the session.

Crucially, rather than at the level of language generation, logging is performed at the level of interaction decisions and state transitions. This guarantees that, regardless of the particular language realization mechanism used, the system behavior will always be transparent, auditable, and reproducible. Without changing the underlying control logic, the system response that is ultimately displayed to the user may be saved when appropriate as a result of the interaction.

Without adding to the user's interaction demands, this structured logging facilitates post-session analysis, system debugging, and future evaluation of interaction patterns [10,25].

4 Interaction Model and User Interface Design

The interaction model of the proposed chatbot is designed to balance structure and flexibility, ensuring predictable behavior while supporting user autonomy and spontaneous interaction [11,15].

4.1 State-Based Interaction Model

Interaction is modeled as a set of discrete states corresponding to different system behaviors. Each state defines a specific set of allowable system actions and user inputs, ensuring clarity and consistency across interaction turns.

Transitions between states are event-driven and may be triggered either by system logic (e.g., completion of a task or achievement of progression criteria) or by explicit user actions (e.g., selecting a different activity or requesting a break). Importantly, the interaction model allows for interruptible state transitions, enabling users to change activities at any time without negative feedback or loss of session continuity. This design choice directly supports user autonomy and self-initiation.

4.2 User-Initiated Actions and Interaction Control

To facilitate spontaneous user engagement, the system provides dedicated mechanisms for user-initiated actions that remain available throughout the session. These include quick-action buttons such as requests to change activities, pause interaction, or express uncertainty. Unlike traditional dialogue systems that constrain users to predefined response paths, the proposed model explicitly accommodates off-path actions without interpreting them as errors.

From an engineering perspective, these user-initiated actions are treated as first-class events within the interaction logic, incrementing initiation counters and triggering appropriate state transitions. This approach ensures that spontaneous interaction is not only permitted but also systematically captured and supported by the system [20].

4.3 Emotion-Aware Interaction

Emotional self-reporting is implemented as a lightweight and optional interaction component, allowing users to indicate their current emotional state through simple visual icons.

Selected emotional states influence subsequent system behavior by modulating interaction pace, feedback tone, and task difficulty. For example, indications of negative affect may result in simplified tasks or the suggestion of a rest state. This emotion-aware adaptation enhances interaction robustness while preserving user control.

4.4 Visual Design and Accessibility Considerations

Visual design prioritizes clarity, consistency, and accessibility. Interactive elements are intentionally limited in number and remain spatially stable across interaction states, reducing the need for visual scanning. Persistent interface components, such as the activity selection panel, ensure that key controls are always visible and accessible [23].

The interface is designed to be suitable for both children and adolescents by avoiding overly childish aesthetics while maintaining simplicity. This design choice supports broader applicability across age ranges without requiring separate system versions.

5 Illustrative Interaction Scenarios

To illustrate how the proposed architecture operates during a typical session, a representative interaction sequence can be described. At session initialization, the system loads the user profile and enters a choice state, where the user can select among several activities such as games, conversation, emotional regulation exercises, or rest. Once an activity is selected, the session engine updates the internal interaction state and initializes the corresponding activity with an appropriate difficulty level derived from the user profile and recent performance. During structured activities, the system evaluates user responses in real time and provides immediate contextual feedback, while progression rules determine whether task complexity should increase through additional cues or constraints.

At any moment, the user can initiate spontaneous actions through persistent quick-action controls, such as requesting a different activity or temporarily pausing the session. These actions are interpreted as valid interaction events and may trigger state transitions without penalties or disruption of session continuity. Additionally, the system allows voluntary emotional self-reporting through visual emotion selectors. The reported emotional state is stored in the session state and can influence subsequent interaction parameters, such as task pacing, feedback tone, or the suggestion of alternative interaction modes (e.g., rest), enabling emotion-aware adaptation while maintaining user autonomy and transparency.

6 Discussion and Conclusions

This paper presented an engineering-oriented framework for designing conversational systems inspired by Pivotal Response Treatment (PRT). Rather than focusing on clinical evaluation, the proposed work translates key PRT principles into explicit engineering requirements and embeds them within a modular, deterministic interaction architecture. By mapping therapeutic concepts such as motivation, self-initiation, and responsiveness to multiple cues to functional requirements, interaction states, and event-driven logic, the framework contributes to improving transparency, reproducibility, and extensibility in conversational systems designed for individuals with ASD.

One of the main strengths of the proposed approach is the explicit separation between therapeutic intent and computational implementation. This separation allows behavioral intervention principles to be operationalized as enforceable software constraints while maintaining a clear and auditable interaction structure. Such an approach facilitates iterative development and supports the comparison of alternative dialogue management strategies or interaction models in future research.

Several limitations should nevertheless be acknowledged. First, the present work describes a proof-of-concept architecture without empirical validation involving end users. Second, although deterministic interaction rules and predefined adaptation criteria enhance predictability and safety, they may reduce conversational flexibility or sustained engagement for certain user profiles.

Future work will focus on extending the system in several directions. Planned developments include the integration of multimodal input sources, such as behavioral or physiological signals, to support richer user-state estimation. In addition, hybrid interaction models combining deterministic control with constrained generative language components will be explored in order to enhance conversational variability while preserving interaction safety. The modular design also facilitates deployment in different contexts, including educational environments and socially assistive robotic platforms.

Acknowledgments. This project has received funding by grant PID2020-115220RB-C22 funded by MCIN/AEI/ 10.13039/501100011033 and, as appropriate, by "ERDF A way of making Europe", by the "European Union" or by the "European Union NextGenerationEU/PRTR", and was funded in part by grants DTS19/00175 and PDC2022-133952-100 from the Spanish "Ministerio de Ciencia, Innovación y Universidades" and by the European Union's Horizon 2020. This work was partially supported by Programa Iberoamericano de Ciencia y Tecnología para el Desarrollo (CYTED) (through Red [225RT0169]) and EPISTEAM: Epistemology in Science, Technology, Engineering, Arts, and Maths.

Disclosure of Interests. The authors have no competing interests to declare that are relevant to the content of this article.

References

1. Acikgoz, E.C., et al.: A Desideratum for Conversational Agents: Capabilities, Challenges, and Future Directions (2025). https://doi.org/10.48550/arXiv.2504.16939, http://arxiv.org/abs/2504.16939, arXiv:2504.16939 [cs]
2. Aghakhani, S., et al.: Qualitative analysis of mental health conversational agents messages about autism spectrum disorder: a call for action. Front. Digit. Health **5**, 1251016 (2023). https://doi.org/10.3389/fdgth.2023.1251016, https://pmc.ncbi.nlm.nih.gov/articles/PMC10728644/
3. Ali, M.R., et al.: A virtual conversational agent for teens with autism: experimental results and design lessons. In: Proceedings of the 20th ACM International

Conference on Intelligent Virtual Agents. pp. 1–8 (2020). https://doi.org/10.1145/3383652.3423900, http://arxiv.org/abs/1811.03046, arXiv:1811.03046 [cs]
4. Boffa, M., You, J.: Large-Scale Constraint Generation – Can LLMs Parse Hundreds of Constraints? (2025). https://doi.org/10.48550/arXiv.2509.24090, http://arxiv.org/abs/2509.24090, arXiv:2509.24090 [cs]
5. Bone, D., Goodwin, M.S., Black, M.P., Lee, C.-C., Audhkhasi, K., Narayanan, S.: Applying Machine Learning to Facilitate Autism Diagnostics: Pitfalls and Promises. J. Autism Dev. Disord. **45**(5), 1121–1136 (2014). https://doi.org/10.1007/s10803-014-2268-6
6. Bölte, S., Golan, O., Goodwin, M.S., Zwaigenbaum, L.: What can innovative technologies do for Autism Spectrum Disorders? Autism Int. J. Res. Pract. **14**(3), 155–159 (2010). https://doi.org/10.1177/1362361310365028
7. Cardei, M., Christopher, J.K., Hartvigsen, T., Kailkhura, B., Fioretto, F.: Constrained Discrete Diffusion (2025). https://doi.org/10.48550/arXiv.2503.09790, http://arxiv.org/abs/2503.09790, arXiv:2503.09790 [cs]
8. Catania, F., Spitale, M., Garzotto, F.: Conversational agents in therapeutic interventions for neurodevelopmental disorders: a survey. ACM Comput. Surv. **55**(10), 209:1–209:34 (2023). https://doi.org/10.1145/3564269, https://dl.acm.org/doi/10.1145/3564269
9. Diehl, J.J., Schmitt, L.M., Villano, M., Crowell, C.R.: The clinical use of robots for individuals with autism spectrum disorders: a critical review. Res. Autism Spectr. Disord. **6**(1), 249–262 (2012). https://doi.org/10.1016/j.rasd.2011.05.006
10. D'Mello, S., Graesser, A.: AutoTutor and Affective AutoTutor: Learning by Talking with Cognitively and Emotionally Intelligent Computers that Talk Back
11. Fischer, G.: User Modeling in Human–Computer Interaction. User Modeling and User-Adapted Interaction **11**(1), 65–86 (2001). https://doi.org/10.1023/A:1011145532042
12. Fletcher-Watson, S.: A targeted review of computer-assisted learning for people with autism spectrum disorder: towards a consistent methodology. Rev. J. Autism Dev. Disord. **1**(2), 87–100 (2014). https://doi.org/10.1007/s40489-013-0003-4, http://link.springer.com/10.1007/s40489-013-0003-4
13. Grynszpan, O., Weiss, P.L.T., Perez-Diaz, F., Gal, E.: Innovative technology-based interventions for autism spectrum disorders: a meta-analysis. Autism Int. J. Res. Pract. **18**(4), 346–361 (2014). https://doi.org/10.1177/1362361313476767
14. Hernández-Leo, D., Martinez-Maldonado, R., Pardo, A., Muñoz-Cristóbal, J.A., Rodríguez-Triana, M.J.: Analytics for learning design: a layered framework and tools. Br. J. Edu. Technol. **50**(1), 139–152 (2019). https://doi.org/10.1111/bjet.12645, https://bera-journals.onlinelibrary.wiley.com/doi/10.1111/bjet.12645
15. Hou, X., Forsyth, C., Rice, J., Cai, Z., Jiang, Y.: An LLM-enhanced Multi-Agent Architecture for Conversation-Based Assessment
16. Imrattanatrai, W., Fukuda, K.: End-to-end task-oriented dialogue systems based on schema. In: Findings of the Association for Computational Linguistics: ACL 2023, pp. 10148–10161. Association for Computational Linguistics, Toronto, Canada (2023). https://doi.org/10.18653/v1/2023.findings-acl.645, https://aclanthology.org/2023.findings-acl.645
17. Knight, V., McKissick, B.R., Saunders, A.: A review of technology-based interventions to teach academic skills to students with autism spectrum disorder. J. Autism Dev. Disord. **43**(11), 2628–2648 (2013). https://doi.org/10.1007/s10803-013-1814-y

18. Kobsa, A.: Privacy-Enhanced Web Personalization. In: Hutchison, D., et al. (eds.) The Adaptive Web, vol. 4321, pp. 628–670. Springer Berlin Heidelberg, Berlin, Heidelberg (2007). https://doi.org/10.1007/978-3-540-72079-9_21, http://link.springer.com/10.1007/978-3-540-72079-9_21, series Title: Lecture Notes in Computer Science
19. Koegel, L.K., Koegel, R.L., Harrower, J.K., Carter, C.M.: Pivotal response intervention I: overview of approach. J. Assoc. Persons Severe Handicaps **24**(3), 174–85 (1999), eRIC Number: EJ599193
20. Koegel, R.L., Koegel, L.K.: Pivotal response treatments for autism: communication, social, & academic development. Pivotal response treatments for autism: Communication, social, & academic development, Paul H. Brookes Publishing Co., Baltimore, MD, US (2006), pages: xiv, 296
21. Lorah, E.R., Parnell, A., Whitby, P.S., Hantula, D.: A systematic review of tablet computers and portable media players as speech generating devices for individuals with autism spectrum disorder. J. Autism Dev. Disord. **45**(12), 3792–3804 (2014). https://doi.org/10.1007/s10803-014-2314-4
22. McDuff, D., Czerwinski, M.: Designing emotionally sentient agents. Commun. ACM **61**(12), 74–83 (2018). https://doi.org/10.1145/3186591
23. Parsons, S., Cobb, S.: State-of-the-art of virtual reality technologies for children on the autism spectrum. Eur. J. Spec. Needs Edu. **26**, 355–366 (2011). https://doi.org/10.1080/08856257.2011.593831
24. Pinho, P.C.R., Silva, R.Z.D., Primo, T.T., Dermeval, D., Bittencourt, I.I., Isotani, S.: Win-win situation: generative AI in educational constrained environments. In: Anais do XXXVI Simpósio Brasileiro de Informática na Educação (SBIE 2025), pp. 1607–1616. Sociedade Brasileira de Computação - SBC, Brasil (2025). https://doi.org/10.5753/sbie.2025.12497, https://sol.sbc.org.br/index.php/sbie/article/view/38530
25. Pohl, K.: Requirements Engineering Fundamentals, 2nd Edition: A Study Guide for the Certified Professional for Requirements Engineering Exam - Foundation Level - IREB compliant. Rocky Nook, Inc. (2016), google-Books-ID: 1VsUDgAAQBAJ
26. Pressman, R.S.: Software engineering: a practitioner's approach. McGraw-Hill Higher Education, New York, 7th edn. (2010)
27. Skinner, B.F.: Science and human behavior. Science and human behavior, p. x, 461. Macmillan, Oxford, England, (1953)
28. Sommerville, I.: Software engineering. Always learning, Pearson, Boston Columbus Indianapolis New York San Francisco Hoboken Amsterdam Cape Town Dubai London, tenth edn. (2016)
29. Young, S., Gasic, M., Thomson, B., Williams, J.D.: POMDP-based Statistical Spoken Dialogue Systems: a Review
30. Zhang, E., Yan, X., Lin, W., Zhang, T., Lu, Q.: Learning Like Humans: Advancing LLM Reasoning Capabilities via Adaptive Difficulty Curriculum Learning and Expert-Guided Self-Reformulation

Author Index

J. M. Ferrández Vicente et al. (Eds.): IWINAC 2026, LNCS 16574, pp. 487–489, 2026.
https://doi.org/10.1007/978-3-032-27314-7